92%

94%

eText

Study
Plan

Pearson eText enhances student learning—both in and outside the classroom. Take notes, highlight, and bookmark important content. Accessible anytime, anywhere via MyLab or the app.

% of students who found
learning tool helpful

86%

of students would tell their instructor to keep using MyLab Management

The **MyLab Gradebook** offers an easy way for students and instructors to view course performance. Item Analysis allows instructors to quickly see trends by analyzing details like the number of students who answered correctly/incorrectly, time on task, and median time spend on a question by question basis. And because it's correlated with the AACSB Standards, instructors can track students' progress toward outcomes that the organization has deemed important in preparing students to be **leaders.**

"I was able to find myself actually learning at home rather than memorizing things for a class."
— Katherine Vicente, Student at County College of Morris

For additional details visit: www.pearson.com/mylab/management

International Business

The Challenges of Globalization

Ninth Edition

Global Edition

John J. **Wild**
University of Wisconsin, Madison

Kenneth L. **Wild**
University of London, England

Pearson

Harlow, England • London • New York • Boston • San Francisco • Toronto • Sydney • Dubai • Singapore • Hong Kong
Tokyo • Seoul • Taipei • New Delhi • Cape Town • Sao Paulo • Mexico City • Madrid • Amsterdam • Munich • Paris • Milan

Vice President, Business, Economics, and UK Courseware:
    Donna Battista
Director of Portfolio Management: Stephanie Wall
Director, Courseware Portfolio Management: Ashley Dodge
Senior Sponsoring Editor: Neeraj Bhalla
Ediorial Assistant: Linda Albelli
Vice President, Product Marketing: Roxanne McCarley
Product Marketer: Kaylee McCarley
Product Marketing Assistant: Marianela Silvestri
Manager of Field Marketing, Business Publishing: Adam Goldstein
Field Marketing Manager: Nicole Price
Vice President, Production and Digital Studio, Arts and
    Business: Etain O'Dea
Director of Production, Business: Jeff Holcomb
Managing Producer, Business: Melissa Feimer
Content Producer: Sugandh Juneja
Content Producer, Global Edition: Nitin Shankar
Associate Acquisitions Editor, Global Edition: Ishita Sinha

Senior Project Editor, Global Edition: Daniel Luiz
Assistant Project Editor, Global Edition: Shasya Goel
Managing Editor, Global Edition: Steven Jackson
Senior Manufacturing Controller, Production, Global
    Edition: Angela Hawksbee
Operations Specialist: Carol Melville
Design Lead: Kathryn Foot
Manager, Learning Tools: Brian Surette
Content Developer, Learning Tools: Lindsey Sloan
Managing Producer, Digital Studio and GLP, Media Production
    and Development: Ashley Santora
Managing Producer, Digital Studio: Diane Lombardo
Digital Studio Producer: Regina DaSilva
Digital Studio Producer: Alana Coles
Project Managers: Nicole Suddeth and Thomas Murphy, SPi Global
Interior Design: Laurie Entringer
Cover Design: Lumina Datamatics, Inc.
Cover Art: PHOTOCREO Michal Bednarek/Shutterstock

Pearson Education Limited
KAO Two
KAO Park
Harlow
CM17 9NA
United Kingdom

and Associated Companies throughout the world

Visit us on the World Wide Web at:
www.pearsonglobaleditions.com

© Pearson Education Limited 2020

ISBN 10: 1-292-26225-7
ISBN 13: 978-1-29-226225-3

British Library Cataloguing-in-Publication Data
A catalogue record for this book is available from the British Library.

10 9 8 7 6 5 4 3 2 1
20 19 18

Typeset in Times LT Pro by SPi Global.

Printed and bound by Vivar, Malaysia.

Brief Contents

Contents

PART 5 International Business Management 294

Dear Friends and Colleagues,

As we roll out the new edition of International Business: The Challenges of Globalization, we thank each of you who provided suggestions to enrich this textbook. This edition reflects the advice and wisdom of many dedicated reviewers and instructors. Together, we have created the most readable, concise, and innovative international business book available today.

As teachers, we know it is important to select the right book for your course. Instructors say this book's clear and lively writing style helps students learn international business. The book's streamlined and clutter-free design is a competitive advantage that will never be sacrificed.

The accompanying cutting-edge technology package also helps students to better understand international business. MyLab Management is an innovative set of course-management tools for delivering all or part of your course online, which makes it easy to add meaningful assessment to your course. Whether you're interested in testing your students on simple recall of concepts and theories or you'd like to gauge how well they can apply their new knowledge to real-world scenarios, MyLab Management offers a variety of activities that are applied and personalized with immediate feedback. You and your students will find these and other components of this book's learning system fun and easy to use.

We owe the success of this book to our colleagues and our students who keep us focused on their changing educational needs. In this time of rapid global change, we must continue to instill in our students a passion for international business and to equip them with the skills and knowledge they need to compete. Please accept our heartfelt thanks and know that your input is reflected in everything we write.

John J. Wild

Kenneth L. Wild

Preface

Welcome to the ninth edition of *International Business: The Challenges of Globalization*. As in previous editions, this book resulted from extensive market surveys, chapter reviews, and correspondence with scores of instructors and students. We are delighted that an overwhelming number of instructors and students agree with our approach to international business. The reception of this textbook in the United States and across the world has exceeded all expectations.

This book is our means of traveling on an exciting tour through the study of international business. It motivates the reader by making international business challenging yet fun. It also embraces the central role of people and their cultures in international business. Each chapter is infused with real-world discussion, while underlying theory appears in the background where it belongs. Terminology is used consistently, and theories are explained in direct and concise terms. This book's visual style is innovative yet subtle and uses photos, illustrations, and features sparingly. The result is an easy-to-read and clutter-free design.

New to This Edition

- Learning Objectives for each chapter now appear in the margins of the text right next to where the corresponding material begins. This allows the reader to better follow the material presented in each chapter and increases student comprehension.
- New material in Chapter 1 includes coverage of highly useful capabilities we call employability skills. Where appropriate, the book presents material that helps students to develop critical thinking skills, refine their sense of business ethics and social responsibility, develop their communication skills, and expand their ability to apply and analyze knowledge.
- Chapter 1 topic of the world's largest companies and its accompanying Figure 1.1 has been updated, as is material on the most globalized nations and the timely and important topic of global inequality.
- The Manager's Briefcase feature in Chapter 1 appears earlier to emphasize the textbook's applied and managerial treatment of material.
- Presentation of national illiteracy rates and its accompanying Table 2.1 are updated to present the most recent data available.
- Figure 3.2 and its discussion reflect recent data on business software piracy rates around the world.
- The most recently available Human Development Index is presented in Table 4.1 along with its updated in-text explanation.
- Table 5.1 presents most recently available data on the world's top exporters and importers, by both US dollar value and share of the world total.
- Chapter 5 discussion of regional merchandise trade has been removed to present the material in a more streamlined and less complicated fashion.
- Chapter 6 contains an update to the discussion of the WTO Doha Round of negotiations.
- Figures 7.1 and 7.2 and their explanations update the annual value of foreign direct investment inflows and cross-border mergers and acquisitions, respectively.
- Chapter 8 presentation of regional trading blocs contains the latest available information on Britain's exit (Brexit) from the European Union, Venezuela's suspension from the Southern Common Market, and other events.
- Chapter 10 updates the discussion of exchange rates among major world currencies, value of the US dollar over time, and the addition of China's currency to the IMF's special drawing right (SDR).
- Table 12.1 updates the ranking of the world's top market research firms.

- Chapter 13 discussion of letter-of-credit financing and its related Figure 13.4 have been revised for precision and a smoother presentation.
- All chapter-opening company profiles and chapter-closing mini-cases are updated to reflect the most recent data and facts available at the time of publication.

Solving Teaching and Learning Challenges

Students who take the international business course can have difficulty seeing the relevance of certain key concepts to their lives and future careers. These topics can include political economy, trade theory, foreign exchange rates, and the international financial system. This can reduce the willingness of a student to prepare for class and be engaged in class.

We use the ever-present and salient subject of culture to present real-world examples and engaging features to bring international business to life and pique student interest. We present complex material in concrete, straightforward terms and illustrate it appropriately to make international business accessible for all students. This approach makes the material interesting and relevant and shows students the importance of these concepts to their future employability and careers. We use the following additional methods and resources to engage students with the content of international business:

Interactive Approach to International Business

Pearson's MyLab Management is now fully integrated into the text. These features are outlined below. The online assessment activities enable you to quiz your students before class so you have more time in class to focus on areas that students find most challenging.

Watch It Cases expose students to life in other cultures by asking them to view a video clip on a key topic. Each video corresponds to the chapter material and is accompanied by multiple choice questions that reinforce student comprehension.

Quick Study Concept Checks appear at the end of each textbook section to verify that students have learned key terms and concepts before moving on. Students obtain immediate feedback on answers they provide in an online environment.

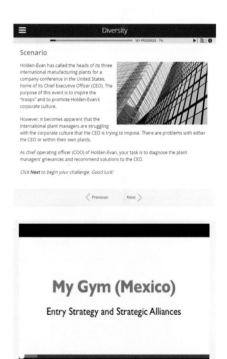

Making International Business Relevant

This textbook captures the real-world characteristics of international business today by emphasizing the importance of cultural influences, sustainable business practices, and managerial implications.

Culture Matters boxes present the relation between culture and a key chapter topic. For example, Chapter 2 presents the importance of businesspeople developing a global mindset and avoiding cultural bias. Another chapter presents the debate over globalization's influence on culture, and another box shows how entrepreneurs succeed by exploiting their knowledge of local cultures.

Global Sustainability boxes present special topics related to economic, social, and environmental sustainability. Today, businesses know that flourishing

---

CULTURE MATTERS | The Culture Debate

The debate about globalization's influence on culture evokes strong opinions. Here are a few main arguments in this debate:

- **Material Desire.** Critics say globalization fosters the "Coca-Colanization" of nations through advertising campaigns that promote material desire. They also argue that global consumer-goods companies destroy cultural diversity (especially in developing nations) by putting local companies out of business.
- **Artistic Influence.** Evidence suggests, however, that the cultures of developing nations are thriving and that the influence of their music, art, and literature has grown (not shrunk) throughout the past century. African cultures, for example, have influenced the works of artists including Picasso, the Beatles, and Sting.
- **Western Values.** International businesses reach far and wide through the Internet, global media, increased business travel, and local marketing. Critics say local values and traditions are being replaced by US companies promoting "Western" values.

- **A Force for Good.** On the positive side, globalization tends to foster two important values: tolerance and diversity. Advocates say nations should be more tolerant of opposing viewpoints and should welcome diversity among their peoples. This view interprets globalization as a potent force for good in the world.
- **Deeper Values.** Globalization can cause consumer purchases and economic ideologies to converge, but these are rather superficial aspects of culture. Deeper values that embody the essence of cultures might be more resistant to a global consumer culture.
- **Want to Know More?.** Visit the globalization page of the Global Policy Forum (www.globalpolicy.org), Globalization 101 (www.globalization101.org), or The Globalist (www.theglobalist.com).

Sources: "Economic Globalization and Culture: A Discussion with Dr. Francis Fukuyama," Merrill Lynch Forum website (www.ml.com); "Globalization Issues," The Globalization website (www.sociology.emory.edu/globalization/index.html); "Cultural Diversity in the Era of Globalization," UNESCO Culture Sector website (www.unesco.org/culture).

GLOBAL SUSTAINABILITY | Three Markets, Three Strategies

A company adapts its business strategy to the nuances of the market it enters. The world's population of 7.5 billion people lives in three different types of markets:

- **Developed Markets.** These include the world's established consumer markets, around *one billion* people. The population is solidly middle class, and people can consume almost any product desired. The infrastructure is highly developed and efficient.
- **Emerging Markets.** These markets, around *two billion* people, are racing to catch up to developed nations. The population is migrating to cities for better pay and is overloading cities' infrastructures. Rising incomes are increasing global demand for resources and basic products.
- **Traditional Markets.** Globalization has bypassed these markets, nearly *four billion* people. The population is mostly rural, the infrastructure is very poor, and there is little credit or collateral. People have almost no legal protections, and corruption prevails.

Like business strategy, sustainability strategies reflect local conditions. Examples of businesses working toward sustainability in these three markets include the following:

- **Toyota** focused on the environment in its *developed markets.* After extensively researching gas-electric hybrid technologies, Toyota launched the Prius. As *Motor Trend*'s Car of the Year, the Prius drove Toyota's profits to record highs and gave it a "green" image.
- **Shree Cement** faced limited access to low-cost energy in India's *emerging market,* so it developed the world's most energy-efficient process for making its products. The world's leading cement companies now visit Shree to learn from its innovations in energy usage.
- **Blommer Chocolate** of the United States works closely with cocoa farmers in *traditional markets.* Blommer received the Rainforest Alliance's "Sustainable Standard-Setter" award for training farmers in safe farming practices, environmental stewardship, and HIV awareness.

Sources: Wang Wen, "Emerging Markets are Set to Lead Globalisation," *Financial Times* (www.ft.com), April 10, 2017; Jeremy Jurgens and Knut Haanæs, "Companies from Emerging Markets Are the New Sustainability Champions," *The Guardian* (www.guardian.co.uk), October 12, 2011; Stuart L. Hart, *Capitalism at the Crossroads, Third Edition* (Upper Saddle River, NJ: Wharton School Publishing, 2010); Daniel C. Esty and Andrew S. Winston, *Green to Gold* (New Haven, CT: Yale University Press, 2006).

MANAGER'S BRIEFCASE | The Keys to Global Success

Making everything from 99-cent hamburgers (McDonald's) to $150 million jumbo jets (Boeing), managers of global companies must overcome obstacles when competing in unfamiliar markets. Global managers acknowledge certain common threads in their approaches to management and offer the following advice:

- **Communicate Effectively** Cultural differences in business relationships and etiquette are central to global business and require cross-cultural competency. Effective global managers welcome uniqueness and ambiguity while demonstrating flexibility, respect, and empathy.
- **Know the Customer** Successful managers understand how a company's different products serve the needs of international customers. Then, they ensure that the company remains flexible and capable enough to customize products that meet those needs.

- **Emphasize Global Awareness** Good global managers integrate foreign markets into business strategy from the outset. They ensure that products and services are designed and built with global markets in mind, and not used as dumping grounds for the home market's outdated products.
- **Market Effectively** The world will beat a path to your door to buy your "better mousetrap" only if it knows about it. A poor marketing effort can cause great products to fade into obscurity while an international marketing blunder can bring unwanted media attention. Top global managers match quality products with excellent marketing.
- **Monitor Global Markets** Successful managers keep a watchful eye on business environments for shifting political, legal, and socioeconomic conditions. They make obtaining accurate information a top priority.

---

markets rely on strong economies, thriving societies, and healthy environments. Topics include the factors that contribute to sustainable development, and how companies can make their supply chains more environmentally friendly.

Manager's Briefcase boxes address issues facing companies active in international business. Issues presented can be relevant to entrepreneurs and small businesses or to the world's largest global companies. Topics include obtaining capital to finance international activities, getting paid for exports, and how to be mindful of personal security while abroad on business.

Uniquely Integrative

International business is not simply a collection of separate business functions and environmental forces. The model shown below (and detailed in Chapter 1) is a unique organizing framework that helps students to understand how the elements of international business are related. It depicts a dynamic, integrated system that weaves together national business environments, the international business environment, and international business management. It also shows that characteristics of globalization (new technologies and falling barriers to trade and investment) are causing greater competition.

Tools for Active Learning

Carefully chosen assignment materials span the full range of complexity to test students' knowledge and ability to apply key principles. Assignment materials are often experiential in nature to help students develop decision-making skills.

Talk About It questions raise important issues currently confronting entrepreneurs, international managers, policy makers, consumers, and others.

Ethical Challenge exercises ask students to assume the role of a manager, government official, or someone else and to make a decision based on the facts presented to them.

Teaming Up projects go beyond the text and require students to collaborate in teams to conduct interviews, research other countries, or hold in-class debates.

Market Entry Strategy Project is an interactive simulation that asks students to research a country as a future market for a new video game system. Working as part of a team, students research and analyze a country, and then recommend a course of action.

Practicing International Management cases ask students to analyze the responses of real-world companies to the issues, problems, and opportunities discussed in each chapter.

TALK ABOUT IT 1

Today, international businesspeople must think globally about production and sales opportunities. Many global managers will eventually find themselves living and working in other cultures, and entrepreneurs might find themselves taking flights to places they had never heard about.

1-1. What can companies do now to prepare their managers for international markets?
1-2. How can entrepreneurs and small businesses with limited resources prepare?

TALK ABOUT IT 2

In the past, national governments influenced the pace of globalization through agreements to lower barriers to international trade and investment.

1-3. Is rapid change now outpacing the capability of governments to manage the global economy?
1-4. Will national governments grow more or less important to international business in the future?

Ethical Challenge

You are the CEO of a global healthcare corporation looking at the possibility of entering some new emerging markets. Market size and potential is actually quite hard to judge, so you need to look at some other way of working out their potential. Ethically, you will avoid markets that seem to have political or social problems as you do not wish your corporation to be tainted with accusations that you are prepared to operate anywhere to make a profit.

12-5. Decisions made about markets are based on secondary data. What ethical issues does this present?

12-6. Is it ethical to be focused on issues such as economic freedom when considering a market?

12-7. What is "country risk," and what types of factors are considered under this variable when assessing market potential? Is it a fair measurement?

Teaming Up

Imagine that you and several of your classmates own a company that manufactures cheap sunglasses. To lower production costs, you decide to move your factory from your developed country to a more cost-effective location.

1-8. Which elements of the national business environment might influence your decision of where to move production?

1-9. What aspects of the globalization of production and marketing do you expect will benefit your company after the move?

✪ Market Entry Strategy Project

This exercise corresponds to the *MESP* online simulation. With several classmates, select a country that interests you. For the country your team researches, integrate your answers to the following questions into your completed *MESP* report.

1-10. Is the nation the home base of any large multinational companies?

1-11. How does globalization influence the country's jobs and wages, its income inequality, and its culture, sovereignty, and physical environment?

1-12. How does the country rank in terms of its degree of globalization?

1-13. What benefits can the country offer to businesses seeking a new market or production base?

PRACTICING INTERNATIONAL MANAGEMENT CASE

Toyota's Strategy for Production Efficiency

Toyota Motor Corporation (www.toyota-global.com) commonly appears in most rankings of the world's most respected companies. One reason for Toyota's strong showing in such rankings is that the company always seems to maintain profitability in the face of economic downturns and slack demand. Another reason is that leaders in a wide range of industries have high regard for Toyota's management and production practices.

Toyota first began producing cars in 1937. In the mid-1950s, a machinist named Taiichi Ohno began developing a new concept of automobile production. Today, the approach known as the Toyota Production System (TPS) has been intensely studied and widely copied throughout the automobile industry. Ohno, who is addressed by fellow employees as *sensei* ("teacher and master"), followed the lead of the family that founded Toyota (spelled Toyoda) by exhibiting high regard for company employees. Ohno also believed that mass production of automobiles was obsolete and that a flexible production system that produced cars according to specific customer requests would be superior.

It was at Toyota that the well-known just-in-time approach to inventory management was developed and perfected. Implementing just-in-time required *kanban*, a simple system of colored paper cards that accompanied the parts as they progressed down the assembly line. *Kanban* eliminates inventory buildup by quickly telling the production personnel which parts are being used and which are not. The third pillar of the TPS was quality circles, groups of workers who discussed ways to improve the work process and make better cars. Finally, the entire system was based on *jidoka*, which literally means "automation." As used at Toyota, however, the word expresses management's faith in the worker as a human being and a thinker.

A simple example illustrates the benefits of Toyota's system. Toyota dealerships found that customers kept returning their vehicles with leaking radiator hoses. When a team of workers at the US plant where the vehicle was made was asked to help find a solution, they found the problem was the clamp on the radiator hose. In assembly, the clamp is put over the hose, a pin on the side is pulled out, and the hose is secured. But sometimes the operator would

forget to pull out the pin. The hose would remain loose and would leak. The team installed a device next to the line that contains a funnel and electric eye. If a pin is not tossed into the funnel (passing the electric eye) every 60 seconds, the device senses that the operator must have forgotten to pull the pin and stops the line. As a result, a warranty problem at the dealerships was eliminated, customer dissatisfaction was reduced, and productivity was increased.

Nearly 50 years after the groundwork for the TPS was first laid, the results speak for themselves. Toyota's superior approach to manufacturing has been estimated to yield a cost advantage of $600 to $700 per car due to more efficient production, plus another $300 savings per car because fewer defects mean less warranty repair work. Ohno's belief in flexible production can also be seen in the fact that Toyota's Sienna minivan is produced on the same assembly line in Georgetown, Kentucky, as the company's Camry models. The Sienna and Camry share the same basic chassis and 50 percent of their parts. Out of 300 different stations on the assembly line, Sienna models require different parts at only 26 stations. Toyota expects to build one Sienna for every three Camrys that come off the assembly line.

Thinking Globally

15-13. Chrysler engineers helped Toyota develop its Sienna minivan. In return, Toyota provided input on automobile production techniques to Chrysler. Why do you think Chrysler was willing to share its minivan know-how with a key competitor?

15-14. Considering financial, marketing, and human resource management issues, what other benefits do you think Toyota obtains from its production system?

Sources: Christoph Rauwald, "Toyota Loses Global Sales Crown to VW as US Trade Barriers Loom," *Automotive News* (www.autonews.com), January 30, 2017; Hirotaka Takeuchi, Emi Osono, and Norihiko Shimizu, "The Contradictions That Drive Toyota's Success," *Harvard Business Review*, June 2008, pp. 96–104; David Welch, "What Could Dull Toyota's Edge," *Bloomberg Businessweek*, April 28, 2008, p. 38.

MyLab Management

Reach every student by pairing this text with MyLab Management MyLab is the teaching and learning platform that empowers you to reach every student. By combining trusted author content with digital tools and a flexible platform, MyLab personalizes the learning experience and improves results for each student. Learn more about MyLab Management at www.pearson.com/mylab/management. This approach helps you reach students who have little international knowledge and experience.

Deliver trusted content You deserve teaching materials that meet your own high standards for your course. That's why we partner with highly respected authors to develop interactive content and course-specific resources that you can trust—and that keep your students engaged. This material piques student interest and engages them with abstract topics, such as the global monetary system.

Empower each learner Each student learns at a different pace. Personalized learning pinpoints the precise areas where each student needs practice, giving all students the support they need—when and where they need it—to be successful. This strategy helps students master difficult concepts, such as foreign exchange rates.

Teach your course your way Your course is unique. So whether you'd like to build your own assignments, teach multiple sections, or set prerequisites, MyLab gives you the flexibility to easily create *your* course to fit *your* needs. You can teach chapters or individual modules in the order you prefer, for example, by covering global economic topics before teaching culture.

Improve student results When you teach with MyLab, student performance improves. That's why instructors have chosen MyLab for over 15 years, touching the lives of over 50 million students.

Developing Employability Skills

Some students enrolled in this course are majoring in international business or a related area. Other students are not business majors and are taking this course to gain insight into how businesses operate in the global economy today. Regardless of the chosen field of study, this course helps students develop useful capabilities we call employability skills.

Critical thinking involves purposeful and goal-directed thinking used to define and solve problems, make decisions, or form judgments related to a set of circumstances. This textbook requires students to use critical thinking skills to, for example, study how a country designs its political, economic, and legal systems into a complex arrangement to achieve a specific set of priorities for the nation and its people.

Business ethics and social responsibility are sets of guiding principles that influence the way individuals and organizations behave within society. Throughout the book students encounter the issues of personal ethical responsibility and reasoning as they read how managers made ethical decisions under specific circumstances and how they fared.

Communication skills involve the use of oral, written, and nonverbal language, and technology to communicate ideas effectively and to listen effectively. This book teaches that articulating one's thoughts and ideas in another language and culture must be done to not offend other's values and beliefs. The reader will encounter many examples of appropriate communication and thoughtless communication.

Knowledge application and analysis refers to one's ability to learn a concept and appropriately apply that knowledge in another setting to achieve a higher level of understanding. Students will apply analytical reasoning and research skills in numerous assignments, projects, mini-cases, and, perhaps, the market entry strategy project developed for use with this textbook.

Instructor Teaching Resources

This program comes with the following teaching resources.

Supplements available to instructors at *www.pearsonglobaleditions.com*	Features of the Supplement
Instructor's Resource Manual authored by John Capela from St. Joseph's College, New York	• Chapter-by-chapter summaries • Examples and activities not in the main book • Learning outlines • Teaching tips • Solutions to all questions and problems in the book
Test Bank authored by John Capela from St. Joseph's College, New York	1600 multiple-choice, true/false, short-answer, and graphing questions with these annotations: • Difficulty level (1 for straight recall, 2 for some analysis, and 3 for complex analysis) • Answer • Skill • Learning outcome • AACSB learning standard (ethical understanding and reasoning; analytical thinking; information technology; diverse and multicultural work; reflective thinking; application of knowledge)
Computerized TestGen®	TestGen allows instructors to: • Customize, save, and generate classroom tests • Edit, add, or delete questions from the Test Item Files • Analyze test results • Organize a database of tests and student results
PowerPoints authored by Carol Heeter from Ivy Tech Community College	Slides include all the figures, tables, maps, and equations in the textbook. PowerPoints meet accessibility standards for students with disabilities. Features include, but not limited to: • Keyboard and screen reader access • Alternative text for images • High color contrast between background and foreground colors

Acknowledgments

We are grateful for the encouragement and suggestions provided by many instructors, professionals, and students in preparing this ninth edition of *International Business: The Challenges of Globalization*. We especially thank the following instructors who provided valuable feedback to improve this and previous editions:

Rob Abernathy	*University of North Carolina, Greensboro*
Hadi S. Alhorr	*Drake University*
Gary Anders	*Arizona State University West*
Madan Annavarjula	*Northern Illinois University*
Ogugua Anunoby	*Lincoln University*
Robert Armstrong	*University of North Alabama*
Wendell Armstrong	*Central Virginia Community College*
Mernoush Banton	*Florida International University*
George Barnes	*University of Texas at Dallas*
Constance Bates	*Florida International University*
Marca Marie Bear	*University of Tampa*
Leta Beard	*University of Washington, Washington*
Tope A. Bello	*East Carolina University*
Robert Blanchard	*Salem State College*
David Boggs	*Eastern Illinois University*
Chuck Bohleke	*Owens Community College*
Erin Boyer	*Central Piedmont Community College*
Todd Brachman	*Marquette University, Wisconsin*
Richard Brisebois	*Everglades University*
Bill Brunsen	*Eastern New Mexico at Portales*
Thierry Brusselle	*Chaffey College*
Mikelle Calhoun	*Ohio State University*
Martin Calkins	*Santa Clara University*
Lisa Cherivtch	*Oakton Community College*
Kenichiro Chinen	*California State University at Sacramento*
Joy Clark	*Auburn University–Montgomery*
Randy Cray	*University of Wisconsin at Stevens Point*
Tim Cunha	*Eastern New Mexico University at Portales*
Robert Engle	*Quinnipiac University*
Herbert B. Epstein	*University of Texas at Tyler*
Blair Farr	*Jarvis Christian College*
Stanley Flax	*St. Thomas University*
Ronelle Genser	*Devry University*
Carolina Gomez	*University of Houston*
Jorge A. Gonzalez	*University of Wisconsin at Milwaukee*
Andre Graves	*SUNY Buffalo*
Kenneth R. Gray	*Florida A&M University*
James Gunn	*Berkeley College*
James Halteman	*Wheaton College*
Alan Hamlin	*Southern Utah University*

Dale Hartley	*Laramie County Community College*
Charles Harvey	*University of the West of England, UK*
M. Anaam Hashmi	*Minnesota State University at Mankato*
Les Jankovich	*San Jose State University*
R. Sitki Karahan	*Montana State University*
Bruce Keillor	*Youngstown State University*
Ken Kim	*University of Toledo*
Ki Hee Kim	*William Paterson University*
Anthony C. Koh	*University of Toledo*
Donald J. Kopka Jr.	*Towson University*
James S. Lawson Jr.	*Mississippi State University*
Ian Lee	*Carleton University*
Tomasz Lenartowicz	*Florida Atlantic University*
Joseph W. Leonard	*Miami University (Ohio)*
Antoinette Lloyd	*Virginia Union University*
Carol Lopilato	*California State University at Dominguez Hills*
Jennifer Malarski	*North Hennepin Community College*
Donna Weaver McCloskey	*Widener University*
James McFillen	*Bowling Green State University*
Mantha Vlahos Mehallis	*Florida Atlantic University*
John L. Moore	*Oregon Institute of Technology*
David Mosby	*University of Texas, Arlington*
Richard T. Mpoyi	*Middle Tennessee State University*
Tim Muth	*Florida Institute of Technology*
Christopher "Kit" Nagel	*Concordia University Irvine*
Rod Oglesby	*Southwest Baptist University*
Sam Okoroafo	*University of Toledo*
Patrick O'Leary	*St. Ambrose University*
Jaime Ortiz	*Texas International Education Consortium*
Yongson Paik	*Loyola Marymount University*
Thomas Passero	*Owens Community College*
Hui Pate	*Skyline College*
Clifford Perry	*Florida International University*
Susan Peterson	*Scottsdale Community College*
Janis Petronis	*Tarleton State University*
William Piper	*William Piedmont College*
Abe Qastin	*Lakeland College*
Krishnan Ramaya	*Pacific University of Oregon*
James Reinnoldt	*University of Washington–Bothell*
Elva A. Resendez	*Texas A&M University*
Nadine Russell	*Central Piedmont Community College*
C. Richard Scott	*Metropolitan State College of Denver*
Deepak Sethi	*Old Dominion University*
Charlie Shi	*Diablo Valley College*
Coral R. Snodgrass	*Canisius College*

Mark J. Snyder	*University of North Carolina*
Rajeev Sooreea	*Penn State—University Park*
John Stanbury	*George Mason University*
William A. Stoever	*Seton Hall University*
Kenneth R. Tillery	*Middle Tennessee State University*
William Walker	*University of Houston*
Paula Weber	*St. Cloud State University*
James E. Welch	*Kentucky Wesleyan College*
Steve Werner	*University of Houston*
David C. Wyld	*Southeastern Louisiana University*
Robert Yamaguchi	*Fullerton College*
Bashar A. Zakaria	*California State University, Sacramento*
Man Zhang	*Bowling Green State University, Kentucky*

It takes a dedicated group of individuals to take a textbook from first draft to final manuscript. We thank our partners at Pearson for their tireless efforts in bringing the ninth edition of this book to fruition. Special thanks on this project go to Stephanie Wall, Editor-in-Chief; Neeraj Bhalla, Senior Sponsoring Editor; Melissa Feimer, Managing Producer, Business; Sugandh Juneja, Content Producer; Nicole Suddeth and Thomas Murphy, Project Managers, SPi Global; Roxanne McCarley, Vice President, Product Marketing; Becky Brown, Senior Product Marketer; Adam Goldstein, Manager of Field Marketing, Business Publishing; and Nicole Price, Field Marketing Manager.

Global Edition Acknowledgments

Pearson would like to thank the following people for their work on the Global Edition:

Contributors

John Bancroft, Oxford Brooks University

Krish Saha, Birmingham City University

Shishank Shishank, Birmingham City University

Diane Sutherland

Jon Sutherland

Reviewers

David Ahlstrom, Chinese University of Hong Kong

Nikhil Celly, University of Houston

Javier Cuervo, University of Macau

Stefania Paladini, Birmingham City University

About the Authors

John J. Wild and Kenneth L. Wild provide a blend of skills uniquely suited to writing an international business textbook. They combine award-winning teaching and research with a global view of business gained through years of living and working in cultures around the world. Their writing makes the topic of international business practical, accessible, and enjoyable.

John J. Wild is a distinguished Professor of Business at the University of Wisconsin at Madison. He previously held appointments at the University of Manchester in England and at Michigan State University. He received his BBA, MS, and PhD degrees from the University of Wisconsin at Madison.

Teaching business courses at both the undergraduate and graduate levels, Professor Wild has received several teaching honors, including the Mabel W. Chipman Excellence-in-Teaching Award, the Teaching Excellence Award from the business graduates of the University of Wisconsin, and a departmental Excellence-in-Teaching Award from Michigan State University. He is a prior recipient of national research fellowships from KPMG Peat Marwick and the Ernst and Young Foundation. Professor Wild is also a frequent speaker at universities and at national and international conferences.

The author of more than 60 publications, in addition to 5 best-selling textbooks, Professor Wild conducts research on a wide range of topics, including corporate governance, capital markets, and financial analysis and forecasting. He is an active member of several national and international organizations, including the Academy of International Business, and has served as associate editor and editorial board member for several prestigious journals.

Kenneth L. Wild is affiliated with the University of London, England. He previously taught at Pennsylvania State University. He received his PhD from the University of Manchester (UMIST) in England and his BS and MS degrees from the University of Wisconsin. Dr. Wild also undertook postgraduate work at École des Affairs Internationale in Marseilles, France.

Having taught students of international business, marketing, and management at both the undergraduate and graduate levels, Dr. Wild is a dedicated contributor to international business education. An active member of several national and international organizations, including the Academy of International Business, Dr. Wild has spoken at major universities and at national and international conferences.

Dr. Wild's research covers a range of international business topics, including market entry modes, country risk in emerging markets, international growth strategies, and globalization of the world economy.

International Business

The Challenges of Globalization

Chapter One

Globalization

Learning Objectives

After studying this chapter, you should be able to

1.1 Identify the types of companies active in international business.

1.2 Explain globalization and how it affects markets and production.

1.3 Detail the forces that drive globalization.

1.4 Outline the debate about globalization's impact on jobs and wages.

1.5 Summarize the debate about income inequality.

1.6 Outline the debate about culture, sovereignty, and the environment.

1.7 Identify how this course will help you to develop skills for your career.

A Look at This Chapter

This chapter defines the scope of international business and introduces us to some of its most important topics. We begin by identifying the key players in international business today. We then present globalization, describing its influence on markets and production, and the forces behind its growth. Next, we analyze each main argument in the debate about globalization in detail. This chapter closes by describing how this course can help develop your employability skills and by explaining a model of an integrated global business environment.

A Look Ahead

Part 2, encompassing Chapters 2, 3, and 4, introduces us to the main features of national business environments. Chapter 2 describes important cultural differences among nations. Chapter 3 examines systems of political economy and philosophies of ethics and social responsibility. Chapter 4 presents issues regarding the economic development of nations.

MyLab Management

✪ IMPROVE YOUR GRADE!

When you see this icon ✪, visit **www.pearson.com/mylab/management** for activities that are applied, personalized, and offer immediate feedback.

Ray-Ban: Looking Good Again

Milan, Italy—As World War II loomed, a medical equipment company named Bausch & Lomb was approached by the U.S. military to develop a pair of sunglasses for pilots that would block glare from the sun without obscuring vision. In 1937, these aviator-style sunglasses were sold to the public, marketed as having the ability to block UV rays—

and thus the world's most iconic brand of sunglasses got their name: Ray-Ban.

The brand received a lot of media coverage over the course of World War II, during which photographs of military personnel donning Ray-Bans became widely publicized, and it gained further global fame and appeal through Hollywood.

However, by 1999, the brand was on the brink of collapse. Outdated production methods led to poor quality, forcing low prices, and to low-end points of sale. In 1999, the brand was sold to Luxottica, for $640 million.

Luxottica rescued Ray-Ban through globalization. Shifting production to its state-of-the-art facility in Italy helped Luxottica to gain access to suppliers

Aleksandrs Muiznieks/Shutterstock

who possessed higher-quality materials. Ray-Bans were sold at higher prices at higher-end department stores; this was achieved by leveraging Luxottica's existing relationship with such vendors. The focus on utility turned into a focus on lifestyle fashion, offering more styles, prescription eyeglasses, and significant customizability.

Globalizing Ray-Ban has not been without its downsides. The brand's desirability has given rise to piracy and to counterfeit Ray-Bans, and the business is further complicated by the inevitable seasonal demand for sunglasses and the impact this has on both production and income streams.

Nevertheless, Ray-Ban is still one of the most ubiquitous brands in fashion, with an estimated global market share of 5 percent. Aided by the high degree of standardization across its markets, globalization has enabled Ray-Ban and the Luxottica Group to produce and sell around the world while keeping production and marketing costs low, boosting its profitability and ultimately its success.[1]

Each of us experiences the results of international business transactions as we go about our daily routines. The General Electric (www.ge.com) alarm clock/radio that woke you this morning was made in *China*. The breaking news buzzing in your ears was produced by *Britain's* BBC radio (www.bbc.co.uk). You slip on your Adidas sandals (www.adidas.com) that were made in *Indonesia*, an Abercrombie & Fitch T-shirt (www.abercrombie.com) made in the *Northern Mariana Islands*, and American Eagle jeans (www.ae.com) made in *Mexico*. As you head out the door, you pull the battery charger off your Apple iPhone (www.apple.com), which was designed in the *United States* and assembled in *China* with parts from *Japan*, *South Korea*, *Taiwan*, and several other nations. You hop into your *Korean* Hyundai (www.hmmausa.com) that was made in *Alabama*, grab your iPod, and play a song by the *English* band Coldplay (www.coldplay.com). You drive to the local Starbucks (www.starbucks.com) to charge your own batteries with coffee brewed from beans harvested in *Colombia* and *Ethiopia*. Your day is just one hour old, but in a way, you've already taken a virtual trip around the world. A quick glance at the "Made in" tags on your jacket, backpack, watch, wallet, or other items with you right now will demonstrate the pervasiveness of international business transactions.

international business

Commercial transaction that crosses the borders of two or more nations.

imports

Goods and services purchased abroad and brought into a country.

exports

Goods and services sold abroad and sent out of a country.

International business is any commercial transaction that crosses the borders of two or more nations. You don't have to set foot outside a small town to find evidence of international business. No matter where you live, you'll be surrounded by **imports**—goods and services purchased abroad and brought into a country. Your counterparts around the world will undoubtedly spend some part of their day using your nation's **exports**—goods and services sold abroad and sent out of a country. Every year, all the nations of the world export goods worth $16.2 trillion and services worth $4.7 trillion. This figure for merchandise exports is around 33 times the annual global revenue of Walmart Stores (www.walmart.com).[2]

People can view the role of international business in society very differently from each other, and they can approach globalization from very different perspectives. A businessperson might see globalization as an opportunity to source goods and services from lower-cost locations and to pry open new markets. An economist might see it as an opportunity to examine the impact of globalization on jobs and standards of living. An environmentalist might be concerned with how globalization affects our ecology. An anthropologist might want to examine the influence of globalization on the culture of a group of people. A political scientist might be concerned with the impact of globalization on the power of governments relative to that of multinational companies. And an employee might view globalization either as an opportunity for new work or as a threat to his or her current job. The different lenses through which we view events around us make globalization a rich and complex topic.

As technology drives down the cost of global communication and travel, globalization increasingly exposes us to the traits and practices of other cultures. Individuals and businesses on the other side of the world can sell us their products and purchase our own easily online. Globalization forces companies to grow more competitive in the face of greater rivalry, which has been brought about by lower barriers to trade and investment. By knitting the world more tightly together, globalization is altering our private lives and transforming the way companies do business. The process of globalization is continuing despite a recent slowdown in some areas of international business activity.[3]

We begin this chapter by examining the key players in international business. Then, we describe globalization's powerful influence on markets and production and explain the forces behind its expansion. Next, we cover each main point in the debate about globalization, including jobs, wages, inequality, culture, and more. Then, we describe employability skills this course can help you develop, such as critical thinking, ethics, communication, and knowledge application and analysis. We also explain why international business is special by presenting an integrated model of the global business environment. Finally, the appendix at the end of this chapter contains a world atlas to be used as a primer for this chapter's discussion and as a reference throughout the remainder of the book.

1.1 Key Players in International Business

1.1 Identify the types of companies active in international business.

Companies of all types and sizes and in all sorts of industries become involved in international business; yet, they vary in the extent of their involvement. A small shop owner might only import supplies from abroad, whereas a large company might have dozens of factories located around the world. Large companies from the wealthiest nations still dominate international business. But firms from emerging markets (such as Brazil, China, India, and South Africa) now vigorously compete for global market share. Small and medium-sized companies are also increasingly active in international business, largely because of advances in technology.

Multinational Corporations

A **multinational corporation (MNC)** is a business that has direct investments (in the form of marketing or manufacturing subsidiaries) abroad in multiple countries. Multinationals generate significant jobs, investment, and tax revenue for the regions and nations they enter. Likewise, they can leave thousands of people out of work when they close or scale back operations. Mergers and acquisitions between multinationals are commonly worth billions of dollars and increasingly involve companies based in emerging markets.

multinational corporation (MNC)

Business that has direct investments abroad in multiple countries.

Some companies have more employees than the number of people living in many small countries and island nations. Walmart, for example, has 2.3 million employees. We see the enormous economic clout of multinational corporations when we compare the revenues of the Global 500 ranking of companies with the value of goods and services that countries generate. Figure 1.1 shows the world's 10 largest companies (measured in revenue) inserted into a ranking of nations according to their national output (measured in GDP). If Walmart (www.walmart.com) were a country, it would weigh in as a rich nation and rank just one place behind Sweden. Even the $21 billion in revenue generated by the 500th largest firm in the world, Old Mutual (www.oldmutual .com), exceeds the annual output of many countries.[4]

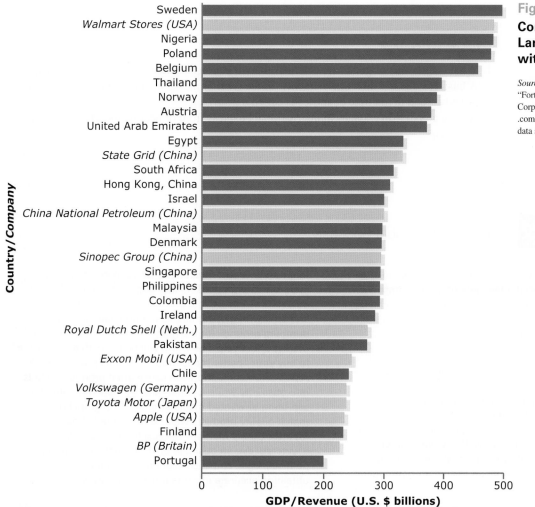

Figure 1.1

Comparing the World's Largest Companies with Select Countries

Source: Based on data obtained from "Fortune Global 500: The 500 Largest Corporations in the World," (www.fortune .com/global500), July 2016; World Bank data set (www.data.worldbank.org).

Entrepreneurs and Small Businesses

born global firm
Company that adopts a global perspective and engages in international business from or near its inception.

International business competition has given rise to a new entity, the **born global firm**—a company that adopts a global perspective and engages in international business from or near its inception. Many of these companies become international competitors in less than three years. Born global firms tend to have *innovative* cultures and *knowledge-based* organizational capabilities. In this age of globalization, companies are exporting earlier and growing faster, often with help from technology.

Small firms selling traditional products benefit from technology that lowers the costs and difficulties of global communication. Vellus Products (www.vellus.com) of Columbus, Ohio, makes and sells pet-grooming products. Some years ago, a dog breeder in Spain became Vellus's first distributor after the breeder received a request for more information about Vellus's products from a man in Bahrain. Sharon Kay Doherty, president of Vellus, says she was stunned that she could so easily process a transaction with someone so far away. Today Vellus has distributors in 35 countries. It is a truly born global business in that, soon after going international, Vellus earned more than half its revenues from international sales.[5]

Electronic distribution for firms that sell digitized products is an effective alternative to traditional distribution channels. Alessandro Naldi's Weekend in Italy website (en.firenze.waf .it) offers visitors more authentic Florentine products than they'll find in the scores of over-priced tourist shops in downtown Florence. A Florentine himself, Naldi established his site to sell high-quality, authentic Italian merchandise made only in the small factories of Tuscany. Weekend in Italy averages 200,000 visitors each month from places as far away as Australia, Canada, Japan, Mexico, and the United States.[6] For additional insights into how small and large companies alike succeed in international markets, see the Manager's Briefcase, titled "The Keys to Global Success."

QUICK STUDY 1

1. What is the value of goods and services that all nations of the world export every year?
2. A business that has direct investments (in the form of marketing or manufacturing subsidiaries) abroad in multiple countries is called a *what*?
3. A born global firm engages in international business from or near its inception and does *what else*?

MANAGER'S BRIEFCASE   The Keys to Global Success

Making everything from 99-cent hamburgers (McDonald's) to $150 million jumbo jets (Boeing), managers of global companies must overcome obstacles when competing in unfamiliar markets. Global managers acknowledge certain common threads in their approaches to management and offer the following advice:

- **Communicate Effectively** Cultural differences in business relationships and etiquette are central to global business and require cross-cultural competency. Effective global managers welcome uniqueness and ambiguity while demonstrating flexibility, respect, and empathy.
- **Know the Customer** Successful managers understand how a company's different products serve the needs of international customers. Then, they ensure that the company remains flexible and capable enough to customize products that meet those needs.

- **Emphasize Global Awareness** Good global managers integrate foreign markets into business strategy from the outset. They ensure that products and services are designed and built with global markets in mind, and not used as dumping grounds for the home market's outdated products.
- **Market Effectively** The world will beat a path to your door to buy your "better mousetrap" only if it knows about it. A poor marketing effort can cause great products to fade into obscurity while an international marketing blunder can bring unwanted media attention. Top global managers match quality products with excellent marketing.
- **Monitor Global Markets** Successful managers keep a watchful eye on business environments for shifting political, legal, and socioeconomic conditions. They make obtaining accurate information a top priority.

We see the result of embracing globalization in this photo of sky-scrapers in the Lujiazui Financial and Trade Zone of the Pudong New Area in Shanghai, China. After years of stunning economic growth and expansion, Shanghai has emerged as a key city for companies entering China's market-place. Pudong was developed to reinvigorate Shanghai as an international trade and financial center, and is now a modern, cosmopolitan district. How has globalization changed the economic landscape of your city and state?

Amanda Hall/Robertharding/Alamy Stock Photo

1.2 What Is Globalization?

Nations historically retained absolute control over the products, people, and capital crossing their borders. But today, economies are becoming increasingly intertwined. This greater interdependence means an increasingly freer flow of goods, services, money, people, and ideas across national borders. **Globalization** is the name we give to this trend toward greater economic, cultural, political, and technological interdependence among national institutions and economies. Globalization is characterized by *denationalization* (national boundaries becoming less relevant) and is different from *internationalization* (entities cooperating across national boundaries).

It is helpful to put today's globalization into context. The first age of globalization extended from the mid-1800s to the 1920s.[7] In those days, labor was highly mobile, with 300,000 people leaving Europe each year in the 1800s and 1 million people leaving each year after 1900.[8] Other than in wartime, nations did not even require passports for international travel before 1914. Like today, workers in wealthy nations feared they might lose their jobs to workers living in other high- and low-wage countries.

Trade and capital flowed more freely than ever during that first age of globalization. Huge companies from wealthy nations built facilities in distant lands to extract raw materials and to produce all sorts of goods. Large cargo ships plied the seas to deliver their manufactures to distant markets. The transatlantic cable (completed in 1866) allowed news between Europe and the United States to travel faster than ever before. The drivers of the first age of globalization included the steamship, telegraph, railroad, and, later, the telephone and airplane.

The first age of globalization was halted abruptly by the arrival of the First World War, the Russian Revolution, and the Great Depression. A backlash to fierce competition in trade and to unfettered immigration in the early 1900s helped to usher in high tariffs and barriers to immigration. The great flows of goods, capital, and people common before the First World War became a mere trickle. For 75 years from the start of the First World War to the end of the Cold War, the world remained divided. There was a geographic divide between East and West and an ideological divide between communism and capitalism. After the Second World War, the West experienced steady economic gains, but international flows of goods, capital, and people were confined to their respective capitalist and communist systems and geographies.

Fast-forward to 1989 and the collapse of the wall separating East and West Berlin. One by one, central and eastern European nations rejected communism and began marching toward democratic institutions and free-market economic systems. Although it took until the 1990s for

1.2 Explain globalization and how it affects markets and production.

globalization
Trend toward greater economic, cultural, political, and technological interdependence among national institutions and economies.

international capital flows, in absolute terms, to recover to levels seen prior to the First World War, the global economy had finally been *reborn*. The drivers of this second age of globalization include communication satellites, fiber optics, microchips, and the Internet.

Let's explore two areas of business in which globalization is having profound effects: the globalization of *markets* and *production*.

Globalization of Markets

Globalization of markets refers to the convergence in buyer preferences in markets around the world. This trend occurs in many product categories, including consumer goods, industrial products, and business services. Clothing retailer L.L. Bean (www.llbean.com), shoe producer Nike (www.nike.com), and electronics maker Vizio (www.vizio.com) are just three companies that sell *global products*—products marketed in all countries essentially without any changes. For example, the iPad qualifies as a global product because of its highly standardized features and because of Apple's global marketing strategy and globally recognized brand.

Global products and global competition characterize many industries and markets, including semiconductors (Intel, Philips), aircraft (Airbus, Boeing), construction equipment (Caterpillar, Mitsubishi), automobiles (Toyota, Volkswagen), financial services (Citicorp, HSBC), air travel (Lufthansa, Singapore Airlines), accounting services (Ernst & Young, KPMG), consumer goods (Procter & Gamble, Unilever), and fast food (KFC, McDonald's). The globalization of markets is important to international business because of the benefits it offers companies. Let's now look briefly at each of those benefits.

REDUCES MARKETING COSTS Companies that sell global products can reduce costs by *standardizing* certain marketing activities. A company selling a global consumer good, such as shampoo, can make an identical product for the global market and then simply design different packaging to account for the language spoken in each market. Companies can achieve further cost savings by keeping an ad's visual component the same for all markets but dubbing TV ads and translating print ads into local languages.

CREATES NEW MARKET OPPORTUNITIES A company that sells a global product can explore opportunities abroad if its home market is small or becomes saturated. China holds enormous potential for online business with more than 700 million Internet users, which is greater than the population of the entire United States. As time goes on, more and more people in China will go online to research and purchase products. The appeal of reaching such a vast audience drives firms from relatively small countries to explore doing business in the Chinese market.

LEVELS UNEVEN INCOME STREAMS A company that sells a product with universal, but seasonal, appeal can use international sales to level its income stream. By supplementing domestic sales with international sales, the company can reduce or eliminate wide variations in sales between seasons and steady its cash flow. For example, a firm that produces suntan and sunblock lotions can match product distribution with the summer seasons in the northern and southern hemispheres in alternating fashion—thereby steadying its income from these global, yet highly seasonal, products.

LOCAL BUYERS' NEEDS In the pursuit of the potential benefits of global markets, managers must constantly monitor the match between the firm's products and markets in order to not overlook the needs of buyers. The benefit of serving customers with an adapted product might outweigh the benefit of a standardized one. For instance, soft drinks, fast food, and other consumer goods are global products that continue to penetrate markets around the world. But sometimes these products require small modifications to better suit local tastes. In southern Japan, Coca-Cola (www.cocacola.com) sweetens its traditional formula to compete with the sweeter-tasting Pepsi (www.pepsi.com). In India, where cows are sacred and the consumption of beef is taboo, McDonald's (www.mcdonalds.com) markets the "Maharaja Mac"—two all-mutton patties on a sesame-seed bun with all the usual toppings.

sustainability
Development that meets the needs of the present without compromising the ability of future generations to meet their own needs.

GLOBAL SUSTAINABILITY Another need that multinationals must consider is the need among all the world's people for **sustainability**—development that meets the needs of the present without compromising the ability of future generations to meet their own needs.[9] Most companies today operate in an environment of increased transparency and scrutiny regarding their business

GLOBAL SUSTAINABILITY   Three Markets, Three Strategies

A company adapts its business strategy to the nuances of the market it enters. The world's population of 7.5 billion people lives in three different types of markets:

- **Developed Markets.** These include the world's established consumer markets, around *one billion* people. The population is solidly middle class, and people can consume almost any product desired. The infrastructure is highly developed and efficient.
- **Emerging Markets.** These markets, around *two billion* people, are racing to catch up to developed nations. The population is migrating to cities for better pay and is overloading cities' infrastructures. Rising incomes are increasing global demand for resources and basic products.
- **Traditional Markets.** Globalization has bypassed these markets, nearly *four billion* people. The population is mostly rural, the infrastructure is very poor, and there is little credit or collateral. People have almost no legal protections, and corruption prevails.

Like business strategy, sustainability strategies reflect local conditions. Examples of businesses working toward sustainability in these three markets include the following:

- **Toyota** focused on the environment in its *developed markets*. After extensively researching gas-electric hybrid technologies, Toyota launched the Prius. As *Motor Trend*'s Car of the Year, the Prius drove Toyota's profits to record highs and gave it a "green" image.
- **Shree Cement** faced limited access to low-cost energy in India's *emerging market*, so it developed the world's most energy-efficient process for making its products. The world's leading cement companies now visit Shree to learn from its innovations in energy usage.
- **Blommer Chocolate** of the United States works closely with cocoa farmers in *traditional markets*. Blommer received the Rainforest Alliance's "Sustainable Standard-Setter" award for training farmers in safe farming practices, environmental stewardship, and HIV awareness.

Sources: Wang Wen, "Emerging Markets are Set to Lead Globalisation," *Financial Times* (www.ft.com), April 10, 2017; Jeremy Jurgens and Knut Haanæs, "Companies from Emerging Markets Are the New Sustainability Champions," *The Guardian* (www.guardian.co.uk), October 12, 2011; Stuart L. Hart, *Capitalism at the Crossroads, Third Edition* (Upper Saddle River, NJ: Wharton School Publishing, 2010); Daniel C. Esty and Andrew S. Winston, *Green to Gold* (New Haven, CT: Yale University Press, 2006).

---

activities. The rise of social media is partly responsible for this trend. Concerned individuals and nongovernmental organizations will very quickly use Internet media to call out any firm caught harming the environment or society.

For years, forward-looking businesses have employed the motto, "reduce, reuse, and recycle." The idea is to *reduce* the use of resources and waste, *reuse* resources with more than a single-use lifespan, and *recycle* what cannot be reduced or reused. The most dedicated managers and firms promote sustainable communities by adding to that motto, "redesign and reimagine." This means *redesigning* products and processes for sustainability and *reimagining* how a product is designed and used to lessen its environmental impact.[10] To read more about the call for more sustainable business practices, see the Global Sustainability feature, "Three Markets, Three Strategies."

Globalization of Production

Globalization of production refers to the dispersal of production activities to locations that help a company achieve its cost-minimization or quality-maximization objectives for a good or service. This includes the sourcing of key production inputs (such as raw materials or products for assembly) as well as the international outsourcing of services. Let's now explore the benefits that companies obtain from the globalization of production.

ACCESS LOWER-COST WORKERS Global production activities allow companies to reduce overall production costs through access to low-cost labor. For decades, companies located their factories in low-wage nations in order to churn out all kinds of goods, including toys, small appliances, inexpensive electronics, and textiles. Yet whereas moving production to low-cost locales traditionally meant *production of goods* almost exclusively, it increasingly applies to the *production of services* such as accounting and research. Although most services must be produced where they are consumed, some services can be performed at remote locations where labor costs are lower. Many European and US businesses have moved their customer service and other nonessential operations to places as far away as India to slash costs by as much as 60 percent.

ACCESS TECHNICAL EXPERTISE Companies also produce goods and services abroad to benefit from technical know-how. Film Roman (www.filmroman.com) produces the TV series *The Simpsons*, but it provides key poses and step-by-step frame directions to AKOM Production Company (www.akomkorea.com) in Seoul, South Korea. AKOM then fills in the remaining poses and links them into an animated whole. But there are bumps along the way, says animation director Mark Kirkland. In one middle-of-the-night phone call, Kirkland was explaining to the Koreans how to draw a shooting gun. "They don't allow guns in Korea; it's against the law," says Kirkland. "So they were calling me [asking]: 'How does a gun work?'" Kirkland and others put up with such cultural differences and phone calls at odd hours to tap a highly qualified pool of South Korean animators.[11]

ACCESS PRODUCTION INPUTS Globalization of production allows companies to access resources that are unavailable or costlier at home. The quest for natural resources draws many companies into international markets. Japan, for example, is a small, densely populated island nation with very few natural resources of its own—especially forests. But Japan's largest paper company, Nippon Seishi, does more than simply import wood pulp. The company owns huge forests and corresponding processing facilities in Australia, Canada, and the United States. This ownership not only gives the firm access to an essential resource but also gives it control over earlier stages in the papermaking process. As a result, the company is guaranteed a steady flow of its key ingredient (wood pulp) that is less subject to the swings in prices and supply associated with buying pulp on the open market. Likewise, to access cheaper energy resources used in manufacturing, a variety of Japanese firms are relocating production to China and Vietnam, where energy costs are lower than in Japan.

QUICK STUDY 2

1. Globalization causes the institutions and economies of nations to become *what*?
2. What *benefits* might companies obtain from the globalization of markets?
3. Sustainability is development that meets current needs without compromising *what*?

1.3 Forces Driving Globalization

1.3 Detail the forces that drive globalization.

Two main forces underlie the globalization of markets and production: *falling barriers to trade and investment* and *technological innovation*. These two features, more than anything else, are increasing competition among nations by leveling the global business playing field. Greater competition is driving companies worldwide into more direct confrontation *and* cooperation. Local industries, once isolated by time and distance, are increasingly accessible to large international companies based many thousands of miles away. Some small- and medium-sized local firms are compelled to cooperate with one another or with larger international firms to remain competitive. Other local businesses revitalize themselves in a bold attempt to survive the competitive onslaught. And on a global scale, consolidation is occurring as former competitors in many industries link up to challenge others on a worldwide basis. Let's now explore the pivotal roles of these two forces driving globalization.

Falling Barriers to Trade and Investment

General Agreement on Tariffs and Trade (GATT)

Treaty designed to promote free trade by reducing both tariffs and nontariff barriers to international trade.

In 1947, political leaders of 23 nations (12 developed and 11 developing economies) made history when they created the **General Agreement on Tariffs and Trade (GATT)**—a treaty designed to promote free trade by reducing tariffs and nontariff barriers to international trade. *Tariffs* are essentially taxes levied on traded goods, and *nontariff barriers* are limits on the quantity of an imported product. The treaty was successful in its early years. After four decades, world merchandise trade had grown 20 times larger, and average tariffs had fallen from 40 percent to 5 percent.

Significant progress occurred again with a 1994 revision of the GATT treaty. Nations that had signed on to the treaty further reduced average tariffs on merchandise trade and lowered subsidies (government financial support) for agricultural products. The treaty's revision also clearly defined *intellectual property rights*. This gave protection to copyrights (including computer programs, databases, sound recordings, and films), trademarks and service marks, and patents (including trade secrets and know-how). A major flaw of the original GATT was that it lacked the power to enforce world trade rules. Thus, the creation of the *World Trade Organization* was likely the greatest accomplishment of the GATT revision.

Today, companies can go almost anywhere in the world to tap favorable business climates. Here, an employee at an Asian subsidiary of a global television maker packages TVs headed for global export markets. US businesses use technology to subcontract work to Chinese companies that write computer code and then email their end product to the US clients. Companies use such tactics to lower costs, increase efficiency, and grow more competitive. How else might technology and global talent facilitate international business activity?

Albert Karimov/123RF.com

WORLD TRADE ORGANIZATION The **World Trade Organization (WTO)** is the international organization that enforces the rules of international trade. The three main goals of the WTO (www .wto.org) are to help the free flow of trade, help negotiate the further opening of markets, and settle trade disputes among its members. It is the power of the WTO to settle trade disputes that sets it apart from its predecessor, the GATT. The various WTO agreements are essentially contracts between member nations that commit them to maintaining fair and open trade policies. Offenders must realign their trade policies according to WTO guidelines or face fines and, perhaps, trade sanctions (penalties). Because of its ability to penalize offending nations, the WTO's dispute-settlement system truly is the spine of the global trading system. The WTO replaced the *institution* of GATT but absorbed all of the former GATT *agreements*. Thus, the GATT institution no longer officially exists. Today, the WTO recognizes 164 members and 21 "observers."

The WTO launched a new round of negotiations in Doha, Qatar, in late 2001. The renewed negotiations were designed to lower trade barriers further and to help poor nations, in particular. Agricultural subsidies that rich countries pay to their own farmers are worth $1 billion per day—more than six times the value of their combined aid budgets to poor nations. Because 70 percent of poor nations' exports are agricultural products and textiles, wealthy nations had intended to further open these and other labor-intensive industries. Poor nations were encouraged to reduce tariffs among themselves and were supposed to receive help in integrating themselves into the global trading system.

Although the Doha round was to conclude by the end of 2004, negotiations are proceeding very slowly. By the middle of 2017, members had made limited progress on a late 2013 deal to improve "trade facilitation" by reducing red tape at borders and setting standards for customs and the movement of goods internationally. Although the agreement marked the first significant achievement for the Doha round, no agreement was reached on agricultural trade issues, tariffs, or quotas.[12]

OTHER INTERNATIONAL ORGANIZATIONS Two other institutions play leading roles in fostering globalization. The **World Bank** is an agency created to provide financing for national economic development efforts. The initial purpose of the World Bank (www.worldbank.org) was to finance European reconstruction following the Second World War. The bank later shifted its focus to the general financial needs of developing countries, and today it finances many economic development projects in Africa, South America, and Southeast Asia.

The **International Monetary Fund (IMF)** is an agency created to regulate fixed exchange rates and to enforce the rules of the international monetary system. Among the purposes of the

World Trade Organization (WTO)

International organization that enforces the rules of international trade.

World Bank

Agency created to provide financing for national economic development efforts.

International Monetary Fund

Agency created to regulate fixed exchange rates and to enforce the rules of the international monetary system.

IMF (www.imf.org) are promoting international monetary cooperation, facilitating the expansion and balanced growth of international trade, avoiding competitive exchange devaluation, and making financial resources temporarily available to members.

REGIONAL TRADE AGREEMENTS In addition to the WTO, smaller groups of nations are integrating their economies by fostering trade and boosting cross-border investment. For example, the *North American Free Trade Agreement (NAFTA)* gathers three nations (Canada, Mexico, and the United States) into a free-trade bloc. The more ambitious *European Union (EU)* combines 28 countries. The *Asia Pacific Economic Cooperation (APEC)* consists of 21 member economies committed to creating a free-trade zone around the Pacific. The aims of each of these smaller trade pacts are similar to those of the WTO but are regional in nature. Moreover, some nations encourage regional pacts because of recent resistance to worldwide trade agreements.

TRADE AND NATIONAL OUTPUT Together the WTO agreements and regional pacts have boosted world trade and cross-border investment significantly. Trade theory tells us that openness to trade helps a nation produce a greater amount of output. Map 1.1 illustrates that growth in national output over a recent 10-year period has been significantly positive. Economic growth has been greater in nations that have recently become more open to trade, such as China, India, and Russia, than it has been in many other countries. Much of South America is also growing rapidly, whereas Africa's experience is mixed.

Let's take a moment in our discussion to define a few terms that we will encounter time and again throughout this book. **Gross domestic product (GDP)** is the value of all goods and services produced by a domestic economy during a one-year period. We can speak in terms of world GDP when we sum all individual nations' GDP figures. GDP is a somewhat narrower figure than **gross national product (GNP)**—the value of all goods and services produced by a country's domestic and international activities during a one-year period. GNP includes a nation's income generated from exports, imports, and the international operations of its companies. A country's **GDP or GNP per capita** is simply its GDP or GNP divided by its population.

gross domestic product (GDP)
Value of all goods and services produced by a domestic economy during a one-year period.

gross national product (GNP)
Value of all goods and services produced by a country's domestic and international activities during a one-year period.

GDP or GNP per capita
Nation's GDP or GNP divided by its population.

Technological Innovation

Although falling barriers to trade and investment encourage globalization, technology is accelerating its pace. Innovations in information technology and transportation methods are making it easier, faster, and less costly to move data, goods, and equipment around the world. Consumers use technology to reach out to the world on the Internet—gathering and sending information and purchasing all kinds of goods and services. Companies use technology to acquire materials and products from distant lands and to sell goods and services abroad.

When businesses or consumers use technology to conduct transactions, they engage in **e-business (e-commerce)**—the use of computer networks to purchase, sell, or exchange products; to service customers; and to collaborate with partners. E-business is making it easier for companies to make their products abroad, not simply to import and export finished goods. Let's examine several innovations that have had a considerable impact on globalization.

e-business (e-commerce)
Use of computer networks to purchase, sell, or exchange products; to service customers; and to collaborate with partners.

EMAIL AND VIDEOCONFERENCING Operating across borders and time zones complicates the job of coordinating and controlling business activities. But technology can speed the flow of information and ease the tasks of coordination and control. Email is an indispensable tool that managers use to stay in contact with international operations and to respond quickly to important matters.

Videoconferencing allows managers in different locations to meet in virtual face-to-face meetings. Primary reasons for 25 percent to 30 percent annual growth in videoconferencing include the lower cost of bandwidth (communication channels) used to transmit information, the lower cost of equipment, and the rising cost of travel for businesses. Videoconferencing equipment can cost as little as several thousand dollars and as much as several hundred thousand dollars. A company that does not require ongoing video-conferencing can pay even less by renting the facilities and equipment of a local conference center. Those willing to videoconference on a computer, tablet, or smartphone (which includes most people today) can explore iMeet (www.imeet.com), which charges $9 per month for its most basic service.[13] And, of course, people with the simplest video conferencing needs can download and use Skype (www.skype.com), Apple's (www.apple.com) FaceTime, or Google's Hangouts (https://hangouts.google.com) applications free of charge.

THE INTERNET Companies use the Internet to quickly and inexpensively contact managers in distant locations—for example, to inquire about production runs, revise sales strategies, and check on distribution bottlenecks. They also use the Internet to achieve longer-term goals, such as sharpen their forecasting, lower their inventories, and improve communication with suppliers. The lower cost of reaching an international customer base especially benefits small firms, which were among the first to use the Internet as a global marketing tool. Additional gains arise from the ability of the Internet to cut postproduction costs by decreasing the number of intermediaries a product passes through on its way to the customer. Eliminating intermediaries greatly benefits online sellers of all sorts of products, including books, music, travel services, and software.

Some innovative companies use online competitions to attract fresh ideas from the brightest minds worldwide. InnoCentive (www.innocentive.com) connects companies and institutions seeking solutions to difficult problems by using a global network of 300,000 creative thinkers. These engineers, scientists, inventors, and businesspeople with expertise in life sciences, engineering, chemistry, math, computer science, and entrepreneurship compete to solve some of the world's toughest problems in return for significant financial awards. InnoCentive is open to anyone, is available in seven languages, and pays cash awards that range from $5,000 to more than $1 million.[14]

COMPANY INTRANETS AND EXTRANETS Internal company websites and information networks (*intranets*) give employees access to company data using personal computers. A particularly effective marketing tool on Volvo Car Corporation's (www.volvocars.com) intranet is a quarter-by-quarter database of marketing and sales information. The cycle begins when headquarters submits its corporate-wide marketing plan to Volvo's intranet. Marketing managers at each subsidiary worldwide then select those activities that apply to their own market, develop their marketing plan, and submit it to the database. This allows managers in every market to view every other subsidiary's marketing plan and to adapt relevant aspects to their own plan. In essence, the entire system acts as a tool for the sharing of best practices across all of Volvo's markets.

Extranets give distributors and suppliers access to a company's database so they can place orders or restock inventories electronically and automatically. These networks permit international companies (along with their suppliers and buyers) to respond to internal and external conditions more quickly and more appropriately.

ADVANCEMENTS IN TRANSPORTATION TECHNOLOGIES Retailers worldwide rely on imports to stock their storerooms with finished goods and to supply factories with raw materials and intermediate products. Innovation in the shipping industry is helping globalize markets and production by making shipping more efficient and dependable. In the past, a cargo ship would sit in port up to 10 days while it was unloaded one pallet at a time. But because cargo today is loaded onto a ship in 20- and 40-foot containers that are unloaded quickly at the destination onto railcars or truck chassis, a 700-foot cargo ship is routinely unloaded in just 15 hours.

Operation of cargo ships is now simpler and safer because of computerized charts that pinpoint a ship's movements on the high seas using Global Positioning System (GPS) satellites. Combining GPS with radio frequency identification (RFID) technology allows continuous monitoring of individual containers from port of departure to destination. RFID can tell whether a container's doors are opened and closed on its journey and can send an alert if a container deviates from its planned route.

These types of advancements allowed Hewlett-Packard (www.hp.com) to seize the rewards of globalization when it built a new low-cost computer server for businesses. HP dispersed its design and production activities throughout a specialized manufacturing system across five Pacific Rim nations and India. This helped the company minimize labor costs, taxes, and shipping delays yet maximize productivity when designing, building, and distributing its new product. Companies use such innovative production and distribution techniques to squeeze inefficiencies out of their international operations and boost their competitiveness.

⭐ **MyLab Management** Watch It Save the Children Social Networking

Apply what you have learned about the use of technology in management. If your instructor has assigned this, go to **www.pearson.com/mylab/management** to watch a video case about how a not-for-profit enterprise uses social media to achieve its goals and answer questions.

Map 1.1
Growth in National Output

Average annual GDP growth rate, (%)

negative
- less than -2.5
- -2.5 to 0
- no data available

positive
- 0 to 1
- 1 to 2
- 2 to 3
- 3 to 4
- 4 to 5
- over 5

TABLE 1.1 Globalization's Top 10

Country	Rank			
	Overall	Economic	Social	Political
Netherlands	1	4	4	5
Ireland	2	2	3	25
Belgium	3	6	6	3
Austria	4	16	5	7
Switzerland	5	22	2	10
Denmark	6	15	9	11
Sweden	7	17	16	4
United Kingdom	8	20	13	6
France	9	30	11	1
Hungary	10	7	23	23

Source: Based on the 2017 KOF Index of Globalization (www.globalization.kof.ethz.ch), April 20, 2017.

Measuring Globalization

Although we intuitively feel that our world is becoming smaller, researchers have created ways to measure the extent of globalization scientifically. One index of globalization is that created by the KOF Swiss Economic Institute (www.kof.ethz.ch). This index ranks nations on 23 variables within three dimensions: economic globalization (trade and investment volumes, trade and capital restrictions), social globalization (dissemination of information and ideas), and political globalization (political cooperation with other countries).[15]

By incorporating a wide variety of variables, the globalization index attempts to cut through cycles occurring in any single category and to capture the broad nature of globalization. Table 1.1 shows the 10 highest-ranking nations according to the KOF Index of Globalization. European nations occupy all top 10 positions, with smaller nations clearly dominating the rankings. The United States appears in 27th place overall, and ranks 54th in economic globalization, 30th in social globalization, and 19th in political globalization. Large nations often do not make it into the higher ranks of globalization indices because a large home market means they tend to depend less on external trade and investment.

The world's least-globalized nations account for about half the world's population and are found in Africa, East Asia, South Asia, Latin America, and the Middle East. Some of the least-globalized nations are characterized by never-ending political unrest and corruption (Bangladesh, Indonesia, and Venezuela). Other nations with large agricultural sectors face trade barriers in developed countries and are subject to highly volatile prices on commodity markets (Brazil, China, and India). Still others are heavily dependent on oil exports but are plagued by erratic prices in energy markets (Iran and Venezuela). Kenya has suffered from recurring droughts, terrorism, and burdensome visa regulations that hurt tourism. Finally, Turkey and Egypt, along with the entire Middle East, suffer from continued concerns about violence and social unrest, high barriers to trade and investment, and heavy government involvement in the economy. To deepen their global links, these nations will need to make great strides forward in their economic, social, and political environments.

QUICK STUDY 3

1. What global organizations have helped expand globalization?
2. What technological innovations are helping to propel globalization?
3. What nation ranks high in terms of globalization?

1.4 Debate about Jobs and Wages

So far, we have read how globalization benefits companies and nations. But not everyone views globalization as having only positive effects. The following pages explain the main debates about globalization. Opposing sides in each debate tend to hold up results of social and economic studies that support their arguments. But many organizations that publish studies about globalization have political agendas, which can make objective consideration of their findings difficult. A group's aims can influence the selection of the data to analyze, the time period to study, the nations to examine, and so forth.

Be that as it may, we open our coverage of the globalization debate with an important topic for both developed and developing countries—the effect of globalization on jobs and wages. We begin with the arguments of those against globalization and then turn our attention to how supporters of globalization respond.

1.4 Outline the debate about globalization's impact on jobs and wages.

Against Globalization

Groups opposed to globalization blame it for eroding standards of living and ruining ways of life. Specifically, they say globalization *eliminates jobs* and *lowers wages* in developed nations and *exploits workers* in developing countries. Let's explore each of these arguments.

ELIMINATES JOBS IN DEVELOPED NATIONS Some groups claim that *globalization eliminates manufacturing jobs in developed nations*. They criticize the practice of sending good-paying manufacturing jobs abroad to developing countries where wages are a fraction of the cost for international firms. They argue that a label reading "Made in China" translates to "Not Made Here." Critics admit that importing products from China (or another low-wage nation) lowers consumer prices for televisions, sporting goods, and so on, but say this is little consolation for workers who lose their jobs.

To illustrate their argument, globalization critics point to the activities of large retailers such as Amazon (www.amazon.com) and Walmart (www.walmart.com). It is difficult to overstate the power of these retail giants and symbols of globalization. Some say that by relentlessly pursuing low-cost goods, these retailers force their suppliers to move to China and other low-wage nations.

LOWERS WAGES IN DEVELOPED NATIONS Opposition groups say *globalization causes worker dislocation that gradually lowers wages*. They allege that when a manufacturing job is lost in a wealthy nation, the new job (assuming new work is found) pays less than the previous one. Those opposed to globalization say this decreases employee loyalty, employee morale, and job security. They say this causes people to fear globalization and any additional lowering of trade barriers.

Large retailers also come under fire in this discussion. Globalization critics say powerful retailers continually force manufacturers in low-wage nations to accept lower profits so that the retailers can slash prices to consumers. Critics charge that these business practices force down wages and working conditions worldwide.

EXPLOITS WORKERS IN DEVELOPING NATIONS Critics charge that *globalization and international outsourcing exploit workers in low-wage nations*. One notable critic of globalization, Naomi Klein, vehemently opposes the outsourced call center jobs of Western companies. Klein says these jobs force young Asians to disguise their nationality, adopt fake Midwestern accents, and work nights when their US customers are awake halfway around the world.[16]

Figure 1.2 illustrates that Western firms can outsource such work to emerging markets for a fraction of what they pay at home. As long as such economic disparities exist, international outsourcing will continue to be popular. The salary of a programmer in the United States is nearly four times that of one in some eastern European nations, including Lithuania.

Globalization critics also say companies locate operations to developing nations where labor regulations are least restrictive and, therefore, least costly. They argue that this diminishes labor's bargaining power and labor laws in all countries as nations compete to attract international firms.

For Globalization

Supporters of globalization credit it with improving standards of living and making possible new ways of life. They argue that globalization *increases wealth and efficiency in all nations*, *generates labor market flexibility in developed nations*, and *advances the economies of developing nations*. Let's examine each of these arguments.

Figure 1.2

Comparing Salaries of Information Technology Workers

Source: Based on data obtained from the *International Average Salary Income Database* (www.worldsalaries.org).

Average annual net income of an Information Technology worker living in:

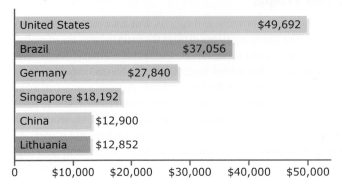

INCREASES WEALTH AND EFFICIENCY IN ALL NATIONS Globalization supporters believe *globalization increases wealth and efficiency in both developed and developing nations.* They argue that openness to international trade increases national production (by increasing efficiency) and raises per capita income (by passing savings on to consumers). For instance, by squeezing inefficiencies out of the retail supply chain, powerful global retailers help restrain inflation and boost productivity. Some economists predict that removing all remaining barriers to free trade would significantly boost worldwide income and greatly benefit developing nations.

GENERATES LABOR MARKET FLEXIBILITY IN DEVELOPED NATIONS Globalization supporters believe *globalization creates positive benefits by generating labor market flexibility in developed nations.* Some claim that there are benefits from worker dislocation, or "churning" as it is called when there is widespread job turnover throughout an economy. Flexible labor markets allow workers to be redeployed rapidly to sectors of the economy where they are highly valued and in demand. This also allows employees, particularly young workers, to change jobs easily with few negative effects. For instance, a young person can gain experience and skills with an initial employer and then move to a different job that provides a better match between employee and employer.

ADVANCES THE ECONOMIES OF DEVELOPING NATIONS Those in favor of globalization argue that *globalization and international outsourcing help to advance developing nations' economies.* India initially became attractive as a location for software-writing operations because of its low-cost, well-trained, English-speaking technicians. Later, young graduates who would not become doctors and lawyers found bright futures in telephone call centers that provide all sorts of customer services. More recently, jobs in business-process outsourcing (including financial, accounting, payroll, and benefits services) is elevating living standards in India.

Today, the relentless march of globalization is bringing call center jobs to the Philippines. Young Filipinos possess an excellent education, a solid grasp of the English language and US culture, and a neutral accent. In fact, top Indian firms, such as Wipro (www.wipro.com), have substantial operations in the Philippines and happily pay as much or more than what they would pay workers in India. The work is not considered low-paying by any means, and instead represents a solid, middle-class job.

The International Labor Organization (www.ilo.org) found no evidence that nations with a strong union presence suffered any loss of investment in their *export-processing zones (EPZs)*— special regions that allow tariff-free importing and exporting. And the World Bank found that the higher occupational safety and health conditions an EPZ had in place, the greater the amount of foreign investment it attracted.[17] The evidence suggests that economic openness and foreign investment advances the economies of developing nations.

Summary of the Jobs and Wages Debate

All parties appear to agree that globalization eliminates some jobs in a nation but creates jobs in other sectors of the nation's economy. Yet, although some people lose their jobs and find new employment, it can be very difficult for others to find new work. The real point of difference between the two sides in the debate, it seems, is whether overall gains that (might or might not) accrue to *national economies* are worth the lost livelihoods that *individuals* (might or might not) suffer. Those in favor of globalization say individual pain is worth the collective gain, whereas those against globalization say it is not.

QUICK STUDY 4

1. In the debate about jobs and wages, opponents of globalization say that it does *what*?
2. In the debate about jobs and wages, supporters of globalization say that it does *what*?

1.5 Debate about Income Inequality

Perhaps no controversy swirling around globalization is more complex than the debate about its effect on income inequality. Here, we focus on three main aspects of the debate: inequality within nations, inequality between nations, and global inequality.

1.5 Summarize the debate about income inequality.

Inequality within Nations

The first aspect of the inequality debate is whether globalization increases income inequality among people *within* nations. Opponents of globalization argue that freer trade and investment allows international companies to close factories in high-wage, developed nations and to move them to low-wage, developing nations. They argue that this increases the wage gap between white-collar and blue-collar occupations in rich nations.

Two studies of *developed and developing nations* find contradictory evidence about this argument. The first study, of 38 countries for almost 30 years, supports the increasing inequality argument. The study found that as a nation increases its openness to trade, income growth among the poorest 40 percent of its population declines, whereas income growth among other groups increases.[18] The second study, of 80 countries for 40 years, failed to support the increasing inequality argument. It found that incomes of the poor rise one-for-one with overall economic growth and concluded that the poor benefit from international trade along with the rest of a nation.[19]

Two studies of *developing nations only* are more consistent in their findings. One study found that an increase in the ratio of trade to national output of 1 percent raised average income levels by 0.5 to 2 percent. Another study showed that incomes of the poor kept pace with growth in average incomes in economies (and periods) of fast trade integration, but that the poor fell behind during periods of declining openness.[20] Results of these two studies suggest that, by integrating their economies into the global economy, developing nations (by far the nations with the most to gain) can boost the incomes of their poorest residents.

Another approach takes a multidimensional view of poverty and deprivation. Proponents of this approach say that the problem with focusing on income alone is that higher income does not necessarily translate into better health or nutrition. The new approach examines 10 basic factors, including whether the family home has a decent toilet and electricity service; whether children are enrolled in school; and whether family members are malnourished or must walk more than 30 minutes to obtain clean drinking water. A household is considered poor if it is "deprived" on more than 30 percent of the indicators. This new approach reveals important differences among poor regions. For example, whereas material measures contribute more to poverty in sub-Saharan Africa, malnutrition is a bigger factor in South Asia.[21]

Inequality between Nations

The second aspect of the inequality debate is whether globalization widens the gap in average incomes *between* rich and poor nations. If we compare average incomes in high-income countries with average incomes in middle- and low-income nations, we do find a widening gap. But *averages* conceal differences between nations.

On closer inspection, it appears the gap between rich and poor nations does not occur everywhere: *One group of poor nations is closing the gap with rich economies, while a second group of poor countries is falling further behind.* For example, China is narrowing the income gap between itself and the United States as measured by GDP per capita, but the gap between Africa and the United States is widening. China's progress is no doubt a result of its integration with the world economy and annual economic growth rates of between 7 percent and 9 percent. Another emerging market, India, also is narrowing its income gap with the United States by embracing globalization.[22]

Developing countries that embrace globalization are increasing personal incomes, extending life expectancies, and improving education systems. In addition, post-communist countries that

Here we see a home along a dirt road in Cambodia where 11 members of a family live. Cambodia is a "traditional" market that has not benefited as much from globalization as have other nations. Living conditions like the plight of the family that lives here incites calls for a wider distribution of the benefits of economic progress. What, if anything, do you think businesses and governments can do to improve the lives of people enduring such harsh living conditions?

Ozgur Yusuf Cagdas/123RF.com

welcomed world trade and investment experienced high growth rates in GDP per capita. But nations that remain closed off from the world economy have performed far worse.

Global Inequality

The third aspect of the inequality debate is whether globalization increases *global inequality*—widening income inequality between all people of the world, no matter where they live. Recent studies paint a promising picture of declining poverty worldwide. The World Bank estimates the percentage of the world's population living on less than $1.90 per day day (a common poverty gauge revised upward from one dollar per day) fell from 42 percent to just below 11 percent between 1981 and 2013. In population figures, whereas 1.9 billion people were extremely poor in 1981, just 767 million people were poor in 2013, taking population growth into account.[23] Much of the decline in global poverty is the direct result of economic progress in China. Today there is little debate about this topic. Most experts agree that global inequality has fallen and might disagree only on the extent of the fall.

The continent of Africa presents the most pressing problem. Africa accounts for just 3 percent of world GDP, but is home to 13 percent of the world's population and more than half the world's extremely poor. What it is like to live on less than $1.90 per day in sub-Saharan Africa, South Asia, or elsewhere is too difficult for most of us to comprehend. Rich nations realize they cannot sit idly by while so many of the world's people live in such conditions. Still, the United Nations' Sustainable Development Goal of reducing global poverty to 3 percent by 2030 will be difficult to meet.

What can be done to help the world's poor? First, rich nations could increase the amount of foreign aid they give to poor nations—foreign aid as a share of donor country GDP is at historically low levels. Second, rich nations can accelerate the process of forgiving some of the debt burdens of the most heavily indebted poor countries (HIPCs). The HIPC initiative is committed to reducing the debt burdens of the world's poorest countries. This initiative would enable these countries to spend money on social services and greater integration with the global economy instead of on interest payments on debt.

SUMMARY OF THE INCOME INEQUALITY DEBATE   For the debate about inequality *within nations*, studies suggest that developing nations can boost incomes of their poorest people by embracing globalization and integrating themselves into the global economy. In the debate about inequality *between nations*, nations open to world trade and investment appear to grow faster than rich nations do. Meanwhile, economies that remain sheltered from the global economy tend to be worse off. Finally, regarding the debate about *global inequality*, although experts agree inequality has fallen in recent decades, they might disagree only on the extent of the drop.

1. Evidence suggests that globalization can help developing nations boost incomes for their poorest people in *what part* of the debate about inequality?
2. In the debate about inequality *between nations*, evidence suggests that developing nations that are open to trade and investment do *what*?
3. Regarding the debate about *global inequality*, experts tend to agree about *what*?

1.6 Debate about Culture, Sovereignty, and the Environment

Coverage of the globalization debate would be incomplete without examining several additional topics in the globalization debate. Let's now look at globalization's effect on a nation's culture, sovereignty, and physical environment.

1.6 Outline the debate about culture, sovereignty, and the environment.

Globalization and Culture

National culture is a strong shaper of a people's values, attitudes, customs, beliefs, and communication. Whether globalization eradicates cultural differences between groups of people or reinforces cultural uniqueness is a hotly debated topic.

Globalization's detractors say that it homogenizes our world and destroys our rich diversity of cultures. They say that in some drab, new world we all will wear the same clothes bought at the same brand-name shops, eat the same foods at the same brand-name restaurants, and watch the same movies made by the same production companies. Blame is usually placed squarely on the largest multinational companies in consumer goods, which typically are based in the United States.

Supporters argue that globalization allows us all to profit from our differing circumstances and skills. Trade allows countries to specialize in producing the goods and services they can produce most efficiently. Nations then can trade with each other to obtain goods and services they desire but do not produce. In this way, France still produces many of the world's finest wines, South Africa yields much of the world's diamonds, and Japan continues to design some of the world's finest-engineered automobiles. Other nations then trade their goods and services with these countries to enjoy the wines, diamonds, and automobiles that they do not, or cannot, produce. To learn more about the interplay between culture and globalization, see the Culture Matters feature, titled, "The Culture Debate."

CULTURE MATTERS   The Culture Debate

The debate about globalization's influence on culture evokes strong opinions. Here are a few main arguments in this debate:

- **Material Desire.** Critics say globalization fosters the "Coca-Colanization" of nations through advertising campaigns that promote material desire. They also argue that global consumer-goods companies destroy cultural diversity (especially in developing nations) by putting local companies out of business.
- **Artistic Influence.** Evidence suggests, however, that the cultures of developing nations are thriving and that the influence of their music, art, and literature has grown (not shrunk) throughout the past century. African cultures, for example, have influenced the works of artists including Picasso, the Beatles, and Sting.
- **Western Values.** International businesses reach far and wide through the Internet, global media, increased business travel, and local marketing. Critics say local values and traditions are being replaced by US companies promoting "Western" values.

- **A Force for Good.** On the positive side, globalization tends to foster two important values: tolerance and diversity. Advocates say nations should be more tolerant of opposing viewpoints and should welcome diversity among their peoples. This view interprets globalization as a potent force for good in the world.
- **Deeper Values.** Globalization can cause consumer purchases and economic ideologies to converge, but these are rather superficial aspects of culture. Deeper values that embody the essence of cultures might be more resistant to a global consumer culture.
- **Want to Know More?** Visit the globalization page of the Global Policy Forum (www.globalpolicy.org), Globalization 101 (www.globalization101.org), or The Globalist (www.theglobalist.com).

Sources: "Economic Globalization and Culture: A Discussion with Dr. Francis Fukuyama," Merrill Lynch Forum website (www.ml.com); "Globalization Issues," The Globalization website (www.sociology.emory.edu/globalization/index.html); "Cultural Diversity in the Era of Globalization," UNESCO Culture Sector website (www.unesco.org/culture).

Globalization and National Sovereignty

National sovereignty generally involves the idea that a nation-state (1) is autonomous, (2) can freely select its government, (3) cannot intervene in the affairs of other nations, (4) can control movements across its borders, and (5) can enter into binding international agreements. Opposition groups allege that globalization erodes national sovereignty and encroaches on the authority of local and state governments. Supporters disagree, saying that globalization spreads democracy worldwide and that national sovereignty must be viewed from a long-term perspective.

GLOBALIZATION: MENACE TO DEMOCRACY? A main argument leveled against globalization is that it empowers supranational institutions at the expense of national governments. It is not in dispute that the WTO, the IMF, and the United Nations are led by appointed, not democratically elected, representatives. What is debatable, however, is whether these organizations unduly impose their will on the citizens of sovereign nations. Critics argue that such organizations undercut democracy and individual liberty by undermining the political and legal authority of national, regional, and local governments.

Opponents of globalization also take issue with the right of national political authorities to enter binding international agreements on behalf of citizens. Critics charge that such agreements violate the rights of local and state governments. For example, state and local governments in the United States had no role in creating the NAFTA. Yet, WTO rules require the US federal government to take all available actions (including enacting preemptive legislation or withdrawing funding) to force local and state compliance with WTO terms. Protesters say that such requirements directly attack the rights and authority of local and state governments.[24]

GLOBALIZATION: GUARDIAN OF DEMOCRACY? Globalization supporters argue that an amazing consequence of globalization has been the spread of democracy worldwide. In recent decades, the people of many nations have become better educated, better informed, and more empowered. Supporters say globalization has not sent democracy spiraling into decline but instead has been instrumental in spreading democracy to the world.

Backers of globalization also contend that it is instructive to take a long-term view on the issue of national sovereignty. Witnessing a sovereign state's scope of authority altered is nothing new, as governments have long given up trying to control issues they could not resolve. In the mid-1600s, governments in Europe surrendered their authority over religion because attempts to control it undermined overall political stability. Also, Greece in 1832, Albania in 1913, and the former Yugoslavian states in the 1990s had to protect minorities in exchange for international recognition. And during the past 50 years, the United Nations has made significant progress on worthy issues such as genocide, torture, slavery, refugees, women's rights, children's rights, forced labor, and racial discrimination. Like the loss of sovereignty over these issues, globalization supporters say lost sovereignty over some economic issues actually might enhance the greater good.[25]

Globalization and the Environment

Some environmental groups say globalization causes a "race to the bottom" in environmental conditions and regulations. Yet studies show that pollution-intensive US firms tend to invest in countries with stricter environmental standards. Many developing nations, including Argentina, Brazil, Malaysia, and Thailand, liberalized their foreign investment environment while simultaneously enacting *stricter* environmental legislation. If large international companies were eager to relocate to nations having poor environmental protection laws, they would not have invested in these countries for decades. Additional evidence that closed, protectionist economies are worse than open ones at protecting the environment includes Mexico before NAFTA, Brazil under military rule, and the former Warsaw Pact of communist nations—all of which had extremely poor environmental records. Again, the evidence refutes claims that economic openness and globalization lessen environmental standards.

Globalization opponents claim that Western firms exploit lax environmental laws abroad to produce goods that are then exported back to the home countries. These claims have no factual basis and might only perpetuate a false image of corporations. In fact, less than 5 percent of US firms invest in developing countries to obtain low-cost resources and then export finished products back to the United States.

Most international firms today support reasonable environmental laws because (if for no other reason) they want to expand future local markets for their goods and services. They recognize that healthy future markets require a sustainable approach to business expansion. Companies today often examine a location for its potential as a future market as well as a production base.

> ### QUICK STUDY 6
>
> 1. People opposed to globalization say that it does *what* to national cultures?
> 2. Regarding national sovereignty, opponents of globalization say that it does *what*?
> 3. Regarding the physical environment, what do globalization supporters argue?

1.7 Developing Skills for Your Career

Some of you taking this course are majoring in international business or a related business area, such as marketing, business administration, or accounting. Others are majoring in political science, economics, history, psychology, and so forth, and are taking this course to gain insight into how businesses operate in the global economy. But as we read at the beginning of this chapter, and regardless of your chosen field of study, international business activities touch all aspects of our lives today. So, although you might not one day become a manager with direct international business responsibilities, this course will help you develop highly useful capabilities we call *employability skills*, regardless of your chosen career.

1.7 Identify how this course will help you to develop skills for your career.

Critical thinking involves purposeful and goal-directed thinking used to define and solve problems, make decisions, or form judgments related to a set of circumstances. This course will help you to develop this key employability skill. For example, you will use critical thinking skills in this course to study how a country designs its political, economic, and legal systems into a complex arrangement to achieve a specific set of priorities for the nation and its people. Throughout the book, you will be able to put yourself in the position of a business manager and make a decision or solve a dilemma that commonly occurs in business today.

A keener sense of *business ethics and social responsibility* is another employability skill that this course will help you to improve. We define these concepts simply as sets of guiding principles that influence the way individuals and organizations behave within society. You will encounter the issues of personal ethical responsibility and reasoning throughout this course as you read how managers made ethical decisions under specific circumstances and how they fared. You will also read about the social responsibilities that companies face regarding topics such as human rights, fair trade, and sustainable development.

This course also will help to improve your *communication skills*, which is another key employability skill. Communication is the use of oral, written, and nonverbal language, and technology to communicate ideas effectively and to listen effectively. International business means doing business across national borders, across languages, and across cultures. Articulating one's thoughts and ideas in another language and culture must be done in a considerate and mindful way so as to not offend another person's values and beliefs. You will read about many situations in which appropriate communication resulted in successful dealings, and thoughtless communication meant failure of one kind or another. You will see how managers who are posted abroad for the first time on international assignment must work effectively with others, remain flexible, and make cultural compromises to succeed.

One other employability skill this course will help you to develop is that of *knowledge application and analysis*. This refers to your ability to learn a concept and appropriately apply that knowledge in another setting to achieve a higher level of understanding. You will be asked to apply your analytical reasoning and research skills in numerous assignments, projects, mini-cases, and, perhaps, the market entry strategy project developed for use with this textbook. You will learn that at the core of global business success is innovation, which we view as a process of experimenting, learning, applying knowledge, and assessing success or failure. For example, throughout the course you will have ample opportunities to explain why a company succeeded or failed because of the actions it did or did not take.

To assist you in developing these and other career skills as you study this course, we created a unique organizing framework to help you conceptualize international business. We call this the global business environment.

The Global Business Environment

As we've already seen in this chapter, international business differs greatly from business in a purely domestic context. The most obvious contrast is that different nations can have entirely different societies and commercial environments. The best way to explain what makes international business special is to introduce a model unique to this book—a model we call the *global business environment*. This model weaves together four distinct elements:

1. The forces of *globalization*
2. The *international* business environment
3. Many *national* business environments
4. International *firm* management.

The model in Figure 1.3 identifies each of these elements and their subparts that together comprise the global business environment. Thinking about international business as occurring within this global system helps us to understand the complexities of international business and

Figure 1.3

The Global Business Environment

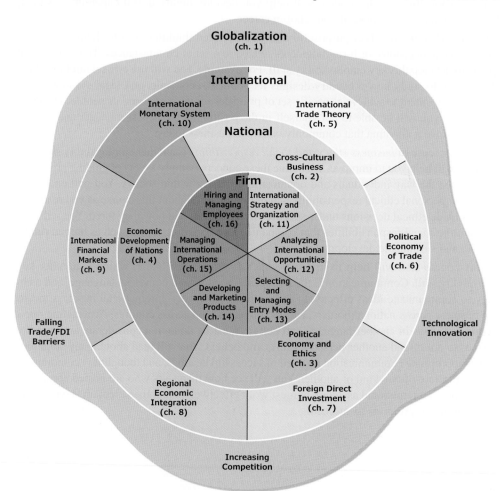

the interrelations between its distinct elements. Let's preview each of the four main components in the global business environment.

Globalization is a potent force transforming our societies and commercial activities in countless ways. Globalization, and the pressures it creates, forces its way into each element shown in Figure 1.3. In this way, the drivers of globalization (technological innovation and falling trade and investment barriers) influence every aspect of the global business environment. The dynamic nature of globalization also creates increasing competition for all firms everywhere, as managers begin to see the entire world as an opportunity. At home and abroad, firms must remain vigilant to the fundamental societal and commercial changes that globalization causes.

The *international business environment* influences how firms conduct their operations in both subtle and not-so-subtle ways. No business is entirely immune to events in the international business environment, as evidenced by the long-term trend toward more porous national borders. The drivers of globalization are causing the flows of trade, investment, and capital to grow and to become more entwined—often causing firms to search simultaneously for production bases *and* new markets. Companies today must keep their fingers on the pulse of the international business environment to see how it might affect their business activities.

Each *national business environment* is composed of unique cultural, political, economic, and legal characteristics that define business activity within that nation's borders. This set of national characteristics can differ greatly from country to country. But as nations open up and embrace globalization, their business environments are being transformed. Globalization can cause powerful synergies and enormous tensions to arise within and across various elements of a society. Company managers must be attentive to such nuances, adapting their products and practices as needed.

International firm management is vastly different from the management of a purely domestic business. Companies must abide by the rules in every market in which they choose to operate. Therefore, the context of international business management is defined by the characteristics of national business environments. Because of widely dispersed production and marketing activities today, firms commonly interact with people in distant locations within the international business environment. Finally, managers and their firms are compelled to be knowledgeable about the nations in which they operate because of the integrating power of globalization. Businesses should try to anticipate events and forces that can affect their operations by closely monitoring globalization, national business environments, and the international business environment.

The Road Ahead for International Business

The coverage of international business in this book follows the model of the global business environment displayed in Figure 1.3. In this chapter, we learned how *globalization* is transforming our world and how elements of the global business environment are becoming increasingly intertwined. As globalization penetrates deeper into the national context, every aspect of international business management is being affected.

In Part 2 (Chapters 2 through 4), we explore how *national business environments* differ from one nation to another. We examine how people's attitudes, values, beliefs, and institutions differ from one culture to another and how this affects business. This part also covers how nations differ in their political, economic, and legal systems. This material is placed early in the text because such differences between countries help frame subsequent topics and discussions, such as how companies modify business practices and strategies abroad.

We describe major components of the *international business environment* in Part 3 (Chapters 5 through 8) and Part 4 (Chapters 9 and 10). Our coverage begins with an examination of trade and investment theories and a discussion of why governments encourage or discourage these two forms of international business. We explore the process of regional economic integration around the world and outline its implications for international business. Finally, we discuss how events in global financial markets affect international business and how the global monetary system functions.

In Part 5 (Chapters 11 through 16), we cover ways in which *international business management* differs from management of a purely domestic firm. We explain how a company creates an international strategy, organizes itself for international business, and analyzes and selects the markets it will pursue. We explore different potential entry modes and then discuss how a firm develops and markets products for specific nations, regions, or the entire world. We then cover how international companies manage their sometimes-far-flung international operations. The book closes by discussing how international firms manage their human resources in the global business environment.

This chapter has only introduced you to the study of international business—we hope you enjoy the rest of your journey!

QUICK STUDY 7

1. What employability skills will this course help you to develop?
2. It helps to think about international business as four elements that occur within a *what*?
3. *How* does managing an international firm differ from managing a purely domestic business?

BOTTOM LINE FOR BUSINESS

The main theme of this chapter is that the world's national economies are becoming increasingly intertwined through the process of globalization. Cultural, political, economic, and legal events in one country increasingly affect the lives of people in other countries. Companies must pay attention to how changes in nations where they do business can affect operations. In this section, we briefly examine several important business implications of globalization.

Harnessing Globalization's Benefits

People opposed to globalization say it negatively affects wages and environmental protection, reduces political freedom, increases corruption, and inequitably rewards various groups. Yet there is evidence that the most globalized nations have the strongest records on equality, the most robust protection of natural resources, the most inclusive political systems, and the lowest levels of corruption. People in the most globalized nations also live the healthiest and longest lives, and women there have achieved the most social, educational, and economic progress.

One thing the debate over globalization has achieved is a dialogue about the merits and demerits of globalization. What has emerged is a more sober, less naïve notion of globalization. Those on each side of the debate understand that globalization can have positive effects on people's lives, but that globalization cannot, by itself, alleviate the misery of the world's poor. Both sides in the debate now often work together to harness the benefits of globalization while minimizing its costs.

Intensified Competition

The two driving forces of globalization (lower trade and investment barriers and increased technological innovation) are taking companies into previously isolated markets and increasing competitive pressures worldwide. And innovation is unlikely to slow any time soon.

As the cost of computing power continues to fall and new technologies are developed, companies will find it easier and less costly to manage widely dispersed marketing activities and production facilities. Technological developments might even strengthen the case for outsourcing more professional jobs to low-cost locations. As competition intensifies, international companies are increasing their cooperation with suppliers and customers.

Wages and Jobs

Some labor groups in wealthy nations contend that globalization forces companies to join the "race to the bottom" in terms of wages and benefits. But to attract investment, a location must offer low-cost, adequately skilled workers in an environment with acceptable levels of social, political, and economic stability.

Rapid globalization of markets and production is making product delivery a complex engineering task. As companies cut costs by outsourcing activities, supply and distribution channels grow longer and more complex. Corporate logistics departments and logistics specialist firms are helping international companies untangle lengthy supply chains, monitor shipping lanes, and forecast weather patterns. High-wage logistics jobs represent the kind of high-value-added employment that results from the "churning" in labor markets caused by globalization.

The Policy Agenda

Countless actions could be taken by developed and developing nations to lessen the negative effects of globalization. The World Bank calls on rich countries to (1) open their markets to exports from developing countries, (2) slash their agricultural subsidies that hurt poor-country exports, and (3) increase development aid, particularly in education and health. It calls on poor countries to improve their investment climates and improve social protection for poor people in a changing economic environment.

The Peterson Institute for International Economics (www.iie .com) proposed a policy agenda for rich nations on two fronts. On the *domestic front*, it proposes (1) establishing on-the-job training to help workers cope with globalization, (2) offering "wage insurance" to workers forced by globalization to take a lower-paying job, (3) subsidizing health insurance costs in case of lost work, and (4) improving education and lifetime learning. On the *international front,* it proposes (1) better enforcing labor

standards, (2) clarifying the relation between international trade and environmental agreements, and (3) reviewing the environmental implications of trade agreements.

MyLab Management

Go to **www.pearson.com/mylab/management** to complete the problems marked with this icon .

Chapter Summary

LO1.1   Identify the types of companies active in international business.
- Most international business is conducted by large *multinational corporations (MNCs),* which have great economic muscle and do deals often worth billions of dollars.
- *Born global firms* adopt a global perspective and conduct international business nearly from the start. They tend to have innovative cultures, knowledge-based capabilities, and become international competitors in less than three years.
- Entrepreneurs and small firms benefit from the Internet and other technologies that help them overcome the hurdles of high advertising and distribution costs.

LO1.2   Explain globalization and how it affects markets and production.
- *Globalization* is the trend toward greater economic, cultural, political, and technological interdependence among national institutions and economies.
- The globalization of *markets* helps a company to (1) reduce costs by standardizing marketing activities, (2) explore international markets if the home market is small or saturated, and (3) level income streams.
- The globalization of *production* helps a company to (1) access low-cost labor and become more price competitive, (2) access technical know-how, and (3) access natural resources nonexistent or too expensive at home.

LO1.3   Detail the forces that drive globalization.
- One major force behind globalization is *falling barriers to trade and investment.*
- Those helping to reduce such barriers include the *World Trade Organization,* the *World Bank,* the *International Monetary Fund,* and regional trading groups.
- Another force behind globalization is *technological innovation.* Specific innovations include email, videoconferencing, firm intranets and extranets, and advancements in transportation technologies such as RFID and GPS.

LO1.4   Outline the debate about globalization's impact on jobs and wages.
- Globalization opponents say it (1) destroys developed-country jobs that are moved to developing countries, (2) lowers wages, job security, and employee morale and loyalty in developed nations, (3) exploits developing-nation workers in outsourced service jobs, and (4) reduces the bargaining power of labor.
- Globalization supporters say it (1) fuels efficiency and greater production that raises consumer income, (2) promotes labor market flexibility that quickly shifts workers to where they are needed, (3) outsources sorely needed jobs to developing nations that elevate living standards, and (4) actually might strengthen labor rights.

LO1.5   Summarize the debate about income inequality.
- Regarding *inequality within nations,* evidence suggests that a developing nation can boost incomes for its poorest residents by integrating itself into the global economy.
- In the debate about *inequality between nations,* studies find that a nation embracing world trade and investment can grow faster than rich nations, whereas a sheltered economy becomes worse off.
- Regarding *global inequality,* groups tend to agree that inequality has fallen in recent decades although they differ about the extent of the drop.

LO1.6 Outline the debate about culture, sovereignty, and the environment.
- Evidence suggests that the *cultures* of developing nations are thriving in an age of globalization and that deeper elements of culture are not easily abandoned, as critics say.
- In terms of *national sovereignty*, the case can be made that globalization has not undermined democracy, but has helped it to spread worldwide and has aided progress on many global issues.
- Regarding the *environment*, it seems globalization has not caused a "race to the bottom," but instead has urged firms to embrace sustainability as a precondition to fostering healthy future markets.

LO1.7 Identify how this course will help you to develop skills for your career.
- The *employability skills* this course can help you develop are critical thinking skills, business ethics and social responsibility, communication, and knowledge application and analysis.
- The *global business environment* model in Figure 1.3 will help you to conceptualize international business today and aid in your skills development.
- The *international business environment* influences how firms conduct operations, while *globalization* further entwines the flows of trade, investment, and capital.
- Separate *national business environments* comprise unique cultural, political, economic, and legal characteristics that define *business* activity within every nation.

Key Terms

born global firm (p. 32)	globalization (p. 33)	International Monetary Fund
e-business (e-commerce) (p. 38)	gross domestic product	(IMF) (p. 37)
exports (p. 30)	(GDP) (p. 38)	multinational corporation (MNC) (p. 31)
GDP or GNP per capita (p. 38)	gross national product (GNP) (p. 38)	sustainability (p. 34)
General Agreement on Tariffs and Trade	imports (p. 30)	World Bank (p. 37)
(GATT) (p. 36)	international business (p. 30)	World Trade Organization (WTO) (p. 37)

✪ TALK ABOUT IT 1

Today, international businesspeople must think globally about production and sales opportunities. Many global managers will eventually find themselves living and working in other cultures, and entrepreneurs might find themselves taking flights to places they had never heard about.

1-1. What can companies do now to prepare their managers for international markets?
1-2. How can entrepreneurs and small businesses with limited resources prepare?

✪ TALK ABOUT IT 2

In the past, national governments influenced the pace of globalization through agreements to lower barriers to international trade and investment.

1-3. Is rapid change now outpacing the capability of governments to manage the global economy?
1-4. Will national governments grow more or less important to international business in the future?

Ethical Challenge

You are the CEO of a smartphone company based in South Africa. You have developed a 10-year relationship with a manufacturer in Indonesia. They currently supply you with 40 percent of your product range. The factory owners have invested heavily in facilities, equipment, and training. The 550 employees work exclusively for your company. Falling sales in handsets mean that production has to be cut by 25 percent. Your South African factories are underutilized. As the CEO, you have to decide whether to close the more expensive but more efficient South African facilities or to end your relationship with the cheaper but less efficient Indonesia sub-contractor.

1-5. Which of the two facilities should you use and why?

1-6. What are the key social and ethical responsibilities facing the CEO if the decision is made to sever ties with the Indonesian contractor?

1-7. Is outsourcing a fundamentally ethical approach to manufacturing? If so, what are the implications for domestic manufacturers?

Teaming Up

Imagine that you and several of your classmates own a company that manufactures cheap sunglasses. To lower production costs, you decide to move your factory from your developed country to a more cost-effective location.

1-8. Which elements of the national business environment might influence your decision of where to move production?

1-9. What aspects of the globalization of production and marketing do you expect will benefit your company after the move?

✪ Market Entry Strategy Project

This exercise corresponds to the *MESP* online simulation. With several classmates, select a country that interests you. For the country your team researches, integrate your answers to the following questions into your completed *MESP* report.

1-10. Is the nation the home base of any large multinational companies?

1-11. How does globalization influence the country's jobs and wages, its income inequality, and its culture, sovereignty, and physical environment?

1-12. How does the country rank in terms of its degree of globalization?

1-13. What benefits can the country offer to businesses seeking a new market or production base?

MyLab Management

✪ Go to **www.pearson.com/mylab/management** for the following assisted-graded writing questions:

1-14. When going international, companies today often research new locations as potential markets as well as potential sites for operations. What specific benefits can companies gain from the globalization of markets and production? Explain.

1-15. Opponents of globalization say that it has many negative consequences for jobs and wages, income inequality, culture, sovereignty, and the environment. What are some positive outcomes of globalization for each of these topics?

PRACTICING INTERNATIONAL MANAGEMENT CASE

IO Interactive—Storytelling Goes Global

Denmark is a country probably best known for its storytelling culture, epitomized by Hans Christian Andersen and his classic folk stories. These fairy tales have delighted youngsters from across the globe for well over a century, seamlessly crossing language and cultural barriers. They are an art form that has inspired the country's largest video game developer, IO Interactive. The 170-strong Copenhagen-based group of programmers, software engineers, animators, and mathematicians has created a number of critically acclaimed games such as *Hitman, Kane & Lynch*, and *Freedom Fighters*, whose dark tales appeal to gamers from Boston to Beijing.

IO Interactive decided soon after it was formed in 1998 that it wanted to target the international market. It did not have to look far to realize that the companies at the top of their game, so to speak, were the ones whose products held a worldwide appeal. Indeed, the perceived wisdom in the highly competitive industry is that the only way to survive, and indeed thrive, is to go for total globalization. This in itself appeals to young people, for whom gaming is a modern medium for the modern age. They love the fact that gaming is capable of hitting all the current buzzwords while crossing borders and encouraging a rich mix of collaboration and user-generated content.

Most game companies have interpreted this as a sign that, in order to successfully market games worldwide, they must limit any overtly culturally distinct elements in their titles. Any references to local traditions, national literature, and musical identity are intentionally kept to a minimum. This is something IO Interactive very much bears in mind when devising its games, but thanks to its rich storytelling roots, the company has been fortunate that it has not had to completely turn its back on its traditions. Indeed, the company has managed to make great use of its native culture of dark humor and fantasy, which perfectly suits the genre of games it designs and which has significant appeal to young gamers worldwide.

This is not to say that IO Interactive has been able to completely ignore the sensibilities of the international audience, and sometimes the search for global appeal means including credible material from abroad. Thus, for the release of *Kane & Lynch 2: Dog Days*, which featured levels based in China, 23 different authentic-sounding Asian songs were written with vocals in Mandarin, backed with musicians performing with Chinese instruments including percussion, Shakuhachi, and Pipa. Game reviewers were bowled over by the international aspect, and one even compared the experience to watching a movie by famed Chinese film director John Woo.

IO Interactive is helped in its quest for international credibility by its highly diverse workforce of specialists hailing from 23 different countries. This is not unusual in this industry. Game developers are used to relocating and frequently transfer to different countries to find the work they want. This inevitably affects both the storylines and content of games as the newcomers are not infused with local traits and have no strong pull to protect national identities.

Likewise, IO Interactive frequently dispatches its game developers to locations around the world to soak up the local culture and reflect it more accurately in their games. According to IO Interactive, the secret to creating good games is to get all the right ingredients together in one big stew and then stir the pot, which for any Hans Christian Andersen fan sounds like a very familiar tale indeed.

Thinking Globally

1-16. Some say globalization is homogenizing the attitudes and spending habits of young consumers worldwide. As one journalist puts it, "It may still be conventional wisdom to 'think globally and act locally,' but in the youth market, it is increasingly a case of 'one size fits all.'" Do you agree or disagree? Why or why not?

1-17. Some critics say that although video games are designed to have a broad appeal, they do reflect a "Westernized" version of life. Is there a danger that teens exposed to large doses of video games will identify less with the cultures of their own societies and that teens in developing countries will want a Western lifestyle and goods they cannot afford?

1-18. It is now the norm for game developers to relocate to work anywhere in the world. Can you think of other social trends and technological innovations that have helped companies to think more globally?

1-19. Advances in technology often spur evolution in the entertainment industry. How might products and services such as the iPhone and YouTube affect entertainment in years to come?

Sources: IO Interactive website (www.ioi.dk); Margaret Robertson, "State of Play, a Wide World of Games," *BBC News* website (http://news.bbc.co.uk), September 11, 2007; "IO Interactive's Thomas Howalt", *GamesIndustry.biz* website (www.gamesindustry.biz), September 4, 2008; Christian Nutt, "IO Style: We Just Want to Entertain People," *Gamasutra* website (www.gamasutra.com), August 17, 2010; Kane & Lynch 2: Dog Days, EMI website (http://www.emisound.com).

Appendix

World Atlas

As globalization marches across the world, international business managers can make more-informed decisions if they know the locations of countries and the distances between them. This atlas presents the world in a series of maps and is designed to assist you in understanding the global landscape of business. We encourage you to return to this atlas frequently to refresh your memory, especially when you encounter the name of an unfamiliar city or country.

Familiarize yourself with each of the maps in this appendix, and then try to answer the following 20 questions. For each question, select all answers that apply.

Map Exercises

1. Which of the following countries border the Atlantic Ocean?
   - a. Bolivia
   - b. Australia
   - c. South Africa
   - d. Japan
   - e. United States

2. Which of the following countries are found in Africa?
   - a. Guyana
   - b. Morocco
   - c. Egypt
   - d. Pakistan
   - e. Niger

3. Which one of the following countries does not border the Pacific Ocean?
   - a. Australia
   - b. Venezuela
   - c. Japan
   - d. Mexico
   - e. Peru

4. Prague is the capital city of:
   - a. Uruguay
   - b. Czech Republic
   - c. Portugal
   - d. Tunisia
   - e. Hungary

5. If transportation costs for getting your product from your market to Japan are high, which of the following countries might be good places to locate a manufacturing facility?
   - a. Thailand
   - b. Philippines
   - c. South Africa
   - d. Indonesia
   - e. Portugal

6. Seoul is the capital city of (capitals are designated with red dots):
   - a. Vietnam
   - b. Cambodia
   - c. Malaysia
   - d. China
   - e. South Korea

7. Turkey, Romania, Ukraine, and Russia border the body of water called the _____ Sea.

8. Thailand shares borders with:
   - a. Cambodia
   - b. Pakistan
   - c. Singapore
   - d. Malaysia
   - e. Indonesia

9. Which of the following countries border no major ocean or sea?
   - a. Austria
   - b. Paraguay
   - c. Switzerland
   - d. Niger
   - e. all of the above

10. Oslo is the capital city of:
    - a. Germany
    - b. Canada
    - c. Brazil
    - d. Australia
    - e. Norway

11. Chile is located in:
    - a. Africa
    - b. Asia
    - c. the Northern Hemisphere
    - d. South America
    - e. Central Europe

12. Saudi Arabia shares borders with:
    - a. Jordan
    - b. Kuwait
    - c. Iraq
    - d. United Arab Emirates
    - e. all of the above

13. The body of water located between Sweden and Estonia is the _____ Sea.

14. Which of the following countries are located on the Mediterranean Sea?
    - a. Italy
    - b. Croatia
    - c. Turkey
    - d. France
    - e. Portugal

15. The distance between Sydney (Australia) and Tokyo (Japan) is shorter than that between:
    - a. Tokyo and Cape Town (South Africa)
    - b. Sydney and Hong Kong (China, SAR)
    - c. Tokyo and London (England)
    - d. Sydney and Jakarta (Indonesia)
    - e. all of the above

16. Madrid is the capital city of:
    - a. Madagascar
    - b. Italy
    - c. Mexico
    - d. Spain
    - e. United States

17. Which of the following countries is not located in central Asia?
    a. Afghanistan
    b. Uzbekistan
    c. Turkmenistan
    d. Kazakhstan
    e. Suriname

18. If you were shipping your products from your production facility in Pakistan to market in Australia, they would likely cross the _____ Ocean.

19. Papua New Guinea, Guinea-Bissau, and Guinea are alternative names for the same country.
    a. true
    b. false

20. Which of the following countries are island nations?
    a. New Zealand
    b. Madagascar
    c. Japan
    d. Australia
    e. all of the above

Answers

(1) c. South Africa, e. United States; (2) b. Morocco, c. Egypt, e. Niger; (3) b. Venezuela; (4) b. Czech Republic; (5) a. Thailand, b. Philippines, d. Indonesia; (6) e. South Korea; (7) Black; (8) a. Cambodia, d. Malaysia; (9) e. all of the above; (10) e. Norway; (11) d. South America; (12) e. all of the above; (13) Baltic; (14) a. Italy, c. Turkey, d. France; (15) a. Tokyo and Cape Town (South Africa), c. Tokyo and London (England); (16) d. Spain; (17) e. Suriname; (18) Indian; (19) b. false; (20) e. all of the above.

Self-Assessment

If you scored 15 correct answers or more, well done! You seem well prepared for your international business journey. If you scored fewer than 8 correct answers, you might wish to review this atlas before moving on to Chapter 2.

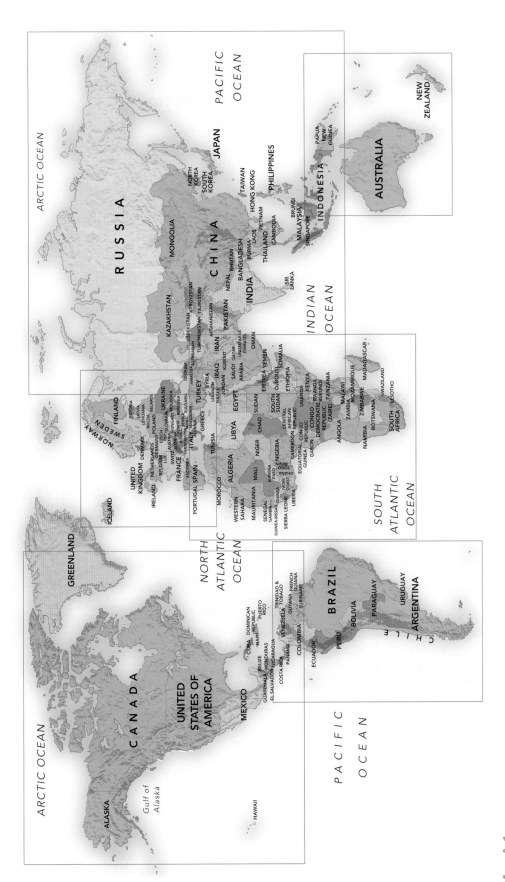

Map A. 1
The World

Map A.2

North America

Map A.3
South America

Map A.4
Europe

Map A.5
Asia

Map A.6
Africa

Map A.7
Oceania

Chapter Two

Cross-Cultural Business

Learning Objectives

After studying this chapter, you should be able to

2.1 Explain culture and the need for cultural knowledge.

2.2 Summarize the cultural importance of values and behavior.

2.3 Describe the roles of social structure and education in culture.

2.4 Outline how the major world religions can influence business.

2.5 Explain the importance of personal communication to international business.

2.6 Describe how firms and culture interact in the global workplace.

A Look Back

Chapter 1 introduced us to international business. We examined the impact of globalization on markets and production, the forces behind globalization's expansion, and each main argument in the debate over globalization. We also profiled the kinds of companies engaged in international business.

A Look at This Chapter

This chapter introduces the important role of culture in international business. We explore the main elements of culture and how they affect business policies and practices. We learn about different frameworks for studying cultures and how they apply to international business.

A Look Ahead

Chapter 3 describes the political economy of nations. We will learn how different political, economic, and legal systems affect the policies and activities of international companies. We also discover how ethics and social responsibility affect international business.

MyLab Management

✪ IMPROVE YOUR GRADE!

When you see this icon ✪, visit **www.pearson.com/mylab/management** for activities that are applied, personalized, and offer immediate feedback.

Hold the Pork, Please!

BONN, Germany—"Kids and grownups love it so, the happy world of Haribo!" So goes the phrase that drives sales of Haribo gummi candies worldwide. Germany-based Haribo (www.haribo.com) gets its name from that of the company's founder, **Ha**ns **Ri**egel **Bo**nn. Haribo CEO Hans Riegel Bonn, Jr. and his brother, Paul, built a global brand out of the tiny candy business started by their father in 1920. Shown here, Haribo puts on a small publicity parade during Le Tour de France.

Radu Razvan/Shutterstock

Haribo candies, with names such as Gold Bears and Horror Mix, are available in 46 shapes, including soda bottles and glowworms. They are often the first export from Germany that children in other countries purchase. Haribo supplies 105 countries from its 15 factories at home and abroad, producing more than 100 million gummi candies a day. But despite its success, Haribo was not meeting the needs of a globally dispersed subculture potentially worth $2 billion annually. The culprit: The pork-based substance that gives the candy its sticky, rubbery feel makes the candy off-limits to Muslims and Jews who adhere to a strict religious diet.

So the company embarked on a four-year mission to create a gummi candy free of the pork-based gelatin. "The first time we made it, we got a marmalade you could spread on bread," reported Neville Finlay, the British exporter who ships the new product under his own brand. "And at the other extreme was something you could fill a swimming pool with and drive a truck across," he added. Haribo found success eventually with a bacteria-based compound commonly used in salad dressings and sauces.

Later, a local supplier committed a language blunder—a common occurrence in international business. The printing on the first packages of candies destined for Hebrew communities was backward—Hebrew is read from right to left, not left to right like English. But today production is going smoothly. Haribo even has a Jewish rabbi (for *kosher* candies) or a Muslim cleric (for *halal* candies) inspect ingredients and oversee production to ensure that it adheres to religious customs. As you read this chapter, consider all the ways culture affects international business and how companies affect cultures around the world.[1]

This chapter is the first of three that describes the links between international business activity and a nation's business environment. We discuss these topics early because they help determine how commerce is conducted in a country. Success in international business can often be traced directly to a deep understanding of some aspect of a people's commercial environment. This chapter explores the influence of *culture* on international business activity. Chapter 3 presents the role of *political economy and ethics* and Chapter 4 explores the *economic development of nations*. Assessment of a nation's overall business climate is typically the first step in analyzing its potential as a host for international commercial activity. This means addressing some important questions, such as the following: What language(s) do the people speak? What is the climate like? Are the local people open to new ideas and new ways of doing business? Do government officials and the people want our business? Is the political situation stable enough so that our assets and employees are not placed at unacceptable levels of risk? Answers to these kinds of questions—plus statistical data on items such as income level and labor costs—allow companies to evaluate the attractiveness of a location as a place for doing business.

We address culture first in our discussion of national business environments because of its pivotal role in all international commercial activity. Whether we are discussing an entrepreneur running a small import/export business or a huge global firm directly involved in more than 100 countries, *people* are at the center of all business activity. When people from around the world come together to conduct business, they bring with them different backgrounds, assumptions, expectations, and ways of communicating—each of which is a key part of *culture*.

We begin this chapter by defining culture and understanding the need for cultural knowledge. Next, we learn the importance of values, attitudes, manners, and customs in any given culture. We then examine the key components of culture, including social institutions, education, religion, and language. We close this chapter with a look at how the richness of culture plays out in the global workplace.

2.1 What Is Culture?

2.1 Explain culture and the need for cultural knowledge.

culture
Set of values, beliefs, rules, and institutions held by a specific group of people.

When traveling in other countries, we often perceive differences in the way people live and work. In the United States, dinner is commonly eaten around 6 p.m.; in Spain, it's not served until 8 or 9 p.m. In the United States, most people shop in large supermarkets once or twice a week; Italians tend to shop in smaller local grocery stores nearly every day. These are just a few visible manifestations of **culture**—the set of values, beliefs, rules, and institutions held by a specific group of people. Culture is a highly complex portrait of a people. It includes everything from high tea in England to the tropical climate of Barbados to Mardi Gras in Brazil.

Rightly or wrongly, we tend to invoke the concept of the *nation–state* when speaking of culture. In other words, we usually refer to British and Indonesian cultures as if all Britons and all Indonesians are culturally identical. We do this because we are conditioned to think in terms of *national culture*. But this is at best a generalization. For example, the British population consists of the English as well as the Scottish and Welsh peoples. And people in remote parts of Indonesia build homes in treetops even as people in the nation's developed regions pursue ambitious economic development projects. Let's take a closer look at the diversity that lies within national cultures.

National Culture

Nation-states *support* and *promote* the concept of national culture by building museums and erecting monuments to preserve the legacies of important events and people. Nation-states also intervene in business to preserve treasures of national culture. Most nations, for example, regulate culturally sensitive sectors of the economy, such as filmmaking and broadcasting. France continues to voice fears that its language is being tainted with English and its media with US programming. To stem the English invasion, French law limits the use of English in product packaging and storefront signs. At peak listening times, at least 40 percent of all radio station programming is reserved for French artists. Similar laws apply to television broadcasting. The French government even fined the local branch of a US university for failing to provide a French translation on its English-language website.

Cities, too, get involved in enhancing national cultural attractions, often for economic reasons. Lifestyle enhancements can help a city attract companies, which then benefit by having an easier task retaining top employees. The Guggenheim Museum in Bilbao, Spain (www.guggenheim-bilbao.es), designed by Frank Gehry, revived that old Basque industrial city. And Hong Kong's

Subculture members define themselves by their style (such as clothing, hair, tattoos) and might rebel against mass consumerism. Here, a young woman poses in "steampunk attire" in front of an old-time steam locomotive. Steampunk is a subculture rooted in science fiction and inspired by mechanical inventions of the late 1800s and early 1900s including, of course, steam-powered machines of all sorts. Businesses such as YouTube and Facebook can help subcultures to spread quickly worldwide. Can you think of a company that targets an international subculture with its products?

Petrenco Natalia/Shutterstock

government enhanced its cultural attractions by building a Hong Kong Disney to lure businesses that might otherwise locate elsewhere in Asia.

Subcultures

A group of people who share a unique way of life within a larger, dominant culture is called a **subculture**. A subculture can differ from the dominant culture in language, race, lifestyle, values, attitudes, or other characteristics.

subculture
A group of people who share a unique way of life within a larger, dominant culture.

Although subcultures exist in all nations, they are often glossed over by our *impressions* of national cultures. For example, the customary portrait of Chinese culture often ignores the fact that China's population includes more than 50 distinct ethnic groups. Decisions regarding product design, packaging, and advertising should consider each group's distinct culture. Marketing campaigns also need to recognize that Chinese dialects spoken in the Shanghai and Canton regions differ from the official Mandarin dialect spoken in the country's interior.

A multitude of subcultures also exists within the United States. Initially, Frito Lay (www .fritolay.com) had trouble convincing 46 million US Latinos to try its Latin-flavored versions of Lay's and Doritos chips. But then Frito Lay brought four popular brands into the US market from its Mexican subsidiary, Sabritas. The gamble paid off and sales of the Sabritas brand doubled to more than $100 million during a two-year period.

Cultural boundaries do not always correspond to political boundaries. In other words, subcultures sometimes exist across national borders. People who live in different nations but who share the same subculture can have more in common with one another than with their fellow nationals. These subcultures can share purchasing behaviors rooted in lifestyle or values that allow marketers to address them with a single worldwide campaign.

Physical Environment

Land features affect personal communication in a culture. Surface features such as navigable rivers and flat plains facilitate travel and contact with others. By contrast, treacherous mountain ranges and large bodies of water that are difficult to navigate discourage contact. Mountain ranges and the formidable Gobi Desert consume two-thirds of China's land surface. Groups living in the valleys of these mountain ranges hold on to their own ways of life and speak their own languages, despite the Mandarin dialect having been decreed the national language many years ago.

The physical environment of a region affects consumers' product needs. For example, there is little market for Honda scooters (www.honda.com) in most mountainous regions because a scooter's engine is too small to climb the steep grades. Such regions are better markets for the company's more rugged, maneuverable, on–off road motorcycles that have more powerful engines.

Climate affects where people settle and the distribution systems they create. In Australia, intensely hot and dry conditions in two large deserts and jungle conditions in the northeast pushed settlement to coastal areas. These conditions, together with the higher cost of land transport, means coastal waters are still used to distribute products between distant cities. Climate can also play a role in determining work habits. The heat of the summer sun grows intense in the early afternoon hours in the countries of southern Europe, northern Africa, and the Middle East. For this reason, people often take afternoon breaks of one or two hours in July and August. They use this time to perform errands or to take short naps before returning to work until about 7 or 8 p.m. Companies operating in these regions must adapt to this local tradition.

Need for Cultural Knowledge

A visual depiction of culture would resemble an iceberg. Cultural features that we can see comprise a very small portion of all that comprises it—it is just the "tip of the iceberg." The vast majority of a people's cultural makeup remains hidden from view and below the surface. It takes knowledge, effort, understanding, and experience to uncover the essence of a culture and to develop a deep appreciation for it.

ethnocentricity

Belief that one's own ethnic group or culture is superior to that of others.

AVOIDING ETHNOCENTRICITY Our thoughts can harbor subconscious, unintentional, and inaccurate perceptions of other cultures. **Ethnocentricity** is the belief that one's own ethnic group or culture is superior to that of others. Ethnocentricity can seriously undermine international business projects. It can cause people to disregard the beneficial characteristics of other cultures. Ethnocentricity played a role in many stories, some retold in this chapter, of companies that failed when they tried to implement a new business practice in a subsidiary abroad. Failure can occur when managers ignore a fundamental aspect of the local culture. This can provoke a backlash from the local population, its government, or nongovernmental groups. As suppliers and buyers increasingly treat the world as a single, interconnected marketplace, managers should eliminate the biases inherent in ethnocentric thinking. To read about how companies can foster a nonethnocentric perspective, see this chapter's Culture Matters feature, titled "Creating a Global Mindset."

cultural literacy

Detailed knowledge about a culture that enables a person to work happily and effectively within it.

DEVELOPING CULTURAL LITERACY As globalization continues, people directly involved in international business increasingly benefit from a certain degree of **cultural literacy**—detailed knowledge about a culture that enables a person to work happily and effectively within it. Cultural literacy improves people's ability to manage employees, market products, and conduct negotiations in other countries. Procter & Gamble (www.pg.com) and Apple (www.apple.com) might have a competitive advantage because consumers know and respect these highly recognizable brand names. Yet, cultural differences often dictate alterations in some aspect of a business to suit

---

CULTURE MATTERS   Creating a Global Mindset

In this era of globalization, companies need employees who function without the blinders of ethnocentricity. Here are some ways managers can develop a *global mindset*:

- **Cultural Adaptability.** Managers need the ability to alter their behavior when working with people from other cultures. The first step in doing this is to develop one's knowledge about unfamiliar cultures. The second step is to act on that knowledge to alter behavior to suit cultural expectations. The manager with a global mindset can evaluate others in a culturally unbiased way and can motivate and lead multicultural teams.
- **Bridging the Gap.** A large gap can emerge between theory and practice when Western management ideas are applied in Eastern cultures. Whereas US management principles are often accepted at face value in businesses throughout the world, US business customs are not. In Asia, for example, Western managers might try implementing "collective leadership" practices more in line with Asian management styles.

- **Building Global Mentality.** Companies can apply personality-testing techniques to measure the global aptitude of managers. A global-mindset test evaluates an individual's openness and flexibility, understanding of global principles, and strategic implementation abilities. It also can identify areas in which training is needed and generate a list of recommended programs.
- **Flexibility Is Key.** The more behavioral the issues, the greater the influence of local cultures. Japanese and Korean managers are more likely than US managers to wait for directions and consult peers about decisions. Western managers posted in the Middle East must learn to work within a rigid hierarchy in order to be successful. And although showing respect for others is universally valued, respect is defined differently from country to country.
- **Want to Know More?** Visit the Center for Creative Leadership (www.ccl.org), The Globalist (www.theglobalist.com), and Transnational Management Associated (www.tmaworld.com).

local tastes and preferences. The culturally literate manager who compensates for local needs and desires brings the company closer to customers and improves its competitiveness.

Globalization is causing cultures to converge to some extent. The successful *Idol* TV series, in which aspiring singers compete for a chance to become a celebrity, is one example of global pop culture. The original British show, *Pop Idol*, spawned 39 clones around the world, including *American Idol* in the United States. The same company helped develop and market *The Apprentice*, another globally successful TV platform.

It is unlikely that the world will ever homogenize into one global culture in which all people share similar lifestyles, values, and attitudes. It seems that just as often as we see signs of an emerging global culture, we discover some new habit that is unique to a single culture. We are then reminded of the pivotal roles of history and tradition in defining any culture. Although cultural traditions are under continually greater pressure from globalization, their transformation will be gradual rather than abrupt because they are so deeply ingrained in society.

As you read through the concepts and examples in this chapter, try to avoid reacting with *ethnocentricity* while developing your own *cultural literacy*. Because cultural literacy is central to the discussion about many international business topics, you will encounter them throughout this book. In the book's final chapter (Chapter 16), we explore specific types of cultural training that companies use to develop their employees' cultural literacy.

QUICK STUDY 1

1. How might a subculture differ from the dominant culture?
2. What do we call the belief that one's own culture is superior to that of others?
3. What do we call detailed knowledge about a culture that enables a person to work happily and effectively within it?

2.2 Values and Behavior

So far, our definition of culture is one that most people intuitively understand. We are familiar with the idea that people in different nations behave differently and that every culture has segments of people with distinct values and behaviors. But culture includes what people consider beautiful and tasteful, their underlying beliefs, their traditional habits, and the ways in which they relate to one another and their surroundings. Let's now go beneath the surface of the "iceberg" for a fuller understanding of the building blocks of society (see Figure 2.1).

2.2 Summarize the cultural importance of values and behavior.

Values

Ideas, beliefs, and customs to which people are emotionally attached are called **values**. Values include concepts such as honesty, freedom, and responsibility. Values are important to business because they affect a people's work ethic and desire for material possessions. For example, whereas people in Singapore value hard work and material success, people in Greece value leisure

values
Ideas, beliefs, and customs to which people are emotionally attached.

Figure 2.1
Components of Culture

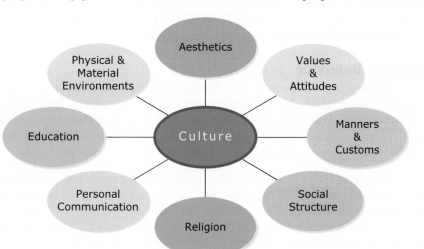

and a modest lifestyle. The United Kingdom and the United States value individual freedom; Japan and South Korea value group consensus.

The influx of values from other cultures can be fiercely resisted. Many Muslims believe drugs, alcohol, and certain kinds of music and literature will undermine conservative values. In Bahrain, the local version of the reality TV program, *Big Brother*, was canceled after people objected to the program's format in which young unmarried adults of both sexes lived under the same roof. The Lebanon-based program *Hawa Sawa* (*On Air Together*) was shut down because its "elimidate" format (a young man gradually eliminates women to finally select a date) was perceived as too Western. Indonesia's National Police denied Lady Gaga a permit to perform there after conservative Muslim groups accused her of corrupting the morals of the country's youth.

Attitudes

attitudes

Positive or negative evaluations, feelings, and tendencies that individuals harbor toward objects or concepts.

Attitudes reflect a people's underlying *values*. **Attitudes** are positive or negative evaluations, feelings, and tendencies that individuals harbor toward objects or concepts. For example, a Westerner would be expressing an attitude if he or she were to say, "I do not like the Japanese purification ritual because it involves being naked in a communal bath." The Westerner quoted here might value modesty and hold conservative beliefs regarding exposure of the body.

Similar to values, attitudes are learned from role models, including parents, teachers, and religious leaders. Attitudes also differ from one country to another because they are formed within a cultural context. But unlike values (which generally concern only important matters), people hold attitudes toward both important and unimportant aspects of life. And whereas values remain quite rigid over time, attitudes are more flexible.

Aesthetics

aesthetics

What a culture considers "good taste" in the arts, the imagery evoked by certain expressions, and the symbolism of certain colors.

What a culture considers "good taste" in the arts (including music, painting, dance, drama, and architecture), the imagery evoked by certain expressions, and the symbolism of certain colors is called **aesthetics**. In other words, it includes the art, images, symbols, colors, and so on that a culture *values*.

Aesthetics are important when a company does business in another culture. The selection of appropriate colors for advertising, product packaging, and even work uniforms can improve the odds of success. For example, companies take advantage of a positive emotional attachment to the color green across the Middle East by incorporating it into a product, its packaging, or its promotion. Across much of Asia, on the other hand, green is associated with sickness. In Europe, Mexico, and the United States, the color of death and mourning is black; in Japan and most of Asia, it's white.

Music is deeply embedded in culture and, when used correctly, can be a clever and creative addition to a promotion; if used incorrectly, it can offend the local population. The architecture of buildings and other structures also should be researched to avoid making cultural blunders attributable to the symbolism of certain shapes and forms.

The importance of aesthetics is just as great when going international using the Internet. When a company decides to globalize its Internet presence, it must consider adapting websites to account for cultural preferences such as color scheme, imagery, and slogans. Entrepreneurs and small businesses can seek advice from specialist firms if they do not have in-house employees who are well versed in other cultures.

Appropriate Behavior

When doing business in another culture, it is important to understand what is considered appropriate behavior. At a minimum, understanding manners and customs helps managers avoid making embarrassing mistakes or offending people. In-depth knowledge, meanwhile, improves the ability to negotiate in other cultures, market products effectively, and manage international operations. Let's explore some important differences in manners and customs around the world.

manners

Appropriate ways of behaving, speaking, and dressing in a culture.

MANNERS Appropriate ways of behaving, speaking, and dressing in a culture are called **manners**. Jack Ma founded Alibaba (www.alibaba.com) as a way for suppliers and buyers to increase efficiency by cutting through layers of intermediaries and trading companies. But he realized early that his Chinese clients needed training in business etiquette to cross the cultural divide and do business with people from Western cultures. So Alibaba offers seminars about business manners that instruct clients to spend more time chitchatting with clients and conversing more casually.[2]

Conducting business during meals is common practice in the United States. In Mexico, however, it is poor manners to bring up business at mealtime unless the host does so first. Business discussions in Mexico typically begin when coffee and brandy arrive. Likewise, toasts in the United States tend to be casual and sprinkled with lighthearted humor. In Mexico, a toast should be philosophical and full of passion.

CUSTOMS When habits or ways of behaving in specific circumstances are passed down through generations, they become **customs**. Customs differ from manners in that they define appropriate habits or behaviors in *specific situations*. For example, the Japanese tradition of throwing special parties for young women and men who turn age 20 is a custom.

Folk and Popular Customs A **folk custom** is behavior, often dating back several generations, that is practiced by a homogeneous group of people. Celebrating the Dragon Boat Festival in China and the art of belly dancing in Turkey are both folk customs. A **popular custom** is behavior shared by a heterogeneous group or by several groups. Wearing blue jeans and playing golf are both popular customs across the globe. Folk customs that spread to other regions develop into popular customs. Despite their appeal, popular customs can be seen as a threat by conservative or xenophobic members of a culture.

We can also distinguish between folk and popular food. Popular Western-style fast food, for instance, is rapidly replacing folk food around the world. Widespread acceptance of "burgers 'n' fries" (born in the United States) and "fish 'n' chips" (born in Britain) is altering deep-seated dietary traditions in many Asian countries, especially among young people. In Asia today, these popular foods are even becoming a part of home-cooked meals.

Gift Giving Customs Although giving token gifts to business and government associates is customary in many countries, the proper type of gift varies. A knife, for example, should not be offered to associates in Russia, France, or Germany, where it signals the severing of a relationship. In Japan, gifts must be wrapped in such a delicate way that it is wise to ask someone trained in the practice to do the honors. It is also Japanese custom for the giver to protest that the gift is small and unworthy of the recipient and for the recipient to not open the gift in front of the giver. This tradition does not endorse trivial gifts but is simply a custom.

Cultures differ in their legal and ethical rules against giving or accepting bribes. Large gifts to business associates are particularly suspicious. The US Foreign Corrupt Practices Act, which prohibits companies from giving large gifts to government officials in order to win business favors, applies to US firms operating at home *and* abroad. Yet in many cultures, bribery is woven into a social fabric that has worn well for centuries. In some cultures, large gifts remain an effective way to obtain contracts, enter markets, and secure protection from competitors. See the Manager's Briefcase, titled "A Globetrotter's Guide to Meetings," for additional pointers on manners and customs when abroad on business.

customs
Habits or ways of behaving in specific circumstances that are passed down through generations in a culture.

folk custom
Behavior, often dating back several generations, that is practiced by a homogeneous group of people.

popular custom
Behavior shared by a heterogeneous group or by several groups.

MANAGER'S BRIEFCASE   A Globetrotter's Guide to Meetings

Large multinationals need top managers who are comfortable living, working, and traveling worldwide. Here are a few guidelines for a manager to follow when meeting colleagues from other cultures:

- **Familiarity** Avoid the temptation to get too familiar too quickly. Use titles such as "doctor" and "mister." Switch to a first-name basis only when invited to do so, and do not shorten people's names from, say, Catherine to Cathy.
- **Personal Space** Culture dictates what is considered the appropriate distance between two people. In Latin America, people close the gap significantly and a man-to-man embrace is common in business.
- **Religious Values** Be cautious so that your manners do not offend people. Former Secretary of State Madeline Albright acquired the nickname "The Kissing Ambassador" for

kissing the Israeli and Palestinian leaders of those two religious peoples.
- **Business Cards** In Asia, business cards are considered an extension of the individual. Business cards in Japan are typically exchanged after a bow, with two hands extended, and the wording facing the recipient. Leave the card on the table for the entire meeting—don't quickly stuff it in your wallet or toss it into your briefcase.
- **Comedy** Use humor cautiously because it often does not translate well. Avoid jokes that rely on wordplay and puns or events in your country, about which local people might have little or no knowledge.
- **Body Language** Do not "spread out" by hanging your arms over the backs of chairs, but don't be too stiff either. Look people in the eye lest they deem you untrustworthy, but don't stare too intently in a challenging manner.

1. What are examples of values?
2. What type of custom might a conservative group oppose in a culture?
3. The law that restricts the gift giving by US firms at home and abroad is called *what*?

2.3 Social Structure and Education

2.3 Describe the roles of social structure and education in culture.

social structure
A culture's fundamental organization, including its groups and institutions, its system of social positions and their relationships, and the process by which its resources are distributed.

social group
Collection of two or more people who identify and interact with each other.

social stratification
Process of ranking people into social layers or classes.

Social structure embodies a culture's fundamental organization, including its groups and institutions, its system of social positions and their relationships, and the process by which its resources are distributed. Social structure plays a role in many aspects of business, including production-site selection, advertising methods, and the costs of doing business in a country. Three important elements of social structure that differ across cultures are social group associations, social status, and social mobility.

Social Group Associations

People in all cultures associate themselves with a variety of **social groups** collections of two or more people who identify and interact with each other. Social groups contribute to each individual's identity and self-image. Two groups that play especially important roles in affecting business activity everywhere are family and gender.

FAMILY There are two different types of family groups. The *nuclear family* consists of a person's immediate relatives, including parents, brothers, and sisters. This concept of family prevails in Australia, Canada, the United States, and much of Europe. The *extended family* broadens the nuclear family and adds grandparents, aunts and uncles, cousins, and relatives through marriage. It is an important social group in much of Asia, the Middle East, North Africa, and Latin America.

Extended families can present some interesting situations for businesspeople unfamiliar with the concept. In some cultures, owners and managers obtain supplies and materials from another company at which someone from the extended family works. Gaining entry into such family arrangements can be difficult because quality and price are not sufficient motives to ignore family ties.

In extended-family cultures, managers and other employees often try to find jobs for relatives inside their own companies. This practice (called nepotism) can present a challenge to the human resource operations of a Western company, which typically must establish explicit policies on the practice.

GENDER *Gender* refers to socially learned habits associated with, and expected of, men or women. It includes behaviors and attitudes such as styles of dress and activity preferences. It is not the same thing as sex, which refers to the biological fact that a person is either male or female. Strictly speaking, gender is a category—people know they share a particular status with others but tend to remain strangers to one another.

Though many countries have made great strides toward gender equality in the workplace, others have not. In countries where women are denied equal opportunity in the workplace, their unemployment rate can easily be double that of men and their pay half that of men in the same occupation. Caring for children and performing household duties are also likely considered women's work in such countries and not the responsibility of the entire family.

Social Status

Another important aspect of social structure is the way a culture divides its population according to *status*—that is, according to positions within the structure. Although some cultures have only a few categories, others have many. The process of ranking people into social layers or classes is called **social stratification**.

Three factors that normally determine social status are family heritage, income, and occupation. In most industrialized countries, royalty, government officials, and top business leaders occupy the highest social layer. Scientists, medical doctors, and others with a university education occupy the middle layer. Next are those with vocational training or a secondary-school education, people who dominate the manual and clerical occupations. Although rankings are fairly stable, they can and do change over time. For example, because Confucianism (a major Chinese religion) stresses a life of learning, not commerce, Chinese culture frowned on businesspeople for centuries. In modern China, however, people who obtain wealth and power through business are considered important role models for younger generations.

✪ **MyLab Management** Watch It Impact of Culture on Business
a Spotlight on China
Apply what you have learned so far about the fundamental aspects of culture. If your instructor has assigned this, go to **www.pearson.com/mylab/management** to watch a video case about doing business in Chinese culture and answer questions.

Social Mobility

Moving to a higher social class is easy in some cultures but difficult or impossible in others. **Social mobility** is the ease with which individuals can move up or down a culture's "social ladder." For much of the world's population today, one of two systems regulates social mobility: a *caste system* or a *class system*.

social mobility
Ease with which individuals can move up or down a culture's "social ladder."

CASTE SYSTEM A **caste system** is a system of social stratification in which people are born into a social ranking, or *caste*, with no opportunity for social mobility. India is the classic example of a caste culture. Although the Indian constitution officially bans discrimination by caste, its influence persists. Little social interaction occurs between castes, and marrying out of one's caste is taboo. Opportunities for work and advancement are defined within the system, and certain occupations are reserved for the members of each caste. For example, a member of a lower caste cannot supervise someone of a higher caste because personal clashes would be inevitable.

caste system
System of social stratification in which people are born into a social ranking, or caste, with no opportunity for social mobility.

The caste system forces Western companies to make some difficult decisions when entering the Indian marketplace. They must decide whether to adapt to local human resource policies in India or to import their own from the home country. As globalization penetrates deeper into Indian culture, both the nation's social system and international companies will face challenges.

CLASS SYSTEM A **class system** is a system of social stratification in which personal ability and actions determine social status and mobility. It is the most common form of social stratification in the world today. But class systems vary in the amount of mobility they allow. Highly class-conscious cultures offer less mobility and, not surprisingly, experience greater class conflict. Across Western Europe, for example, wealthy families have retained power for generations by restricting social mobility. Companies doing business there must sometimes deal with class conflict in the form of labor–management disputes that can increase the cost of doing business.

class system
System of social stratification in which personal ability and actions determine social status and mobility.

Conversely, lower levels of class-consciousness encourage mobility and lessen conflict. A more cooperative atmosphere in the workplace tends to prevail when people feel that a higher social standing is within their reach. For example, most US citizens share the belief that hard work can improve their standard of living and social status, with relatively less regard for family background.

Education

Education is crucial for passing on traditions, customs, and values. Each culture educates its young people through schooling, parenting, religious teachings, and group memberships. Families and other groups provide informal instruction about customs and how to socialize with others. In most cultures, intellectual skills such as reading and mathematics are taught in formal educational settings.

Data that a government provides about its people's education level must be taken with a grain of salt. Comparisons from country to country can be difficult because many nations rely on literacy tests of their own design. Although some countries administer standardized tests, others require only a signature as proof of literacy. Yet searching for untapped markets or new factory locations can force managers to rely on such undependable benchmarks. As you can see from Table 2.1, some countries have further to go than others to increase national literacy rates. Around 800 million adults remain illiterate globally.

Countries with poorly educated populations attract the lowest-paying manufacturing jobs. Nations with excellent programs for basic education tend to attract relatively good-paying industries. Those that invest in worker training are usually repaid in productivity increases and rising incomes. Meanwhile, countries with highly educated workforces can attract the highest-paying jobs.

Emerging economies in Asia owe much of their rapid economic development to solid education systems. They focus on rigorous mathematical training in primary and secondary schooling. University education concentrates on the hard sciences and aims to train engineers, scientists, and managers.

brain drain
Departure of highly educated people from one profession, geographic region, or nation to another.

THE "BRAIN DRAIN" PHENOMENON The quality of a nation's education system is related to its level of economic development. **Brain drain** is the departure of highly educated people from one profession, geographic region, or nation to another. Over the years, political unrest and economic hardship has forced many Indonesians to flee their homeland for other nations, particularly Hong Kong, Singapore, and the United States. Most of Indonesia's brain drain has occurred among Western-educated professionals in finance and technology—exactly the people needed for economic development.

Many countries in Eastern Europe experienced high levels of brain drain early in their transition to market economies. Economists, engineers, scientists, and researchers in all fields fled westward to escape poverty. But as these nations continue their long transition from communism, some of them are luring professionals back to their homelands—a process known as *reverse brain drain*.

TABLE 2.1 Illiteracy Rates of Selected Countries

Country	Adult Illiteracy Rate (% of People Age 15 and Up)
Burkina Faso	64
Pakistan	42
Nigeria	40
Morocco	31
Cambodia	23
Zimbabwe	13
Brazil	7
Peru	5
Colombia	5
Mexico	5
Portugal	4
Philippines	4

Source: Based on The World Factbook dataset, Washington, DC: Central Intelligence Agency, (https://www.cia.gov/library/publications/the-world-factbook/index.html).

1. Social structure embodies a culture's fundamental organization, including *what*?
2. A person and his or her immediate relatives including parents and siblings, is called a *what*?
3. The departure of highly educated people from one profession, region, or nation to another is called *what*?

2.4 Religion

Human values often originate from religious beliefs. Different religions take different views of work, savings, and material goods. Identifying why they do so can help us understand business practices in other cultures. Knowing how religion affects business is especially important in countries with religious governments.

2.4 Outline how the major world religions can influence business.

Map 2.1 (on pages 78–79) shows where the world's major religions are practiced. Religion is not confined to national political boundaries but can exist in different regions of the world simultaneously. It is also common for several or more religions to be practiced within a single nation. In the following sections, we explore Christianity, Islam, Hinduism, Buddhism, Confucianism, Judaism, and Shinto. We examine their potential effects, both positive and negative, on international business activity.

Christianity

Christianity was born in Palestine around 2,000 years ago among Jews who believed that God sent Jesus of Nazareth to be their savior. Although Christianity boasts more than 300 denominations, most Christians belong to the Roman Catholic, Protestant, or Eastern Orthodox churches. With 2 billion followers, Christianity is the world's single largest religion. The Roman Catholic faith asks its followers to refrain from placing material possessions above God and others. Protestants believe that salvation comes from faith in God and that hard work gives glory to God—a tenet known widely as the "Protestant work ethic." Many historians believe this conviction was a main factor in the development of capitalism and free enterprise in nineteenth-century Europe.

Christian organizations sometimes get involved in social causes that affect business policy. For example, some conservative Christian groups have boycotted the Walt Disney Company (www.disney.com), charging that, in portraying young people as rejecting parental guidance, Disney films impede the moral development of young viewers worldwide.

The Catholic Church itself has been involved in some highly publicized controversies. Ireland-based Ryanair (www.ryanair.com), Europe's leading low-fare airline, ruffled the feathers of the Roman Catholic Church with an ad campaign. The ad depicted the pope (the head of the Catholic Church) claiming that the fourth secret of Fatima was Ryanair's low fares. The Church sent out a worldwide press release accusing the airline of blaspheming the pope. But much to the Church's dismay, the press release generated an enormous amount of free publicity for Ryanair.

Hyundai (www.hyundai.com) offended the Catholic Church when it ran a TV commercial during World Cup soccer matches. The spot showed a "church" in Argentina with a stained-glass window of a soccer ball, a soccer ball topped with a crown of thorns, and parishioners receiving slices of pizza instead of communion hosts. The Catholic Church took offense at the images of people worshipping soccer and at the mocking of its practice of receiving Holy Communion. Hyundai put a stop to the ad two days after it began airing.

Islam

With 1.3 billion adherents, Islam is the world's second-largest religion. The prophet Muhammad founded Islam around AD 600 in Mecca, the holy city of Islam located in Saudi Arabia. Islam thrives in North Africa, the Middle East, Central Asia, Pakistan, and some Southeast Asian nations, including Indonesia. Muslim concentrations are also found in most European and US cities. *Islam* means "submission to Allah," and *Muslim* means "one who submits to Allah." Islam revolves around the "five pillars": (1) reciting the *Shahada* (profession of faith), (2) giving to the poor, (3)

Map 2.1
World Religions

OCEAN

RUSSIA

KAZAKHSTAN

MONGOLIA

CHINA

INDIA

PACIFIC
OCEAN

INDIAN
OCEAN

AUSTRALIA

NEW
ZEALAND

- Christianity
- Judaism
- Hinduism
- Islam
- Buddhism
- Nature religion
- Chinese religion
- Other groups

praying five times daily, (4) fasting during the holy month of *Ramadan*, and (5) making the *Hajj* (pilgrimage) to the Saudi Arabian city of Mecca at least once in a person's lifetime.

Religion strongly affects the kinds of goods and services acceptable to Muslim consumers. Islam, for example, prohibits the consumption of alcohol and pork. Popular alcohol substitutes are soft drinks, coffee, and tea. Substitutes for pork include lamb, beef, and poultry (all of which must be slaughtered in a prescribed way so as to meet *halal* requirements). Markets for hot coffee and tea are quite large in Muslim culture because they often play ceremonial roles. And because usury (charging interest for money lent) violates the laws of Islam, credit card companies collect management fees rather than interest, and each cardholder's credit line is limited to an amount held on deposit.

Nations governed by Islamic law (see Chapter 3) sometimes segregate the sexes at certain activities and in locations such as schools. In Saudi Arabia, women cannot drive cars on public streets. In orthodox Islamic nations, men cannot conduct market research surveys with women at their homes unless they are family members. Women visiting Islamic cultures need to be especially sensitive to Islamic beliefs and customs. Although the issue of *hejab* (Islamic dress) is hotly debated, both Muslim and non-Muslim women are officially expected to wear body-concealing garments and scarves over their hair.

Hinduism

Hinduism formed around 4,000 years ago in present-day India, where more than 90 percent of Hinduism's 900 million adherents live. It is also the majority religion of Nepal and a secondary religion in Bangladesh, Bhutan, and Sri Lanka. Considered by some to be a way of life rather than a religion, Hinduism recalls no founder and recognizes no central authority or spiritual leader. Integral to the Hindu faith is the caste system described earlier in this chapter.

Hindus believe in reincarnation—the rebirth of the human soul at the time of death. For many Hindus, the highest goal of life is *moksha*—escaping from the cycle of reincarnation and entering a state of eternal happiness called *nirvana*. Hindus tend to disdain materialism. Strict Hindus do not eat or willfully harm any living creature because it might be a reincarnated human soul. Because Hindus consider cows to be sacred animals, they do not eat beef. Yet, consuming cow's milk is considered a means of religious purification. Firms such as McDonald's (www.mcdonalds.com) must work closely with government and religious officials in India in order to respect Hindu beliefs. In many regions, McDonald's has removed all beef products from its menu and prepares vegetable and fish products in separate kitchen areas. And for those Indians who do eat red meat (but not cows because of their sacred status), the company sells the Maharaja Mac, made of lamb, in place of the Big Mac.

In India, there have been attacks on Western consumer-goods companies in the name of preserving Indian culture and Hindu beliefs. Some companies such as Pepsi-Cola (www.pepsi.com) have been vandalized, and local officials even shut down a KFC restaurant (www.kfc.com) for a time. Although it currently operates in India, Coca-Cola (www.cocacola.com) once left the market completely rather than succumb to demands that it reveal its secret formula to authorities. India's investment environment has improved greatly in recent years. Yet labor–management relations sometimes deteriorate to such a degree that strikes cut deeply into productivity.

Buddhism

Buddhism was founded about 2,600 years ago in India by a Hindu prince named Siddhartha Gautama, who later became the Buddha. Today, Buddhism has around 380 million followers, mostly in China, Tibet, Korea, Japan, Vietnam, and Thailand, with pockets of Buddhists in Europe and the Americas. Although founded in India, Buddhism has relatively few adherents there. Unlike Hinduism, Buddhism rejects the caste system of Indian society. But like Hinduism, Buddhism promotes a life centered on spiritual rather than worldly matters. Buddhism also teaches that seeking pleasure for the human senses causes suffering. In a formal ceremony, Buddhists take refuge in the "three jewels": the Buddha, the *dharma* (his teachings), and the *sangha* (community of enlightened beings). They seek *nirvana* (escape from reincarnation) through charity, modesty, compassion for others, restraint from violence, and general self-control.

Although monks at many temples are devoted to lives of solitary meditation and discipline, many other Buddhist priests are dedicated to lessening the burden of human suffering. They finance schools and hospitals across Asia and are active in worldwide peace movements. In Tibet, most people

Buddhism instructs its followers to live a simple life void of materialistic ambitions. But as globalization pries open Asia's markets, the products of Western multinational corporations are streaming in. Here, a Buddhist monk takes a selfie with a group of Italian children. Do you think Asian cultures can modernize while retaining their traditional values and beliefs?

Gari Wyn Williams/Alamy Stock Photo

still acknowledge the exiled Dalai Lama as the spiritual and political head of the Buddhist culture. In the United States, a coalition of religious groups and human rights advocates continue to press the US Congress to apply economic sanctions against countries that are seen as practicing religious persecution.

Confucianism

An exiled politician and philosopher named Kung-fu-dz (pronounced "Confucius" in English) began teaching his ideas in China nearly 2,500 years ago. Today, China is home to most of Confucianism's 225 million followers. Confucian thought is also ingrained in the cultures of Japan, South Korea, and nations with large numbers of ethnic Chinese, such as Singapore.

South Korean business practice reflects Confucian thought in its rigid organizational structure and unswerving reverence for authority. Korean employees do not question strict chains of command. Yet, efforts to apply Korean-style management in overseas subsidiaries have caused some high-profile disputes with US executives and confrontations with factory workers in Vietnam.

Some observers contend that the Confucian work ethic and a commitment to education helped spur East Asia's phenomenal economic growth, but others respond that the link between culture and economic growth is weak. They argue that economic, historical, and international factors are at least as important as culture. They say that Chinese leaders had distrusted Confucianism for centuries because they believed that it stunted economic growth. Many ordinary Chinese, however, despised merchants and traders because their main objective (earning money) violated Confucian beliefs. As a result, many Chinese businesspeople moved to Indonesia, Malaysia, Singapore, and Thailand, where they launched successful businesses.

Judaism

More than 3,000 years old, Judaism was the first religion to preach belief in a single God. Nowadays, Judaism has roughly 18 million followers worldwide. In Israel, Orthodox ("fully observant") Jews make up 12 percent of the population and constitute an increasingly important economic segment. In Jerusalem, there is even a modeling agency that specializes in casting Orthodox Jews in ads aimed both inside and outside the Orthodox community. Models include scholars and one rabbi. Targeting specific groups, however, must be done carefully. The Israeli branch of Swedish furniture retailer, IKEA, targeted ultra-Orthodox Jews with an advertising catalog purposely containing no images of women. IKEA pulled the catalog and headquarters in Sweden issued an apology, saying " . . . we have been very clear that this is not what the IKEA brand stands for."[3]

Employers and human resource managers must be aware of important days in the Jewish faith. Because the Sabbath lasts from sundown on Friday to sundown on Saturday, work schedules might need adjustment. Devout Jews want to be home before sundown on Fridays. On the Sabbath itself, they do not work, travel, or carry money. Several other important observances are Rosh Ha-Shanah (the two-day Jewish New Year, in September or October), Yom Kippur (the Day of Atonement, 10 days after New Year), Passover (which celebrates the Exodus from Egypt, in March or April each year), and Hanukkah (which celebrates an ancient victory over the Syrians, usually in December).

Marketers must take into account foods that are banned among strict Jews. Pork and shellfish (such as lobster and crab) are prohibited. Meat is stored and served separately from milk. Other meats must be slaughtered according to a practice called *shehitah*. Meals prepared according to Jewish dietary traditions are called *kosher*. Most airlines offer kosher meals for Jewish passengers on their flights.

Shinto

Shinto (meaning "way of the gods") arose as the native religion of the Japanese. But today, Shinto can claim only about 4 million strict adherents in Japan. Because modern Shinto preaches patriotism, it is sometimes said that the religion of Japan is nationalism. Shinto teaches sincere and ethical behavior, loyalty and respect toward others, and enjoyment of life.

Shinto beliefs are reflected in the workplace through the traditional practice of lifetime employment (although this is waning today) and through the traditional trust extended between firms and customers. Japanese competitiveness in world markets has benefited from loyal workforces, low employee turnover, and good labor–management cooperation. The phenomenal success of many Japanese companies in recent decades gave rise to the concept of a Shinto work ethic, certain aspects of which have been emulated by Western managers.

QUICK STUDY 4

1. Which denomination of Christianity has a "work ethic" named after it?
2. India is home to more than 90 percent of the adherents of *which* religion?
3. The Dalai Lama is the spiritual and political head of *which* religion?

2.5 Personal Communication

2.5 Explain the importance of personal communication to international business.

communication
System of conveying thoughts, feelings, knowledge, and information through speech, writing, and actions.

People in every culture have a **communication** system to convey thoughts, feelings, knowledge, and information through speech, writing, and actions. Understanding a culture's spoken language gives us great insight into why people think and act the way they do. Understanding a culture's body language helps us avoid sending unintended or embarrassing messages. Let's examine each of these forms of communication more closely.

Spoken and Written Language

Spoken and written language is the most obvious difference we notice when traveling in another country. We overhear and engage in many conversations and read many signs and documents to find our way. Knowledge about a people's language is the key to deeply understanding a culture.

Linguistically different segments of a population are often culturally, socially, and politically distinct. Malaysia's population is composed of Malay (60 percent), Chinese (30 percent), and Indian (10 percent) peoples. Although Malay is the official national language, each ethnic group speaks its own language and continues its traditions. The United Kingdom includes England, Northern Ireland, Scotland, and Wales. The native languages of Ireland and Scotland are dialects of *Gaelic*, and the speaking of *Welsh* in Wales predates the use of English in Britain. After decades of decline, Gaelic and Welsh are staging comebacks on radio and television and in school curricula.

The global reach of media today, increased travel for tourism and business, and aging populations mean that some cultures face the possibility of losing their native languages. Read the Global Sustainability feature, titled "Speaking in Fewer Tongues," to see how a lack of social sustainability can endanger languages around the world.

GLOBAL SUSTAINABILITY   Speaking in Fewer Tongues

One day this year, somewhere in the world, an old man or woman will die and his or her language will die, too. Dozens of languages have just one native speaker still living. Here are the facts, the consequences, and what can be done.

- **Some Are Losing.** Of the world's roughly 6,000 languages, about 90 percent have fewer than 100,000 speakers. By the end of this century, more than half of the world's languages might be lost; perhaps fewer than 1,000 will survive. One endangered language is Aramaic, a 2,500-year-old Semitic language that was once the major language in the Middle East.
- **Some Are Gaining.** Even as minority languages die out, three languages continue to grow in popularity: Mandarin, Spanish, and English. English has emerged as the universal language of business, higher education, diplomacy, science, popular music, entertainment, and international travel. More than 70 nations give special status to English, and roughly one-quarter of the world's population is fluent or competent in it.

- **The Consequences.** The loss of a language can diminish the richness of a people's cultural, spiritual, and intellectual life. What is lost includes prayers, myths, humor, poetry, ceremonies, conversational styles, and terms for emotions, behaviors, and habits. When a language dies, all these must be expressed in a new language with different words, sounds, and grammar.
- **What Can Be Done?** Linguists are concerned that such a valuable part of human culture could vanish, so they are busily creating videotapes, audiotapes, and written records of endangered tongues before they disappear. Communities are also taking action. In New Zealand, Maori communities set up nursery schools called *kohanga reo*, or "language nests," that are staffed by elders and conducted entirely in Maori.
- **Want to Know More?** Visit Enduring Voices (http://travel.nationalgeographic.com/travel/enduring-voices), Living Tongues (www.livingtongues.org), and the Foundation For Endangered Languages (www.ogmios.org).

IMPLICATIONS FOR MANAGERS The importance of understanding local languages is becoming increasingly apparent on the Internet. Roughly one-half to two-thirds of all web pages are in English, but about three-fourths of all Internet users are nonnative English speakers. Software-solutions providers assist companies from English-speaking countries to adapt their websites for global e-business. Consumers across the globe bring their tastes, preferences, and buying habits online with them in search of an enjoyable buying experience.

Language proficiency is crucial in production facilities where nonnative managers supervise local employees. One US manager in Mexico was confused when his seemingly relaxed and untroubled workers went on strike. The problem lay in different cultural perspectives. Mexican workers generally do not take the initiative in problem solving and workplace complaints. Workers concluded that the plant manager knew, but did not care, about their concerns because he did not question employees about working conditions. Likewise, employees in the west often question their bosses or seek additional explanation if something doesn't seem quite right. But western managers working in China must work hard at ascertaining what local workers think because they might not be accustomed to speaking up and questioning authority figures.

Marketers prize insights into the interests, values, attitudes, and habits of teenagers to better target their promotions. Habbo (www.habbo.com), the world's largest virtual hangout for teens, says teens worldwide communicate with friends primarily through Facebook (www.facebook.com), its Messenger app, and other instant messaging apps. They tend to reserve email for non-personal needs such as school, work, and correspondence with family members.

LANGUAGE BLUNDERS Advertising slogans and company documents must be translated carefully so that messages are received precisely as intended. If they are not carefully translated, a company can make a language blunder in its international business dealings. In Sweden, Kellogg (www.kellogg.com) had to rename its Bran Buds cereal because the Swedish translation came out roughly as "burned farmer." And then there's the entrepreneur in Miami who tried to make the most of a visit to the United States by the Pope of the Roman Catholic Church. He quickly printed T-shirts for Spanish-speaking Catholics that should have read, "I saw the Pope (el Papa)." But a gender error on the noun resulted in T-shirts proclaiming, "I saw the Potato (la Papa)"! Other translation blunders include:

- An English-language sign in a Moscow hotel read, "You are welcome to visit the cemetery where famous Russian composers, artists, and writers are buried daily except Thursday."

- A sign for English-speaking guests in a Tokyo hotel read, "You are respectfully requested to take advantage of the chambermaids."
- An airline ticket office in Copenhagen read in English, "We take your bags and send them in all directions."
- A Japanese knife manufacturer labeled its exports to the United States with "Caution: Blade extremely sharp! Keep out of children."
- Braniff Airlines' English-language slogan "Fly in Leather" was translated into "Fly Naked" in Spanish.

Such blunders are not the exclusive domain of humans. The use of machine translation—computer software used to translate one language into another—is booming along with the explosion in the number of nonnative English speakers using the Internet. One search engine allows its users to search the Internet in English and Asian languages, translate web pages, and compose an email in one language and send it in another. The computers attempted a translation of the following: "The Chinese Communist Party is debating whether to drop its ban on private-enterprise owners being allowed to join the party." And it came up with this in Chinese: "The Chinese Communist Party is debating whether to deny its ban in join the Party is allowed soldier enterprise owners on." Various other machine translators turned the French version of "I don't care" ("*Je m'en fou*") into "I myself in crazy," "I of insane," and "Me me in madman."

lingua franca

Third or "link" language understood by two parties who speak different native languages.

LINGUA FRANCA A **lingua franca** is a third or "link" language understood by two parties who speak different native languages. The original *lingua franca* arose to support ancient trading activities and contained a mixture of Italian and French, along with Arabic, Greek, and Turkish. Although only 5 percent of the world's population speaks English as a first language, it is the most common *lingua franca* used in international business, followed closely by French and Spanish.

The Cantonese dialect of Chinese spoken in Hong Kong and the Mandarin dialect spoken in Taiwan and on the Chinese mainland are so different that a *lingua franca* is often preferred. And, although India's official language is Hindi, its *lingua franca* among the multitude of dialects is English because it was once a British colony. Many young people speak what is referred to as "Hinglish"—a combination of Hindi, Tamil, and English words mixed within a single sentence.

Multinational corporations also sometimes choose a *lingua franca* for official internal communications because they operate in many nations, each with its own language. Companies that use English for internal correspondence include Philips (www.philips.com; a Dutch electronics firm), Asea Brown Boveri (www.abb.com; a Swiss industrial giant), Alcatel-Lucent (www.alcatel-lucent.com; a French telecommunications firm), and Rakuten (www.rakuten.co.jp; a Japanese Internet shopping site). English plays a prominent role in international business because just five countries (Australia, Canada, New Zealand, the United Kingdom, and the United States) account for one-quarter of global economic output, despite having just 6 percent of the world's population. These five nations also boast some of the highest standards of living in the world.[4]

Body Language

body language

Language communicated through unspoken cues, including hand gestures, facial expressions, physical greetings, eye contact, and the manipulation of personal space.

Body language communicates through unspoken cues, including hand gestures, facial expressions, physical greetings, eye contact, and the manipulation of personal space. Similar to spoken language, body language communicates both information and feelings and differs greatly from one culture to another. Italians, French, Arabs, and Venezuelans, for example, tend to animate conversations with lively hand gestures and other body motions. Japanese and Koreans, although more reserved, can communicate just as much information through their own body languages; a look of the eye can carry as much or more meaning as two flailing arms.

Most body language is subtle and takes time to recognize and interpret. For example, navigating the all-important handshake in international business can be tricky. In the United States, a firm grip and several pumps of the arm is usually the standard. But in the Middle East and Latin America, a softer clasp of the hand with little or no arm pump is the custom. And in some countries, such as Japan, people do not shake hands at all but bow to one another. Bows of respect carry different meanings, usually depending on the recipient. Associates of equal standing bow about 15 degrees toward one another. But proper respect for an elder requires a bow of about 30 degrees. Bows of remorse or apology should be about 45 degrees.

Proximity is an extremely important element of body language to consider when meeting someone from another culture. If you stand or sit too close to your counterpart (from their

Forming the thumb-and-index finger circle in most of Europe and in the United States means "okay"; in Germany, it's a rude gesture. Tapping one's nose in England and Scotland means "You and I are in on the secret"; in Wales, it means "You're very nosy." Tapping one's temple in much of Western Europe means "You're crazy"; in the Netherlands, it means "You're very clever."

leungchopan/Shutterstock; Lorenz Timm/Shutterstock; Borjaika/Shutterstock

perspective), you might invade their personal space and appear aggressive. If you remain too far away, you risk appearing untrustworthy. For North Americans, a distance of about 19 inches is about right between two speakers. For Western Europeans, 14 to 16 inches seems appropriate, but someone from the United Kingdom might prefer about 24 inches. Koreans and Chinese are likely to be comfortable about 36 inches apart; people from the Middle East will close the distance to about 8 to 12 inches.

Physical gestures often cause the most misunderstanding between people of different cultures because they can convey very different meanings. For example, the thumbs-up sign is vulgar in Italy and Greece but means "all right" or even "great" in the United States.

QUICK STUDY 5

1. Every culture has a communication system that it uses to convey *what*?
2. A special language understood by two parties who speak different native languages is called *what*?
3. An interesting fact about body language is *what*?

2.6 Culture in the Global Workplace

So far in this chapter, we learned about the key components of culture and read examples from around the world about how each one influences international business. Likewise, the workplace holds a prominent position in a culture. In addition to providing a way to earn a living, work supplies people with an avenue to give their lives meaning, structure, and identity.[5] Let's now take a closer look at how specific aspects of a people's beliefs and behaviors affect activities in the global workplace.

2.6 Describe how firms and culture interact in the global workplace.

Perception of Time

People in many Latin American and Mediterranean cultures are casual about their use of time. They maintain flexible schedules and would rather enjoy their time than sacrifice it to unbending efficiency. Businesspeople, for example, might arrive after the scheduled meeting time and prefer to build personal trust before discussing business. Not surprisingly, it usually takes longer to conduct business in these parts of the world than in the United States or northern Europe.

By contrast, people in Japan and the United States typically arrive promptly for meetings, keep tight schedules, and work long hours. The emphasis on using time efficiently reflects the underlying value of hard work in both these countries. Yet, people in Japan and the United States sometimes differ in how they use their time at work. For example, US employees strive toward workplace efficiency and might leave work early if the day's tasks are done, reflecting the value placed on producing individual results. But in Japan, although efficiency is prized, it is equally important to look busy in the eyes of others even when business is slow. A Japanese employee would not leave work early even if he or she finished the day's task ahead of schedule. Japanese workers want to demonstrate their dedication to superiors and coworkers—an attitude grounded in values such as the concern for group cohesion, loyalty, and harmony.

View of Work

Some cultures display a strong work ethic; others stress a more balanced pace in juggling work and leisure. People in southern France like to say they work to live, whereas people in the United States live to work. The French say work is a means to an end for them, whereas work is an end in itself in the United States. Not surprisingly, the lifestyle in southern France is slower-paced. People tend to concentrate on earning enough money to enjoy a relaxed, quality lifestyle. Businesses practically close down during August, when many workers take month-long paid holidays, often outside the country.

In European countries, start-ups are considered quite risky, and capital for entrepreneurial ventures can be scarce. Moreover, if an entrepreneur's venture goes bust, he or she can find it very difficult to obtain financing for future projects because of the stigma of failure. This remains true despite some recent progress. By contrast, in the United States, a prior bankruptcy is sometimes considered a valuable learning experience (assuming lessons were learned) when referenced in a business plan. As long as US bankers or venture capitalists see promising business plans, they are generally willing to loan money. Today, many European nations are trying to encourage entrepreneurial activity.

Material Culture

material culture

All the technology used in a culture to manufacture goods and provide services.

All the technology used in a culture to manufacture goods and provide services is called its **material culture**. Material culture is often used to measure the technological advancement of a nation's markets or industries. Generally, a firm enters a new market only if demand for its products has developed or the infrastructure can support production operations. Some nations lack the most basic elements of a modern society's material culture. Yet, technology is helping countries at the bottom of the global economic pyramid break down barriers that keep their people mired in poverty.

Material culture often displays uneven development across a nation's geography, markets, and industries. For example, Shanghai has long played an important role in China's international trade because of its strategic location and its superb harbor on the East China Sea. Although it is home to only 1 percent of the total population, Shanghai accounts for about 5 percent of China's total output—including about 12 percent of both its industrial production and its financial-services output. Likewise, Bangkok, the capital city of Thailand, houses only 10 percent of the nation's population but accounts for about 40 percent of its economic output. Meanwhile, the northern parts of the country remain rural, consisting mostly of farms, forests, and mountains.

Cultural diffusion is a powerful force of cultural change. Traditional cultures can be especially susceptible to change when they are introduced to the lifestyles of people in wealthy, industrialized nations. Satellite TV and the Internet are highly effective at exposing people to the cultural traits of other societies. Do you think the family living in this traditional thatch hut in India view the world any differently since they acquired satellite television?

Mikhail Vorobiev/123RF.com

Cultural Change

A **cultural trait** is anything that represents a culture's way of life, including gestures, material objects, traditions, and concepts. Such traits include bowing to show respect in Japan (gesture), a Buddhist temple in Thailand (material object), celebrating the Day of the Dead in Mexico (tradition), and practicing democracy in the United States (concept).

The process whereby cultural traits spread from one culture to another is called **cultural diffusion**. As new traits are accepted and absorbed into a culture, *cultural change* occurs naturally and, as a rule, gradually. Globalization and technological advances are increasing the pace of both cultural diffusion and cultural change. The global spread of media today, along with the expanding reach of the Internet and services such as YouTube and Facebook, plays a role in cultural diffusion. These forces expose people, some of whom are extremely isolated, to the traits and ideas of other cultures.

WHEN COMPANIES CHANGE CULTURES International companies are often agents of cultural change. As trade and investment barriers fall, for example, US consumer-goods and entertainment companies are moving into untapped markets. Critics sometimes charge that, in exporting the products of such firms, the United States is practicing **cultural imperialism**—the replacement of one culture's traditions, folk heroes, and artifacts with substitutes from another.

Fears of cultural imperialism still drive some French to oppose the products of the Walt Disney Company (www.disney.com) and its Disneyland Paris theme park. They fear "Mickey and Friends" could replace traditional characters rooted in French culture. McDonald's (www.mcdonalds.com) is also sometimes charged with cultural imperialism. It is reported that the average Japanese child thinks McDonald's was invented in Japan and exported to the United States. Chinese children consider "Uncle" McDonald to be "funny, gentle, kind, and understanding." Meanwhile, politicians in Russia decry the "Snickerization" of their culture—a snide term that refers to the popularity of the Snickers candy bar made by Mars Incorporated (www.mars.com). And when the Miss World Pageant was held in India, conservative groups criticized Western corporate sponsors for spreading the message of consumerism and portraying women as sex objects.

Sensitivity to the cultures in which they operate can help companies avoid charges of cultural imperialism. Firms must focus not only on meeting people's product needs but also on how their activities and products affect people's traditional ways and habits. Rather than view their influence on culture as the inevitable consequence of doing business, companies can take several steps to soften those effects. For example, policies and practices that are at odds with deeply held beliefs can be introduced gradually. Managers could also seek the advice of highly respected local individuals such as elders, who fulfill key societal roles in many emerging markets. And businesses should always make clear to local workers the benefits of any proposed changes that are closely linked to cultural traits.

An area in which US companies might be changing the workplace in other cultures is how workers are treated. As US companies outsource jobs to other nations, they are being held accountable for how these subcontractors treat their employees. In the process, US companies are exporting the values of the US workplace.

WHEN CULTURES CHANGE COMPANIES Culture often forces companies to adjust business policies and practices. Managers from the United States, for example, often encounter cultural differences that force changes in how they motivate employees in other countries. Managers sometimes use *situational management*—a system in which a supervisor walks an employee through every step of an assignment or task and monitors the results at each stage. This technique helps employees fully understand the scope of their jobs and clarifies the boundaries of their responsibilities.

Cultural differences can force other changes to suit local culture. In Vietnam, individual criticism should be delivered privately to save employees from "losing face" among coworkers. Individual praise for good performance can be delivered either in private or in public, if done carefully. The Vietnamese place great value on group harmony, so an individual can be embarrassed if singled out publicly as being superior to the rest of the work unit. And Vietnam's traditional, agriculture-based economy means that people's concept of time revolves around the seasons. The local "timepiece" is the monsoon, not the clock. Western managers need to take a patient, long-term view of business activity there.

cultural trait
Anything that represents a culture's way of life, including gestures, material objects, traditions, and concepts.

cultural diffusion
Process whereby cultural traits spread from one culture to another.

cultural imperialism
Replacement of one culture's traditions, folk heroes, and artifacts with substitutes from another.

Overseas Chinese youth learn to perform Tai Chi during the "Chinese Root-Seeking Tour" summer camp in Beijing, the capital of China. The camp attracts more than 6,000 overseas Chinese youths from 54 countries and regions each year. It is designed to educate young people in the cultural traditions of their Chinese ancestors. Organizers hope that by gaining a better understanding about Chinese history and culture, these youths will grow up to become good cross-cultural communicators between China and other nations.

Xinhua/Alamy Stock Photo

Studying Culture in the Workplace

When discussing culture's role in the global workplace, we need to discuss two frameworks developed to differentiate between cultures. These frameworks examine characteristics such as values, attitudes, social structures, and so on. Let's now take a detailed look at each of these tools.

KLUCKHOHN-STRODTBECK FRAMEWORK Two researchers by the names of Florence Kluckhohn and Fred Strodtbeck compared cultures and believed they differ along six dimensions. The **Kluckhohn-Strodtbeck** framework studies a given culture by asking each of the following questions:[6]

Kluckhohn–Strodtbeck framework
Framework for studying cultural differences along six dimensions, such as focus on past or future events and belief in individual or group responsibility for personal well-being.

- Do people believe that their environment controls them, that they control the environment, or that they are part of nature?
- Do people focus on past events, on the present, or on the future implications of their actions?
- Are people easily controlled and not to be trusted, or can they be trusted to act freely and responsibly?
- Do people desire accomplishments in life, carefree lives, or spiritual and contemplative lives?
- Do people believe that individuals or groups are responsible for each person's welfare?
- Do people prefer to conduct most activities in private or in public?

Case: Japanese Culture By providing answers to each of these six questions, we can apply the Kluckhohn–Strodtbeck framework to Japanese culture:

1. *Japanese believe in a delicate balance between people and environment that must be maintained.* Suppose an undetected flaw in a company's product harms customers using it. In many countries, a high-stakes class-action lawsuit would be filed against the manufacturer on behalf of the victims' families. This scenario rarely plays out in Japan. Japanese culture does not hold that individuals can possibly control every situation but that accidents happen. Japanese victims would receive heartfelt apologies, a promise it won't happen again, and a relatively small damage award.

2. *Japanese culture emphasizes the future.* Because Japanese culture emphasizes strong ties between people and groups, including companies, forming long-term relationships with people is essential when doing business there. Throughout the business relationship, Japanese companies remain in close, continuous contact with buyers to ensure that their needs are being met. This relationship also forms the basis of a communication channel by

which suppliers learn about the types of products and services buyers would like to see in the future.

3. ***Japanese culture treats people as quite trustworthy.*** Business dealings among Japanese companies are based heavily on trust. After an agreement to conduct business is made, it is difficult to break unless there are extreme, uncontrollable factors at work. This is because of the fear of "losing face" if one cannot keep a business commitment. In addition to business applications, society at large reflects the Japanese concern for trustworthiness. Crime rates are quite low, and the streets of Japan's largest cities are very safe to walk at night.

4. ***Japanese are accomplishment-oriented—not necessarily for themselves, but for their employers and work units.*** Japanese children learn the importance of groups early by contributing to the upkeep of their schools. They share duties such as mopping floors, washing windows, cleaning chalkboards, and arranging desks and chairs. They carry such habits learned in school into the adult workplace, where management and labor tend to work together toward company goals. Japanese managers make decisions only after considering input from subordinates. Also, materials buyers, engineers, designers, factory floor supervisors, and marketers cooperate closely throughout each stage of a product's development.

5. ***Japanese culture emphasizes individual responsibility to the group and group responsibility to the individual.*** This trait has long been a hallmark of Japanese corporations. Traditionally, subordinates promise hard work and loyalty, and top managers provide job security. But to remain competitive internationally, Japanese companies have eliminated jobs and moved production to China and Vietnam and other low-wage nations. As the tradition of job security falls by the wayside, more Japanese workers now consider working for non-Japanese companies, whereas others find work as temporary employees. Although this trait of loyalty is diminishing somewhat in business, it remains a very prominent feature in other aspects of Japanese society, especially family.

6. ***The culture of Japan tends to be public.*** You will often find top Japanese managers located in the center of a large, open-space office surrounded by the desks of many employees. In comparison, Western executives are often secluded in walled offices located on the perimeter of workspaces. This characteristic reaches deep into Japanese society— consider, for example, Japan's tradition of bathing in public bathhouses.

HOFSTEDE FRAMEWORK Psychologist and researcher, Geert Hofstede, created another way to differentiate cultures.[7] He initially developed the **Hofstede framework** from a study of more than 110,000 people working in IBM subsidiaries (www.ibm.com) in 40 countries. Later research expanded the framework so that it now contains a total of six dimensions:[8]

Hofstede framework
Framework for studying cultural differences along five dimensions, such as individualism versus collectivism and equality versus inequality.

1. ***Individualism versus collectivism.*** This dimension identifies the extent to which a culture emphasizes the individual versus the group. Individualist cultures (those scoring high on this dimension) value hard work and promote entrepreneurial risk-taking, thereby fostering invention and innovation. Although people are given freedom to focus on personal goals, they are held responsible for their actions. That is why responsibility for poor business decisions is placed squarely on the shoulders of the individual in charge. At the same time, higher individualism might be responsible for higher rates of employee turnover. You can see how a sample of nations scored on this and the remaining Hofstede dimensions in Table 2.2.

   People in collectivist cultures (those scoring low on this dimension) feel a strong association to groups, including family and work units. The goal of maintaining group harmony is probably most evident in the family structure. People in collectivist cultures tend to work toward collective rather than personal goals and are responsible to the group for their actions. In turn, the group shares responsibility for the well-being of each of its members. Thus, in collectivist cultures, success or failure tends to be shared among the people in the work unit, rather than any individual receiving all the praise or blame. All social, political, economic, and legal institutions reflect the group's critical role.

2. ***Power distance.*** This dimension conveys the degree to which a culture accepts social inequality among its people. A culture with large power distance tends to be characterized by much inequality between superiors and subordinates. Organizations tend also to be

TABLE 2.2 National Scores on the Hofstede Dimensions

Country	Individualism	Power Distance	Uncertainty Avoidance	Masculinity	Long-Term Orientation	Indulgence
Argentina	46	49	86	56	20	62
Australia	90	36	51	61	21	71
Brazil	38	69	76	49	44	59
Canada	80	39	48	52	36	68
Chile	23	63	86	28	31	68
China	20	80	30	66	87	24
France	71	68	86	43	63	48
Germany	67	35	65	66	83	40
Great Britain	89	35	35	66	51	69
Hong Kong	25	68	29	57	61	17
India	48	77	40	56	51	26
Japan	46	54	92	95	88	42
South Korea	18	60	85	39	100	29
Mexico	30	81	82	69	24	97
Netherlands	80	38	53	14	67	68
Norway	69	31	50	8	35	55
Russia	39	93	95	36	81	20
Spain	51	57	86	42	48	44
Sweden	71	31	29	5	53	78
United States	91	40	46	62	26	68

Source: Based on the dataset at (http://geerthofstede.com/dimension-data-matrix).

more hierarchical, with power deriving from prestige, force, and inheritance. Executives and upper management in cultures with large power distance often enjoy special recognition and privileges. On the other hand, cultures with small power distance display a greater degree of equality, with prestige and rewards more equally shared between superiors and subordinates. Power in these cultures is seen to derive more from hard work and entrepreneurial drive and is therefore often considered more legitimate.

3. *Uncertainty avoidance.* This dimension identifies the extent to which a culture avoids uncertainty and ambiguity. A culture with large uncertainty avoidance values security and places its faith in strong systems of rules and procedures in society. Not surprisingly, perhaps, cultures with large uncertainty avoidance normally have lower employee turnover, more formal rules for regulating employee behavior, and more difficulty implementing change. Cultures scoring low on uncertainty avoidance tend to be more open to change and new ideas. This helps explain why individuals in this type of culture tend to be entrepreneurial and organizations tend to welcome the best business practices from other cultures. Because people tend to be less fearful of change, however, these cultures can also suffer from higher levels of employee turnover.

4. *Masculinity versus femininity.* This dimension captures the extent to which a culture emphasizes masculinity versus femininity. According to Hofstede, cultures scoring high on masculinity tend to be characterized more by personal assertiveness and the accumulation of wealth, typically translating into an entrepreneurial drive. Cultures scoring low on this dimension (greater tendency toward femininity) generally have more relaxed lifestyles, wherein people are more concerned about caring for others as opposed to material gain.

5. *Long-term orientation.* This dimension indicates a society's perception of time and its attitudes about overcoming obstacles with time, if not with will and strength. It attempts to capture the differences between Eastern and Western cultures. A high-scoring culture (strong long-term orientation) values respect for tradition, thrift, perseverance, and a sense

of personal shame. These cultures tend to have a strong work ethic because people expect long-term rewards from today's hard work. A low-scoring culture is characterized by individual stability and reputation, fulfillment of social obligations, and reciprocation of greetings and gifts. These cultures can change more rapidly because tradition and commitment are not insurmountable impediments to change.

6. *Indulgence versus restraint.* This dimension captures the extent to which a society allows free expression. An indulgent society (one scoring high on this dimension) allows people to rather freely satisfy human needs related to enjoying life and having fun. By contrast, a restrained society uses varying degrees of social norms to suppress the free satisfaction of such needs. Indulgent societies tend to value individual happiness, leisure, freedom, and personal control. Restrained societies are less concerned with each of these and tend to believe that certain aspects of life are predestined. Employees in an indulgent society might be more forthcoming with frank opinions and more likely to quit an unsatisfying job. And whereas service workers in indulgent societies are expected to offer customers a genuine smile and friendly demeanor, such overt expressions could appear artificial in a restrained society.[9]

QUICK STUDY 6

1. People living in different cultures often have different views regarding their *what*?
2. *What* is an example of cultural imperialism?
3. The Kluckhohn-Strodtbeck framework does *not* directly investigate whether people do *what*?
4. In the Hofstede framework the term "power distance" refers to *what*?

BOTTOM LINE FOR BUSINESS

As globalization continues to draw companies into the international arena, understanding local culture can give a company an advantage over rivals. By avoiding ethnocentric thinking, managers can avoid mistakenly disregarding the beneficial aspects of other cultures. Culturally literate managers who understand local needs and desires bring their companies closer to customers and, therefore, increase their competitiveness. They can become more-effective marketers, negotiators, and production managers. Let's explore several areas in which culture has a direct impact on international business activity.

Marketing and Cultural Literacy
Many international companies operating in local markets abroad take advantage of the public relations value of supporting national culture. Companies are helping India's government to maintain some of the nation's most precious historical monuments and sites and, in the process, are earning the goodwill of the people.

This chapter introduced the Kluckhohn–Strodtbeck and Hofstede frameworks for classifying cultures. Local culture is

important for a company exploring international markets for its products. We can see the significance of power distance in the export of luxury items. A nation with a large power distance accepts greater inequality among its people and tends to have a wealthy upper class that can afford luxury goods. Thus, companies marketing products such as expensive jewelry, high-priced cars, and even yachts could find wealthy market segments within relatively poor nations.

Work Attitudes and Cultural Literacy
National differences in work attitudes are complex and involve other factors in addition to culture. Perceived opportunity for financial reward is no doubt a strong element in attitudes toward work in any culture. Research suggests both US and German employees work longer hours when there is a greater likelihood that good performance will lead to promotion and increased pay. Yet this appears relatively less true in Germany, where wages are less variable and job security and jobless benefits (such as free national health care) are greater. Thus, other aspects of German society are at least as important as culture in determining work

attitudes. The culturally literate manager understands the complexity of national workplace attitudes and incorporates this knowledge into reward systems.

Expatriates and Cultural Literacy

As stated in our discussion of classifying cultures, people living in broadly different cultures tend to respond differently in similar business situations. This is why companies that send personnel abroad to unfamiliar cultures are concerned with cultural differences. For example, a Norwegian manager working in Japan for a European car manufacturer, but whose colleagues were mostly Japanese, soon became frustrated with the time needed to make decisions and take action. The main cause for his frustration was that the uncertainty avoidance index for Japan is much larger than in his native Norway (see Table 2.2). In Japan, a greater aversion to uncertainty led to the need for a greater number of consultations than would have been needed in the home market. The frustrated manager eventually left Japan and returned to Norway.

Gender and Cultural Literacy

In Japan, men have traditionally held nearly all positions of responsibility. Women have generally served as office clerks and administrative assistants until their mid- to late 20s, when they were expected to marry and then focus on tending to family needs. Although this is still largely true today, progress is being made in expanding the role of women in Japan's business community. Women own nearly a quarter of all businesses in Japan, but many of these businesses are very small and have little economic influence. Greater gender equality prevails in Australia, Canada, Germany, and the United States, but women in these countries still tend to earn less money than men in similar positions.

MyLab Management

Go to **www.pearson.com/mylab/management** to complete the problem marked with this icon .

Chapter Summary

LO2.1 Explain culture and the need for cultural knowledge.
- *Culture* is the set of values, beliefs, rules, and institutions held by a specific group of people. Work habits and product preferences can be influenced by the physical environment.
- We tend to equate a nation–state and its people with a single culture. But most nations are home to numerous *subcultures*—groups of people who share a unique way of life within a larger, dominant culture.
- Managers try to avoid *ethnocentricity* (the tendency to view one's own culture as superior to others) and to develop *cultural literacy* (detailed knowledge necessary to function happily and effectively in another culture).

LO2.2 Summarize the cultural importance of values and behavior.
- A culture's *values and attitudes* are important because they affect work ethic and material desires. Understanding the *aesthetics* that a people value can help improve effectiveness and avoid blunders.
- *Manners* are appropriate behaviors, speech, and dress in a culture, whereas *customs* are appropriate behaviors in specific circumstances. Knowing these can improve performance and help avoid sending unintended messages.

LO2.3 Describe the roles of social structure and education in culture.
- *Social structure* embodies a culture's fundamental organization. It affects the cost of doing business and business decisions such as site selection and which advertising methods to use.
- *Social status* and *mobility* in a culture guide people's desire for material things and their emphasis on work. Firms also consider the influence of family and gender on people's purchase and work decisions.
- *Education* level affects the quality of the workforce and a people's standard of living. Wages in a society are determined to a large extent by a people's educational attainment.

LO2.4 Outline how the major world religions can influence business.
- Different *religions* view work, savings, and material goods differently. Protestants believe that hard work glorifies God, which is known as the "Protestant work ethic."
- Strict Hindus disdain materialism and believe in the caste system, which constrains consumer markets and can affect work ethic. Western restaurants must adapt to the fact that many Hindus are vegetarians or don't eat beef.
- Islamic governments often ban alcohol consumption so coffee, tea, and soft drinks are popular substitutes. Judaism's religious holidays are often crucial to observe and food must often be *kosher* for believers.

LO2.5 Explain the importance of personal communication to international business.
- *Personal communication* conveys thoughts, feelings, knowledge, and information through speech, writings, and actions. Understanding a people's system of communication provides insight into their values and behavior.
- Language proficiency can help avoid misunderstandings when nonnative managers supervise local employees. It can also help avoid translation blunders in marketing and advertising efforts.
- Most body language (including personal space, hand gestures, and handshakes) is subtle and takes time to interpret. English is a common *lingua franca* in this era of globalization.

LO2.6 Describe how firms and culture interact in the global workplace.
- Attributes such as a culture's perception of time, view of work, and material culture affect many aspects of business, including management styles, work scheduling, and reward systems.
- *Cultural change* occurs when people integrate the gestures, material objects, traditions, or concepts of another culture through *cultural diffusion*. Companies might change culture when they import new products, policies, and practices into a country.
- The two main frameworks used to compare cultures are the *Kluckhohn–Strodtbeck framework* and the *Hofstede framework*. These frameworks help firms understand many aspects of a culture, including risk taking, innovation, job mobility, team cooperation, pay levels, and hiring practices.

Key Terms

aesthetics (p. 72)
attitudes (p. 72)
body language (p. 84)
brain drain (p. 76)
caste system (p. 75)
class system (p. 75)
communication (p. 82)
cultural diffusion (p. 87)
cultural imperialism (p. 87)

cultural literacy (p. 70)
cultural trait (p. 87)
culture (p. 68)
customs (p. 73)
ethnocentricity (p. 70)
folk custom (p. 73)
Hofstede framework (p. 89)
Kluckhohn–Strodtbeck framework (p. 88)
lingua franca (p. 84)

manners (p. 72)
material culture (p. 86)
popular custom (p. 73)
social group (p. 74)
social mobility (p. 75)
social stratification (p. 74)
social structure (p. 74)
subculture (p. 69)
values (p. 71)

✪ TALK ABOUT IT 1

Two students are discussing why they are not studying international business. "International business doesn't affect me," declares the first student. "I'm going to stay here, not work in some foreign country." "Yeah, me neither," agrees the second. "Besides, some cultures are really strange. The sooner other countries start doing business our way, the better."

2-1. What arguments can you present to counter these students' perceptions?

✪ TALK ABOUT IT 2

Imagine that you and several classmates are the top managers of a company seeking new international markets. Select your company's industry and product line, and then choose a country to enter.

2-2. Is it important for the company to balance the need for global efficiency through large-scale production with the need for cultural responsiveness through local product adaption?

2-3. Will cultural differences between the home and host countries require alterations in personnel or corporate practices?

Ethical Challenge

You are the CEO of a Chinese recycling company. You are finding it difficult to attract domestic employees to your plants based in several remote locations outside five cities across the country. Your usual source of migrant workers is not as plentiful as in the past, and government rules put low-skilled workers from rural areas at a disadvantage. Over 30 percent of your workers are recent migrants and they have adjusted to their new employment and life very quickly.

2-4. Taking China as an example, what types of migrant employees can work in the country? Why does the government set limits?

2-5. What additional costs might impact the business if they employ migrant employees?

Teaming Up

Two groups of four students each will debate the benefits and drawbacks of individualist versus collectivist cultures. After the first student from each side has spoken, the second student will question the opponent's arguments, looking for holes and inconsistencies. The third student will attempt to answer these arguments. The fourth student will present a summary of each side's arguments. Finally, the class will vote on which team has offered the more compelling argument.

✪ Market Entry Strategy Project

This exercise corresponds to the *MESP* online simulation. For the country your team is researching, integrate your answers to the following questions into your completed *MESP* report.

2-6. What are the various ethnicities that reside in the nation?

2-7. List several of the values that people hold dear.

2-8. What are several of the culture's identifiable manners and customs?

2-9. Describe in broad terms the nation's social structure.

2-10. How would you describe people's perception of time and work?

2-11. Is the culture relatively open or closed to cultural change?

MyLab Management

✪ Go to **www.pearson.com/mylab/management** for the following assisted-graded writing questions:

2-12. Iran's religious government banned access to the WhatsApp messaging site because, officials said, it is owned by Jewish "American Zionist" Mark Zuckerberg. Might the ban have more to do with the government's fear of social media's power to spread information and ideas quickly? Explain.

2-13. The first time Swedish furniture company, IKEA, searched outside Scandinavia for new design inspiration, it looked to China. The resulting product line, called Trendig, was a cultural collaboration between Swedish and Chinese artisans. What cultural and global business factors may have inspired IKEA to seek design aesthetics in China?

A Tale of Two Cultures

Many cultures in Asia are in the midst of an identity crisis. In effect, they are being torn between two worlds. Pulling in one direction is a traditional value system derived from agriculture-based communities and extended families—that is, elements of a culture in which relatives take care of one another and state-run welfare systems are unnecessary. Pulling from the opposite direction is a new set of values emerging from manufacturing- and finance-based economies—elements of a culture in which workers must often move to faraway cities to find work, sometimes leaving family members to fend for themselves.

For decades, Western multinational corporations set up factories across Southeast Asia to take advantage of relatively low-cost labor. Later, local companies sprang up and became competitive global players in their own right. Spectacular rates of economic growth in a few short decades elevated living standards beyond what was thought possible. Young people in Malaysia and Thailand felt the lure of "Western" brands. Gucci handbags (www.gucci.com), Harley-Davidson motorcycles (www.harley-davidson.com), and other global brands became common symbols of success. Many parents felt that brand-consciousness among their teenage children signaled familywide success.

Despite the growing consumer society, polls of young people show them holding steadfast to traditional values such as respect for family and group harmony. Youth in Hong Kong, for example, overwhelmingly believe that parents should have a say in how hard they study, in how they treat family members and elders, and in their choice of friends.

The practice of outsourcing non-essential tasks helped create an Indian IT industry worth $140 billion. As outsourcing continues to wash over India, a social revolution is occurring among India's graduates of technical colleges and universities. Unlike in India's traditional high-tech service jobs, young call-center staffers are in direct contact with Western consumers, answering inquiries on items such as tummy crunchers and diet pills. For these young, mostly female staffers, the work means money, independence, and freedom—sometimes far away from home in big cities such as Bangalore and Mumbai. But in addition to the training in American accents and geography, these workers are learning new ideas about family, materialism, and relationships.

Parents are suspicious of call-center work because it must typically be performed at night in India, when consumers are awake in Canada, Europe, or the United States. When her parents objected, Binitha Venugopal quit her call-center job in favor of a "regular" daytime job. Binitha says her former coworkers' values are changing and that dating and live-in relationships among them are

common. Indian tradition dictates that young adults live with their parents at least until they get married (typically to someone their parents choose). Perhaps facilitating shifting values in India is an influx of Western professionals, such as lawyers, who accepted good-paying jobs there that could not be found back home during the global recession.

Roopa Murthy works for an Indian company that offers call-center and back-office services. Roopa moved to Bangalore from her native Mysore armed with an accounting degree. She now earns $400 per month, which is several times what her father earned before he retired from his government job. Roopa cut her hair short and tossed aside her *salwar kameez*, the traditional loose-fitting clothing she wore back home, in favor of designer-labeled Western attire.

Although she once shunned drinking and her curfew at home was 9 p.m., Roopa now frequents a pub called Geoffrey's, where she enjoys dry martinis and rum, and The Club, a suburban disco. Roopa confesses that she is "seeing someone" but that her parents would disapprove, adding, "It is difficult to talk to Indian parents about things like boyfriends." She said she sometimes envies her callers' lives but that she hopes her job will help her succeed. "I may be a small-town girl, but there is no way I'm going back to Mysore after this," she said. Many observers wonder whether Asia can embrace modernization and yet retain traditional values.

Thinking Globally

2-14. If you worked for an international firm doing business in Asia, is there anything you would suggest to ease the tensions these cultures are experiencing? Be specific.

2-15. Social ills in any country are normally born from a multitude of factors. What role, if any, do you think globalization is having in higher reported rates of divorce, crime, and drug abuse in Asia?

2-16. Broadly defined, Asia comprises more than 60 percent of the world's population—a population that practices Buddhism, Confucianism, Hinduism, Islam, and numerous other religions. Do you think it is possible to carry on a valid discussion of "Asian" values? Explain.

Sources: "Reboot: Indian Outsourcing Specialists Must Reboot Their Strategies," *The Economist*, January 21, 2017, pp. 56–57; Stephanie Overby, "Cloud Services Now Account for a Third of IT Outsourcing Market," *CIO* magazine (www.cio.com), July 22, 2016; Heather Timmons, "Outsourcing to India Draws Western Lawyers," *New York Times* (www.nytimes.com), August 4, 2010; Lisa Tsering, "NBC Picks up Series 'Outsourced' for Fall 2010," Indiawest.com website (www.indiawest.com), May 27, 2010.

Chapter Three

Political Economy and Ethics

Learning Objectives

After studying this chapter, you should be able to

3.1 Describe the key features of each form of political system.

3.2 Explain how the three types of economic systems differ.

3.3 Summarize the main elements of each type of legal system.

3.4 Outline the global legal issues facing international firms.

3.5 Describe the main issues of global ethics and social responsibility.

A Look Back

Chapter 2 explored the main components of culture and showed how they relate to business practices. We learned about different methods used to study cultures and how these methods are applied in business.

A Look at This Chapter

This chapter first explores the political economy of nations. We examine the main types of political, economic, and legal systems in practice around the world. We then examine key legal issues for international firms and explore the importance of ethical behavior and social responsibility.

A Look Ahead

Chapter 4 presents the economic development of nations. We feature several large emerging markets and explore key challenges facing countries that are transforming their economies into free market systems.

MyLab Management
✪ IMPROVE YOUR GRADE!

When you see this icon ✪, visit **www.pearson.com/mylab/management** for activities that are applied, personalized, and offer immediate feedback.

PepsiCo's Global Challenge

PURCHASE, New York—Entrepreneurial despite its enormity, PepsiCo's (www.pepsico.com) sales have grown an amazing 13 percent annually for nearly half a century. To keep profits bubbling, PepsiCo is targeting international sales, which comprise 40 percent of total revenue, and is investing aggressively in India, which ranks among PepsiCo's top 10 markets and its three fastest-growing countries. Shown here is an Iranian consumer holding a can of Pepsi Cola written in Persian script.

Like all companies operating internationally, PepsiCo must carefully navigate political, economic, and legal systems in other countries. For example, the company needed to obtain the approval of India's government before it could increase its investment there by nearly one-third. PepsiCo also showed its respect for the importance of local politics and law in China. Rather than trying to force China to accept wholly owned subsidiaries, executives formed strategic alliances with local Chinese business partners. PepsiCo knows that companies are expected to be model citizens wherever they operate and that their conduct directly affects their bottom line.

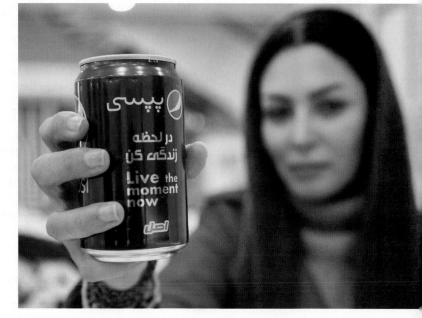

Bertrand Gardel/Hemis/Alamy Stock Photo

PepsiCo's CEO, Indra Nooyi, is moving the company's product line in healthier directions. She introduced the motto "Performance with Purpose" to reflect how the company is transforming its global businesses. She wants the company to balance its drive for profits with making healthier "guilt-free" snacks, decreasing its impact on the environment, and taking care of its workforce. In fact, healthier foods comprise as much as 45 percent of PepsiCo's revenue today. Born and raised in India, Nooyi believes it is essential that "we use corporations as a productive player in addressing some of the big issues facing the world."

Nooyi also helped spark "green" initiatives at PepsiCo. She has proved that investments in water- and heat-related conservation projects can be worthy endeavors. In addition to their environmental benefits, those projects now save the company $55 million annually. Nooyi says, "Companies today are bigger than many economies. We are little republics. We are engines of efficiency. If companies don't do [responsible] things, who is going to?" As you read this chapter, consider how companies adapt to political, economic, and legal systems worldwide while fulfilling their ethical and social responsibilities.[1]

As business men and women venture abroad, they can encounter social and economic environments that are unlike anything they've ever experienced. In Chapter 2 we learned how important it is for employees of a company to have cultural knowledge when doing business with people from other countries. Another crucial element of international business success is an understanding of other countries' political, economic, and legal systems.

political economy

Study of how a country manages its affairs by using its political, economic, and legal systems.

Political economy is the study of how a country manages its affairs by using its political, economic, and legal systems. Any nation's political economy reflects how its people put their preferred political, economic, and legal theories into practice and the institutions they create. Political economy forms within a cultural context, which is why they vary from nation to nation in their degree of openness, individualism, equality, transparency, flexibility, and so on.

Individualism is a belief that the concerns of individuals should be placed above the group's welfare. *Collectivism*, on the other hand, stresses the primacy of the group over individual needs. As we learned in Chapter 2, no nation is either completely individualist or completely collectivist in its *cultural* orientation. Likewise, the *political economy* of every nation displays a unique blend of individual and group values. In other words, no political economy is entirely focused on individual needs at the expense of social well-being, and vice versa.

Firms involved in international business should understand how different systems of political economy operate. This applies not only to companies with traditional, brick-and-mortar subsidiaries abroad, but also to Internet-based companies and many types of service firms. Rupert Murdoch's News Corp. (www.newscorp.com) removed BBC news (www.bbc.co.uk) from its Asian lineup of television stations after it criticized China. Barnes & Noble (www.barnesandnoble.com) and Amazon (www.amazon.com) stopped selling the English-language version of Adolf Hitler's *Mein Kampf* to Germans when the German government complained (although it's illegal only to sell the German-language version). A statement by Barnes & Noble read, "Our policy with regard to censorship remains unchanged. But as responsible corporate citizens, we respect the laws of the countries where we do business."[2]

Google (www.google.com) had to skillfully handle protests by German politicians and citizens who decried its plan to introduce its Street View mapping service in that country. Memories of secret police prying into personal lives under past dictatorial regimes make Germans fearful of allowing the entire world to see photos of their homes and gardens on the Internet.[3] Knowing how different political economies function can help companies avoid trouble and be more effective in their operations.

In this chapter, we present the basic differences among the main types of political, economic, and legal systems around the world. We also discuss several legal topics that hold special importance for international business activities. We close this chapter with a look at key issues of ethical behavior and social responsibility.

Google's Street View project in Germany had already censored car number license plates and people's faces by blurring them, but that wasn't enough. Google modified its policies in Germany, and offers people who do not wish to have their property's photos published online the option to request blurring of an image. Part of the problem is that Google's cameras snap photos from atop cars and so peer over top privacy hedges and walls. What is your personal view on this matter?

Randy Miramontez/Alamy Stock Photo

3.1 Political Systems

Understanding the nature of political systems in other countries can reduce the risks of conducting international business there. A **political system** includes the structures, processes, and activities by which a nation governs itself. Japan's political system, for instance, features a *Diet* (Parliament) that chooses a prime minister to carry out the operations of government with the help of Cabinet ministers. The *Diet* consists of two houses of elected representatives who enact the nation's laws. These laws affect the personal lives of people living in and visiting Japan, as well as the activities of companies doing business there.

A country's political system is rooted in the history and culture of its people. Factors such as population, age and race composition, and per capita income influence a country's political system. In Switzerland, the political system actively encourages all eligible members of society to vote. By means of *public referendums*, Swiss citizens vote directly on many national issues. The Swiss system works because Switzerland consists of a relatively small population living in a small geographic area. Contrast this practice with that of most other democracies, in which representatives of the people, not the people themselves, vote on national issues.

We can arrange the world's three political ideologies on a horizontal scale, with one on either end and one in the middle. At the one extreme lies *anarchism*—the belief that only individuals and private groups should control a nation's political activities. An anarchist views public government as unnecessary and unwanted because it tramples personal liberties.

At the other extreme lies *totalitarianism*—the belief that every aspect of people's lives must be controlled for a nation's political system to be effective. Totalitarianism disregards individual liberties and treats people as slaves of the political system. The state reigns supreme over institutions such as family, religion, business, and labor. Totalitarian political systems include authoritarian regimes such as communism and fascism.

Between those two extremes lies *pluralism*—the belief that both private and public groups play important roles in a nation's political activities. Each group (consisting of people with different ethnic, racial, class, and lifestyle backgrounds) serves to balance the power that can be gained by the others. Pluralistic political systems include democracies, constitutional monarchies, and some aristocracies.

To better understand how elements of politics influence international business, let's take a detailed look at the different forms of the two most common political systems: totalitarianism and democracy.

Totalitarianism

In a **totalitarian system**, individuals govern without the support of the people, tightly control people's lives, and do not tolerate opposing viewpoints. Nazi Germany under Adolf Hitler and the former Soviet Union under Joseph Stalin are historical examples of totalitarian governments. Today, North Korea is the most prominent example of a totalitarian government. Totalitarian leaders attempt to silence those with opposing political views and, therefore, require the near-total centralization of political power. But a "pure" form of totalitarianism is not possible because no totalitarian government is capable of entirely silencing all its critics.

Totalitarian governments tend to share three features:

* *Imposed Authority*   An individual or group forms the political system without the explicit or implicit approval of the people. Leaders often acquire and retain power through military force or fraudulent elections. In some cases, they come to power through legitimate means but then remain in office after their terms expire.
* *Lack of Constitutional Guarantees*   Totalitarian systems deny citizens the constitutional guarantees woven into the fabric of democratic practice. They limit, abuse, or reject concepts such as freedom of expression, periodically held elections, guaranteed civil and property rights, and minority rights.
* *Restricted Participation*   Political representation is limited to parties sympathetic to the government or to those who pose no credible threat. In most cases, political opposition is completely banned, and political dissidents are severely punished.

3.1 Describe the key features of each form of political system.

political system
Structures, processes, and activities by which a nation governs itself.

totalitarian system
Political system in which individuals govern without the support of the people, tightly control people's lives, and do not tolerate opposing viewpoints.

theocracy
Political system in which a country's religious leaders are also its political leaders.

theocratic totalitarianism
Political system under the control of totalitarian religious leaders.

secular totalitarianism
Political system in which leaders rely on military and bureaucratic power.

communism
Belief that social and economic equality can be obtained only by establishing an all-powerful Communist Party and by granting the government ownership and control over all types of economic activity.

socialism
Belief that social and economic equality is obtained through government ownership and regulation of the means of production.

THEOCRATIC TOTALITARIANISM A political system in which a country's religious leaders are also its political leaders is called a **theocracy**. The religious leaders enforce a set of laws and regulations based on religious beliefs. A political system under the control of totalitarian religious leaders is called **theocratic totalitarianism**.

Iran is a prominent example of a theocratic totalitarian state. Iran has been an Islamic state since the 1979 revolution in which the reigning monarch was overthrown. Today, many young Iranians appear disenchanted with the strict code imposed on many aspects of their public and private lives, including stringent laws against products and ideas deemed too "Western." They may not question their religious beliefs, but they do yearn for a more open society.

SECULAR TOTALITARIANISM A political system in which political leaders rely on military and bureaucratic power is called **secular totalitarianism**. It takes three forms: *communist*, *tribal*, and *right-wing*.

Under *communist totalitarianism* (referred to here simply as *communism*), the government maintains sweeping political and economic powers. The Communist Party controls all aspects of the political system, and opposition parties are given little or no voice. In general, each party member holding office is required to support all government policies, and dissension is rarely permitted. **Communism** is the belief that social and economic equality can be obtained only by establishing an all-powerful Communist Party and by instituting **socialism**— a system in which the government owns and controls all types of economic activity. This includes granting the government ownership of the means of production (such as capital, land, and factories) and the power to decide what the economy produces and the prices at which goods are sold.

However, important distinctions separate communism from socialism. Communists follow the teachings of Karl Marx and Vladimir Lenin, believe that a violent revolution is needed to seize control over resources, and wish to eliminate political opposition. Socialists believe in none of these. Thus, communists are socialists, but socialists are not necessarily communist.

Under *tribal totalitarianism*, one tribe (or ethnic group) imposes its will on others with whom it shares a national identity. Tribal totalitarianism characterizes the governments of several African nations, including Burundi and Rwanda. When the European colonial powers departed Africa, many national boundaries were created with little regard to ethnic differences among the people. People of different ethnicities found themselves living in the same nation, whereas members of the same ethnicity found themselves living in different nations. In time, certain ethnic groups gained political and military power over other groups. Animosity among them often erupted in bloody conflict.

Nations mired in military conflict pay a hefty price in terms of sustainability. Over the decades, civil war has inflicted enormous human, social, and environmental costs on many African nations. To explore the costs of civil wars (particularly in Africa) and how developed nations can help put an end to them, see the Global Sustainability feature, titled "From Civil War to Civil Society."

Under *right-wing totalitarianism*, the government endorses private ownership of property and a market-based economy but grants few (if any) political freedoms. Leaders generally strive for economic growth while opposing *left-wing totalitarianism* (communism). Argentina, Brazil, Chile, and Paraguay all had right-wing totalitarian governments in the 1980s.

Despite the inherent contradictions between communism and right-wing totalitarianism, China's current political system is a mix of the two ideologies. China's leaders are engineering high economic growth by implementing certain characteristics of a capitalist economy while retaining a hard line in the political sphere. The Chinese government is selling off money-losing, state-run companies and encouraging the investment needed to modernize its factories. But China's government still has little patience for dissidents who demand greater political freedom, and it does not allow a completely free press.

DOING BUSINESS IN TOTALITARIAN COUNTRIES What are the costs and benefits of doing business in a totalitarian nation? On the plus side, international companies can be relatively less concerned with local political opposition to their activities. On the negative side, they might need to pay bribes and kickbacks to government officials. Refusal to pay could result in loss of market access or even forfeiture of investments in the country.

| GLOBAL SUSTAINABILITY | From Civil War to Civil Society |

Today, most wars occur *within* nations that were once controlled and stabilized by colonial powers. If these nations are to prosper from globalization, they must break the vicious cycle whereby conflict causes poverty and poverty causes conflict.

- **War's Root Causes.** Although tribal or ethnic rivalry is typically blamed for starting civil wars, the most common causes are poverty, low economic growth, and dependency on natural resource exports. In fact, the poorest one-sixth of humanity endures four-fifths of the world's civil wars. Still, religious differences increasingly underlie civil conflicts.
- **What's at Stake.** It appeared that ethnic conflict was the root of pitched battles in Bunia, in the eastern part of Democratic Republic of the Congo. Yet the Hema and the Lendu tribes began fighting each other only when neighboring Uganda, which wanted to control mineral-rich Bunia, started arming rival militias in 1999. In the Darfur region of Sudan, Arab Muslims battled black non-Muslims. Depending on whom you ask, the conflict began as a fight over pastures and livestock or over the oil beneath them. Meanwhile, foreign investors remain wary.
- **What Is Lost.** On average, a civil conflict lasts eight years. And apart from the terrible human cost in lives and health, there is also a financial cost. Health costs are $5 billion per conflict because of collapsed health systems and forced

migrations (which worsen and spread disease). Gross domestic product (GDP) falls by 2.2 percent, and another 18 percent of income is spent on arms and militias. Full economic recovery takes a decade, which reduces output by about 105 percent of the nation's prewar GDP.

- **What to Do.** Because the risk of civil war is cut in half when income per person doubles, conflicts might be *prevented* by funneling more aid to poor nations. Also, war might be *limited* by restricting a nation in conflict from spending the proceeds from its exports on munitions or by lowering the world market price of those exports. Finally, to *halt* nations from slipping back into civil war, health and education aid could be increased after war ends, or a foreign power could intervene to keep the peace.
- **Want to Know More?** Visit the Centre for the Study of African Economies (www.csae.ox.ac.uk), Copenhagen Consensus Center (www.copenhagenconsensus.com), and World Bank Conflict Prevention and Reconstruction unit (www.worldbank.org).

Sources: Patrick Kanyangara, "Conflict in the Great Lakes Region: Root Causes, Dynamics and Effects," ETH Zurich Center for Security Studies (www.css.ethz.ch), May 26, 2016; "A New Depth of Horror," *The Economist* (www.economist.com), April 26, 2014; Paul Collier and Anke Hoeffler, *The Challenge of Reducing the Global Incidence of Civil War* (Oxford: Copenhagen Consensus, March 2004); Copenhagen Consensus Center website (www.copenhagenconsensus.com).

In any case, doing business in a totalitarian country can be a risky proposition. In a country such as the United States, laws regarding the resolution of contractual disputes are quite specific. In totalitarian nations, the law can be either vague or nonexistent, and people in powerful government positions can interpret laws largely as they please. In China, for instance, it may not matter so much what the law states but rather how individual bureaucrats interpret the law. The arbitrary nature of totalitarian governments makes it hard for companies to know how laws will be interpreted and applied to their particular business dealings.

Companies that operate in totalitarian nations are sometimes criticized for lacking compassion for people hurt by the oppressive policies of their hosts. Executives must decide whether to refrain from investing in totalitarian countries—and miss potentially profitable opportunities—or invest and bear the brunt of potentially damaging publicity. There are no simple answers to this controversial issue, which amounts to an ethical dilemma (we cover ethics later in this chapter).

Democracy

A **democracy** is a political system in which government leaders are elected directly by the wide participation of the people or by their representatives. Democracy differs from totalitarianism in nearly every respect. The foundations of modern democracy go back at least as far as the ancient Greeks.

democracy
Political system in which government leaders are elected directly by the wide participation of the people or by their representatives.

The Greeks tried to practice a *pure* democracy, one in which all citizens participate freely and actively in the political process. But a pure democracy is more an ideal than a workable system for several reasons. Some people have neither the time nor the desire to get involved in the political process. Also, citizens are less able to participate completely and actively as a population grows and as the barriers of distance and time increase. Finally, leaders in a pure democracy may find it difficult or impossible to form cohesive policies because direct voting can lead to conflicting popular opinion.

REPRESENTATIVE DEMOCRACY For practical reasons, most nations resort to a **representative democracy**, in which citizens elect individuals from their groups to represent their political

representative democracy
Democracy in which citizens elect individuals from their groups to represent their political views.

views. These representatives then help govern the people and pass laws. The people reelect representatives of whom they approve and replace those they no longer want representing them.

Representative democracies strive to provide some or all of the following:

- *Freedom of Expression*   A constitutional right in most democracies, freedom of expression ideally grants the right to voice opinions freely and without fear of punishment.
- *Periodic Elections*   Each elected representative serves for a period of time, after which the people (or electorate) decide whether to retain that representative. Two examples of periodic elections include the US presidential elections (held every four years) and the French presidential elections (held every five years).
- *Full Civil and Property Rights*   Civil rights include freedom of speech, freedom to organize political parties, and the right to a fair trial. Property rights are the privileges and responsibilities of owners of property (homes, cars, businesses, and so forth).
- *Minority Rights*   In theory, democracies try to preserve peaceful coexistence among groups of people with diverse cultural, ethnic, and racial backgrounds. Ideally, the same rights and privileges extend legally to each group, no matter how few its members.
- *Nonpolitical Bureaucracies*   The bureaucracy is the part of government that implements the rules and laws passed by elected representatives. In *politicized bureaucracies*, bureaucrats tend to implement decisions according to their own political views rather than those of the people's representatives. This clearly contradicts the purpose of the democratic process.

Despite such shared principles, countries vary greatly in the practice of representative democracy. Britain, for example, practices *parliamentary democracy*. The nation divides itself into geographical districts, and people in each district vote for competing *parties* rather than individual candidates. But the party that wins the greatest number of legislative seats in an election does not automatically win the right to run the country. Rather, a party must gain an *absolute majority*—that is, the number of representatives that a party gets elected must exceed the number of representatives elected among all other parties.

If the party with the largest number of representatives lacks an absolute majority, it can join with one or more other parties to form a *coalition government*. In a coalition government, the strongest political parties share power by dividing government responsibilities among themselves. Coalition governments are often formed in Italy, Israel, and the Netherlands, where a large number of political parties make it difficult for any single party to gain an absolute majority.

Nations also differ in the relative power that each political party commands. In some democratic countries, a single political party has effectively controlled the system for decades. In

Freedom of expression and political participation are rights that democracies strive to uphold. Supporters of the opposition party in Cambodia's capital, Phnom Penh, defied road blocks and a jail threat to hold a march in a last-gasp push for an independent probe into an election they say was fixed to favor the ruling party. In what ways do you think upholding freedom of expression and having a politically engaged populace can benefit a society?

REUTERS/Alamy Stock Photo

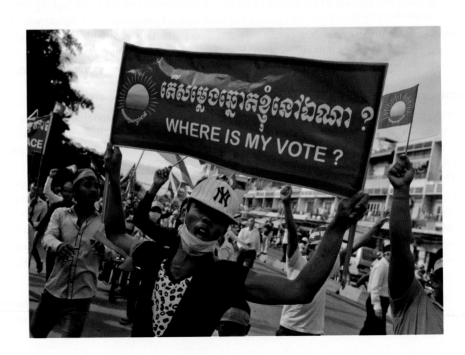

MANAGER'S BRIEFCASE Your Global Security Checklist

- **Getting There** Take nonstop flights when possible, as accidents are more likely during takeoffs and landings. Move quickly from an airport's public and check-in areas to more secure areas beyond passport control. Report abandoned packages to airport security.
- **Getting Around** Kidnappers watch for daily routines. Vary the exits you use to leave your house, office, and hotel, and vary the times that you depart and arrive. Drive with your windows up and doors locked. Swap cars with others occasionally, or take a cab one day and ride the tram/subway the next. Be discreet regarding your itinerary.
- **Keep a Low Profile** Don't draw attention by pulling out a large wad of currency or paying with large denominations. Avoid public demonstrations. Dress like the locals when possible and leave expensive jewelry at home. Avoid loud conversation and being overheard. If you rent an automobile, avoid the flashy car and choose a local, common model.

- **Guard Personal Data** Be friendly but cautious when answering questions about you, your family, and your employment. Keep answers short and vague when possible. Give out your work number only—all family members should do the same. Do not list your home or mobile phone numbers in directories. Do not carry items in your purse or wallet that contain your home address.
- **Use Caution** Be cautious if a local asks directions or the time—it could be a mugging ploy. When possible, travel with others and avoid walking alone after dark. Avoid narrow, dimly lit streets. If you get lost, act as if you know where you are, and ask directions from a place of business, not passersby. Beware of offers by drivers of unmarked or poorly marked cabs.
- **Know Emergency Procedures** Be familiar with the local emergency procedures before trouble strikes. Keep the phone numbers of police, fire, your hotel, your nation's embassy, and a reputable taxi service in your home and with you at all times.

Japan, for example, the Liberal Democratic Party (which is actually conservative) has enjoyed nearly uninterrupted control of the government since the 1950s. In Mexico, the Institutional Revolutionary Party (PRI) ran the country for 71 years until 2001 when the conservative National Action Party (PAN) won the presidency. The PRI returned to power in the presidential election of 2012.

DOING BUSINESS IN DEMOCRACIES Democracies maintain stable business environments primarily through laws that protect individual property rights. In theory, commerce prospers when the **private sector** includes independently owned firms that seek to earn profits. **Capitalism** is the belief that ownership of the means of production belongs in the hands of individuals and private businesses. Capitalism is also frequently referred to as the *free market*.

private sector
Segment of the economic environment comprising independently owned firms that seek to earn profits.

Although participative democracy, property rights, and free markets tend to encourage economic growth, they do not always do so. For instance, although India is the world's largest democracy, it experienced slow economic growth for decades until recently. Meanwhile, some countries achieved rapid economic growth under political systems that were not truly democratic. The four tigers of Asia—Hong Kong, Singapore, South Korea, and Taiwan—built strong market economies in the absence of truly democratic practices.

capitalism
Belief that ownership of the means of production belongs in the hands of individuals and private businesses.

Wherever in the world a business man or woman goes, whether to a democracy or to a totalitarian nation, it is essential that he or she be mindful of personal safety. Certainly, advancements in technology and transportation make it easier to do business globally. But because globalization also can increase efficiency for people with ulterior motives, trouble can arise spontaneously almost anywhere. For ways to keep a low profile and stay safe while on business abroad, see this chapter's Manager's Briefcase feature, titled "Your Global Security Checklist."

QUICK STUDY 1

1. What features characterize the political ideology called pluralism?
2. Communists believe that a violent revolution is needed to seize control over resources, wish to eliminate political opposition, and do *what else*?
3. What does a representative democracy strive to provide for its people?
4. By what other name is capitalism often referred?

3.2 Economic Systems

3.2 Explain how the three types of economic systems differ.

economic system
Structure and processes that a country uses to allocate its resources and conduct its commercial activities.

A country's **economic system** consists of the structure and processes that it uses to allocate its resources and conduct its commercial activities. Every economy displays a *tendency* toward individualist or collectivist economic values that reflects the nation's culture. For example, one culture might prefer theories grounded in individual freedom and responsibility and create a capitalist economic system. Meanwhile, another culture might value collectivist ideas and build a socialist, or even communist, system.

We can arrange national economies on a horizontal scale that is anchored by two extremes. At one end of the scale is a theoretical pure *centrally planned economy*, at the other end is a theoretical pure *market economy*, and in between is a *mixed economy* (see Figure 3.1).

Centrally Planned Economy

centrally planned economy
Economic system in which a nation's land, factories, and other economic resources are owned by the government, which plans nearly all economic activity.

A **centrally planned economy** is a system in which the government owns the nation's land, factories, and other economic resources. The government makes nearly all economy-related decisions—including who produces what and the prices of products, labor, and capital. Central planning agencies specify production goals for factories and other production units, and they even decide prices. In the former Soviet Union, for example, communist officials set prices for milk, bread, eggs, and other essential goods. The ultimate goal of central planning is to achieve a wide range of political, social, and economic objectives by taking complete control over the production and distribution of a nation's resources.

ORIGINS OF THE CENTRALLY PLANNED ECONOMY Central planning is rooted in the ideology of collectivism. Just as collectivist cultures emphasize group goals over individual ones, a centrally planned economy strives to achieve economic and social equality for the sake of the collective, not the individual.

German philosopher Karl Marx popularized the idea of central economic planning in the nineteenth century. Marx formulated his ideas while witnessing the hardship endured by working-class people in Europe during and after the Industrial Revolution. Marx argued that the economy could not be reformed, but that it must be overthrown and replaced with a more equitable "communist" system.

Different versions of Marx's ideas were implemented in the twentieth century by means of violent upheaval. Revolutions installed totalitarian economic and political systems in Russia in 1917, in China and North Korea in the late 1940s, and in Cuba in 1959. By the 1970s, central planning was the economic law in lands stretching across Central and Eastern Europe (Albania, Bulgaria, Czechoslovakia, East Germany, Hungary, Poland, Romania, and Yugoslavia), Asia (Cambodia, China, North Korea, and Vietnam), Africa (Angola and Mozambique), and Latin America (Cuba and Nicaragua).

DECLINE OF CENTRAL PLANNING In the late 1980s, nation after nation began to dismantle communist central planning in favor of market-based economies. Shortly after the former Soviet Union implemented its twin policies of *glasnost* (political openness) and *perestroika* (economic reform), its totalitarian government crumbled. Communist governments in Central and Eastern Europe fell soon after, and today countries such as the Czech Republic, Hungary, Poland, Romania, and Ukraine have republican governments. There are far fewer communist nations than there were two decades ago, although Cuba and North Korea remain hardline communist nations. Let's now examine several factors that economists, historians, and political scientists say contributed to the decline of centrally planned economies.

Figure 3.1
Range of Economic Systems

Although farming is a high-tech endeavor in the world's most advanced nations today, it is labor intensive and inefficient in North Korea. The government's failed communist economic policies hamper development and are at the root of its inability to afford fertilizers and modern machinery that could boost food production. Seemingly endless famines and economic collapse have cut North Korea's life expectancy to 67 years for men and 75 years for women.

Prevost Vincent/Hemis/Alamy Stock Photo

Failure to Create Economic Value Central planners paid little attention to the task of producing quality goods and services at the lowest possible cost. In other words, they failed to see that commercial activities succeed when they create economic value for customers. Along the way, scarce resources were wasted in the pursuit of commercial activities that were not self-sustaining.

Failure to Provide Incentives Government ownership of economic resources drastically reduced incentives for businesses to maximize the output obtained from those resources. Except for aerospace, nuclear power, and other sciences (in which government scientists excelled), there were few incentives to create new technologies, new products, and new production methods. The result was little or no economic growth and consistently low standards of living.

As the world's most closed economy, North Korea has earned its nickname, "The Hermit Kingdom." For the most part, North Korea's policy of *juche* (self-reliance) is causing extreme hardship for its citizens. The combination of recurring floods and droughts, a shortage of fertilizers, and a lack of farm machinery keep the nation from reaching its peak food-production potential. As a result, North Korea often must rely on aid from abroad to feed its people.

Failure to Achieve Rapid Growth Leaders in communist nations took note of the high rates of economic growth in countries such as Hong Kong, Singapore, South Korea, and Taiwan—called Asia's four tigers. That a once-poor region of the world had so rapidly achieved such astounding growth awakened central planners to the possibilities. They realized that an economic system based on private ownership fosters growth much better than one hampered by central planning.

North Korea, once again, provides us with a good example. Each year for a decade until 1999, the North Korean economy contracted. Out of desperation, the country's leaders quietly allowed limited free market reforms, and small bazaars soon dotted the countryside. Street-corner currency exchanges sprang up to help facilitate a tiny but growing trade with bordering Chinese merchants. Impoverished North Koreans could buy mobile phones and found hope for a better life in DVDs of South Korean soap operas. But a disastrous attempt to reform its currency dealt a serious setback to North Korea's experiment with the free market.

Failure to Satisfy Consumer Needs People in centrally planned economies were tired of a standard of living that had slipped far below that found in market economies. Ironically, although central planning was conceived to create a more equitable system of distributing wealth, too many central planners failed to provide even basic necessities such as adequate food, housing, and medical care. Underground (shadow) economies for all kinds of goods and services flourished and, in some cases, even outgrew "official" economies. Prices of goods on the black market were much higher than the official (and artificial) prices set by governments.

Mixed Economy

mixed economy
Economic system in which land, factories, and other economic resources are rather equally split between private and government ownership.

A **mixed economy** is a system in which land, factories, and other economic resources are rather equally split between private and government ownership. In a mixed economy, the government owns fewer economic resources than does the government in a centrally planned economy. Yet in a mixed economy, the government tends to control the economic sectors that it considers important to national security and long-term stability. Such sectors usually include iron and steel manufacturing (for building military equipment), oil and gas production (to guarantee continued manufacturing and availability), and automobile manufacturing (to guarantee employment for a large portion of the workforce). Many mixed economies also maintain generous welfare systems to support the unemployed and to provide health care for the general population.

Mixed economies are found all around the world: Denmark, France, Norway, Spain, and Sweden in Western Europe; India, Indonesia, Malaysia, Pakistan, and South Korea in Asia; Argentina in South America; and South Africa. Although all the governments of these nations do not centrally plan their economies, they all influence economic activity by means of special incentives, including hefty subsidies to key industries, and through significant government involvement in the economy.

ORIGINS OF THE MIXED ECONOMY Advocates of mixed economies contend that a successful economic system not only must be efficient and innovative but also should protect society from the excesses of unchecked individualism and organizational greed. The goal is to achieve low unemployment, low poverty, steady economic growth, and an equitable distribution of wealth by means of the most effective policies.

Proponents of mixed economies point out that European and US rates of productivity and growth were almost identical for decades after the Second World War. Although the United States has created more jobs, it has done so at the cost of widening social inequality, proponents say. They argue that nations with mixed economies should not dismantle their social-welfare institutions but should modernize them so that they contribute to national competitiveness. Austria, the Netherlands, and Sweden are taking this route. In the Netherlands, labor unions and the government agreed to an epic deal involving wage restraint, shorter working hours, budget discipline, new tolerance for part-time and temporary work, and the trimming of social benefits. As a result, unemployment in the Netherlands hovers around 6 percent. By comparison, the average jobless rate for all nations in the Euro currency area is around 10 percent.[4]

DECLINE OF MIXED ECONOMIES Many mixed economies are remaking themselves to more closely resemble free markets. When assets are owned by the government, there seems to be less incentive to eliminate waste or to practice innovation. Extensive government ownership on a national level tends to result in a lack of accountability, rising costs, and slow economic

Unlike communist North Korea, South Korea's economy is grounded in capitalist principles. The quality of life in South Korea is so notably better versus North Korea that life expectancy is 10 years longer (77) for men and nine years longer (84) for women. By 2030 South Korea may lead the world in life expectancy and achieve 84 years for men and 91 for women. Contrast this with expectations in North Korea of just 70 for men and 78 for women.

Noppasin Wongchum/Alamy Stock Photo

growth. Many government-owned businesses in mixed economies need large infusions of tax-payer money to survive as world-class competitors, which raises taxes and prices for goods and services. Underpinning the move toward market-based systems is the sale of government-owned businesses.

Move toward Privatization As discussed earlier, citizens of many European nations prefer a combination of rich benefits and higher unemployment to the low jobless rates and smaller social safety net of the United States. In France, for instance, the electorate continues to hold fast to a deeply embedded tradition of social welfare and job security in government-owned firms. Many French believe the social security and cohesion benefits of a more collectivist economy outweigh the efficiency advantages of an individualist one. Yet such attitudes are costly in terms of economic efficiency.

The selling of government-owned economic resources to private operators is called **privatization**. Privatization helps eliminate subsidized materials, labor, and capital formerly provided to government-owned companies. It also curtails the practice of appointing managers for political reasons rather than for their professional expertise. To survive, newly privatized companies must produce competitive products at fair prices because they are subject to the forces of the free market. The overall aim of privatization is to increase economic efficiency, boost productivity, and raise living standards.

privatization
Policy of selling government-owned economic resources to private operators.

Market Economy

In a **market economy**, most of a nation's land, factories, and other economic resources are privately owned, either by individuals or businesses. This means that who produces what and the prices of products, labor, and capital in a market economy are determined by the interplay of two forces:

- **Supply**: the quantity of a good or service that producers are willing to provide at a specific selling price
- **Demand**: the quantity of a good or service that buyers are willing to purchase at a specific selling price.

As supply and demand change for a good or service, so does its selling price. The lower a product's price, the greater demand will be; the higher its price, the lower demand will be. Likewise, the lower a product's price, the smaller the quantity that producers will supply; the higher the price, the greater the quantity they will supply. In this respect, what is called the "price mechanism" (or "market mechanism") dictates supply and demand.

Market forces and uncontrollable natural forces also influence product prices. Chocolate lovers, for example, should consider how the interplay of several forces affects the price of cocoa, the principal ingredient in chocolate. Suppose cocoa consumption suddenly rises in large cocoa-consuming nations such as Britain, Japan, and the United States. Suppose further that disease and pests plague crops in cocoa-producing countries such as Brazil, Ghana, and the Ivory Coast. As worldwide consumption of cocoa begins to outstrip production, market pressure is felt on both the demand side (consumers) and the supply side (producers). Falling worldwide reserves of cocoa then force the price of cocoa higher.

market economy
Economic system in which most of a nation's land, factories, and other economic resources are privately owned, either by individuals or businesses.

supply
Quantity of a good or service that producers are willing to provide at a specific selling price

demand
Quantity of a good or service that buyers are willing to purchase at a specific selling price.

ORIGINS OF THE MARKET ECONOMY Market economics is rooted in the belief that individual concerns should be placed above group concerns. According to this view, the entire group benefits when individuals receive incentives and rewards to act in certain ways. It is argued that people take better care of property they own and that individuals have fewer incentives to care for property under a system of public ownership.

Laissez-Faire Economics For many centuries, the world's dominant economic philosophy supported government control of a significant portion of a society's assets and government involvement in its international trade. But in the mid-1700s a new approach to national economics called for less government interference in commerce and greater individual economic freedom. This approach became known as a *laissez-faire* system, loosely translated from French as "allow them to do [without interference]."

Canada and the United States are examples of contemporary market economies. It is no accident that both these countries have individualist cultures (although Canada to a somewhat lesser extent than the United States). Just as an emphasis on individualism fosters a democratic form of government, it also supports a market economy.

FEATURES OF A MARKET ECONOMY   To function smoothly and properly, a market economy requires three things: *free choice*, *free enterprise*, and *price flexibility*.

- *Free choice* gives individuals access to alternative purchase options. In a market economy, few restrictions are placed on consumers' ability to make their own decisions and exercise free choice. For example, a consumer shopping for a new car is guaranteed a variety from which to choose. The consumer can choose among dealers, models, sizes, styles, colors, and mechanical specifications such as engine size and transmission type.
- *Free enterprise* gives companies the ability to decide which goods and services to produce and the markets in which to compete. Companies are free to enter new and different lines of business, select geographic markets and customer segments to pursue, hire workers, and advertise their products. They are, therefore, guaranteed the right to pursue interests profitable to them.
- *Price flexibility* allows most prices to rise and fall to reflect the forces of supply and demand. By contrast, nonmarket economies often set and maintain prices at stipulated levels. Interfering with the price mechanism violates a fundamental principle of the market economy.

GOVERNMENT'S ROLE IN A MARKET ECONOMY   In a market economy, the government has far less direct involvement in business than it does in centrally planned or mixed economies. Even so, government in a market economy plays four important roles.

Enforcing Antitrust Laws   When one company is able to control a product's supply—and, therefore, its price—it is considered a monopoly. **Antitrust (antimonopoly) laws** prevent companies from fixing prices, sharing markets, and gaining unfair monopoly advantages. They are designed to encourage the development of industries with as many competing businesses as the market will sustain. In competitive industries, the forces of competition keep prices low. By enforcing antitrust laws, governments prevent trade-restraining monopolies and business combinations that exploit consumers and constrain the growth of commerce.

The Federal Trade Commission (FTC) of the US government seeks to ensure the competitive and efficient functioning of the nation's markets. But the FTC (www.ftc.gov) can also evaluate proposed deals outside the United States when the US market is likely to be affected. In fact, if the FTC fears potential anticompetitive effects, it can force companies to sell parts of a proposed combined business to third parties in return for agency approval.

Preserving Property Rights   A smoothly functioning market economy rests on a legal system that safeguards individual property rights. By preserving and protecting individual property rights, governments encourage individuals and companies to take risks such as investing in technology, inventing new products, and starting new businesses. Strong protection of property rights ensures entrepreneurs that their claims to assets and future earnings are legally safeguarded. This protection also supports a healthy business climate in which a market economy can flourish.

Providing a Stable Fiscal and Monetary Environment   Unstable economies are often characterized by high inflation and unemployment. These forces create general uncertainty about a nation's suitability as a place to do business. Governments can help control inflation through effective *fiscal policies* (policies regarding taxation and government spending) and *monetary policies* (policies controlling money supply and interest rates). A stable economic environment helps companies make better forecasts of costs, revenues, and the future of the business in general. Such conditions reduce the risks associated with future investments, such as new product development and business expansion.

Preserving Political Stability   A market economy depends on a stable government for its smooth operation and, indeed, for its future existence. Political stability helps businesses engage in activities without worrying about terrorism, kidnappings, and other political threats to their operations. (See Chapter 4 for extensive coverage of political risk and stability.)

---

antitrust (antimonopoly) laws

Laws designed to prevent companies from fixing prices, sharing markets, and gaining unfair monopoly advantages.

ECONOMIC FREEDOM So far, we have discussed the essence of market economies as being grounded in freedom: free choice, free enterprise, free prices, and freedom from direct intervention by government. Map 3.1 (on pages 110–111) classifies countries according to their levels of economic freedom. Factors making up each country's rating include trade policy, government intervention in the economy, property rights, black markets, and wage and price controls. Most developed economies are completely or mostly free, but most emerging markets and developing nations are far less free.

Earlier, we learned that the connection between political freedom and economic growth is not at all certain. Likewise, we can say only that countries with the greatest economic freedom *tend to have* the highest standards of living, whereas those with the lowest freedom *tend to have* the lowest standards of living. But greater economic freedom does not *guarantee* a high per capita income. A country can rank very low on economic freedom yet have a higher per capita income than a country with far greater freedom.

QUICK STUDY 2

1. What factors contributed to the decline of centrally planned economies?
2. *Which* economic system strives toward low unemployment, low poverty, steady economic growth, and an equitable distribution of wealth?
3. *Laissez-faire* economics calls for less government interference in commerce and *what else*?
4. Countries with the greatest amount of economic freedom tend to have *what*?

3.3 Legal Systems

A country's **legal system** is its set of laws and regulations, including the processes by which its laws are enacted and enforced and the ways in which its courts hold parties accountable for their actions. Many cultural factors—including ideas about social mobility, religion, and individualism—influence a nation's legal system. Likewise, many laws and regulations are enacted to safeguard cultural values and beliefs. For several examples of how legal systems differ from nation to nation, see this chapter's Culture Matters feature, titled "Playing by the Rules."

A country's political system also influences its legal system. Totalitarian governments tend to favor public ownership of economic resources and enact laws limiting entrepreneurial behavior.

3.3 Summarize the main elements of each type of legal system.

legal system
Set of laws and regulations, including the processes by which a country's laws are enacted and enforced and the ways in which its courts hold parties accountable for their actions.

CULTURE MATTERS Playing by the Rules

Understanding legal systems in other countries begins with an awareness about cultural differences. Here are snapshots of several nations' legal environments:

- *Japan*. Japan's harmony-based, consensus-driven culture considers court battles to be a last resort. But with growing patent disputes and a rise in cross-border mergers, Japan is discovering the value of lawyers. Japan has just 22,000 licensed attorneys compared with more than one million in the United States. So Japan is minting thousands of new lawyers every year. Japanese businesses now litigate disputes that once might have been settled between parties.
- *Saudi Arabia*. Islam permeates every aspect of life in Saudi Arabia and affects its laws, politics, economics, and social development. Islamic law is grounded in religious teachings contained in the Koran and governs both criminal and civil cases. The Koran, in fact, is considered Saudi Arabia's constitution. The king and the council of ministers exercise all executive and legislative authority within the framework of Islamic law.

- *China*. Factory workers in China must sometimes endure military-style drills, verbal abuse, and mockery. But labor groups are winning higher wages, better working conditions, and better housing from a flock of lawyers and law students who hold free seminars and argue labor cases in China's courts. Inadequate protection of workers' rights is giving way to better conditions for China's 169 million factory workers.
- *Want to Know More?* Visit the Law Library of Congress (www.loc.gov/law/help/guide/nations/japan.php), the Royal Embassy of Saudi Arabia (www.saudiembassy.net), and China Gate (en.chinagate.cn).

Sources: "Stability v. Rights: Balancing Act," *The Economist* (www.economist.com), January 18, 2014; David Barboza, "After Suicides, Scrutiny of China's Grim Factories," *New York Times* (www.nytimes.com), June 6, 2010; "Saudi Arabia: Our Women Must Be Protected," *The Economist*, April 24, 2008, pp. 64–65; "Japan: Lawyers Wanted. No, Really," *Bloomberg Businessweek* (www.businessweek.com), April 2, 2006.

Map 3.1
**Countries Ranked
by Level of Economic
Freedom**

Level of economic freedom

- 80-100% free
- 70-79.9% free
- 60-69.9% free
- 50-59.9% free
- 0-49.9% free
- Not ranked

nationalism

Devotion of a people to their nation's interests and advancement.

By contrast, democracies tend to encourage entrepreneurial activity and protect business with strong property-rights laws. The rights and responsibilities of parties to business transactions also differ from nation to nation. Political systems and legal systems, therefore, are naturally interlocked. A country's political system inspires and endorses its legal system, and its legal system legitimizes and supports its political system.

Legal systems are frequently influenced by political moods and upsurges of **nationalism**—the devotion of a people to their nation's interests and advancement. Nationalism typically involves intense national loyalty and cultural pride and is often associated with drives toward national independence. In India, for example, most business laws originated when the country was struggling for "self-sufficiency." As a result, the legal system tended to protect local businesses from international competition. Although years ago India had nationalized many industries and closely scrutinized business applications, today its government is embracing globalization by enacting pro-business laws. With that brief introduction, let's now examine the key characteristics of *common law*, *civil law*, and *theocratic law*.

✪ **MyLab Management** Watch It Olympic Athletes' Outfits Made in China

Apply what you have learned so far about political economy and nationalism. If your instructor has assigned this, go to **www.pearson.com/mylab/management** to watch a video case about the outfits of US Olympic athletes being made in China and answer questions.

Common Law

common law

Legal system based on a country's legal history (tradition), past cases that have come before its courts (precedent), and how laws are applied in specific situations (usage).

The practice of common law originated in eleventh-century England and was adopted in that nation's territories worldwide. The US legal system, therefore, is based largely on the common law tradition (although it integrates some aspects of civil law). A **common law** legal system reflects three elements:

- *Tradition* A country's legal history
- *Precedent* Past cases that have come before the courts
- *Usage* How laws are applied in specific situations.

The justice system decides cases by interpreting the law based on tradition, precedent, and usage. Yet each law may be interpreted somewhat differently in each case to which it is applied. In turn, each new interpretation sets a precedent that may be followed in later cases. As new precedents arise, laws are altered to clarify vague wording or to accommodate situations not previously considered.

Business contracts tend to be lengthy in common-law nations (especially the United States) because they must consider many possible contingencies and many possible interpretations of the law in case of a dispute. Companies devote considerable time to devising clear contracts and spend large sums of money on legal advice. On the positive side, common-law systems are flexible. Instead of applying uniformly to all situations, laws take into account particular situations and circumstances. The common-law tradition prevails in Australia, Britain, Canada, Ireland, New Zealand, the United States, and some nations of Asia and Africa.

Civil Law

civil law

Legal system based on a detailed set of written rules and statutes that constitute a legal code.

The origins of the civil law tradition can be traced to Rome in the fifth century B.C. It is the world's oldest and most common legal tradition. A **civil law** system is based on a detailed set of written rules and statutes that constitute a legal *code*. Civil law can be less adversarial than common law because there tends to be less need to interpret what a particular law states. Because all laws are codified and concise, parties to contracts tend to be more concerned only with the explicit wording of the code. All obligations, responsibilities, and privileges follow directly from the relevant code. Less time and money are typically spent, therefore, on legal matters. But civil law systems can ignore the unique circumstances of particular cases. Civil law is practiced in Cuba, Puerto Rico, Quebec, all of Central and South America, most of Western Europe, and many nations in Asia and Africa.

Theocratic Law

A legal tradition based on religious teachings is called **theocratic law**. Three prominent theocratic legal systems are Islamic, Hindu, and Jewish law. Although Hindu law was restricted by India's 1950 constitution, in which the state appropriated most legal functions, it does persist as a cultural and spiritual force. Likewise, although Jewish law remains a strong religious force, it has served few legal functions since the eighteenth century, when most Jewish communities lost their judicial autonomy.

Islamic law is the most widely practiced theocratic legal system today. Islamic law was initially a code governing moral and ethical behavior and was later extended to commercial transactions. It restricts the types of investments companies can make and sets guidelines for business transactions. According to Islamic law, for example, banks cannot charge interest on loans or pay interest on deposits. Instead, banks receive a portion of the profits earned by investors who borrow funds and pay depositors from these earnings. Likewise, because the products of alcohol- and tobacco-related businesses violate Islamic beliefs, firms abiding by Islamic law cannot invest in such companies.

theocratic law
Legal system based on religious teachings.

QUICK STUDY 3

1. Which legal system decides cases by interpreting the law based on tradition, precedent, and usage?
2. Which legal system is based on a detailed set of written rules and statutes that constitute a legal code?
3. A legal tradition based on faithless teaching is called *what*?

3.4 Global Legal Issues

Earlier in this chapter, we saw how international companies work to overcome obstacles that an unfamiliar political system presents. Firms must adapt to dissimilar legal systems in global markets because there is no clearly defined body of international law that all nations accept. There is a movement toward *standardizing* the interpretation and application of laws in more than one country, but this does not involve standardizing entire legal systems. Enduring differences in legal systems, therefore, can force companies to continue the costly practice of hiring legal experts in each country where they operate.

Still, international treaties and agreements exist in intellectual property rights, antitrust regulation, taxation, contract arbitration, and general matters of trade. International organizations that promote standardization include the **United Nations** (UN; www.un.org), the Organization for Economic Cooperation and Development (OECD; www.oecd.org), and the International Institute for the Unification of Private Law (www.unidroit.org). The European Union is standardizing parts of its members' legal systems to facilitate commerce in Western Europe. Let's now examine the key legal issues facing companies that are active in international business.

3.4 Outline the global legal issues facing international firms.

United Nations (UN)
International organization formed after World War II to provide leadership in fostering peace and stability around the world.

Intellectual Property

Property that results from people's intellectual talent and abilities is called **intellectual property**. It includes graphic designs, novels, computer software, machine-tool designs, and secret formulas, such as that for making Coca-Cola.

Most national legal systems protect **property rights**—the legal rights to resources and any income they generate. Similar to other types of property, intellectual property can be traded, sold, and licensed in return for fees and/or royalty payments. Intellectual property laws are designed to compensate people whose property rights are violated.

Intellectual property laws differ greatly from nation to nation. Business Software Alliance (BSA; www.bsa.org), the trade body for business software makers, conducts an annual study of software piracy rates around the globe. Where illegal copies of business software recently made up 17 percent of the US domestic market (the lowest in the world), pirated software made up 90 percent of the market in both Libya and Zimbabwe (the highest worldwide). Globally, business software piracy averages around 39 percent and costs business software makers nearly $52 billion annually.[5] Figure 3.2 shows piracy rates for some of the nations included in the BSA study.

intellectual property
Property that results from people's intellectual talent and abilities.

property rights
Legal rights to resources and any income they generate.

Figure 3.2

Business Software Piracy

Source: Based on the BSA Global Software Survey (Washington, D.C.; Business Software Alliance, May 2016), pp. 8–9, available at www.bsa.org/globalstudy.

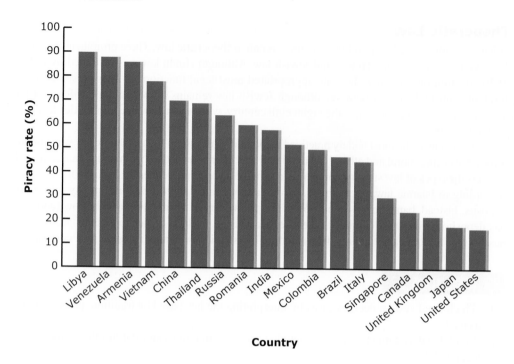

As these figures suggest, the laws (or the enforcement of such laws) of some countries are softer on piracy than the laws of some other nations. Although peddlers of pirated CDs and DVDs operate openly from sidewalk kiosks in China, China's government is doing more to tackle piracy recently. Software companies in the United States and the European Union continually lobby their governments to pressure other nations to adopt stronger laws.

Technically, intellectual property results in *industrial property* (in the form of either a *patent* or a *trademark*) or *copyright* and confers a limited monopoly on its holder.

industrial property

Patents and trademarks.

INDUSTRIAL PROPERTY **Industrial property** includes patents and trademarks, which are often a firm's most valuable assets. Laws protecting industrial property are designed to reward inventive and creative activity. Industrial property is protected internationally under the Paris Convention for the Protection of Industrial Property (www.wipo.int), to which nearly 100 countries are signatories.

patent

Property right granted to the inventor of a product or process that excludes others from making, using, or selling the invention.

A **patent** is a right granted to the inventor of a product or process that excludes others from making, using, or selling the invention. Current US patent law went into effect on June 8, 1995, and is in line with the systems of most developed nations. Its provisions are those of the World Trade Organization (WTO), the international organization that regulates trade between nations. The WTO (www.wto.org) typically grants patents for a period of 20 years. The 20-year term begins when a patent application is filed with a country's patent office, not when it is finally granted. Patents can be sought for any invention that is new, useful, and not obvious to any individual of ordinary skill in the relevant technical field. Patents motivate companies to pursue inventions and make them available to consumers because they protect investments that companies make in research and development.

trademark

Property right in the form of words or symbols that distinguish a product and its manufacturer.

Trademarks are words or symbols that distinguish a product and its manufacturer. The Nike (www.nike.com) "swoosh" is a trademark, as is the name "Lexus" (www.lexus.com). Trademark law creates incentives for manufacturers to invest in developing new products. It also benefits consumers because they know what to expect when they buy a particular brand. In other words, you would not expect a canned drink labeled "Monster" to taste like one labeled "Sprite."

Trademark protection typically lasts indefinitely, provided the word or symbol continues to be *distinctive*. Ironically, this stipulation presents a problem for companies such as Coca-Cola (www.coca-cola.com) and Xerox (www.xerox.com), whose trademarks "Coke" and "Xerox" have evolved into *generic* terms for all products in their respective categories. Trademark laws differ from country to country, though some progress toward standardization is occurring. The European Union, for example, opened a trademark-protection office to police trademark infringement against firms that operate in any European Union country.

Designers who own trademarks, such as Chanel (www.chanel.com), Christian Dior (www .dior.com), and Gucci (www.gucci.com), have long been plagued by shoddily made counterfeit handbags, shoes, shirts, and other products. But recently, pirated products of equal or nearly equal quality are turning up, especially in Italy. Most Italian owners of luxury, brand-name leather goods and jewelry, for example, outsource production to small manufacturers. It is not hard for these same artisans to counterfeit extra copies of a high-quality product. Bootleg copies of a Prada (www.prada.com) backpack that costs $500 in New York can be bought for less than $100 in Rome. Jewelry shops in Milan can buy fake watches labeled Bulgari (www.bulgari.com) and Rolex (www.rolex.com) for $300 and sell them retail for $2,500.

COPYRIGHTS **Copyrights** give creators of original works the freedom to publish or dispose of them as they choose. A copyright is typically denoted by the well-known symbol ©, a date, and the copyright holder's name. A copyright holder has the legal rights to:

copyright
Property right giving creators of original works the freedom to publish or dispose of them as they choose.

- Reproduce the copyrighted work.
- Derive new works from the copyrighted work.
- Sell or distribute copies of the copyrighted work.
- Perform the copyrighted work.
- Display the copyrighted work publicly.

Copyright holders include artists, photographers, painters, literary authors, publishers, musical composers, and software developers. Works created after January 1, 1978, are automatically copyrighted for the creator's lifetime plus 50 years. Publishing houses receive copyrights for either 75 years from the date of publication or 100 years after creation, whichever comes first. Copyrights are protected under the **Berne Convention** (www.wipo.int), which is an international copyright treaty to which the United States is a member, and the 1954 Universal Copyright Convention. More than 50 countries abide by one or both of these treaties.

Berne Convention
International treaty that protects copyrights.

A copyright is granted for the *tangible expression* of an idea, not for the idea itself. For example, no one can copyright the idea for a movie about the sinking of the *Titanic*. But once a film is made that expresses its creator's treatment of the subject, that film can be copyrighted.

Perhaps the most well-known song around the world, "Happy Birthday to You," is actually protected by US copyright law. The song was composed in 1859 and copyrighted in 1935. Although the copyright was set to expire in 2010 on the song's 75th copyright birthday, the US Congress extended it until 2030. Time Warner owns the copyright and stands to gain as much as $20 million from the extension.

Product Safety and Liability

Product safety laws in most countries set standards that manufactured products must meet. **Product liability** holds manufacturers, sellers, individuals, and others responsible for damage, injury, or death caused by defective products. Injured parties can sue for monetary compensation through *civil* lawsuits and for fines or imprisonment through *criminal* lawsuits.

product liability
Responsibility of manufacturers, sellers, individuals, and others for damage, injury, or death caused by defective products.

Developed nations have the toughest product liability laws, whereas developing and emerging countries have the weakest laws. Business insurance costs and legal expenses are greater in nations with strong product liability laws, where damage awards can be large. Likewise, enforcement of product liability laws differs from nation to nation. In the most developed nations, for example, tobacco companies are regularly under attack for the negative health effects of tobacco and nicotine. Critics say that the tobacco industry markets aggressively to women and children in developing countries where regulations are weak and many people do not know that smoking is dangerous.[6]

Taxation

National governments use income and sales taxes for many purposes. They use tax revenue to pay government salaries, build military capabilities, and shift earnings from people with high incomes to the poor. Nations may also tax imports in order to make them more expensive and give locally made products an advantage among price-sensitive consumers.

Nations pass indirect taxes, called "consumption taxes," which help pay for the consequences of using particular products. Consumption taxes on products such as alcohol and tobacco help pay the health-care costs of treating illnesses that result from using these products. Similarly,

TABLE 3.1 Effect of Value Added Taxes (VAT)

Production Stage	Selling Price	Value Added	10% VAT	Total VAT
Shrimper	$1.00	$1.00	$0.10	$0.10
Processor	1.70	0.70	0.07	0.17
Wholesaler	2.80	1.10	0.11	0.28
Retailer	3.80	1.00	1.10	0.38

value added tax (VAT)

Tax levied on each party that adds value to a product throughout its production and distribution.

gasoline taxes help pay for the road and bridge repairs needed to counteract the effects of traffic and weathering.

Many countries impose a **value added tax (VAT)**—a tax levied on each party that adds value to a product throughout its production and distribution. The United States has not previously implemented a VAT tax, but the nation's considerable debt level is causing speculation that it may impose one. Supporters of the VAT system contend that it distributes taxes on retail sales more evenly between producers and consumers. Suppose, for example, that a shrimper sells the day's catch of shrimp for $1 per pound and that the country's VAT is 10 percent (see Table 3.1). The shrimper, processor, wholesaler, and retailer pay taxes of $0.10, $0.07, $0.11, and $0.10, respectively, for the value that each adds to the product as it makes its way to consumers. Consumers pay no additional tax at the point of sale because the government has already collected taxes from each party in the value chain. Still, consumers end up paying the tax because producers and distributors must increase prices to compensate for their tax burdens. So that the poor are not overly burdened, many countries exclude the VAT on certain items such as children's clothing.

Antitrust Regulations

Antitrust laws try to provide consumers with a wide variety of products at fair prices. The United States and the European Union are the world's strictest antitrust regulators. In Japan, the Fair Trade Commission enforces antitrust laws but is often ineffective because *absolute proof* of wrongdoing is needed to bring charges.

Companies based in strict antitrust countries often argue that they are at a disadvantage against competitors whose home countries condone *market sharing*, whereby competitors agree to serve only designated segments of a certain market. That is why firms in strict antitrust countries often lobby for exemptions in certain international transactions. Small businesses also argue that they could better compete against large international companies if they could join forces without fear of violating antitrust laws.

In the absence of a global antitrust enforcement agency, international companies must concern themselves with the antitrust laws of each nation where they do business. In fact, a nation (or group of nations) can block a merger or acquisition between two nondomestic companies if those companies do a good deal of business there. This happened to the proposed $43 billion merger between General Electric (GE; www.ge.com) and Honeywell (www.honeywell.com). GE wanted to marry its manufacture of airplane engines to Honeywell's production of advanced electronics for the aviation industry. Although both companies are based in the United States, together they employed 100,000 Europeans. GE alone earned $25 billion in Europe the year before the proposed merger. The European Union blocked the merger because it believed the result would be higher prices for customers, particularly airlines.

QUICK STUDY 4

1. What are some examples of intellectual property?
2. What are the different types of industrial property?
3. Laws that hold manufacturers, sellers, individuals, and others responsible for damage, injury, or death caused by defective products are called *what*?

3.5 Ethics and Social Responsibility

We learned in Chapter 2 that when a company goes global its managers encounter many unfamiliar cultural rules that govern human behavior. Although legal systems set clearly defined *boundaries* for lawful individual and corporate behavior, they are inadequate for dilemmas of ethics and social responsibility. Ethical issues and social responsibility are related to, but are not the same as, legal issues. When laws are silent about a particular matter, international businesspeople step into a gray area of personal ethics and business responsibility.

Ethical behavior is personal behavior in accordance with guidelines for good conduct or morality. Ethical dilemmas are not legal questions. When a law exists to guide a manager toward a legally correct action, that path must be followed. In an ethical dilemma, there is no right or wrong decision. There are alternatives, however, that may be equally valid in ethical terms depending on one's perspective.

In addition to the need for individual managers to behave ethically, businesses are expected to exercise **corporate social responsibility**—the practice of going beyond legal obligations to actively balance commitments to investors, customers, other companies, and communities. Corporate social responsibility (or CSR, as it is known) includes a wide variety of activities, including giving to the poor, building schools in developing countries, and protecting the global environment. Most conscientious business leaders realize that the futures of their companies rest on healthy workforces and environments worldwide. For example, soft drink makers support all sorts of environmental initiatives because they understand that their futures depend on an ample supply of clean drinking water. But firms should not produce public relations campaigns that present a business as socially responsible if it does not truly embrace CSR principles.

We can think of CSR as consisting of three layers of activity. The first layer is *traditional philanthropy*, whereby a corporation donates money and, perhaps, employee time toward a specific social cause. The second layer is related to *risk management*, whereby a company develops a code of conduct that it will follow in its global operations and agrees to operate with greater transparency. The third layer is *strategic CSR*, in which a business builds social responsibility into its core operations to create value and build competitive advantage.[7]

Philosophies of Ethics and Social Responsibility

Business ethics and social responsibility have four commonly cited philosophies. The *Friedman view*—named for its main supporter, the late economist Milton Friedman—says that a company's sole responsibility is to maximize profits for its owners (or shareholders) while operating within the law.[8] Imagine a company that moves its pollution-generating operations from a country having strict and expensive environmental-protection laws to a country having no such laws. Managers subscribing to the Friedman philosophy would applaud this decision. They would argue that the company is doing its duty to increase profits for its owners and is operating within the law in the foreign country. Many people disagree with this argument and say the discussion is not *whether* a company has CSR obligations but *how* it will fulfill them.

The *cultural relativist view* says that a company should adopt local ethics wherever it operates because all belief systems are determined within a cultural context. Cultural relativism sees truth, itself, as relative and argues that right and wrong are determined within a specific situation. The expression "When in Rome, do as the Romans do" captures the essence of cultural relativism. Consider a company that opens a factory in a developing market and, following local customs, employs child laborers. The cultural relativist manager would argue that this company is acting appropriately and in accordance with local standards of conduct. Many people strongly oppose this line of ethical reasoning.

The *righteous moralist view* says that a company should maintain its home-country ethics wherever it operates because the home-country's view of ethics and responsibility is superior to others' views. Imagine a company that expands from its developed-country base to an emerging market where local managers commonly bribe officials. Suppose headquarters detests the act of bribery and instructs its subsidiary managers to refrain from bribing any local officials. In this situation, headquarters is imposing its righteous moralist view on local managers.

3.5 Describe the main issues of global ethics and social responsibility.

ethical behavior
Personal behavior in accordance with guidelines for good conduct or morality.

corporate social responsibility
Practice of companies going beyond legal obligations to actively balance commitments to investors, customers, other companies, and communities.

The *utilitarian view* says that a company should behave in a way that maximizes "good" outcomes and minimizes "bad" outcomes wherever it operates. The utilitarian manager asks the question, "What outcome should I aim for?" and answers, "That which produces the best outcome for all affected parties." In other words, utilitarian thinkers say the right behavior is that which produces the greatest good for the greatest number. Consider, again, the righteous moralist company above that instructs its employees not to bribe local officials in the emerging market. Now suppose a manager learns that, by bribing a local official, the company will finally obtain permission to expand its factory and create 100 well-paying jobs for the local community. If the manager pays the bribe based on his or her calculations that more people will benefit than will be harmed by the outcome, he or she is practicing utilitarian ethics.

Although businesses can create policies regarding ethics and social responsibility, issues arise daily that can cause dilemmas for international managers. Let's now learn more about several of these key issues.

Bribery and Corruption

Similar to other cultural and political elements, the prevalence of corruption varies from nation to nation. In certain countries, bribes are routinely paid to distributors and retailers in order to push a firm's products through distribution channels. Bribes can mean the difference between obtaining an important contract and being completely shut out of a market. But corruption is detrimental to society and business. Among other things, corruption can send resources toward inefficient uses, hurt economic development, distort public policy, and damage national integrity.

Map 3.2 on pages 120–125 shows how countries rate on their perceived levels of corruption. The higher a country's score on the corruption perceptions index (CPI), the less corrupt it is perceived to be by international managers. What stands out immediately on this map is that the poorer and least developed nations tend to be perceived as being most corrupt (such as Russia, much of Africa, and areas in the Middle East). This reflects the hesitancy on the part of international companies about investing in corrupt economies.

Enron Corporation made history when it acknowledged in a federal filing that it had overstated its earnings. Investors fled in droves as Enron stock became worthless and the company went bankrupt. Although executives had earned millions over the years in salaries and bonuses, Enron's rank-and-file employees saw their retirement savings disappear as the firm disintegrated. European banks lost around $2 billion that they had lent to Enron and its subsidiaries. Chairman of the board Kenneth Lay (now deceased) and CEO Jeffrey Skilling were convicted on criminal charges. Then a criminal indictment was filed against accounting firm Arthur Andersen, Enron's auditor, for shredding documents related to its work for Enron. With its reputation irreparably damaged, Andersen also collapsed.

The financial losses and diminished confidence in business that resulted from Enron's collapse prompted the US Congress to pass the *Sarbanes–Oxley Act* (Sarbox) on corporate governance. The law established new, stringent accounting standards and reporting practices for firms. Around the world, governments, accounting standards boards, other regulators, and interest groups won the fight for higher standards and more transparent financial reporting by companies. Businesses worldwide received the message that fudging the accounting numbers, misrepresenting the firm's financial health, and running a company in that gray area between right and wrong is unethical and, now, illegal.

Some people believe Sarbox needs to be reformed because of the financial burden that companies face in conforming to the act's requirements. Regulators, securities experts, and scholars (who largely praise Sarbox) are pitted against chief financial officers—many of whom say that the act should be reformed or repealed because its costs outweigh its benefits.

Labor Conditions and Human Rights

To fulfill their responsibilities to society, companies are monitoring the actions of their own employees and the employees of companies with which they conduct business. Pressure from human rights activists drove conscientious apparel companies to introduce codes of conduct and monitoring mechanisms for their international suppliers. Levi-Strauss (www.levistrauss.com) pioneered the use of practical codes to control working conditions at contractors' facilities. The company does business only with partners who meet its "Terms of Engagement," which sets minimal guidelines regarding ethical behavior, environmental and legal requirements, employment standards, and community involvement.[9]

Consider one case publicized by human rights and labor groups investigating charges of worker abuse at the factory of one of Nike's Vietnamese suppliers. Twelve of 56 female employees reportedly fainted when a supervisor forced them to run around the factory as punishment for not wearing regulation shoes. Nike confirmed the report and, in suspending the supervisor, took steps to implement practices more in keeping with the company's home-country ethics.

International law says that only nations can be held liable for human rights abuses. But activist groups can file a lawsuit against a US business for an alleged human rights violation under the Alien Tort Claims Act by alleging a company's complicity in the abuse. Yahoo (www.yahoo.com) felt the power of this law when two Chinese dissidents were jailed after the company gave data it had on them to Chinese authorities. Yahoo reached an out-of-court settlement with the families of the jailed men. And despite denials of any responsibility in the matter, US oil company Unocal, now part of Chevron (www.chevron.com), settled out of court over allegations of complicity in government soldiers' abuse of villagers during construction of an oil pipeline in Myanmar in the 1990s.[10]

Fair Trade Practices

Starbucks (www.starbucks.com) works hard to operate in a socially responsible manner by trying to ease the plight of citizens in poor coffee-producing countries. Starbucks does this by building schools, health clinics, and coffee-processing facilities to improve the well-being of families in coffee-farming communities. The company also sells what it calls "fair trade coffee." Fair trade products are those that involve companies working with suppliers in more equitable, meaningful, and sustainable ways. For Starbucks, this means ensuring that coffee farmers earn a fair price for their coffee crop and helping them farm in environmentally friendly ways.[11]

Fair Trade USA (www.fairtradeusa.org) is the nonprofit organization that independently certifies fair trade products such as Starbucks coffee. The Fair Trade model of international trade benefits more than one million farmers and farm laborers in 58 developing countries across Africa, Asia, and Latin America. Fair Trade products now include coffee, tea, herbs, cocoa, chocolate, fruit, rice, sugar, flowers, honey, and spices. Fair Trade USA certifies that a product meets the following criteria:[12]

- *Fair Prices*   Producer groups receive a guaranteed minimum floor price.
- *Fair Labor Conditions*   Farms do not employ children, and workers are given freedom of association, safe working conditions, and a living wage.
- *Direct Trade*   Whenever possible, importers purchase from producer groups to eliminate intermediaries.
- *Democratic Community Development*   Farmers and workers decide how to spend their Fair Trade premiums in social and business development projects.
- *Environmental Sustainability*   Farming methods protect the health of farmers and preserve ecosystems.

Environment

Concern for the environment and ecosystem is no longer left to government agencies and nongovernmental organizations. Today companies pursue "green" initiatives to reduce their toll on the environment *and* to reduce operating costs and boost profit margins. **Carbon footprint** is the

carbon footprint
Environmental impact of greenhouse gases (measured in units of carbon dioxide) that results from human activity.

Map 3.2

Corruption Perception Index

CPI Score

- 9.0 to 10.0
- 8.0 to 8.9
- 7.0 to 7.9
- 6.0 to 6.9
- 5.0 to 5.9
- 4.0 to 4.9
- 3.0 to 3.9
- 2.0 to 2.9
- 1.0 to 1.9
- no data available

Many people believe that globalization and economic development take a toll on the environment. Here, an electric Tesla Roadster charges up near London, England. Some Tesla chargers can provide half a charge in as little as 20 minutes. All sorts of companies are working to create "green" products to reduce the human impact on our ecosystem. Besides car manufacturers, what other companies are growing more environmentally responsible?

Gavin Rodgers/Alamy Stock Photo

environmental impact of greenhouse gases (measured in units of carbon dioxide) that result from human activity. It consists of two components:[13]

- *Primary Footprint*   Direct carbon dioxide emissions from the burning of fossil fuels, including domestic energy consumption and transportation (such as electricity and gasoline).
- *Secondary Footprint*   Indirect carbon dioxide emissions from the whole life cycle of products (from their manufacture to eventual breakdown).

Companies at the leading edge of the green movement are printing a number on their products that represents the grams of carbon dioxide emitted from producing and shipping them to retailers. The number signifies the environmental impact of all the materials, chemicals, and so on, used in producing and distributing a good. For example, the United Kingdom's No. 1 selling snack food brand, Walker (www.walkers-crisps.co.uk), stamps "75g" on its packets of cheese- and onion-flavored potato chips, or *crisps*—meaning 75 grams of carbon dioxide were emitted in producing and shipping each packet. Footwear and clothing maker Timberland (www.timberland.com) labels its products with a score ranging from 0 to 10. A score of "0" means producing and shipping a product emitted less than 2.5 kilograms of carbon dioxide; a product with a score of "10" emitted 100 kilograms of carbon dioxide—roughly equivalent to driving a car 240 miles.[14]

Another trendsetter in reducing its carbon footprint is Marriott International (www.marriott.com). The hotel company's employee cafeteria replaced paper and plastic containers with real plates and biodegradable potato-based containers called Spudware. Marriott gives employees reusable plastic water bottles and lets them exchange burned-out regular light bulbs, from work or home, for the latest energy-saving bulbs. And the company has "green ambassadors" who remind employees to print documents double-sided and to turn off lights and electronic devices not in use.[15]

Boisset Family Estates (www.boisset.com), France's third-largest winery, initiated an eco-smart alternative to the glass bottle. Boisset uses aluminum-coated paperboard similar to containers commonly used for juices and milk. Besides protecting the product from oxidation and making it easier to chill, the new packaging helps the environment and improves company profits. It used to take 28 trucks to haul enough empty glass bottles to the winery to package the same volume of wine that today takes just one truck of empty cartons. After the cartons are filled, one truck now hauls away what used to take three trucks. The savings in materials, fuel, and equipment are significant.[16]

On a national level, the German government has gone greener than most others. Germany's energy law guarantees operators of windmills and solar generators prices that are above the market rate for as long as 20 years. That law, combined with German expertise in aerodynamics, is making the country a global leader in renewable energy. Today, 60 companies in Germany specialize in wind systems. The former East Germany is nicknamed Solar Valley because of the large number of companies that manufacture solar cells there. Germany's green-energy sector employs more than 235,000 people and generates $33 billion in sales annually.[17]

QUICK STUDY 5

1. The essence of which philosophy is captured by the expression, "When in Rome, do as the Romans do"?
2. Possible consequences of corruption include *what*?
3. What are some criteria a product must meet in order to be Fair Trade certified?
4. The environmental impact of greenhouse gases that result from human activity is called *what*?

BOTTOM LINE FOR BUSINESS

Differences in political economy among nations present both opportunities and risks for international companies. Gaining complete control over events in even the most stable national business environment is extremely difficult because of the intricate connections among politics, economics, law, and culture. Still, understanding these connections is the first step in managing the risks of doing business in unfamiliar environments.

Implications for Business in Totalitarian Nations
Political opposition to business from nongovernmental organizations is extremely unlikely if a totalitarian nation sanctions a particular commercial activity. Bribery and kickbacks to government officials will likely prevail, and refusal to pay is generally not an option. As such, business activities in totalitarian nations are inherently risky. Business law in totalitarian nations is either vague or nonexistent, and interpretation of the law is highly subjective. Finally, certain groups criticize companies for doing business in or with totalitarian nations, saying they are helping sustain oppressive political regimes.

Implications for Business in Democracies
Democracies tend to provide stable business environments through laws that protect individual property rights. Commerce should prosper when the private sector comprises independently owned firms that exist to make profits. Although participative democracy, property rights, and free markets tend to encourage economic growth, they do not always do so. India is the world's largest democracy, yet its economy grew very slowly for decades. Meanwhile, some countries achieved rapid economic growth under political systems that were not genuinely democratic.

Which Type of Government Is Best for Business?
Although democracies pass laws to protect individual civil liberties and property rights, totalitarian governments could also grant such rights. The difference is that, whereas democracies strive to guarantee such rights, totalitarian governments retain the power to repeal them whenever they choose. As for a nation's rate of economic growth, a democracy does not guarantee high rates of economic growth, and totalitarianism does not doom a nation to slow economic growth. An economy's growth rate is influenced by many additional factors.

Implications of Legal Issues for Companies
A nation's political economy is naturally intertwined with its legal system. Its political economy inspires and endorses its legal system, which legitimizes and supports the political economy. Flexible business strategies help companies operate within the political economy frameworks of nations. Managers will benefit if they have a solid grasp of how such frameworks affect company operations and strategy.

Implications of Ethical Issues for Companies
Probably every international company of at least moderate size has a policy for corporate social responsibility (CSR). Traditionally, companies practiced CSR through old-fashioned philanthropy. Indeed, donating money and time toward solving social problems helped society and bolstered a company's public image. Companies later developed codes of conduct for their global operations to ensure they were good citizens wherever they operated. Today, companies search for ways to use CSR to create value and build competitive advantage.

MyLab Management

Go to **www.pearson.com/mylab/management** to complete the problems marked with this icon .

Chapter Summary

LO3.1 Describe the key features of each form of political system.
- In a *totalitarian system* individuals govern without the support of the people, tightly control people's lives, and do not tolerate opposing viewpoints.
- *Theocratic totalitarianism* means that order is kept with laws based on religious and totalitarian beliefs. In *secular totalitarianism* political leaders rely on military and bureaucratic power for control.
- In a *democratic system* leaders are elected by the people or by their representatives. *Representative democracies* strive to provide freedom of expression, periodic elections, civil and property rights, minority rights, and nonpolitical bureaucracies.

LO3.2 Explain how the three types of economic systems differ.
- In a *centrally planned economy*, the government owns land, factories, and other economic resources and plans nearly all economic activities. Economic and social equality are paramount and the needs of the group are above those of the individual.
- In a *mixed economy*, land, factories, and other economic resources are split between private and government ownership. Efficiency is strived for but society is protected from unchecked greed.
- In a *market economy*, private individuals or businesses own most of the land, factories, and other economic resources. The entire group is thought to benefit when individuals receive incentives and rewards. Government is subdued and prices are set by *supply* and *demand*.

LO3.3 Summarize the main elements of each type of legal system.
- A *legal system* is a country's set of laws and regulations, including the processes by which its laws are enacted and enforced and how its courts hold parties accountable.
- *Common law* is a legal system based on a country's legal history (tradition), past cases tried in the courts (precedent), and how laws are applied in specific situations (usage).
- *Civil law* is a system based on a detailed set of written rules and statutes that constitute a legal code, from which flows all obligations, responsibilities, and privileges.
- *Theocratic law* is a system based on religious teachings.

LO3.4 Outline the global legal issues facing international firms.
- Firms must work hard to protect their *property rights* (legal rights to resources and income generated) and *intellectual property* (that which results from intellectual talent and abilities) against violations of patents, trademarks, and copyrights.
- Companies must know *product liability laws* (responsibility for damage, injury, or death caused by defective products) and taxation requirements wherever they operate.
- Businesses need to know how *antitrust laws* (designed to stop companies from fixing prices, sharing markets, and gaining unfair monopoly advantages) influence operations.

LO3.5 Describe the main issues of global ethics and social responsibility.
- Managers often encounter different views toward bribery and corruption in a host country, and must abide by stringent accounting standards and reporting practices.
- Firms can guarantee good working conditions and protect human rights by monitoring the actions of their own employees and those of companies with whom they do business.
- Companies active in developing countries can foster social responsibility in those markets by encouraging fair-trade practices.
- Businesses can pursue "green" initiatives that reduce operating costs and boost profits while protecting the environment.

Key Terms

antitrust (antimonopoly) laws (p. 108)
Berne Convention (p. 115)
capitalism (p. 103)
carbon footprint (p. 119)
centrally planned economy (p. 104)
civil law (p. 112)
common law (p. 112)
communism (p. 100)
copyright (p. 115)
corporate social responsibility (p. 117)
demand (p. 107)
democracy (p. 101)
economic system (p. 104)

ethical behavior (p. 117)
industrial property (p. 114)
intellectual property (p. 113)
legal system (p. 109)
market economy (p. 107)
mixed economy (p. 106)
nationalism (p. 112)
patent (p. 114)
political economy (p. 98)
political system (p. 99)
private sector (p. 103)
privatization (p. 107)
product liability (p. 115)

property rights (p. 113)
representative democracy (p. 101)
secular totalitarianism (p. 100)
socialism (p. 100)
supply (p. 107)
theocracy (p. 100)
theocratic law (p. 113)
theocratic totalitarianism (p. 100)
totalitarian system (p. 99)
trademark (p. 114)
United Nations (p. 113)
value added tax (VAT) (p. 116)

✪ TALK ABOUT IT 1

The Internet and the greater access to information it provides are disrupting traditional ways of doing things in almost every sphere of life. Unsurprisingly, perhaps, government seems to be among the slowest economic sectors to undergo change.

3-1. How might the Internet change, if at all, totalitarian governments such as North Korea?

3-2. Can you think of ways that technology might change the way democracies function? Explain.

✪ TALK ABOUT IT 2

Under a totalitarian government, the Indonesian economy grew strongly for 30 years. Meanwhile, the economy of the largest functioning democracy, India, performed poorly for decades until recently.

3-3. Do you think the Indonesian economy grew despite or because of a totalitarian regime?

3-4. What might explain India's relatively poor performance under a democratic political system?

Ethical Challenge

You are the CEO of a manufacturing facility in the Eastern Cape, South Africa. You manufacture automotive parts under license for two Chinese corporations. Last year, two of your senior managers resigned and set up their own factory inland. It is not uncommon for senior managers to leave and establish their own businesses, but within six months you started receiving alarming news from the automotive market in South Africa. It seems that the new company is producing cloned parts and selling them directly into the market at prices that undercut your licensed parts. The packaging looks suspiciously similar to the original product, and you are deeply concerned.

3-5. As the CEO, what would be your first reaction to this problem, and how would you respond?

3-6. Should you contact the Chinese corporations and tell them about the problem or is it better to try to solve the problem yourself? Explain your decision.

3-7. Research the legal position in South Africa and investigate any legal remedies that might be useful to you in this case. What is the likelihood of success in terms of legal proceedings?

Teaming Up

In groups of three or four, consider the ethical implications of doing business in a country where bribery and corruption are not only endemic but also part of the accepted norm. If it is impossible to do business without paying bribes, should the business consider not operating there at all? Draw up a list of key points and then share your ideas with the rest of the class.

✪ Market Entry Strategy Project

This exercise corresponds to the *MESP* online simulation. For the country your team is researching, integrate your answers to the following questions into your completed *MESP* report.

3-8. How would you classify the nation's political, economic, and legal systems?
3-9. Is government heavily involved in the nation's economy?
3-10. Is the legal system effective and impartial?
3-11. Does its political economy suggest that the country could be a potential market?
3-12. What is the level of corruption throughout the political economy?
3-13. Is legislation pending that might be relevant to international companies?

MyLab Management

✪ Go to **www.pearson.com/mylab/management** for the following assisted-graded writing questions:

3-14. Consider the following statement: "Democratic political systems, as opposed to totalitarian ones, provide international companies with more stable environments in which to do business." Do you agree or disagree with this statement, and why?

3-15. Many companies get involved in environmental, or "green," issues to demonstrate their social responsibility. How might a company align its social responsibility efforts with its strategy? Provide specific examples.

Pirates of Globalization

It pays to remember that old Latin phrase, *caveat emptor* ("let the buyer beware"), when tackling the production of counterfeit products on a global scale. Sophisticated pirates routinely violate patents, trademarks, and copyrights to churn out high-quality fakes of the best-known brands. Trademark counterfeiting amounts to between 5 percent and 7 percent of world trade, or around $500 billion a year. Phony products appear in many industries, including computer software, films, books, music CDs. Fake computer chips, broadband routers, and computers cost the electronics industry alone up to $100 billion annually. And the global market for fake pharmaceutical drugs is now a multibillion-dollar industry that poses a direct threat to the good health of folks everywhere.

Traditionally peddled by sidewalk vendors and in back-street markets, counterfeiters now employ the latest technology. Just as honest businesses do, they use the Internet to slash the cost of distributing their fake goods. All merchandise on some Internet sites is counterfeit, and even legitimate website operators, such as eBay (www.ebay.com), have difficulty rooting out pirates.

New York retailer Tiffany & Company (www.tiffany.com) sued eBay when counterfeits of its products appeared on eBay's website. In the complaint, Tiffany said that, of the 186 jewelry pieces bearing the Tiffany name that it randomly purchased on eBay, 73 percent were phony. Tiffany argued that eBay should bear responsibility for the sale of counterfeit merchandise on its site because it profits significantly from the sale of fake merchandise, provides a forum for such sales, and promotes it. Others disagree, saying it is impractical to require online auctioneers to verify the authenticity of every product sold on its site.

Pirates have not ignored the market for automotive parts, which loses around $12 billion annually to phony goods. Car manufacturers list harmful fakes such as brake linings made of compressed sawdust and transmission fluid that is nothing more than cheap oil with added dye. Boxes bearing legitimate-looking labels make it difficult for consumers to tell the difference between a fake and the real deal. The problem is causing fears of lawsuits because of malfunctioning counterfeits and concerns of lost revenue for producers of the genuine articles. For example, if someone is in an accident because of a counterfeit product, legitimate manufacturers need to prove the product is not their own.

Lax antipiracy regulations and booming economies in emerging markets mean potential intellectual-property traps await companies doing business there. For example, Indian law gives international pharmaceutical firms five- to seven-year patents on *processes used to manufacture drugs*—but *not on the drugs themselves*. This lets Indian companies modify the patented production processes of international pharmaceutical companies to create drugs that are only slightly different.

In China, political protection for pirates of intellectual property remains fairly common. Government officials, people working for the government, and even the People's Liberation Army (China's national army) operate factories that churn out pirated goods. An international company has difficulty fighting piracy in China because filing a lawsuit can severely damage its business relations there.

Yet, opinion is divided on the root causes of intellectual property violations in China. Some argue that Chinese legislation is vaguely worded and difficult to enforce. Others say China's intellectual property laws and regulations are fine, but poor enforcement is to blame for high rates of piracy. Amazingly, China's regulatory body sometimes allows a counterfeiter to remove an infringing trademark and still sell the substandard good. Technology companies said to have been harmed by China's weak intellectual property laws include Microsoft (www.microsoft.com), which claims that its software is widely pirated, and Cisco Systems (www.cisco.com), which sued a Chinese hardware maker for allegedly copying and using Cisco networking software.

Thinking Globally

3-16. What more do you think the international business community could do to protect its intellectual property rights?

3-17. Are international companies simply afraid to speak out against counterfeiting in potentially lucrative emerging markets for fear of being denied access to them?

3-18. By using the latest technologies, people can often create perfect clones of original works. How are the Internet and the latest digital technologies influencing intellectual property laws?

3-19. Locate information about the Tiffany versus eBay lawsuit and identify each side's arguments and who prevailed. What are the implications of that lawsuit for the sale of counterfeits in online auctions?

Sources: Tom Espiner, "The Slimming Pills that Put Me In Hospital," *BBC News* (www.bbc.com), May 10, 2017; Sarah E. Needleman and Kathy Chu, "Entrepreneurs Bemoan Counterfeit Goods," *Wall Street Journal* (www.wsj.com), April 28, 2014; "Counterfeit Drugs: Fake Pharma," *The Economist* (www.economist.com), February 15, 2012; Rachel Metz, "eBay Beats Tiffany in Court Case over Trademarks," *USA Today* (www.usatoday.com) July 14, 2008.

Chapter Four

Economic Development of Nations

Learning Objectives

After studying this chapter, you should be able to

4.1 Explain economic development and how it is measured.

4.2 Describe economic transition and its main obstacles.

4.3 Outline the various sources of political risk.

4.4 Explain how companies can manage political risk.

4.5 Describe China's and Russia's experiences with economic transition.

A Look Back

Chapter 3 explored the political economy of nations and the main types of political, economic, and legal systems around the world. We also examined key legal issues for international firms and the importance of ethical behavior and social responsibility.

A Look at This Chapter

This chapter presents the economic development of nations and the main ways to measure development. We then explore economic transition, political risk and how it can be managed, and China's and Russia's experiences with economic transition.

A Look Ahead

Chapter 5 introduces us to a major form of international business activity—international trade. We examine the patterns of international trade and outline several theories that attempt to explain why nations conduct trade.

MyLab Management
✪ IMPROVE YOUR GRADE!

When you see this icon ✪, visit **www.pearson.com/mylab/management** for activities that are applied, personalized, and offer immediate feedback.

Foxconn: Contracting for Growth

NEW TAIPEI, Taiwan—Hai Precision Industry Co., trading as Foxconn Technology Group, is a Taiwanese multinational company. It opened its very first production facilities in 1988 in Shenzhen, China, and 30 years later, the company is one of China's largest private employers and the world's largest contract manufacturer of consumer electronics, with over one million employees and annual revenues amounting to more than $150 billion. Perhaps best known for assembling Apple's iPhones, Foxconn provides electronic products and components to companies globally and has operations worldwide. However, this achievement owes much to serendipitous initiatives led by the Chinese government to boost economic development.

China's fast-paced economic development and growth has been made possible thanks to its expansion as a manufacturer of all things, underpinned by governmental support and access to an abundant supply of competitive and efficient labor. Crucial elements of China's exponential development were the way they positioned themselves internationally as a producer of goods and their open welcome to the flood of foreign investment that followed.

ROPI/Alamy Stock Photo

Previously hostile toward foreign firms, the Chinese government reversed that policy in December 1978, when it announced an "open door" policy welcoming outside investment. Deng Xiaoping recognized China's need for advanced technology and investment to spur its economic development and instituted a top-down movement from the Chinese government to that end. It was also at this point that China's economic strategy began to develop its focus on the production of goods for overseas consumption.

China's journey toward successful economic development has not been without its problems. Some argue that its legal system lags behind some other developing economies and that there is an inherent protectionist bias favoring domestic companies at the cost of international counterparts. The recent tariffs imposed by the United States on $50 billion worth of Chinese goods is a response to estimated losses resulting from domestic firms stealing the intellectual property of foreign companies producing in China, either through counterfeit markets or through mandatory joint ventures.

Serious concerns have also been raised about the costs of the country's economic development and the dreadful conditions that workers are exposed to daily. Foxconn, no stranger to this criticism, became famous globally in 2010 after a group of its workers threatened to throw themselves off a company building in 2010.

economic development
Increase in the economic well-being, quality of life, and general welfare of a nation's people.

In Chapter 2, we saw that one defining element of a culture is its tendency toward individualism or collectivism. In Chapter 3, we saw how this tendency and a society's history influence the formation of its political economy. In this chapter, we investigate the linkages between political economy and **economic development**—an increase in the economic well-being, quality of life, and general welfare of a nation's people. Similar to how systems of political economy differ from country to country, so too do levels of economic development.

National culture can have a strong impact on a nation's economic development. In turn, the development of a country's economy can dramatically influence many aspects of its culture. Economic systems in individualist cultures tend to provide incentives and rewards for individual business initiative. Collectivist cultures tend to offer fewer such incentives and rewards. For example, in individualist cultures, *entrepreneurs*—businesspeople who accept the risks and opportunities involved in creating and operating new business ventures—tend to be rewarded with relatively low tax rates that encourage their activities.

We begin this chapter by introducing categories in which we place countries depending on their level of economic development. We then examine several indicators of national economic development. Next, we look at how countries in transition are implementing market-based reforms to encourage economic development and learn about the obstacles they face. We then cover the nature of political risk because of its potential impact on economic development and see how firms manage this type of risk. We conclude this chapter with a look at how two *emerging markets* are faring in their economic development efforts.

4.1 Economic Development

4.1 Explain economic development and how it is measured.

Economic development includes economic improvements in people's lives as well as progress on physical health, safety, life expectancy, education and literacy, poverty, critical infrastructure, environmental sustainability, and so forth. As such, the concept incorporates both quantitative and qualitative features.

Yet, economic development requires *economic growth*, which is a quantifiable increase in the goods and services that a society produces. Economic growth, in turn, depends on gains in *productivity*, which is simply the ratio of outputs (what is created) to inputs (resources used to create output). We can speak about the productivity of a business, an industry, or an entire economy. For a business to boost its productivity it must increase the value of its outputs using the same amount of inputs, create the same value of outputs with fewer inputs, or do both at the same time. Businesses increase their productivity through *entrepreneurial activities* and *innovation*, in all their forms.

Classifying Countries

Differences in political economy among nations can cause great differences in economic development. Development is an increasingly important topic as international companies pursue business opportunities in emerging markets. Although much of the population in these countries is poor, there is often a thriving middle class and ambitious programs toward economic development.

Nations are commonly classified as being *developed, newly industrialized*, or *developing* based on a quantifiable economic measure. Such measures include figures on national production, the portion of the economy devoted to agriculture, the amount of exports in the form of industrial goods, and overall economic structure. There is no single, agreed-on list of countries in each category, however, and borderline countries are often classified differently in different listings.

developed country
Country that is highly industrialized and highly efficient, and whose people enjoy a high quality of life.

DEVELOPED COUNTRIES Countries that are highly industrialized and highly efficient, and whose people enjoy a high quality of life, are **developed countries**. People in developed countries usually receive the finest health care and benefit from the best educational systems in the world. Most developed nations also support aid programs for helping poorer nations to improve their economies and standards of living. Countries in this category include Australia, Canada, Japan, New Zealand, the United States, and all western European nations.

NEWLY INDUSTRIALIZED COUNTRIES Countries that have recently increased the portion of their national production and exports derived from industrial operations are

newly industrialized countries (NICs). The NICs are located primarily in Asia and Latin America. Most listings of NICs include Asia's "four tigers" (Hong Kong, South Korea, Singapore, and Taiwan), Brazil, China, India, Malaysia, Mexico, South Africa, and Thailand. Depending on the pivotal criteria used for classification, a number of other countries could be placed in this category, including Argentina, Brunei, Chile, the Czech Republic, Hungary, Indonesia, the Philippines, Poland, Russia, Slovakia, Turkey, and Vietnam.

When we combine newly industrialized countries with countries that have the potential to become newly industrialized, we arrive at a category often called **emerging markets**. Generally, emerging markets have developed some (but not all) of the operations and export capabilities associated with NICs. Debate continues, however, over the defining characteristics of such classifications as *newly industrialized country* and *emerging market*.

DEVELOPING COUNTRIES Nations with the poorest infrastructures and lowest personal incomes are called **developing countries** (also called *less-developed countries*). These countries often rely heavily on one or a few sectors of production, such as agriculture, mineral mining, or oil drilling. They might show potential for becoming newly industrialized countries, but typically lack the necessary resources and skills to do so. Most lists of developing countries include many nations in Africa, the Middle East, and the poorest formerly communist nations in Eastern Europe and Asia.

Developing countries (and NICs as well) are sometimes characterized by a high degree of **technological dualism**—use of the latest technologies in some sectors of the economy coupled with the use of outdated technologies in others. By contrast, developed countries typically incorporate the latest technological advancements in all manufacturing sectors.

When exploring potential markets, managers can use a variety of measures to estimate a country's level of economic development. But it is wise to examine a combination of measures because each one has advantages and disadvantages. Let's now look at the main gauges of economic development.

National Production

Recall from Chapter 1 that *gross domestic product (GDP)* is the value of all goods and services produced by a domestic economy over a one-year period. GDP is a narrower figure than *gross national product (GNP)* in that it excludes a nation's income generated from exports, imports, and the international operations of its companies. A country's *GDP per capita* is simply its GDP divided by its population to measure a nation's income per person. Map 4.1 on pages 132–133 shows how the World Bank (www.worldbank.org) classifies countries according to *gross national income (GNI)* per capita—a measure that is similar to GNP per capita.

Marketers often use GDP or GNP per capita figures to determine whether a country's population is wealthy enough to begin purchasing its products. For example, the Asian nation of Myanmar, with a GDP per capita of about $1,500 per year, is very poor. You won't find many computer companies marketing laptops or designer-apparel firms selling expensive clothing there. Yet several large makers of personal-care products are staking out territory in Myanmar. Companies like Colgate-Palmolive (www.colgate.com) and Unilever (www.unilever.com) are traditional explorers of uncertain but promising markets in which they can offer relatively inexpensive, everyday items such as soap and shampoo. As multinational companies enter such markets, they often try to satisfy the needs of people who live at the *bottom of the pyramid*—the world's poorest populations with the least purchasing power.

Although GDP and GNP are the most popular indicators of economic development, they have several important drawbacks.

UNCOUNTED TRANSACTIONS For a variety of reasons, many of a nation's transactions do not get counted in either GDP or GNP. Some activities not included are:

- Volunteer work
- Unpaid household work
- Illegal activities such as gambling and black market (underground) transactions
- Unreported transactions conducted in cash

newly industrialized country (NIC)
Country that has recently increased the portion of its national production and exports derived from industrial operations.

emerging markets
Newly industrialized countries plus those with the potential to become newly industrialized.

developing country
Nation that has a poor infrastructure and extremely low personal incomes. Also called less-developed countries.

technological dualism
Use of the latest technologies in some sectors of the economy coupled with the use of outdated technologies in other sectors.

Map 4.1
Gross National Income

C OCEAN

NORWAY
SWEDEN
FINLAND
ESTONIA
LATVIA
DIMARK
LITHUANIA
RUSSIA
BELARUS
NDS
POLAND
GERMANY
CZECH
JURG
REP. SLOVAKIA
UKRAINE
HT
AUSTRIA
SLOVENIA
HUNGARY
MOLDOVA
CROATIA
ROMANIA
BOSNIA
SERBIA AND
HERZEGOVINA
MONTENEGRO
BULGARIA
ITALY
MACEDONIA
GEORGIA
ALBANIA
ARMENIA
AZERBAIJAN
UZBEKISTAN
KYRGYZSTAN
GREECE
TURKEY
TURKMENISTAN
TAJIKISTAN
NISIA
CYPRUS
SYRIA
LEBANON
IRAQ
IRAN
AFGHANISTAN
ISRAEL
JORDAN
KUWAIT
PAKISTAN
LIBYA
EGYPT
QATAR
UNITED ARAB
EMIRATES
SAUDI
ARABIA
OMAN
NEPAL
BHUTAN
BANGLADESH
GER
CHAD
SUDAN
INDIA
MYANMAR
(BURMA)
LAOS
ERITREA
YEMEN
THAILAND
VIETNAM
ERIA
SOUTH
SUDAN
DJIBOUTI
SOMALIA
CAMBODIA
CENTRAL AFRICAN
REPUBLIC
ETHIOPIA
SRI
LANKA
AMEROON
AL
CONGO
REPUBLIC
UGANDA
KENYA
BON
CONGO
DEMOCRATIC
REPUBLIC
(ZAIRE)
RWANDA
BURUNDI
TANZANIA
ANGOLA
ZAMBIA
MALAWI
MOZAMBIQUE
NAMIBIA
ZIMBABWE
MADAGASCAR
MAURITIUS
BOTSWANA
RÉUNION
SWAZILAND
SOUTH
AFRICA
LESOTHO

RUSSIA

KAZAKHSTAN

MONGOLIA

CHINA

NORTH
KOREA

SOUTH
KOREA

JAPAN

TAIWAN

PACIFIC
OCEAN

INDIAN
OCEAN

BRUNEI
MALAYSIA
SINGAPORE

PHILIPPINES

INDONESIA

PAPUA
NEW
GUINEA

SOLOMON
ISLANDS

VANUATU

FIJI

NEW
CALEDONIA

AUSTRALIA

NEW
ZEALAND

GNI in US dollars

- 7,490 or more
- 2,350 – 7,490
- 1,110 – 2,350
- 430 – 1,110
- less than 430
- no data available

In some cases, the unreported (shadow) economy is so large and prosperous that official statistics such as GDP per capita are almost meaningless. Government statistics can mask a thriving shadow economy driven by differences between official and black-market currency exchange rates. In many wealthy nations, the shadow economy is from one-tenth to one-fifth as large as the official economy. But in more than 50 countries, the shadow economy is at least 40 percent the size of the documented GDP. In the Eurasian country of Georgia, for example, unreported transactions are estimated to equal as much as 73 percent of reported transactions. So, whereas Georgia's official GDP is around $15 billion, its shadow economy could be worth nearly $11 billion.

One way in which goods and services flow through shadow economies is through *barter*—the exchange of goods and services for other goods and services instead of money. In one classic incident, Pepsi-Cola (www.pepsi.com) traded soft drinks in the former Soviet Union for 17 submarines, a cruiser, a frigate, and a destroyer. Pepsi then converted its payment into cash by selling the military goods as scrap metal.[2] Russians still use barter extensively because of a lack of currency. In another classic, and bizarre, case, the Russian government paid 8,000 teachers in the Altai republic (1,850 miles east of Moscow) their monthly salaries with 15 bottles of vodka each. Teachers had previously refused an offer to receive part of their salaries in toilet paper and funeral accessories.[3]

QUESTION OF GROWTH Gross product figures do not tell us whether a nation's economy is growing or shrinking—they are simply a snapshot of one year's economic output. Managers will want to supplement this data with information on expected future economic performance. A nation with moderate GDP or GNP figures attracts more investment if its expected growth rate is high.

PROBLEM OF AVERAGES Recall that per capita numbers give an average figure for an entire country. These numbers are helpful in estimating national quality of life, but averages do not give us a very detailed picture of development. Urban areas in most countries are more developed and have higher per capita income than rural areas. In less advanced nations, regions near good harbors or other transportation facilities are usually more developed than interior regions. Likewise, an industrial park that boasts companies with advanced technology in production or design can generate a disproportionate share of a country's earnings.

For example, GDP or GNP per capita figures for China are misleading because Shanghai and coastal regions of China are far more developed than the country's interior. Although luxury cars are sold in many of China's large cities and coastal regions, bicycles and simple vehicles are still the transportation of choice in China's interior.

PITFALLS OF COMPARISON Country comparisons using gross product figures can be misleading. When comparing gross product per capita, the currency of each nation being compared must be translated into another currency unit (usually the dollar) at official exchange rates. But official exchange rates only tell us how many units of one currency it takes to buy one unit of another. They do not tell us what that currency can buy in its home country. Therefore, to understand the true value of a currency in its home country, we apply the concept of *purchasing power parity*.

Purchasing Power Parity

Using gross product figures to compare production across countries does not account for the different cost of living in each country. **Purchasing power** is the value of goods and services that can be purchased with one unit of a country's currency. **Purchasing power parity (PPP)** is the relative ability of two countries' currencies to buy the same "basket" of goods in those two countries. This basket of goods is representative of ordinary, daily-use items such as apples, rice, soap, toothpaste, and so forth. Estimates of gross product per capita at PPP allow us to see what a currency can actually buy in real terms.

Let's see what happens when we compare the wealth of several countries to that of the United States by adjusting GDP per capita to reflect PPP. If we convert Swiss francs to dollars at official exchange rates, we estimate Switzerland's GDP per capita at $47,900. This is higher than the official GDP per capita of the United States ($39,700). But adjusting Switzerland's GDP per capita for PPP gives us a revised figure of $34,700, which is lower than the US GDP figure of $39,700. Why the difference? GDP per capita at PPP is lower in Switzerland because of that nation's higher cost of living. It simply costs more to buy the same basket of goods in Switzerland than it does in the United States. The opposite phenomenon occurs in the case of the Czech Republic. Because

purchasing power

Value of goods and services that can be purchased with one unit of a country's currency.

purchasing power parity (PPP)

Relative ability of two countries' currencies to buy the same "basket" of goods in those two countries.

the cost of living there is lower than in the United States, the Czech Republic's GDP per capita rises from \$10,600 to \$18,600 when PPP is considered.[4] We discuss PPP in greater detail in Chapter 10.

Human Development

So far we see that adjusting figures on national production for purchasing power provide numerical measures for comparing nations. But we also see that they do not capture development's qualitative aspects. Also, the PPP concept does a fairly decent job of revealing different levels of economic development, but is *a poor indicator of a people's total well-being*. Table 4.1 shows how selected countries rank according to the United Nations' **human development index (HDI)**—the measure of the extent to which a government equitably provides its people with a long and healthy life, an education, and a decent standard of living.

Table 4.1 also illustrates the disparity that can be present between a nation's wealth and the HDI. For example, we see that Germany ranks 17th in terms of gross national income (GNI) per capita yet ranks 4th (a disparity of plus 13) in providing health care, education, and a decent standard of living. The disparity is negative 30 for South Africa; the country ranks 89th in terms of GNI per capita but ranks 119th in terms of HDI. Perhaps most striking is the column showing each nation's life expectancy at birth. We see that the people of first-ranked Norway have a life expectancy that is 30 years longer than the people of last-ranked Central African Republic.

Unlike other measures we have discussed, the HDI looks beyond financial wealth. By stressing the human aspects of economic development, it demonstrates that high national income alone does not guarantee human progress. However, the importance of national income should

human development index (HDI)

Measure of the extent to which a government equitably provides its people with a long and healthy life, an education, and a decent standard of living.

TABLE 4.1 Human Development Index (HDI)

HDI Rank	Country	HDI Value	GNI per Capita Rank	Life Expectancy at Birth (Years)
Very High Human Development				
1	Norway	0.949	6	81.7
2	Switzerland	0.939	9	83.1
4	Germany	0.926	17	81.1
10	Canada	0.920	22	82.2
10	United States	0.920	11	79.2
16	United Kingdom	0.909	26	80.8
21	France	0.897	25	82.4
27	Spain	0.884	34	82.8
45	Argentina	0.827	57	76.5
High Human Development				
49	Russia	0.804	50	70.3
77	Mexico	0.762	68	77.0
90	China	0.738	83	76.0
Medium Human Development				
111	Egypt	0.691	104	71.3
119	South Africa	0.666	89	57.7
139	Bangladesh	0.579	147	72.0
Low Human Development				
152	Nigeria	0.527	129	53.1
188	Central African Rep.	0.352	192	51.5

Source: Based on data obtained from Human Development Report 2016 (New York: United Nations Development Programme, 2016), Table 1, pp. 198–201, available at www.undp.org.

not be underestimated. Countries need money to build good schools, provide quality health care, support environmentally friendly industries, and underwrite other programs designed to improve the quality of life.

QUICK STUDY 1

1. An increase in the economic well-being, quality of life, and general welfare of a nation's people is called *what*?
2. What are the drawbacks of using national production to measure economic development?
3. The human development index measures what aspects of a nation's development?

4.2 Economic Transition

4.2 Describe economic transition and its main obstacles.

economic transition
Process by which a nation changes its fundamental economic organization and creates new free-market institutions.

Over the past two decades, countries with centrally planned economies have been remaking themselves in the image of stronger market economies. This process, called **economic transition**, involves changing a nation's fundamental economic organization and creating entirely new free-market institutions. Some nations take transition further than others do, but the process typically involves several key reform measures to promote economic development:

- Stabilizing the economy, reducing budget deficits, and expanding credit availability
- Allowing prices to reflect supply and demand
- Legalizing private business, selling state-owned companies, and supporting property rights
- Reducing barriers to trade and investment and allowing currency convertibility

Transition from central planning to free-market economies generates tremendous international business opportunities. Yet, difficulties arising from years of socialist economic principles hamper development efforts from the start, and some countries still endure high unemployment rates. Governments of former centrally planned economies in Eastern Europe continue to sell state-owned companies in order to boost productivity and competitiveness and to raise living standards. Let's examine the key obstacles for countries in transition.

Managerial Expertise

In central planning, there was little need for production, distribution, and marketing strategies or for trained individuals to devise them. Central planners decided all aspects of the nation's commercial activities. There was no need to investigate consumer wants and no need for market research. Little thought was given to product pricing or to the need for experts in operations, inventory, distribution, or logistics. Factory managers at government-owned firms had only to meet production requirements set by central planners. In fact, some products rolled off assembly lines merely to be stacked outside the factory because knowing where they were to go after production—and who took them there—was not the factory manager's job.

Recent years, however, are seeing higher-quality management in transition countries. Reasons for this trend include improved education, opportunities to study and work abroad, and changes in work habits caused by foreign companies investing locally. Some managers from former communist nations are even finding managerial opportunities in Western Europe and the United States with large multinational corporations.

Shortage of Capital

Not surprisingly, economic transition and development are expensive undertakings. To facilitate the process and ease the pain, governments usually spend a great deal of money to:

- Develop a telecommunications and infrastructure system, including highways, bridges, rail networks, and sometimes subways.
- Create financial institutions, including stock markets and a banking system.
- Educate people in the ways of market economics.

The governments of many countries in transition cannot afford all the investments required of them. Outside sources of capital are available, however, including national and international companies, other governments, and international financial institutions, such as the World Bank, the International Monetary Fund (IMF), and the Asian Development Bank. Some transition countries owe substantial amounts of money to international lenders, but this is becoming less of a problem today than it was earlier in the era of transition economies.

Cultural Differences

Economic transition and development reforms make deep cultural impressions on a nation's people. As we saw in Chapter 2, some cultures are more open to change than others. Likewise, certain cultures welcome economic change more easily than others do. Transition replaces dependence on the government with greater emphasis on individual responsibility, incentives, and rights. But sudden deep cuts in welfare payments, unemployment benefits, and guaranteed government jobs can present a major shock to a nation's people.

Importing modern management practices into the culture of a transition country can be difficult. South Korea's Daewoo Motors (www.daewoo.com) faced a culture clash when it entered Central Europe. Korea's management system is based on a rigid hierarchical structure and an intense work ethic. Managers at Daewoo's car plants in South Korea arrived early for work to stand and greet workers at the company gates. But problems arose when Daewoo's managers did not fully comprehend the culture at its factories in Central Europe. Daewoo bridged the cultural and workplace gaps by sending central European workers to staff assembly lines in Korea and sent Korean managers and technicians to work in Central and Eastern Europe.

Sustainability

The economic and social policies of former communist governments in Central and Eastern Europe were disastrous for the natural environment. The direct effects of environmental destruction were evident in high levels of sickness and disease, including asthma, blood deficiencies, and cancer—which lowered productivity in the workplace. Countries in transition often suffer periods during which the negative effects of a market economy seem to outweigh its benefits. But as transition and development efforts continue, the wider population begins to enjoy the benefits of a market economy.

Nations that lived under central planning have had to overcome one of central planning's lasting legacies—lack of a topnotch healthcare system. The spread of communicable diseases in the world's poorest nations is especially worrying. Diseases such as HIV/AIDS, tuberculosis, and malaria still infect many people in Southeast Asia, Eastern Europe, and elsewhere. These diseases cause human and economic loss, social disintegration, and political instability. The health care costs required to combat such diseases can significantly impair efforts toward sustainable development. To read about the costs of three particularly lethal diseases, see the Global Sustainability feature, titled "Public Health Goes Global" on page 140.

> **QUICK STUDY 2**
>
> 1. What does the economic transition process involve?
> 2. What are the key obstacles for countries in transition?
> 3. Transition replaces dependence on the government with greater emphasis on *what*?

4.3 Political Risk

All companies doing business domestically or internationally confront **political risk**—the likelihood that a society will undergo political change that negatively affects local business activity. Political risk abroad affects different types of companies in different ways. It can threaten the market of an exporter, the production facilities owned by a foreign manufacturer, or the ability of a firm to extract a profit from a country in which it was earned. A solid grasp of local values, customs, and traditions can help reduce a company's exposure to political risk.

Map 4.2 (on pages 138–139) shows that political risk levels vary from nation to nation. Some of the factors included in the assessment of political risk levels include government stability,

4.3 Outline the various sources of political risk.

political risk
Likelihood that a society will undergo political change that negatively affects local business activity.

Map 4.2
Political Risk around the World

Level of risk

- very high
- high
- moderate
- low
- very low
- no data available

GLOBAL SUSTAINABILITY | Public Health Goes Global

Beyond the human suffering, three communicable diseases put a drag on economic development and social sustainability.

- **HIV/AIDS.** This disease killed nearly as many people as the plague that struck fourteenth-century Europe. AIDS has already killed at least 22 million worldwide, and at least 40 million are infected with HIV. In Africa alone, 20 million have died and 30 million are infected. The disease cut GDP growth by 2.6 percent in some African countries and could *decrease* South Africa's average household income by 8 percent.

- **Tuberculosis.** Each year, tuberculosis (TB) kills 1.7 million people and sickens another 8 million. More than 90 percent of TB cases occur in low- and lower-middle-income countries across Southeast Asia, Eastern Europe, and sub-Saharan Africa. TB is on the rise because of economic hardship, broken health systems, and the emergence of drug-resistant TB. This disease depletes the incomes of the poorest nations by about $12 billion.

- **Malaria.** Each year, malaria kills one million people and indirectly causes the deaths of up to three million. Malaria is prevalent in Vietnam's Mekong Delta, central Africa, and Brazil's Amazon Basin. Central and sub-Saharan Africa

account for 90 percent of all malaria deaths (mostly children and pregnant women) and is where around 20 percent of all children die of malaria before age five. In the worst-affected African nations, malaria costs about 1.3 percent of GDP.

- **The Challenge.** To combat *HIV/AIDS*, rich nations could donate money to train doctors and nurses in poor nations and could invest more in research. To battle *tuberculosis*, more aid money could purchase drugs that cost just $10 per person for the full six-to-eight-month treatment. To fight *malaria*, better distribution of insecticide-treated bed nets could reach the 98 percent of Africa's children who do not sleep under such nets.

- **Want to Know More?** Visit the Global Business Coalition (www.gbchealth.org); the Global Fund to fight AIDS, Tuberculosis, and Malaria (www.theglobalfund.org); the Malaria Foundation International (www.malaria.org); and the World Health Organization TB site (www.who.int/gtb).

Sources: "Altogether Now," The Economist (www.economist.com), June 3, 2010; Tom Randall, "J&J, Sanofi, Pfizer Speed Testing for New Tuberculosis Drug," Bloomberg Businessweek (www.businessweek.com), March 18, 2010; "Twenty-Five Years of AIDS," The Economist, June 3, 2006, pp. 24–25; Malaria Foundation International (www.malaria.org), various reports.

---

internal and external conflict, military and religious involvement in politics, corruption, law and order, and the quality of a government's bureaucracy.

Two broad categories of political risk reflect the range of companies each affects. *Macro risk* threatens the activities of all domestic and international companies in every industry. Examples include an ongoing threat of violence against corporate assets in a nation and a rising level of government corruption. *Micro risk* threatens companies only within a particular industry (or more narrowly defined group). For example, an international trade war in steel affects the operations of steel producers and companies that require steel as an input to their business activities.

The main sources of political risk include:

- Conflict and violence
- Terrorism and kidnapping
- Property seizure
- Policy changes
- Local content requirements

Conflict and Violence

Local conflict can discourage international companies from investing in a nation and set back economic development significantly. Violent disturbances impair a company's ability to manufacture and distribute products, obtain materials and equipment, and recruit talented personnel. Open conflict threatens a company's physical assets (such as offices and factories) and the lives of its employees. Conflict also harms the economic development of nations.

There are at least three main origins of conflict. First, it may arise from people's resentment toward their own government. When peaceful resolution of disputes between people (or factions) and the government fails, violent attempts to change political leadership can ensue. ExxonMobil (www.exxonmobil.com) suspended production of liquid natural gas at its facility in Indonesia's Aceh province when separatist rebels targeted the complex with violence.

Second, conflict can arise over territorial disputes between countries. For example, a dispute over the Kashmir territory between India and Pakistan resulted in major armed conflict between their two peoples several times. And a border dispute between Ecuador and Peru caused these South American nations to go to war three times.

Third, disputes among ethnic, racial, and religious groups may erupt in violent conflict. Indonesia comprises 13,000 islands, more than 300 ethnic groups, and some 450 languages. Years ago, Indonesia's government relocated people from crowded, central islands to less populated, remote ones without regard to ethnicity and religion. Violence among them later displaced more than one million people.

Terrorism and Kidnapping

Terrorist activities are a means of making political statements. Groups dissatisfied with the current political or social situation sometimes resort to terrorist tactics in order to force change through fear and destruction. On September 11, 2001, the world witnessed terrorism on a scale like never before. Two passenger planes were flown into the twin towers of the World Trade Center in New York City, one plane was crashed into the Pentagon in Washington, DC, and one plane crashed in a Pennsylvania field. The terrorist group Al-Qaida claimed responsibility for those US attacks and for more recent attacks around the world. The terror organization's stated goals are to drive Western influence out of Muslim nations and to implement Islamic law. The destructive power of those terrorist acts and the expensive wars that followed in Afghanistan and Iraq exacted a heavy economic toll on many nations.

Kidnapping and the taking of hostages for ransom may be used to fund a terrorist group's activities. Executives of large international companies are often prime targets for kidnappers because their employers have "deep pockets" to pay large ransoms. Latin American countries have some of the world's highest kidnapping rates, and Mexico City is at or near the top of the list of cities with the highest kidnapping rates. Annual security costs for a company with a sales office in Bogotá, Colombia, can be $125,000 and up to $1 million for a company with operations in rebel-controlled areas. Top executives are forced to spend about a third of their time coordinating their company's security in Colombia. Although some policies can cost as little as $500, a medium-sized firm that has 5 to 10 employees traveling to Latin America for a week at a time could expect to pay around $5,000 a year for $10 million of kidnap and ransom insurance.

When high-ranking executives are required to enter countries with high kidnapping rates, they should enter unannounced, meet with only a few key people in secure locations, and leave just as quickly and quietly. Some companies purchase kidnap, ransom, and extortion insurance, but security experts say that training people to avoid trouble in the first place is a far better investment.

Property Seizure

Governments sometimes seize the assets of companies doing business within their borders. Asset seizures fall into one of three categories: *confiscation*, *expropriation*, or *nationalization*.

The forced transfer of assets from a company to the government *without compensation* is called **confiscation**. The former owners typically have no legal basis for requesting compensation or the return of assets. The 1996 Helms–Burton Law allows US businesses to sue companies from other nations that use their property confiscated by Cuba in its 1959 communist revolution. For example, the Cuban government faces nearly 6,000 company claims valued at $20 billion. But US presidents repeatedly waive the law so as not to harm its relations with other countries.

The forced transfer of assets from a company to the government *with compensation* is called **expropriation**. The expropriating government normally determines the amount of compensation. There is no framework for legal appeal, and compensation is typically far below market value. Today, governments rarely resort to confiscation or expropriation because these acts can jeopardize investment in the country. Still, it does happen. Argentina expropriated 51 percent of that country's largest energy firm, named Yacimientos Petroliferos Fiscales (YPF). The move isolated Argentina internationally and caused even greater uncertainty for international investors. Buenos Aires Waterworks and Aerolineas Argentinas are two other entities in Argentina that saw increasing losses after they were nationalized a second time.[5]

Whereas expropriation involves one or several companies in an industry, **nationalization** means government takeover of an *entire* industry. Nationalization is more common than confiscation and expropriation. Likely candidates for nationalization include industries important to a nation's security and those that generate large revenues. Venezuela's late President Hugo Chavez nationalized that country's telephone, electricity, and oil industries and threatened to nationalize many more. Businesses from other countries reacted to these moves by not investing in Venezuela. In general, a government may nationalize an industry to:

* Use subsidies to protect an industry for ideological reasons.
* Save local jobs in an ailing industry to gain political clout.

confiscation
Forced transfer of assets from a company to the government without compensation.

expropriation
Forced transfer of assets from a company to the government with compensation.

nationalization
Government takeover of an entire industry.

- Control industry profits so they cannot be transferred to low tax-rate countries.
- Invest in sectors, such as public utilities, that private companies cannot afford.

Confiscation, expropriation, and nationalization can have the short term effect of saving jobs, boosting currency reserves, or helping the government or the economy in other ways. But the long-term result of this form of political risk is usually slower economic development because foreign investors are more reluctant to invest in the country.

Policy Changes

Government policy changes are the result of a variety of influences, including the ideals of newly empowered political parties, political pressure from special interests, and civil or social unrest. One common policy tool restricts ownership to domestic companies or limits ownership by non-domestic firms to a minority stake. This type of policy restricted PepsiCo's (www.pepsico.com) ownership of local companies to 49 percent when it first entered India. If a company decides to withhold investment from a nation because of such policies, they can be seen as impairing economic development.

Other policy changes can reduce political risk, such as those related to cross-border investments. Facing a slowdown in the technology sector, Taiwan's businesses and politicians called for a scrapping of the nation's "go slow, be patient" policy with China. That policy capped investments in mainland China at $50 million and banned investments in infrastructure and industries sensitive for national security reasons. Taiwan's government created a new policy called "active opening, effective management," which reduced restrictions on cross-border investment. These actions improved ties between China and Taiwan and promoted economic development.

Local Content Requirements

local content requirements
Laws stipulating that a specified amount of a good or service be supplied by producers in the domestic market.

Laws stipulating that a specified amount of a good or service be supplied by producers in the domestic market are called **local content requirements**. These requirements can force companies to use locally available raw materials, procure parts from local suppliers, or employ a minimum number of local workers. They ensure that international companies foster local business activity and help ease regional or national unemployment. They also help governments maintain some degree of control over international companies without resorting to extreme measures such as confiscation and expropriation. These efforts can help the economic development of a nation when used skillfully, or slow development if used carelessly.

We must also acknowledge that local content requirements can jeopardize an international firm's long-term survival. First, a company required to hire local personnel might be forced to take on an inadequately trained workforce or take on excess workers. Second, a company made to obtain raw materials or parts locally can find its production costs rise or its product quality decline.

People rally in the streets of Buenos Aires, Argentina. The Argentinian government nationalized 51 percent of its biggest oil company, YPF, with the overwhelming support of its people and lawmakers. The move rattled foreign investors and trade partners. The Spanish firm, Repsol, accepted $5 billion in compensation for its stake in YPF, which was far below the $10.5 billion it was demanding.

Corina Cohen/Alamy Stock Photo

1. How does political risk abroad affect companies?
2. Companies fear open violence and conflict abroad because it can threaten the ability to do *what*?
3. What is the name given to the forced transfer of assets from a company to the government with compensation?

4.4 Managing Political Risk

International companies benefit from monitoring and attempting to predict political changes that can negatively affect their activities. When an international business opportunity arises in an environment plagued by extremely high risk, simply not investing in the location may be the wisest course of action. Yet when risk levels are moderate and the local market is attractive, international companies can find ways to manage political risk. In this way, private sector investment from foreign companies helps advance a nation's economic development. The three main methods of managing political risk are *adaptation, information gathering*, and *political influence*.

4.4 Explain how companies can manage political risk.

Adaptation

Adaptation means incorporating risk into business strategies, often with the help of local officials. Companies can incorporate risk in four ways.

First, *partnerships* help companies leverage expansion plans. They can be informal arrangements or include joint ventures, strategic alliances, and cross-holdings of company stock. Partnering helps a company to share the risk of loss, which is especially important in emerging markets. If partners own shares (*equity*) in local operations, they get cuts of the profits; if they loan cash (*debt*), they receive interest. Local partners who can help keep political forces from interrupting operations include firms, trade unions, financial institutions, and government agencies.

Second, *localization* entails modifying operations, the product mix, or some other business element—even the company name—to suit local tastes and culture. Consider how MTV (www .mtv.com) demonstrates its sensitivity to local cultural and political issues by localizing its programming to suit regional and national tastes.

Third, *development assistance* allows an international business to assist the host country or region in improving the quality of life for locals. For example, by developing distribution and communications networks, both a company and a nation benefit. Royal Dutch/Shell (www.shell.com), the oil company, is working in Kenya to increase the incomes of poor villagers and to triple the average period of food security.[6] Canon (www.canon.com), the Japanese copier and printer maker, practices *kyosei* ("spirit of cooperation") to press local governments into making social and political reforms.

Fourth, *insurance* against political risk can be essential to companies entering risky business environments. The *Overseas Private Investment Corporation* (www.opic.gov) insures US companies that invest abroad against loss and can provide project financing. Some policies protect companies when local governments restrict the convertibility of local money into home-country currency, whereas others insure against losses created by violent events, including war and terrorism. The *Foreign Credit Insurance Association* (www.fcia.com) also insures US exporters against loss due to a variety of causes.

Information Gathering

International firms attempt to gather information that will help them predict and manage political risk. There are two sources that companies use to conduct accurate political risk forecasting. *Current employees* who have worked in a country long enough to gain insight into local culture and politics are often good sources of information. Individuals who formerly had decision-making authority while on international assignment probably had contact with local politicians and other officials. Yet it is important that an employee's international experience be recent because political power in a nation can shift rapidly and dramatically.

Second, *agencies specialized in providing political-risk services* include banks, political consultants, news publications, and risk-assessment services. Many of these agencies publish reports detailing national levels and sources of political risk. Small companies that cannot afford to pay for these services can consider the many free sources of information available, notably from their federal governments. Government intelligence agencies are excellent and inexpensive sources to consult.

Political Influence

lobbying

Policy of hiring people to represent a company's views on political matters.

Managers must work within the established rules and regulations of each national business environment. Business law in most nations undergoes frequent change, with new laws being enacted and existing ones modified. Influencing local politics means dealing with local lawmakers and politicians directly or through lobbyists. **Lobbying** is the policy of hiring people to represent a company's views on political matters. Lobbyists meet with a local public official to influence his or her position on issues relevant to the company. The ultimate goal of the lobbyists is to get favorable legislation enacted and unfavorable legislation rejected. Lobbyists also work to convince local officials that a company benefits economic development, sustainability efforts, workforce skills, and so on.

Foreign Corrupt Practices Act

Law that forbids US companies from bribing government officials or political candidates in other nations.

Bribes often represent attempts to gain political influence. Years ago, the president of US-based Lockheed Corp., now Lockheed Martin (www.lockheedmartin.com), bribed Japanese officials in order to obtain large sales contracts. Public disclosure of the incident resulted in passage of the **Foreign Corrupt Practices Act**, which forbids US companies from bribing government officials or political candidates in other nations (except when a person's life is in danger). A bribe constitutes "anything of value"—money, gifts, and so forth—and cannot be given to any "foreign government official" empowered to make a "discretionary decision" that may be to the payer's benefit. The law also requires firms to keep accounting records that reflect their international activities and assets.

International Relations

Our coverage shows that relations between countries can influence the political economy of nations and the pace of economic development. Although governments, not companies, are directly responsible for managing international relations, the actions of business can cause relations to improve or worsen. So, in this sense, managers do have a role to play in helping to manage international relations.

Favorable and strong political relationships foster stable business environments. Stability then enhances international cooperation in sectors such as the development of international communications and distribution infrastructures. Strong legal systems through which disputes are resolved quickly and fairly further promote stability and cooperation. Simply put, favorable political relations among countries expand business opportunities, lower risk, and promote economic development.

To generate stable business environments, some countries have turned to *multilateral agreements*—treaties concluded among several nations, each of whom agrees to abide by treaty terms even if tensions develop. According to the European Union's founding treaty, goods, services, and citizens of member nations are free to move across members' borders. Every nation must continue to abide by such terms even if it has a conflict with another member. For instance, although Germany and France may disagree on many issues, neither can treat goods, services, and citizens coming and going between their two nations any differently than it treats any other member nation's goods, services, and citizens. See Chapter 8 for a detailed presentation of the European Union.

The United Nations

Although individual nations sometimes have the power to influence the course of events in certain parts of the world, they cannot monitor political activities everywhere at once. The United Nations (UN; www.un.org) was formed after the Second World War to provide leadership in fostering peace and stability around the world. The UN and its many agencies provide food and medical supplies, educational supplies and training, and financial resources to poorer member nations. The UN receives its funding from member contributions based primarily on gross national product (GNP). Practically all nations in the world are UN members—except for several small countries and territories that have observer status.

The UN is headed by a secretary general who is elected by all members and who serves for a five-year term. The UN system consists of six main bodies:

- All members have an equal vote in the *General Assembly*, which discusses and recommends action on any matter that falls within the UN Charter. It approves the UN budget and the makeup of the other bodies.
- The *Security Council* consists of 15 members. Five (China, France, the United Kingdom, Russia, and the United States) are permanent. Ten others are elected by the General Assembly for two-year terms. The council is responsible for ensuring international peace and security, and all UN members are supposed to be bound by its decisions.
- The *Economic and Social Council*, which is responsible for economics, human rights, and social matters, administers a host of smaller organizations and specialized agencies.
- The *Trusteeship Council* consists of the five permanent members of the Security Council and administers all trustee territories under UN custody.
- The *International Court of Justice* consists of 15 judges elected by the General Assembly and Security Council. It can hear disputes only between nations, not cases brought against individuals or corporations. It has no compulsory jurisdiction, and its decisions can be, and have been, disregarded by specific nations.
- Headed by the secretary general, the *Secretariat* administers the operations of the UN.

An important body within the UN Economic and Social Council is the United Nations Conference on Trade and Development (UNCTAD; unctad.org). The organization has a broad mandate in the areas of international trade and economic development. It hosts conferences on pressing development issues including entrepreneurship, poverty, and national debt. Certain conferences are designed to develop the business management skills of individuals in developing nations.

QUICK STUDY 4

1. How can a company incorporate political risk into its business strategies?
2. What is a good source of information to help conduct accurate political risk forecasting?
3. What might result from unfavorable political relations among countries?

4.5 Emerging Markets and Economic Transition

In this section, we learn more about the experiences of two emerging markets that are transforming their political economies. Both China and Russia continue to undergo economic transition away from central planning and toward more market-based economies. We first explore the history of transition for China and the main issues it confronts today. We then explore Russia's experience with transition and the challenges it faces.

4.5 Describe China's and Russia's experiences with economic transition.

China's Profile

China began its experiment with central planning in 1949, after the communists defeated nationalists in a long and bloody civil war. Following the war, China imprisoned or exiled most of its capitalists. From 1949 until reforms were initiated in the late 1970s, China had a unique economic system. Agricultural production was organized into groups of people who formed production "brigades" and production "units." Communes were larger entities responsible for planning agricultural production quotas and industrial production schedules. Rural families owned their homes and parcels of land on which to produce particular crops. Production surpluses could be consumed by the family or sold at a profit on the open market.

In 1979, China initiated agricultural reforms that strengthened work incentives in this sector. Family units could then grow whatever crops they chose and could sell the produce at market

Chinese migrants work at a construction site in Beijing, China. The government is luring 90 million rural residents to higher-paid jobs in cities and boost urbanization of its 1.4 billion-strong population. The current migration wave brings more than 43,000 people a day to China's cities. The government hopes to increase domestic consumption to make up for slower growth in China's export markets.

View Stock/Alamy Stock Photo

prices. At about the same time, township and village enterprises (TVEs) began to appear. Each TVE relied on the open market for materials, labor, and capital and used a nongovernmental distribution system. Each TVE employed managers who were directly responsible for profits and losses. The government initially regarded TVEs as illegal and unrelated to the officially sanctioned communes. But they were legalized in 1984 and helped lay additional groundwork for a market economy. Today, private businesspeople can even join China's Communist Party, and workers can elect local representatives to the official trade union.

China has done more for its people economically over the past two decades than perhaps any other nation on earth. Today, China's leaders describe its economic philosophy as "socialism with Chinese characteristics," and glistening skyscrapers dominate the Shanghai and Beijing cityscapes. The country's immense population, rising incomes, and expanding opportunities attract huge sums of investment.

More recently, China has relaxed government control over private property. China began selling "land-use rights" for residential use (up to 70 years), commercial use (up to 40 years), and other uses (50 years) in 1988 to raise capital and formalized the practice into law in 1994. Buyers paid an upfront fee for the right to use the land for specific period of time. But the holders of these land-use rights wanted clarity on whether they could renew their rights for another 70 years upon expiration. To assuage these concerns, China's 2007 Property Law clarified that renewal of any leases would be "automatic" but said nothing about if a fee would be involved. In 2017, Chinese Premier, Li Keqiang, stated that the government will permit perpetual and free renewals. In other words, a 70-year land-use right whose renewal is automatic and free implies a perpetual right to use the land. In a capitalist economy this is called private land ownership.[7]

Chinese Patience and *Guanxi*

If there is one trait that is needed by all private companies in China, it is patience. Despite obvious ideological differences between itself and the private sector, China's Communist Party is trying very hard to appear well suited to running the country. Karl Marx once summed up communism as the "abolition of private property," and the name of China's Communist Party (in Chinese characters) literally means "common property party." But today, private property is an accepted concept and encourages Chinese companies to invest in innovation. Leading Chinese multinationals, such as Huawei (www.huawei.com), now rank among the world's largest applicants for patents.

An interesting facet of doing business in China is *guanxi*—the Chinese term for "personal relationships." We can see how this works by exploring the role of *guanxi* in China's approach to innovation. First, *flexible networks* fueled by *guanxi* help companies to reduce costs and increase flexibility. Chinese companies spread their production contracts over a large number of parts suppliers and can then increase or decrease orders as demand dictates. Second, some companies exploit China's lax enforcement of property rights to quickly copy new, pricey global products and make cheaper versions available to Chinese consumers. These companies employ *bandit* or *guerilla innovation* to continually learn innovative ways to produce goods at lower cost, though they are clearly violating the original producer's property rights.[8]

A personal touch is a necessary ingredient for foreign companies to achieve success in China. Initially, and in line with communist ideology, non-Chinese companies were restricted from participating in China's economy. But today, outsiders enjoy ever-greater opportunities to create joint ventures with local partners. To learn more about the need for personal relationships, or *guanxi*, in China, see this chapter's Culture Matters feature, titled "Guidelines for Good *Guanxi*."

China's Challenges

China's economy continued to grow throughout the global recession and is expanding at rates of between 7 and 9 percent today. But China's leadership must deal with increasingly rapid economic and social change and carefully manage *political and social problems* that threaten China's future economic performance. In general, the nation's leadership has poor relations with ethnic minorities and skirmishes between secular and Muslim Chinese in western provinces still occur. Meanwhile, political leaders restrict advanced democratic reforms for the most part. Protests arise sporadically whenever ordinary Chinese citizens grow impatient with political progress.

Another potential problem is *unemployment*, largely the result of the collapse of state-owned industry, intensified competition, and the entry of international companies into China. These forces are placing greater emphasis on efficiency and cutting payrolls in some industries. China's social safety net struggles to cope with the needs of millions of unemployed people.

The biggest contributor to the unemployed sector seems to be migrant workers. Hundreds of thousands of workers have left their farms and now go from city to city searching for better-paying factory work or construction jobs. Unhappiness with economic progress in the countryside and the difficulties migrant workers face are potential sources of social unrest for the Chinese government.

Another key issue is *reunification* of "greater China." China regained control of Hong Kong in 1997 after 99 years under British rule. For the most part, China has kept its promise of "one country, two systems." Although the economic (and, to a lesser extent, political) freedoms of people in

---

CULTURE MATTERS   Guidelines for Good *Guanxi*

- **Importance of Contacts, Not Contracts.** In China, face-to-face communication and personal relationships take priority over written contracts. Mu Dan Ping of Ernst & Young (www.ey.com) offers this diagram to show the different priorities:

    United States: Reason → Law → Relationship
    China: Relationship → Reason → Law

    Managers from the United States look for rationale or reason first, wondering if there is a market with profit potential. If so, they want a legal contract before spending time on a business relationship. But the Chinese need to establish a trust relationship first and then look for common goals as a reason for doing business. For them, legal contracts are just a formality, serving to ensure mutual understanding.

- **Pleasure before Business.** Experts advise managers to leave the sales pitch on the back burner and to follow the lead of their Chinese hosts. If seeking partnerships in China, one cannot overlook the importance of personal relationships. Companies that send their top performers to wow Chinese businesspeople with savvy sales pitches can return empty-handed—friendship comes before business in China.

- **Business Partners Are Family Members, Too.** The importance of family means that visiting managers should never

turn down invitations to partake in a Chinese executive's family life. Lauren Hsu, market analyst for Kohler Company (www.kohler.com), was responsible for researching and identifying potential joint venture partners in China. She once went bowling with the partner's daughter and then to a piano concert with the entire family. Two years of meetings and visits to get acquainted eventually resulted in a joint venture deal.

- **Cultural Sensitivity.** China is not a single market but many different regional markets with different cultures and even different languages. Bob Wilner, of McDonald's Corporation (www.mcdonalds.com), went to China to learn how Chinese people are managed. He explained that although McDonald's cooks its hamburgers exactly the same way worldwide, it is sensitive to local culture in how it manages, motivates, rewards, and disciplines employees. Wilner and other McDonald's managers developed that sensitivity only through repeated visits to China.

Source: "The Panda Has Two Faces," *The Economist*, April 3, 2010, p. 70 Paul Maidment, "China's Legal Catch-22," *Forbes* (www.forbes.com), February 17, 2010; Frederik Balfour, "You Say *Guanxi*, I Say Schmoozing," *Bloomberg Businessweek* (www.businessweek.com), November 18, 2007.

Hong Kong would remain largely intact, the rest of China would continue along lines drawn by the communist leadership. In addition, China regained control of its southern coastal territory of Macao in 1999. Only a one-hour ferry ride from Hong Kong, Macao had been under Portuguese administration since it was founded in 1557. Although Macao's main function used to be that of trading post, today it serves mainly as a gambling outpost and is referred to as "Asia's Vegas."

Any chance of Taiwan's eventual reunification with the Chinese mainland depends on how China manages Hong Kong and Macao. For now, reunification seems more likely as economic ties between China and Taiwan grow steadily. Taiwan scrapped a 50-year ban that capped the size of investments in China and eased restrictions on direct financial flows between Taiwan businesses and the mainland. Also, the entry of both China and Taiwan into the World Trade Organization (www.wto.org) is encouraging further integration of their two economies.

✪ **MyLab Management** Watch It Yongshua USA, LLC the Value of Yuan in China

Apply what you have learned so far about China and its economic development. If your instructor has assigned this, go to **www.pearson.com/mylab/management** to watch a video case about how manufacturing is propelling China's economy and answer questions.

Russia's Profile

Russia's experience with communism began in 1917. For the next 75 years, factories, distribution, and all other facets of operations, including the prices of labor, capital, and products, were controlled by Russia's government. While China was experimenting with private farm ownership and a limited market-price system, Russia and other nations in the Soviet Union remained staunchly communist under a system of complete government ownership.

In the 1980s, the former Soviet Union entered a new era of freedom of thought, freedom of expression, and economic restructuring. For the first time since 1917, people could speak freely about their lives under economic socialism, and speak freely they did. People vented their frustrations over a general lack of consumer goods, poor-quality products, and long lines at banks and grocery stores.

Transition away from government ownership and central planning was challenging. Except for politicians, bureaucrats, and wealthy businesspeople (called the "oligarchs"), ordinary people had difficulty maintaining their standard of living and affording many basic items. Some Russians are now doing well financially because they were factory managers under the old system and retained their jobs in the new system. Others have turned to the black market to amass personal wealth. Still others are working hard to build legitimate companies but find themselves forced into making "protection" payments to organized crime. Today, Russia is far more stable as it has made progress on corruption although a good deal undoubtedly remains.

A somewhat opaque legal system, a fair amount of corruption, and shifting business laws make Russia a place where non-Russian businesspeople must still operate cautiously. Yet some ambitious managers and foreign entrepreneurs are not put off by such obstacles. For some insights on how to do business in today's Russia, see the Manager's Briefcase feature, titled "Russian Rules of the Game."

Russia's Challenges

As in so many other transitional economies, Russia must continue to foster *managerial talent*. Years of central planning delayed the development of managerial skills needed in a market-based economy. Russian managers could do well to advance their skills in every facet of management practice, including financial control, research and development, human resource management, and marketing strategy.

Political instability, especially in the form of intensified nationalist sentiment, is another potential threat to progress. Strong ethnic and nationalist sentiments in the region can cause misunderstandings to spiral out of control quickly. Russia and Georgia had a military confrontation in the summer of 2008 over two of Georgia's restive republics that wanted to draw closer to Russia. Then, in 2014, Russia annexed the Ukraine's peninsula of Crimea, arguing that the

MANAGER'S BRIEFCASE   Russian Rules of the Game

Although business in Russia can be brutal at times, some go-getting entrepreneurs and brave managers are venturing into this rugged land. If you are one of them, or just an interested observer, here are a few pointers on doing business in Russia:

- **Getting Started** A visit to your country's local chamber of commerce in Russia should be high on your list. The best organized and managed of these hold regularly scheduled luncheons at which you can make contacts with Russians and others wanting to do business. They might also offer programs on getting acquainted with the business climate in Russia. Many businesses get started in Moscow, St. Petersburg, or Vladivostok, depending in part on their line of business.
- **Be Adventurous** The kind of person who will succeed in Russia thrives on adventure and enjoys a challenge. He or she also should not demand predictability in day-to-day activities—Russia is anything but predictable. Initially, knowledge of Russian is helpful, though not essential, but

eventual proficiency will be necessary. Prior experience working and living in Eastern Europe would be a big plus.
- **Office Space** Doing business in Russia demands a personal touch. Locating an office in Russia is crucial if you eventually want to receive income from your operations. Your office does not need to be a suite off Red Square. Almost any local address will do, and a nice flat can double as an office at the start. For business services, upscale hotels commonly have business centers in them. Eventually, renting an average Russian-style office would be more than adequate.
- **Making Deals** Business in Russia takes time and patience. The Russian negotiating style, like the country itself, is tough and ever changing. During negotiations, emotional outbursts, walkouts, or threats to walk out from your Russian counterparts should not be unexpected. Finally, signed contracts in Russia are not always followed to the letter, as your Russian associate may view new circumstances as a chance to renegotiate terms. All in all, the personalities of individuals involved in business deals count for much in Russia.

ethnically Russian people in Crimea voted to break away from Ukraine and to become part of Russia. Many nations swiftly rebuked Russia's actions and some, including the United States, imposed political and economic sanctions. Russia remains undeterred, however, and is strengthening its presence in Crimea, other neighboring countries, and as far away as the Middle East.

Russia's *unstable investment climate* is another concern among international businesses. Tense uneasiness between Russia's government and its business community stems from the government's attacks on business owners who disagree with official policy and on firms that it wants to control. The root of many of Russia's problems appears to be *corrupt law enforcement*. Officials of the government, such as the Russian Interior Ministry, are accused of raiding the offices of companies for documents and computers. Records are then falsified and signatures forged to make it appear that another company—one controlled by government officials—has massively overpaid taxes and is due a government refund. Meanwhile, the owners and managers of the raided businesses often find themselves in prison.

The Russian government has little patience or sympathy for reformers inside the country. Ordinary Russians never cared much for the wealthy "oligarchs, as they were called, and saw them as corrupt businesspeople who gained wealth at the expense of the people. Some wealthy individuals tried to create a better Russia by encouraging formation of a new class of people who would one day push for political reforms. They financed boarding schools for orphans, computer classes for village schools, and civil-society programs for journalists and politicians. But such actions made them a threat to the state and they often found themselves imprisoned on charges of tax evasion, fraud, and so forth. If Russia truly wishes to become a location of choice for international companies, it will need to respect the sovereignty of other nations, meddle less in business, and better safeguard property rights.

QUICK STUDY 5

1. During what time period did China undergo its most rigorous experience with central planning?
2. What challenges might pose a threat to China's future economic performance?
3. Over what aspects of Russia's centrally-planned economy did planners exercise control?
4. What might challenge Russia's future economic prospects?

BOTTOM LINE FOR BUSINESS

This completes our three-chapter coverage of national business environments. Nations are removing unnecessary regulations and government interference in the hope of advancing their economic development. Formerly centrally planned economies continue free-market reforms in order to drive domestic entrepreneurial activity and attract international investors. These trends are changing the face of global capitalism. Two topics are likely to dominate conversations on development—the race between China and India and the productivity gap between the United States and Europe.

Economic Development in China versus India

Both China and India have immense potential for growth, and it is only a matter of time before each has a middle class larger than the entire US population. Whether the organic-led path of India or the investment-led path of China is best for a particular nation depends on that nation's circumstances.

Every nation on earth has so far followed a path to development that relied on its natural resources and/or its relatively cheap labor—the model China is following. China's top-down approach to development and India's bottom-up approach reflect their political systems: India is a democracy, whereas China is not. Although China is growing rapidly, it needs homegrown entrepreneurs and advanced managerial skills to take it to the next level of global competitiveness.

If India can achieve sustained economic growth, it will become the first developing nation to advance economically by relying on the brainpower of its people. India's growth came largely from native competitive firms in cutting-edge, knowledge-based industries. Although India has a long reputation for high taxes and burdensome regulations, it also has had the foundations of a market economy, such as private enterprise, democratic government, and Western accounting practices. India also has a relatively advanced legal system, fairly efficient capital markets, and many talented entrepreneurs.

Productivity in the United States versus Europe

Productivity growth is a key driver of living standards in any nation. Although productivity growth in Europe kept pace with that in the United States for decades, it has fallen behind in recent years. But why is there a productivity gap at all?

Several explanations have been proposed. First, despite its benefits, information technology (IT) spending in Europe lags behind that in the United States. Europeans may be discouraged from spending on IT for reasons related to European business law. Second, stronger labor laws in Europe relative to the United States make it more difficult and costly to shed workers. Thus, even if European companies invest in IT to increase labor productivity, overall productivity gains may be hampered by their inability to rid themselves of excess workers. Third, whereas the US tech sector is a big driver behind higher US productivity growth, the tech sector in Europe is far smaller by comparison. Fourth, Europe spends far less overall on research and development, even though such spending is a big boost to productivity growth.

Strong productivity growth will translate to a higher level of economic development. Many European officials are calling for a greater shift toward free-market reform to boost productivity. European officials understand that robust productivity growth is the only way for their citizens to close the gap with their US counterparts.

MyLab Management

Go to **www.pearson.com/mylab/management** to complete the problems marked with this icon .

Chapter Summary

LO4.1 Explain economic development and how it is measured.
- *Economic development* refers to an increase in the economic well-being, quality of life, and general welfare of a nation's people.
- One measure of economic development is *national production*, including *gross national product* and *gross domestic product*.
- Another method is *purchasing power parity*, the relative ability of two countries' currencies to buy the same "basket" of goods in those two countries.
- A third method is the *human development index*, or the extent to which a people's needs are satisfied and addressed equally across the population.

LO4.2 Describe economic transition and its main obstacles.
- *Economic transition* is the process whereby a nation changes its fundamental economic organization to create free-market institutions.
- One obstacle is a *lack of managerial expertise* because central planners made nearly all business decisions.

- There is a *shortage of capital* to pay for communications, infrastructure, financial institutions, and education.
- *Cultural differences* between transition economies and western nations can make it difficult to introduce modern management practices.
- And *unsustainable* practices lowered productivity due to lax environmental standards and poor healthcare.

LO4.3 Outline the various sources of political risk.
- *Political risk* is the likelihood that a society will undergo political change that negatively affects local business activity. *Macro risk* threatens all companies alike whereas *micro risk* threatens one industry or group of companies.
- The five main sources of political risk are conflict and violence, terrorism and kidnapping, property seizure, policy changes, and local content requirements.
- Property seizure can take the form of *confiscation* (without compensation), *expropriation* (with compensation), or *nationalization* (takeover of an entire industry).

LO4.4 Explain how companies can manage political risk.
- Managers can reduce the effects of political risk through *adaptation* (incorporating risk into business strategies), *information gathering* (monitoring local political events), and *political influence* (such as by *lobbying* local political leaders).
- Firms can also manage political risk to some extent by ensuring that their actions do not harm international relations.
- Supporting economic development efforts of international organizations, such as the United Nations, can also help mitigate political risk.

LO4.5 Describe China's and Russia's experiences with economic transition.
- China has had tremendous economic success for over two decades with its economic philosophy called, "socialism with Chinese characteristics." The country's immense population, rising incomes, and expanding opportunities attract huge sums of investment. Potential threats to China's pace of development are political and social problems, high migrant unemployment, and a rocky reunification with Taiwan.
- Russia's experience with communism extended from 1917 until it began its economic restructuring in the 1980s. Transition away from central planning was challenging for common Russians and corruption became the norm. Challenges facing Russia are the need to foster *managerial talent* suited to a market-based economy, *political instability* in the form of intense nationalism, and an *unstable investment climate*.

Key Terms

confiscation (p. 141)
developed country (p. 130)
developing country (also called *less-developed country*) (p. 131)
economic development (p. 130)
economic transition (p. 136)
emerging markets (p. 131)

expropriation (p. 141)
Foreign Corrupt Practices Act (p. 144)
human development index (HDI) (p. 135)
lobbying (p. 144)
local content requirements (p. 142)
nationalization (p. 141)

newly industrialized country (NIC) (p. 131)
political risk (p. 137)
purchasing power (p. 134)
purchasing power parity (PPP) (p. 134)
technological dualism (p. 131)

✪ TALK ABOUT IT 1

The Internet and mobile technologies have penetrated nearly all aspects of life in developed countries, unlike many developing countries. This leads some people to say that technology widens the development gap between rich and poor countries.

4-1. Do you agree that technology is widening the economic development gap between rich and poor nations? Explain.

4-2. In what ways might the poorest of countries use technology as a tool for economic development?

⊛ TALK ABOUT IT 2

Imagine that you are the new director of a major international lending institution that gets its funding from member countries. You are evaluating your organization's lending policies and priorities.

4-3. What one aspect of people's lives would you prioritize for receiving aid in developing economies?

4-4. Might the funding of certain aspects of society cause a backlash from any groups or member nation(s)? Explain.

Ethical Challenge

You are the CEO of a French-German dairy product manufacturer. You have processing plants in France, Germany, Greece, the United Kingdom, and Sweden. You have grave concerns about the political and economic risks both in the United Kingdom and Greece, particularly in consideration of their relationship with the European Union. With the United Kingdom leaving the European Union in 2019 and the continuing social, political, and economic situation in Greece, it may be time to make contingency plans.

4-5. The United Kingdom will begin the process of leaving the European Union. What is the current position of the United Kingdom, and how is it affecting business?

4-6. The Greek economy is fragile and reliant on loans from the European Union and other sources. Is it wise to continue to operate in the country?

4-7. Some board members favor relocating production to countries hoping to join the European Union in the near future. Which countries have applied, and is this a good idea?

Teaming Up

In groups of three or four, look at the political risk map featured in this chapter. Focus on Africa and consider which of the countries would represent a reasonable political risk in terms of investment. Suggest reasons why you have drawn up your short list. Are there borderline countries whose political risk is outweighed by opportunity or those that are simply too unstable? Compare your suggestions with those of the rest of the class.

⊛ Market Entry Strategy Project

This exercise corresponds to the *MESP* online simulation. For the country your team is researching, integrate your answers to the following questions into your completed *MESP* report.

4-8. Is it a developed, newly industrializing, emerging, or developing country?

4-9. What is its GDP, GDP per capita, and GDP at PPP?

4-10. How does the country rank in the human development index?

4-11. Has it undergone economic transition within the past 20 years?

4-12. Does any form of political risk pose a threat to the nation's economic development?

4-13. How would you describe the country's international relations?

MyLab Management

⊛ Go to **www.pearson.com/mylab/management** for the following assisted-graded writing questions:

4-14. Two students are discussing the pros and cons of different measures of economic development. "The productivity of a nation's workforce," declares the first, "is the only true measure of how developed a country's economy is." The second student counters, "I disagree. The only true measure of development is GDP per capita." What information can you provide each of these students so they can refine their positions?

4-15. Political risk affects different countries and companies in countless ways. Imagine that your firm's CEO says to you, "The reason we went global by entering Safeland first is because our firm is immune to all political risk there." What would you say to your CEO?

PRACTICING INTERNATIONAL MANAGEMENT CASE

The Role of Social and Political Factors in the Lebanese Economy

Lebanon is a nation that tolerates and respects multiple cultures, religions, and ethnicities, and its economy today tries to keep to its traditional preferences of favoring strong fiscal and monetary freedoms as well as developing a labor market that is highly flexible.

Prior to the Lebanese Civil War between 1975 and 1990, the country had enjoyed relative calm and prosperity. Tourism, agriculture, small- and medium-sized manufacturers, education, and banking all promoted a successful economy. Lebanon became known as the finance and banking capital of the Arab world and the "Paris of the Middle East." Before the war, Lebanon had a competitive and free market environment and a strong laissez-faire commercial tradition. There were no restrictions on foreign exchange or capital movement. Bank secrecy was strictly enforced, and there were practically no restrictions on foreign investment. Corporate tax rates and inflation were relatively low. The financial sector was well developed prior to the civil war and has since developed again into a system aligned to fit the demands of the region, including a range of private banks and services.

The civil war seriously damaged Lebanon's economic infrastructure, cut national output by half, and ruined a wide range of businesses in service and manufacturing sectors. It ultimately ended Lebanon's position as a Middle Eastern banking hub. The subsequent period of relative peace enabled the central government to restore control in Beirut. How was this achieved?

Steps were taken to reestablish its taxation system and to regain access to key port and government facilities. Furthermore, economic recovery was aided by a financially sound banking system and resilient small- and medium-sized enterprises, with family remittances, banking services, manufactured and farm exports, and international aid as the main sources of foreign exchange.

Immediately after the end of the civil war, there were extensive efforts to revive the economy and rebuild the national infrastructure. By early 2006, a considerable degree of stability had been achieved in most parts of the country, Beirut's reconstruction was almost complete, and an increasing number of foreign tourists from all around the world were beginning to head toward Lebanon's resorts. As a result, the per-capita GDP increased from $4,158 in 1990 to $10,751 in 2006 (an increase of nearly 160 percent in 16 years), and unemployment dropped to 8.1 percent in 2004.

But a new shock to the country's economy occurred in 2006. After only a month of fighting with Israel in July 2006, Lebanon suffered significant damage to businesses and infrastructure. Many countries struggled to get as many of their citizens as possible out of the country safely and quickly. The tourism industry suffered a massive loss. Lebanon was in crisis again. In September 2006,

Rafiq Hariri International Airport in Beirut reopened, and efforts to revive the Lebanese economy were to begin once more. Major investors in the reconstruction of Lebanon included the European Union and Saudi Arabia as well as many other countries across the world. Lebanon's recent economic history has been a series of instances of taking one step forward and two steps back, yet there is still promise for a bright future if peace can be maintained.

Toward achieving its targets, Lebanon has received external support as well. International support in humanitarian programs and victim-assistance programs have been significant. Moreover, there are external contributions and involvements in the reconstruction of Lebanon. Since 2006, the United States alone has provided more than $2 billion in bilateral foreign assistance. In addition to this, the United States has also provided $1.8 billion in humanitarian assistance (to support Lebanese assistance for Syrian refugees). Since 2008, the United States has funded over $170 million in basic education programs and an additional $160 million in higher education programs.

From an internal perspective, liberalization of the economy, investment, and business activities are confronted by other challenges. Intrusive bureaucracy and chaotic regulatory regimes slow down local businesses and discourage foreign investment. Besides, fair adjudication of property rights is not guaranteed because the Lebanese courts are subject to significant influence from Lebanese security services, the government, and even the police. More importantly, in order to create a productive and stable business environment, it is essential for Lebanon to work diligently on improving its ability to stamp out fraud; for example, Lebanon has recently adopted new laws to combat money laundering.

Thinking Globally

4-16. Why do you think Lebanon is in need of foreign direct investment (FDI)? Discuss the enablers and barriers to foreign direct investment in Lebanon.

4-17. Do some research on Lebanon and its current socioeconomic status. Discuss how social and political situations may affect the Lebanese economy.

4-18. How do you think the transition to a normal economy in Lebanon after the war in 2006 differs from the experiences of European countries after World War II?

4-19. The Lebanese government prohibited all imports from Israel. Discuss the socioeconomic aspects of this decision.

Sources: Kirk D. Hoppe, "Case Study on Lebanon: Can the U.S. Build upon Socio-Economic Influences in Order to Foster Good Citizenship versus Insurgency?", Naval Postgraduate School, Monterey, California (2007).

Chapter Five

International Trade Theory

Learning Objectives

After studying this chapter, you should be able to

5.1 Describe the benefits, volume, and patterns of international trade.

5.2 Explain how mercantilism worked and identify its inherent flaws.

5.3 Detail the theories of absolute advantage and comparative advantage.

5.4 Summarize the factor proportions theory of trade.

5.5 Explain the international product life cycle theory.

5.6 Outline the new trade theory and the first-mover advantage.

5.7 Describe the national competitive advantage theory and the Porter diamond.

A Look Back

Chapters 2, 3, and 4 examined cultural, political, legal, and economic differences among countries. We covered these differences early in the book because of their important influence on international business activities.

A Look at This Chapter

This chapter begins our study of the international trade and investment environment. We explore the oldest form of international business activity—international trade. We discuss the benefits, volume, and patterns of international trade and explore the major theories that attempt to explain why trade occurs.

A Look Ahead

Chapter 6 explains the political economy of international trade. We explore both the motives and methods of government intervention in trade and how the global trading system works to promote free trade.

MyLab Management

⭐ IMPROVE YOUR GRADE!

When you see this icon ⭐, visit **www.pearson.com/mylab/management** for activities that are applied, personalized, and offer immediate feedback.

From Bentonville to Beijing

BENTONVILLE, Arkansas—Walmart (www.walmart.com) first became an international company in 1991 when it built a new store near Mexico City, Mexico. Today, Walmart has around 5,300 stores in the United States and approximately 6,200 stores in 27 other countries. With nearly $486 billion in sales globally, Walmart is one of the world's largest companies—yet it is based in a state in which chickens outnumber people.

Ambitious global expansion by Walmart (and similar firms) is helping boost international trade. To fulfill its promise to deliver the lowest priced goods around the world, Walmart sources inexpensive merchandise from low-cost production locations such as China. The discount retailer has played a big part in increasing Chinese imports to the United States in recent years. In fact, if Walmart were a country, it would be China's sixth-largest trading partner. The actions of Walmart and other global firms have propelled world exports of goods and services to record levels.

Growth in international trade is increasing interdependence between China and other nations. Chinese companies and businesses around the world quickly transformed China into

Testing/Shutterstock

the world's factory. China's international trade is expanding at a rate that is about two to three times faster than trade growth for the rest of the world. Around 18 percent of Japan's imports come from China, and about 12 percent of all goods imported by the United States are Chinese-made. China's imports are also growing. From the United States, China imports everything from steel that feeds its booming construction industry to x-ray machines and other devices to improve its people's health. China is also becoming a larger market for Walmart and other Western consumer-goods businesses. As you read this chapter, consider why nations trade and how the ambitions of firms such as Walmart are driving growth in world trade.[1]

People around the world are accustomed to purchasing goods and services produced in other countries. In fact, many consumers get their first taste of another country's culture through merchandise purchased from that country. Chanel No. 5 perfume (www.chanel.com) evokes the romanticism of France. The fine artwork on Imari porcelain conveys the Japanese attention to detail and quality. And American Eagle jeans (www.ae.com) portray the casual lifestyle of people in the United States.

In this chapter, we explore international trade in goods and services. We begin by examining the benefits, volume, and patterns of international trade. We then explore a number of important theories that attempt to explain why nations trade with one another.

5.1 Benefits, Volume, and Patterns of International Trade

5.1 Describe the benefits, volume, and patterns of international trade.

international trade
Purchase, sale, or exchange of goods and services across national borders.

The purchase, sale, or exchange of goods and services across national borders is called **international trade**. This is in contrast to domestic trade, which occurs between different states, regions, or cities within a country.

In recent years, nations that embrace globalization are seeing trade grow in importance for their economies. One way to measure the importance of trade to a nation is to examine the volume of an economy's trade relative to its total output. Map 5.1 on pages (on pages 158–159) shows each nation's trade volume as a share of its gross domestic product (GDP). Trade as a share of GDP is defined as the sum of exports and imports (of goods and services) divided by GDP. Recall that GDP is the value of all goods and services produced by a domestic economy over a one-year period. Map 5.1 demonstrates that the value of trade passing through some nations' borders actually exceeds the amount of goods and services they produce (the "over 100%" category).

Benefits of International Trade

International trade provides a country's people with a greater choice of goods and services. For example, because Finland has a cool climate, it cannot be expected to grow cotton. But it can sell paper and other products made from lumber (which it has in abundance) to the United States. Finland can then use the proceeds from the sale of products derived from lumber to buy US-grown Pima cotton. Thus, people in Finland get cotton they otherwise would not have. Likewise, although the United States has vast forests, the wood-based products from Finland might be of a certain quality that fills a gap in the US marketplace.

International trade is also an important engine for job creation in many countries. The US Department of Commerce (www.commerce.gov) calculates that for every $1 billion increase in exports, 22,800 jobs are created in the United States. It is also estimated that 12 million US jobs depend on exports and that these jobs pay on average from 13 to 18 percent more than those not related to international trade.[2] Expanded trade benefits other countries similarly.

Volume of International Trade

The value and volume of international trade continues to increase. Today, world merchandise exports are valued at $16.5 trillion, and service exports are worth $4.8 trillion.[3] Table 5.1 shows the world's largest exporters of merchandise and services. Perhaps not surprisingly, the United States ranks first in commercial services exports and ranks second in merchandise exports (behind China).

Most of world merchandise trade is composed of trade in manufactured goods. The dominance of manufactured goods in the trade of merchandise has persisted over time and will likely continue to do so. The reason is its growth is much faster than trade in the two other classifications of merchandise—mining and agricultural products. Trade in services accounts for around 22 percent of total world trade. Although the importance of trade in services is growing for many nations, it tends to be relatively more important for the world's richest countries.

The level of world output in any given year influences the level of international trade in that year. Slower world economic output slows the volume of international trade, and higher output propels greater trade. Trade slows in times of economic recession because when people are less certain about their own financial futures they buy fewer domestic and imported products. Another reason output and trade move together is that a country in recession also often has a currency that is weak relative to other nations. This makes imports more expensive relative to domestic products. (We discuss the relationship between currency values and trade at length in Chapter 10.) In addition to international trade and world output moving in lockstep fashion, trade has consistently grown faster than output.

TABLE 5.1 World's Top Exporters

World's Top Merchandise Exporters				World's Top Service Exporters			
Rank	Exporter	Value (US $ billions)	Share of World Total (%)	Rank	Exporter	Value (US $ billions)	Share of World Total (%)
1	China	2,275	13.8	1	United States	690	14.5
2	United States	1,505	9.1	2	United Kingdom	345	7.3
3	Germany	1,329	8.1	3	China	285	6.0
4	Japan	625	3.8	4	Germany	247	5.2
5	Netherlands	567	3.4	5	France	240	5.0
6	South Korea	527	3.2	6	Netherlands	178	3.7
7	Hong Kong	511	3.1	7	Japan	158	3.3
8	France	506	3.1	8	India	155	3.3
9	United Kingdom	460	2.8	9	Singapore	139	2.9
10	Italy	459	2.8	10	Ireland	128	2.7

Source: Based on *World Trade Statistical Review 2016* (Geneva, Switzerland: World Trade Organization, October 2016), Tables A.6 and A.8, available at www.wto.org.

International Trade Patterns

Exploring the volume of international trade and world output provides useful insights into the international trade environment, but it does not tell us who trades with whom. It does not reveal whether trade occurs primarily between the world's richest nations or whether there is significant trade activity involving poorer nations.

Customs agencies in most countries record the destination of exports, the source of imports, and the physical quantities and values of goods crossing their borders. Customs data reflects overall trade patterns among nations, but this type of data is sometimes misleading. For example, governments sometimes deliberately distort the reporting of trade in military equipment or other sensitive goods. In other cases, extensive trade in unofficial (underground) economies can distort the real picture of trade between nations.

Large ocean-going cargo vessels are needed to support these patterns in international trade and deliver merchandise from one shore to another. In fact, Greek and Japanese merchant ships own more than 30 percent of the world's total capacity (measured in tons shipped, or tonnage) of merchant ships. Yet, global merchant-shipping companies are feeling the pinch of higher oil prices. And as importers must absorb a portion of higher shipping costs, they may begin producing goods closer to home and reduce the need for additional merchant-ship capacity.[4]

There has been a persistent pattern of merchandise trade among nations. Trade between the world's high-income economies accounts for roughly 60 percent of total world merchandise trade. Two-way trade between high-income countries and low- and middle-income nations accounts for about 34 percent of world merchandise trade. Meanwhile, merchandise trade between low- and middle-income nations accounts for only about 6 percent of total world trade. These figures reveal the low purchasing power of the world's poorest nations and indicate their general lack of economic development.

Asia's role in merchandise trade is increasing as the region's economies continue to expand. Some economists call this century the "Pacific century," referring to the expected growth of Asian economies and the resulting shift in the majority of trade flows from the Atlantic Ocean to the Pacific. It will be increasingly important for managers to understand the varying and rich cultures in Asia. For some pointers on doing business in Pacific Rim nations, see this chapter's Culture Matters feature, titled "Business Culture in the Pacific Rim."

TRADE INTERDEPENDENCE Trade between most nations is characterized by a degree of interdependency. Companies in developed nations trade a great deal with companies in other developed nations. The level of interdependency between pairs of countries often reflects the amount of trade that occurs between a company's subsidiaries in the two nations. Emerging markets that share borders with developed countries are often dependent on their wealthier neighbors.

Map 5.1
Importance of Trade

Trade as a percent of GDP

- over 100%
- 75%–100%
- 50%–74%
- 25%–49%
- less than 25%
- no data available

CULTURE MATTERS | Business Culture in the Pacific Rim

Asian customers are as diverse as their cultures and aggressive sales tactics do not work. Before visiting these countries, it is helpful for managers to review some general rules:

- **Make Use of Contacts.** Asians prefer to do business with people they know. Cold calls and other direct-contact methods seldom work. Meeting the right people in an Asian company often depends on having the right introduction. If the person with whom you hope to do business respects your intermediary, chances are that he or she will respect you.
- **Carry Bilingual Business Cards.** To make a good first impression, have bilingual cards printed, even though many Asians speak English. It shows both respect for the language and a commitment to doing business in a country. It also translates your title into the local language. Asians generally are not comfortable until they know what your position is and whom you represent.

- **Respect, Harmony, and Consensus.** Asian cultures command respect for their achievements in music, art, science, philosophy, business, and more. Asian businesspeople are tough negotiators, but they dislike argumentative exchanges. Harmony and consensus are the bywords in Asia, so be patient but firm.
- **Drop the Legal Language.** Legal documents are subordinate to personal relationships. Asians tend to dislike detailed contracts. Agreements are often left flexible so that adjustments can be made easily in order to fit changing circumstances. It's important to foster good relations based on mutual trust and benefit. The importance of a contract in many Asian societies is not what it stipulates but rather who signed it.
- **Build Personal Rapport.** Social ease and friendship are prerequisites to doing business across much of Asia. As much business is transacted at informal dinners as it is in corporate settings, so accept invitations, and be sure to reciprocate.

Trade dependency has been a blessing for many Central and Eastern European nations. Germany recently had more than 6,000 joint ventures in Hungary alone. And Germany is the single most important trading partner of many Central and Eastern European nations that belong to the European Union (www.europa.eu). To gain an advantage over competitors, German firms combine homegrown technology with relatively low-cost labor in Central and Eastern Europe. For example, Opel (www.opel.com), the German division of General Motors Corporation (www.gm.com), built a $440 million plant in Szentgotthard, Hungary, to make parts for and assemble its Astra hatchbacks destined for export markets.

TRADE DEPENDENCE The dangers of trade dependency become apparent when a nation experiences economic recession or political turmoil, which then harms dependent nations. For many years, Mexico was a favorite location for the production and assembly operations of US companies making all sorts of products, including refrigerators, mobile phones, and textiles. But then some companies abandoned Mexico for cheaper production locations in Asia, which left empty factories and unemployed workers behind. But today, as labor costs continue to climb in China, some US companies are relocating their factories back to Mexico. The best way for Mexico to deal with its dependency on the United States is to boost its competitiveness and make itself a top choice among emerging markets.

> ✪ **MyLab Management** Watch It Made in America and Mexico
> Apply what you have learned about international trade basics. If your instructor has assigned this, go to **www.pearson.com/mylab/management** to watch a video case about trade between the United States and Mexico and answer questions.

QUICK STUDY 1

1. List several benefits of international trade.
2. World merchandise exports are valued at *how many times* the value of worldwide service exports?
3. What portion of total world merchandise trade is accounted for by two-way trade between high-income economies?
4. What term often describes the nature of trade between a developing nation and a neighboring wealthy one?

5.2 Mercantilism

Trade between different groups of people has occurred for many thousands of years. But it was not until the fifteenth century that people began trying to explain why trade occurs and how trade can benefit both parties to an exchange. Figure 5.1 shows a timeline of when the main theories of international trade were proposed.

The trade theory that nations should accumulate financial wealth, usually in the form of gold, by encouraging exports and discouraging imports is called **mercantilism**. It states that other measures of a nation's well-being, such as living standards or human development, are irrelevant. Nation-states in Europe followed this economic philosophy from about 1500 to the late 1700s. The most prominent mercantilist nations included Britain, France, the Netherlands, Portugal, and Spain.

How Mercantilism Worked

When navigation was a fairly new science, Europeans explored the world by sea and claimed the lands they encountered in the name of the European monarchy that financed their voyage. Early explorers landed in Africa, Asia, and the Americas, where they established colonies. Colonial trade was conducted for the benefit of mother countries, and the appeal of the colonies was their abundant resources.

In recent times, former colonies have struggled to diminish their reliance on the former colonial powers. For example, in an effort to decrease their dependence on their former colonial powers, African nations are welcoming trade relationships with partners from Asia and North America. But because of geographic proximity, the European Union is still often preferred as a trading partner.

Just how did countries implement mercantilism? The practice of mercantilism rested on three essential pillars: trade surpluses, government intervention, and colonialism.

TRADE SURPLUSES Nations believed they could increase their wealth by maintaining a **trade surplus**—the condition that results when the value of a nation's exports is greater than the value of its imports. In mercantilism, a trade surplus means that a country takes in more gold on the sale of its exports than it pays out for its imports. A **trade deficit** is the opposite condition—one that results when the value of a country's imports is greater than the value of its exports. In mercantilism, trade deficits are to be avoided at all costs. (We discuss the importance of national trade balance at length in Chapter 7.)

GOVERNMENT INTERVENTION Governments actively intervened in international trade in order to maintain a trade surplus. According to mercantilism, the accumulation of wealth depends on increasing a nation's trade surplus, not necessarily expanding its total value or volume of trade. The governments of mercantilist nations did this by either banning certain imports or imposing various restrictions on them, such as tariffs or quotas. At the same time, the nations subsidized industries based in the home country in order to expand exports. Governments also typically outlawed the removal of their gold and silver to other nations.

COLONIALISM Mercantilist nations acquired territories (colonies) around the world to serve as sources of inexpensive raw materials and as markets for higher-priced finished goods. These colonies were the source of essential raw materials, including tea, sugar, tobacco, rubber, and cotton.

5.2 Explain how mercantilism worked and identify its inherent flaws.

mercantilism

Trade theory that nations should accumulate financial wealth, usually in the form of gold, by encouraging exports and discouraging imports.

trade surplus

Condition that results when the value of a nation's exports is greater than the value of its imports.

trade deficit

Condition that results when the value of a country's imports is greater than the value of its exports.

Figure 5.1

Trade Theory Timeline

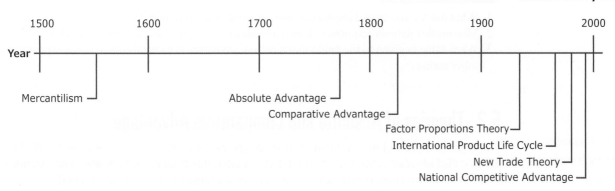

Mexico churns out all sorts of products that are then shipped to ports all around the United States in shipping containers like those shown here. For decades, trade with the United States has brought well-paying jobs to ordinary Mexicans, who build cars, stoves, refrigerators, and all sorts of equipment. Yet, when multinationals in Mexico move to cheaper locations, such as China and Vietnam, Mexico experiences the negative effects of its dependence on US trade.

John C Panella jr/123RF.com

These resources would be shipped to the mercantilist nation, where they were incorporated into finished goods such as clothing, cigars, and other products. These finished goods would then be sold to the colonies. Trade between mercantilist countries and their colonies were a huge source of profits for the mercantilist powers. The colonies received low prices for basic raw materials but paid high prices for finished goods.

The mercantilist and colonial policies greatly expanded the wealth of nations that implemented them. This wealth allowed nations to build armies and navies to control their far-flung colonial empires and to protect their shipping lanes from attack by other nations. It was a source of a nation's economic power that in turn increased its political power relative to other countries. Today, countries seen by others as trying to maintain a trade surplus and expand their national treasuries at the expense of other nations are accused of practicing *neomercantilism* or *economic nationalism*.

Flaws of Mercantilism

Despite its seemingly positive benefits for any nation implementing it, mercantilism is inherently flawed. Mercantilist nations believed that the world's wealth was limited and that a nation could increase its share of the pie only at the expense of its neighbors—a situation called a *zero-sum game*. The main problem with mercantilism is that, if all nations were to barricade their markets from imports and push their exports onto others, international trade would be severely restricted. In fact, trade in all nonessential goods would likely cease altogether.

In addition, paying colonies little for their exports but charging them high prices for their imports impaired their economic development. Thus, their appeal as markets for goods was less than it would have been if they had been allowed to accumulate greater wealth.

> **QUICK STUDY 2**
>
> 1. What did the successful implementation of mercantilism require?
> 2. Mercantilist nations acquired colonies around the world to serve as sources of *what*?
> 3. What name is given to the belief that a nation can increase its wealth only at the expense of other nations?

5.3 Theories of Absolute and Comparative Advantage

5.3 Detail the theories of absolute advantage and comparative advantage.

The negative aspects of mercantilism were made apparent by a trade theory developed in the late 1700s called *absolute advantage*. Several decades later, this theory was built upon and extended into what is called *comparative advantage*. Let's now examine these two theories in detail.

Absolute Advantage

Scottish economist Adam Smith first put forth the trade theory of absolute advantage in 1776.[5] The ability of a nation to produce a good more efficiently than any other nation is called an **absolute advantage**. In other words, a nation with an absolute advantage can produce a greater output of a good or service than other nations using the same amount of, or fewer, resources.

Among other things, Smith reasoned that international trade should not be banned or restricted by tariffs and quotas but allowed to flow as dictated by market forces. If people in different countries were able to trade as they saw fit, no country would need to produce all the goods it consumed. Instead, a country could concentrate on producing the goods in which it holds an absolute advantage. It could then trade with other nations to obtain the goods it needs but does not produce.

Suppose a talented CEO wants to install a hot tub in her home. Should she do the job herself or hire a professional installer to do it for her? Suppose the CEO (who has never installed a hot tub before) would have to take one month off from work and forgo $80,000 in salary in order to complete the job. On the other hand, the professional installer (who is not a talented CEO) can complete the job for $5,000 and do it in two weeks. Whereas the CEO has an absolute advantage in running a company, the installer has an absolute advantage in installing hot tubs. It takes the CEO one month to do the job the installer can do in two weeks. Thus, the CEO should hire the professional to install the hot tub to save both time and money resources.

Let's now apply the absolute advantage concept to an example of two trading countries to see how trade can increase production and consumption in both nations.

absolute advantage
Ability of a nation to produce a good more efficiently than any other nation.

CASE: RICELAND AND TEALAND Suppose that we live in a world of just two countries (Riceland and Tealand), with two products (rice and tea), and that transporting goods between these two countries costs nothing. Riceland and Tealand currently produce and consume their own rice and tea. The following table shows the number of units of resources (labor) each country expends in creating rice and tea. In Riceland, just one resource unit is needed to produce a ton of rice, but five units of resources are needed to produce a ton of tea. In Tealand, six units of resources are needed to produce a ton of rice, whereas three units are needed to produce a ton of tea.

	Units Required for Production	
	Rice	Tea
Riceland	1	5
Tealand	6	3

Another way of stating each nation's efficiency in the production of rice and tea is:

- In Riceland, 1 unit of resources = 1 ton of rice or 1/5 ton of tea
- In Tealand, 1 unit of resources = 1/6 ton of rice or 1/3 ton of tea

These numbers also tell us one other thing about rice and tea production in these two countries. Because one unit of resources produces one ton of rice in Riceland compared with Tealand's output of only 1/6 ton of rice, Riceland has an absolute advantage in rice production—it is the more efficient rice producer. However, because one resource unit produces 1/3 ton of tea in Tealand compared with Riceland's output of just 1/5 ton, Tealand has an absolute advantage in tea production.

GAINS FROM SPECIALIZATION AND TRADE Suppose now that Riceland specializes in rice production to maximize the output of rice in our two-country world. Likewise, Tealand specializes in tea production to maximize the world output of tea. Although each country now specializes and world output increases, both countries face a problem. Riceland can consume only its rice production, and Tealand can consume only its tea production. The problem can be solved if the two countries trade with each other to obtain the good that it needs but does not produce.

Suppose that Riceland and Tealand agree to trade rice and tea on a one-to-one basis—a ton of rice costs a ton of tea, and vice versa. Thus, Riceland can produce one extra ton of rice with an additional resource unit and can trade with Tealand to get one ton of tea. This is much better than the 1/5 ton of tea that Riceland would have gotten by investing that additional resource unit in making tea for itself. Thus, Riceland definitely benefits from the trade. Likewise, Tealand can

Figure 5.2

Gains from Specialization and Trade: Absolute Advantage

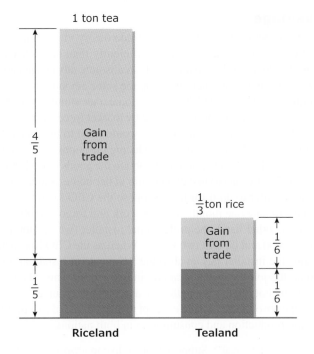

produce 1/3 extra ton of tea with an additional resource unit and trade with Riceland to get 1/3 ton of rice. This is twice as much as the 1/6 ton of rice it could have produced using that additional resource unit to make its own rice. Thus, Tealand also benefits from the trade. The gains resulting from this simple trade are shown in Figure 5.2.

Although Tealand does not gain as much as Riceland does from the trade, it does get more rice than it would without trade. The gains from trade for actual countries would depend on the total number of resources each country has at its disposal and the demand for each good in each country.

As this example shows, the theory of absolute advantage destroys the mercantilist idea that international trade is a *zero-sum game*. Instead, because there are gains to be had by both countries party to an exchange, international trade is a *positive-sum game*. The theory also calls into question the objective of national governments to acquire wealth through restrictive trade policies. It argues that nations should instead open their doors to trade so that their people can obtain a greater quantity of goods more cheaply. The theory does not measure a nation's wealth by how much gold and silver it has on reserve but by the living standards of its people.

Despite the power of the theory of absolute advantage in showing the gains from trade, there is one potential problem. What happens if a country does not hold an absolute advantage in the production of any product? Are there still benefits to trade, and will trade even occur? To answer these questions, let's take a look at an extension of absolute advantage: the theory of *comparative advantage*.

Comparative Advantage

comparative advantage

Inability of a nation to produce a good more efficiently than other nations but an ability to produce that good more efficiently than it does any other good.

An English economist named David Ricardo developed the theory of comparative advantage in 1817.[6] He proposed that if one country (in our example of a two-country world) held absolute advantages in the production of both products, specialization and trade could still benefit both countries. A country has a **comparative advantage** when it is unable to produce a good more efficiently than other nations but produces the good more efficiently than it does any other good. In other words, *trade is still beneficial even if one country is less efficient in the production of two goods, as long as it is less inefficient in the production of one of the goods.*

Let's return to our hot tub example. Now suppose that the talented CEO has previously installed many hot tubs and can do the job in one week—twice as fast as the hot tub installer. Thus, the CEO now holds absolute advantages in both running a company and hot tub installation. Although the professional installer is at an absolute disadvantage in both hot tub installation and running a company, he is less inefficient in hot tub installation. Despite her absolute advantage in both areas, however, the CEO would still have to give up $20,000 (one week's pay) to take time off from running the company to complete the work. Is this a wise decision? No. The CEO should hire the professional installer to do the work for $5,000. The installer earns money he would not earn if the CEO did the job herself. And the CEO earns more money by focusing on running the company than she would save by installing the hot tub herself.

GAINS FROM SPECIALIZATION AND TRADE To see how the theory of comparative advantage works with international trade, let's return to our example of Riceland and Tealand. In our earlier discussion, Riceland had an absolute advantage in rice production, and Tealand had an absolute advantage in tea production. Suppose that Riceland now holds absolute advantages in the production of both rice *and* tea. The following table shows the number of units of resources each country now expends in creating rice and tea. Riceland still needs to expend just one resource unit to produce a ton of rice, but now it needs to invest only two units of resources (instead of five) to produce one ton of tea. Tealand still needs six units of resources to produce a ton of rice and three units to produce a ton of tea.

	Units Required for Production	
	Rice	Tea
Riceland	1	2
Tealand	6	3

Another way of stating each nation's efficiency in the production of rice and tea is:

- In Riceland, 1 unit of resources = 1 ton of rice or 1/2 ton of tea
- In Tealand, 1 unit of resources = 1/6 ton of rice or 1/3 ton of tea

Thus, for every unit of resource used, Riceland can produce more rice and tea than Tealand can. Riceland has *absolute* advantages in the production of both goods. But Riceland can still gain from trading with a less-efficient producer. Although Tealand has absolute disadvantages in both rice and tea production, it has a *comparative* advantage in tea. In other words, although Tealand is unable to produce either rice or tea more efficiently than Riceland, it produces tea more efficiently than it produces rice.

Assume once again that Riceland and Tealand decide to trade rice and tea on a one-to-one basis. Tealand could use one unit of resources to produce 1/6 ton of rice. But it would do better to produce 1/3 ton of tea with this unit of resources and trade with Riceland to get 1/3 ton of rice. By specializing and trading, Tealand gets twice as much rice as it could get if it were to produce the rice itself. There are also gains from trade for Riceland despite its dual absolute advantages. Riceland could invest one unit of resources in the production of 1/2 ton of tea. It would do better, however, to produce one ton of rice with the one unit of resources and trade that rice to Tealand in exchange for one ton of tea. Thus, Riceland gets twice as much tea through trade than if it were to produce the tea itself. This is in spite of the fact that it is a more efficient producer of tea than Tealand.

The benefits for each country from this simple trade are shown in Figure 5.3. Again, the benefits actual countries obtain from trade depend on the amount of resources at their disposal and each market's desired level of consumption of each product.

ASSUMPTIONS AND LIMITATIONS Throughout the discussion of absolute and comparative advantage, we made several important assumptions that limit real-world application of the theories. First, we assumed that countries are driven only by the maximization of production and consumption. This is often not the case. Governments often get involved in international trade out of a concern for workers or consumers. (We discuss the role of government in international trade in Chapter 6.)

Second, the theories assume that there are only two countries engaged in the production and consumption of just two goods. This is obviously not the situation that exists in the real world. There currently are more than 180 countries and a countless number of products being produced, traded, and consumed worldwide.

Figure 5.3

Gains from Specialization and Trade: Comparative Advantage

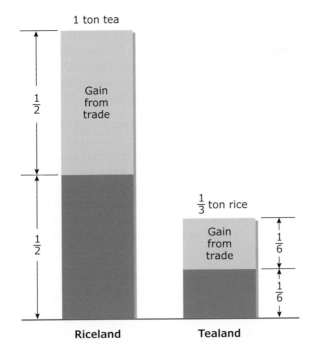

Third, it is assumed that there are no costs for transporting traded goods from one country to another. In reality, transportation costs are a major expense of international trade for some products. If transportation costs for a good are higher than the savings generated through specialization, trade will not occur.

Fourth, the theories consider labor to be the only resource used in the production process because labor accounted for a large portion of the total production cost of goods at the time the theories were developed. Moreover, it is assumed that resources are mobile within each nation but cannot be transferred between nations. But labor and natural resources can be transferred between nations, although doing so can be difficult and costly.

Finally, it is assumed that specialization in the production of one particular good does not result in gains in efficiency. But we know that specialization results in increased knowledge of a task and perhaps even future improvements in how that task is performed. Thus, the amount of resources needed to produce a specific amount of a good should decrease over time.

Despite the assumptions made in the theory of comparative advantage, research reveals that it appears to be supported by a substantial body of evidence. Nevertheless, economic researchers continue to develop and test new theories to explain international trade.

QUICK STUDY 3

1. A nation that is able to produce a good more efficiently than other nations is said to have *what*?
2. What does a nation have when it is unable to produce a good more efficiently than other nations but it can produce the good more efficiently than it can any other good?
3. The theories of absolute advantage and comparative advantage say that nations benefit from trading because of the gains from *what*?

5.4 Factor Proportions Theory

5.4 Summarize the factor proportions theory of trade.

In the early 1900s, an international trade theory emerged that focused attention on the proportion (supply) of resources in a nation. The cost of any resource is simply the result of supply and demand: Factors in great supply relative to demand will be less costly than factors in short supply relative to demand. **Factor proportions theory** states that countries produce and export goods that require resources (factors) that are abundant and import goods that require resources in short supply.[7] The theory resulted from the research of two economists, Eli Heckscher and Bertil Ohlin, and is therefore sometimes called the Heckscher–Ohlin theory.

factor proportions theory
Trade theory stating that countries produce and export goods that require resources (factors) that are abundant and import goods that require resources in short supply.

Factor proportions theory differs considerably from the theory of comparative advantage. Recall that the theory of comparative advantage states that a country specializes in producing the good that it can produce more efficiently than any other good. Thus, the focus of the theory (and absolute advantage, as well) is on the *productivity* of the production process for a particular good. By contrast, factor proportions theory says that a country specializes in producing and exporting goods using the factors of production that are most *abundant* and thus *cheapest*—not the goods in which it is most productive.

Labor Versus Land and Capital Equipment

Factor proportions theory breaks a nation's resources into two categories: labor on the one hand, land and capital equipment on the other. It predicts that a country will specialize in products that require labor if the cost of labor is low relative to the cost of land and capital. Alternatively, a country will specialize in products that require land and capital equipment if their cost is low relative to the cost of labor.

Factor proportions theory is conceptually appealing. For example, Australia has a great deal of land (nearly 60 percent of which is meadows and pastures) and a small population relative to its size. Australia's exports consist largely of mined minerals, grain, beef, lamb, and dairy products—products that require a great deal of land and natural resources. Australia's imports, on the other hand, consist mostly of manufactured raw materials, capital equipment, and consumer goods—things needed in capital-intensive mining and modern agriculture. But instead of looking only at anecdotal evidence, let's see how well factor proportions theory stands up to scientific testing.

Evidence on Factor Proportions Theory: The Leontief Paradox

Despite its conceptual appeal, factor proportions theory is not supported by studies that examine the trade flows of nations. The first large-scale study to document such evidence was performed by a researcher named Wassily Leontief in the early 1950s.[8] Leontief tested whether the United States, which uses an abundance of capital equipment, exports goods requiring capital-intensive production and imports goods requiring labor-intensive production. Contrary to the predictions of the factor proportions theory, his research found that US exports require more labor-intensive production than its imports. This apparent paradox between the predictions using the theory and the actual trade flows is called the *Leontief paradox*. Leontief's findings are supported by more-recent research on the trade data of a large number of countries.

What might account for the paradox? One possible explanation is that factor proportions theory considers a country's production factors to be homogeneous—particularly labor. But we know that labor skills vary greatly within a country—more highly skilled workers emerge from training and development programs. When expenditures on improving the skills of labor are taken into account, the theory seems to be supported by actual trade data. Further studies examining international trade data will help us better understand what reasons actually account for the Leontief paradox.

Because of the drawbacks of each of the international trade theories mentioned so far, researchers continue to propose new ones. Let's now examine a theory that attempts to explain international trade based on the life cycle of products.

QUICK STUDY 4

1. What is the name of the theory that says countries produce and export goods that require resources that are abundant and import goods that require resources in short supply?
2. Factor proportions theory divides a nation's resources into what two categories?

5.5 International Product Life Cycle

5.5 Explain the international product life cycle theory.

international product life cycle

Theory stating that a company will begin by exporting its product and later undertake foreign direct investment as the product moves through its life cycle.

Raymond Vernon put forth an international trade theory for manufactured goods in the mid-1960s. His **international product life cycle theory** says that a company will begin by exporting its product and later undertake foreign direct investment as the product moves through its life cycle. The theory also says that, for a number of reasons, a country's export eventually becomes its import.[9]

Although Vernon developed his model around the United States, we can generalize it to apply to any developed and innovative market such as Australia, the European Union, and Japan. Let's examine how this theory attempts to explain international trade flows.

Stages of the Product Life Cycle

The international product life cycle theory follows the path of a good through its life cycle (from new to maturing to standardized product) in order to determine where it will be produced (see Figure 5.4). In Stage 1, the *new product stage*, the high purchasing power and demand of buyers in an industrialized country drive a company to design and introduce a new product concept. Because the exact level of demand in the domestic market is highly uncertain at this point, the company keeps its production volume low and based in the home country. Keeping production where initial research and development occurred and staying in contact with customers allow the company to monitor buyer preferences and to modify the product as needed. Although initially there is virtually no export market, exports do begin to pick up late in the new product stage.

In Stage 2, the *maturing product stage*, the domestic market and markets abroad become fully aware of the existence of the product and its benefits. Demand rises and is sustained over a fairly lengthy period of time. As exports begin to account for an increasingly greater share of total product sales, the innovating company introduces production facilities in the countries with the highest demand. Near the end of the maturity stage, the product begins generating sales in developing nations, and perhaps some manufacturing presence is established there.

In Stage 3, the *standardized product stage*, competition from other companies selling similar products pressures companies to lower prices in order to maintain sales levels. As the market becomes more price sensitive, the company begins searching aggressively for low-cost production bases in developing nations to supply a growing worldwide market. Furthermore, as most production now takes place outside the innovating country, demand in the innovating country is supplied with imports from developing countries and other industrialized nations. Late in this stage, domestic production might even cease altogether.

Limitations of the Theory

Vernon developed his theory at a time when most new products were being developed and sold first in the United States. One reason US companies were strong globally in the 1960s was that their domestic production bases were not destroyed during the Second World War, as was the case in Europe (and to some extent Japan). In addition, during the war, the production of many durable goods in the United States, including automobiles, was shifted to the production of military transportation and weaponry. This laid the foundation for enormous postwar demand for new capital-intensive consumer goods, such as automobiles and home appliances. Furthermore, advances in

Figure 5.4

International Product Life Cycle

Source: Adapted from Raymond Vernon and Louis T. Wells Jr., *The Economic Environment of International Business*, 5th ed. (Upper Saddle River, NJ: Prentice Hall, 1991), p. 85.

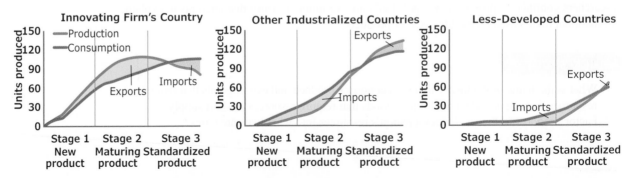

technology that were originally developed with military purposes in mind were integrated into consumer goods. A wide range of new and innovative products like TVs, photocopiers, and computers met the seemingly insatiable appetite of consumers in the United States.

The theory seemed to explain world trade patterns quite well when the United States dominated world trade. But today, the theory's ability to accurately depict the trade flows of nations is weak. The United States is no longer the sole innovator of products in the world. New products spring up everywhere as companies continue to globalize their research-and-development activities.

Furthermore, companies today design new products and make product modifications at a very quick pace. The result is quicker product obsolescence and a situation in which companies replace their existing products with new product introductions. This is forcing companies to introduce products in many markets simultaneously in order to recoup a product's research-and-development costs before sales decline and the product is dropped. The theory has a difficult time explaining the resulting trade patterns.

In fact, older theories might better explain today's global trade patterns. Much production in the world today more closely resembles what is predicted by the theory of comparative advantage. Boeing's (www.boeing.com) assembly plant in Everett, Washington, assembles its 787 Dreamliner wide-body aircraft. But companies around the world build the parts used in the 787. Cargo doors arrive stamped "Made in Sweden" and are supplied by Saab Aerostructures. The plane's lavatories are made by Jamco in Japan, its flight deck seats are supplied by Ipeco of the United Kingdom, its landing gear is made by Messier-Bugatti-Dowty of France, and so forth.[10] Components are later assembled in a chosen location. This pattern resembles the theory of comparative advantage in that a product's components are made in the country that can produce them at a high level of productivity.

Finally, the theory is challenged by the fact that more companies are operating in international markets from their inception. Many small companies are teaming up with companies in other markets to develop new products or production technologies. This strategy is particularly effective for small companies that would otherwise be unable to participate in international production or sales. French company Ingenico (www.ingenico.com) is a leading global supplier of secure transaction systems, including terminals and their associated software. The company began small and worked with a global network of entrepreneurs who acted as Ingenico's local agents and helped it to conquer local markets. The cultural knowledge embedded in Ingenico's global network helped it to design and sell products appropriate for each market.[11]

The Internet also makes it easier for companies of all sizes to reach a global audience. For a discussion of several pitfalls companies can avoid in fulfilling their international orders taken on the Internet, see the Manager's Briefcase, titled "Five Fulfillment Mistakes."

MANAGER'S BRIEFCASE   Five Fulfillment Mistakes

Although there's no way to completely foolproof logistics when selling online, a company should enjoy greater customer satisfaction if it can avoid these five key mistakes:

- **Mistake 1: Misunderstanding the Supply Chain** How many orders can fulfillment centers fill in an hour, a day, and a week? How long does it take a package to reach a customer from the fulfillment center using standard, non-expedited delivery? And how much inventory can the centers receive on any given day? If a company doesn't know the answers, it could be in serious danger of making delivery promises it can't keep.

- **Mistake 2: Overpromising on Delivery** The entrepreneur owner/manager should not advertise aggressive delivery times without a qualifier for uncontrollable factors, such as the weather. Care must also be taken to ensure that a customer is not promised an unrealistically quick order-turnaround time. Flexibility must be built into fulfillment operations.

- **Mistake 3: Not Planning for Returns** Handling customer returns well can increase repeat business. The internal returns process needs to be organized, and returns should not wait to go out until products start coming back to fulfillment centers. Prompt credit to customers can reward the entrepreneurial firm with a reputation as standing behind its products.

- **Mistake 4: Misunderstanding Customer Needs** Many Internet shoppers are willing to sacrifice shipping speed in exchange for lower shipping costs. Balancing this cost–service differential is an opportunity for online marketers to cut order-fulfillment costs.

- **Mistake 5: Poor Internal Communication** Marketing departments must communicate with logistics people. A public relations nightmare can result if logistics professionals are not told and the big planned marketing push crashes the company website.

1. The international product life cycle theory says that a company will begin by exporting its product and later undertake *what* as the product moves through its life cycle?
2. List the three stages that a product goes through according to the international product life cycle theory.
3. Whenever optimizing productivity determines where a product's components are manufactured and where it is assembled, the resulting pattern of activities resembles that predicted by *which* theory?

5.6 New Trade Theory

5.6 Outline the new trade theory and the first-mover advantage.

During the 1970s and 1980s, another theory emerged to explain trade patterns.[12] The **new trade theory** states that (1) there are gains to be made from specialization and increasing economies of scale, (2) the companies first to market can create barriers to entry, and (3) government may play a role in assisting its home companies. Because the theory emphasizes productivity rather than a nation's resources, it is in line with the theory of comparative advantage but at odds with factor proportions theory.

new trade theory
Trade theory stating that (1) there are gains to be made from specialization and increasing economies of scale, (2) the companies first to market can create barriers to entry, and (3) government may play a role in assisting its home companies.

First-Mover Advantage

According to the new trade theory, as a company increases the extent to which it specializes in the production of a particular good, output rises because of gains in efficiency. Regardless of the amount of a company's output, it has fixed production costs such as the cost of research and development and the plant and equipment needed to produce the product. The theory states that, as specialization and output increase, companies can realize economies of scale, thereby pushing the unit costs of production lower. That is why as many companies expand, they lower prices to buyers and force potential new competitors to produce at a similar level of output if they want to be competitive in their pricing. Thus, the presence of large economies of scale can create an industry that supports only a few large firms.

first-mover advantage
Economic and strategic advantage gained by being the first company to enter an industry.

A **first-mover advantage** is the economic and strategic advantage gained by being the first company to enter an industry. This first-mover advantage can create a formidable barrier to entry for potential rivals. The new trade theory also states that a country may dominate in the export of a certain product because it has a home-based firm that has acquired a first-mover advantage.[13]

Because of the potential benefits of being the first company to enter an industry, some businesspeople and researchers make a case for government assistance to companies. They say that by working together to target potential new industries, a government and its home companies can take advantage of the benefits of being the first mover in an industry. Government involvement has always been widely accepted in undertakings such as space exploration for national security reasons, but has been less so in purely commercial ventures. But the fear that governments of other countries might participate with industry to gain first-mover advantages drives many governments into action.

1. What is the main thrust of the new trade theory?
2. The economic and strategic advantage gained by being the first company to enter an industry is called *what*?

5.7 National Competitive Advantage

5.7 Describe the national competitive advantage theory and the Porter diamond.

What aspects of a nation's economic development can supply it with a national competitive advantage? The poorest nations tend to invest in the fundamental drivers of productivity growth (such as basic infrastructure). The richest nations typically exploit the latest technological advancements in order to boost productivity. Research into how nations achieve sustainable economic development has examined the potential roles of (1) culture, (2) geography, and (3) innovation.

To read more about whether these factors drive economic growth, see this chapter's Global Sustainability feature, titled "Foundations of Development."

A related question researchers have tried to answer is, How do firms in certain nations develop competitive advantage in specific industries? Michael Porter put forth a theory in 1990 to explain why certain countries are leaders in the production of certain products.[14] His **national competitive advantage theory** states that a nation's competitiveness in an industry depends on the capacity of the industry to innovate and upgrade. Porter's work incorporates certain elements of previous international trade theories but also makes some important new discoveries.

Porter is not preoccupied with explaining the export and import patterns of nations but rather with explaining why some nations are more competitive in certain industries. He identifies four elements that are present to varying degrees in every nation and that form the basis of national competitiveness. The *Porter diamond* consists of (1) factor conditions, (2) demand conditions, (3) related and supporting industries, and (4) firm strategy, structure, and rivalry. Let's look at these elements and see how they interact to support national competitiveness.

national competitive advantage theory

Trade theory stating that a nation's competitiveness in an industry depends on the capacity of the industry to innovate and upgrade.

Factor Conditions

Factor proportions theory considers a nation's resources, such as a large labor force, natural resources, climate, or surface features, as paramount factors in what products a country will produce and export. Porter acknowledges the value of such resources, which he terms *basic* factors, but he also discusses the significance of what he calls *advanced* factors.

ADVANCED FACTORS Advanced factors include the skill levels of different segments of the workforce and the quality of the technological infrastructure in a nation. Advanced factors are the result of investments in education and innovation, including worker training and technological research and development. Whereas basic factors can be the initial spark for why an economy begins producing a certain product, advanced factors account for the sustained competitive advantage a country enjoys in that product.

Today, for example, Japan has an advantage in automobile production and the United States in the manufacture of airplanes. In the manufacture of computer components, Taiwan reigns supreme, although China is an increasingly important competitor. These countries did not attain their status in their respective areas because of basic factors. For example, Japan did not acquire its advantage in automobiles because of its natural resources of iron ore—it has virtually none and must import most of the iron it needs. These countries developed their productivity and advantages in producing these products through deliberate efforts.

GLOBAL SUSTAINABILITY   Foundations of Development

Which aspects of a nation influence its path toward sustainable economic development? Researchers point to a host of different factors, including the following:

- **Culture.** Some researchers believe cultural differences among nations can explain differences in development, material well-being, and socioeconomic equity. They argue that any culture can attain high productivity and economic growth if it values the benefits that development brings. Critics say that this perspective unfairly judges other cultures. They argue that each culture defines its own values, practices, goals, and ethics, and that Western nations should not impose their concept of "progress" on other cultures.

- **Geography.** Other researchers claim geography is central to productivity and economic development. Factors thought to hinder development include being a landlocked nation far from the coast, having poor access to markets, possessing few natural resources, and having a tropical climate. But Hong Kong, Singapore, South Korea, and Taiwan built competitive market economies despite their small size and lack

of vast natural resources. Each of these nations also threw off dependence on a colonial power.

- **Innovation.** Nations that want to join the European Union must satisfy strict and innovative requirements. This is pulling Eastern Europe's culture closer to Western Europe's, along with shifting habits, attitudes, and values. In emerging markets today, innovation is being driven by ambition to improve one's lot in life and the fear of being replaced by an even cheaper production location. Homegrown businesses in emerging markets have developed very inexpensive yet highly functional automobiles, computers, and mobile phones that appeal to consumers at home and abroad.

- **Want to Know More?** Visit the Culturelink Network (www.culturelink.org), the Observatory of Cultural Policies in Africa (ocpa.irmo.hr), and the North-South Institute (www.nsi-ins.ca).

Sources: Mark Johnson, "Innovation in Emerging Markets," Bloomberg Businessweek (www.businessweek.com), May 28, 2010; "The World Turned Upside Down," The Economist, April 17, 2010, pp. 3–6; William Fischer, "Dealing with Innovation from Emerging Markets," IMD website (www.imd.org), November 2008.

An architecture student completes a project using a 3D printer. Advanced factors in Porter's theory of national competitive advantage result from investments in education and innovation, such as worker training and research and development. We do not know the full impact of 3D printing, but it is likely to reduce distribution costs for some products that can be made entirely at a home or business or made in local shops and then picked up by a customer.

luchschen/123RF.com

Demand Conditions

Sophisticated buyers in the home market are also important to national competitive advantage in a product area. A sophisticated domestic market drives companies to add new design features to products and to develop entirely new products and technologies. Companies in markets with sophisticated buyers should see the competitiveness of the entire group improve. For example, the sophisticated US market for computer software has helped give companies based in the United States an edge in developing new software products.

Related and Supporting Industries

Companies that belong to a nation's internationally competitive industries do not exist in isolation. Rather, supporting industries spring up to provide the inputs required by the industry. This happens because companies that can benefit from the product or process technologies of an internationally competitive industry begin to form clusters of related economic activities in the same geographic area. Each industry in the cluster serves to reinforce the productivity and, therefore, competitiveness of every other industry within the cluster. For example, Italy is home to a successful cluster in the footwear industry that greatly benefits from the country's closely related leather-tanning and fashion-design industries. And within the United States, Phoenix, Arizona, is home to companies that specialize in semiconductors, optics, and electronic testing—all heavily incorporated into the activities of Boeing (www.boeing.com) and Motorola (www.motorola.com), which have a significant presence there.

A relatively small number of clusters usually account for a major share of regional economic activity. They also often account for an overwhelming share of the economic activity that is "exported" to other locations. *Exporting clusters*—those that export products or make investments to compete outside the local area—are the primary source of an area's long-term prosperity. Although demand for a local industry is inherently limited by the size of the local market, an exporting cluster can grow far beyond that limit.[15]

Firm Strategy, Structure, and Rivalry

The strategies of firms and the actions of their managers have lasting effects on future competitiveness. Essential to successful companies are managers who are committed to producing quality products valued by buyers while maximizing the firm's market share and/or financial returns. Equally as important is the industry structure and rivalry between a nation's companies. The more intense the struggle to survive between a nation's domestic companies, the greater will be their competitiveness. This heightened competitiveness helps them to compete against imports and against companies that might develop a production presence in the home market.

Government and Chance

Apart from the four factors identified as part of the diamond, Porter identifies the roles of government and chance in fostering the national competitiveness of industries.

First, governments, by their actions, can often increase the competitiveness of firms and perhaps even entire industries. Governments of emerging markets could increase economic growth by increasing the pace of privatization of state-owned companies, for example. Privatization forces those companies to grow more competitive in world markets if they are to survive.

Second, although chance events can help the competitiveness of a firm or an industry, it can also threaten it. McDonald's (www.mcdonalds.com) holds a clear competitive advantage worldwide in the fast-food industry. But its overwhelming dominance was threatened by the discovery of mad cow disease several years ago. To keep customers from flocking to the nonbeef substitute products of competitors, McDonald's introduced the McPork sandwich and other nonbeef products.

There are important implications for companies and governments if Porter's theory accurately identifies the important drivers of national competitiveness. For instance, government policies should not be designed to protect national industries that are not internationally competitive but should develop the components of the diamond that contribute to increased competitiveness.

QUICK STUDY 7

1. The national competitive advantage theory states that a nation's competitiveness in an industry depends on the capacity of the industry to do *what*?
2. The four main components of the Porter diamond are: (1) factor conditions, (2) demand conditions, (3) firm strategy, structure, and rivalry, and *what else*?
3. A group of related industries that spring up in a geographic area to support a nation's internationally competitive industry is called a *what*?

BOTTOM LINE FOR BUSINESS

Trade can liberate the entrepreneurial spirit and bring economic development to a nation and its people. As the value and volume of trade continue to expand worldwide, new theories will likely emerge to explain why countries trade and why nations have advantages in producing certain products.

Globalization and Trade

An underlying theme of this book is how companies are adapting to globalization. Globalization and the increased competition it causes are forcing companies to locate particular operations to where they can be performed most efficiently. Firms are doing this either by relocating their own production facilities to other nations or by outsourcing certain activities to companies abroad. Companies undertake such action in order to boost competitiveness.

The relocation and outsourcing of business activities are altering international trade in both goods and services. In this chapter's opening company profile, we saw that Walmart relies on the sourcing of products from low-cost production locations such as China to deliver low-priced goods. Hewlett-Packard also makes use of globalization and international trade to minimize costs while maximizing output. The company dispersed the design and production of a new computer server throughout an increasingly specialized electronics-manufacturing system. HP conceptualized and designed the computer in Singapore, engineered and manufactured many parts for it in Taiwan, and assembled it in Australia, China, India, and Singapore. Companies are using such production and distribution techniques to maximize efficiency.

Not only is the production of goods being sent to distant locations, but so too is the delivery of business services, including financial accounting, data processing, and the handling of credit card and insurance inquiries. Even jobs requiring higher-level skills such as engineering, computer programming, and scientific research are migrating to distant locations. The motivation for companies is the same as when they send manufacturing jobs to more cost-effective locations—remaining viable in the face of increasing competitive pressure.

Supporting Free Trade

International trade theory is fundamentally no different when it comes to the relocation of services production as compared with the production of goods. As we've seen in this chapter, trade theory tells us that if a refrigerator bound for a Western market can be made more cheaply in China, it should be. The same reasoned logic tells us that if a credit card inquiry from a Western market can be more cheaply (but adequately) processed in India, it should be. In both cases, the importing country benefits from a less-expensive product, and the exporting country benefits from inward-flowing investment and more numerous and better-paying jobs.

Finally, there are policy implications for governments. Although employment in developed countries should not be negatively affected in the aggregate, job dislocation is a concern. Many governments are encouraging lifelong education among workers to guard against the possibility that an individual may become "obsolete" in terms of lacking marketable skills relative to workers in other nations. And no matter how loud the calls for protectionism grow in the service sector, governments will do well to resist such temptations. Experience tells us that erecting barriers to competition results in less competitive firms and industries, greater job losses, and lower standards of living than would be the case under free trade.

MyLab Management

Go to **www.pearson.com/mylab/management** to complete the problems marked with this icon .

Chapter Summary

LO5.1 Describe the benefits, volume, and patterns of international trade.

- Trade provides a country's people with a greater choice of goods and services and is an important engine for job creation in many countries.
- Nations export $16.5 trillion of merchandise and $4.8 trillion of services each year, with trade flows following the pace of world economic output.
- Wealthy nations account for around 60 percent of world merchandise trade. Trade between wealthy nations on the one hand and middle- and low-income countries on the other accounts for around 34 percent. Trade between low-income and middle-income nations accounts for around 6 percent.

LO5.2 Explain how mercantilism worked and identify its inherent flaws.

- *Mercantilism* says that nations should accumulate financial wealth in the form of gold by encouraging exports and discouraging imports.
- Governments believed that they should intervene actively in international trade in order to maintain a trade surplus, mainly by acquiring colonies to serve as sources of inexpensive raw materials and as markets for higher-priced finished goods.
- Mercantilism is flawed because it assumes that a nation increases its wealth only at the expense of other nations (a zero-sum game), and it restricts the economic development of colonies—thus, limiting the amount of goods they could purchase from the wealthy nation.

LO5.3 Detail the theories of absolute advantage and comparative advantage.

- The ability of a nation to produce a good more efficiently than any other nation is called an *absolute advantage*, which advocates letting market forces dictate trade flows.
- Absolute advantage allows a country to produce goods in which it holds an absolute advantage and trade with other nations to obtain goods it needs but does not produce (a positive-sum game).
- A nation holds a *comparative advantage* in production of a good when it is unable to produce the good more efficiently than other nations but can produce it more efficiently than it can any other good.
- Thus, trade is still beneficial if one country is less efficient in the production of two goods, so long as it is less inefficient in the production of one of the goods.

LO5.4 Summarize the factor proportions theory of trade.

- The *factor proportions theory* states that countries produce and export goods that require resources (factors) that are abundant and import goods that require resources that are in short supply.
- Factor proportions theory predicts that a country will specialize in products that require labor if its cost is low relative to the cost of land and capital, and vice versa.
- The apparent paradox between predictions of the theory and actual trade flows is called the *Leontief paradox*.

LO5.5 Explain the international product life cycle theory.

- The *international product life cycle theory* says that a company will begin exporting its product and later undertake foreign direct investment as the product moves through its life cycle.

- In the *new product stage*, production remains based in the home country; in the *maturing product stage*, production begins in countries with the highest demand; and in the *standardized product stage*, production moves to low-cost locations to supply a global market.

LO5.6 Outline the new trade theory and the first-mover advantage.

- The *new trade theory* argues that, as specialization and output increase, companies realize economies of scale that push the unit costs of production lower.
- This forces potential new entrants to an industry to produce a similar level of output if they want to be competitive in their pricing.
- The economies of scale in production help a firm to gain a *first-mover advantage*— the economic and strategic advantage gained by being the first company to enter an industry.

LO5.7 Describe the national competitive advantage theory and the Porter diamond.

- *National competitive advantage theory* states that a nation's competitiveness in an industry (and, therefore, trade flows) depends on the capacity of the industry to innovate and upgrade.
- The *Porter diamond* identifies four elements that form the basis of national competitiveness: (1) *factor conditions (basic and advanced)*, (2) *demand conditions*, (3) *related and supporting industries*, and (4) *firm strategy, structure, and rivalry.*
- The actions of *governments* and the occurrence of *chance events* can also affect the competitiveness of a nation's companies.

Key Terms

absolute advantage (p. 163)
comparative advantage (p. 164)
factor proportions theory (p. 167)
first-mover advantage (p. 170)

international product life cycle theory (p. 168)
international trade (p. 156)
mercantilism (p. 161)

national competitive advantage theory (p. 171)
new trade theory (p. 170)
trade deficit (p. 161)
trade surplus (p. 161)

✪ TALK ABOUT IT 1

Imagine that the nations of the world were to suddenly cut off all trade with one another and the people in each nation were able to consume only products their own nation produced.

5-1. What products previously imported would no longer be available in your country?
5-2. What products would people in a country other than your own need to do without?

✪ TALK ABOUT IT 2

Companies shift physical resources and capital among national markets with relative ease. They can move production operations to where labor is cheaper, but laborers generally cannot move to markets where wages are higher.

5-3. Why does labor remain the most restricted component of production in terms of its international mobility? Explain.
5-4. Do you agree with those who say this locks poor people to their poor geographies and gives them little hope for advancement? Explain.

Ethical Challenge

You are a member of a World Trade Organization task force that is reviewing the nine-year banana conflict between the United States and the European Union. The European Union was giving preferential treatment to banana exporters from Africa, the Caribbean, and the Pacific island nations. But the United States challenged what it saw as unfair trading practices and the World Trade Organization agreed. The US action gained support from global fruit companies Dole, Chiquita, and Del Monte, which account for nearly two-thirds of the fruit traded worldwide. The European Union argued it was supporting struggling economies for which bananas make up a large portion of their income.

5-5. Should international trade be left to private enterprise only, or should governments openly manage it to benefit poorer nations?

5-6. Would you have argued on behalf of the United States or the European Union? Explain.

5-7. What are the pros and cons of each side's arguments?

Teaming Up

Poor nations invest in the fundamental drivers of productivity growth, while rich nations try to use technological advancements to boost productivity. In groups of three or four, consider your own country and think about whether it has any particular national competitive advantages. Your deliberations should extend to both basic and extended advantages. List all the competitive advantages. Now share your list with the rest of the class to create a definitive list.

✪ Market Entry Strategy Project

This exercise corresponds to the *MESP* online simulation. For the country your team is researching, integrate your answers to the following questions into your completed *MESP* report.

5-8. How important is trade to the nation (trade as a share of GDP)?

5-9. What products and services does it export and import?

5-10. Is there a concerted effort to stimulate the economy by promoting exports?

5-11. With whom does the nation trade?

5-12. Is it dependent on any particular nation for trade, or does another nation depend on it?

5-13. Does the nation trade only with high-income countries or also with low- and middle-income countries?

MyLab Management

✪ Go to **www.pearson.com/mylab/management** for the following assisted-graded writing questions:

5-14. Many economists believe that China will soon achieve "superpower" status because of its economic reforms, along with the work ethic and high education of its population. How is the rise of China affecting trade patterns among Asia, Europe, and North America?

5-15. Despite its abundance of natural resources, Brazil was once considered an economic "basket case." Yet in recent years, Brazil's economy has performed well. Employing the national competitive advantage theory, what factors might be behind Brazil's economic progress?

BT in Local and International Markets

Dating back to the nineteenth century, BT Group PLC (BT) is the world's oldest telecommunications company. Based in the United Kingdom, it is the largest telecommunications service company in the world and has operations in more than 170 countries. Customers include individuals and small businesses as well as multinational corporations. Its operations and market, however, are not limited solely to the United Kingdom.

BT has made strategic alliances with telecommunications companies worldwide, giving BT access to overseas markets and facilitating its international operations. In June 1994, BT launched a new $1 billion joint venture company named Concert Communications Services. The joint venture was with MCI Communication Corporation, the second-largest carrier of long-distance telecommunications services in the United States. The alliance provides BT with a global network of end-to-end connectivity for advanced business services. In 1999, BT also entered into another joint venture with AT&T, the American telecommunications giant, to serve the needs of its business and individual customers.

Acquisition has been another strategy employed by BT to expand its global market share. In 2005, BT acquired Infonet (rebranded as BT Infonet), a world-leading provider of voice and data network services to corporate customers. In the same year, BT bought Radianz (renamed as BT Radianz later). Moreover, BT acquired Albacom, the second-largest telecommunications operator in the Italian business market. The acquisitions expanded BT's coverage and increased its ability to supply networked IT services to international organizations and financial markets across the globe. Furthermore, they provided BT with more buying power in certain countries and enhanced its position as a leading provider of communication solutions across the world.

In local markets, BT has always tried to be a leader and first mover. In the broadband service market, BT launched its commercial broadband service in March 2000 and achieved its target of 6 million broadband lines by the summer of 2005. Thanks to its well-structured and well-distributed network across the United Kingdom, in 2000, BT provided other telecommunications operators with access to its copper local loops (i.e., the connection between the customer's premises and the exchange) to connect directly with their customers. By mid-2005, more than 100,000 lines had been unbundled.

In 2004, BT launched a very ambitious and radical next-generation network transformation program called 21st Century Network (21CN), which facilitates communications between an extensive range of devices including computers, laptops, PDAs, mobile phones, and home phones.

BT, however, is confronted with many challenges in the British market these days. It has lost its market share to other network owners, new arrivals, innovative companies, and low-cost followers. Since then, in the residential broadband service market, BT has taken time to improve its services and reputation.

By the end of 2016, BT managed to attract some 9.28 million UK subscribers. BT is responsible for the Broadband UK (BDUK) project, which aims to expand the fiber and standard broadband networks. By the beginning of 2017, superfast FTTC broadband access had reached some 4.3 million UK homes. This was at considerable cost, estimated by 2017 to be $5.2 billion. BT seems to be on target to reach 95 percent coverage by 2018 (they had achieved 90 percent by the end of 2016, compared to 82 percent in 2015).

First financial and operating results for 2018 suggest continued success for BT. They reported mobile customers up by 4 percent, revenue at nearly $31 billion (though actually 2 percent down as a result of regulated price reductions).

In May 2018, BT announced plans to cut 13,000 jobs over the next three years, close its ageing London headquarters, and save nearly $2 billion. In 2017, BT had cut 4,000 jobs, mainly in global services. The most significant move for BT was the acquisition of UK Premier League football rights up to 2021–22. The rights package cost BT $384 million, but this has had a huge impact on BT's consumer portfolio. Despite shedding some job roles, BT plans to hire 6,000 employees to support customer service and network deployment, and in 2017, the corporation also announced its intention to recruit 3,500 trainee engineers.

Thinking Globally

5-16. As the first to set up telecommunication infrastructures, systems, and services in the United Kingdom, BT is recognized as a first-mover in the telecommunication industry. Discuss the advantages and disadvantages of being a first mover like BT.

5-17. Compare and contrast being a first mover in a service sector (e.g., telecommunications) and in a manufacturing sector (e.g., Sony or Airbus). Discuss opportunities and threats for first movers in each sector.

5-18. When it comes to global expansion and setting up affiliates abroad, how is a service company's focus different from that of a manufacturing company? What elements are necessary for a service company to achieve global success? What are the obstacles to global expansion?

5-19. Why do you think BT is losing its market share to smaller companies in the United Kingdom? Explain.

5-20. What challenges do you expect for BT in international markets?

Sources: "United Kingdom—Telecom Country Profile 2010," Research and Markets website, (www.researchandmarkets.com); "BT vs Virgin Media vs Cable and Wireless vs Talk Talk," Cloud Net website (www.cloudnetuk.com), April 8, 2010; BT website (www.BT.com); TalkTalk website (www.talktalkgroup.com).

Chapter Six

Political Economy of Trade

Learning Objectives

After studying this chapter, you should be able to

6.1 Explain why governments sometimes intervene in trade.

6.2 Outline the instruments that governments use to promote trade.

6.3 Describe the instruments that governments use to restrict trade.

6.4 Summarize the main features of the global trading system.

A Look Back

Chapter 5 explored theories that have been developed to explain the pattern international trade should take. We examined the important concept of comparative advantage and the conceptual basis for how international trade benefits nations.

A Look at This Chapter

This chapter discusses the active role of national governments in international trade. We examine the motives for government intervention and the tools that nations use to accomplish their goals. We then explore the global trading system and show how it promotes free trade.

A Look Ahead

Chapter 7 continues our discussion of the international business environment. We explore recent patterns of foreign direct investment, theories that try to explain why it occurs, and how governments influence investment flows.

MyLab Management

✪ IMPROVE YOUR GRADE!

When you see this icon ✪, visit **www.pearson.com/mylab/management** for activities that are applied, personalized, and offer immediate feedback.

Regulating the Global Textile and Clothing Trade

Governments often formulate international trade regulations to manage a balance between the exports and imports of commodities. The U.S., EU, and Canadian governments used the Multi-Fiber Arrangement (MFA) between 1974 and 2004 to regulate the imports of cheaper textile and clothing (TC) from emerging countries such as China and India. The MFA restricted the amount of cheaper imports to safeguard American and European TC manufacturing businesses from price-based competition. The manufacturing cost of the American and European companies was much higher compared to their competitors primarily due to higher labor cost. Unrestricted cheaper imports were a threat to the survival of these businesses.

Africa Studio/Shutterstock

Nonetheless, to facilitate their economic growth, the import restriction was not applied to poorer TC manufacturing countries such as Bangladesh, Vietnam, and Sri Lanka. As a result, these countries have gained substantive comparative advantages in clothing exports. Bangladesh, the third-highest manufacturer, exported $28 billion worth of clothing in 2016. The industry employs more than four million Bangladeshi workers, of whom 70 percent are women who had essentially been unpaid labor for centuries. Large clothing retailers such as H&M, M&S, Primark, Walmart, and Tesco procure a significant proportion of their merchandise from Bangladesh. Ha-meem, Beximco, Opex Sinha, DBL, Square, Knit Asia, and Epyllion are some of the Bangladeshi businesses that have emerged as leading clothing manufacturers worldwide by optimizing the MFA and similar trade regulations.

When the MFA expired in January 2005, China emerged as the principal beneficiary due to its economy of scale. Chinese products could now enter into the American and European clothing market without much restriction. The TC industries from other countries that had survived mainly due to the MFA failed to take advantage of the safeguards to build up sustainability. For example, clothing exports from El Salvador decreased by approximately 30 percent immediately after the expiry of the MFA. It was also expected that the TC industry of the Dominican Republic would lose up to 40 percent of its employment opportunities. Such a level of reduction in export revenue and job displacement can be a severe threat to developing economies.

The MFA is an example of government intervention on trade and the global impact of such interference. As you read this chapter, consider all the cultural, political, and economic reasons why governments regulate international trade.[1]

Chapter 5 presented theories that describe what the patterns of international trade *should* look like. The theory of comparative advantage says that the country that has a comparative advantage in the production of a certain good will produce that good when barriers to trade do not exist. But this ideal does not accurately characterize trade in today's global marketplace. Despite efforts by organizations such as the World Trade Organization (www.wto.org) and smaller groups of countries, nations still retain many barriers to trade.

In this chapter, we investigate the political economy of trade. We first explain why nations erect barriers to trade by exploring their cultural, political, and economic motives. We then examine the instruments countries use to restrict imports and exports. Efforts to promote trade by reducing barriers within the context of the global trading system are then presented. In Chapter 8 we discuss how smaller groups of countries are eliminating barriers to both trade and investment.

6.1 Why do Governments Intervene in Trade?

6.1 Explain why governments sometimes intervene in trade.

free trade
Pattern of imports and exports that occurs in the absence of trade barriers.

The pattern of imports and exports that occurs in the absence of trade barriers is called **free trade**. Despite the advantages of open and free trade among nations, governments have long intervened in the trade of goods and services. Governments impose restrictions on free trade for political, economic, or cultural reasons. For example, countries often intervene in trade by strongly supporting their domestic companies' exporting activities. But the more emotionally charged intervention occurs when a nation's economy is underperforming. In tough economic times, businesses and workers often lobby their governments for protection from imports that are eliminating jobs in the domestic market. Let's take a closer look at the political, economic, and cultural motives for intervention.

Political Motives

Government officials often make trade-related decisions based on political motives because a politician's career can depend on pleasing voters and getting reelected. Yet, a trade policy based purely on political motives is seldom wise in the long run. The main political motives behind government intervention in trade include protecting jobs, preserving national security, responding to other nations' unfair trade practices, and gaining influence over other nations.

PROTECT JOBS Short of an unpopular war, nothing will oust a government faster than high rates of unemployment. Thus, practically all governments become involved when free trade creates job losses at home. For example, Ohio lost around 215,000 manufacturing jobs over a recent 14-year period. Most of those jobs went to China and the nations of Central and Eastern Europe. The despair of unemployed workers and the pivotal role of Ohio in presidential elections lured politicians to the state, who promised Ohio lower income taxes, expanded worker retraining, and greater investment in the state's infrastructure.

But political efforts to protect jobs can draw attention away from free trade's real benefits. General Electric (GE) certainly sent many jobs from the United States to Mexico over the years. GE now employs 30,000 Mexicans at 35 factories that manufacture all sorts of its appliances and other goods. But less known is that GE also sold Mexican companies $350 million worth of its turbines made in Texas, 100 of its locomotives made in Pennsylvania, and dozens of its US-made aircraft engines. Mexico specializes in making products that require less-expensive labor, and the United States specializes in producing goods that require advanced technology and a large investment of capital.[2]

PRESERVE NATIONAL SECURITY Human, economic, and environmental security are closely related to national security. The globalization of markets and production creates new security risks for companies. To read about these risks, see this chapter's Global Sustainability feature, titled "Managing Security in the Age of Globalization."

National Security and Imports Certain imports can be restricted in the name of preserving national security. In the event of war, governments must have access to a domestic supply of certain items such as weapons, fuel, and air, land, and sea transportation in case their availability is restricted. Many nations continue to search for oil within their borders in case war disrupts its flow from outside sources. Legitimate national security reasons for intervention can be difficult to argue against, particularly when they have the support of most of a country's people.

| GLOBAL SUSTAINABILITY | Managing Security in the Age of Globalization |

As well as the need to secure lengthy supply chains and distribution channels, companies must secure their facilities, information systems, and reputations.

- **Facilities Risk.** Large companies with top-notch property risk-management programs produce more stable earnings. Companies practicing weak risk management experience 55 times greater risk of property loss due to fire and 29 times greater risk of property loss caused by natural hazards. Planning and facilities assessment (around $12,000 for a midsize company, $1 million for a large firm) can be well worth the cost.
- **Information Risk.** Computer viruses, software worms, malicious code, and cyber criminals cost companies around the world many billions of dollars each year. Disgruntled employees, dishonest competitors, and hackers who steal customers' personal and financial data can then sell it to the highest bidder. Upon termination, employees sometimes leave with digital devices containing confidential memos, competitive data, and private e-mails.
- **Reputational Risk.** News today travels worldwide quickly. Reputational risk is anything that can harm a firm's image,

including product recalls, workers' rights violations, and lawsuits. The damaged reputation of Goldman Sachs following a $550 million settlement with the Securities and Exchange Commission for its actions before and during recent financial crises cost the firm 40 percent ($6 billion) of its brand value in one year.
- **What to Do.** Like the risks themselves, the challenges are varied. Companies should identify all potential risks to their facilities and then develop a best-practice property risk program. It sounds simple, but employees must change passwords frequently, safeguard their computers and mobile devices from attack, and return company-owned digital devices when leaving the firm. Finally, ever-increasing scrutiny means that companies should act ethically and within the law to protect their reputations.
- **Want to Know More?** Visit Sustainable Security (sustainablesecurity.org), the Foundation for Environmental Security and Sustainability (www.fess-global.org), Kroll (www.krollworldwide.com), and Check Point Software Technologies (www.checkpoint.com).

Some countries claim that national security is the reason for fierce protection of their agricultural sector, since food security is essential at a time of war. France was criticized by many nations for ardently protecting its agricultural sector. French agricultural subsidies are intended to provide a fair financial return for French farmers, who traditionally operate on a small scale and therefore have high production costs and low profit margins. But many developed nations are exposing agribusiness to market forces and prompting their farmers to discover new ways to manage risk and increase efficiency. Innovative farmers are experimenting with more intensive land management, high-tech precision farming, and greater use of biotechnology.

Yet, protection from import competition does have its drawbacks. Perhaps the main one is the added cost of continuing to produce a good or provide a service domestically that could be supplied more efficiently from abroad. Also, a policy of protection may remain in place much longer than necessary once it is adopted. Thus, policy makers should consider whether an issue truly is a matter of national security before intervening in trade.

National Security and Exports Governments also have national security motives for banning certain defense-related goods from export to other nations. Most industrialized nations have agencies that review requests to export technologies or products that are said to have *dual uses*—meaning they have both industrial and military applications. Products designated as dual use are classified as such and require special governmental approval before export can take place.

Products on the dual-use lists of most nations include nuclear materials, technological equipment, certain chemicals and toxins, some sensors and lasers, and specific devices related to weapons, navigation, aerospace, and propulsion. Bans on the export of dual-use products were strictly enforced during the Cold War years between the West and the former Soviet Union. Whereas many countries relaxed enforcement of these controls in recent years, the continued threat of terrorism and fears of weapons of mass destruction are renewing support for such bans.

Nations also place certain companies and organizations in other countries on a list of entities that are restricted from receiving their exports. For example, the owner of an electronics firm pleaded guilty to charges of conspiracy to illegally export dual-use items from the United States to India for possible use in ballistic missiles, space launch vehicles, and fighter jets. The individual admitted that he provided the components to government entities in India, including two companies on the US Department of Commerce's "Entity List" and received a 35-month jail sentence and was fined $60,000.

RESPOND TO "UNFAIR" TRADE Many observers argue that it makes no sense for one nation to allow free trade if other nations actively protect their own industries. Governments often threaten to close their ports to another nation's ships or to impose extremely high tariffs on its goods if the other nation does not concede on some trade issue that is seen as being unfair. In other words, if one government thinks another nation is not "playing fair," it will often threaten to retaliate unless certain concessions are made.

GAIN INFLUENCE Governments of the world's largest nations may become involved in trade to gain influence over smaller nations. The United States goes to great lengths to gain and maintain control over events in all of Central, North, and South America, and the Caribbean basin.

In 1962, the United States banned all trade and investment with Cuba in the hope of exerting political influence against its communist leaders. Designed to pressure Cuba's government to change, the policy unintentionally caused suffering among Cuba's citizens. But change is occurring in Cuba, albeit slowly. Even the concept of performance-related pay was introduced. These seemingly trivial freedoms represent monumental change to ordinary Cubans, who now hope for continually greater freedom.

Economic Motives

Although governments intervene in trade for highly charged cultural and political reasons, they also have economic motives for their intervention. The most common economic reasons for nations' attempts to influence international trade are the protection of young industries from competition and the promotion of a strategic trade policy.

PROTECT INFANT INDUSTRIES According to the *infant industry argument,* a country's emerging industries need protection from international competition during their development phase until they become sufficiently competitive internationally. This argument is based on the idea that infant industries need protection because of a steep learning curve. In other words, only as an industry grows and matures does it gain the knowledge it needs to become more innovative, efficient, and competitive.

Although this argument is conceptually appealing, it does have several problems. First, it requires governments to distinguish between industries that are worth protecting and those that are not. This is difficult, if not impossible, to do. For years, Japan targeted infant industries for protection, low interest loans, and other benefits. Its performance on assisting these industries was very good through the early 1980s but was less successful since then. Until the government

All types of crops today, including corn, soybeans, and wheat, are grown with genetically enhanced seed technology to resist insects and disease. Genetically modified plants like those shown here have had their DNA genetically altered in laboratories. Many people in Europe fiercely resist efforts by the United States to export genetically modified crops to their markets. Do you believe Europeans are right to be wary of the importation of genetically modified crops?

Hero Images Inc./Alamy Stock Photo

achieves future success in identifying and targeting industries, supporting this type of policy remains questionable.

Second, protection from international competition can cause domestic companies to become complacent toward innovation. This can limit a company's incentives to obtain the knowledge it needs to become more competitive. The most extreme examples of complacency are industries within formerly communist nations. When their communist protections collapsed, nearly all companies that were run by the state were decades behind their competitors from capitalist nations. To survive, many government-owned businesses required financial assistance in the form of infusions of capital or outright purchase.

Third, protection can do more economic harm than good. Consumers often end up paying more for products because a lack of competition typically creates fewer incentives to cut production costs or improve quality. Meanwhile, companies become less competitive and more reliant on protection. Protection in Japan created a two-tier economy where, in one tier, highly competitive multinational corporations faced rivals in overseas markets and learned to become strong competitors. In the other tier, domestic industries were made noncompetitive through protected markets, high wages, and barriers to imports.

Fourth, the infant industry argument also says that it is not always possible for small, promising companies to obtain funding in capital markets, and thus they need financial support from their government. However, international capital markets today are far more sophisticated than in the past, and promising business ventures can normally obtain funding from private sources.

PURSUE STRATEGIC TRADE POLICY Recall from our discussion in Chapter 5 that new trade theorists believe government intervention can help companies take advantage of economies of scale and become the first movers in their industries. First-mover advantages arise because economies of scale in production limit the number of companies that an industry can sustain.

Benefits of Strategic Trade Policy Supporters of strategic trade policy argue that it results in increased national income. Companies should earn a good profit if they obtain first-mover advantages and solidify positions in their markets around the world. Advocates claim that strategic trade policies helped South Korea build global conglomerates (called *chaebol*) that dwarf competitors. For years, South Korean shipbuilders received a variety of government subsidies, including low-cost financing. The *chaebol* helped South Korea to emerge strongly from the recent global economic crisis because of their market power and the wide range of industries in which they compete. Such policies had spin-off effects on related industries, and local suppliers to the *chaebol* are now thriving.[3]

Drawbacks of Strategic Trade Policy Although it sounds as if strategic trade policy only has benefits, there can be drawbacks as well. Lavish government assistance to domestic companies in the past caused inefficiency and high costs for both South Korean and Japanese companies. Large government concessions to local labor unions hiked wages and forced Korea's *chaebol* to accept low profit margins. Yet, over time, the chaebol overcame these difficulties.

In addition, when governments decide to support specific industries, their choice is often subject to political lobbying by the groups seeking government assistance. It is possible that special interest groups could capture all the gains from assistance with no benefit for consumers. If this were to occur, consumers could end up paying more for goods of lower-quality than they could otherwise obtain.

Cultural Motives

Nations often restrict trade in goods and services to achieve cultural objectives, the most common being protection of national identity. Culture and trade are intertwined and greatly affect one another. The cultures of countries are slowly altered by exposure to the people and products of other cultures. Unwanted cultural influence in a nation can cause great distress and force a government to block imports that it believes are harmful (recall our discussion of *cultural imperialism* in Chapter 2).

French law bans foreign-language words from virtually all business and government communications, radio and TV broadcasts, public announcements, and advertising messages—at least whenever a suitable French alternative is available. You can't advertise a *best seller*; it has to be a *succès de librairie*. You can't sell *popcorn* at *le cinéma*; French moviegoers must snack on *maïs soufflé*. The Higher Council on French Language works against the inclusion of so-called

Franglais phrases such as *le marketing, le cash flow*, and *le brainstorming* into commerce and other areas of French culture. Not to be outdone by neighboring France, German bureaucrats exchanged governmental use of English words with German ones, for example, replacing *brainstorming* with *ideensammlung* and *meeting points* with *treffpukte*.[4]

Canada also tries to mitigate the cultural influence of entertainment products imported from the United States. Canada requires at least 35 percent of music played over Canadian radio to be by Canadian artists. In fact, many countries are considering laws to protect their media programming for cultural reasons. The downside of such restrictions is they reduce the selection of products available to consumers.

CULTURAL INFLUENCE OF THE UNITED STATES   International trade is the vehicle by which the English language swiftly infiltrates the cultures of other nations. International trade in all sorts of goods and services is exposing people around the world to new words, ideas, products, and ways of life. Still, as international trade continues to expand, many governments try to limit potential adverse effects on their cultures and economies.

The United States, more than any other nation, is seen by many around the world as a threat to local culture. The reason is the global strength of the United States in entertainment and media (such as movies, magazines, and music) and consumer goods. These products are highly visible to all consumers and cause groups of various kinds to lobby government officials for protection from their cultural influence. Domestic producers find it easy to join in the calls for protection because the rhetoric of protectionism often receives widespread public support.

Oddly, many small businesses capable of exporting have not yet begun to do so. By some estimates, only 10 percent of US companies with fewer than 100 employees export. Encouraging greater export activity may require US companies to undergo a cultural shift in mindset. Although a lack of investment capital can be a real obstacle to exporting for small businesses, some common myths in the business culture create artificial obstacles. To explore some of these myths and the facts that dispute them, see this chapter's Culture Matters feature, titled "Myths of Small Business Exporting."

QUICK STUDY 1

1. Free trade is the pattern of imports and exports that occurs in the *what*?
2. For what political reasons does a government intervene in trade?
3. What are some economic reasons why a government intervenes in trade?
4. Some people see the products of what country as the greatest threat to local cultures around the world?

CULTURE MATTERS   Myths of Small Business Exporting

- **Myth 1:** Only large companies can export successfully.
  Fact: Most exporters are small and medium-sized enterprises with fewer than 50 employees. Exporting can reduce the dependency of small firms on domestic markets and can help them avoid seasonal sales fluctuations. A product popular domestically, or perhaps even unsuccessful at home, may be wanted elsewhere in the global market.
- **Myth 2:** Small businesses can find little export advice.
  Fact: Novice and experienced exporters alike can receive comprehensive export assistance from federal agencies (www.export.gov). International trade specialists can help small businesses locate and use federal, state, local, and private-sector programs. They are also an excellent source of market research, trade leads, financing, and trade events.

- **Myth 3:** Licensing requirements needed to export are too complicated.
  Fact: Most products do not need export licenses. Exporters need only to write "NLR" for "no license required" on their Shipper's Export Declaration. A license is generally needed only for high-tech or defense-related goods or when the receiving country is under a US embargo or other restriction.
- **Myth 4:** Small businesses cannot obtain export financing.
  Fact: The Small Business Administration (www.sba.gov) and the Export-Import Bank (www.exim.gov) work together in lending money to small businesses. Whereas the SBA is responsible for loan requests below $750,000, the Export-Import Bank handles transactions more than $750,000. The Trade and Development Agency (www.ustda.gov) also helps small and medium-sized firms obtain financing for international projects.

6.2 Instruments of Trade Promotion

The previous discussion alluded to the types of instruments governments use to promote or restrict trade with other nations. The most common instruments that governments use are shown in Table 6.1. In this section, we examine methods of trade promotion. We cover methods of trade restriction in the next section.

6.2 Outline the instruments that governments use to promote trade.

Subsidies

Financial assistance to domestic producers in the form of cash payments, low-interest loans, tax breaks, product price supports, or other forms is called a **subsidy**. Regardless of the form a subsidy takes, it is intended to assist domestic companies in fending off international competitors. This can mean becoming more competitive in the home market or increasing competitiveness in international markets through exports. It is extremely difficult to calculate the amount of subsidies a country offers its producers because of the many forms that subsidies take. This makes the work of the World Trade Organization difficult when it is called on to settle arguments over subsidies (the World Trade Organization is discussed later in this chapter).

subsidy
Financial assistance to domestic producers in the form of cash payments, low-interest loans, tax breaks, product price supports, or other forms.

DRAWBACKS OF SUBSIDIES Critics say that subsidies encourage inefficiency and complacency by covering costs that truly competitive industries should be able to absorb on their own. Many believe subsidies benefit companies and industries that receive them but harm consumers because they tend to be paid for with income and sales taxes. Thus, although subsidies provide short-term relief to companies and industries, whether they help a nation's citizens in the long term is questionable.

Some observers say that far more devastating is the effect of subsidies on farmers in developing and emerging markets. We've already seen that many wealthy nations award subsidies to their farmers to ensure an adequate food supply for their people. It is said that these subsidies, worth billions of dollars, make it difficult if not impossible for farmers from poor countries to sell their unsubsidized (i.e., more expensive) food on world markets. Compounding the plight of these farmers is the fact that their nations are being forced to eliminate trade barriers by international organizations. The economic consequences for poor farmers in Africa, Asia, and Latin America are higher unemployment and poverty.

Subsidies can lead to an overuse of resources, negative environmental effects, and higher costs for commodities. Subsidies tend to drive fuel prices higher and eliminate incentives to conserve fuel. A period of rising fuel prices gave researches to examine the effects of subsidies on fuel usage. Research supported the notion that whereas countries without fuel subsidies saw steady or falling demand, subsidizing countries saw rising demand that threatened to outstrip growth in global fuel supplies.

Export Financing

Governments often promote exports by helping companies finance their export activities. They can offer loans that a company could otherwise not obtain or can charge them an interest rate that is lower than the market rate. Another option is for a government to guarantee that it will repay the loan of a company if the company should default on repayment; this is called a *loan guarantee*.

TABLE 6.1 Instruments of Trade Policy

Trade Promotion	Trade Restriction
Subsidies	Tariffs
Export financing	Quotas
Foreign trade zones	Embargoes
Special government agencies	Local content requirements
	Administrative delays
	Currency controls

Many nations have special agencies dedicated to helping their domestic companies obtain export financing. For example, a very well-known institution is called the *Export-Import Bank of the United States—or Ex-Im Bank* for short. The Ex-Im Bank (www.exim.gov) finances the export activities of companies in the United States and offers insurance on foreign accounts receivable. Another US government agency, the *Overseas Private Investment Corporation (OPIC)*, also provides insurance services but for investors. Through OPIC (www.opic.gov), companies that invest abroad can insure against losses due to (1) expropriation, (2) currency inconvertibility, and (3) war, revolution, and insurrection.

Receiving financing from government agencies is often crucial to the success of small businesses that are just beginning to export. Taken together, small businesses account for more than 80 percent of all transactions handled by the Ex-Im Bank. For instance, the Ex-Im Bank guaranteed to cover a loan of nearly $4 million to help fund development of an amusement park in Accra, Ghana. The investment in Africa is in response to rising demand for world-class amusement parks across West Africa. The park will employ at least 175 local Ghanaians under the supervision of US expatriate managers. For more on how the Ex-Im Bank helps businesses gain export financing, see the Manager's Briefcase, titled "Experts in Export Financing."

Foreign Trade Zones

foreign trade zone (FTZ)

Designated geographic region through which merchandise is allowed to pass with lower customs duties (taxes) and/or fewer customs procedures.

Most countries promote trade with other nations by creating what is called a **foreign trade zone (FTZ)**—a designated geographic region through which merchandise is allowed to pass with lower customs duties (taxes) and/or fewer customs procedures. Increased employment is often the intended purpose of FTZs, with a by-product being increased trade. A good example of a foreign trade zone is Turkey's Aegean Free Zone, in which the Turkish government allows companies to conduct manufacturing operations free from taxes.

Customs duties increase the total amount of a good's production cost and increase the time needed to get it to market. Companies can reduce such costs and time by establishing a facility inside an FTZ. A common purpose of many companies' facilities in such zones is final product assembly. The US Department of Commerce (www.commerce.gov) administers dozens of FTZs within the United States. Many of these zones allow components to be imported at a discount from the normal duty. Once assembled, the finished product can be sold within the US market with no further duties charged. State governments welcome such zones in order to obtain the jobs that the assembly operations create.

China established a number of large FTZs in order to reap the employment advantages they offer. Goods imported into these zones do not require import licenses or other documents, nor are

---

MANAGER'S BRIEFCASE Experts in Export Financing

Several Ex-Im Bank (www.exim.gov) programs can help US businesses expand abroad:

- **City/State Program** This program brings financing services to small and medium-sized US companies that are ready to export. This program currently exists with 38 state and local government offices and private sector organizations.
- **Working Capital Guarantee Program** This program encourages commercial banks to loan money to companies with export potential. The guarantee covers 90 percent of the loan's principal and accrued interest. The guaranteed financing can help purchase finished products for export or pay for raw materials, for example.
- **Credit Information Services** The Ex-Im Bank supplies credit information to US exporters and commercial lenders. It provides information on a country or specific company abroad. But the bank does not divulge either confidential financial data on non-US buyers to whom it has extended credit or confidential information on specific conditions in other countries.

- **Credit Insurance** This program helps US exporters by protecting them against loss should a non-US buyer or debtor default for political or commercial reasons. The proceeds of the policy can be used as collateral and therefore can make obtaining export financing easier.
- **Guarantee Program** This program provides repayment protection for private sector loans made to creditworthy buyers of US capital equipment, projects, and services. The bank guarantees the principal and interest on the loan if the borrower defaults. Most guarantees provide comprehensive coverage against political and commercial risks.
- **Loan Program** The bank makes loans directly to non-US buyers of US exports and intermediary loans to creditworthy parties that provide loans to non-US buyers. The program provides fixed-interest-rate financing for export sales of US-made capital equipment and related services.

Source: Export-Import Bank of the United States website (www.exim.gov).

they subject to import duties. International companies can also store goods in these zones before shipping them to other countries without incurring taxes in China. Moreover, five of these zones are located within specially designated economic zones in which local governments can offer additional opportunities and tax breaks to international investors.

Another country that enjoys the beneficial effects of FTZs is Mexico. Decades ago, Mexico established such a zone along its northern border with the United States. Creation of the zone caused development of companies called *maquiladoras* along the border inside Mexico. The *maquiladoras* import materials or parts from the United States duty free, process them to some extent, and export them back to the United States, which charges duties only on the value added to the product in Mexico. The program expanded rapidly over the five decades since its inception, employing hundreds of thousands of people from all across Mexico who move north looking for work.

Special Government Agencies

Learning the government regulations of other countries can be a daunting task. A company must know whether its product is subject to a tariff or quota, for example. Governments of most nations, therefore, have special agencies responsible for promoting exports. Such agencies can be particularly helpful to small and medium-sized businesses that have limited financial resources.

Government trade-promotion agencies often organize trips for trade officials and businesspeople to visit other countries in order to meet potential business partners and generate contacts for new business. They also typically open trade offices in other countries. These offices are designed to promote the home country's exports and introduce businesses to potential partners in the host nation. Government trade-promotion agencies typically do a great deal of advertising in other countries promoting the nation's exports. For example, Chile's Trade Commission, ProChile, has commercial offices in 40 countries and a website (www.chileinfo.com).

Governments not only promote trade by encouraging exports but also encourage imports that the nation does not or cannot produce. For example, the Japan External Trade Organization (JETRO; www.jetro.go.jp) is a trade-promotion agency of the Japanese government. The agency coaches small and medium-sized overseas businesses on the protocols of Japanese deal making, arranges meetings with suitable Japanese distributors and partners, and even assists in finding temporary office spaces.

QUICK STUDY 2

1. Financial assistance from a government to domestic producers is called a *what*?
2. What are the hoped-for outcomes of a foreign trade zone?
3. What are some of the ways that governments provide export financing?

6.3 Instruments of Trade Restriction

Earlier in this chapter, we read about the political, economic, and cultural reasons for governmental intervention in trade. In this section, we discuss the methods governments can use to restrict unwanted trade. There are two general categories of trade barriers available to governments: tariffs and nontariff barriers. A **tariff** is a government tax levied on a product as it enters or leaves a country. A tariff increases the price of an imported product *directly* and, therefore, reduces its appeal to buyers. A nontariff barrier limits the availability of an imported product, which increases its price *indirectly* and, therefore, reduces its appeal to buyers. Let's take a closer look at tariffs and the various types of nontariff barriers.

6.3 Describe the instruments that governments use to restrict trade.

tariff
Government tax levied on a product as it enters or leaves a country.

Tariffs

We can classify a tariff into one of three categories. An *export tariff* is levied by the government of a country that is exporting a product. Countries can use export tariffs when they believe an export's price is lower than it should be. Developing nations whose exports consist mostly of low-priced natural resources often levy export tariffs. A *transit tariff* is levied by the government of a country that a product is passing through on its way to its final destination. Transit tariffs have been almost entirely eliminated worldwide through international trade agreements. An *import tariff* is levied by the government of a country that is importing a product. The import tariff is by far the most common tariff used by governments today.

We can further break down the import tariff into three subcategories based on the manner in which it is calculated. An **ad valorem tariff** is levied as a percentage of the stated price of an imported product. A **specific tariff** is levied as a specific fee for each unit (measured by number, weight, etc.) of an imported product. A **compound tariff** is levied on an imported product and calculated partly as a percentage of its stated price and partly as a specific fee for each unit. Let's now discuss the two main reasons why countries levy tariffs.

ad valorem tariff
Tariff levied as a percentage of the stated price of an imported product.

specific tariff
Tariff levied as a specific fee for each unit (measured by number, weight, etc.) of an imported product.

compound tariff
Tariff levied on an imported product and calculated partly as a percentage of its stated price and partly as a specific fee for each unit.

PROTECT DOMESTIC PRODUCERS Nations can use tariffs to protect domestic producers. For example, an import tariff raises the cost of an imported good and increases the appeal of domestically produced goods. In this way, domestic producers gain a protective barrier against imports. Although producers that receive tariff protection can gain a price advantage, in the long run protection can keep them from increasing efficiency. A protected industry can be devastated if protection encourages complacency and inefficiency and it is later thrown into the lion's den of international competition. Mexico began reducing tariff protection in the mid-1980s as a prelude to NAFTA negotiations, and many Mexican producers went bankrupt despite attempts to grow more efficient.

GENERATE REVENUE Tariffs are also a source of government revenue, but mostly among developing nations. The main reason is that less-developed nations tend to have less-formal domestic economies that lack the capability to record domestic transactions accurately. The lack of accurate record keeping makes collection of sales taxes within the country extremely difficult. Nations solve the problem by simply raising their needed revenue through import and export tariffs. As countries develop, however, they tend to generate a greater portion of their revenues from taxes on income, capital gains, and other economic activity.

The discussion so far leads us to question who benefits from tariffs. We've already learned the two principal reasons for tariff barriers—protecting domestic producers and raising government revenue. On the surface, it appears that governments and domestic producers benefit. We also saw that tariffs raise the price of a product because importers typically charge a higher price to recover the cost of this additional tax. Thus, it appears on the surface that consumers do not benefit. As we also mentioned earlier, there is the danger that tariffs will create inefficient domestic producers that may go out of business once protective import tariffs are removed. Analysis of the total cost to a country is far more complicated and goes beyond the scope of our discussion. Suffice it to say that tariffs tend to exact a cost on countries as a whole because they lessen the gains that a nation's people obtain from trade.

Quotas

A restriction on the amount (measured in units or weight) of a good that can enter or leave a country during a certain period of time is called a **quota**. After tariffs, quotas are the second most common type of trade barrier. Governments typically administer their quota systems by granting quota licenses to the companies or governments of other nations (in the case of import quotas) and domestic producers (in the case of export quotas). Governments normally grant such licenses on a year-by-year basis.

quota
Restriction on the amount (measured in units or weight) of a good that can enter or leave a country during a certain period of time.

REASON FOR IMPORT QUOTAS A government may impose an *import quota* to protect its domestic producers by placing a limit on the amount of goods allowed to enter the country. This helps domestic producers maintain their market shares and prices because competitive forces are restrained. In this case, domestic producers win because their market is protected. Consumers lose because of higher prices and limited selection attributable to lower competition. Other losers include domestic producers whose own production requires the import subjected to a quota. Companies relying on the importation of so-called intermediate goods will find the final cost of their own products increase.

Historically, countries placed import quotas on the textile and apparel products of other countries under the Multi-Fiber Arrangement. This arrangement at one time affected countries accounting for more than 80 percent of world trade in textiles and clothing. When that arrangement expired in 2005, many textile producers in poor nations feared the loss of jobs to China.

A young woman works in a garment factory in Phnom Penh, Cambodia. Across Cambodia and much of the rest of Southeast Asia, small clothing factories have thrived following removal of a worldwide system allowed under the Multi-Fiber Agreement. Under this agreement, wealthy nations guaranteed imports of textiles and garments from poor countries under a quota system. Under what conditions do you think nations should be allowed to impose import quotas?

Dennis Drenner/Alamy Stock Photo

But some countries with a large textile industry, such as Bangladesh, are benefiting from cheap labor and the reluctance among purchasers to rely exclusively on China for all supplies.

REASONS FOR EXPORT QUOTAS There are at least two reasons why a country imposes *export quotas* on its domestic producers. First, it may wish to maintain adequate supplies of a product in the home market. This motive is most common among countries that export natural resources that are essential to domestic business or the long-term survival of a nation.

Second, a country may limit the export of a good in order to restrict its supply on world markets, thereby increasing the international price of the good. This is the motive behind the formation and activities of the Organization of Petroleum Exporting Countries (OPEC; www.opec.org). This group of nations from the Middle East and Latin America attempts to restrict the world's supply of crude oil in order to earn greater profits.

VOLUNTARY EXPORT RESTRAINTS A unique version of the export quota is called a **voluntary export restraint (VER)**—a quota that a nation imposes on its own exports, usually at the request of another nation. Countries normally self-impose a voluntary export restraint in response to the threat of an import quota or a total ban on the product by an importing nation. The classic example of the use of a voluntary export restraint is from the 1980s when Japanese carmakers were making significant market-share gains in the United States. The closing of US carmakers' production facilities in the United States was creating a volatile anti-Japan sentiment among the population and the US Congress. Fearing punitive legislation if Japan did not limit its automobile exports to the United States, the Japanese government and its carmakers self-imposed a voluntary export restraint on cars headed for the United States.

Consumers in the country that imposes an export quota benefit from lower-priced products (due to their greater supply) as long as domestic producers do not curtail production. Producers in an importing country benefit because the goods of producers from the exporting country are restrained, which may allow them to increase prices. Export quotas hurt consumers in the importing nation because of reduced selection and perhaps higher prices. Yet export quotas might allow these same consumers to retain their jobs if imports were threatening to put domestic producers out of business. Again, detailed economic studies are needed to determine the winners and losers in any particular export quota case.

TARIFF-QUOTAS A hybrid form of trade restriction is called a **tariff-quota**—a lower tariff rate for a certain quantity of imports and a higher rate for quantities that exceed the quota. Imports entering a nation under a quota limit of, say, 1,000 tons are charged a 10-percent tariff. But

voluntary export restraint (VER)
Unique version of export quota that a nation imposes on its exports, usually at the request of an importing nation.

tariff-quota
Lower tariff rate for a certain quantity of imports and a higher rate for quantities that exceed the quota.

Figure 6.1

How a Tariff-Quota Works

Source: World Trade Organization Website
(www.wto.org).

subsequent imports that do not make it under the quota limit of 1,000 tons are charged a tariff of 80 percent. Figure 6.1 shows how a tariff-quota actually works. Tariff-quotas are used extensively in the trade of agricultural products. Many countries implemented tariff-quotas in 1995 after their use was permitted by the World Trade Organization, the agency that regulates trade among nations.

Embargoes

embargo

Complete ban on trade (imports and exports) in one or more products with a particular country.

A complete ban on trade (imports and exports) in one or more products with a particular country is called an **embargo**. An embargo may be placed on one or a few goods, or it may completely ban trade in all goods. It is the most restrictive nontariff trade barrier available, and it is typically applied to accomplish political goals. Embargoes can be decreed by individual nations or by supranational organizations such as the United Nations. Because they can be very difficult to enforce, embargoes are used less today than they have been in the past. One example of a total ban on trade with another country is the US embargo on trade with Cuba.

After a military coup ousted elected President Aristide of Haiti in the early 1990s, restraints were applied to force the military junta either to reinstate Aristide or to hold new elections. One restraint was an embargo by the Organization of American States. Because of difficulties in enforcing the embargo and after two years of fruitless United Nations diplomacy, the embargo failed. The United Nations then stepped in with a ban on trade in oil and weapons. Despite some smuggling through the Dominican Republic, which shares the island of Hispaniola with Haiti, the embargo was generally effective and Aristide was eventually reinstated.

Local Content Requirements

Recall from Chapter 4 that *local content requirements* are laws stipulating that producers in the domestic market must supply a specified amount of a good or service. These requirements can state that a certain portion of the end product must consist of domestically produced goods or that a certain portion of the final cost of a product must come from domestic sources.

The purpose of local content requirements is to force companies from other nations to use local resources in their production processes—particularly labor. Similar to other restraints on imports, such requirements help protect domestic producers from the price advantage of companies based in other, low-wage countries. Today, many developing countries use local content requirements as a strategy to boost industrialization. Companies often respond to local content requirements by locating production facilities inside the nation that stipulates such restrictions.

For example, although many people consider music to be the universal language, not all cultures are equally open to the world's diverse musical influences. To prevent Anglo-Saxon music from invading French culture, French law requires radio programs to include at least 40-percent French content. Such local content requirements are intended to protect both the French cultural identity and the jobs of French artists against other nations' pop culture that may wash up on French shores.

Administrative Delays

administrative delays

Regulatory controls or bureaucratic rules designed to impair the flow of imports into a country.

Regulatory controls or bureaucratic rules designed to impair the flow of imports into a country are called **administrative delays**. This nontariff barrier includes a wide range of government actions, such as requiring international air carriers to land at inconvenient airports, requiring product inspections that damage the product itself, purposely understaffing customs offices to cause unusual time delays, and requiring special licenses that take a long time to obtain. The objective of all such administrative delays for a country is to discriminate against imported products—it is, in a word, protectionism.

Currency Controls

Restrictions on the convertibility of a currency into other currencies are called **currency controls**. A company that wishes to import goods generally must pay for those goods in a common, internationally acceptable currency such as the US dollar, European Union euro, or Japanese yen. Generally, it must also obtain the currency from its nation's domestic banking system. Governments can require companies that desire such a currency to apply for a license to obtain it. Thus, a country's government can discourage imports by restricting who is allowed to convert the nation's currency into the internationally acceptable currency.

currency controls
Restrictions on the convertibility of a currency into other currencies.

Another way governments apply currency controls to reduce imports is by stipulating an exchange rate that is unfavorable to potential importers. Because the unfavorable exchange rate can force the cost of imported goods to an impractical level, many potential importers simply give up on the idea. Meanwhile, the country will often allow exporters to exchange the home currency for an international currency at favorable rates to encourage exports.

✪ **MyLab Management** Watch It Government Intervention
   a Spotlight on China and Germany

Apply what you have learned so far about government intervention in trade. If your instructor has assigned this, go to **www.pearson.com/mylab/management** to watch a video case to learn how China and Germany intervened in world trade to advance their economies and answer questions.

QUICK STUDY 3

1. Why might a government impose a tariff on a product?
2. Why might a government impose a quota on a product?
3. A stipulation that a portion of a product be sourced domestically is called a *what*?

6.4 Global Trading System

The global trading system certainly has seen its ups and downs. World trade volume reached a peak in the late 1800s, only to be devastated when the United States passed the Smoot–Hawley Act in 1930. The act represented a major shift in US trade policy from one of free trade to one of protectionism. The act set off round after round of competitive tariff increases among the major trading nations. Other nations felt that, if the United States was going to restrict its imports, they were not going to give exports from the United States free access to their domestic markets. The Smoot–Hawley Act, and the global trade wars that it helped to usher in, crippled the economies of the industrialized nations and helped spark the Great Depression. Living standards around the world were devastated throughout most of the 1930s.

6.4 Summarize the main features of the global trading system.

We begin this section by looking at early attempts to develop a global trading system—the *General Agreement on Tariffs and Trade*—and then examine its successor, the *World Trade Organization*.

General Agreement on Tariffs and Trade (GATT)

Attitudes toward free trade changed markedly in the late 1940s. For the previous 50 years, extreme economic competition among nations and national quests to increase their resources for production helped create two world wars and the worst global economic recession ever. As a result, economists and policy makers proposed that the world band together and agree on a trading system that would help to avoid similar calamities in the future. A system of multilateral agreements was developed that became known as the *General Agreement on Tariffs and Trade (GATT)*—a treaty designed to promote free trade by reducing both tariff and nontariff barriers to international trade. The GATT was formed in 1947 by 23 nations—12 developed and 11 developing economies—and came into force in January 1948.[5]

The GATT was highly successful throughout its early years. Between 1947 and 1988, it helped to reduce average tariffs from 40 percent to 5 percent and to multiply the volume of international trade by a factor of 20. But by the middle to late 1980s, rising nationalism worldwide and trade conflicts led to a nearly 50 percent increase in nontariff barriers to trade. Also, services (not covered by the original GATT) had become increasingly important and had grown to account for a much greater share of total world trade. It was clear that a revision of the treaty was necessary, and in 1986 a new round of trade talks began.

URUGUAY ROUND OF NEGOTIATIONS The ground rules of the GATT resulted from periodic "rounds" of negotiations among its members. Though relatively short and straightforward in the early years, negotiations later became protracted as issues grew more complex. Table 6.2 shows the eight completed negotiating rounds that occurred under the auspices of the GATT. Note that whereas tariffs were the only topic of the first five rounds of negotiations, other topics were added in subsequent rounds.

The Uruguay Round of GATT negotiations, begun in 1986 in Punta del Este, Uruguay (hence its name), was the largest trade negotiation in history. It was the eighth round of GATT talks within a span of 40 years and took more than 7 years to complete. The Uruguay Round made significant progress in reducing trade barriers by revising and updating the 1947 GATT. In addition to developing plans to further reduce barriers to merchandise trade, the negotiations modified the original GATT treaty in several important ways.

AGREEMENT ON SERVICES Because of the ever-increasing importance of services to the total volume of world trade, nations wanted to include GATT provisions for trade in services. The General Agreement on Trade in Services (GATS) extended the principle of nondiscrimination to cover international trade in all services, although talks regarding some sectors were more successful than were others. The problem is that, although trade in goods is a straightforward concept—goods are exported from one country and imported to another—defining exactly what a service is can be difficult. Nevertheless, the GATS created during the Uruguay Round identifies four different forms that international trade in services can take:

1. *Cross-border supply:* Services supplied from one country to another (for example, international telephone calls).
2. *Consumption abroad:* Consumers or companies using a service while in another country (for example, tourism).

TABLE 6.2 Completed Rounds of GATT

Year	Site	Number of Countries Involved	Topics Covered
1947	Geneva, Switzerland	23	Tariffs
1949	Annecy, France	13	Tariffs
1951	Torquay, England	38	Tariffs
1956	Geneva	26	Tariffs
1960–1961	Geneva (Dillon Round)	26	Tariffs
1964–1967	Geneva (Kennedy Round)	62	Tariffs, antidumping measures
1973–1979	Geneva (Tokyo Round)	102	Tariffs, nontariff measures, "framework agreements"
1986–1994	Geneva (Uruguay Round)	123	Tariffs, nontariff measures, rules, services, intellectual property, dispute settlement, investment measures, agriculture, textiles and clothing, natural resources, creation of the World Trade Organization

Source: Based on *About the WTO*, World Trade Organization website (www.wto.org).

3. *Commercial presence:* A company establishing a subsidiary in another country in order to provide a service (for example, banking operations).
4. *Presence of natural persons:* Individuals traveling to another country in order to supply a service (for example, business consultants).

Agreement on Intellectual Property Like services, products consisting entirely or largely of intellectual property are accounting for an increasing portion of international trade. Recall from Chapter 3 that *intellectual property* refers to property resulting from people's intellectual talent and abilities. Products classified as intellectual property are supposed to be legally protected by copyrights, patents, and trademarks.

Although international piracy continues, the Uruguay Round took an important step toward getting it under control. It created the Agreement on Trade-Related Aspects of Intellectual Property (TRIPS) to help standardize intellectual property rules around the world. The TRIPS Agreement acknowledges that protection of intellectual property rights benefits society because it encourages the development of new technologies and other creations. It supports the articles of both the Paris Convention and the Berne Convention (see Chapter 3) and in certain instances takes a stronger stand on intellectual property protection.

Agreement on Agricultural Subsidies Trade in agricultural products was a bone of contention for most of the world's trading partners at one time or another. Some of the more popular barriers that countries use to protect their agricultural sectors include import quotas and subsidies paid directly to farmers. The Uruguay Round addressed the main issues of agricultural tariffs and nontariff barriers in its Agreement on Agriculture. The result is increased exposure of national agricultural sectors to market forces and increased predictability in international agricultural trade. The agreement forces countries to convert all nontariff barriers to tariffs—a process called "tariffication." It then calls on developed and developing nations to cut agricultural tariffs significantly, but it places no requirements on the least-developed economies.

World Trade Organization (WTO)

Perhaps the greatest achievement of the Uruguay Round was the creation of the *World Trade Organization (WTO)*—the international organization that regulates trade among nations. The three main goals of the WTO (www.wto.org) are to help the free flow of trade, to help negotiate further opening of markets, and to settle trade disputes among its members. One key component of the WTO that was carried over from the GATT is the principle of nondiscrimination called **normal trade relations** (formerly called "most favored nation status")—a requirement that WTO members extend the same favorable terms of trade to all members that they extend to any single member. For example, if Japan were to reduce its import tariff on German automobiles to 5 percent, it must reduce the tariff it levies against automobile imports from all other WTO nations to 5 percent.

normal trade relations (formerly "most favored nation status") Requirement that WTO members extend the same favorable terms of trade to all members that they extend to any single member.

The WTO replaced the *institution* of the GATT but absorbed the GATT *agreements* (such as on services, intellectual property, and agriculture) into its own agreements. Thus, the GATT institution no longer officially exists. The WTO recognizes 164 members and 21 observers.

DISPUTE SETTLEMENT IN THE WTO The power of the WTO to settle trade disputes is what really sets it apart from the GATT. Under the GATT, nations could file a complaint against another member and a committee would investigate the matter. If appropriate, the GATT would identify the unfair trade practices, and member countries would pressure the offender to change its ways. In reality, most nations simply ignored GATT rulings, which were usually made only after very long investigative phases that sometimes lasted years.

By contrast, the various WTO agreements are essentially contracts between member nations that commit them to maintaining fair and open trade policies. When one WTO member files a complaint against another, the Dispute Settlement Body of the WTO moves into action. Decisions are to be rendered in less than one year—although within nine months if the case is urgent and 15 months if the case is appealed. The WTO dispute settlement system is not only faster and automatic, but its rulings cannot be ignored or blocked by members. Offenders must realign their trade policies according to WTO guidelines or suffer financial penalties and perhaps trade sanctions. Because of its ability to penalize offending member nations, the WTO's dispute settlement system is the spine of the global trading system.

dumping

Exporting a product at a price either lower than the price that the product normally commands in its domestic market or lower than the cost of production.

antidumping duty

Additional tariff placed on an imported product that a nation believes is being dumped on its market.

countervailing duty

Additional tariff placed on an imported product that a nation believes is receiving an unfair subsidy.

DUMPING AND THE WTO The WTO also gets involved in settling disputes that involve "dumping" and the granting of subsidies. When a company exports a product at a price that is either lower than the price normally charged in its domestic market or lower than the cost of production, it is said to be **dumping**. Charges of dumping are made (fairly or otherwise) against companies from almost every nation at one time or another and can occur in any type of industry. For example, Western European plastic producers considered retaliating against Asian competitors whose prices were substantially lower in European markets than at home. More recently, US steel producers and their powerful union charged that steelmakers in Brazil, Japan, and Russia were dumping steel on the US market at low prices. The problem arose as those nations tried to improve their economies through increased exporting of all products, including steel.

The WTO cannot punish the country in which the company accused of dumping is based because dumping is an act by a company, not a country. The WTO can respond only to the actions of a country that retaliates against a company that is dumping. The WTO allows a nation to retaliate against dumping if it can show that dumping is actually occurring, can calculate the damage to its own companies, and can show that the damage is significant. The normal way a country retaliates is to charge an **antidumping duty**—an additional tariff placed on an imported product that a nation believes is being dumped on its market. But such measures must expire within five years of the time they are initiated unless a country can show that circumstances warrant their continuation. A large number of antidumping cases have been brought before the WTO in recent years.

SUBSIDIES AND THE WTO Governments often retaliate when the competitiveness of their companies is threatened by a subsidy that another country pays its own domestic producers. Like antidumping measures, nations can retaliate against product(s) that receive an unfair subsidy by charging a **countervailing duty**—an additional tariff placed on an imported product that a nation believes is receiving an unfair subsidy. Unlike dumping, because payment of a subsidy is an action by a country, the WTO regulates the actions of the government that reacts to the subsidy as well as those of the government that originally paid the subsidy.

DOHA ROUND OF NEGOTIATIONS The WTO launched a new round of negotiations in Doha, Qatar, in late 2001. The renewed negotiations were designed to lower trade barriers further and to help poor nations in particular. Agricultural subsidies that rich countries pay to their own farmers are worth $1 billion per day—more than six times the value of their combined aid budgets to poor nations. Because 70 percent of the exports of poor nations are agricultural products and textiles, wealthy nations had intended to open these and other labor-intensive industries further. Poor nations were encouraged to reduce tariffs among themselves and were to receive help from rich nations in integrating themselves into the global trading system.

The Doha round was to conclude by the end of 2004 but negotiations are proceeding very slowly. By the middle of 2017 members had made limited progress on a late 2013 deal to improve "trade facilitation" by reducing red tape at borders and setting standards for customs and the movement of goods internationally. Although the agreement marked the first significant achievement for the Doha round, no agreement was reached on agricultural trade issues, tariffs, or quotas.[6]

WTO AND THE ENVIRONMENT Steady gains in global trade and rapid industrialization in many developing and emerging economies have generated environmental concerns among both governments and special interest groups. Of concern to many people are levels of carbon dioxide emissions—the principal greenhouse gas believed to contribute to global warming. Most carbon dioxide emissions are created from the burning of fossil fuels and the manufacture of cement.

The WTO has no separate agreement that deals with environmental issues. The WTO explicitly states that it is not to become a global environmental agency responsible for setting environmental standards. It leaves such tasks to national governments and the many intergovernmental organizations that already exist for such purposes. The WTO works alongside existing international agreements on the environment, including the Montreal Protocol for protection of the ozone layer, the Basel Convention on international trade or transport of hazardous waste, and the Convention on International Trade in Endangered Species.

Nevertheless, the preamble to the agreement that established the WTO does mention the objectives of environmental protection and sustainable development. The WTO also has an internal committee called the Committee on Trade and Environment. The committee's responsibility is to study the relationship between trade and the environment and to recommend possible changes in the WTO trade agreements.

In addition, the WTO does take explicit positions on some environmental issues related to trade. Although the WTO supports national efforts at labeling "environmentally friendly" products as such, it states that labeling requirements or policies cannot discriminate against the products of other WTO members. Also, the WTO supports policies of the least developed countries that require full disclosure of potentially hazardous products entering their markets for reasons of public health and environmental damage.

QUICK STUDY 4

1. The first system of multilateral agreements to promote free trade was called *what*?
2. What are the main goals of the World Trade Organization (WTO)?
3. Exporting a product at a price that is lower than that normally charged domestically or one that is lower than production costs can expose a firm to charges of *what*?

BOTTOM LINE FOR BUSINESS

Despite the theoretical benefits of free trade, nations do not simply throw open their doors to trade and force their domestic businesses to sink or swim. This chapter explained why governments protect their industries and how they go about it. The WTO tries to strike a balance between national desires for protection and international desires for free trade.

Implications of Trade Protection

Free trade allows firms to move production to locations that maximize efficiency. Yet, government interference in the free flow of trade has implications for production efficiency and firm strategy. *Subsidies* often encourage complacency on the part of companies receiving them because they discourage competition. Subsidies can be thought of as a redistribution of wealth in society whereby international firms not receiving subsidies are at a disadvantage. Unsubsidized firms either must cut production and distribution costs or must differentiate in some way to justify a higher selling price.

Import tariffs raise the cost of an imported good and make domestically produced goods more attractive to consumers. But because a tariff can create inefficient domestic producers, deteriorating competitiveness may offset the benefits of import tariffs. Companies trying to enter markets having high import tariffs often produce within that market. *Import quotas* help domestic producers maintain market share and prices by restraining competitive forces. Domestic producers protected by the quota win because the market is protected. Other producers that require the import subjected to a quota lose because they will need to pay more for their intermediate products or locate production outside the market imposing the quota.

Local content requirements protect domestic producers from producers based in low-cost countries. A firm trying to sell to a market imposing local content requirements may have no alternative but to produce locally. The objective of *administrative delays* is to discriminate against imported products, but it can discourage efficiency. *Currency controls* can require firms to apply for a license to obtain an internationally accepted currency. The nation thus discourages imports by restricting who is allowed to obtain such a currency to pay for imports. A government may also block imports by stipulating an exchange rate that is unfavorable to potential importers. The unfavorable exchange rate forces the cost of imported goods to an impractical level. The same country then often stipulates an exchange rate that is favorable for exporters.

Government subsidies are typically paid for by levying taxes across the economy. Whether subsidies help a nation's people long term is questionable, and they may actually harm a nation. Import tariffs also hurt consumers because they raise the price of imports and protect domestic firms that may raise prices. Import quotas hurt consumers because they lessen competition, boost prices, and decrease selection. Protection tends to lessen the long-term gains a people can obtain from free trade.

Implications of the Global Trading System

Development of the global trading system benefits international companies by promoting free trade through the reduction of both tariffs and nontariff barriers to international trade. The GATT treaty was successful in its early years, and its revision significantly improved the climate for trade. Average tariffs on merchandise trade were reduced and subsidies for agricultural products were lowered. Firms also benefited from an agreement that extended the principle of nondiscrimination to cover trade in services. The revision of the GATT also clearly defined intellectual property rights—giving protection to copyrights, trademarks and service marks, and patents.

(continued)

This encourages firms to develop new products and processes because they know their rights to the property will be protected.

Creation of the WTO is also good for international firms because the various WTO agreements commit member nations to maintaining fair and open trade policies. Both domestic and international firms based in relatively poor nations should benefit most from future rounds of trade negotiations. Firms from poor nations that export agricultural products and textiles will benefit if wealthy nations reduce barriers to imports in these sectors. Companies based in poor countries should also benefit from better cooperation among poor countries and their further integration into the global trading system.

MyLab Management

Go to **www.pearson.com/mylab/management** to complete the problems marked with this icon .

Chapter Summary

LO6.1   Explain why governments sometimes intervene in trade.
- *Political* reasons for trade intervention include to: (a) protect jobs, (b) preserve national security, (c) respond to other nations' unfair trade practices, and (d) gain influence over other nations.
- *Economic* reasons include to: (a) protect infant industries from global competition until they are sufficiently competitive, and (b) promote a strategic trade policy in which companies are assisted in taking advantage of economies of scale and being first movers in their industries.
- The most common *cultural* reason for trade intervention is protection of national identity. Unwanted cultural influence in a nation can cause great distress and force a government to block imports that it believes are harmful.

LO6.2   Outline the instruments that governments use to promote trade.
- A *subsidy* is financial assistance to domestic producers in the form of cash payments, low-interest loans, tax breaks, product price supports, and other forms. Subsidies can fend off international competitors, although critics say they amount to corporate welfare.
- *Export financing* includes loans at below-market interest rates, loans that are otherwise unavailable, and *loan guarantees* that a government will repay a loan if a firm defaults.
- A *foreign trade zone (FTZ)* allows merchandise to pass through a geographic region with lower customs duties (taxes) and/or fewer customs procedures.
- *Special government agencies* organize international trips for trade officials and businesspeople and create offices abroad to promote home country exports.

LO6.3   Describe the instruments that governments use to restrict trade.
- A *tariff* is a government tax levied on a product that enters, transits across, or leaves a country. An import tariff can be an *ad valorem tariff*, a *specific tariff*, or a *compound tariff*.
- *Quotas* restrict the amount of a good that can enter or leave a country during a certain period of time. *Import quotas* protect domestic producers. *Export quotas* maintain adequate supplies domestically or raise the global price of a product.
- An embargo completely bans trade with a country. *Local content requirements* stipulate that a good or service be supplied by domestic producers. Imports can also be discouraged with *administrative delays* or *currency controls* (restrictions on currency convertibility).

LO6.4   Summarize the main features of the global trading system.
- The *General Agreement on Tariffs and Trade (GATT)* treaty promoted free trade by reducing tariff and nontariff barriers. The *Uruguay Round* of GATT negotiations (a) covered trade in services, (b) defined intellectual property rights, (c) reduced trade barriers in agriculture, and (d) created the *World Trade Organization (WTO)*.
- The three goals of the WTO are to help the free flow of trade, to help negotiate further opening of markets, and to settle trade disputes among its members.

- A key component of the WTO is the principle of nondiscrimination, called *normal trade relations,* which requires WTO members to treat all members equally.
- *Dumping* is said to occur if a company exports a product at a price either lower than the price it normally charges in its domestic market or lower than the cost of production.

Key Terms

administrative delays (p. 190)

ad valorem tariff (p. 188)

antidumping duty (p. 194)

compound tariff (p. 188)

countervailing duty (p. 194)

currency controls (p. 191)

dumping (p. 194)

embargo (p. 190)

foreign trade zone (FTZ) (p. 186)

free trade (p. 180)

normal trade relations (p. 193)

quota (p. 188)

specific tariff (p. 188)

subsidy (p. 185)

tariff (p. 187)

tariff-quota (p. 189)

voluntary export restraint (VER) (p. 189)

✪ TALK ABOUT IT 1

Most countries create a list of "hostile" countries that require exporters to obtain special permission before the export is allowed to proceed.

6-1. Which countries and products would you place on such a list for your nation? Explain.

6-2. On which countries' lists do you think your nation would appear? Explain.

✪ TALK ABOUT IT 2

Two students are discussing environmentalists' claims that trade harms the environment. One student says, "Sure, there may be pollution effects, but they're a small price to pay for a higher standard of living." The other student agrees, saying, "Yeah, those 'tree-huggers' are always exaggerating those effects anyway. Who cares if a toad in the Amazon goes extinct?"

6-3. What arguments can you offer to counter these students' opinions?

6-4. What specific actions could firms take to ensure that trade does not harm the environment?

Ethical Challenge

You are the CEO of a chain of automobile dealerships across Australia. Australia imposes a 5 percent tariff on all imported automobiles. Since you only sell new imported cars, it is in your interest that this tariff is removed. The Australian Minister for Transport and Infrastructure has suggested that the idea of the removal of the tariff has some merit. The Australian Automobile Association supports the move on the grounds that Australian drivers would have cheaper access to newer and safer automobiles. His preference is for the government to offer subsidies to consumers to make cars cheaper. Others support the idea of a financial incentive or subsidy to be provided to automobile buyers, arguing that the tariff is a barrier to Australian buyers obtaining imported automobiles with safer technology that can prevent road deaths.

6-5. Research the automobile tariff situation in Australia. Is the tariff really a barrier to safer automobiles?

6-6. What is the case for a country such as Australia to impose a tariff on imported automobiles?

6-7. How has the protection from tariffs affected the domestic automobile manufacturing industry?

Teaming Up

In groups of three or four, take the role of board members of a global business faced with increasingly difficult trading conditions in a country you have been operating in for some years. It is becoming increasingly apparent that the country's government is trying to force you out of the market for political and economic reasons.

6-8. They are demanding that you incorporate a minimum of 40 percent local content in your products. Discuss what this means.

6-9. They are blaming staff shortages in customs for import delays. What are they doing?

6-10. What are your general recommendations to the business in this situation?

✪ Market Entry Strategy Project

This exercise corresponds to the *MESP* online simulation. For the country your team is researching, integrate your answers to the following questions into your completed *MESP* report.

6-11. To what extent does the national government intervene in trade?

6-12. What are some of its political, economic, or cultural motives for intervention?

6-13. What instruments does the country use to promote exports?

6-14. What instruments does it use to restrict imports?

6-15. Does the nation maintain a free trade zone within its borders?

6-16. Has the country filed a complaint with the WTO against another nation?

MyLab Management

✪ Go to **www.pearson.com/mylab/management** for the following assisted-graded writing questions:

6-17. Suppose you are the president of a sugar company based in southern Florida. Poor sugar harvests in the Caribbean Islands means your firm is struggling to meet demand and prices are rising. Cuba is having a bumper sugar harvest but you cannot import from Cuba because of the Helms–Burton Act and the US embargo on Cuba. A powerful US senator from Florida serves on a committee in Washington, DC, that is reviewing the embargo. What arguments do you make to your senator to eliminate the embargo?

6-18. Imagine that a majority of people in your country believe international trade harms their wages and jobs, and that your task is to change their minds. How would you go about educating people about the benefits of trade?

The New Protectionism

Economic crisis is well known in the literature for provoking a renewal of aggressive measures in international trade, and sometimes (as in the Great Depression of 1929) even for provoking commercial wars. Amid the global economic and financial crisis that began in 2008, many feared that one of its main consequences would be the breaking down of WTO rules and even the start of trade wars among some of the countries worst hit by the crisis. However, things have turned out to be more complicated than that.

Although the economic slowdown and rising levels of unemployment in many countries have led several governments to try to protect some sectors with a wide array of protectionist measures, they have done so in an unexpected way. This resurgent protectionism, also labeled "creeping" or "murky protectionism," is characterized by a number of factors, the first being fundamentally different from what was experienced during the Great Depression. This is because, with very few exceptions, the protective measures now introduced are not in violation of agreements taken multilaterally in the WTO; therefore, some countries may double or even triple import duties without incurring penalties, given that the threshold negotiated under the WTO framework is much higher than what is normally imposed.

Another important difference from 1929—and the effect of the recession on international trade—is the greater prevalence of vertical trade, or trade between countries, which creates a chain of production across various borders. The existence of these close links in the cycle of production of many countries means that those with greater openness cannot increase duties indiscriminately without damaging domestic companies. Vertical trade and reduction in countries' demand could be one reason for the severity and speed of international decline in trade flows and perhaps also the motivation that has most helped to keep protectionist pressures under control. Once the value chain crumbles, as it certainly could in the event of renewed difficulties to export, recreating the links and the infrastructure would be expensive and would risk slowing down the global recovery further.

Between October 2008 and February 2009, 78 procedures were initiated, including 66 measures restrictive to trade, of which 47 entered into force. Only a third of these measures were related to increased tariffs, in some cases taking the form of nontariff restrictions such as export bans. These measures are as follows:

1. *Import duty (imposition of new ones or increasing existing ones) imposed on a wide range of products.* However, this traditional instrument has been used in only a minority of cases, whereas others were far more common.

2. *Import ban.* This is the kind of measure that so far has hit emerging countries—China, for instance—more seriously. A good example is represented by the six-month ban imposed by the Indian government in January 2009 on Chinese toys, causing protests not only by Chinese exporters but even by the domestic Indian industry due to the huge increase in retail prices that this measure provoked.

3. *Nontariff barriers.* This kind of measure has generally been fairly popular and is now applied extensively by such countries as Argentina and Indonesia.

4. *Subsidies to industries in crisis.* Subsidies have been granted virtually everywhere, although the details and the areas concerned have been very different among countries. Some examples are the EU subsidies on food products, including butter, cheese, and milk powder, and increased tax rebates on exports from China and India. China in 2008 and 2009 revised tax rebates upward seven times on more than 2,600 products.

5. *Increase in antidumping procedures.* The crisis is evident when considering the antidumping procedures submitted to the WTO. According to WTO data, there were a total of 208 antidumping procedures in the year 2008 alone, an increase of 31 percent compared with 2007. Data in 2009 and 2010 showed the same worrying upward trend.

Although not all the procedures started have led to the imposition of duties, what seems obvious is the need for a multilateral review and for the establishment of more binding and strict rules, without which it is likely that their use will become more generalized. The real danger here is that a mechanism created to stop exceptional cases of unfair competition is instead used as weapons of trade policy and retaliation.

Thinking Globally

6-19. One of the dangers of the new protectionism is its impact on the vertical integration of companies and its effects on the global supply chain. Can you figure out the economic impact of the new protectionism on global corporations such as Apple, which manufactures its components in a series of different countries and then assembles them in a unique product? How can high tariff barriers change this system?

6-20. The WTO website publishes updated figures about antidumping procedures every six months. Which countries are more exposed to antidumping procedures being brought against them? Why, in your opinion?

6-21. Important, comparatively recent, features of protectionism measures are the so-called voluntary restrictive measures, in which a country agrees to limit its exports voluntarily. In which way are these measures different from the old, more traditional ones?

Sources: "Trade Protection: Incipient but Worrisome Trends," *World Bank Trade Notes,* no. 37 (http://web.worldbank.org/WBSITE/EXTERNAL/TOPICS/ TRADE/0, contentMDK:20115046~menuPK:267122~pagePK: 148956~piPK: 216618~theSitePK:239071,00.html), March 2, 2009; S. Paladini, "Il Nuovo Protezionismo," *Italian Foreign Trade Report 2008–2009,* Italian Trade Commission, 2009; R. Baldwin and S. Evenett, *The Collapse of Global Trade, Murky Protectionism, and the Crisis: Recommendations for the G20,* March 5, 2009, available at www.VoxEU.org; C. Bown, (2009) "Protectionism is on the Rise: Antidumping Import Investigations," Chapter 11 in *The Collapse of Global Trade, Murky Protectionism, and the Crisis: Recommendations for the G20,* March 5, 2009, available at www.VoxEU.org.

Chapter Seven

Foreign Direct Investment

Learning Objectives

After studying this chapter, you should be able to:

7.1 Describe the worldwide pattern of foreign direct investment (FDI).

7.2 Summarize each theory that attempts to explain why FDI occurs.

7.3 Outline the important management issues in the FDI decision.

7.4 Explain why governments intervene in FDI.

7.5 Describe the policy instruments governments use to promote and restrict FDI.

A Look Back

Chapter 6 explained the political economy of trade in goods and services. We explored the motives and instruments of government intervention. We also examined the global trading system and how it promotes free trade.

A Look at This Chapter

This chapter examines another significant form of international business: foreign direct investment (FDI). We explore the patterns of FDI and the theories on which it is based. We also learn why and how governments intervene in FDI activity.

A Look Ahead

Chapter 8 explores the trend toward greater regional integration of national economies. We explore the benefits of closer economic cooperation and examine prominent regional trading blocs around the world.

MyLab Management

✪ IMPROVE YOUR GRADE!

When you see this icon ✪, visit **www.pearson.com/mylab/management** for activities that are applied, personalized, and offer immediate feedback.

Das Auto

FRANKFURT, Germany—The Volkswagen Group (www.vw.com) owns 10 of the most prestigious and best-known automotive brands in the world, including Audi, Bentley, Bugatti, Lamborghini, Porsche, and Volkswagen. From its 48 production facilities worldwide, the company produces and sells around 8 million cars annually to more than 150 countries. Volkswagen is the top-selling manufacturer in South America and China and has been active in China since 1985. In fact, around 30 percent of VW's total sales come from China. Shown here a young couple enjoys their classic VW bus.

Volkswagen also has ambitious goals for its US expansion. It is adapting designs to domestic tastes, cutting prices, and adding inexpensive production capacity. VW uses a *modular strategy* in production that lets it use the same key components in 16 different vehicles and seven million units across its brands. The strategy cuts product development and parts costs by 20 percent and reduces production time by 30 percent. And as part of its punishment for falsifying the mileage its diesel cars get, VW will invest $2 billion in the United States

Dmytro Sobokar/123RF.com

by the year 2028 in electric vehicle charging stations and in promoting the use of electric vehicles.

Volkswagen, like companies everywhere, received plenty of help in getting where it is today. Until recently, Volkswagen received special protection from its own legislation known as the VW Law. The law gave the German state of Lower Saxony, which owns 20.1 percent of Volkswagen, the power to block any takeover attempt that threatened local jobs and the economy. Volkswagen's special treatment lies in the close ties between government and management in Germany and its importance to the nation's economy, where it employs tens of thousands of people. As you read this chapter, consider all the issues that affect the foreign investment decisions of companies.[1]

Many early trade theories were created at a time when most production factors (such as labor, financial capital, capital equipment, and land or natural resources) either could not be moved or could not be moved easily across national borders. But today, all those production factors except land are internationally mobile and flow across borders to wherever they are needed. Financial capital is readily available from international financial institutions to finance corporate expansion, and whole factories can be picked up and moved to another country. Even labor is more mobile than in years past, although many barriers restrict the complete mobility of labor.

foreign direct investment (FDI)

Purchase of physical assets or a significant amount of the ownership (stock) of a company in an-other country to gain a measure of management control.

International flows of capital are at the core of **foreign direct investment (FDI)**—the purchase of physical assets or a significant amount of the ownership (stock) of a company in another country in order to gain a measure of management control. But there is wide disagreement on what exactly constitutes FDI. Nations set different thresholds at which they classify an international capital flow as FDI. The US Commerce Department sets the threshold at 10 percent of stock ownership in a company abroad, but most other governments set it at anywhere from 10 to 25 percent. By contrast, an investment that does not involve obtaining a degree of control in a company is called a **portfolio investment**.

portfolio investment

Investment that does not involve obtaining a degree of control in a company.

In this chapter, we examine the importance of FDI to the operations of international companies. We begin by exploring the growth of FDI in recent years and investigating its sources and destinations. We then look at several theories that attempt to explain FDI flows. Next, we turn our attention to several important management issues that arise in most decisions about whether a company should undertake FDI. This chapter closes by discussing the reasons why governments encourage or restrict FDI and the methods they use to accomplish these goals.

7.1 Pattern of Foreign Direct Investment

7.1 Describe the worldwide pattern of foreign direct investment (FDI).

Just as international trade displays a distinct pattern (see Chapter 5), so too does FDI. In this section, we first look at the factors that have propelled growth in FDI over the past decade. We then turn our attention to the destinations and sources of FDI.

Ups and Downs of FDI

FDI inflows grew around 20 percent per year in the first half of the 1990s and expanded about 40 percent per year in the second half of the decade. As shown in Figure 7.1, global FDI inflows averaged $548 billion annually between 1994 and 1999. FDI inflows peaked at around $1.4 trillion in 2000 and then slowed. FDI inflows benefitted from strong economic performance and high corporate profits in many countries between 2004 and 2007, at which point it reached an all-time record of more than $1.9 trillion.

Global recession meant declining FDI inflows in 2008 and 2009. FDI inflows climbed higher in 2010 and 2011; then dipped in 2012, 2013, and 2014; and then rose to nearly $1.8 trillion in 2015 as the world emerged from recession. Significant uncertainty surrounds

Figure 7.1

Yearly Foreign Direct Investment Inflows

Source: Based on *World Investment Report* (Geneva, Switzerland: UNCTAD), various years.

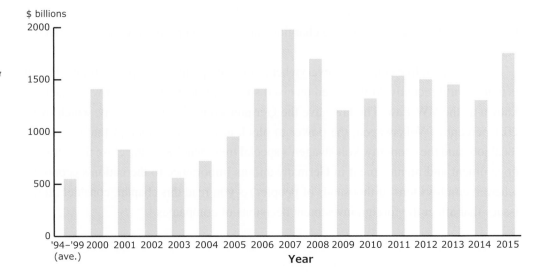

medium-term FDI flows, but the long-term trend points toward greater FDI inflows world-wide. The two main drivers of FDI flows are *globalization* and international *mergers and acquisitions*.

GLOBALIZATION Recall from Chapter 6 that barriers to trade were not being reduced years ago, and new, creative barriers seemed to be popping up in many nations. This presented a problem for companies that were trying to export their products to markets around the world. A wave of FDI began as many companies entered promising markets to get around growing trade barriers. Then the Uruguay Round of GATT negotiations created renewed determination to further reduce barriers to trade. As countries lowered their trade barriers, companies realized that they could now produce in the most efficient and productive locations and simply export to their markets worldwide. This set off another wave of FDI flows into low-cost emerging markets. The forces behind globalization are, therefore, part of the reason for long-term growth in FDI.

Increasing globalization is also causing a growing number of international companies from emerging markets to undertake FDI. For example, companies from Taiwan began investing heavily in other nations two decades ago. Acer (www.acer.com), headquartered in Singapore but founded in Taiwan, manufactures personal computers and computer components. Just 20 years after it opened for business, Acer had spawned 10 subsidiaries worldwide and had become an industry player in many emerging markets.

MERGERS AND ACQUISITIONS The number of *mergers and acquisitions (M&As)* and their rising values over time also underlie long-term growth in FDI. In fact, cross-border M&As are the main vehicle through which companies undertake FDI. Companies based in developed nations have historically been the main participants behind cross-border M&As. Yet, firms from emerging markets are accounting for an ever greater share of global M&A activity. The value of cross-border M&As peaked in 2000 at around $1.2 trillion (see Figure 7.2), accounting for about 3.7 percent of the market capitalization of all stock exchanges worldwide. Reasons previously mentioned for the ups and downs of FDI inflows also cause the pattern we see in cross-border M&A deals. After three years of falling FDI, the value of cross-border M&As rose to around $1 trillion by 2007. M&A activity then cooled in 2008 and then fell significantly in 2009 due to the global recession. The value of cross-border M&A activity then fluctuated for several years before climbing back to $721 billion by 2015.

Many cross-border M&A deals are driven by the desire of companies to:

- Get a foothold in a new geographic market.
- Increase a firm's global competitiveness.
- Fill gaps in companies' product lines in a global industry.
- Reduce costs of research and development, production, distribution, and so forth.

Entrepreneurs and small businesses also play a role in the expansion of FDI inflows. There is no data on the portion of FDI contributed by small businesses, but we know from anecdotal evidence that these companies are engaged in FDI. Unhindered by many of the constraints of a large company, entrepreneurs investing in other markets often demonstrate an inspiring can-do spirit mixed with ingenuity and bravado. Another advantage individuals can possess is an understanding

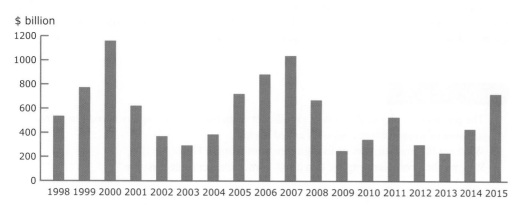

Figure 7.2

Value of Cross-Border Mergers and Acquisitions

Source: Based on *World Investment Report* (Geneva, Switzerland: UNCTAD), various years.

CULTURE MATTERS   The Cowboy of Manchuria

Tom Kirkwood turned his dream of introducing his grandfather's taffy to China into a fast-growing business. Kirkwood's story—his hassles and hustling—provides some lessons on the purest form of global investing. The basics that small investors in China can follow are as rudimentary as they get. Find a product that's easy to make, widely popular, and cheap to sell, and then choose the least expensive, investor-friendliest place to make it.

Kirkwood, whose family runs the Shawnee Inn, a ski and golf resort in Shawnee-on-Delaware, Pennsylvania, decided to make candy in Manchuria—China's gritty, heavily populated, industrial northeast. Chinese people often give individually wrapped candies as a gift, and Kirkwood reckoned that China's rising, increasingly prosperous urbanites would have a lucrative sweet tooth. Kirkwood realized that he could not beat M&Ms or Reese's Pieces at their own game. But he did not want to produce no-name candy to be sold in bulk bins at the grocery store, either. He wanted to find a niche and own it, because a niche in China can be worth an entire market in another country.

Kirkwood concluded early on that he wanted to do business in China. In the mid-1980s after prep school, he spent a year in Taiwan and China learning Chinese and working in a Shanghai engineering company. The experience gave him a taste for adventure capitalism on the frontier of China's economic development. Using $400,000 of Kirkwood's family money, Kirkwood and his friend Peter Moustakerski bought equipment and rented a factory in Shenyang, a city of six million people in the heart of Manchuria. Roads and rail transport were convenient, and wages were low. The local government seemed amenable to a 100 percent foreign-owned factory, and the Shenyang Shawnee Cowboy Food Company was born.

Although it's a small operation, it now has 89 employees and is growing. Kirkwood is determined to succeed selling his candies with names such as Longhorn Bars. As he boarded a flight to Beijing for a meeting with a distributor recently, Kirkwood realized he had a bag full of candy. He offered one to a flight attendant. When lunch is over, he vowed, "Everybody on this plane will know Cowboy Candy."

---

of the local language and culture of the market being entered. For a day-in-the-life look at a young entrepreneur who is realizing his dreams in China, see the Culture Matters feature, titled "The Cowboy of Manchuria."

Worldwide Flows of FDI

Driving FDI growth are more than 100,000 multinational companies with more than 900,000 affiliates abroad, roughly half of which are in developing countries.[2] In 2014, for the first time ever, developing countries attracted greater FDI inflows than did developed countries. In 2014, FDI inflows to developing countries were around 55 percent ($699 billion) of total world FDI inflows ($1.28 trillion). By comparison, developed countries accounted for 41 percent ($522 billion) of total global FDI inflows. The remaining roughly four percent of global FDI went into countries across Southeast Europe in various stages of transition from communism to capitalism. FDI inflows reverted back to their traditional pattern in 2015 whereby developing economies attracted less FDI (44 percent of the world total) than developed nations did (55 percent).

Among developed countries, European Union (EU) nations, the United States, and Japan account for the majority of world FDI inflows. Behind the large FDI figure for the EU is consolidation among large national competitors and further efforts at EU regional integration.

Developing nations had varying experiences with FDI in 2015. Inflows to developing nations in Asia were $541 billion, with China attracting $136 billion of that total. India, the largest recipient on the Asian subcontinent, had inflows of nearly $44 billion. Elsewhere, all of Africa drew in $54 billion of FDI in 2015, or about 2 percent of the world's total. FDI flows into Latin America and the Caribbean were $168 billion, or nearly 10 percent of the total world FDI. It is important to note that FDI *outflows from* developing Asian nations is also rising, coinciding with the rise of these nations' own global competitors.

QUICK STUDY 1

1. The purchase of physical assets or significant ownership of a company abroad to gain a measure of management control is called a *what*?
2. What are the main drivers of foreign direct investment flows?
3. Why might a company engage in a cross-border merger or acquisition?

7.2 Theories of Foreign Direct Investment

So far, we have examined the flows of FDI, but we have not investigated explanations for why FDI occurs. Let's now investigate the four main theories that attempt to explain why companies engage in FDI.

7.2 Summarize each theory that attempts to explain why FDI occurs.

International Product Life Cycle

Although we introduced it in Chapter 5 in the context of international trade, the international product life cycle is also used to explain FDI.[3] The **international product life cycle** theory states that a company begins by exporting its product and then later undertakes FDI as a product moves through its life cycle. In the *new product stage*, a good is produced in the home country because of uncertain domestic demand and to keep production close to the research department that developed the product. In the *maturing product stage*, the company directly invests in production facilities in countries where demand is great enough to warrant its own production facilities. In the final *standardized product stage*, increased competition creates pressures to reduce production costs. In response, a company builds production capacity in low-cost developing nations to serve its markets around the world.

international product life cycle
Theory stating that a company begins by exporting its product and then later undertakes foreign direct investment as the product moves through its life cycle.

Despite its conceptual appeal, the international product life cycle theory is limited in its power to explain why companies choose FDI over other forms of market entry. A local firm in the target market could pay for (license) the right to use the special assets needed to manufacture a particular product. In this way, a company could avoid the additional risks associated with direct investments in the market. The theory also fails to explain why firms choose FDI over exporting activities. It might be less expensive to serve a market abroad by increasing output at the home country factory rather than by building additional capacity within the target market.

The theory explains why the FDI of some firms follows the international product life cycle of their products. But it does not explain why other market entry modes are inferior or less advantageous options.

Market Imperfections (Internalization)

A market that is said to operate at peak efficiency (prices are as low as they can possibly be) and where goods are readily and easily available is said to be a *perfect market*. But perfect markets are rarely, if ever, seen in business because of factors that cause a breakdown in the efficient operation of an industry—called *market imperfections*. **Market imperfections** theory states that when an imperfection in the market makes a transaction less efficient than it could be, a company will undertake FDI to internalize the transaction and thereby remove the imperfection. There are two market imperfections that are relevant to this discussion—trade barriers and specialized knowledge.

market imperfections
Theory stating that when an imperfection in the market makes a transaction less efficient than it could be, a company will undertake foreign direct investment to internalize the transaction and thereby remove the imperfection.

TRADE BARRIERS Tariffs are a common form of market imperfection in international business. For example, the North American Free Trade Agreement stipulates that a sufficient portion of a product's content must originate within Canada, Mexico, or the United States for the product to avoid tariff charges when it is imported to any of these three markets. That is why a large number of Korean manufacturers invested in production facilities in Tijuana, Mexico, just south of Mexico's border with the state of California. By investing in production facilities in Mexico, Korean companies were able to skirt the North American tariffs that would have been imposed if they were to export goods from Korean factories. The presence of a market imperfection (tariffs) caused those companies to undertake FDI.

SPECIALIZED KNOWLEDGE The unique competitive advantage of a company sometimes consists of specialized knowledge. This knowledge could be the technical expertise of engineers or the special marketing abilities of managers. When the knowledge is technical expertise, companies can charge a fee to companies in other countries for use of the knowledge in producing the same or a similar product. But when a company's specialized knowledge is embodied in its employees, the only way to exploit a market opportunity in another nation may be to undertake FDI.

The possibility that a company will create a future competitor by charging others a fee for access to its knowledge is another market imperfection that encourages FDI. Rather than trade a short-term gain (the fee charged another company) for a long-term loss (lost competitiveness),

At one time, Boeing aircraft were made entirely in the United States. Today, Boeing can source its landing gear doors from Northern Ireland, wings from Japan, outboard wing flaps from Italy, wing tip assemblies from Korea, and rudders from Australia. The parts are all shipped to Everett, Washington, in the United States for assembly.

Shutterbas/123RF.com

a company will prefer to undertake investment. For example, as Japan rebuilt its industries following the Second World War, many Japanese companies paid Western firms for access to the special technical knowledge embodied in their products. Those Japanese companies became adept at revising and improving many of these technologies and became leaders in their industries, including electronics and automobiles.

Eclectic Theory

eclectic theory
Theory stating that firms undertake foreign direct investment when the features of a particular location combine with ownership and internalization advantages to make a location appealing for investment.

The **eclectic theory** states that firms undertake FDI when the features of a particular location combine with ownership and internalization advantages to make a location appealing for investment.[4] A *location advantage* is the advantage of locating a particular economic activity in a specific location because of the characteristics (natural or acquired) of that location.[5] These advantages have historically been natural resources such as oil in the Middle East, timber in Canada, or copper in Chile. But the advantage can also be an acquired one, such as a productive workforce. An *ownership advantage* refers to company ownership of some special asset, such as brand recognition, technical knowledge, or management ability. An *internalization advantage* is one that arises from internalizing a business activity rather than leaving it to a relatively inefficient market. The eclectic theory states that when all of these advantages are present, a company will undertake FDI.

Market Power

market power
Theory stating that a firm tries to establish a dominant market presence in an industry by undertaking foreign direct investment.

Firms often seek the greatest amount of power possible relative to rivals in their industries. The **market power** theory states that a firm tries to establish a dominant market presence in an industry by undertaking FDI. The benefit of market power is greater profit because the firm is far better able to dictate the cost of its inputs and/or the price of its output.

vertical integration
Extension of company activities into stages of production that provide a firm's inputs (backward integration) or that absorb its output (forward integration).

One way a company can achieve market power (or dominance) is through **vertical integration**—the extension of company activities into stages of production that provide a firm's inputs (*backward integration*) or that absorb its output (*forward integration*). Sometimes a company can effectively control the world supply of an input needed by its industry if it has the resources or ability to integrate backward into supplying that input. Companies may also be able to achieve a great deal of market power if they can integrate forward to increase control over output. For example, they could perhaps make investments in distribution to leapfrog channels of distribution that are tightly controlled by competitors.

QUICK STUDY 2

1. What imperfections are relevant to the discussion of market imperfections theory?
2. Location, ownership, and internalization advantages combine in which FDI theory?
3. Which FDI theory depicts a firm establishing a dominant market presence in an industry?

7.3 Management Issues and Foreign Direct Investment

Decisions about whether to engage in FDI involve several important issues regarding management of the company and its market. Some of these issues are grounded in the inner workings of firms that undertake FDI, such as the control desired over operations abroad or the firm's cost of production. Others are related to the market and the industry in which a firm competes, such as the preferences of customers or the actions of rivals. Let's now examine each of these important issues.

7.3 Outline the important management issues in the FDI decision.

Control

Many companies investing abroad are greatly concerned with controlling the activities that occur in the local market. Perhaps the company wants to be certain that its product is being marketed in the same way in the local market as it is at home. Or maybe it wants to ensure that the selling price remains the same in both markets. Some companies try to maintain ownership of a large portion of the local operation, say, even up to 100 percent, in the belief that greater ownership gives them greater control.

Yet for a variety of reasons, even complete ownership does not *guarantee* control. For example, the local government might intervene and require a company to hire some local managers rather than bringing them all in from the home office. Companies may need to prove a scarcity of skilled local managerial talent before the government will let them bring managers in from the home country. Governments might also require that all goods produced in the local facility be exported so that they do not compete with products of the country's domestic firms.

PARTNERSHIP REQUIREMENTS Many companies have strict policies regarding how much ownership they take in firms abroad because of the importance of maintaining control. In the past, IBM (www.ibm.com) strictly required that the home office own 100 percent of all international subsidiaries. But companies must sometimes abandon such policies if a country demands shared ownership in return for market access.

Some governments saw shared ownership requirements as a way to shield their workers from exploitation and their industries from domination by large international firms. Companies would sometimes sacrifice control in order to pursue a market opportunity, but frequently they did not. Most countries today do not take such a hard-line stance and have opened their doors to investment by multinational companies. Mexico used to make decisions on investment by multinational corporations on a case-by-case basis. IBM was negotiating with the Mexican government for 100 percent ownership of a facility in Guadalajara and got the go-ahead only after the company made numerous concessions in other areas.

BENEFITS OF COOPERATION Many nations have grown more cooperative toward international companies in recent years. Governments of developing and emerging markets realize the benefits of investment by multinational corporations, including decreased unemployment, increased tax revenues, training to create a more highly skilled workforce, and the transfer of technology. A country known for overly restricting the operations of multinational enterprises can see its inward investment flow dry up. Indeed, the restrictive policies of India's government hampered FDI inflows for many years.

Cooperation also frequently opens important communication channels that help firms to maintain positive relationships in the host country. Both parties tend to walk a fine line—cooperating most of the time, but holding fast on occasions when the stakes are especially high.

A Belgian brewery benefited from its cooperation with a local partner and respect for national pride in Central Europe when it acquired a local brewery in Hungary formerly owned by the government. From the start, the Belgian company wisely insisted that it would move ahead with its purchase only if local management would remain in charge. The company also assisted local management with technical, marketing, sales, distribution, and general management training.

Purchase-or-Build Decision

Another important matter for managers is whether to purchase an existing business or to build a subsidiary abroad from the ground up—called a *greenfield investment*. An acquisition generally provides the investor with an existing plant, equipment, and personnel. The acquiring firm may also benefit from the goodwill the existing company has built up over the years and, perhaps, the existing firm's brand recognition. The purchase of an existing business can also allow for alternative methods of financing the purchase, such as an exchange of stock ownership between the companies. Factors that reduce the appeal of purchasing existing facilities include obsolete equipment, poor relations with workers, and an unsuitable location. For insight into several issues managers consider when deciding to build or purchase operations, see the Manager's Briefcase, titled "Surprises of Investing Abroad."

Mexico's Cemex, S.A. (www.cemex.com), is a multinational company that made a fortune buying struggling, inefficient plants around the world and turning them around. Chairman Lorenzo Zambrano has long figured that the overriding principle is "Buy big globally, or be bought." The success of Cemex in using FDI confounded, even rankled, its competitors in developed nations. For example, Cemex shocked global markets when it carried out a $1.8 billion purchase of Spain's two largest cement companies, Valenciana and Sanson.

But adequate facilities in the local market are sometimes unavailable, and a company must go ahead with a greenfield investment. For example, because Poland is a source of skilled and inexpensive labor, it is an appealing location for automobile manufacturers. But the country had little in the way of advanced automobile-production facilities when General Motors (www.gm.com) considered investing there. So, GM built a facility in Poland's Silesian region. The factory has the potential to produce 200,000 units annually—some of which are destined for export to profitable markets in Western Europe. However, greenfield investments can have their share of headaches. Obtaining the necessary permits, financing, and hiring local personnel can be a real problem in some markets.

Production Costs

Many factors contribute to production costs in every national market. Labor regulations can add significantly to the overall cost of production. Companies may be required to provide benefits

---

MANAGER'S BRIEFCASE   Surprises of Investing Abroad

The decision of whether to build facilities in a market abroad or to purchase existing operations in the local market can be a difficult one. Managers can minimize risk by preparing their companies for a number of surprises they might face:

- **Human Resource Policies** Companies cannot always import home country policies without violating local laws or offending local customs. Countries have differing requirements for plant operations and have their own regulations regarding business operations.
- **Mandated Benefits** These include company-supplied clothing and meals, required profit sharing, guaranteed employment contracts, and generous dismissal policies. These costs can exceed an employee's wages and are typically not negotiable.
- **Labor Costs** France has a minimum wage of about $12 an hour, whereas Mexico has a minimum wage of nearly $5 a day. But Mexico's real minimum wage is nearly double that

due to government-mandated benefits and employment practices. Such differences are not always obvious.

- **Labor Unions** In some countries, organized labor is found in nearly every industry and at almost every company. Rather than dealing with a single union, managers may need to negotiate with five or six different unions, each of which represents a distinct skill or profession.
- **Information** Sometimes there simply is no reliable data on factors such as labor availability, cost of energy, and national inflation rates. These data are generally high quality in developed countries but suspect in emerging and developing ones.
- **Personal and Political Contacts** These contacts can be extremely important in developing and emerging markets and can be the only way to establish operations. But complying with locally accepted practices can cause ethical dilemmas for managers.

packages for their employees that are over and above hourly wages. More time than was planned for might be required to train workers adequately in order to bring productivity up to an acceptable standard. Although the cost of land and the tax rate on profits can be lower in the local market (or purposely lowered to attract multinational corporations), the fact that they will remain constant cannot be assumed. Companies from around the world using China as a production base have witnessed rising wages erode their profits as the nation continues to industrialize. Some companies are therefore finding that Vietnam is now their low-cost location of choice.

RATIONALIZED PRODUCTION One approach companies use to contain production costs is called **rationalized production**—a system of production in which each of a product's components is produced where the cost of producing that component is lowest. All the components are then brought together at one central location for assembly into the final product. Consider the typical stuffed animal made in China whose components are all imported to China (with the exception of the polycore thread with which it's sewn). The stuffed animal's eyes are molded in Japan. Its outfit is imported from France. The polyester-fiber stuffing comes from either Germany or the United States, and the pile-fabric fur is produced in Korea. Only final assembly of these components occurs in China.

Although this production model is highly efficient, a potential problem is that a work stoppage in one country can bring the entire production process to a standstill. For example, the production of automobiles is highly rationalized, with parts coming in from a multitude of countries for assembly. When the United Auto Workers (www.uaw.org) union held a strike for weeks against GM (www.gm.com), many of GM's international assembly plants were threatened. The UAW strategically launched their strike at GM's plant that supplied brake pads to virtually all of its assembly plants throughout North America.

MEXICO'S MAQUILADORA Stretching 2,000 miles from the Pacific Ocean to the Gulf of Mexico lies a 130-mile-wide strip along the US–Mexican border that comprises a special economic region. The region's economy encompasses 11 million people and $150 billion in output. The combination of a low-wage economy nestled next to a prosperous giant is now becoming a model for other regions that are split by wage or technology gaps. Some analysts compare the US–Mexican border region with that between Hong Kong and its manufacturing realm, China's Guangdong province. Officials from cities along the border between Germany and Poland studied the US–Mexican experience to see what lessons could be applied to their unique situation.

COST OF RESEARCH AND DEVELOPMENT As technology becomes an increasingly powerful competitive factor, the soaring cost of developing subsequent stages of technology has led multinational corporations to engage in cross-border alliances and acquisitions. For instance, huge multinational pharmaceutical companies are intensely interested in the pioneering biotechnology work done by smaller, entrepreneurial start-ups. Cadus Pharmaceutical Corporation of New York discovered the function of 400 genes related to what are called receptor molecules. Many disorders are associated with the improper functioning of these receptors—making them good targets for drug development. Britain's SmithKline Beecham (www.gsk.com) then invested around $68 million in Cadus in return for access to its research knowledge.

One indicator of technology's significance in FDI is the amount of research and development (R&D) conducted by company affiliates in other countries. The globalization of innovation and the phenomenon of foreign investment in R&D are not necessarily motivated by demand factors such as the size of local markets. They instead appear to be encouraged by supply factors, including gaining access to high-quality scientific and technical human capital.

rationalized production
System of production in which each of a product's components is produced where the cost of producing that component is lowest.

✪ MyLab Management Watch It Bringing Jobs Back to the United States
Apply what you have learned so far about foreign direct investment. If your instructor has assigned this, go to **www.pearson.com/mylab/management** to watch a video case to learn more about why companies decide to make products in a particular country and its effects on people's livelihoods.

Customer Knowledge

The behavior of buyers is frequently an important issue in the decision of whether to undertake FDI. A local presence can help companies gain valuable knowledge about customers that could not be obtained from the home market. For example, when customer preferences for a product differ a great deal from country to country, a local presence might help companies better understand such preferences and tailor their products accordingly.

Some countries have quality reputations in certain product categories. German automotive engineering, Italian shoes, French perfume, and Swiss watches impress customers as being of superior quality. Because of these perceptions, it can be profitable for a firm to produce its product in the country with the quality reputation, even if the company is based in another country. For example, a cologne or perfume producer might want to bottle its fragrance in France and give it a French name. This type of image appeal can be strong enough to encourage FDI.

Following Clients

Firms commonly engage in FDI when the firms they supply have already invested abroad. This practice of "following clients" is common in industries in which producers source component parts from suppliers with whom they have close working relationships. The practice tends to result in companies clustering within close geographic proximity to each other because they supply each other's inputs (see Chapter 5). When Mercedes (www.mercedes.com) opened its first international car plant in Tuscaloosa County, Alabama, automobile-parts suppliers also moved to the area from Germany—bringing with them additional investment in the millions of dollars.

With firms working closely together to deliver a product on a global basis, they get to know one another rather well. And the movement toward making business activities more environmentally, economically, and socially sustainable means that companies sometimes pressure their suppliers and their clients to "green" their activities. For several examples of how businesses have done this, read this chapter's Global Sustainability feature, titled "Greening the Supply Chain."

Following Rivals

FDI decisions frequently resemble a "follow the leader" scenario in industries that have a limited number of large firms. In other words, many of these firms believe that choosing not to make a move parallel to that of the "first mover" might result in being shut out of a potentially lucrative market. When firms based in industrial countries moved back into South Africa after the end of apartheid, their competitors followed. Of course, each market can sustain only a certain number

---

GLOBAL SUSTAINABILITY Greening the Supply Chain

- The Rainforest Action Network (RAN) wanted to get paper and wood products manufacturer Boise Cascade (www.bc.com) to protect endangered forests. Instead of approaching Boise Cascade directly, RAN contacted 400 of its customers, including Home Depot. RAN convinced Home Depot (www.homedepot.com) to phase out wood products not certified as originating from well-managed forests. It also convinced FedEx Office (www.fedex.com/us/office) to drop Boise Cascade as a supplier. The strategy encouraged Boise Cascade to adopt an environmental policy, part of which involved no longer harvesting US virgin forests.

- When furniture manufacturer Herman Miller (www.hermanmiller.com) started creating its environmentally friendly chair the Mirra, it asked potential suppliers to provide a list of ingredients that went into the part it would supply. Every material and chemical inside each component was assigned a color code of green (environmentally friendly), yellow (neutral), or red (like PVC plastic). The goal was to avoid red-coded materials, minimize yellows, and

maximize the greens. Herman Miller bought components only from companies that (1) supplied its list of ingredients, and (2) had "greener" components than competitors had.

- When Apple (www.apple.com) decided to pull its products from the Electronic Product Environmental Assessment Tool (EPEAT) environmental registry, it expected no one would notice. But some major Apple customers, like educational institutions and governments, must make most or all of their technology purchases from products on the EPEAT-certified list, comprising $65 billion worth of goods annually. The backlash from consumers, corporations, and government agencies forced Apple to backtrack. Apple said its products would again be submitted for certification and that its relationship with EPEAT "has become stronger as a result of this experience."

Sources: Jon Fortt, "EPEAT CEO: Apple's Exit Spurred a Customer Backlash," CNBC website (www.cnbc.com), July 13, 2012; Peter Senge, *The Necessary Revolution* (New York: Broadway Books, 2010), pp. 107–108; Daniel C. Esty and Andrew S. Winston, *Green to Gold* (New Haven, CT: Yale University Press, 2006), pp. 84–85, 176–177.

of rivals and firms that cannot compete often choose to exit the market. This seems to have been the case for Pepsi (www.pepsi.com), which went back into South Africa in the 1990s but withdrew three years later after being crushed there by Coke (www.cocacola.com).

In this section, we have presented several key issues managers consider when investing abroad. We will have more to say on this topic in Chapter 15, when we learn how companies take on this ambitious goal.

QUICK STUDY 3

1. When adequate facilities are not present in a market, a firm may decide to undertake a *what*?
2. A system in which a product's components are made where the cost of producing a component is lowest is called *what*?
3. What do we call the situation in which a company engages in FDI because the firms it supplies have already invested abroad?

7.4 Why Governments Intervene in FDI

Nations often intervene in the flow of FDI in order to protect their cultural heritages, domestic companies, and jobs. They can enact laws, create regulations, or construct administrative hurdles that companies from other nations must overcome if they want to invest in the nation. Yet, rising competitive pressure is forcing nations to compete against each other to attract multinational companies. The increased national competition for investment is causing governments to enact regulatory changes that encourage investment.

In a general sense, a bias toward protectionism or openness is rooted in a nation's culture, history, and politics. Values, attitudes, and beliefs form the basis for much of a government's position regarding FDI. For example, South American nations with strong cultural ties to a European heritage (such as Argentina) are generally enthusiastic about investment received from European nations. South American nations with stronger indigenous influences (such as Ecuador) are generally less enthusiastic.

Opinions vary widely on the appropriate amount of FDI a country should encourage. At one extreme are those who favor complete economic self-sufficiency and who oppose any form of FDI. At the other extreme are those who favor no governmental intervention and who favor booming FDI inflows. Between these two extremes lie most countries, which believe a certain amount of FDI is desirable to raise national output and enhance the standard of living for their people.

Besides philosophical ideals, countries intervene in FDI for a host of very practical reasons. But to fully appreciate those reasons, we must first understand what is meant by a country's *balance of payments*.

7.4 Explain why governments intervene in FDI.

Balance of Payments

A country's **balance of payments** is a national accounting system that records all receipts coming into the nation and all payments to entities in other countries. International transactions that result in inflows from other nations add to the balance of payments accounts. International transactions that result in outflows to other nations reduce the balance of payments accounts. Table 7.1 shows the balance of payments accounts for the United States, which has two major components—the *current account* and the *capital account*. The balances of the current and capital accounts should be equal.

balance of payments
National accounting system that records all receipts coming into the nation and all payments to entities in other countries.

CURRENT ACCOUNT The **current account** is a national account that records transactions involving the export and import of goods and services, income receipts on assets abroad, and income payments on foreign assets inside the country. The *merchandise* account in Table 7.1 covers tangible goods such as computer software, electronic components, and apparel. An "Export" of merchandise is assigned a positive value in the balance of payments because income is received. An "Import" is assigned a negative value because money is paid to a firm abroad.

The *services* account involves tourism, business consulting, banking, and other services. Suppose a business in the United States receives payment for consulting services provided to a company in another country. The receipt is recorded as an "Export" of services and is assigned a

current account
National account that records transactions involving the export and import of goods and services, income receipts on assets abroad, and income payments on foreign assets inside the country.

TABLE 7.1 US Balance of Payments Accounts

CURRENT ACCOUNT			
Exports of goods and services and income receipts	+		
Merchandise	+		
Services	+		
Income receipts on US assets abroad	+		
Imports of goods and services and income payments			−
Merchandise			−
Services			−
Income payments on foreign assets in United States			−
Unilateral transfers			−
Current account balance		+/−	
CAPITAL ACCOUNT			
Increase in US assets abroad (capital outflow)			−
US official reserve assets			−
Other US government assets			−
US private assets			−
Foreign assets in the United States (capital inflow)	+		
Foreign official assets	+		
Other foreign assets	+		
Capital account balance		+/−	

positive value. An "Import" of services requires money to be sent out of a nation and therefore receives a negative value.

The *income receipts* account is income earned on US assets held abroad. When a US company's subsidiary abroad remits profits back to the parent in the United States, it is recorded as an "Income receipt" and is assigned a positive value.

Finally, the *income payments* account is money paid to entities in other nations that was earned on assets held in the United States. For example, when a French company's US subsidiary sends its profits back to the parent company in France, the transaction is recorded as an "Income payment" and is assigned a negative value.

A **current account surplus** occurs when a country exports more goods and services and receives more income from abroad than it imports and pays abroad. Conversely, a **current account deficit** occurs when a country imports more goods and services and pays more abroad than it exports and receives from abroad.

current account surplus

When a country exports more goods and services and receives more income from abroad than it imports and pays abroad.

current account deficit

When a country imports more goods and services and pays more abroad than it exports and receives from abroad.

capital account

National account that records transactions involving the purchase and sale of assets.

CAPITAL ACCOUNT The **capital account** is a national account that records transactions involving the purchase and sale of assets. Suppose a US citizen buys shares of stock in a Mexican company on Mexico's stock market. The transaction is recorded as an "Increase in US assets abroad (capital outflow)" and is assigned a negative value. If a Mexican investor buys real estate in the United States, the transaction increases "Foreign assets in the United States (capital inflow)" and is assigned a positive value.

Reasons for Intervention by the Host Country

There are a number of reasons why governments intervene in FDI. Let's look at the two main reasons—to control the *balance of payments* and *to obtain resources and benefits*.

CONTROL BALANCE OF PAYMENTS Many governments see intervention as the only way to keep their balance of payments under control. First, because FDI inflows are recorded as additions to the balance of payments, a nation gets a balance-of-payments boost from an initial FDI inflow. Second, countries can impose local content requirements on investors from other nations for the purpose of local production. This gives local companies the chance to become suppliers to the production operation, which can help the nation to reduce imports and improve its balance of payments. Third, exports (if any) generated by the new production operation can have a favorable impact on the host country's balance of payments.

When companies repatriate profits back to their home countries, however, they deplete the foreign exchange reserves of their host countries. These capital outflows decrease the balance of payments of the host country. To shore up its balance of payments, the host nation may prohibit or restrict the nondomestic company from removing profits to its home country.

Alternatively, host countries conserve their foreign exchange reserves when international companies reinvest their earnings. Reinvesting in local manufacturing facilities can also improve the competitiveness of local producers and boost a host nation's exports—thus improving its balance-of-payments position.

OBTAIN RESOURCES AND BENEFITS Beyond balance-of-payments reasons, governments might intervene in FDI flows to acquire resources and benefits such as technology, management skills, and employment.

ACCESS TO TECHNOLOGY Investment in technology, whether in products or processes, tends to increase the productivity and the competitiveness of a nation. That is why host nations have a strong incentive to encourage the importation of technology. For years, developing countries in Asia were introduced to expertise in industrial processes as multinational corporations set up factories within their borders. But today, some of them are trying to acquire and develop their own technological expertise. When German industrial giant Siemens (www.siemens.com) chose Singapore as the site for an Asia-Pacific microelectronics design center, Singapore gained access to valuable technology. Singapore also accessed valuable semiconductor technology by joining with US-based Texas Instruments (www.ti.com) and others to set up the country's first semiconductor-production facility.

MANAGEMENT SKILLS AND EMPLOYMENT As we saw in Chapter 4, former communist nations lack some of the management skills needed to succeed in the global economy. By encouraging FDI, these nations can attract talented managers to come in and train locals and thereby improve the international competitiveness of their domestic companies. Furthermore, locals who are trained in modern management techniques may eventually start their own local businesses—further expanding employment opportunities. Yet, detractors argue that although FDI can create jobs it can also destroy jobs if less-competitive local firms are forced out of business.

Reasons for Intervention by the Home Country

Home nations (those from which international companies launch their investments) may also seek to encourage or discourage *outflows* of FDI for a variety of reasons. But home nations tend to have fewer concerns because they are often prosperous, industrialized nations. For these countries, an outward investment seldom has a national impact—unlike the impact on developing or emerging nations that receive the FDI. Nevertheless, the following are among the most common reasons for discouraging outward FDI:

* *Investing in other nations sends resources out of the home country.* As a result, fewer resources are used for development and economic growth at home. On the other hand, profits earned on assets abroad that are returned home increase both a home country's balance of payments and its available resources.
* *Outgoing FDI may ultimately damage a nation's balance of payments by taking the place of its exports.* This can occur when a company creates a production facility in a market abroad, the output of which replaces exports that used to be sent there from the home country. For example, if a Volkswagen (www.vw.com) plant in the United States fills a demand that US buyers would otherwise satisfy with purchases of German-made automobiles,

Club Med's resort in Guilin, China, was its first culture-focused resort in Asia for the French resort operator. The resort boasts 116 acres of private grounds and two stylish hotels. China's liberal economic policies have caused its inward FDI to surge. The investments of multinational corporations bring badly needed jobs to China's 130 million migrant workers. How might foreign direct investments, such as vacation resorts, impact China's balance of payments?

View Stock/Alamy Stock Photo

Germany's balance of payments is correspondingly decreased. Still, Germany's balance of payments would be positively affected when Volkswagen repatriates US profits, which helps negate the investment's initial negative balance-of-payments effect. Thus, an international investment might make a positive contribution to the balance-of-payments position of the country in the long term and offset an initial negative impact.

- *Jobs resulting from outgoing investments may replace jobs at home.* This is often the most contentious issue for home countries. The relocation of production to a low-wage nation can have a strong impact on a locale or region. However, the impact is rarely national, and its effects are often muted by other job opportunities in the economy. In addition, there may be an offsetting improvement in home country employment if additional exports are needed to support the activity represented by the outgoing FDI. For example, if Hyundai (www.hyundai-motor.com) of South Korea builds an automobile manufacturing plant in Brazil, Korean employment may increase in order to supply the Brazilian plant with parts.

FDI is not always a negative influence on home nations. In fact, countries promote outgoing FDI for the following reasons:

- *Outward FDI can increase long-term competitiveness.* Businesses today frequently compete on a global scale. The most competitive firms tend to be those that conduct business in the most favorable locations anywhere in the world, continuously improve their performance relative to competitors, and derive technological advantages from alliances formed with other companies. Japanese companies have become masterful at benefiting from FDI and cooperative arrangements with companies from other nations. The key to their success is that Japanese companies see every cooperative venture as a learning opportunity.

- *Nations may encourage FDI in industries identified as "sunset" industries.* Sunset industries are those that use outdated and obsolete technologies or those that employ low-wage workers with few skills. These jobs are not greatly appealing to countries having industries that pay skilled workers high wages. By allowing some of these jobs to go abroad and by retraining workers in higher-paying skilled work, they can upgrade their economies toward "sunrise" industries. This represents a trade-off for governments between a short-term loss of jobs and the long-term benefit of developing workers' skills.

QUICK STUDY 4

1. The national accounting system that records all receipts coming into a nation and all payments to entities in other countries is called *what*?
2. Why might a *host* country intervene in foreign direct investment?
3. Why might a *home* country intervene in foreign direct investment?

7.5 Government Policy Instruments and FDI

Over time, both host and home nations have developed a range of methods either to promote or to restrict FDI (see Table 7.2). Governments use these tools for many reasons, including improving balance-of-payments positions, acquiring resources, and, in the case of outward investment, keeping jobs at home. Let's take a look at these methods.

7.5 Describe the policy instruments governments use to promote and restrict FDI.

Host Countries: Promotion

Host countries offer a variety of incentives to encourage FDI inflows. These take two general forms—financial incentives and infrastructure improvements.

FINANCIAL INCENTIVES Host governments of all nations grant companies financial incentives to invest within their borders. One method includes tax incentives, such as lower tax rates or offers to waive taxes on local profits for a period of time—extending as far out as five years or more. A country may also offer *low-interest loans* to investors.

The downside of these types of incentives is that they can allow multinational corporations to create bidding wars between locations that are vying for the investment. In such cases, the company typically invests in the most appealing region after the locations endure rounds of escalating incentives. Companies have even been accused of engaging other governments in negotiations to force concessions from locations already selected for investment. The cost to taxpayers of attracting FDI can be several times what the actual jobs themselves pay—especially when nations try to one-up each other to win investment.

INFRASTRUCTURE IMPROVEMENTS Because of the problems associated with financial incentives, some governments are taking an alternative route to luring investment. Lasting benefits for communities surrounding the investment location can result from making local *infrastructure improvements*—better seaports suitable for containerized shipping, improved roads, and advanced telecommunications systems. For instance, Malaysia is carving an enormous Multimedia Super Corridor (MSC) into a region's forested surroundings. The MSC promises a paperless government, an intelligent city called Cyberjaya, two telesuburbs, a technology park, a multimedia university, and an intellectual property–protection park. The MSC is dedicated to creating the most advanced technologies in telecommunications, medicine, distance learning, and remote manufacturing.

TABLE 7.2 Instruments of FDI Policy

	FDI Promotion	FDI Restriction
Host Countries	Tax incentives	Ownership restrictions
	Low-interest loans	Performance demands
	Infrastructure improvements	
Home Countries	Insurance	Differential tax rates
	Loans	Sanctions
	Tax breaks	
	Political pressure	

Host Countries: Restriction

Host countries also have a variety of methods to restrict incoming FDI. Again, these take two general forms—ownership restrictions and performance demands.

OWNERSHIP RESTRICTIONS Governments can impose *ownership restrictions* that prohibit nondomestic companies from investing in certain industries or from owning certain types of businesses. Such prohibitions typically apply to businesses in cultural industries and companies vital to national security. For example, as some cultures try to protect traditional values, accepting investment by multinational companies can create controversy among conservatives, moderates, and liberals. Also, most nations do not allow FDI in their domestic weapons or national defense firms. Another ownership restriction is a requirement that nondomestic investors hold less than a 50 percent stake in local firms when they undertake FDI.

But nations sometimes eliminate such restrictions when a firm can choose another location that has no such restriction in place. When GM was deciding whether to invest in an aging automobile plant in Jakarta, Indonesia, the Indonesian government scrapped its demand of an eventual forced sale to Indonesians because China and Vietnam were also courting GM for the same financial investment.

PERFORMANCE DEMANDS More common than ownership requirements are *performance demands* that influence how international companies operate in the host nation. Although typically viewed as intrusive, most international companies allow for them in the same way they allow for home-country regulations. Performance demands include ensuring that a portion of the product's content originates locally, stipulating that a portion of the output must be exported, or requiring that certain technologies be transferred to local businesses.

Home Countries: Promotion

To encourage outbound FDI, home-country governments can do any of the following:

* Offer *insurance* to cover the risks of investments abroad, including, among others, insurance against expropriation of assets and losses from armed conflict, kidnappings, and terrorist attacks.
* Grant *loans* to firms wishing to increase their investments abroad. A home-country government may also guarantee the loans that a company takes from financial institutions.
* Offer *tax breaks* on profits earned abroad or negotiate special tax treaties. For example, several multinational agreements reduce or eliminate the practice of double taxation—profits earned abroad being taxed both in the home and host countries.
* Apply *political pressure* on other nations to get them to relax their restrictions on inbound investments. Non-Japanese companies often find it very difficult to invest inside Japan. The United States, for one, repeatedly pressures the Japanese government to open its market further to FDI. But because such pressure has achieved little success, many US companies cooperate with local Japanese businesses when entering Japan's markets.

Home Countries: Restriction

On the other hand, to limit the effects of outbound FDI on the national economy, home governments may exercise either of the following two options:

* Impose *differential tax rates* that charge income from earnings abroad at a higher rate than domestic earnings;
* Impose outright *sanctions* that prohibit domestic firms from making investments in certain nations.

QUICK STUDY 5

1. What policy instruments can *host* countries use to promote FDI?
2. What policy instruments can *home* countries use to promote FDI?
3. Ownership restrictions and performance demands are policy instruments used by *whom* to do *what*?
4. Differential tax rates and sanctions are policy instruments used by *whom* to do *what*?

BOTTOM LINE FOR BUSINESS

Companies ranging from massive global corporations to adventurous entrepreneurs all contribute to FDI flows, and the long-term trend in FDI is upward. Here we briefly discuss the influence of national governments on FDI flows and the flow of FDI in Asia and Europe.

National Governments and Foreign Direct Investment

The actions of national governments have important implications for business. Companies can either be thwarted in their efforts or be encouraged to invest in a nation, depending on the philosophies of home and host governments. The balance-of-payments positions of both home and host countries are also important because FDI flows affect the economic health of nations. To attract investment, a nation must provide a climate conducive to business operations, including pro-growth economic policies, a stable regulatory environment, and a sound infrastructure, to name just a few.

Increased competition for investment by multinational corporations has caused nations to make regulatory changes more favorable to FDI. Moreover, just as nations around the world are creating free trade agreements (covered in Chapter 8), they are also embracing bilateral investment treaties. These bilateral investment treaties are becoming prominent tools used to attract investment. Investment provisions within free trade agreements are also receiving greater attention than in the past. These efforts to attract investment have direct implications for the strategies of multinational companies, particularly when it comes to deciding where to locate production, logistics, and back-office service activities.

Foreign Direct Investment in Europe

FDI inflows into the developing (transition) nations of Southeast Europe and the Commonwealth of Independent States hit an all-time high in 2008. Countries that recently entered the European Union did particularly well. They saw less investment in areas supporting low-wage, unskilled occupations and greater investment in higher value-added activities that take advantage of a well-educated workforce.

The main reason for the fast pace at which FDI is occurring in Western Europe is regional economic integration. Some of the foreign investment reported by the European Union certainly went to the relatively less-developed markets of the new Central and Eastern European members. But much of the activity occurring among Western European companies is industry consolidation brought on by the opening of markets and the tearing down of barriers to free trade and investment. Change in the economic landscape across Europe is creating a more competitive business climate there.

Foreign Direct Investment in Asia

China attracts the majority of Asia's FDI, luring companies with a lower-wage workforce and access to an enormous domestic market. Many companies already active in China are upping their investment further, and companies not yet there are developing strategies for how to include China in their future plans. The "offshoring" of services will likely propel continued FDI in the coming years, for which India is the primary destination. India's attraction is its well-educated, low-cost, and English-speaking workforce.

An aspect of national business environments that has implications for future business activity is the natural environment. By their actions, businesses lay the foundation for people's attitudes in developing nations toward FDI by multinational corporations. For example, some early cases of FDI in China were characterized by a lack of control over people's actions due to greater decentralization in China's politics and increased power in the hands of local Communist Party bosses and bureaucrats. These individuals were often more motivated by their personal financial gain than they were concerned with the wider impact on society. But China's government is increasing its spending on the environment, and multinational corporations are helping in cleaning up the environment.

MyLab Management

Go to **www.pearson.com/mylab/management** to complete the problems marked with this icon .

Chapter Summary

LO7.1 Describe the worldwide pattern of foreign direct investment (FDI).

- In 2014, for the first time, developing countries attracted a greater share of global FDI inflows (about 55 percent) than developed countries attracted (41 percent).
- Among developed countries, the EU, the United States, and Japan account for the majority of FDI inflows.
- FDI to developing Asian nations was nearly $541 billion in 2015, with China attracting more than $136 billion and India attracting nearly $44 billion. FDI to Latin America and the Caribbean accounted for about 10 percent of the world total.
- *Globalization* and *mergers and acquisitions* are the two main drivers of global FDI.

LO7.2   Summarize each theory that attempts to explain why FDI occurs.
- The *international product life cycle theory* says that a company begins by exporting its product and then later undertakes FDI as the product moves through its life cycle.
- *Market imperfections theory* says that a company undertakes FDI to internalize a transaction and remove an imperfection in the marketplace that is causing inefficiencies.
- The *eclectic theory* says that firms undertake FDI when the features of a location combine with ownership and internalization advantages to make for an appealing investment.
- The *market power theory* states that a firm tries to establish a dominant market presence in an industry by undertaking FDI.

LO7.3   Outline the important management issues in the FDI decision.
- Companies investing abroad often wish to *control* activities in the local market, but even 100 percent ownership may not guarantee control.
- Acquisition of an existing business is preferred when it has updated equipment, good relations with workers, and a suitable location.
- A company might need to undertake a *greenfield investment* when adequate facilities are unavailable in the local market.
- Firms often engage in FDI when it gives them valuable knowledge of local *buyer behavior*, or when it locates them close to *client* firms and *rival* firms.

LO7.4   Explain why governments intervene in FDI.
- *Host nations* receive a *balance-of-payments* boost from initial FDI and from any exports the FDI generates, but they see a decrease in balance of payments when a company sends profits to the home country.
- FDI in *technology* brings in people with *management skills* who can train locals and increase a nation's productivity and competitiveness.
- *Home countries* can restrict a FDI outflow because it lowers the balance of payments, but profits earned on assets abroad and sent home increase the balance of payments.
- FDI outflows may replace jobs at home that were based on exports to the host country, and may damage a home nation's balance of payments if they reduce prior exports.

LO7.5   Describe the policy instruments governments use to promote and restrict FDI.
- Host countries promote FDI inflows by offering companies *tax incentives*, extending *low interest loans,* and making local *infrastructure improvements*.
- Host countries restrict FDI inflows by imposing *ownership restrictions*, and by creating *performance demands* that influence how a company operates.
- Home countries promote FDI outflows by offering *insurance* to cover investment risk, granting loans to firms investing abroad, guaranteeing company loans, offering *tax breaks* on profits earned abroad, negotiating special tax treaties, and applying *political pressure* on other nations to accept FDI.
- Home countries restrict FDI outflows by imposing *differential tax rates* that charge income from earnings abroad at a higher rate than domestic earnings and by imposing *sanctions* that prohibit domestic firms from making investments in certain nations.

Key Terms

balance of payments (p. 211)
capital account (p. 212)
current account (p. 211)
current account deficit (p. 212)
current account surplus (p. 212)

eclectic theory (p. 206)
foreign direct investment (FDI) (p. 202)
international product life cycle (p. 205)
market imperfections (p. 205)
market power (p. 206)

portfolio investment (p. 202)
rationalized production (p. 209)
vertical integration (p. 206)

✪ TALK ABOUT IT 1

You overhear your supervisor tell another manager in the company, "I'm fed up with our nation's companies sending jobs abroad to lower-wage nations. Don't they have any national pride?" The other manager responds, "I disagree. It's every company's duty to make as much profit as possible for its owners. If that means going abroad to reduce costs, so be it."

7-1. Do you agree with either of these managers? Explain.

7-2. Which FDI policy instruments might each manager support? Be specific.

✪ TALK ABOUT IT 2

The global automaker you work for has decided to invest in building a *greenfield* automobile assembly facility in Costa Rica with a local partner.

7-3. Which FDI theory presented in this chapter might explain your company's decision?

7-4. In what areas might your company want to exercise control, and in what areas might it cede control to the partner? Be specific.

Ethical Challenge

You are a minister in the government of the Republic of Ireland, an EU member state and a country with a stable economy but very reliant on the activities of overseas investors. The statistics seem to suggest that Irish manufacturing (approximately 36 percent of the economy), for example, is dominated by US companies, which have employed over 10 percent of the Irish workforce. According to the European Commission, only 3 percent of small Irish businesses is involved in manufacturing; this compares unfavorably to 10 percent across the European Union as a whole. Some 75 percent of all Irish exports is accounted for by non-Irish multinationals. It does make the economy one of the most globalized in the world, but it also means that the country is over-reliant on potentially volatile FDI. There is a fear that any rise in corporation tax will see an exodus of FDI.

7-5. Why do countries such as the Republic of Ireland seek to attract FDI?

7-6. Why might FDIs fall if the Republic of Ireland increases corporation tax?

7-7. How would you advise the government on managing the imbalanced nature of FDI going forward?

Teaming Up

In a group of three or four, in the role of advisors to a developed country, you have been asked to outline some of the downsides of outward FDI. Consider the following questions and then share your ideas with the rest of the class.

7-8. In the view of the group, what are the resource implications of investing in other countries?

7-9. What is the group's view that outward FDI might actually damage the balance of payment as they are taking the place of exports?

7-10. Theoretically, outward FDI can only lead to many job losses at home. Discuss.

✪ Market Entry Strategy Project

This exercise corresponds to the *MESP* online simulation. For the country your team is researching, integrate your answers to the following questions into your completed *MESP* report.

7-11. Does the country attract a large amount of FDI?
7-12. Is the country a major source of FDI for other nations?
7-13. Have any of the nation's large firms merged with, or acquired, a firm in another country?
7-14. Do labor unions have a weak, moderate, or strong presence in the nation?
7-15. Does the nation have healthy balance-of-payments accounts?
7-16. What policy instruments, if any, does the government use to promote or restrict FDI?

MyLab Management

✪ Go to **www.pearson.com/mylab/management** for the following assisted-graded writing questions:

7-17. Sometimes a company has a reputation for quality that is inextricably linked to the home country where it is made. What can a company do to reduce the risk of tarnishing its reputation for quality if it begins making its products abroad?

7-18. Developing nations and emerging markets are increasingly important to the global economy, not only as markets for goods but also as sources of FDI. How is the rise of developing and emerging markets changing the pattern of worldwide FDI flows?

Driving the Green Car Market in Australia

High fuel costs and concerns over climate change are just two factors that have caused Australia's once-booming automotive industry to stall in recent years. Although car exports stood at a respectable $5.2 billion in 2008, making it one of the country's top ten export earners ahead of more traditional exports such as wine, wheat, and wool, there has been a significant change in consumer preferences. While the market was once dominated by demand for large passenger cars, consumers both domestically and abroad now want smaller cars with lower fuel consumption.

As well as demands for change from car buyers, the industry has also been facing the double whammy of pressures on costs from within. Longstanding plans to cut trade tariffs and quotas that had protected the industry since 1985 have been causing alarm about what the future might hold because there is now even less incentive to build cars locally. Although the automotive industry around the world has been suffering in the deep financial downturn of the time, any further pressure on Australian car manufacturing would undoubtedly have a devastating effect. Australian carmakers build about 320,000 vehicles a year and employ about 65,000 people. Many others are also engaged in associated industries that benefit from the large market.

When Mitsubishi closed the last of its manufacturing plants in 2008, leaving just three automakers operating in the country (local subsidiaries of Ford, Toyota, and General Motors), the government could see it was time to act. To add a sense of urgency, Ford Australia announced plans to cut 450 jobs, as industry figures showed car sales down 11 percent from the year before.

The solution was a proposal to spend $3.4 billion between 2011 and 2020 on a fund to transform the Australian automotive industry into the green car market. The intention is to use the fund to help the manufacturers still involved in that country with the costs of developing new technologies for alternative energy vehicles and encourage them to make any existing environmentally friendly models in Australia.

The initiative caught the attention of Japanese car giant Toyota, which is one of the many international automakers racing to offer more fuel-efficient models in the wake of fuel prices hitting record highs around the world as well as increased environmental concerns. Toyota's business plan is to reach a target of selling 1 million hybrid cars by the early part of the next decade, and to accomplish this goal, it needs to more than double production of the vehicles. The Japanese company was already building its Camry hybrid in Japan, as well as in Kentucky in the United States and in a joint venture factory in China. In 2008, thanks in part to the strength of the Australian dollar, it had been weighing an alternative plan to import engines to Australia from its Kamigo plant in Japan.

In September 2010, after months of discussion, Toyota announced a $300 million upgrade of its plant in western Melbourne. Under the investment, which has been partly funded by taxpayers through a $63 million payment from the Green Car Innovation Fund, as well as an injection of cash from the local Victorian administration, the Altona engine plant was aiming to produce 100,000 hybrid engines and four-cylinder new generation engines each year from the second half of 2012. The plan was that the Australian-made engines would be exported into other countries that manufacture Toyota's Camry and Hybrid Camry. Toyota's more environmentally sustainable engines will consume 4.5 percent less fuel and produce 5 percent fewer greenhouse gas emissions than the current equivalent. The Australian government claimed that the initiative would secure as many as 3,300 jobs, including existing direct and indirect jobs, and would anchor Toyota's operations in the country for years to come. According to Toyota executives, the support provided by the Green Car Innovation Fund was the major factor in the project going ahead when they weighed it against other alternatives, including transferring production to the home market in Japan.

Thinking Globally

7-19. What do you think were the chief factors involved in Toyota's decision to undertake FDI in Australia rather than build its hybrids in Japan?

7-20. Why do you think Toyota decided to adapt the existing plant in Melbourne rather than build one from the ground up elsewhere in Australia? List as many reasons as you can, and explain your answer.

7-21. What do you think the decision to manufacture in Australia rather than in its domestic factories will do to the company's reputation at home? How much attention do international customers pay to the location where their automotives are assembled?

7-22. What do you see as the pros and cons of Toyota's approach to managing FDI?

[*Sources:* "Japanese Auto Manufacturers in the Australian Market and the Government Industry Assistance Spending" *The Otemon Journal of Australian Studies,* 34, 2008; "Toyota Plant to Deliver Greener Engines" Drive website (www.drive.com.au), September 10, 2010; "Review of Australia's Automotive Industry" Australian Policy Online website (www.apo.org.au), July 22, 2008.]

Chapter Eight

Regional Economic Integration

Learning Objectives

After studying this chapter, you should be able to

8.1 Outline the levels of economic integration and its debate.

8.2 Describe integration in Europe and its enlargement.

8.3 Describe integration in the Americas and its prospects.

8.4 Summarize integration in Asia and elsewhere.

A Look Back

Chapter 7 examined recent patterns of foreign direct investment. We explored the theories that try to explain why foreign direct investment occurs and discussed how governments influence investment flows.

A Look at This Chapter

This chapter explores the trend toward greater integration of national economies. We first examine the reasons why nations are making significant efforts at regional integration. We then study the most prominent regional trading blocs in place around the world today.

A Look Ahead

Chapter 9 begins our inquiry into the international financial system. We describe the structure of the international capital market and explain how the foreign exchange market operates.

MyLab Management

✪ IMPROVE YOUR GRADE!

When you see this icon ✪, visit **www.pearson.com/mylab/management** for activities that are applied, personalized, and offer immediate feedback.

Nestlé's Global Recipe

VEVEY, Switzerland—Nestlé (www.nestle.com) is the largest food company in the world and is active in nearly every country on the planet. It earns just 2 percent of its sales at home in Switzerland, and it operates across cultural borders 24 hours a day.

Nestlé has a knack for turning humdrum products like bottled water and pet food into well-known global brands. It also takes regional products to the global market when the opportunity arises. For example, Nestlé launched a cereal bar for diabetics first in Asia under the brand name Nutren Balance and then introduced it to other markets worldwide.

Food is integral to every culture's social fabric. Nestlé must carefully navigate the cultural landscape in other countries in order to remain sensitive to local dietary traditions. Nestlé learned from past mistakes and now tries to ensure that mothers in developing nations use purified water to mix its baby milk formulas, for example. As Nestlé expands into emerging markets, it watches for changes in consumer attitudes that result from greater cross-cultural contact caused by regional integration.

Tofino/Alamy Stock Photo

Nestlé also needs to tread carefully when it comes to global sustainability. Greenpeace charged that Nestlé (and others) source palm oil for their products from delicate Indonesian rainforests and peatlands. Nestlé stopped purchasing such palm oil and now ensures that all its palm oil is certified sustainable. The company also recently announced that it will be reducing the sugar content in its snack foods by 40 percent or more in order to make them more nutritious.

When Nestlé and Coca-Cola announced a joint venture to develop coffee and tea drinks, they first had to show the European Union (EU) Commission that they would not stifle competition across the region. Firms operating within the EU must also abide by EU environmental protection laws. Nestlé works with governments to minimize packaging waste that results from the use of its products by developing and managing waste-recovery programs. As you read this chapter, consider all the business implications of nations banding together in regional trading blocs.[1]

Regional trade agreements are changing the landscape of the global marketplace. Companies like Nestlé of Switzerland are finding that these agreements lower trade barriers and open new markets for goods and services. Markets otherwise off-limits because tariffs made imported products too expensive can become quite attractive once tariffs are lifted. But trade agreements can be double-edged swords for countries, companies, and consumers. Not only do regional trade agreements allow domestic companies to seek new markets abroad, but they also let competitors from other nations enter the domestic market. Such mobility increases competition in all markets that participate in an agreement.

We began Part 3 of this book by discussing the gains resulting from specialization and trade. We now close this part of the book by showing how groups of countries are cooperating to dismantle barriers that threaten these potential gains. In this chapter, we focus on regional efforts to encourage freer trade and investment. We begin by defining regional economic integration and describing each of its five levels. We then examine the case for and against regional economic integration. In the remainder of the chapter, we explore several long-established trade agreements and several agreements in the early stages of development.

8.1 Levels of Integration and the Debate

8.1 Outline the levels of economic integration and its debate.

regional economic integration (regionalism)
Process whereby countries in a geographic region cooperate to reduce or eliminate barriers to the international flow of products, people, or capital.

free trade area
Economic integration whereby countries seek to remove all barriers to trade among themselves but where each country determines its own barriers against nonmembers.

The process whereby countries in a geographic region cooperate to reduce or eliminate barriers to the international flow of products, people, or capital is called **regional economic integration (regionalism)**. A group of nations in a geographic region undergoing economic integration is called a *regional trading bloc*.

Nations have banded together to reap the potential gains of international trade in a variety of ways. Figure 8.1 shows five potential levels (or degrees) of economic and political integration for regional trading blocs. A *free trade area* is the lowest extent of national integration; *political union* is the greatest. Each level of integration incorporates the properties of those levels that precede it.

Free Trade Area

Economic integration whereby countries seek to remove all barriers to trade among themselves but where each country determines its own barriers against nonmembers is called a **free trade area**. A free trade area is the lowest level of economic integration that is possible between two or more countries. Countries belonging to the free trade area strive to remove all tariffs and nontariff

Figure 8.1

Levels of Regional Integration

barriers, such as quotas and subsidies, on international trade in goods and services. However, each country is able to maintain whatever policy it sees fit against nonmember countries. These policies can differ widely from country to country. Countries belonging to a free trade area also typically establish a process by which trade disputes can be resolved.

Customs Union

Economic integration whereby countries remove all barriers to trade among themselves and set a common trade policy against nonmembers is called a **customs union**. Thus, the main difference between a free trade area and a customs union is that the members of a customs union agree to treat trade with all nonmember nations in a similar manner. Countries belonging to a customs union might also negotiate as a single entity with other supranational organizations, such as the World Trade Organization (WTO).

customs union
Economic integration whereby countries remove all barriers to trade among themselves and set a common trade policy against nonmembers.

Common Market

Economic integration whereby countries remove all barriers to trade and to the movement of labor and capital among themselves and set a common trade policy against nonmembers is called a **common market**. Thus, a common market integrates the elements of free trade areas and customs unions and adds the free movement of important factors of production—people and cross-border investment. This level of integration is very difficult to attain because it requires members to cooperate to at least some extent on economic and labor policies. Furthermore, the benefits to individual countries can be uneven because skilled labor may move to countries where wages are higher, and investment capital may flow to areas where returns are greater.

common market
Economic integration whereby countries remove all barriers to trade and to the movement of labor and capital among themselves and set a common trade policy against nonmembers.

Economic Union

Economic integration whereby countries remove barriers to trade and the movement of labor and capital among members, set a common trade policy against nonmembers, and coordinate their economic policies is called an **economic union.** An economic union goes beyond the demands of a common market by requiring member nations to harmonize their tax, monetary, and fiscal policies and to create a common currency. Economic unions require that member countries concede a certain amount of their national autonomy (or sovereignty) to the supranational union of which they are a part.

economic union
Economic integration whereby countries remove barriers to trade and the movement of labor and capital among members, set a common trade policy against non-members, and coordinate their economic policies.

Political Union

Economic and political integration whereby countries coordinate aspects of their economic *and* political systems is called a **political union**. A political union requires member nations to accept a common stance on economic and political matters regarding nonmember nations. However, nations are allowed a degree of freedom in setting certain political and economic policies within their territories. Individually, Canada and the United States provide examples of political unions early in their histories. In both these nations, smaller states and provinces combined to form larger entities. A group of nations currently taking steps in this direction is the European Union—discussed later in this chapter.

political union
Economic and political integration whereby countries coordinate aspects of their economic and political systems.

Table 8.1 identifies the members of every regional trading bloc presented in this chapter. As you work through this chapter, refer back to this table for a quick summary of each bloc's members.

The Case for Regional Integration

Few topics in international business are as hotly contested and involve as many groups as the effects of regional trade agreements on people, jobs, companies, cultures, and living standards. On one side of the debate are people who see the positive effects that regional trade agreements cause; on the other side, those who see the negative effects.

The goals of nations pursuing economic integration are not only to increase cross-border trade and investment but also to raise living standards for their people. We saw in Chapter 5, for example, how specialization and trade create real gains in terms of greater choice, lower prices, and increased productivity. Regional trade agreements are designed to help nations accomplish these objectives. Regional economic integration sometimes has additional goals, such as protection of intellectual property rights or the environment, or even eventual political union.

TABLE 8.1 The World's Main Regional Trading Blocs

EU	**European Union**
	Austria, Belgium, Bulgaria, Croatia, Czech Republic, Denmark, Estonia, Finland, France, Germany, Greece, Greek Cyprus (southern portion), Hungary, Ireland, Italy, Latvia, Lithuania, Luxembourg, Malta, the Netherlands, Poland, Portugal, Romania, Slovakia, Slovenia, Spain, Sweden, and the United Kingdom (until it exits)
EFTA	**European Free Trade Association**
	Iceland, Liechtenstein, Norway, and Switzerland
NAFTA	**North American Free Trade Agreement**
	Canada, Mexico, and United States
CAFTA-DR	**Central American Free Trade Agreement**
	Costa Rica, El Salvador, Guatemala, Honduras, Nicaragua, Dominican Republic, and United States
CAN	**Andean Community**
	Bolivia, Colombia, Ecuador, and Peru
MERCOSUR	**Southern Common Market**
	Argentina, Brazil, Paraguay, Uruguay, and Venezuela (suspended in 2016). Associate members are Bolivia, Chile, Colombia, Ecuador, Peru, and Suriname.
CARICOM	**Caribbean Community and Common Market**
	Antigua and Barbuda, Bahamas, Barbados, Belize, Dominica, Grenada, Guyana, Haiti, Jamaica, Montserrat, St. Kitts and Nevis, St. Lucia, St. Vincent and the Grenadines, Suriname, and Trinidad and Tobago
CACM	**Central American Common Market**
	Costa Rica, Guatemala, Honduras, Nicaragua, and El Salvador
FTAA	**Free Trade Area of the Americas**
	34 nations from Central, North, and South America and the Caribbean
ASEAN	**Association of Southeast Asian Nations**
	Brunei, Cambodia, Indonesia, Laos, Malaysia, Myanmar, the Philippines, Singapore, Thailand, and Vietnam
APEC	**Asia Pacific Economic Cooperation**
	Australia, Brunei, Canada, Chile, China, Hong Kong, Indonesia, Japan, South Korea, Malaysia, Mexico, New Zealand, Papua New Guinea, Peru, the Philippines, Russia, Singapore, Taiwan, Thailand, United States, and Vietnam
CER	**Closer Economic Relations Agreement**
	Australia and New Zealand
GCC	**Gulf Cooperation Council**
	Bahrain, Kuwait, Oman, Qatar, Saudi Arabia, and United Arab Emirates
ECOWAS	**Economic Community of West African States**
	Benin, Burkina Faso, Cape Verde, Gambia, Ghana, Guinea, Guinea-Bissau, Ivory Coast, Liberia, Mali, Niger, Nigeria, Senegal, Sierra Leone, and Togo
AU	**African Union**
	Total of 55 nations on the continent of Africa

trade creation

Increase in the level of trade between nations that results from regional economic integration.

TRADE CREATION Economic integration removes barriers to trade and/or investment for nations belonging to a trading bloc. The increase in the level of trade between nations that results from regional economic integration is called **trade creation.** One result of trade creation is that consumers and industrial buyers in member nations are faced with a wider selection of goods and services not previously available. For example, the United States has many popular brands of bottled water, including Coke's Dasani (www.dasani.com) and Pepsi's Aquafina (www.pepsi.com). But grocery and convenience stores inside the United States stock a wide variety of lesser-known imported brands of bottled water, such as Stonepoint from Canada. Certainly, the free trade agreement between Canada, Mexico, and the United States (discussed later in this chapter) created export opportunities for this and other Canadian brands.

Trade creation can also increase aggregate demand in an economy. The wider selection of products that results from trade creation can lower prices. Lower product prices then increase purchasing power, which in turn tend to increase demand for goods and services.

GREATER CONSENSUS In Chapter 6, we saw how the WTO works to lower barriers on a global scale. Efforts at regional economic integration differ in that they comprise smaller groups of nations—ranging from several countries to as many as 30 or more. The benefit of trying to eliminate trade barriers in smaller groups of countries is that it can be easier to gain consensus from fewer members as opposed to, say, the 164 countries that comprise the WTO.

POLITICAL COOPERATION There can also be *political* benefits from efforts toward regional economic integration. A group of nations can have significantly greater political weight than each nation has individually. Thus, the group, as a whole, can have more say when negotiating with other countries in forums such as the WTO. Integration involving political cooperation can also reduce the potential for military conflict between member nations. In fact, peace was at the center of early efforts at integration in Europe in the 1950s. The devastation of two world wars in the first half of the twentieth century caused Europe to see integration as one way of preventing further armed conflicts.

EMPLOYMENT OPPORTUNITIES Regional integration can expand employment opportunities by enabling people to move from one country to another to find work or, simply, to earn a higher wage. Regional integration opened doors for young people in Europe. Forward-looking young people have abandoned extreme nationalism and have taken on what can only be described as a "European" attitude that embraces a shared history. Those with language skills and a willingness to pick up and move to another EU country get to explore a new culture's way of life while earning a living. As companies seek their future leaders in Europe, they will hire people who can think across borders and across cultures.

CORPORATE SAVINGS Trade agreements can allow companies to alter their strategies, sometimes radically. For example, nations in the Americas may eventually create a free trade area that runs from the northern tip of Alaska to the southern tip of South America. Companies that do business throughout this region could save millions of dollars annually from the removal of import tariffs under an eventual agreement. Multinational corporations could also save money by supplying entire regions from just a few regional factories, rather than having a factory in each nation. Savings can then be passed on to consumers in the form of lower prices.

The Case Against Regional Integration

Opposite those who argue the case for regional economic integration are those who see the companies who have packed up and moved abroad, leaving unemployed workers in their wake. Let's now look at the main arguments of those pushing the case against regional economic integration.

TRADE DIVERSION The flip side of trade creation is **trade diversion**—the diversion of trade away from nations not belonging to a trading bloc and toward member nations. Trade diversion can occur after the formation of a trading bloc because of the lower tariffs charged among member nations. It can result in increased trade with a less-efficient producer within the trading bloc and in reduced trade with a more efficient, nonmember producer. So, economic integration can unintentionally reward a less efficient producer within the trading bloc. Unless there is other internal competition for the producer's good or service, buyers will likely pay more after trade diversion because of the inefficient production methods of the producer.

trade diversion
Diversion of trade away from nations not belonging to a trading bloc and toward member nations.

A World Bank report caused a stir over the results of the free trade bloc among Latin America's largest countries, MERCOSUR (discussed later in this chapter). The report suggested that the bloc's formation only encouraged free trade in the lowest-value products of local origin, while deterring competition for more sophisticated goods manufactured outside the market. Closer analysis showed that, while imports from one member state to another tripled during the period studied, imports from the rest of the world also tripled. Thus, the net effect of the agreement was trade creation, not trade diversion, as critics had charged. Also, the Australian Department of Foreign Affairs and Trade released the results of a study that examined the impact of the

North American Free Trade Agreement (NAFTA) on Australia's trade with and investment in North America. The study found no evidence of trade diversion following the agreement's formation.[2]

SHIFTS IN EMPLOYMENT Perhaps the most controversial aspect of regional economic integration is its effect on people's jobs. The formation of a trading bloc promotes efficiency by significantly reducing or eliminating barriers to trade among its members. The surviving producer of a particular good or service, then, is likely to be the bloc's most efficient producer. Industries requiring mostly unskilled labor, for example, tend to respond to the formation of a trading bloc by shifting production to a low-wage nation within the bloc.

Yet, figures on jobs lost or gained as a result of trading bloc formation vary depending on the source. The US government contends that rising US exports to Mexico and Canada create jobs overall. But the AFL-CIO (www.aflcio.org), the federation of US unions, disputes these figures and claims a loss of jobs due to NAFTA. Trade agreements do cause dislocations in labor markets; some jobs are lost while others are gained.

It is likely that once trade and investment barriers are removed, countries protecting low-wage domestic industries from competition will see these jobs move to the country where wages are lower. This can be an opportunity for workers who lose their jobs to upgrade their skills and gain more advanced job training. This can help nations increase their competitiveness because a more educated and skilled workforce attracts higher-paying jobs than does a less skilled workforce.

LOSS OF NATIONAL SOVEREIGNTY There is also a cultural element of such agreements. Some people argue that they will lose their unique national identity if their nation cooperates too much with others. As we saw in this chapter's opening company profile, Nestlé tries to be sensitive to cultural differences across markets. But such large global companies are often lightning rods for nationalist forces and those warning of cultural homogenization.

Successive levels of integration require that nations surrender more of their national sovereignty. The least amount of sovereignty that must be surrendered to the trading bloc occurs in a free trade area. By contrast, a political union requires nations to give up a high degree of sovereignty in foreign policy. This is why a political union is so hard to achieve. Long histories of cooperation or animosity between nations do not become irrelevant when a group of countries forms a union. Because one member nation may have very delicate ties with a nonmember nation with which another member may have very strong ties, the setting of a common foreign policy can be extremely tricky.

Economic integration is taking place throughout the world because of the benefits and despite the drawbacks of regional trade agreements. Europe, the Americas, Asia, the Middle East, and Africa are all undergoing integration to varying degrees (see Map 8.1 on pages 230–231). Let's now begin our coverage of specific efforts toward economic integration by exploring Europe, which has the longest history and highest level of integration to date.

QUICK STUDY 1

1. What is it called when countries in a region cooperate to reduce or eliminate barriers to the international flow of products, people, or capital?
2. What are the names of the lowest and highest levels of regional economic integration?
3. An increase in trade between nations as a result of regional economic integration is called *what*?
4. Trade shifting away from nations not belonging to a trading bloc and toward member nations is called *what*?

8.2 Integration in Europe

8.2 Describe integration in Europe and its enlargement.

The most sophisticated and advanced example of regional integration that we can point to today is occurring in Europe. European efforts at integration began shortly after the Second World War as a cooperative endeavor among a small group of countries and involved a few select industries. Regional integration now encompasses practically all of Western Europe and all industries.

European Union

In the middle of the twentieth century, many would have scoffed at the idea that European nations, which had spent so many years at war with one another, could present a relatively unified whole more than 50 years later. Let's investigate how Europe came so far in such a relatively brief time.

EARLY YEARS A war-torn Europe emerged from the Second World War in 1945 facing two challenges: (1) It needed to rebuild itself and avoid further armed conflict, and (2) it needed to increase its industrial strength to stay competitive with an increasingly powerful United States. Cooperation seemed to be the only way of facing these challenges. Belgium, France, West Germany, Italy, Luxembourg, and the Netherlands signed the Treaty of Paris in 1951, creating the *European Coal and Steel Community*. These nations were determined to remove barriers to trade in coal, iron, steel, and scrap metal in order to coordinate coal and steel production among themselves, thereby controlling the postwar arms industry.

The members of the European Coal and Steel Community signed the Treaty of Rome in 1957, creating the *European Economic Community*. The Treaty of Rome outlined a future common market for these nations. It also aimed to establish common transportation and agricultural policies among members. In 1967, the community's scope was broadened to include additional industries, notably atomic energy, and it changed its name to the *European Community*. As the goals of integration continued to expand, so too did the bloc's membership. Waves of enlargement occurred in 1973, 1981, 1986, 1995, 2004, and 2007. In 1994, the bloc once again changed its name to the *European Union (EU)*. Today, the 28-member EU (www.europa.eu) has a population of more than 500 million people and a gross domestic product (GDP) of around $16 trillion (see Map 8.2 on page 232). After the United Kingdom completes its planned exit there will be 27 members.

In recent years, two important milestones contributed to the continued progress of the EU: the *Single European Act* and the *Maastricht Treaty*.

Single European Act By the mid-1980s, EU member nations were frustrated by remaining trade barriers and a lack of progress on several important matters, including taxation, law, and regulations. The important objective of harmonizing laws and policies was beginning to appear unachievable. A commission that was formed to analyze the potential for a common market by the end of 1992 put forth several proposals. The goal was to remove remaining barriers, increase harmonization, and thereby enhance the competitiveness of European companies. The proposals became the *Single European Act (SEA)*, which went into effect in 1987.

A wave of mergers and acquisitions swept across Europe as companies took advantage of the opportunities that the SEA offered. Large firms combined their special understanding of European needs, capabilities, and cultures with their advantage of economies of scale. Small and medium-sized companies networked with one another to increase their competitiveness.

Maastricht Treaty Some members of the EU wanted to take European integration further still. A 1991 summit meeting of EU member nations took place in Maastricht, the Netherlands. The meeting resulted in the *Maastricht Treaty*, which went into effect in 1993.

The Maastricht Treaty had three aims. First, it called for banking in a single, common currency after January 1, 1999, and circulation of coins and paper currency on January 1, 2002. Second, the treaty set up monetary and fiscal targets for countries that wished to take part in monetary union. Third, the treaty called for political union of the member nations—including development of a common foreign and defense policy and common citizenship. Member countries will hold off further political integration until they gauge the success of the final stages of economic and monetary union. Let's take a closer look at monetary union in Europe.

EUROPEAN MONETARY UNION As stated previously, EU leaders were determined to create a single, common currency. **European monetary union** is the EU plan that established its own central bank and currency in January 1999. The Maastricht Treaty stated the economic criteria with which member nations must comply in order to partake in the single currency, the *euro*. First, consumer price inflation must be below 3.2 percent and must not exceed that of the three best-performing countries by more than 1.5 percent. Second, the debt of government must be no higher than 60 percent of GDP. An exception is made if the ratio is diminishing and approaching the 60 percent mark.

European monetary union
European Union plan that established its own central bank and currency.

Map 8.1

Most Active Economic Blocs

The most active economic blocs

EU
EFTA
NAFTA

MERCOSUR
CARICOM
CAN

ASEAN
APEC
CER

Map 8.2
Economic Integration In Europe

Third, the general government deficit must be no higher than 3.0 percent of GDP. An exception is made if the deficit is close to 3.0 percent or if the deviation is temporary and unusual. Fourth, interest rates on long-term government securities must not exceed, by more than 2.0 percent, those of the three countries with the lowest inflation rates. Meeting these criteria better aligned countries' economies and paved the way for smoother policy making under a single European Central Bank. The 19 EU member nations that adopted the single currency are Austria, Belgium, Cyprus, Estonia, Finland, France, Germany, Greece, Ireland, Italy, Latvia, Lithuania, Luxembourg, Malta, the Netherlands, Portugal, Slovakia, Slovenia, and Spain.

Members of the EU were not immune to the recent global financial crisis and recession. The countries that had amassed the largest debts relative to their GDPs included Greece, Ireland, Italy, Portugal, and Spain. In 2012, the EU supported the economies of Greece and Spain with emergency funding when they began to buckle due to a lack of confidence in their banking and finance sectors. The EU later announced that it would act as a lender of last resort for troubled countries and pledged to create a banking union in order to support the financial institutions of the weakest economies. These moves halted the spread of Europe's financial crisis. The newly pledged banking union may, in fact, serve as a stepping stone to a future fiscal union in the EU.[3]

Management Implications of the Euro The move to a single currency influences the activities of companies within the EU. First, the euro removes financial obstacles created by the use of multiple currencies. It completely eliminates exchange-rate risk for business deals between member nations using the euro. The euro also reduces transaction costs by eliminating the cost of converting from one currency to another. In fact, the EU leadership estimates the financial gains to Europe could eventually be 0.5 percent of GDP. The efficiency of trade between participating members resembles that of interstate trade in the United States because only a single currency is involved.

Second, the euro makes prices between markets more transparent, making it difficult to charge different prices in adjoining markets. As a result, shoppers feel less of a need to travel to other countries to save money on high-ticket items. For example, shortly before monetary union, a Mercedes-Benz S320 (www.mercedes.com) cost $72,614 in Germany but only $66,920 in Italy. A Renault Twingo (www.renault.com) that sold for $13,265 in France cost $11,120 in Spain. Automobile brokers and shopping agencies even sprang up specifically to help European consumers reap such savings. The euro greatly reduced or eliminated this type of situation.

ENLARGEMENT OF THE EUROPEAN UNION One of the most historic events across Europe in recent memory was the EU enlargement that added 12 new members in 2007. Croatia was the most recent country to join the EU in 2013. Albania, Montenegro, Serbia, the Former Yugoslav Republic of Macedonia, and Turkey remain candidates for EU membership and are to become members after they meet certain demands laid down by the EU. These so-called *Copenhagen Criteria* require each country to demonstrate that it:

- Has stable institutions, which guarantee democracy, the rule of law, human rights, and respect for and protection of minorities.
- Has a functioning market economy, capable of coping with competitive pressures and market forces within the EU.
- Is able to assume the obligations of membership, including adherence to the aims of economic, monetary, and political union.
- Has the ability to adopt the rules and regulations of the community, the rulings of the European Court of Justice, and the treaties.

Although it has applied for membership, negotiations for Turkey are expected to be difficult. One reason for Turkey's lack of support in the EU is charges (fair or not) of human rights abuses with regard to its Kurdish minority. Another reason is intense opposition by Greece, Turkey's longtime foe. Turkey does have a customs union with the EU, however, and trade between them is growing. Despite disappointment among some EU hopefuls and despite intermittent setbacks in the enlargement process, integration is progressing. To read about how culture affects business activities in one EU country, see the Culture Matters feature, titled "Czech List."

The countries of Central and Eastern Europe that belong to the EU represent a land of opportunity. But like doing business anywhere, understanding local culture can be a big advantage. Successful businesspeople in the Czech Republic offer the following advice:

- **Formalities.** Czech society is rather formal, and it is best to tend toward the more formal unless you know your colleague well. This includes using titles like "Doctor" and "Mister." It's rarely appropriate to use first names unless you're close friends.
- **Business Relationships.** Making money is obviously important and is the ultimate goal for any business. Still, building personal relationships, establishing good references, and doing favors for others can smooth the way for newcomers.

- **Czech Partners.** Being communist for 40 years before it became a capitalist democracy left its mark on the Czech people and their culture. Finding a local partner who can handle the inevitable cultural difficulties that arise is crucial.
- **Local Professionals.** It is a good idea to hire a Czech accountant or someone familiar with Czech laws, taxes, and red tape. An attorney who is bilingual can also interpret differences between Czech and US laws.
- **The *Jednatel*.** Companies need a "responsible person" (or *jednatel* in Czech) who is in charge of all aspects of the business. Some Czechs still feel more comfortable working with this *jednatel* rather than with foreign and unfamiliar company reps.

STRUCTURE OF THE EU Five EU institutions play particularly important roles in monitoring and enforcing economic and political integration. Other EU institutions that fulfill secondary and support roles are not discussed here.

European Parliament Every five years each member nation votes into office its representatives to the European Parliament. As such, they are expected to voice their constituency's political views on EU matters. The European Parliament fulfills its role of adopting EU law by debating and amending legislation proposed by the European Commission. It exercises political supervision over all EU institutions—giving it the power to supervise commissioner appointments and to censure the commission. It also has veto power over some laws (including the annual budget of the EU). There is a call for increased democratization within the EU, and some believe this could be achieved by strengthening the powers of the Parliament. The Parliament conducts its activities in Belgium (in the city of Brussels), France (in the city of Strasbourg), and Luxembourg.

Council of the EU The council is the legislative body of the EU. When it meets, it brings together representatives of member states at the ministerial level. The configuration of the council changes depending on which topic is under discussion. For example, when the topic is agriculture, the council is composed of the ministers of agriculture from each member nation. No proposed legislation becomes EU law unless the council votes it into law. Although passage into law for sensitive issues such as immigration and taxation still requires a unanimous vote, some legislation today requires only a simple majority to win approval. The council also concludes, on behalf of the EU, international agreements with other nations or international organizations. The council is headquartered in Brussels, Belgium.

European Commission The commission is the executive body of the EU. It is comprised of one commissioner from each member country. Member nations appoint the president and commissioners after being approved by the European Parliament. The commission has the right to draft legislation, is responsible for managing and implementing policy, and monitors member nations' implementation of, and compliance with, EU law. Each commissioner is assigned a specific policy area, such as competitive policy or agricultural policy. Although commissioners are appointed by their national governments, they are expected to behave in the best interest of the EU as a whole, not in the interest of their own country. The European Commission is headquartered in Brussels, Belgium.

Court of Justice The Court of Justice is the court of appeals of the EU and is composed of one judge from each member nation and a smaller number of advocates general who hold renewable six-year terms. One type of case that the Court of Justice hears is one in which a member nation is accused of not meeting its treaty obligations. Another type is one in which the commission or council is charged with failing to live up to its responsibilities under the terms of a treaty. Like the commissioners, justices are required to act in the interest of the EU as a whole, not in the interest of their own countries. The Court of Justice is located in Luxembourg.

Court of Auditors The Court of Auditors is made up of one individual per each member nation appointed for renewable six-year terms. The court is assigned the duty of auditing the EU accounts and implementing its budget. It also aims to improve financial management in the EU and to report to member nations' citizens on the use of public funds. As such, it issues annual reports and statements on the implementation of the EU budget. The court employs a large number of subordinate auditors and staff to assist it in carrying out its functions. The Court of Auditors is based in Luxembourg.

⭐ **MyLab Management** Watch It Regional Economic Integration
Outlook for the European Union

Apply what you have learned so far about regional economic integration. If your instructor has assigned this, go to **www.pearson.com/mylab/management** to watch a video case to learn more about the the European Union and answer questions.

European Free Trade Association (EFTA)

Certain nations in Europe were reluctant to join in the ambitious goals of the EU, fearing destructive rivalries and a loss of national sovereignty. Some of these nations did not want to be part of a common market but instead wanted the benefits of a free trade area. In 1960, several countries banded together and formed the *European Free Trade Association (EFTA)* to focus on trade in industrial, not consumer, goods. Because some of the original members joined the EU and some new members joined EFTA (www.efta.int), today the group consists of only Iceland, Liechtenstein, Norway, and Switzerland (see Map 8.2).

The population of EFTA is around 13.5 million, and it has a combined GDP of around $800 billion. Despite its relatively small size, members remain committed to free trade principles and raising standards of living for their people. The EFTA and the EU created the *European Economic Area (EEA)* to cooperate on matters such as the free movement of goods, persons, services, and capital among member nations. The two groups also cooperate in other areas, including the environment, social policy, and education.

QUICK STUDY 2

1. What is the name of the official single currency of the European Union?
2. A country may receive membership in the European Union once it meets what are called the *what*?
3. Why did nations belonging to the European Free Trade Association not want to join the European Union?

8.3 Integration in the Americas

Europe's success at economic integration caused other nations to consider the benefits of forming their own regional trading blocs. Latin American countries began forming regional trading arrangements in the early 1960s, but they made substantial progress only in the 1980s and 1990s. North America was about three decades behind Europe in taking major steps toward economic integration. Let's now explore the major efforts toward economic integration in North, South, and Central America, beginning with North America.

8.3 Describe integration in the Americas and its prospects.

North American Free Trade Agreement

There has always been a good deal of trade between Canada and the United States. Canada and the United States had in the past established trade agreements in several industrial sectors of their economies, including automotive products. In January 1989, the *US–Canada Free Trade Agreement* went into effect. The goal was to eliminate all tariffs on bilateral trade between Canada and the United States by 1998.

Accelerating integration in Europe caused new urgency in the task of creating a North American trading bloc that included Mexico. Mexico joined what is now the World Trade Organization in 1987 and began privatizing state-owned enterprises in 1988. Talks among Canada, Mexico, and the United States in 1991 eventually resulted in the formation of the *North American Free Trade Agreement (NAFTA)*. NAFTA (www.nafta-sec-alena.org) became effective in January 1994 and superseded the US–Canada Free Trade Agreement. Today NAFTA comprises a market with 480 million consumers and a GDP of around $21 trillion (see Map 8.1).

As a free trade agreement, NAFTA has eliminated all tariffs and nontariff trade barriers on goods originating within North America. The agreement also calls for liberalized rules regarding government procurement practices, the granting of subsidies, and the imposition of countervailing duties (see Chapter 6). Other provisions deal with issues such as trade in services, intellectual property rights, and standards of health, safety, and the environment.

LOCAL CONTENT REQUIREMENTS AND RULES OF ORIGIN While NAFTA encourages free trade among Canada, Mexico, and the United States, manufacturers and distributors must abide by local content requirements and rules of origin. Although producers and distributors rarely know the precise origin of every part or component in a piece of industrial equipment, they are responsible for determining whether a product has sufficient North American content to qualify for tariff-free status. The producer or distributor must also provide a NAFTA "certificate of origin" to an importer to claim an exemption from tariffs. Four criteria determine whether a good meets NAFTA rules of origin:

- Goods wholly produced or obtained in the NAFTA region
- Goods containing nonoriginating inputs but meeting Annex 401 origin rules (which covers regional input)
- Goods produced in the NAFTA region wholly from originating materials
- Unassembled goods and goods classified in the same harmonized system category as their parts that do not meet Annex 401 rules but that have sufficient North American regional value content

EFFECTS OF NAFTA Since NAFTA came into effect, trade among the three participating nations has increased markedly, with the greatest gains occurring between Mexico and the United States. Today, the United States exports more to Mexico than it does to Britain, France, Germany, and Italy combined. In fact, Mexico is the third largest source of US imports (behind China and Canada) and is the second largest market for US exports (behind Canada).

Overall, NAFTA has helped trade among the three countries to grow from $297 billion in 1993 to around $1.6 trillion. Since the start of NAFTA, Mexico's exports to the United States have jumped to around $280 billion, and US exports to Mexico have grown to more than $226 billion.[4] Over the same period, Canada's exports to the United States more than doubled to nearly $332 billion, and US exports to Canada grew to $300 billion. As these numbers suggest, the United States has developed a trade deficit with Canada and Mexico. Canada and Mexico traded very little with each other before NAFTA. But within a few years, Canada's exports to Mexico grew to $3.9 billion and Mexico's exports to Canada grew from $1.5 billion to $5.2 billion.[5]

The agreement's effect on employment and wages is not as easy to determine. The US Trade Representative Office claims that exports to Mexico and Canada support 2.9 million US jobs (900,000 more than in 1993), which pay 13 to 18 percent more than national averages for production workers.[6] But the AFL-CIO group of unions disputes this claim; it argues that, since its formation, NAFTA has cost the United States more than one million jobs and job opportunities.[7]

In addition to claims of job losses, opponents claim that NAFTA has damaged the environment, particularly along the United States–Mexico border. Although the agreement included provisions for environmental protection, Mexico is making some headway in dealing with the environmental impact of greater economic activity. Mexico's *Instituto Nacional de Ecologia* (www.ine.gob.mx) has developed an industrial waste–management program, including an incentive system to encourage waste reduction and recycling. The US and Mexican federal governments have invested several billion dollars in environmental protection efforts since the creation of NAFTA.[8]

EXPANSION OF NAFTA Continued ambivalence among union leaders and environmental watchdogs regarding the long-term effects of NAFTA are partly responsible for delays in the possible expansion of NAFTA. The pace at which it expands will depend to a large extent on whether the US Congress grants successive US presidents trade-promotion ("fast track") authority.

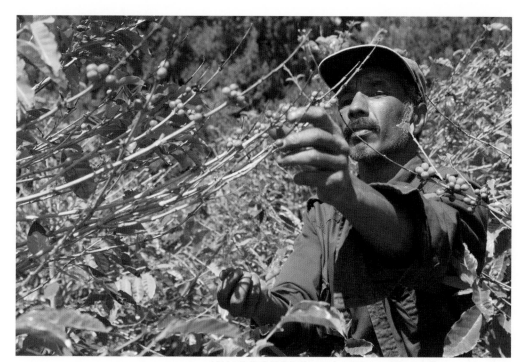

Coffee is a main crop for small farmers across Central America. Like other free trade agreements, CAFTA-DR has supporters as well as detractors. Supporters say the agreement will encourage trade efficiency and promote investment that will bring good-paying jobs to the region. Others fear that the agreement will benefit large U.S. companies and badly damage small businesses and farmers across Central America.

Darrin Henry/123RF.com

Trade-promotion authority allows a US administration to engage in all necessary talks surrounding a trade deal without the official involvement of Congress. After details of the deal are decided, Congress then simply votes yes or no on the deal and cannot revise the treaty's provisions.

If the pace of expansion accelerates for NAFTA, it is possible that the North American economies will one day adopt a single currency. As trade among Canada, Mexico, and the United States strengthens, a single currency (likely the US dollar) would benefit companies in these countries with reduced exposure to changes in exchange rates. Although this would be difficult for Canada and Mexico to accept politically, in the long run we could see one currency for all of North America.

Central American Free Trade Agreement (CAFTA-DR)

The potential benefits from freer trade induced another trading bloc between the United States and six far smaller economies. The *Central American Free Trade Agreement (CAFTA-DR)* was established in 2006 between the United States and Costa Rica, El Salvador, Guatemala, Honduras, Nicaragua, and, later, the Dominican Republic.

Prior to its creation, CAFTA-DR nations had already traded a great deal. The Central American nations and the Dominican Republic are already the second-largest US export market in Latin America behind Mexico. The CAFTA-DR nations represent a US export market larger than India, Indonesia, and Russia combined. Likewise, nearly 80 percent of exports from the Central American nations and the Dominican Republic already enter the United States tariff free. And Central American nations have already cut average tariffs from 45 percent in 1985 to around 7 percent today. The combined value of goods traded between the United States and the six other CAFTA-DR countries is around $50 billion.[9]

The agreement benefits the United States in several ways. CAFTA-DR aims to reduce tariff and nontariff barriers against US exports to the region. It also ensures that US companies are not disadvantaged by Central American nations' trade agreements with Mexico, Canada, and other countries. The agreement also requires the Central American nations and the Dominican Republic to reform their legal and business environments to encourage competition and investment, protect intellectual property rights, and promote transparency and the rule of law. CAFTA-DR is also designed to support US national security interests by advancing regional integration, peace, and stability.

Andean Community (CAN)

Attempts at integration among Latin American countries had a rocky beginning. The first try, the *Latin American Free Trade Association (LAFTA)*, was formed in 1961. The agreement first called for the creation of a free trade area by 1971 but then extended that date to 1980. Yet because of a crippling debt crisis in South America and a reluctance of member nations to do away with protectionism, the agreement was doomed to an early demise. Disappointment with LAFTA led to the creation of two other regional trading blocs—the Andean Community and the Latin American Integration Association.

Formed in 1969, the *Andean Community* (in Spanish *Comunidad Andina de Naciones*, or *CAN*) includes four South American countries located in the Andes mountain range—Bolivia, Colombia, Ecuador, and Peru (see Map 8.1). Today, the Andean Community (www.comunidadandina.org) comprises a market of around 100 million consumers and a combined GDP of about $600 billion. The main objectives of the group include tariff reduction for trade among member nations, a common external tariff, and common policies in both transportation and certain industries. The Andean Community had the ambitious goal of establishing a common market by 1995, but delays mean that it remains a somewhat incomplete customs union.

Several factors hamper progress. Political ideology among member nations is somewhat hostile to the concept of free markets and favors a good deal of government involvement in business affairs. Also, inherent distrust among members makes lower tariffs and more open trade hard to achieve. The common market will be difficult to implement within the framework of the Andean Community. One reason is that each country has been given significant exceptions in the tariff structure that they have in place for trade with nonmember nations. Another reason is that countries continue to sign agreements with just one or two countries outside the Andean Community framework. Independent actions impair progress internally and hurt the credibility of the Andean Community with the rest of the world.

Southern Common Market (MERCOSUR)

The *Southern Common Market* (in Spanish *El Mercado Comun del Sur*, or *MERCOSUR*) was established in 1988 between Argentina and Brazil but expanded to include Paraguay and Uruguay in 1991 and Venezuela in 2006. Venezuela's membership was later suspended in 2016. Associate members of MERCOSUR (www.mercosur.int) include Bolivia, Chile, Colombia, Ecuador, Peru, and Suriname (see Map 8.1). Mexico has been granted observer status in the bloc.

Today, MERCOSUR acts as a customs union and boasts a market of more than 290 million consumers (nearly half of Latin America's total population) and a GDP of around $4 trillion. Its first years of existence were very successful, with trade among members growing nearly fourfold. MERCOSUR is progressing on trade and investment liberalization and is emerging as the most powerful trading bloc in all of Latin America. Latin America's large consumer base and its potential as a low-cost production platform for worldwide export appeal to both the European Union and the United States.

Central America and the Caribbean

Attempts at economic integration in Central American countries and throughout the Caribbean basin have been much more modest than efforts elsewhere in the Americas. Nevertheless, let's look at two efforts at integration in these two regions—CARICOM and CACM.

CARIBBEAN COMMUNITY AND COMMON MARKET (CARICOM) The *Caribbean Community and Common Market (CARICOM)* trading bloc was formed in 1973. There are 15 full members, 5 associate members, and 8 observers active in CARICOM (www.caricom.org). Although the Bahamas is a member of the community, it does not belong to the common market. As a whole, CARICOM has a combined GDP of nearly $30 billion and a market of almost 16 million people.

A key CARICOM agreement calls for the establishment of a Single Market, which would permit the free movement of factors of production including goods, services, capital, and labor. The main difficulty CARICOM will continue to face is that most members trade more with nonmembers than they do with one another simply because members do not have the imports each other needs.

CENTRAL AMERICAN COMMON MARKET (CACM) The *Central American Common Market (CACM)* was formed in 1961 to create a common market. Today, its members are Costa Rica, El Salvador, Guatemala, Honduras, and Nicaragua. Together, the members of CACM comprise a market of 30 million consumers and have a combined GDP of about $200 billion. The common market was never realized, however, because of a long war between El Salvador and Honduras and guerrilla conflicts in several countries. Yet, renewed peace is creating more business confidence and optimism, which is driving double-digit growth in trade between members.

Furthermore, the group has not yet created a customs union. External tariffs among members range between 4 and 12 percent. The tentative nature of cooperation was obvious when Honduras and Nicaragua slapped punitive tariffs on each other's goods during a recent dispute. But officials remain positive, saying that their ultimate goal is European-style integration, closer political ties, and adoption of a single currency—probably the dollar. In fact, El Salvador has adopted the US dollar as its official currency, and Guatemala already uses the dollar alongside its own currency, the quetzal.

Free Trade Area of the Americas (FTAA)

A truly daunting trading bloc would be the creation of a *Free Trade Area of the Americas (FTAA)*. The objective of the FTAA (www.alca-ftaa.org) is to create the largest free trade area on the planet, stretching from the northern tip of Alaska to the southern tip of Tierra del Fuego, in South America. The FTAA would comprise 34 nations and 830 million consumers, with Cuba being the only Western Hemisphere nation excluded from participating. The FTAA would work alongside existing trading blocs throughout the region.

The first official meeting, the 1994 Summit of the Americas, created the broad blueprint for the agreement. Nations reaffirmed their commitment to the FTAA at the Second Summit of the Americas four years later when negotiations began. The Third Summit of the Americas in 2001 met with fierce protests. The ambitious plan of the FTAA means that it will likely be many years before such an agreement would be realized.

> **QUICK STUDY 3**
>
> 1. Canada, Mexico, and the United States belong to the regional trading bloc called *what*?
> 2. What countries belong to the regional trading bloc called CAFTA-DR?
> 3. What is the name of Latin America's most powerful regional trading bloc?

8.4 Integration in Asia and Elsewhere

Efforts toward economic and political integration outside Europe and the Americas tend to be looser arrangements. Let's take a look at important coalitions in Asia, the Middle East, and Africa.

8.4 Summarize integration in Asia and elsewhere.

Association of Southeast Asian Nations (ASEAN)

Indonesia, Malaysia, the Philippines, Singapore, and Thailand formed the *Association of Southeast Asian Nations (ASEAN)* in 1967. Brunei joined in 1984, Vietnam in 1995, Laos and Myanmar in 1997, and Cambodia in 1998 (see Map 8.1). Together, the 10 ASEAN (www.asean.org) countries comprise a market of nearly 600 million consumers and a GDP of nearly $2.4 trillion. The three main objectives of the alliance are to (1) promote economic, cultural, and social development in the region; (2) safeguard the region's economic and political stability; and (3) serve as a forum in which differences can be resolved fairly and peacefully.

The decision to admit Cambodia, Laos, and Myanmar was criticized by some Western nations. The concern regarding Laos and Cambodia being admitted stems from their roles in supporting the communists during the Vietnam War. The quarrel with Myanmar centered on evidence cited by the West of its human rights violations. Yet, ASEAN felt that adding these countries to the coalition could help it to counter China's rising strength with its abundance of inexpensive labor and raw materials.

Companies involved in Asia's developing economies are likely to be doing business with an ASEAN member. This is even a more likely prospect as China, Japan, and South Korea accelerate their efforts to join ASEAN. China's admission would allow the club to bridge the gap between less advanced and more advanced economies. Some key facts about ASEAN that companies should consider are contained in the Manager's Briefcase, titled "The Ins and Outs of ASEAN."

Asia Pacific Economic Cooperation (APEC)

The organization for *Asia Pacific Economic Cooperation (APEC)* was formed in 1989. Begun as an informal forum among 12 trading partners, APEC (www.apec.org) now has 21 members

MANAGER'S BRIEFCASE   The Ins and Outs of ASEAN

Businesses unfamiliar with operating in ASEAN countries should exercise caution in their dealings. Some inescapable facts about ASEAN that warrant consideration are the following:

- **Diverse Cultures and Politics** The Philippines is a representative democracy, Brunei is an oil-rich sultanate, and Vietnam is a state-controlled country. Business policies and protocols must be adapted to suit each country.
- **Economic Competition** Many ASEAN nations are feeling the effects of China's power to attract investment from multinational corporations worldwide. Whereas ASEAN members used to attract around 30 percent of foreign direct investment into Asia's developing economies, they now attract about half that amount.
- **Corruption and Shadow Markets** Bribery and shadow (unofficial) markets are common in many ASEAN countries,

including Indonesia, Myanmar, the Philippines, and Vietnam. Studies typically place these countries very high on the list of nations surveyed for corruption.
- **Political Change and Turmoil** Several nations in the region recently elected new leaders and some go through presidents at a fast clip. Companies must remain alert to shifting political winds and laws regarding trade and investment.
- **Border Disputes** Parts of Thailand's borders with Cambodia and Laos are tested frequently. Hostilities break out sporadically between Thailand and Myanmar over border alignment and ethnic Shan rebels operating along the border.
- **Lack of Common Tariffs and Standards** Doing business in ASEAN nations can be costly. Harmonized tariffs, quality and safety standards, customs regulations, and investment rules could cut transaction costs significantly.

(see Map 8.1). Together, the APEC nations account for more than 44 percent of world trade and have a combined GDP of nearly $36 trillion.

The stated aim of APEC is not to build another trading bloc. Instead, it desires to strengthen the multilateral trading system and expand the global economy by simplifying and liberalizing trade and investment procedures among member nations. In the long term, APEC hopes to have completely free trade and investment throughout the region.

THE RECORD OF APEC APEC has succeeded in halving its members' tariff rates from an average of 15 to 7.5 percent. The early years saw the greatest progress, but liberalization received a setback when the Asian financial crisis struck in the late 1990s. APEC is at least as much a political body as it is a movement toward freer trade. After all, APEC certainly does not have the focus or the record of accomplishments of NAFTA or the EU. Nonetheless, open dialogue and attempts at cooperation should continue to encourage progress, however slow.

Further progress may create some positive benefits for people doing business in APEC nations. APEC is changing the granting of business visas so that businesspeople can travel throughout the region without obtaining multiple visas. It is recommending mutual recognition agreements on professional qualifications so that engineers, for example, can practice in any APEC country, regardless of nationality. And APEC is ready to simplify and harmonize customs procedures. Eventually, businesses could use the same customs forms and manifests for all APEC economies.

Closer Economic Relations (CER) Agreement

Australia and New Zealand created a free trade agreement in 1966 and formed the *Closer Economic Relations (CER) Agreement* in 1983 to further advance free trade and integrate their two economies (see Map 8.1). The CER completely eliminated tariffs and quotas between Australia and New Zealand in 1990, five years ahead of schedule. Each nation allows goods (and most services) to be sold within its borders that can be legally sold in the other country. Each nation also recognizes most professionals who are registered to practice their occupation in the other country.

Gulf Cooperation Council (GCC)

Several Middle Eastern nations formed the *Gulf Cooperation Council (GCC)* in 1980. Members of the GCC are Bahrain, Kuwait, Oman, Qatar, Saudi Arabia, and the United Arab Emirates. The primary purpose of the GCC at its formation was to cooperate with the EU and EFTA. But it evolved to become as much a political entity as an economic one. Its cooperative thrust allows citizens of member countries to travel freely in the GCC without visas. It also permits citizens of one member nation to own land, property, and businesses in any other member nation without the need for local sponsors or partners.

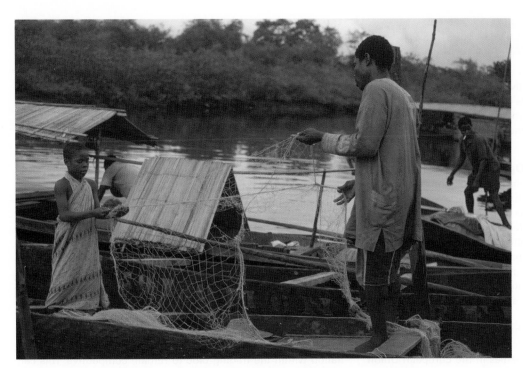

A Nigerian fisherman and child attend to fishing nets on their boat. Nigeria participates in the regional trading bloc—known as ECOWAS—in order to improve the lives of its people. The latest food crisis to hit Africa brought participants to Lagos from 25 African countries to exchange ideas with international organizations. Africa is the only region in the world where fish consumption is falling, which led to calls for massive investment in fish farms.

Sarah Errington/Hutchison Archive/Eye Ubiquitous/Alamy Stock Photo

Economic Community of West African States (ECOWAS)

The *Economic Community of West African States (ECOWAS)* was formed in 1975 but its efforts at economic integration were restarted in 1992 because of a lack of early progress. The most important goals of ECOWAS (www.ecowas.int) include the formation of a customs union, an eventual common market, and a monetary union. The ECOWAS nations comprise a large portion of the economic activity in sub-Saharan Africa, but progress on market integration is almost nonexistent. In fact, the value of trade occurring among ECOWAS nations is just 11 percent of the value that the trade members undertake with third parties. But ECOWAS made progress in the free movement of people, construction of international roads, and development of international telecommunication links. Some of its main problems are due to political instability, poor governance, weak national economies, poor infrastructure, and poor economic policies.

African Union (AU)

A group of 55 nations on the African continent joined forces in 2002 to create the *African Union (AU)*. Heads of state of the nations belonging to the Organization of African Unity paved the way for the AU (www.au.int.en/) when they signed the Sirte Declaration in 1999.

The AU is based on the vision of a united and strong Africa and on the need to build a partnership among governments and all segments of civil society in order to strengthen cohesion among the peoples of Africa. Its ambitious goals are to promote peace, security, and stability across Africa and to accelerate economic and political integration while addressing problems compounded by globalization. Specifically, the stated aims of the AU are to (1) rid the continent of the remaining vestiges of colonialism and apartheid, (2) promote unity and solidarity among African states, (3) coordinate and intensify cooperation for development, (4) safeguard the sovereignty and territorial integrity of members, and (5) promote international cooperation within the framework of the United Nations. Although it is too early to judge the success of the AU, there is no shortage of opportunities for it to demonstrate its capabilities.

QUICK STUDY 4

1. What are the stated aims of the Association of Southeast Asian Nations (ASEAN)?
2. The stated aim of which organization is not to build a trading bloc but instead to strengthen the multilateral trading system?
3. What is the name of the grouping of 55 nations across the continent of Africa?

BOTTOM LINE FOR BUSINESS

Regional economic integration can expand buyer selection, lower prices, increase productivity, and boost national competitiveness. Yet, integration has its drawbacks, and governments and independent organizations work to counter those negative effects. Here we review regional integration as it relates to business operations and employment.

Integration and Business Operations

Regional trade agreements are changing the landscape of the global marketplace. They are lowering trade barriers and opening up new markets for goods and services. Markets otherwise off-limits because tariffs made imported products too expensive can become attractive after tariffs are lifted. Trade agreements can also be double-edged swords for companies. Not only do they allow domestic companies to seek new markets abroad, they also let competitors from other nations enter the domestic market. Such mobility increases competition in every market that participates in such an agreement.

Despite increased competition that often accompanies regional integration, there can be economic benefits, such as those provided by a single currency. Companies in the European Union clearly benefit from its common currency, the euro. First, charges for converting from one member nation's currency to that of another can be avoided. Second, business owners need not worry about potential losses due to shifting exchange rates on cross-border deals. Not having to cover such costs and risks frees up capital for greater investment. Third, the euro makes prices between markets more transparent, making it more difficult to charge different prices in different markets. This helps companies compare prices among suppliers of a raw material, intermediate product, or service.

Another benefit is lower tariffs or none at all. This allows a multinational company to reduce its number of factories that supply a region and thereby reap economies of scale benefits. This is possible because a company can produce in one location and then ship products throughout the low-tariff region at little additional cost. This lowers costs and increases productivity.

One potential drawback of regional integration is that lower tariffs between members of a trading bloc can result in trade diversion. This can increase trade with less-efficient producers within the trading bloc and reduce trade with more-efficient non-member producers. Unless there is other internal competition for the producer's good or service, buyers will likely pay more after trade diversion.

Integration and Employment

Perhaps most controversial is the impact of regional integration on jobs. Companies can affect the job environment by contributing to dislocations in labor markets. The nation that supplies a particular good or service within a trading bloc is likely to be the most-efficient producer. When that product is labor intensive, the cost of labor in that market is likely to be quite low. Competitors in other nations may shift production to that relatively lower-wage nation within the trading bloc to remain competitive. This can mean lost jobs in the relatively higher-wage nation.

Yet job dislocation can be an opportunity for workers to upgrade their skills and gain more advanced training. This can help nations increase their competitiveness because a more educated and skilled workforce attracts higher-paying jobs. An opportunity for a nation to improve its competitiveness, however, is little consolation to people finding themselves suddenly out of work.

Although there are drawbacks to integration, there are potential gains from increased trade such as raising living standards. Regional economic integration efforts are likely to continue rolling back barriers to international trade and investment because of their potential benefits.

MyLab Management

Go to **www.pearson.com/mylab/management** to complete the problems marked with this icon .

Chapter Summary

LO8.1 Outline the levels of economic integration and its debate.
- There are five levels of regional economic integration, with each level signifying greater cooperation among nations: *free trade area, customs union, common market, economic union,* and *political union.*
- Arguments for free trade include: (1) trade creation expands buyer selection, decreases prices, increases productivity, and boosts national competitiveness; (2) greater consensus to reduce barriers among smaller groups of nations; (3) political cooperation can enhance negotiating power, and reduce potential military conflict; and (4) corporate savings can arise from modifying strategies and eliminating duplicate factories.
- Arguments against free trade include: (1) trade diversion can result in increased trade with a less-efficient producer within the trading bloc; (2) jobs are lost when factories close and jobs move to lower-wage nations; and (3) cultural identity and national sovereignty is diminished due to increased exposure to other cultures.

LO8.2   Describe integration in Europe and its enlargement.
- The *European Coal and Steel Community* formed in 1951 to remove trade barriers for coal, iron, steel, and scrap metal among members. After waves of expansion, broadenings of its scope, and name changes, the community is now called the European Union (EU) and currently has 28 members.
- Five main institutions of the EU are the European Parliament, European Commission, Council of the European Union, Court of Justice, and Court of Auditors. The EU single currency has been adopted by 19 member nations, which benefit from no exchange-rate risk and currency conversion costs within the euro zone.
- The *European Free Trade Association (EFTA)* has four members and was created to focus on trade in industrial goods.

LO8.3   Describe integration in the Americas and its prospects.
- The *North American Free Trade Agreement (NAFTA)* began in 1994 among Canada, Mexico, and the United States; it seeks to eliminate all tariffs and nontariff trade barriers on goods originating from within North America. The *Central American Free Trade Agreement (CAFTA-DR)* was established in 2006 between the United States and six Central American nations to boost the efficiency of trade.
- The *Andean Community* was formed in 1969 and calls for tariff reduction for trade among member nations, a common external tariff, and common policies in transportation and certain industries. The *Southern Common Market (MERCOSUR)*, established in 1988, acts as a customs union.
- The *Caribbean Community and Common Market (CARICOM)* trading bloc was formed in 1973, and the *Central American Common Market (CACM)* was formed in 1961.

LO8.4   Summarize integration in Asia and elsewhere.
- The *Association of Southeast Asian Nations (ASEAN)* formed in 1967 and seeks to: (1) promote economic, cultural, and social development; (2) safeguard economic and political stability; and (3) serve as a forum to resolve differences peacefully.
- The organization for *Asia Pacific Economic Cooperation (APEC)* was formed in 1989 and strives to strengthen the multilateral trading system and expand the global economy. The *Closer Economic Relations (CER) Agreement* in 1983 between Australia and New Zealand totally eliminated tariffs and quotas between the two economies.
- The *Gulf Cooperation Council (GCC)* of 1980 allows citizens of Middle Eastern countries to travel freely without visas and to own properties in other member nations. The *African Union (AU)* was started in 2002 among 55 nations to promote peace, security, and stability and to accelerate economic and political integration across Africa.

Key Terms

common market (p. 225)
customs union (p. 225)
economic union (p. 225)
European monetary union (p. 229)

free trade area (p. 224)
political union (p. 225)
regional economic integration (regionalism) (p. 224)

trade creation (p. 226)
trade diversion (p. 227)

✪ TALK ABOUT IT 1

Some people believe that the rise of regional trading blocs threatens free trade progress made by the World Trade Organization (WTO).

8-1. What arguments can you present to *counter* this point of view?
8-2. Do you think regional trading blocs promote or undermine regional or global stability? Explain.

⭐ TALK ABOUT IT 2

Some governments across the Americas are strong supporters of the Free Trade Area of the Americas (FTAA). This is true despite evidence that small companies typically have difficulty competing against large multinationals when their nations take part in regional trading blocs.

8-3. Do you think the FTAA would improve living standards in small countries (such as Ecuador and Nicaragua) or benefit only the largest nations such as Canada and the United States? Explain.

8-4. What can national governments do to help small companies compete in large trading blocs like the FTAA?

Ethical Challenge

You are an economic advisor to Papua New Guinea, a prospective member of the Association of Southeast Asian Nations (ASEAN). The group was founded in 1967 when the Bangkok Declaration was signed by the original five members. Since then the membership has grown to 10. Members are expected to agree to all the treaties, declarations, and agreements of ASEAN. There are no conditions to membership other than being located in Southeast Asia. There are no expectations regarding the government, ideology, development status, or economic policy. ASEAN acknowledges the fact that there are diverse types of country in the region.

8-5. Is ASEAN taking the right approach by not setting any pre-conditions to membership?

8-6. Why might Papua New Guinea not yet be a member of ASEAN?

8-7. How might membership be disadvantageous to the domestic industries in Papua New Guinea?

Teaming Up

Two groups of four students each will debate the merits of an Eastern European country joining the European Union. After the first student from each side has spoken, the second student will question the opponent's arguments, looking for holes and inconsistencies. The third student will attempt to answer these arguments. The fourth student will present a summary of each side's arguments. Finally, the class will vote on which team has offered the more compelling argument.

⭐ Market Entry Strategy Project

This exercise corresponds to the *MESP* online simulation. For the country your team is researching, integrate your answers to the following questions into your completed *MESP* report.

8-8. Is the nation participating in any regional integration efforts?

8-9. What other nations are members of the group?

8-10. What economic, political, and social objectives are driving the integration efforts?

8-11. So far, what have been the positive and negative results of integration?

8-12. How are international companies coping?

8-13. Are companies' coping strategies succeeding or failing?

MyLab Management

⭐ Go to **www.pearson.com/mylab/management** for the following assisted-graded writing questions:

8-14. Supporters of free trade agreements are winning the argument as nations continue to form bilateral and multilateral agreements with other nations. When do you think the proliferation of regional trading blocs and the integration process will stop, if ever? Explain.

8-15. Certain groups of countries, particularly in Africa, are far less economically developed than other regions, such as Europe and North America. What sort of integration arrangement do you think developed countries could create with less developed nations to improve living standards?

Global Food Trade: Fair Trade or Safe Consumption?

Today, Europeans thousands of miles away from India can put Indian-grown mangoes on their breakfast cereal. U.S. citizens braving a freezing Minnesota winter can indulge their cravings for summer-fresh raspberries with fruit brought in from Mexico. Japanese shoppers can buy apples that were grown in New Zealand and South Africa. Advances in logistics and communication technologies and increasing regional trade pacts have given consumers around the world greater choices of food products. Unfortunately, these forces have also made it more likely that consumers will contract illnesses from food-borne pathogens.

In recent years, several outbreaks linked to the burgeoning global trade in produce have made headlines. One serious case occurred when 2,300 people were victims of a parasite called *Cyclospora* that had hitched a ride on raspberries grown in Guatemala. Outbreaks of hepatitis A and *Salmonella* from tainted strawberries and alfalfa sprouts, respectively, have also sickened consumers. The outbreak of severe acute respiratory syndrome (SARS) killed hundreds and sickened hundreds more, mainly in China, Singapore, and Canada. Some scientists believe a fair amount of those cases might actually have been cases of H5N1, also called avian (bird) flu. Avian flu is particularly virulent and can cross barriers between species. It is most likely transmitted through poor sanitation and the handling of poultry.

Although health officials say that there is no evidence that imports are inherently more dangerous, they do cite several reasons for concern. For one thing, produce is often imported from less-advanced countries where food hygiene and sanitation are lacking. Also, some microbes that cause no damage in their home country can be deadly when introduced in other countries. Finally, the longer the journey from farm to table, the greater the chance of contamination. Just consider the journey taken by the salmonella-ridden alfalfa sprouts: the seeds for the sprouts were bought from Uganda and Pakistan, among other nations, shipped through the Netherlands, flown into New York, trucked to retailers across the United States, and then purchased by consumers.

Incidences of food contamination show no signs of abating. Since the creation of the European Union in 1993, cross-border trade between the growing number of member states has skyrocketed. So too have the incidences of food scares. A horse meat scandal in Ireland and the United Kingdom broke in 2013 in the Republic of Ireland and soon spread to involve several EU countries. The problem was traced back to the French company Comigel, which had a very complex supply chain linked to 16 countries. It has since been established that the horse meat entered the supply chain at abattoirs in Romania, where it was wrongly labeled as beef.

As the influence of individual food-monitoring administrations in European countries has diminished, food-buying groups have set up their own regulatory powers. The Euro Retailer Produce Working Group, or EUREP, which began in Europe, now includes giant food companies worldwide. However, critics say that the food groups are more interested in commercial concerns and can easily drown out the efforts of administrative agencies such as the EU's European Food Safety Authority (EFSA).

Although it isn't feasible for the EU to plant EFSA inspectors in every country that imports and exports food, options are available. The EU could place further bans on imports from countries that fail to meet accepted food-safety standards. Better inspections could be made of farming methods and government safety systems in other countries. The World Health Organization also proposes new policies for food safety, such as introducing food irradiation and other technologies.

Thinking Globally

8-16. How do you think countries with a high volume of exports to the European Union would respond to the introduction of any stricter food-safety rules? Do you think such measures are a good way to stem the tide of food-related illnesses? Why or why not?

8-17. Sue Doneth of Marshall, Michigan, is a mother of a schoolchild who was exposed to the hepatitis A virus after eating tainted frozen strawberry desserts. Speaking before Congress, she said, "We are forcing consumers to trade the health and safety of their families for free trade. That is not fair trade. NAFTA is not a trade issue: it is a safety issue." Do you think food-safety regulations should be built into an extension of NAFTA or the EFSA? Why or why not? What are the benefits and drawbacks of putting food-safety regulations into international trade pacts?

8-18. The lack of harmonized food-safety practices and standards is just one of the challenges faced by the food industry as it becomes more global. What other challenges face the food industry in an era of economic integration and opening markets?

Sources: "Food Safety and Foodborne Illness," World Health Organization Fact Sheet No. 237, March 2007; "Preparing for a Pandemic," *Harvard Business Review*, Special Report, May 2006, pp. 20–40; "Dioxin Crisis Widens in Belgium, Netherlands," *Food Production Daily*, February 2006; "Food, the Law and Public Health: Three Models of the Relationship" (www.nuffieldtrust.org.uk.).

Chapter Nine

International Financial Markets

Learning Objectives

After studying this chapter, you should be able to

9.1 Explain the importance of the international capital market.

9.2 Describe the main components of the international capital market.

9.3 Outline the functions of the foreign exchange market.

9.4 Explain the different types of currency quotes and exchange rates.

9.5 Describe the instruments and institutions of the foreign exchange market.

A Look Back

Chapter 8 introduced the most prominent efforts at regional economic integration occurring around the world. We saw how international companies are responding to the challenges and opportunities that regional integration is creating.

A Look at This Chapter

This chapter introduces us to the international financial system by describing the structure of international financial markets. We learn first about the international capital market and its main components. We then turn to the foreign exchange market, explaining how it works and outlining its structure.

A Look Ahead

Chapter 10 concludes our study of the international financial system. We discuss the factors that influence exchange rates and explain why and how governments and other institutions try to manage exchange rates. We also present recent monetary problems in emerging markets worldwide.

MyLab Management
✪ IMPROVE YOUR GRADE!

When you see this icon ✪, visit **www.pearson.com/mylab/management** for activities that are applied, personalized, and offer immediate feedback.

Wii Is the Champion

KYOTO, Japan—Nintendo (www.nintendo.com) has been feeding the addiction of video-gaming fans worldwide since 1989. One hundred years earlier, in 1889, Fusajiro Yamauchi started Nintendo when he began manufacturing *Hanafuda* playing cards in Kyoto, Japan. Today, Nintendo produces and sells mobile gaming devices and home gaming systems, including Switch, Wii, Nintendo DS, GameCube, and Game Boy Advance, which feature such global icons as Mario, Donkey Kong, Pokémon, and others.

Nintendo took the global gaming industry by storm when it introduced the Wii with its wireless motion-sensitive remote controllers, built-in Wi-Fi, and other features. Nintendo's Wii Fit forces players through 40 exercises consisting of yoga, strength training, cardio, and even the hula-hoop. Amazingly, Nintendo has sold more than 100 million Wii units. Nintendo's newer Switch gaming system allows players to unplug their home-based system and take it with them for on-the-go fun. Retail stores

Elena Nichizhenova/123RF.com

sold out of the devices within a few hours of receiving a shipment, leaving some to fear "customer tantrums" when Nintendo released its flagship, Mario Odyssey.

Nintendo's marketing and game-design talents are not all that affect its performance—so, too, do exchange rates between the Japanese yen (¥) and other currencies. The earnings of Nintendo's subsidiaries and affiliates outside Japan must be integrated into consolidated financial statements at the end of each year. Translating subsidiaries' earnings from other currencies into a strong yen decreases Nintendo's stated earnings in yen.

Nintendo recently reported an annual net income of ¥ 257.3 billion ($2.6 billion), but also reported that its income included a foreign exchange loss of ¥ 92.3 billion ($923.5 million). A rise of the yen against foreign currencies prior to the translation of subsidiaries' earnings into yen caused the loss. As you read this chapter, consider how shifting currency values affect financial performance and how managers can reduce their impact.[1]

Well-functioning financial markets are an essential element of the international business environment. They funnel money from organizations and economies with excess funds to those with shortages. International financial markets also allow companies to exchange one currency for another. The trading of currencies and the rates at which they are exchanged are crucial to international business.

Suppose you purchase an MP3 player imported from a company based in the Philippines. Whether you realize it or not, the price you paid for that MP3 player was affected by the exchange rate between your country's currency and the Philippine *peso*. Ultimately, the Filipino company that sold you the MP3 player must convert the purchase made in your currency into Philippine *pesos*. Thus, the profit earned by the Filipino company is also influenced by the exchange rate between your currency and the peso. Managers must understand how changes in currency values—and thus in exchange rates—affect the profitability of their international business activities. Among other things, our hypothetical company in the Philippines must know how much to charge you for its MP3 player.

In this chapter, we launch our study of the international financial system by exploring the structure of the international financial markets. The two interrelated systems that comprise the international financial markets are the international capital market and foreign exchange market. We start by examining the purposes of the international capital market and tracing its recent development. We then take a detailed look at the international bond, equity, and Eurocurrency markets, each of which helps companies to borrow and lend money internationally. Later, we take a look at the functioning of the foreign exchange market—an international market for currencies that facilitates international business transactions. We close this chapter by exploring how currency convertibility affects international transactions.

9.1 Importance of the International Capital Market

9.1 Explain the importance of the international capital market.

capital market
System that allocates financial resources in the form of debt and equity according to their most efficient uses.

A **capital market** is a system that allocates financial resources in the form of debt and equity according to their most efficient uses. Its main purpose is to provide a mechanism through which those who wish to borrow or invest money can do so efficiently. Individuals, companies, governments, mutual funds, pension funds, and all types of nonprofit organizations participate in capital markets. For example, an individual might want to buy her first home, a midsized company might want to add production capacity, and a government might want to support the development of a new wireless communications system. Sometimes, these individuals and organizations have excess cash to lend, and, at other times, they need funds.

A customer shows the Philippine pesos he just converted from U.S. dollars at a moneychanger in Manila, the Philippines. The foreign exchange market gives Filipinos working overseas a safe way to wire money to relatives back home. The prices of currencies on the foreign exchange market also help determine the prices of imports and exports. And exchange rates affect the amount of profit a company receives when it translates revenue earned abroad into the home currency.

Paul Jan Hilton/Alamy Stock Photo

Purposes of National Capital Markets

There are two primary means by which companies obtain external financing: *debt* and *equity*. National capital markets help individuals and institutions borrow the money that other individuals and institutions want to lend. Although in theory borrowers could search individually for various parties who are willing to lend or invest, this would be an extremely inefficient process.

ROLE OF DEBT **Debt** consists of loans, for which the borrower promises to repay the borrowed amount (the *principal*) plus a predetermined rate of *interest*. Company debt normally takes the form of **bonds**—instruments that specify the timing of principal and interest payments. The holder of a bond (the *lender*) can force the borrower into bankruptcy if the borrower fails to pay on a timely basis. Bonds issued for the purpose of funding investments are commonly issued by private-sector companies and by municipal, regional, and national governments.

ROLE OF EQUITY **Equity** is part ownership of a company in which the equity holder participates with other part owners in the company's financial gains and losses. Equity normally takes the form of **stock**—shares of ownership in a company's assets that give *shareholders (stockholders)* a claim on the company's future cash flows. Shareholders may be rewarded with *dividends*—payments made out of surplus funds—or by increases in the value of their shares. Of course, they may also suffer losses due to poor company performance and thus experience a decrease in the value of their shares. Dividend payments are not guaranteed but are determined by the company's board of directors and are based on financial performance. In capital markets, shareholders can sell one company's stock for that of another or can *liquidate* them—exchange them for cash. **Liquidity**, which is a feature of both debt and equity markets, refers to the ease with which bondholders and shareholders can convert their investments into cash.

Purposes of the International Capital Market

The **international capital market** is a network of individuals, companies, financial institutions, and governments that invest and borrow across national boundaries. It consists of both formal exchanges (in which buyers and sellers meet to trade financial instruments) and electronic networks (in which trading occurs anonymously). This market makes use of unique and innovative financial instruments specially designed to fit the needs of investors and borrowers located in different countries. Large international banks play a central role in the international capital market. They gather the excess cash of investors and savers around the world and then channel this cash to borrowers across the globe.

EXPANDS THE MONEY SUPPLY FOR BORROWERS The international capital market is a conduit for joining borrowers and lenders in different national capital markets. A company that is unable to obtain funds from investors in its own nation can seek financing from investors elsewhere. The option of going outside the home nation is particularly important to firms in countries with small or developing capital markets of their own.

REDUCES THE COST OF MONEY FOR BORROWERS An expanded money supply reduces the cost of borrowing. Similar to the prices of potatoes, wheat, and other commodities, the "price" of money is determined by supply and demand. If its supply increases, its price—in the form of interest rates—falls. That is why excess supply creates a borrower's market, forcing down interest rates and the cost of borrowing. Projects regarded as infeasible because of low expected returns might be viable at a lower cost of financing.

REDUCES RISK FOR LENDERS The international capital market expands the available set of lending opportunities. In turn, an expanded set of opportunities helps reduce risk for lenders (investors) in two ways:

1. *Investors enjoy a greater set of opportunities from which to choose.* They can thus reduce overall portfolio risk by spreading their money over a greater number of debt and equity instruments. In other words, if one investment loses money, the loss can be offset by gains elsewhere.
2. *Investing in international securities benefits investors because some economies are growing while others are in decline.* For example, the prices of bonds in Thailand may follow a pattern that is different from bond-price fluctuations in the United States. Thus, investors reduce risk by holding international securities whose prices move independently.

debt
Loan in which the borrower promises to repay the borrowed amount (the principal) plus a predetermined rate of interest.

bond
Debt instrument that specifies the timing of principal and interest payments.

equity
Part ownership of a company in which the equity holder participates with other part owners in the company's financial gains and losses.

stock
Shares of ownership in a company's assets that give shareholders a claim on the company's future cash flows.

liquidity
Ease with which bondholders and shareholders may convert their investments into cash.

international capital market
Network of individuals, companies, financial institutions, and governments that invest and borrow across national boundaries.

GLOBAL SUSTAINABILITY   Big Results from Microfinance

Developing nations are teeming with budding entrepreneurs who need a bit of start-up capital to get going. A practice called microfinance has several key characteristics.

- **Overcoming Obstacles.** If a person in a developing country is lucky enough to obtain a loan, it is typically from a loan shark, whose sky-high interest rates devour most of the entrepreneur's profits. Thus, microfinance is an increasingly popular alternative to lend money to low-income entrepreneurs at competitive interest rates (around 10 to 20 percent) without requiring collateral. Now institutions are warming to the idea of "microsavings" so that people can manage their small but highly uneven flows of income over time.
- **One for All, and All for One.** Sometimes a loan is made to a group of entrepreneurs who sink or swim together. If one member fails to pay off a loan, all members of the group may lose future credit. Peer pressure and support often defend against defaults, however. Support networks in developing countries often incorporate extended family ties. One bank in Bangladesh boasts 98 percent on-time repayment.

- **No Glass Ceiling Here.** Although outreach to male borrowers is increasing, most microfinance borrowers are female. Women tend to be better at funneling profits into family nutrition, clothing, and education, as well as into business expansion. The successful use of microfinance in Bangladesh has increased wages, community income, and the status of women. The microfinance industry is estimated at around $8 billion worldwide.
- **Developed Country Agenda.** The microfinance concept was pioneered in Bangladesh as a way for developing countries to create the foundation for a market economy. It now might be a way to spur economic growth in depressed areas of developed nations, such as in decaying city centers. But whereas microfinance loans in developing countries typically average a few hundred dollars, those in developed nations would need to be significantly larger.

Sources: "A Better Mattress," The Economist, March 13, 2010, pp. 75–76; Steve Hamm, "Setting Standards for Microfinance," Bloomberg Businessweek (www.businessweek.com), July 28, 2008; Jennifer L. Schenker, "Taking Microfinance to the Next Level," Bloomberg Businessweek (www.businessweek.com), February 26, 2008; Grameen Bank website (www.grameen-info.org), select reports.

Would-be borrowers in developing nations often face difficulties trying to secure loans. Interest rates are often high, and borrowers typically have little or nothing to put up as collateral. For some unique methods of getting capital to small business owners in developing nations, see this chapter's Global Sustainability feature, titled "Big Results from Microfinance."

Forces Expanding the International Capital Market

Around 40 years ago, national capital markets functioned largely as independent markets. But since that time, the amount of debt, equity, and currencies traded internationally has increased dramatically. This rapid growth can be traced to three main factors:

- *Information Technology* Information is the lifeblood of every nation's capital market because investors need information about investment opportunities and their corresponding risk levels. Large investments in information technology over the past two decades have drastically reduced the costs, in both time and money, of communicating around the globe. Investors and borrowers can now respond in record time to events in the international capital market. The introduction of electronic trading that can occur after the daily close of formal exchanges also facilitates faster response times.
- *Deregulation* Deregulation of national capital markets has been instrumental in the expansion of the international capital market. The need for deregulation became apparent in the early 1970s, when heavily regulated markets in the largest countries were facing fierce competition from less regulated markets in smaller nations. Deregulation increased competition, lowered the cost of financial transactions, and opened many national markets to global investing and borrowing. But the pendulum swung the other direction when legislators tightened regulation to help avoid another global financial crisis like that of 2008–2009. More recently, the United States has loosened some of the most stringent regulations enacted during that time.
- *Financial Instruments* Greater competition in the financial industry is creating the need to develop innovative financial instruments. One result of the need for new types of financial instruments is **securitization**—the unbundling and repackaging of hard-to-trade financial assets into more liquid, negotiable, and marketable financial instruments (or *securities*). For example, a mortgage loan from a bank is not liquid or negotiable because it is a customized

securitization

Unbundling and repackaging of hard-to-trade financial assets into more liquid, negotiable, and marketable financial instruments (or *securities*).

contract between the bank and the borrower. But agencies of the US government, such as the Federal National Mortgage Association (www.fanniemae.com), guarantee mortgages against default and accumulate them as pools of assets. Securities that are backed by these mortgage pools are then sold in capital markets to raise capital for investment.

Securitization is criticized for the excessive debt that financial institutions took on in the boom years prior to 2007. When investors lost faith in securities backed by sub-prime mortgages, they sold their investments and helped spark the global credit crisis of 2008–2009. Although the trigger for the crisis was lost value in mortgage-backed securities, legislators soon began exploring the option of placing reasonable limits on securitization in order to discourage an appetite for excessive levels of debt.

✪ MyLab Management Watch It Root Capital International Strategy

Apply what you have learned so far about international capital markets. If your instructor has assigned this, go to **www.pearson.com/mylab/management** to watch a video case about how one organization lends money to businesses that fall through the cracks of traditional capital markets and answer questions.

World Financial Centers

The world's three most important financial centers are London, New York, and Tokyo. But traditional exchanges may become obsolete unless they continue to modernize, cut costs, and provide new customer services. In fact, trading over the Internet and other systems might increase the popularity of *offshore financial centers*.

OFFSHORE FINANCIAL CENTERS An **offshore financial center** is a country or territory whose financial sector features very few regulations and few, if any, taxes. These centers tend to be economically and politically stable and tend to provide access to the international capital market through an excellent telecommunications infrastructure. Most governments protect their own currencies by restricting the amount of activity that domestic companies can conduct in foreign currencies. So, companies that find it hard to borrow funds in foreign currencies can turn to offshore centers. Offshore centers are sources of (usually cheaper) funding for companies with multinational operations.

Offshore financial centers fall into two categories:

- *Operational centers* see a great deal of financial activity. Prominent operational centers include London (which does a good deal of currency trading) and Switzerland (which supplies a great deal of investment capital to other nations).
- *Booking centers* are usually located on small island nations or territories with favorable tax and/or secrecy laws. Little financial activity takes place here. Rather, funds simply pass through on their way to large operational centers. Booking centers are typically home to offshore branches of domestic banks that use them merely as bookkeeping facilities to record tax and currency-exchange information. Some important booking centers are the Cayman Islands and the Bahamas in the Caribbean; Gibraltar, Monaco, and the Channel Islands in Europe; Bahrain and Dubai in the Middle East; and Singapore in Southeast Asia.

offshore financial center
Country or territory whose financial sector features very few regulations and few, if any, taxes.

QUICK STUDY 1

1. What is the purpose of the international capital market?
2. Unbundling and repackaging hard-to-trade financial assets into more marketable financial instruments is called *what*?
3. What is a characteristic of an offshore financial center?

9.2 International Capital Market Components

Now that we have covered the basic features of the international capital market, let's take a closer look at its main components: the international bond, international equity, and Eurocurrency markets.

International Bond Market

international bond market

Market consisting of all bonds sold by issuing companies, governments, or other organizations outside their own countries.

The **international bond market** consists of all bonds sold by issuing companies, governments, or other organizations *outside their own countries*. Issuing bonds internationally is an increasingly popular way to obtain needed funding. Typical buyers include medium-sized to large banks, pension funds, mutual funds, and governments with excess financial reserves. Large international banks typically manage the sales of new international bond issues for corporate and government clients.

Eurobond

Bond issued outside the country in whose currency it is denominated.

TYPES OF INTERNATIONAL BONDS One instrument used by companies to access the international bond market is called a **Eurobond**—a bond issued outside the country in whose currency it is denominated. In other words, a bond issued by an Australian company, denominated in US dollars, and sold in Britain, France, Germany, and the Netherlands (but not available in the United States or to its residents) is a Eurobond. Because this Eurobond is denominated in US dollars, the Australian borrower both receives dollars and makes its interest payments in dollars.

Eurobonds are popular (accounting for 75 to 80 percent of all international bonds) because the governments of countries in which they are sold do not regulate them. The absence of regulation substantially reduces the cost of issuing a bond. Unfortunately, it increases its risk level—a fact that may discourage some potential investors. The traditional markets for Eurobonds are Europe and North America.

foreign bond

Bond sold outside the borrower's country and denominated in the currency of the country in which it is sold.

Companies also obtain financial resources by issuing so-called **foreign bonds**—bonds sold outside the borrower's country and denominated in the currency of the country in which they are sold. For example, a *yen*-denominated bond issued by the German carmaker BMW in Japan's domestic bond market is a foreign bond. Foreign bonds account for about 20 to 25 percent of all international bonds.

Foreign bonds are subject to the same rules and regulations as the domestic bonds of the country in which they are issued. Countries typically require issuers to meet certain regulatory requirements and to disclose details about company activities, owners, and upper management. Thus BMW's *samurai bonds* (the name for foreign bonds issued in Japan) would need to meet the same disclosure and other regulatory requirements that Toyota's bonds in Japan must meet. Foreign bonds in the United States are called *yankee bonds*, and those in the United Kingdom are called *bulldog bonds*. Foreign bonds issued and traded in Asia outside Japan (and normally denominated in dollars) are called *dragon bonds*.

INTEREST RATES: A DRIVING FORCE Today, low interest rates (the cost of borrowing) fuel growth in the international bond market. Unfortunately, low interest rates in developed nations mean that investors earn relatively little interest on bonds in those markets. So, banks, pension funds, and mutual funds are seeking higher returns in emerging markets, where higher interest payments reflect the greater risk of the bonds. At the same time, corporate and government borrowers in emerging markets badly need capital to invest in corporate expansion plans and public works projects.

This situation raises an interesting question: How can investors who are seeking higher returns and borrowers who are seeking to pay lower interest rates both come out ahead? The answer, at least in part, lies in the international bond market:

- By issuing bonds in the international bond market, borrowers from emerging markets can borrow money from other nations where interest rates are lower.
- By the same token, investors in developed countries buy bonds in emerging markets in order to obtain higher returns on their investments (although they also accept greater risk).

Despite the attraction of the international bond market, many emerging markets see the need to develop their own national markets because of volatility in the global currency market. A currency whose value is rapidly declining can wreak havoc on companies that earn profits in, say, Indonesian rupiahs but must pay off debts in dollars. Why? A drop in a country's currency forces borrowers to shell out more local currency in order to pay off the interest owed on bonds denominated in a stable currency.

International Equity Market

The **international equity market** consists of all stocks bought and sold outside the issuer's home country. Companies and governments frequently sell shares in the international equity market. Buyers include other companies, banks, mutual funds, pension funds, and individual investors. The stock exchanges that list the greatest number of companies from outside their own borders are Frankfurt, London, and New York. Large international companies frequently list their stocks on several national exchanges simultaneously and sometimes offer new stock issues only outside their country's borders. Four factors are responsible for much of the past growth in the international equity market, discussed in the following sections.

international equity market
Market consisting of all stocks bought and sold outside the issuer's home country.

SPREAD OF PRIVATIZATION As many countries abandoned central planning and socialist-style economics, the pace of privatization accelerated worldwide. A single privatization often places billions of dollars of new equity on stock markets. When the government of Peru sold its 26-percent share of the national telephone company, Telefonica del Peru (www.telefonica.com.pe), it raised $1.2 billion. Of the total value of the sale, 26 percent went to domestic retail and institutional investors in Peru, but 48 percent was sold to investors in the United States and 26 percent was sold to other international investors.

ECONOMIC GROWTH IN EMERGING MARKETS Continued economic growth in emerging markets is contributing to growth in the international equity market. Companies based in these economies require greater investment as they succeed and grow. The international equity market becomes a major source of funding because only a limited supply of funds is available in these nations.

ACTIVITY OF INVESTMENT BANKS Global banks facilitate the sale of a company's stock worldwide by bringing together sellers and large potential buyers. Increasingly, investment banks are searching for investors outside the national market in which a company is headquartered. In fact, this method of raising funds is becoming more common than listing a company's shares on another country's stock exchange.

ADVENT OF CYBERMARKETS The automation of stock exchanges is encouraging growth in the international equity market. The term *cybermarkets* denotes stock markets that have no central geographic locations. Rather, they consist of global trading activities conducted on the Internet. Cybermarkets (consisting of supercomputers, high-speed data lines, satellite uplinks, and individual personal computers) match buyers and sellers in nanoseconds. They allow companies to list their stocks worldwide through an electronic medium in which trading takes place 24 hours a day.

Eurocurrency Market

All the world's currencies that are banked outside their countries of origin are referred to as *Eurocurrency* and trade on the **Eurocurrency market**. Thus, US dollars deposited in a bank in Tokyo are called *Eurodollars*, and British pounds deposited in New York are called *Europounds*. Japanese yen deposited in Frankfurt are called *Euroyen*, and so forth.

Eurocurrency market
Market consisting of all the world's currencies (referred to as "Eurocurrency") that are banked outside their countries of origin.

Because the Eurocurrency market is characterized by very large transactions, only the very largest companies, banks, and governments are typically involved. Deposits originate primarily from four sources:

• Governments with excess funds generated by a prolonged trade surplus
• Commercial banks with large deposits of excess currency
• International companies with large amounts of excess cash
• Extremely wealthy individuals

Eurocurrency originated in Europe during the 1950s—hence the "Euro" prefix. Governments across Eastern Europe feared they might forfeit dollar deposits made in US banks if US citizens were to file claims against them. To protect their dollar reserves, they deposited them in banks across Europe. Banks in the United Kingdom began lending these dollars to finance international trade deals, and banks in other countries (including Canada and Japan) followed suit. The Euro-currency market is valued at around $6 trillion, with London accounting for about 20 percent of all deposits. Other important markets include Canada, the Caribbean, Hong Kong, and Singapore.

APPEAL OF THE EUROCURRENCY MARKET Governments tend to strictly regulate commercial banking activities in their own currencies within their borders. For example, they often force banks to pay deposit insurance to a central bank, where they must keep a certain portion of all deposits "on reserve" in noninterest-bearing accounts. Although such restrictions protect investors, they add costs to banking operations. By contrast, the main appeal of the Eurocurrency market is the complete absence of regulation, which lowers the cost of banking. The large size of transactions in this market further reduces transaction costs. Thus, banks can charge borrowers less, pay investors more, and still earn healthy profits.

interbank interest rates
Interest rates that the world's largest banks charge one another for loans.

Interbank interest rates—rates that the world's largest banks charge one another for loans—are determined in the free market. The most commonly quoted rate of this type in the Eurocurrency market is the *London Interbank Offer Rate (LIBOR)*—the interest rate that London banks charge other large banks that borrow Eurocurrency. The *London Interbank Bid Rate (LIBID)* is the interest rate offered by London banks to large investors for Eurocurrency deposits.

An unappealing feature of the Eurocurrency market is greater risk; government regulations that protect depositors in national markets are nonexistent here. Despite the greater risk of default, however, Eurocurrency transactions are fairly safe because the banks involved are large, with well-established reputations.

QUICK STUDY 2

1. What type of financial instrument is traded in the international bond market?
2. The market of all stocks bought and sold outside the issuer's home country is called *what*?
3. What does the Eurocurrency market consist of?

9.3 The Foreign Exchange Market

9.3 Outline the functions of the foreign exchange market.

Unlike domestic transactions, international transactions involve the currencies of two or more nations. To exchange one currency for another in international transactions, companies rely on a mechanism called the **foreign exchange market**—a market in which currencies are bought and sold and their prices are determined. Financial institutions can convert currencies using an **exchange rate**—the rate at which one currency is exchanged for another. Rates depend on the size of the transaction, the trader conducting it, general economic conditions, and, sometimes, government mandate.

foreign exchange market
Market in which currencies are bought and sold and their prices determined.

exchange rate
Rate at which one currency is exchanged for another.

The forces of supply and demand determine currency prices, and transactions are conducted through a process of *bid* and *ask quotes*. If someone asks for the current exchange rate of a certain currency, the bank does not know whether it is dealing with a prospective buyer or seller so it quotes two rates. The *bid quote* is the price at which the bank will buy. The *ask quote* is the price at which the bank will sell. For example, say that the British pound is quoted in US dollars at $1.5054. The bank may then bid $1.5052 to *buy* British pounds and offer to *sell* them at $1.5056. The difference between the two rates is the *bid–ask spread*. Naturally, banks will buy currencies at a lower price than they sell them and earn their profits from the bid–ask spread.

Functions of the Foreign Exchange Market

The foreign exchange market is not really a source of corporate finance. Rather, it facilitates corporate financial activities and international transactions. Investors use the foreign exchange market for four main reasons, as discussed in the following sections.

CURRENCY CONVERSION Companies use the foreign exchange market to convert one currency into another. Suppose a Malaysian company sells a large number of computers to a customer in France. The French customer wants to pay for the computers in euros, the European Union currency, whereas the Malaysian company wants to be paid in its own *ringgit*. How do the two parties resolve this dilemma? They turn to banks that will exchange the currencies for them.

China and Japan began direct trading between their currencies in Tokyo, Japan, and Shanghai, China, in 2012. Average daily turnover on Tokyo's foreign exchange market is about $240 billion. While impressive, this is significantly lower than trading volume in the U.K. market ($1.33 trillion) and the U.S. market ($618 billion). Around $3.2 trillion worth of currency is traded on global foreign exchange markets every day.

Gumpanat Thavankitdumrong/Alamy Stock Photo

Companies also must convert to local currencies when they undertake foreign direct investment. Later, when a firm's international subsidiary earns a profit and the company wants to return some of it to the home country, it must convert the local money into the home currency.

CURRENCY HEDGING The practice of insuring against potential losses that result from adverse changes in exchange rates is called **currency hedging**. International companies commonly use hedging for one of two purposes:

1. To lessen the risk associated with international transfers of funds.
2. To protect themselves in credit transactions in which there is a time lag between billing and receipt of payment.

currency hedging
Practice of insuring against potential losses that result from adverse changes in exchange rates.

Suppose a South Korean automaker has a subsidiary in Britain. The parent company in Korea knows that in 30 days—say, on February 1—its British subsidiary will be sending it a payment in British pounds. Because the parent company is concerned about the value of that payment in South Korean won a month in the future, it wants to insure against the possibility that the pound's value will fall over that period—meaning, of course, that it will receive less money. Therefore, on January 2, the parent company contracts with a financial institution, such as a bank, to exchange the payment in one month at an agreed-upon exchange rate specified on January 2. In this way, as of January 2, the Korean company knows exactly how many won the payment will be worth on February 1.

CURRENCY ARBITRAGE Currency arbitrage is the instantaneous purchase and sale of a currency in different markets for profit. Suppose a currency trader in New York notices that the value of the European Union euro is lower in Tokyo than it is in New York. The trader can buy euros in Tokyo, sell them in New York, and earn a profit on the difference. High-tech communication and trading systems allow the entire transaction to occur within seconds. But note that the trade is not worth making if the difference between the value of the euro in Tokyo and the value of the euro in New York is not greater than the cost of conducting the transaction.

currency arbitrage
Instantaneous purchase and sale of a currency in different markets for profit.

Currency arbitrage is a common activity among experienced traders of foreign exchange, very large investors, and companies in the arbitrage business. Firms whose profits are generated primarily by another economic activity, such as retailing or manufacturing, take part in currency arbitrage only if they have very large sums of cash on hand.

Interest arbitrage is the profit-motivated purchase and sale of interest-paying securities denominated in different currencies. Companies use interest arbitrage to find better interest rates abroad than those that are available in their home countries. The securities involved in such transactions include government treasury bills, corporate and government bonds, and even bank

interest arbitrage
Profit-motivated purchase and sale of interest-paying securities denominated in different currencies.

deposits. Suppose a trader notices that the interest rates paid on bank deposits in Mexico are higher than those paid in Sydney, Australia (after adjusting for exchange rates). He can convert Australian dollars to Mexican pesos and deposit the money in a Mexican bank account for, say, one year. At the end of the year, he converts the pesos back into Australian dollars and earns more in interest than the same money would have earned had it remained on deposit in an Australian bank.

currency speculation

Purchase or sale of a currency with the expectation that its value will change and generate a profit.

CURRENCY SPECULATION **Currency speculation** is the purchase or sale of a currency with the expectation that its value will change and generate a profit. The shift in value might be expected to occur suddenly or over a longer period. The foreign exchange trader may bet that a currency's price will go either up or down in the future. Suppose a trader in London believes that the value of the Japanese *yen* will increase over the next three months. She buys yen with pounds at today's current price, intending to sell them in 90 days. If the price of yen rises in that time, she earns a profit; if it falls, she takes a loss. Speculation is much riskier than arbitrage because the value, or price, of currencies is quite volatile and is affected by many factors. Similar to arbitrage, currency speculation is commonly the realm of foreign exchange specialists rather than the managers of firms engaged in other endeavors.

A classic example of currency speculation unfolded in Southeast Asia in 1997. After news emerged in May about Thailand's slowing economy and political instability, currency traders sprang into action. They responded to poor economic growth prospects and an overvalued currency, the Thai baht, by dumping the baht on the foreign exchange market. When the supply glutted the market, the value of the baht plunged. Meanwhile, traders began speculating that other Asian economies were also vulnerable. From the time the crisis first hit until the end of 1997, the value of the Indonesian rupiah fell by 87 percent, the South Korean won by 85 percent, the Thai baht by 63 percent, the Philippine peso by 34 percent, and the Malaysian ringgit by 32 percent.[2] Although many currency speculators made a great deal of money, the resulting hardship experienced by these nations' citizens caused some to question the ethics of currency speculation on such a scale.

QUICK STUDY 3

1. What is the market in which currencies are bought and sold and their prices are determined?
2. Insuring against potential losses that may result from adverse changes in exchange rates is called *what*?
3. What do we call the instantaneous purchase and sale of a currency in different markets to make a profit?

9.4 Currency Quotes and Rates

9.4 Explain the different types of currency quotes and exchange rates.

Because of the importance of foreign exchange to trade and investment, businesspeople must understand how currencies are quoted in the foreign exchange market. Managers must know what financial instruments are available to help them protect the profits earned by their international business activities. And they must be aware of government restrictions that may be imposed on the convertibility of currencies and know how to work around these and other obstacles.

Quoting Currencies

quoted currency

The numerator in a quoted exchange rate, or the currency with which another currency is to be purchased.

There are two components to every quoted exchange rate: the quoted currency and the base currency. If an exchange rate quotes the number of Japanese yen needed to buy one US dollar (¥/$), the yen is the **quoted currency** and the dollar is the **base currency**. When you designate any exchange rate, the quoted currency is always the *numerator* and the base currency is the *denominator*. For example, if you were given a yen/dollar exchange rate quote of 90/1 (meaning that 90 yen are needed to buy one dollar), the numerator is 90 and the denominator is 1. We can also designate this rate as ¥ 90/$.

base currency

The denominator in a quoted exchange rate, or the currency that is to be purchased with another currency.

DIRECT AND INDIRECT RATE QUOTES Table 9.1 lists exchange rates between the US dollar and a number of other currencies. The columns under the heading "Currency per US $" tell us how many units of each listed currency can be purchased with one US dollar. For example, in the row

TABLE 9.1 Exchange Rates of Major Currencies

Country (Currency)	Currency per US $
Argentina (peso)	3.9512
Australia (dollar)	1.1189
Bahrain (dinar)	0.3770
Brazil (real)	1.7559
Britain (pound)	0.6515
Canada (dollar)	1.0645
Chile (peso)	502.75
China (yuan)	6.8090
Colombia (peso)	1,826.45
Czech Rep. (koruna)	19.5210
Denmark (krone)	5.8684
Ecuador (US dollar)	1
Egypt (pound)	5.7055
Euro area (euro)	0.7883
Hong Kong (dollar)	7.7788
Hungary (forint)	226.3250
India (rupee)	47.0750
Indonesia (rupiah)	9040.0
Israel (shekel)	3.8147
Japan (yen)	84.3770
Jordan (dinar)	0.7057
Kenya (shilling)	81.0200
Kuwait (dinar)	0.2885
Lebanon (pound)	1,507.39
Malaysia (ringgit)	3.1405
Mexico (peso)	13.2040
New Zealand (dollar)	1.4286
Norway (krone)	6.3030
Pakistan (rupee)	85.470
Peru (new sol)	2.7970
Philippines (peso)	45.2250
Poland (zloty)	3.1551
Romania (leu)	3.3659
Russia (ruble)	30.8040
Saudi Arabia (riyal)	3.7509
Singapore (dollar)	1.3546
Slovak Rep (koruna)	23.7470
South Africa (rand)	7.3872
South Korea (won)	1,191.55
Sweden (krona)	7.3773
Switzerland (franc)	1.0163
Taiwan (dollar)	32.0250
Thailand (baht)	31.2170
Turkey (lira)	1.5266

(continued)

Table 9.1 Continued	
Country (Currency)	Currency per US $
U.A.E. (dirham)	3.6724
Uruguay (peso)	20.83
Venezuela (b. fuerte)	4.2946
Vietnam (dong)	19,495

labeled "Japan (yen)," we see that 84.3770 Japanese yen can be bought with one US dollar. We state this exchange rate as ¥ 84.3770/$. Because the yen is the quoted currency, we say that this is a *direct quote* on the yen and an *indirect quote* on the dollar. Note that the exchange rate for a nation participating in the single currency (euro) of the European Union is found on the line in the table that reads "Euro area (euro)."

When we have a direct quote on a currency and wish to calculate the indirect quote, we simply divide the currency quote into the numeral 1. The following formula is used to derive a direct quote from an indirect quote:

$$\text{Direct quote} = \frac{1}{\text{Indirect quote}}$$

And for deriving an indirect quote from a direct quote:

$$\text{Indirect quote} = \frac{1}{\text{Direct quote}}$$

In the previous example, we were given an indirect quote on the US dollar of ¥ 84.3770/$. To find the direct quote on the dollar we simply divide ¥ 84.3770 into $1:

$$\$1 \div ¥ 84.3770 = \$0.011852/¥$$

This means that it costs $0.011852 to purchase one yen (¥)—slightly more than one US cent. We state this exchange rate as $0.011852/¥. In this case, because the dollar is the quoted currency, we have a direct quote on the dollar and an indirect quote on the yen.

Businesspeople and foreign exchange traders track currency values over time because changes in currency values can benefit or harm international transactions. **Exchange-rate risk (foreign exchange risk)** is the risk of adverse changes in exchange rates. Managers develop strategies to minimize this risk by tracking percentage changes in exchange rates. To see how to calculate percentage change in the value of currencies, read this chapter's appendix on page 269.

CROSS RATES International transactions between two currencies other than the US dollar often use the dollar as a vehicle currency. For example, a retail buyer of merchandise in the Netherlands might convert its euros (recall that the Netherlands uses the European Union currency) to US dollars and then pay its Japanese supplier in US dollars. The Japanese supplier may then take those US dollars and convert them to Japanese *yen*. This process was more common years ago, when fewer currencies were freely convertible and when the United States greatly dominated world trade. Today, a Japanese supplier may want payment in euros. In this case, both the Japanese and the Dutch companies need to know the exchange rate between their respective currencies. To find this rate using their respective exchange rates with the US dollar, we calculate what is called a **cross rate**—an exchange rate calculated using two other exchange rates.

Cross rates between two currencies can be calculated using both currencies' indirect or direct exchange rates with a third currency. For example, suppose we want to know the cross rate between the currencies of the Netherlands and Japan. Looking at Table 9.1 again, we see that the direct quote on the euro is € 0.7883/$. The direct quote on the Japanese yen is ¥ 84.3770/$. To find the cross rate between the euro and the yen, with the yen as the base currency, we simply divide € 0.7883/$ by ¥ 84.3770/$:

$$€ 0.7883/\$ \div ¥ 84.3770/\$ = € 0.0093/¥$$

Thus, it costs 0.0093 euros to buy 1 yen.

Table 9.2 shows the cross rates for major world currencies. When finding cross rates using direct quotes, currencies down the left-hand side represent quoted currencies; those across the top

exchange-rate risk (foreign exchange risk)

Risk of adverse changes in exchange rates.

cross rate

Exchange rate calculated using two other exchange rates.

TABLE 9.2 Key Currency Cross Rates

	Dollar	Euro	Yen	Pound	Swiss Franc	Canadian Dollar
Canada	1.0646	1.3505	0.0126	1.6345	1.0476	. . .
Switzerland	1.0163	1.2892	0.0120	1.5603	. . .	0.9546
Britain	0.6513	0.8262	0.0077	. . .	0.6409	0.6118
Japan	84.454	107.13	. . .	129.66	83.102	79.330
Euro area	0.7883	. . .	0.0093	1.2103	0.7757	0.7405
United States	. . .	1.2686	0.0118	1.5354	0.9840	0.9393

represent base currencies. Conversely, when finding cross rates using indirect quotes, currencies down the left side represent base currencies; those across the top represent quoted currencies. Look at the intersection of the "Euro area" row (the quoted currency in our example) and the "Yen" column (our base currency). Note that the solution we calculated above for the cross rate between euro and *yen* match the listed rate of 0.0093 euros to the *yen*.

Naturally, the exchange rate between the euro and the *yen* is quite important to both the Japanese supplier and Dutch retailer we mentioned earlier. If the value of the euro falls relative to the yen, the Dutch company must pay more in euros for its Japanese products. This situation will force the Dutch company to take one of two steps: either increase the price at which it resells the Japanese product (perhaps reducing sales) or keep prices at current levels (thus reducing its profit margin).

Ironically, the Japanese supplier will suffer if the *yen* rises too much. Why? Under such circumstances, the Japanese supplier can do one of two things: allow the exchange rate to force its euro prices higher (thus maintaining profits) or reduce its *yen* prices to offset the decline of the euro (thus reducing its profit margin).

Both the Japanese supplier and the Dutch buyer can absorb exchange rate changes by squeezing profits—but only to a point. After that point is passed, they will no longer be able to trade. The Dutch buyer will be forced to look for a supplier in a country with a more favorable exchange rate or for a supplier in its own country (or another European country that uses the euro).

Spot Rates

All the exchange rates we've discussed so far are called **spot rates**—exchange rates that require delivery of the traded currency within two business days. Exchange of the two currencies is said to occur "on the spot," and the **spot market** is the market for currency transactions at spot rates. The spot market assists companies in performing any one of three functions:

1. Converting income generated from sales abroad into their home-country currency;
2. Converting funds into the currency of an international supplier;
3. Converting funds into the currency of a country in which they wish to invest.

BUY AND SELL RATES The spot rate is available only for trades worth millions of dollars. That is why it is available only to banks and foreign exchange brokers. If you are traveling to another country and want to exchange currencies at your local bank before departing, you will not be quoted the spot rate. Rather, you will receive a quote that includes a markup to cover the costs your bank incurs when performing this transaction for you.

Suppose you are taking a business trip to Spain and need to buy some euros. The bank will quote you exchange-rate terms, such as $1.268/78 per €, which means that the bank will buy US dollars at the rate of $1.268/€ and sell them at the rate of $1.278/€.

Forward Rates

When a company knows that it will need a certain amount of foreign currency on a certain future date, it can exchange currencies using a **forward rate**—an exchange rate at which two parties agree to exchange currencies on a specified future date. Forward rates represent the expectations of currency traders and bankers regarding a currency's future spot rate. Reflected in these

spot rate
Exchange rate requiring delivery of the traded currency within two business days.

spot market
Market for currency transactions at spot rates.

forward rate
Exchange rate at which two parties agree to exchange currencies on a specified future date.

expectations are a country's present and future economic conditions (including inflation rate, national debt, taxes, trade balance, and economic growth rate) as well as its social and political situation. The **forward market** is the market for currency transactions at forward rates.

To insure themselves against unfavorable exchange-rate changes, companies commonly turn to the forward market. It can be used for all types of transactions that require future payment in other currencies, including credit sales or purchases, interest receipts or payments on investments or loans, and dividend payments to stockholders in other countries. But not all nations' currencies trade in the forward market, such as countries experiencing high inflation or currencies not in demand on international financial markets.

FORWARD CONTRACTS Suppose a Brazilian bicycle maker imports parts from a Japanese supplier. Under the terms of their contract, the Brazilian importer must pay 100 million Japanese *yen* in 90 days. The Brazilian firm can wait until one or two days before payment is due, buy *yen* in the spot market, and pay the Japanese supplier. But in the 90 days between the contract date and the due date the exchange rate will likely change. What if the value of the Brazilian real goes down? In that case, the Brazilian importer will have to pay more *reais* (plural of real) to get the same 100 million Japanese yen. Therefore, our importer may want to pay off the debt before the 90-day term. But what if it does not have the cash on hand? What if it needs those 90 days to collect accounts receivable from its own customers?

To decrease its exchange-rate risk, our Brazilian importer can enter into a **forward contract**—a contract that requires the exchange of an agreed-on amount of a currency on an agreed-on date at a specified exchange rate. Forward contracts are commonly signed for 30, 90, and 180 days into the future, but customized contracts (say, for 76 days) are possible. Note that a forward contract *requires* the exchange to occur: The bank must deliver the yen, and the Brazilian importer must buy them at the prearranged price. Forward contracts belong to a family of financial instruments called **derivatives**—instruments whose values derive from other commodities or financial instruments. These include not only forward contracts but also currency swaps, options, and futures (presented next in this chapter).

In our example, the Brazilian importer can use a forward contract to pay yen to its Japanese supplier in 90 days. It is always possible, of course, that in 90 days, the value of the real will be lower than its current value. But by locking in at the forward rate, the Brazilian firm protects itself against the less favorable spot rate at which it would have to buy yen in 90 days. In this case, the Brazilian company protects itself from paying more to the supplier at the end of 90 days than if it were to pay at the spot rate in 90 days. Thus, it protects its profit from further erosion if the spot rate becomes even more unfavorable over the next three months. Remember, too, that such a contract prevents the Brazilian importer from taking advantage of any increase in the value of the Brazilian real in 90 days that would reduce what the company owed its Japanese supplier.

Swaps, Options, and Futures

In addition to forward contracts, three other types of currency instruments are used in the forward market: currency swaps, options, and futures.

CURRENCY SWAPS A **currency swap** is the simultaneous purchase and sale of foreign exchange for two different dates. Currency swaps are an increasingly important component of the foreign exchange market. Suppose a Swedish automaker imports parts from a subsidiary in Turkey. The Swedish company must pay the Turkish subsidiary in Turkish lira for the parts when they are delivered today. The company also expects to receive Turkish liras for automobiles sold in Turkey in 90 days. Our Swedish company exchanges kronor for lira in the spot market today to pay its subsidiary. At the same time, it agrees to a forward contract to sell Turkish lira (and buy Swedish kronor) in 90 days at the quoted 90-day forward rate for lira. In this way, the Swedish company uses a swap both to reduce its exchange-rate risk and to lock in the future exchange rate. In this sense, we can think of a currency swap as a more complex forward contract.

CURRENCY OPTIONS Recall that, once it is entered into, a forward contract requires an exchange of currencies. By contrast, a **currency option** is a right, or option, to exchange a specified amount of a currency on a specified date at a specified rate.

Suppose a company buys an option to purchase Swiss francs at SF 1.02/$ in 30 days. If, at the end of the 30 days, the exchange rate is SF 1.05/$, the company would *not* exercise its currency

forward market
Market for currency transactions at forward rates.

forward contract
Contract that requires the exchange of an agreed-on amount of a currency on an agreed-on date at a specified exchange rate.

derivative
Financial instrument whose value derives from other commodities or financial instruments.

currency swap
Simultaneous purchase and sale of foreign exchange for two different dates.

currency option
Right, or option, to exchange a specified amount of a currency on a specified date at a specified rate.

option. Why? It could get SF 0.03 more for every dollar by exchanging at the spot rate in the currency market rather than at the stated rate of the option. Companies often use currency options to hedge against exchange-rate risk or to obtain foreign currency.

CURRENCY FUTURES CONTRACTS Similar to a currency forward contract is a **currency futures contract**—a contract requiring the exchange of a specified amount of currency on a specified date at a specified exchange rate, with all conditions fixed and not adjustable.

currency futures contract
Contract requiring the exchange of a specified amount of currency on a specified date at a specified exchange rate, with all conditions fixed and not adjustable.

> ### QUICK STUDY 4
>
> 1. The numerator in a quoted exchange rate, or the currency with which another currency is to be purchased, is called a *what*?
> 2. What is the name given to the risk of adverse changes in exchange rates?
> 3. What do we call an exchange rate requiring delivery of a traded currency within two business days?
> 4. What instruments are used in the forward market?

9.5 Market Instruments and Institutions

The foreign exchange market is actually an electronic network that connects the world's major financial centers. In turn, each of these centers is a network of foreign exchange traders, currency trading banks, and investment firms. The daily trading volume on the foreign exchange market (comprising currency swaps and spot and forward contracts) amounts to around $4 trillion—an amount greater than the yearly gross domestic product of many small nations.[3] Several major trading centers and several currencies dominate the foreign exchange market.

9.5 Describe the instruments and institutions of the foreign exchange market.

Trading Centers

Most of the world's major cities participate in trading on the foreign exchange market. In recent years, just three countries have come to account for more than half of all global currency trading: the United Kingdom, the United States, and Japan. Accordingly, most of this trading takes place in the financial capitals of London, New York, and Tokyo.

London dominates the foreign exchange market for historic and geographic reasons. The United Kingdom was once the world's largest trading nation. British merchants needed to exchange currencies of different nations, and London naturally assumed the role of financial trading center. London quickly came to dominate the market and still does so because of its location halfway between North America and Asia. A key factor is its time zone. Because of differences in time zones, London is opening for business as markets in Asia close trading for the day. When New York opens for trading in the morning, trading is beginning to wind down in London. Also, most large banks active in foreign exchange employ overnight traders to ensure continuous trading (see Figure 9.1).

Important Currencies

Although the United Kingdom is the major location of foreign exchange trading, the US dollar is the currency that dominates the foreign exchange market. The US dollar's dominance makes it a **vehicle currency**—a currency used as an intermediary to convert funds between two other currencies. The currencies most often involved in currency transactions are the US dollar, European Union euro, Japanese yen, and British pound.

vehicle currency
Currency used as an intermediary to convert funds between two other currencies.

One reason the US dollar is a vehicle currency is because the United States is the world's largest trading nation. Many companies and banks maintain dollar deposits, making it easy to exchange other currencies with dollars. Another reason is that, following the Second World War, all of the world's major currencies were tied indirectly to the dollar because it was the most stable currency. In turn, the dollar's value was tied to a specific value of gold—a policy that held wild currency swings in check. Although world currencies are no longer linked to the value of gold (see Chapter 10), the stability of the dollar, along with its resistance to inflation, sometimes helps people and organizations maintain their purchasing power better than their own national currencies.

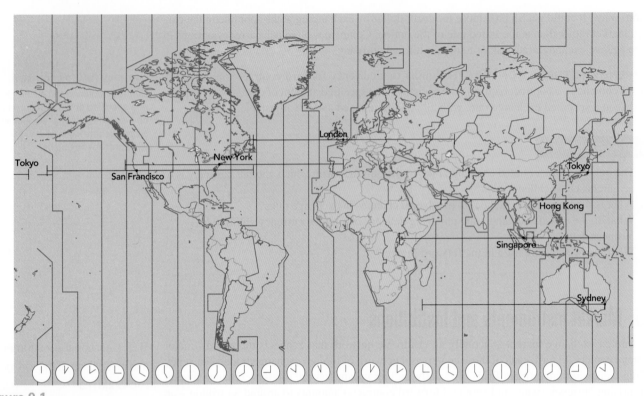

Figure 9.1

Financial Trading Centers by Time Zone

interbank market

Market in which the world's largest banks exchange currencies at spot and forward rates.

clearing

Process of aggregating the currencies that one bank owes another and then carrying out the transaction.

securities exchange

Exchange specializing in currency futures and options transactions.

Interbank Market

It is in the **interbank market** that the world's largest banks exchange currencies at spot and forward rates. Companies tend to obtain foreign exchange services from the bank where they do most of their business. Banks satisfy client requests for exchange quotes by obtaining quotes from other banks in the interbank market. For transactions that involve commonly exchanged currencies, the largest banks often have sufficient currency on hand. Yet, rarely exchanged currencies are not typically kept on hand and may not even be easily obtainable from another bank. In such cases, banks turn to *foreign exchange brokers*, who maintain vast networks of banks through which they obtain seldom-traded currencies.

In the interbank market, then, banks act as agents for client companies. In addition to locating and exchanging currencies, banks commonly offer advice on trading strategy, supply a variety of currency instruments, and provide other risk-management services. Banks also help their clients manage exchange-rate risk by supplying information on rules and regulations around the world.

Large banks in the interbank market use their influence in currency markets to get better rates for their largest clients. Small and medium-sized businesses often cannot get the best exchange rates because they deal only in small volumes of currencies and do so rather infrequently. A small company might get better exchange rate quotes from a discount international payment service.

CLEARING MECHANISMS Clearing mechanisms are an important element of the interbank market. Foreign exchange transactions among banks and foreign exchange brokers happen continuously. The accounts are not settled after each individual trade but are settled following a number of completed transactions. The process of aggregating the currencies that one bank owes another and then carrying out that transaction is called **clearing**. Years ago, banks performed clearing every day or every two days, and they physically exchanged currencies with other banks. Nowadays, clearing is performed more frequently and occurs digitally, which eliminates the need to trade currencies physically.

Securities Exchanges

Securities exchanges specialize in currency futures and options transactions. Buying and selling currencies on these exchanges entails the use of securities *brokers*, who facilitate transactions by transmitting and executing clients' orders. Transactions on securities exchanges are much smaller than those in the interbank market and vary with each currency. The leading exchange that deals in most major asset classes of futures and options is the CME Group, Inc. (www.cmegroup.com). The CME Group merged the futures and options operations of the Chicago Board of Trade, the Chicago Mercantile Exchange, and the New York Mercantile Exchange. The CME Group's foreign exchange marketplace is the world's second largest electronic foreign exchange marketplace, with more than $80 billion in daily liquidity.[4]

Another exchange is the London International Financial Futures Exchange (www.euronext .com), which trades futures and options for major currencies. In the United States, trading in currency *options* occurs only on the Philadelphia Stock Exchange (www.nasdaqtrader.com). It deals in both standardized options and customized options, allowing investors flexibility in designing currency option contracts.[5]

Over-the-Counter Market

The **over-the-counter (OTC) market** is a decentralized exchange encompassing a global computer network of foreign exchange traders and other market participants. All foreign exchange transactions can be performed in the OTC market, where the major players are large financial institutions.

The over-the-counter market has grown rapidly because it offers distinct benefits for business. It allows businesspeople to search freely for the institution that provides the best (lowest) price for conducting a transaction. It also offers opportunities for designing customized transactions. For additional ways companies can become more adept in their foreign exchange activities, see this chapter's Manager's Briefcase, titled "Managing Foreign Exchange."

over-the-counter (OTC) market
Decentralized exchange encompassing a global computer network of foreign exchange traders and other market participants.

CURRENCY RESTRICTION A **convertible (hard) currency** is traded freely in the foreign exchange market, with its price determined by the forces of supply and demand. Countries that allow full convertibility are those that are in strong financial positions and that have adequate reserves of foreign currencies. Such countries have no reason to fear that people will sell their own currency for that of another. Still, many newly industrialized and developing countries do not permit the free convertibility of their currencies.

convertible (hard) currency
Currency that trades freely in the foreign exchange market, with its price determined by the forces of supply and demand.

Governments impose currency restrictions to achieve several goals. One goal is to preserve a country's reserve of hard currencies with which to repay debts owed to other nations. Developed nations, emerging markets, and some countries that export natural resources tend to have the greatest amounts of foreign exchange. Without sufficient reserves (liquidity), a country could default on its loans and thereby discourage future investment flows. This is precisely what happened to Argentina several years ago when the country defaulted on its international public debt.

MANAGER'S BRIEFCASE   Managing Foreign Exchange

- **Match Needs to Providers** Analyze your foreign exchange needs and the range of service providers available. Find a provider that offers the transactions you undertake in the currencies you need, and consolidate repetitive transfers. Many businesspeople naturally look to local bankers when they need to transfer funds abroad, but this may not be the cheapest or best choice. A mix of service providers sometimes offers the best solution.
- **Work with the Majors** Money-center banks (those located in financial centers) that participate directly in the foreign exchange market can have cost and service advantages over local banks. Dealing directly with a large trading institution is often more cost effective than dealing with a local bank because it avoids the additional markup that the local bank charges for its services.
- **Consolidate to Save** Save money by timing your international payments to consolidate multiple transfers into one large transaction. Open a local currency account abroad against which you can write drafts if your company makes

multiple smaller payments in the same currency. Consider allowing foreign receivables to accumulate in an interest-bearing account locally until you repatriate them in a lump sum to reduce service fees.
- **Get the Best Deal Possible** If your foreign exchange activity is substantial, develop relationships with two or more money-center banks to get the best rates. Also, monitor the rates your company gets over time, as some banks raise rates if you're not shopping around. Obtain real-time market rates provided by firms like Reuters and Bloomberg.
- **Embrace Information Technology** Every time an employee phones, e-mails, or faxes in a transaction, human error could delay getting funds where and when your company needs them. Embrace information technology in your business's international wire transfers and drafts. Automated software programs available from specialized service providers reduce the potential for errors while speeding the execution of transfers.

A second goal of currency restriction is to preserve hard currencies in order to pay for imports and to finance trade deficits. Recall from Chapter 5 that a country runs a trade deficit when the value of its imports exceeds the value of its exports. Currency restrictions help governments maintain inventories of foreign currencies with which to pay for such trade imbalances. They also make importing more difficult because local companies cannot obtain foreign currency to pay for imports. The resulting reduction in imports directly improves the country's trade balance.

A third goal is to protect a currency from speculators. For example, in the wake of the Asian financial crisis years ago, some Southeast Asian nations considered controlling their currencies to limit the damage done by economic downturns. Malaysia stemmed the outflow of foreign money by preventing local investors from converting their Malaysian holdings into other currencies. Although the move also curtailed currency speculation, it effectively cut off Malaysia from investors elsewhere in the world.

A fourth (less common) goal is to keep resident individuals and businesses from investing in other nations. These policies can generate more rapid economic growth in a country by forcing investment to remain at home. Unfortunately, although this might work in the short term, it normally slows long-term economic growth. The reason is that there is no guarantee that domestic funds held in the home country will be invested there. Instead, they might be saved or even spent on consumption. Ironically, increased consumption can mean further increases in imports, making a trade deficit even worse.

Instruments for Restricting Currencies

Certain government policies are frequently used to restrict currency convertibility. Governments can require that all foreign exchange transactions be performed at or approved by the country's central bank. They can also require import licenses for some or all import transactions. These licenses help the government control the amount of foreign currency leaving the country.

Some governments implement systems of *multiple exchange rates*, specifying a higher exchange rate on the importation of certain goods or on imports from certain countries. The government can thus reduce importation while ensuring that important goods still enter the country. It also can use such a policy to target the goods of countries with which it is running a trade deficit.

Other governments issue *import deposit requirements* that require businesses to deposit certain percentages of their foreign exchange funds in special accounts before being granted import licenses. In addition, *quantity restrictions* limit the amount of foreign currency that residents can take out of the home country when traveling to other countries as tourists, students, or medical patients.

countertrade
Practice of selling goods or services that are paid for, in whole or in part, with other goods or services.

One way to get around national restrictions on currency convertibility is **countertrade**—the practice of selling goods or services that are paid for, in whole or in part, with other goods or services. One simple form of countertrade is a *barter* transaction, in which goods are exchanged for others of equal value. Parties exchange goods and then sell them in world markets for hard currency. For example, Cuba once exchanged $60 million worth of sugar for cereals, pasta, and vegetable oils from the Italian firm Italgrani. And Boeing (www.boeing.com) has sold aircraft to Saudi Arabia in return for oil. We detail the many different forms of countertrade in Chapter 13.

QUICK STUDY 5

1. Where does more than half of all global currency trading take place?
2. A currency used as an intermediary to convert funds between two other currencies is called a *what*?
3. What is another name for a freely convertible currency?
4. Why do governments sometimes engage in currency restriction?

BOTTOM LINE FOR BUSINESS

Well-functioning financial markets are essential to conducting international business. International financial markets supply companies with the mechanism they require to exchange currencies, and more. Here we focus on the main implications of these markets for international companies.

International Capital Market and Businesses

The international capital market joins borrowers and lenders from different national capital markets. A company unable to obtain funds in its own nation may use the international capital market to obtain financing elsewhere and allow the firm to undertake an otherwise impossible project. This option can be especially important for firms in countries with small or emerging capital markets.

Similar to the prices of any other commodity, the "price" of money is determined by supply and demand. If the supply increases, the price (in the form of interest rates) falls. The international capital market opens up additional sources of financing for companies, possibly financing projects previously regarded as not feasible. The international capital market also expands lending opportunities, which reduces risk for lenders by allowing them to spread their money over a greater number of debt and equity instruments and to benefit from the fact that securities markets do not move up and down in tandem.

International Financial Market and Businesses

Companies must convert to local currencies when they undertake foreign direct investment. Later, when a firm's international subsidiary earns a profit and the company wishes to return profits to the home country, it must convert the local money into the home currency. The prevailing exchange rate at the time profits are exchanged influences the amount of the ultimate profit or loss.

This raises an important aspect of international financial markets—fluctuation. International companies can use hedging in foreign exchange markets to lessen the risk associated with international transfers of funds and to protect themselves in credit transactions in which there is a time lag between billing and receipt of payment. Some firms take part in currency arbitrage when they have large sums of cash on hand. Companies can also use interest arbitrage to find better interest rates abroad than those available in their home countries.

Businesspeople are also interested in tracking currency values over time because changes in currency values affect their international transactions. Profits earned by companies that import products for resale are influenced by the exchange rate between their currency and that of the nation from which they import. Managers who understand that changes in these currencies' values affect the profitability of their international business activities can develop strategies to minimize risk.

In the next chapter, we extend our coverage of the international financial system to see how market forces (including interest rates and inflation) have an impact on exchange rates. We also conclude our study of the international financial system by looking at the roles of government and international institutions in managing movements in exchange rates.

MyLab Management

Go to **www.pearson.com/mylab/management** to complete the problems marked with this icon .

Chapter Summary

LO9.1 Explain the importance of the international capital market.

- The international capital market is meant to (1) expand the supply of capital for borrowers, (2) lower interest rates for borrowers, and (3) lower risk for lenders.
- Growth in the international capital market is due mainly to (1) advances in *information technology*, (2) *deregulation* of capital markets, and (3) innovation in *financial instruments*.
- London, New York, and Tokyo are the world's most important financial centers. *Offshore financial centers* handle less business than the world's most important financial centers but have few regulations and few, if any, taxes.

LO9.2 Describe the main components of the international capital market.

- The *international bond market* consists of all bonds sold by issuers outside their own countries. It is growing as investors in developed markets search for higher rates from borrowers in emerging markets, and vice versa.
- The *international equity market* consists of all stocks bought and sold outside the home country of the issuing company. Factors driving its growth are (1) privatization, (2) increased activity by companies in emerging nations, (3) global reach of investment banks, and (4) global electronic trading.
- The *Eurocurrency market* consists of all the world's currencies banked outside their countries of origin. Its appeal is a lack of government regulation and a lower cost of borrowing.

LO9.3 Outline the functions of the foreign exchange market.

- One function is to *convert* one currency into another for individuals, companies, and governments.
- Second, it is used as a hedging device to *insure against* adverse changes in exchange rates.

- Third, it is used to *earn a profit* from currency arbitrage or other interest-paying security in different markets.
- Fourth, it is used to *speculate* about a change in the value of a currency and thereby earn a profit.

LO9.4 Explain the different types of currency quotes and exchange rates.

- An *exchange-rate quote* between currency A and currency B (A/B) of 10/1 means that it takes 10 units of currency A to buy 1 unit of currency B (this is a *direct quote* of currency A and an *indirect quote* of currency B).
- Exchange rates can also be found using two currencies' exchange rates with a common currency, which results in a *cross rate*.
- An exchange rate that requires delivery of a traded currency within two business days is called a *spot rate*.
- A *forward rate* is the rate at which two parties agree to exchange currencies on a specified future date.

LO9.5 Describe the instruments and institutions of the foreign exchange market.

- The *interbank market* is where the world's largest banks locate and exchange currencies for companies. *Securities exchanges* are physical locations at which currency futures and options are bought and sold (in smaller amounts than those traded in the interbank market).
- Goals of currency restriction include (1) preserve hard currency reserves for repaying debts owed to other nations, (2) preserve hard currency to pay for needed imports or to finance a trade deficit, (3) protect a currency from speculators, and (4) keep badly needed currency from being invested abroad.
- Instruments used to restrict currencies include (1) government approval for currency exchange, (2) imposed import licenses, (3) a system of multiple exchange rates, and (4) imposed quantity restrictions.

Key Terms

base currency (p. 256)
bond (p. 249)
capital market (p. 248)
clearing (p. 262)
convertible (hard) currency (p. 263)
countertrade (p. 264)
cross rate (p. 258)
currency arbitrage (p. 255)
currency futures contract (p. 261)
currency hedging (p. 255)
currency option (p. 260)
currency speculation (p. 256)
currency swap (p. 260)
debt (p. 249)

derivative (p. 260)
equity (p. 249)
Eurobond (p. 252)
Eurocurrency market (p. 253)
exchange rate (p. 254)
exchange-rate risk
   (foreign exchange risk) (p. 258)
foreign bond (p. 252)
foreign exchange market (p. 254)
forward contract (p. 260)
forward market (p. 260)
forward rate (p. 259)
interbank interest rates (p. 254)
interbank market (p. 262)

interest arbitrage (p. 255)
international bond market (p. 252)
international capital market (p. 249)
international equity market (p. 253)
liquidity (p. 249)
offshore financial center (p. 251)
over-the-counter (OTC) market (p. 263)
quoted currency (p. 256)
securities exchange (p. 262)
securitization (p. 250)
spot market (p. 259)
spot rate (p. 259)
stock (p. 249)
vehicle currency (p. 261)

⭐ TALK ABOUT IT 1

The microfinance concept has been a blessing for many people in developing countries. Its success there is prompting some to wonder if it can spur growth in poor areas of developed nations, such as in some poverty-stricken city centers.

9-1. What do you think is at the root of the success of such programs in developing nations?

9-2. What, if any, cultural or commercial obstacles do you foresee derailing this concept in developed nations?

✪ TALK ABOUT IT 2

Offshore financial centers operate with little oversight, few regulations, and often fewer taxes. Many governments complain that these centers sometimes facilitate money laundering.

9-3. Do you think that electronic commerce makes it easier or harder to launder money and camouflage other illegal activities?

9-4. Should offshore financial centers be allowed to operate as freely as they do now, or do you favor regulation? Explain.

Ethical Challenge

In groups of three or four, consider the ethical dimensions of currency speculation. If sufficient funds are available, a great deal of money can be made from buying and selling currency; in fact, the exchange rates can be manipulated. Some countries have found themselves the target of currency speculation. It has had a profound impact on the economy. People's savings have been drastically affected. To what extent is this legitimate business activity? Is this just a version of gambling with no real ethics attached to it? Discuss whether you think it is ethical and then share your thoughts with the rest of the class.

Teaming Up

You are the senior accountant for a business that regularly imports spare parts for a range of your products from overseas suppliers. You have been instructed by the CEO to look at ways you can save money on the transactions when you pay these overseas suppliers. He is convinced that there are ways in which you can organize the transaction so that you maximize the opportunities with fluctuating exchange rates. He has been reading about spot rates and is a little confused about the way it works and whether it is strictly legal or ethical. He wants you to explain the processes involved in organizing forward rates and how the business can take advantage of them.

9-5. When we pay an overseas supplier, should we wait until the last minute to pay?

9-6. How far in advance can we organize these forward contracts? Is the timing of the arrangement crucial?

9-7. Now suppose that, having arranged a forward contract, we don't want to go ahead with it. What happens then?

✪ Market Entry Strategy Project

This exercise corresponds to the *MESP* online simulation. For the country your team is researching, integrate your answers to the following questions into your completed *MESP* report.

9-8. Is the nation home to a city that is an important financial center?

9-9. What volume of bonds is traded on the country's bond market?

9-10. How has its stock market(s) performed over the past year?

9-11. What is the exchange rate between its currency and that of your own country?

9-12. What factors are responsible for the stability or volatility in that exchange rate?

9-13. Are there any restrictions on the exchange of the nation's currency?

MyLab Management

✪ Go to **www.pearson.com/mylab/management** for the following assisted-graded writing questions:

9-14. Past growth in the international capital market has been fueled by advancements in information technology, deregulation, and securitization. What factors do you think are holding back the creation of a truly *global* capital market?

9-15. The use of different national currencies creates a barrier to further growth in international business activity due to conversion costs and exchange-rate risk. What are the pros and cons, among companies *and* governments, of replacing national currencies with regional currencies, or even a global currency?

The Effect of the Asian Crisis on Southeast Asian Corporations

In the summer of 1997, after a couple of months fighting to defend the value of the baht, pegged to the U.S. dollar, the government of Thailand decided to abandon the battle and let its currency flow freely. This move marked the onset of what is now known as the Asian Financial Crisis, which heavily affected the economies of the region such as Malaysia, Indonesia, and South Korea.

To this day, there are ongoing debates about the dynamics of the Asian Financial Crisis. A series of causes have been pinpointed as relevant. Among them were the high level of corporate debt of some of the local corporations (caused by the access to cheap credit they were enjoying in the 1990s), bad government policies, the impact of derivatives and financial speculation, and the increase in competition from China. Some economists have also mentioned other, more indirect factors, such as the Chinese currency devaluation in 1994 and the handover of Hong Kong to China in 1997.

While the affected countries tried to tackle the crisis with a series of measures of fiscal rigor, the international community decided to act to prevent worldwide contagion. The International Monetary Fund (IMF) intervened and poured in a first tranche of a $40 billion program to help stabilize the local currencies most affected by the economic downturn, mainly Thailand, Indonesia, and South Korea. These efforts, heavily criticized in the region, had mixed effects and, at least in the case of Indonesia, were not successful in their aim. A full-fledged economic crisis and widespread riots in Indonesia led to the collapse of the Suharto government. The value of the Indonesian rupiah fell dramatically, from 1 USD = 2,600 INR before the crisis to 1 USD = 14,000 INR during the crisis. By 2012, 15 years after the start of the crisis, the country had certainly recovered from the recession, yet the exchange rate was still below pre-crisis levels (at 1 USD = 9,200 INR).

Other countries, such as Malaysia, decided to oust the IMF and closed their financial market to avoid capital flight. The then Prime Minister of Malaysia, Mahatir Mohamad, adopted a series of restrictions and led the regional opposition to the intervention of foreign institutions. His measures proved successful in the circumstances, and Malaysia managed to recover faster than other countries from the crisis.

The consequences, however, were felt worldwide, and for years these economies did not recover to their pre-crisis levels of growth. Some big corporations, such as the Korean Daewoo, who before the crisis were considered too big to fail, were dismantled by their governments in the crisis' aftermath.

Now, nearly two decades after those events, the countries involved look like they have completely recovered from the downturn. The price paid has been in some cases quite high, and virtually no economy in the region has come out unscathed, with the exception of China and economies strongly linked to it (e.g., Hong Kong and Taiwan). Arguably, the lessons that these countries can learn from this are to invest in quality, strengthen the economic fundamentals, and try to reduce dependence on foreign direct investments (FDIs).

However, the crisis had some important, lasting macroeconomic consequences, the most relevant being the shift of economic weight within the region. Whereas in the 1990s the "Asian Tigers" and the countries generally known as NIEs and Japan were the focus of FDIs, in the 2000s, this role clearly passed to new emerging superpowers, such as China and India, which are now the leading new East Asian economies.

Thinking Globally

9-16. A good starting point for exploring the local currencies of the region is look at a financial newspaper, such as the *Financial Times*. What is the value of the local currencies with respect to the U.S. dollar at the moment? Do you think it was wise for the countries' governments to let the currencies float freely in 1997? Why did they peg their currencies' value to the U.S. dollar in the first place? Do you think that the link with the U.S. dollar had any effect on the Asian Crisis? Explain.

9-17. One of the causes of the Asian crisis has been traced back to the devaluation of the Chinese renminbi in 1994, which, according to some economists, put a strain on the export-led economies of Southeast Asia and eventually made them more vulnerable to the crisis. Do you think this theory is valid? Argue your point with reasons.

9-18. How can export-led economies, such as the countries in Southeast Asia, make themselves more resilient and less dependent on the weakness of their currencies for boosting their exports? Choose one country and one company to illustrate your answer.

Sources: Joseph Stiglitz, "Some Lessons from the East Asian Miracle," *The World Bank Research Observer*, 11 (no. 2), 1996, pp. 151–177; Paul Krugman, "The Myth of Asia's Miracle," *Foreign Affairs*, 73 (no. 6), 1994, 62–78; "The Death of Daewoo," *Economist*, (www.economist.com/node/233562?story_id=233562), August 19, 1999.

Appendix

Calculating Percent Change in Exchange Rates

Businesspeople and foreign exchange traders track currency values over time as measured by exchange rates because changes in currency values can benefit or harm current and future international transactions. Managers develop strategies to minimize exchange-rate risk (foreign exchange risk) by tracking percent changes in exchange rates.

For example, take P_N as the exchange rate at the end of a period (the currency's *new* price) and P_O as the exchange rate at the beginning of that period (the currency's *old* price). We now can calculate percent change in the value of a currency with the following formula:

$$\text{Percent change } (\%) = \frac{P_n - P_o}{P_o} \times 100$$

Note: This equation yields the percent change in the base currency, not in the quoted currency.

Let's illustrate the usefulness of this calculation with a simple example. Suppose that on February 1 of the current year, the exchange rate between the Norwegian *krone* (NOK) and the US dollar was NOK 5/$. On March 1 of the current year, suppose the exchange rate stood at NOK 4/$. What is the change in the value of the base currency, the dollar? If we plug these numbers into our formula, we arrive at the following change in the value of the dollar:

$$\text{Percent change } (\%) = \frac{4 - 5}{5} \times 100 = -20\%$$

Thus, the value of the dollar has fallen 20 percent. In other words, one US dollar buys 20 percent fewer Norwegian krone on March 1 than it did on February 1.

To calculate the change in the value of the Norwegian krone, we must first calculate the indirect exchange rate on the krone. This step is necessary because we want to make the krone our base currency. Using the formula presented earlier in this chapter we obtain an exchange rate of $.20/NOK ($1 \div$ NOK 5) on February 1 and an exchange rate of $.25/NOK ($1 \div$ NOK 4) on March 1. Plugging these rates into our percent-change formula, we get:

$$\text{Percent change } (\%) = \frac{.25 - .20}{.20} \times 100 = 25\%$$

Thus, the value of the Norwegian krone has risen 25 percent. One Norwegian krone buys 25 percent more US dollars on March 1 than it did on February 1.

How important is this difference to businesspeople and exchange traders? Consider that the typical trading unit in the foreign exchange market (called a *round lot*) is $5 million. Therefore, a $5 million purchase of krone on February 1 would yield NOK 25 million. But because the dollar has lost 20 percent of its buying power by March 1, a $5 million purchase would fetch only NOK 20 million—5 million fewer krone than a month earlier.

Chapter Ten

International Monetary System

Learning Objectives

After studying this chapter, you should be able to

10.1 Describe the importance of exchange rates to business activities.

10.2 Outline the factors that help determine exchange rates.

10.3 Explain attempts to construct a system of fixed exchange rates.

10.4 Describe efforts to create a system of floating exchange rates.

A Look Back

Chapter 9 examined how the international capital market and foreign exchange market operate. We also learned how exchange rates are calculated and how different rates are used in international business.

A Look at This Chapter

This chapter extends our knowledge of exchange rates and international financial markets. We examine factors that help determine exchange rates and explore rate-forecasting techniques. We discuss international attempts to manage exchange rates and review recent currency problems in various emerging markets.

A Look Ahead

Chapter 11 introduces the topic of the last part of this book—international business management. We will explore the specific strategies and organizational structures that companies use in accomplishing their international business objectives.

Euro Rollercoaster

BRUSSELS, Belgium—"Europe's Big Idea," "Ready, Set, Euros!" cried the headlines that greeted the launch of Europe's single currency, the euro. Not since the time of the Roman Empire has a currency circulated so widely in Europe. Greece even gave up its drachma, a currency it had used for nearly 3,000 years. The euro is the official currency for 19 European countries and is accepted as legal tender in a number of other European nations.

The euro initially traded at around one-for-one against the dollar. Its value began to rise significantly, and a euro soon could buy around $1.57. The rise of the euro demonstrated confidence in the future expected growth and development of nations in the euro zone. It also boosted the status of the euro as a global currency, one that could perhaps rival the US dollar.

But the global credit crisis and subsequent recession exposed Europe's economies that were carrying too much national debt. By late 2017, the euro could buy only around $1.10. The euro rollercoaster rose and fell with each new revelation about the economic health of European nations. But financial markets stabilized and the euro's future again seemed secure. Analysts who

Daniel Kaesler/123RF.com

once predicted the dollar and euro would move toward one-to-one parity forecast that a euro would soon buy $1.18. The passage of time would determine the accuracy of this forecast.

The euro holds long-term benefits for European companies. Using a common currency in business transactions eliminates exchange-rate risk for companies in the euro zone and improves financial planning. It boosts competitiveness as synergies and economies of scale arise from mergers and acquisitions. Europe's exporters benefit from a weak euro because it lowers their prices on world markets. Some European companies who lost market share abroad when their currency was strong could perhaps win back some of those customers. As you read this chapter, consider how the international monetary system affects managerial decisions and firm performance.[1]

In Chapter 9, we explained the fundamentals of how exchange rates are calculated and how different types of exchange rates are used. This chapter extends our understanding of the international financial system by exploring factors that determine exchange rates and various international attempts to manage them. We begin by learning how exchange-rate movements affect a company's activities and the importance of forecasting exchange rates. We then examine the factors that help determine currency values and, in turn, exchange rates. Next, we learn about different attempts to create a system of fixed exchange rates. We conclude this chapter by exploring efforts to develop a system of floating exchange rates and reviewing several recent financial crises.

10.1 Importance of Exchange Rates

10.1 Describe the importance of exchange rates to business activities.

Exchange rates influence demand for a company's products in the global marketplace. A country with a currency that is *weak* (valued low relative to other currencies) will see a decline in the price of its exports and an increase in the price of its imports. Lower prices for the country's exports on world markets can give companies the opportunity to take market share away from companies whose products are priced high in comparison.

Furthermore, a company improves profits if it sells its products in a country with a *strong* currency (one that is valued high relative to other currencies) while sourcing from a country with a weak currency. For example, if a company pays its workers and suppliers in a falling local currency and sells its products in a rising currency, the company benefits by generating revenue in the strong currency while paying expenses in the weak currency. Yet, managers must take care not to view this type of price advantage as permanent because doing so can jeopardize a company's long-term competitiveness.

Exchange rates also affect the amount of profit a company earns from its international subsidiaries. The earnings of international subsidiaries are typically integrated into the parent company's financial statements *in the home currency*. Translating subsidiary earnings from a weak *host* country currency into a strong *home* currency *reduces* the amount of these earnings when stated in the home currency. Likewise, translating earnings into a weak home currency increases stated earnings in the home currency. Figure 10.1 shows exchange rates between the US dollar and several major currencies.

The intentional lowering of the value of a currency by the nation's government is called **devaluation**. The reverse, the intentional raising of the value of a currency by the nation's government, is called **revaluation**. These concepts are not to be confused with the terms *weak currency* and *strong currency*, although their effects are similar.

devaluation
Intentionally lowering the value of a nation's currency.

revaluation
Intentionally raising the value of a nation's currency.

Figure 10.1
Exchange Rates of Major World Currencies

Source: Based on *Economic Report of the President*, Table B110, multiple years.

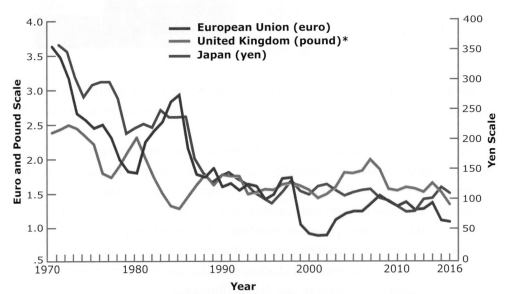

*Value is U.S. dollars per pound.
Prior to 1999, data for the Euro represents the German mark.

Devaluation lowers the price of a country's exports on world markets and increases the price of its imports because the value of the country's currency is now lower on world markets. A government might devalue its currency to give its domestic companies an edge over competition from other countries. But devaluation reduces the buying power of consumers in the nation. It can also allow inefficiencies to persist in domestic companies because there would then be less pressure to contain production costs. Revaluation has the opposite effects: It increases the price of exports and reduces the price of imports.

Desire for Predictability and Stability

Unfavorable movements in exchange rates can be costly for businesses. As the unpredictability of exchange rates increases, so too does the cost of insuring against the accompanying risk. By contrast, *stable* exchange rates improve the accuracy of financial planning and make cash-flow forecasts more precise.

Managers also prefer that movements in exchange rates be *predictable*. Predictable exchange rates reduce the likelihood that companies will be caught off guard by sudden and unexpected rate changes. They also reduce the need for costly insurance (usually by currency hedging) against possible adverse movements in exchange rates. Companies would be better off spending money on more productive activities, such as developing new products or designing more-efficient production methods.

Figure 10.2 shows how the value of the US dollar has changed over time. The figure reveals the dollar's periods of instability, which challenged the financial management capabilities of international companies. Before undertaking any international business activity, managers should forecast future exchange rates and consider the impact of currency values on earnings.

Efficient versus Inefficient Market View

A great deal of debate revolves around the issue of whether markets themselves are efficient or inefficient when it comes to forecasting exchange rates. A market is *efficient* if prices of financial instruments quickly reflect new public information made available to traders. The **efficient market view** states that prices of financial instruments reflect all publicly available information at any given time. As applied to exchange rates, this means that forward exchange rates are accurate forecasts of future exchange rates.

efficient market view
View that prices of financial instruments reflect all publicly available information at any given time.

Recall from Chapter 9 that a *forward exchange rate* reflects a market's expectations about the future values of two currencies. In an efficient currency market, forward exchange rates reflect all relevant publicly available information at any given time; they are considered the best possible predictors of exchange rates. Proponents of this view hold that there is no other publicly available information that could improve the forecast of exchange rates over that provided by forward rates.

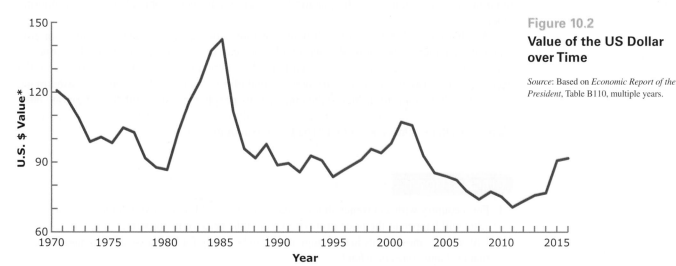

Figure 10.2

Value of the US Dollar over Time

Source: Based on *Economic Report of the President*, Table B110, multiple years.

* Multilateral trade-weighted value of the U.S. dollar. (March 1973 = 100)

inefficient market view
View that prices of financial instruments do not reflect all publicly available information.

But there is always a certain amount of deviation between forward and actual exchange rates, and this inspires companies to search for more-accurate forecasting techniques.

The **inefficient market view** states that prices of financial instruments do not reflect all publicly available information. Proponents of this view believe that companies can search for new pieces of information to improve forecasting. But the cost of searching for further information must not outweigh the benefits of its discovery.

Naturally, the inefficient market view is more compelling when the existence of private information is considered. Suppose that a single currency trader holds privileged information regarding a future change in a nation's economic policy—information that she believes will affect that nation's exchange rate. Because the market is unaware of this information, it is not reflected in forward exchange rates. Our trader will no doubt earn a profit by acting on her store of private information.

Forecasting Techniques

As we have already seen, some analysts believe that forecasts of exchange rates can be improved by uncovering information not reflected in forward exchange rates. In fact, companies exist to provide exactly this type of service. There are two main forecasting techniques based on this belief in the value of added information—fundamental analysis and technical analysis.

fundamental analysis
Technique that uses statistical models based on fundamental economic indicators to forecast exchange rates.

Fundamental analysis uses statistical models based on fundamental economic indicators to forecast exchange rates. These models are often quite complex, with many variations reflecting different possible economic conditions. These models include economic variables such as inflation, interest rates, money supply, tax rates, and government spending. Such analyses also often consider a country's balance-of-payments situation (see Chapter 7) and its tendency to intervene in markets to influence the value of its currency.

technical analysis
Technique that uses charts of past trends in currency prices and other factors to forecast exchange rates.

Technical analysis uses charts of past trends in currency prices and other factors to forecast exchange rates. Using highly statistical models and charts of past data trends, analysts examine conditions that prevailed during changes in exchange rates and try to estimate the timing, magnitude, and direction of future changes. Many forecasters combine the techniques of both fundamental and technical analyses to arrive at potentially more-accurate forecasts.

Difficulties of Forecasting

The business of forecasting exchange rates is a rapidly growing industry. But forecasting exchange rates is not a pure science, despite highly sophisticated statistical techniques in the hands of well-trained analysts. Few, if any, forecasts are ever completely accurate because of unexpected events that occur throughout the forecast period.

Beyond the problems associated with the data used by these techniques, failings can be traced to the human element involved in forecasting. For example, people can miscalculate the importance of economic news by placing too much emphasis on some elements and ignoring others.

Another factor that adds to the difficulty of forecasting exchange rates is changes in government regulation of business. Regulatory changes can improve or detract from the economic outlook for a nation's economy. As forecasts predict economic improvement or worsening, the exchange rate between a nation's currency and that of other nations also changes. Furthermore, a nation's culture tends to influence the emphasis its people place on regulation of private business. To read about several agencies responsible for the enforcement of US business laws, see this chapter's Culture Matters box, titled "The Long Arm of the Law."

QUICK STUDY 1

1. For a country with a currency that is weakening (valued low relative to other currencies), what will happen to the price of its exports and the price of its imports?
2. Unfavorable movements in exchange rates can be costly for businesses, so managers prefer that exchange rates be *what*?
3. The view that prices of financial instruments reflect all publicly available information at any given time is called *what*?

CULTURE MATTERS	The Long Arm of the Law

Culture can affect the degree of oversight that a government imposes on its business environment. Here are several US agencies that monitor business activity:

- **US Patent and Trademark Office (USPTO).** The USPTO is a noncommercial federal bureau within the Department of Commerce. By issuing patents, it provides incentives to invent, invest in, and disclose new technologies worldwide. By registering trademarks, it protects business investment and safeguards consumers against confusion and deception. By disseminating patent and trademark information, it facilitates the development and sharing of new technologies worldwide.
- **US International Trade Commission (USITC).** The USITC is an independent, quasi-judicial federal agency. It provides trade expertise to both the legislative and executive branches of government, determines the impact of imports on US industries, and directs actions against certain unfair trade practices such as patent, trademark, and copyright infringement. The agency has broad investigative powers on matters of trade and is a national resource where trade data are gathered and analyzed.
- **Federal Trade Commission (FTC).** The FTC enforces a variety of federal antitrust and consumer protection laws. It seeks to ensure that the nation's markets function competitively and are vigorous, efficient, and free of undue restrictions. The commission also works to enhance the smooth operation of the marketplace by eliminating acts or practices that are unfair or deceptive. In general, the commission's efforts are directed toward stopping actions that threaten consumers' opportunities to exercise informed choice.
- **US Consumer Product Safety Commission (CPSC).** The CPSC is an independent federal regulatory agency created to protect the public from injury and death associated with some 15,000 types of consumer products, including car seats, bicycles and bike helmets, lawnmowers, toys, and walkers. It also provides information for businesses regarding the export of noncompliant, misbranded, or banned products.
- **Want to Know More?** Visit the websites of the following government agencies: USPTO (www.uspto.gov), USITC (www.usitc.gov), FTC (www.ftc.gov), and CPSC (www.cpsc.gov).

Sources: Federal Trade Commission website (www.ftc.gov); US Consumer Product Safety Commission website (www.cpsc.gov); US Patent and Trademark Office website (www.uspto.gov); US International Trade Commission website (www.usitc.gov).

10.2 What Factors Determine Exchange Rates?

To improve our knowledge of the factors that help determine exchange rates, we must first understand two important concepts: the *law of one price* and *purchasing power parity*. Each of these concepts tells us the level at which an exchange rate *should* be. While discussing these concepts, we will examine some factors that affect *actual* levels of exchange rates.

10.2 Outline the factors that help determine exchange rates.

Law of One Price

An exchange rate tells us how much of one currency we must pay to receive a certain amount of another. But it does not tell us whether a specific product will actually cost us more or less in a particular country (as measured in our own currency). When we travel to another country, we discover that our own currency buys more or less than it does at home. In other words, we quickly learn that exchange rates do not guarantee or stabilize the buying power of our currency. Thus, we can lose purchasing power in some countries while gaining it in others. For example, a restaurant meal for you and a friend that costs $60 in New York might cost you 7,000 yen (about $80) in Japan and 400 pesos (about $30) in Mexico. Compared with your meal in New York, you've suffered a loss of purchasing power in Japan but benefited from increased purchasing power in Mexico.

The **law of one price** stipulates that an identical product must have an identical price in all countries when the price is expressed in a common currency. For this principle to apply, products must be identical in quality and content in each country and be entirely produced within each country.

For example, suppose coal mined in the United States and in Germany is of similar quality. But suppose that one pound of coal costs €1.5 in Germany and $1 in the United States. Therefore, the law of one price calculates the *expected* exchange rate between the euro and dollar to be €1.5/$. However, suppose the *actual* euro/dollar exchange rate on currency markets is €1.2/$. To pay for German coal *with dollars denominated after the change in the exchange rate*, one must convert not just $1 into euros, but $1.25 (which is the expected exchange rate divided by the actual exchange rate, or €1.5 ÷ $1.2). So, German coal costs $1.25 and US coal costs $1, *when the price is expressed in a common currency*, which in this case is the dollar.

law of one price

Principle that an identical item must have an identical price in all countries when the price is expressed in a common currency.

Because the law of one price is being violated in our example, an *arbitrage* opportunity arises—that is, an opportunity to buy a product in one country and sell it in a country where it has a higher value. For example, one could earn a profit by buying US coal at $1 per pound and selling it in Germany for $1.25 (€1.5) per pound. But note that as traders begin buying in the United States and selling in Germany, greater demand drives *up* the price of US coal, whereas greater supply drives *down* the price of German coal. Eventually, the price of coal in both countries will settle somewhere between the previously low US price and the previously high German price.

MCCURRENCY The usefulness of the law of one price is that it helps us determine whether a currency is overvalued or undervalued. *The Economist* magazine publishes what it calls its "Big Mac Index" of exchange rates. This index uses the law of one price to determine the exchange rate that *should* exist between the US dollar and other major currencies. The McDonald's Big Mac is suitable to test the law of one price because each one is fairly identical in quality and content across national markets and is almost entirely produced within the nation in which it is sold. (Recall that the law of one price states that an identical product must have an identical price in all countries when the price is expressed in a common currency.)

A recent Big Mac Index found that the average price of a McDonald's Big Mac was $3.73 in the United States but $1.95 in China. According to the Big Mac Index, China's yuan is undervalued. By contrast, a Big Mac cost $7.20 in Norway and means that Norway's krone is overvalued.[2]

Such large discrepancies between a currency's exchange rate on currency markets and the rate predicted by the Big Mac Index are not surprising. For one thing, the selling price of food is affected by subsidies for agricultural products in most countries. Also, a Big Mac is not a "traded" product in the sense that one can buy Big Macs in low-priced countries and sell them in high-priced countries. Prices can also be affected because Big Macs are subject to different marketing strategies in different countries. Finally, countries impose different levels of sales tax on restaurant meals.

The drawbacks of the Big Mac Index reflect the fact that applying the law of one price to a single product is too simplistic a method for estimating exchange rates. Nonetheless, academic studies find that currency values tend to change in the direction suggested by the Big Mac Index.

Purchasing Power Parity

We introduced the concept of purchasing power parity (PPP) in Chapter 4 in the context of economic development. Although the law of one price holds for single products, PPP theory is meaningful only when applied to a *basket* of goods.

Economic forces, says PPP theory, will push the actual market exchange rate toward that determined by PPP. If they do not, arbitrage opportunities will arise. PPP holds for internationally traded products that are not restricted by trade barriers and that entail few or no transportation costs. To earn a profit, arbitrageurs must be certain that the basket of goods purchased in the low-cost country would still be lower-priced in the high-cost country *after* adding transportation costs, tariffs, taxes, and so forth.

NUMERICAL EXAMPLE The PPP concept is also useful in determining at what level an exchange rate should be. Suppose 650 baht in Thailand will buy a bag of groceries that costs $30 in the United States. What do these two numbers tell us about the economic conditions of people in Thailand as compared with people in the United States? First, they help us compare the *purchasing power* of a Thai consumer with that of a consumer in the United States. But the question remains, Are Thai consumers better off or worse off than their counterparts in the United States? To address this question, suppose the *gross national product (GNP) per capita* of each country is as follows:

Thai GNP/capita = 122,277 baht
US GNP/capita = 26,980 dollars

Suppose also that the *exchange rate* between the two currencies is 41.45 baht = 1 dollar. With this figure, we can translate 122,277 baht into dollars: 122,277 ÷ 41.45 = $2,950. We can now restate our question: Do prices in Thailand enable a Thai consumer with $2,950 to buy more or less than a consumer in the United States with $26,980?

We already know that 650 baht will buy in Thailand what $30 will buy in the United States. Thus, we calculate 650 ÷ 30 = 21.67 baht per dollar. Note that, whereas the exchange rate on currency markets is 41.45 baht/$, the *purchasing power parity rate* of the baht is 21.67/$. Let's now use this figure to calculate a different comparative rate between the two currencies. We can now recalculate Thailand's GNP per capita at PPP as follows: 122,277 ÷ 21.67 = 5,643. Thai consumers on average are not nearly as affluent as their counterparts in the United States. But when we consider the goods and services that they can purchase with their baht—not the amount of US dollars that they can buy—we see that a GNP per capita at PPP of $5,643 more accurately portrays the real purchasing power of Thai consumers.

Our new calculation considers *price levels* in adjusting the relative values of the two currencies. In the context of exchange rates, the principle of purchasing power parity can be interpreted as the exchange rate between two nations' currencies that is equal to the ratio of their price levels. In other words, PPP tells us that a consumer in Thailand needs 21.67 units (not 41.45) of Thai currency to buy the same amount of products as a consumer in the United States can buy with one dollar. As we can see in this example, the exchange rate at PPP (21.67/$) is different from the actual exchange rate in financial markets (41.45/$).

ROLE OF INFLATION Inflation is the result of the supply and demand for a currency. If additional money is injected into an economy that is not producing greater output, people will have more money to spend on the same amount of products as before. As growing demand for products outstrips stagnant supply, prices will rise and devour any increase in the amount of money that consumers have to spend. Therefore, inflation erodes people's purchasing power.

Impact of Money-Supply Decisions Governments try to manage the supply of and demand for their currencies because of inflation's damaging effects. They do this through the use of two types of policies designed to influence a nation's money supply. *Monetary policy* refers to activities that directly affect a nation's interest rates or money supply. Selling government securities reduces a nation's money supply because investors pay money to the government's treasury to acquire the securities. Conversely, when the government buys its own securities on the open market, cash is infused into the economy and the money supply increases.

Fiscal policy involves using taxes and government spending to influence the money supply indirectly. For example, to reduce the amount of money in the hands of consumers, governments increase taxes—people are forced to pay money to the government coffers. Conversely, lowering taxes increases the amount of money in the hands of consumers. Governments can also step up their own spending activities in order to increase the amount of money circulating in the economy or can cut government spending to reduce it.

Impact of Unemployment and Interest Rates Key factors in the inflation equation are a country's unemployment and interest rates. When unemployment rates are low, there is a shortage

Zimbabwe's inflation rate rocketed to more than 100,000 percent shortly before the government abandoned its currency in 2009 and lead to these $1 billion, $10 trillion, and $100 trillion banknotes. The Reserve Bank of Zimbabwe was forced to allow transactions in foreign currencies, including the South African rand, Botswana pula, British pound, and the U.S. dollar. A loaf of bread at that time cost about 6 million ZWD. Zimbabwe's poor economic policies were to blame and caused shortages of necessities, such as food and fuel.

Steve AllenUK/123RF.com

of labor and employers pay higher wages to attract employees. To maintain reasonable profit margins with higher labor costs, companies then usually raise the prices of their products, passing the cost of higher wages on to the consumer and causing inflation.

Interest rates (discussed in detail later in this chapter) affect inflation because they affect the cost of borrowing money. Low interest rates encourage people to take out loans to buy items such as homes and cars and to run up debt on credit cards. High interest rates prompt people to cut down on the amount of debt they carry because higher rates mean larger monthly payments on debt. Thus, one way to cool off an inflationary economy is to raise interest rates. Raising the cost of debt reduces consumer spending and makes business expansion more costly.

How Exchange Rates Adjust to Inflation An important component of the concept of PPP is that exchange rates adjust to different rates of inflation in different countries. Such adjustment is necessary to maintain PPP between nations. Suppose that at the beginning of the year the exchange rate between the Mexican *peso* and the US dollar is 8 pesos/$ (or $0.125/peso). Also suppose that inflation is pushing consumer prices higher in Mexico at an annual rate of 20 percent, whereas prices are rising just 3 percent per year in the United States. To find the new exchange rate (E_e) at the end of the year, we use the following formula:

$$E_e = E_b(1 + i_1) / (1 + i_2)$$

where E_b is the exchange rate at the beginning of the period, i_1 is the inflation rate in Country 1, and i_2 is the inflation rate in Country 2. Plugging the numbers for this example into the formula, we get the following:

$$E_e = 8_{pesos/\$}[(1 + 0.20) / (1 + 0.03)] = 9.3_{pesos/\$}$$

It is important to remember that because the numerator of the exchange rate is in pesos, the inflation rate for Mexico must also be placed in the numerator for the ratio of inflation rates. Thus, we see that the exchange rate adjusts from 8 pesos/$ to 9.3 pesos/$ because of the higher inflation rate in Mexico and the corresponding change in currency values. Higher inflation in Mexico reduces the number of US dollars that a peso will buy and increases the number of pesos that a dollar will buy. In other words, whereas it had cost only 8 pesos to buy a dollar at the beginning of the year, it now costs 9.3 pesos.

In our example, companies based in Mexico must pay more in pesos for any supplies bought from the United States. But US companies will pay less, in dollar terms, for supplies bought from Mexico. Also, tourists from the United States will be delighted, as vacationing in Mexico will be less expensive, but Mexicans will find the cost of visiting the United States is more expensive.

This discussion illustrates at least one of the difficulties facing countries with high rates of inflation. Both consumers and companies in countries experiencing rapidly increasing prices see their purchasing power eroded. Developing countries and countries in transition are those most often plagued by rapidly increasing prices.

ROLE OF INTEREST RATES To see how interest rates affect exchange rates between two currencies, we must first review the connection between inflation and interest rates within a single economy. We distinguish between two types of interest rates: *real interest rates* and *nominal interest rates*. Let's say that your local bank quotes you an interest rate on a new car loan. That rate is the nominal interest rate, which consists of the real interest rate plus an additional charge for inflation. The reasoning behind this principle is simple: The lender must be compensated for the erosion of its purchasing power during the loan period caused by inflation.

Fisher Effect Suppose your bank lends you money to buy a delivery van for your home-based business. Let's say that, given your credit-risk rating, the bank would normally charge you 5 percent annual interest. But if inflation is expected to be 2 percent over the next year, your annual rate of interest will be 7 percent: 5 percent real interest plus 2 percent to cover inflation. The principle that relates inflation to interest rates is called the **Fisher effect**—the principle that the nominal interest rate is the sum of the real interest rate and the expected rate of inflation over a specific period. We write this relation between inflation and interest rates as follows:

Fisher effect
Principle that the nominal interest rate is the sum of the real interest rate and the expected rate of inflation over a specific period.

Nominal Interest Rate = Real Interest Rate + Inflation Rate

If money were free from all controls when transferred internationally, the real rate of interest should be the same in all countries. To see why this is true, suppose that real interest rates are 4 percent in Canada and 6 percent in the United States. This situation creates an arbitrage opportunity: Investors could borrow money in Canada at 4 percent, lend it in the United States at 6 percent, and earn a profit on the 2 percent spread in interest rates. If enough people took advantage of this opportunity, interest rates would go up in Canada, where demand for money would become heavier, and down in the United States, where the money supply was growing. Again, the arbitrage opportunity would disappear because of the same activities that made it a reality. That is why real interest rates must theoretically remain equal across countries.

We saw earlier the relation between inflation and exchange rates. The Fisher effect clarifies the relation between inflation and interest rates. Now, let's investigate the relation between exchange rates and interest rates. To illustrate this relation, we refer to the **international Fisher effect**—the principle that a difference in nominal interest rates supported by two countries' currencies will cause an equal but opposite change in their *spot exchange rates*. Recall from Chapter 9 that the spot rate is the rate quoted for delivery of the traded currency within two business days.

Because real interest rates are theoretically equal across countries, any difference in interest rates in two countries must be due to different expected rates of inflation. A country that is experiencing inflation higher than that of another country should see the value of its currency fall. If so, the exchange rate must be adjusted to reflect this change in value. For example, suppose nominal interest rates are 5 percent in Australia and 3 percent in Canada. Expected inflation in Australia, then, is 2 percent higher than in Canada. The international Fisher effect predicts that the value of the Australian dollar will fall by 2 percent against the Canadian dollar.

international Fisher effect
Principle that a difference in nominal interest rates supported by two countries' currencies will cause an equal but opposite change in their spot exchange rates.

EVALUATING PPP PPP is better at predicting long-term exchange rates (more than 10 years), but accurate forecasts of short-term rates are more beneficial to international managers. Even short-term plans must assume certain things about future economic and political conditions in different countries, including added costs, trade barriers, and investor psychology.

Impact of Added Costs There are many possible reasons for the failure of PPP to predict exchange rates accurately. For example, PPP assumes no transportation costs. Suppose that the same basket of goods costs $100 in the United States and 950 kroner ($150) in Norway. Seemingly, one could make a profit through arbitrage by purchasing these goods in the United States and selling them in Norway. However, if it costs another $60 to transport the goods to Norway, the total cost of the goods once they arrive in Norway will be $160. Thus, no shipment will occur. Because no arbitrage opportunity exists after transportation costs are added, there will be no leveling of prices between the two markets and the price discrepancy will persist. Thus, even if PPP predicts that the Norwegian *krone* is overvalued, the effect of transportation costs will keep the dollar/*krone* exchange rate from adjusting. In a world in which transportation costs exist, PPP does not always correctly predict shifts in exchange rates.

Impact of Trade Barriers PPP also assumes that there are no barriers to international trade. However, such barriers certainly do exist. Governments establish trade barriers for many reasons, including helping domestic companies remain competitive and preserving jobs for their citizens. Suppose the Norwegian government in our earlier example imposes a 60 percent tariff on the $100 basket of imported goods or makes its importation illegal. Because no leveling of prices or exchange-rate adjustment will occur, PPP will fail to predict exchange rates accurately.

Impact of Business Confidence and Psychology Finally, PPP overlooks the human aspect of exchange rates—the role of people's confidence and beliefs about a nation's economy and the value of its currency. Many countries gauge confidence in their economies by conducting a *business confidence survey*. The largest survey of its kind in Japan is called the *tankan* survey. It gauges business confidence four times each year among 10,000 companies.

Investor confidence in the value of a currency plays an important role in determining its exchange rate. Suppose several currency traders believe that the Indian rupee will increase in value. They will buy Indian rupees at the current price, sell them if the value increases, and earn a profit. However, suppose that all traders share the same belief and all follow the same course of action. The activity of the traders themselves will be sufficient to push the value of the Indian rupee higher. It does not matter why traders believed the price would increase. As long as enough people act on a similar belief regarding the future value of a currency, its value will change accordingly.

That is why nations try to maintain the confidence of investors, businesspeople, and consumers in their economies. Lost confidence causes companies to put off investing in new products and technologies and to delay the hiring of additional employees. Consumers tend to increase their savings and not increase their debts if they have lost confidence in an economy. These kinds of behaviors act to weaken a nation's currency.

QUICK STUDY 2

1. The principle that an identical item must have an identical price in all countries when price is expressed in a common currency is called *what*?
2. A unique aspect of purchasing power parity in the context of exchange rates is that it is only useful when applied to *what*?
3. What is the impact on purchasing power when growing demand for products outstrips a stagnant supply?
4. What factors influence the power of purchasing power parity to accurately predict exchange rates?

10.3 Fixed Exchange Rate Systems

10.3 Explain attempts to construct a system of fixed exchange rates.

So far in this chapter, we have read about the benefits of predictable and stable exchange rates. We also know that inflation and interest rates affect currency values and, in turn, exchange rates. For these and other reasons, governments have created formal and informal agreements to control exchange rates. The present-day **international monetary system** is the collection of agreements and institutions that govern exchange rates. In this section, we summarize attempts to construct a system of fixed exchange rates.

international monetary system
Collection of agreements and institutions that govern exchange rates.

The Gold Standard

In the earliest days of international trade, gold was the internationally accepted currency for payment of goods and services. Using gold as a medium of exchange in international trade had several advantages. First, the limited supply of gold made it a commodity in high demand. Second, because gold is highly resistant to corrosion, it was able to be traded and stored for hundreds of years. Third, because it could be melted into either small coins or large bars, gold was a good medium of exchange for both small and large purchases.

But gold also had its disadvantages. First, the weight of gold made transporting it expensive. Second, when a transport ship sank at sea, the gold also sank to the ocean floor and was lost. Thus, merchants wanted a new way to make their international payments without the need to haul large amounts of gold around the world. The solution was found in the **gold standard**—an international monetary system in which nations linked the value of their paper currencies to specific values of gold. Britain was the first nation to implement the gold standard in the early 1700s.

gold standard
International monetary system in which nations link the value of their paper currencies to specific values of gold.

PAR VALUE The gold standard required a nation to fix the value (price) of its currency to an ounce of gold. The value of a currency expressed in terms of gold is called its *par value*. Each nation then guaranteed to convert its paper currency into gold for anyone demanding it at its par value. The calculation of each currency's par value was based on the concept of purchasing power parity. This provision made the purchasing power of gold the same everywhere and maintained the purchasing power of currencies across nations.

All nations fixing their currencies to gold also indirectly linked their currencies to one another. Because the gold standard *fixed* nations' currencies to the value of gold, it is called a **fixed exchange-rate system**—one in which the exchange rate for converting one currency into another is fixed by international governmental agreement. This system and the use of par values made calculating exchange rates between any two currencies a very simple matter. For example, under the gold standard, the US dollar was originally fixed at $20.67/oz of gold and the British pound at £4.2474/oz. The exchange rate between the dollar and pound was $4.87/£ (which is $20.67 ÷ £4.2474).

fixed exchange-rate system
System in which the exchange rate for converting one currency into another is fixed by international agreement.

ADVANTAGES OF THE GOLD STANDARD The gold standard was quite successful in its early years of operation. In fact, this early record of success is causing some economists and policy makers to call for its rebirth today. Three main advantages of the gold standard underlie its early success.

First, the gold standard drastically reduced the risk in exchange rates because it maintains highly fixed exchange rates between currencies. Deviations that did arise were much smaller than they are under a system of freely floating currencies. The more stable the exchange rates are, the less companies are affected by actual or potential adverse changes in them. Because the gold standard significantly reduced the risk in exchange rates and, therefore, the risks and costs of trade, international trade grew rapidly following its introduction.

Second, the gold standard imposed strict monetary policies on all countries that participated in the system. Recall that the gold standard required governments to convert paper currency into gold if demanded by holders of the currency. If all holders of a nation's paper currency decided to trade it for gold, the government must have an equal amount of gold reserves to pay them. That is why a government could not allow the volume of its paper currency to grow faster than the growth in its reserves of gold. By limiting the growth of a nation's money supply, the gold standard also was effective in controlling inflation.

Third, the gold standard could help correct a nation's trade imbalance. Suppose Australia was importing more than it was exporting (experiencing a trade deficit). As gold flowed out of Australia to pay for imports, its government had to decrease the supply of paper currency in the domestic economy because it could not have paper currency in excess of its gold reserves. As the money supply fell, so did prices of goods and services in Australia because demand was falling (consumers had less to spend)—whereas the supply of goods was unchanged. Meanwhile, falling prices of Australian-made goods caused Australian exports to become cheaper on world markets. Exports rose until Australia's international trade was once again in balance. The exact opposite occurred in the case of a trade surplus: The inflow of gold supported an increase in the supply of paper currency, which increased demand for, and therefore the cost of, goods and services. Thus, exports fell in reaction to their higher price until trade was once again in balance.

COLLAPSE OF THE GOLD STANDARD Nations involved in the First World War needed to finance their enormous war expenses, and they did so by printing more paper currency. This certainly violated the fundamental principle of the gold standard and forced nations to abandon the standard. The aggressive printing of paper currency caused rapid inflation for these nations. When the United States returned to the gold standard in 1934, it adjusted its par value from \$20.67/oz of gold to \$35.00/oz to reflect the lower value of the dollar that resulted from inflation. Thus, the US dollar had undergone devaluation. Yet Britain returned to the gold standard several years earlier at its previous level, which did not reflect the effect inflation had on its currency.

Because the gold standard links currencies to one another, devaluation of one currency in terms of gold affects the exchange rates between currencies. The decision of the United States to devalue its currency and Britain's decision not to do so lowered the price of US exports on world markets and increased the price of British goods imported into the United States. For example, whereas it had previously required \$4.87 to purchase one British pound, it now required \$8.24 (which is \$35.00 ÷ £4.2474). This forced the cost of a £10 tea set exported from Britain to the United States to go from \$48.70 before devaluation to \$82.40 after devaluation. This drastically increased the price of imports from Britain (and other countries), lowering its export earnings. As countries devalued their currencies in retaliation, a period of "competitive devaluation" resulted. To improve their trade balances, nations chose arbitrary par values to which they devalued their currencies. People quickly lost faith in the gold standard because it was no longer an accurate indicator of a currency's true value. By 1939, the gold standard was effectively dead.

Bretton Woods Agreement

In 1944, representatives from 44 nations met in the New Hampshire resort town of Bretton Woods to lay the foundation for a new international monetary system. The resulting **Bretton Woods Agreement** was an accord among nations to create a new international monetary system based on the value of the US dollar. The new system was designed to balance the strict discipline of the gold standard with the flexibility that countries needed in order to deal with temporary domestic monetary difficulties. Let's briefly explore the most important features of this system.

Bretton Woods Agreement
Agreement (1944) among nations to create a new international monetary system based on the value of the US dollar.

FIXED EXCHANGE RATES The Bretton Woods Agreement incorporated fixed exchange rates by tying the value of the US dollar directly to gold and the value of other currencies to the value of the dollar. The par value of the US dollar was fixed at $35/oz of gold. Other currencies were then given par values against the US dollar instead of gold. For example, the par value of the British pound was established as $2.40/£. Member nations were expected to keep their currencies from deviating more than 1 percent above or below their par values. The Bretton Woods Agreement also improved on the gold standard by extending the right to exchange gold for dollars only to national governments, rather than to anyone who demanded it.

fundamental disequilibrium

Economic condition in which a trade deficit causes a permanent negative shift in a country's balance of payments.

BUILT-IN FLEXIBILITY The new system also incorporated a degree of built-in flexibility. For example, although competitive currency devaluation was ruled out, large devaluation was allowed under the extreme set of circumstances called **fundamental disequilibrium**—an economic condition in which a trade deficit causes a permanent negative shift in a country's balance of payments. In this situation, a nation can devalue its currency more than 10 percent. Yet devaluation under these circumstances should accurately reflect a permanent economic change for the country in question, not temporary misalignments.

WORLD BANK To provide funding for countries' efforts toward economic development, the Bretton Woods Agreement created the *World Bank*—officially called the International Bank for Reconstruction and Development (IBRD). The immediate purpose of the World Bank (www .worldbank.org) was to finance European reconstruction following the Second World War. It later shifted its focus to the general financial needs of developing countries. The World Bank finances many types of economic development projects in Africa, South America, and Southeast Asia. The World Bank also offers funds to countries that are unable to obtain capital from commercial sources for some projects that are considered too risky. The bank often undertakes projects to develop transportation networks, power facilities, and agricultural and educational programs.

INTERNATIONAL MONETARY FUND In addition, the Bretton Woods Agreement established the *International Monetary Fund (IMF)* as the agency to regulate the fixed exchange rates and to enforce the rules of the international monetary system. At the time of its formation, the IMF (www.imf.org) had just 29 members—189 countries belong today. Included among the main purposes of the IMF are:[3]

- Promoting international monetary cooperation;
- Facilitating expansion and balanced growth of international trade;
- Promoting exchange stability, maintaining orderly exchange arrangements, and avoiding competitive exchange devaluation;
- Making the resources of the fund temporarily available to members;
- Shortening the duration and lessening the degree of disequilibrium in the international balance of payments of member nations.

special drawing right (SDR)

IMF asset whose value is based on a "weighted basket" of five currencies.

Special Drawing Right World financial reserves of dollars and gold grew scarce in the 1960s, at a time when the activities of the IMF demanded greater amounts of dollars and gold. The IMF reacted by creating what is called a **special drawing right (SDR)**—an IMF asset whose value is based on a weighted "basket" of five currencies, including the US dollar, European Union (EU) euro, Chinese renminbi, Japanese yen, and British pound. Figure 10.3 shows the "weight" each currency contributes to the overall value of the SDR. The value of the SDR is set daily and changes with increases and declines in the values of its underlying currencies. Today there are more than 204 billion SDRs in existence worth slightly more than $285 billion (1 SDR equals about $1.40).[4] The significance of the SDR is that it is the unit of account for the IMF. Each nation is assigned a quota based on the size of its economy when it enters the IMF. Payment of this quota by each nation provides the IMF with the funds it needs to make short-term loans to members.

COLLAPSE OF THE BRETTON WOODS AGREEMENT The system developed at Bretton Woods worked quite well for about 20 years—an era that boasted unparalleled stability in exchange rates. But in the 1960s, the Bretton Woods system began to falter. The main problem was that the United States was experiencing a trade deficit (imports were exceeding exports) and a budget deficit (expenses were outstripping revenues). Governments that were holding dollars began to doubt that the US government had an adequate amount of gold reserves to redeem all

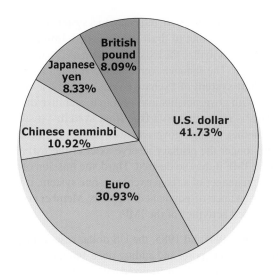

Figure 10.3

Valuation of the Special Drawing Right (SDR)

Source: Based on IMF website (www.imf.org), Special Drawing Rights data section.

its paper currency held outside the country. When they began demanding gold in exchange for dollars, a large sell-off of dollars on world financial markets followed.

Smithsonian Agreement In August 1971, the US government held less than one-fourth of the amount of gold needed to redeem all US dollars in circulation. In late 1971, the United States and other countries reached the so-called **Smithsonian Agreement** to restructure and strengthen the international monetary system. The three main accomplishments of the Smithsonian Agreement were (1) to lower the value of the dollar in terms of gold to $38/oz, (2) to increase the values of other countries' currencies against the dollar, and (3) to increase to 2.25 percent from 1 percent the band within which currencies were allowed to float.

Smithsonian Agreement
Agreement (1971) among IMF members to restructure and strengthen the international monetary system created at Bretton Woods.

Final Days The success of the Bretton Woods system relied on the US dollar remaining a strong reserve currency. High inflation and a persistent trade deficit in the United States kept the dollar weak, however, which demonstrated a fundamental flaw in the system. The weak US dollar strained the capabilities of central banks in Japan and most European countries to maintain exchange rates with the dollar. Because these nations' currencies were tied to the US dollar, as the dollar continued to fall, so too did their currencies. Britain left the system in the middle of 1972 and allowed the pound to float freely against the dollar. The Swiss abandoned the system in early 1973. In January 1973, the dollar was again devalued, this time to around $42/oz of gold. But even this move was not enough. As nations began dumping their reserves of the dollar on a massive scale, currency markets were temporarily closed to prevent further selling of the dollar. When markets reopened, the values of most major currencies were floating against the US dollar. The era of an international monetary system based on *fixed* exchange rates was over.

QUICK STUDY 3

1. The gold standard is an example of what type of international monetary system?
2. What were the main advantages of the gold standard?
3. What is the name of the international monetary system that formed in 1944 following the demise of the gold standard?

10.4 System of Floating Exchange Rates

The Bretton Woods system collapsed because of its heavy dependence on the stability of the dollar. As long as the dollar remained strong, it worked well. But when the dollar weakened, it failed to perform properly. Originally, the new system of *floating* exchange rates was viewed as a temporary solution to the shortcomings of the Bretton Woods and Smithsonian Agreements. But no new coordinated international monetary system was forthcoming. Rather, there emerged several independent efforts to manage exchange rates.

10.4 Describe efforts to create a system of floating exchange rates.

Jamaica Agreement
Agreement (1976) among IMF members to formalize the existing system of floating exchange rates as the new international monetary system.

managed float system
Exchange-rate system in which currencies float against one another, with governments intervening to stabilize their currencies at particular target exchange rates.

free float system
Exchange-rate system in which currencies float freely against one another, without governments intervening in currency markets.

JAMAICA AGREEMENT By January 1976, returning to a system of fixed exchange rates seemed unlikely. Therefore, world leaders met to draft the so-called **Jamaica Agreement**—an accord among members of the IMF to formalize the existing system of floating exchange rates as the new international monetary system. The Jamaica Agreement contained several main provisions. First, it endorsed a **managed float system** of exchange rates—that is, a system in which currencies float against one another, with governments intervening to stabilize their currencies at particular target exchange rates. This is in contrast to a **free float system**—a system in which currencies float freely against one another without governments intervening in currency markets.

Second, gold was no longer the primary reserve asset of the IMF. Member countries could retrieve their gold from the IMF if they so desired. Third, the mission of the IMF was augmented: Rather than being only the manager of a fixed exchange-rate system, it was now also a "lender of last resort" for nations with balance-of-payment difficulties. Member contributions were increased to support the newly expanded activities of the IMF.

LATER ACCORDS Between 1980 and 1985, the US dollar rose dramatically against other currencies, pushing up prices of US exports and adding once again to a US trade deficit. A solution was devised by the world's five largest industrialized nations, known as the "G5" (Britain, France, Germany, Japan, and the United States). The *Plaza Accord* was a 1985 agreement among the G5 nations to act together in forcing down the value of the US dollar. The Plaza Accord caused traders to sell the dollar, and its value fell.

By February 1987, the industrialized nations were concerned that the value of the US dollar was in danger of falling too low. Meeting in Paris, leaders of the "G7" nations (the G5 plus Italy and Canada) drew up another agreement. The *Louvre Accord* was a 1987 agreement among the G7 nations that affirmed that the US dollar was appropriately valued and that they would intervene in currency markets to maintain its current market value. Once again, currency markets responded, and the dollar stabilized.

Today's Exchange-Rate Arrangements

Today's international monetary system remains in large part a managed float system, whereby most nations' currencies float against one another and governments engage in limited intervention to realign exchange rates. Within the larger monetary system, however, certain countries try to maintain more-stable exchange rates by tying their currencies to other currencies. Let's take a brief look at two ways nations attempt to do this.

PEGGED EXCHANGE-RATE ARRANGEMENT Think of one country as a small lifeboat tethered to a giant cruise ship as it navigates choppy monetary waters. Many economists argue that rather than let their currencies face the tides of global currency markets alone, developing economies should tie them to other, more stable currencies. Pegged exchange-rate arrangements "peg" a country's currency to a more stable and widely used currency in international trade. Countries then allow the exchange rate to fluctuate within a specified margin (usually 1 percent) around a central rate.

Many small countries peg their currencies to the US dollar, the EU euro, the special drawing right (SDR) of the IMF, or another individual currency. Belonging to this first category are the Bahamas, El Salvador, Iran, Malaysia, Netherlands Antilles, and Saudi Arabia. Other nations peg their currencies to groups, or "baskets," of currencies. For example, Bangladesh and Burundi tie their currencies (the taka and Burundi franc, respectively) to those of their major trading partners. Other members of this second group are Botswana, Fiji, Kuwait, Latvia, Malta, and Morocco.

currency board
Monetary regime based on an explicit commitment to exchange domestic currency for a specified foreign currency at a fixed exchange rate.

CURRENCY BOARD A **currency board** is a monetary regime that is based on an explicit commitment to exchange domestic currency for a specified foreign currency at a fixed exchange rate. The government with a currency board is legally bound to hold an amount of foreign currency that is at least equal to the amount of domestic currency. Because a currency board restricts a government from issuing additional domestic currency unless it has the foreign reserves to back it, it helps cap inflation. Thus, survival of a currency board depends on wise budget policies.

Thanks to a currency board, the country of Bosnia-Herzegovina built itself a strong and stable currency. Argentina had a currency board from 1991 until it was abandoned in early 2002, when the *peso* was allowed to float freely on currency markets. Other nations with currency boards include Brunei Darussalam, Bulgaria, Djibouti, and Lithuania.

MANAGER'S BRIEFCASE   Adjusting to Currency Swings

A strong and rising currency makes a nation's exports more expensive. Here's how companies can export successfully despite a strong currency:

- **Prune Operations** Cut costs and boost efficiency by downsizing staff and reworking factories at home to maintain production levels, and pursue customers abroad when export earnings decline.
- **Adapt Products** Win customer business and loyalty by tailoring your products to the needs of global customers, and your company may retain its business despite your higher prices.
- **Source Abroad** Source abroad for raw materials and other inputs to the production process—your supplier will likely earn an extra profit, and you'll get a better deal than is available domestically.
- **Freeze Prices** A last resort may be to freeze prices of goods in foreign markets—this might boost overall profits if sales improve.

A weak and falling currency makes a nation's imports more expensive. Here's how companies can adjust to a weak currency:

- **Source Domestically** Source domestically for raw materials and components to lower the cost of production inputs, to avoid exchange-rate risk, and to shorten the supply chain.
- **Grow at Home** Fight for the business of domestic customers now that imported products of foreign competitors are priced high because of their relatively strong currencies.
- **Push Exports** Exploit the price advantage you get from your country's weak currency by expanding your reach and depth abroad—people love a good bargain in all countries.
- **Reduce Expenses** Counteract the rising cost of imported energy by using the latest communication and transportation technologies to reduce air travel, cut utility bills, and slash shipping costs.

Doing business in an era of a managed float international monetary system means that companies need to monitor currency values. For a look at several approaches companies can use to counter the effects of a strong currency and of a weak currency, see this chapter's Manager's Briefcase, titled "Adjusting to Currency Swings."

European Monetary System

Following the collapse of the Bretton Woods system, leaders of many EU nations did not give up hope for a system that could stabilize currencies and reduce exchange-rate risk. Their efforts became increasingly important as trade between EU nations continued to expand. In 1979, these nations created the *European monetary system (EMS)*. The EMS was established to stabilize exchange rates, promote trade among nations, and keep inflation low through monetary discipline. The system was phased out when the EU adopted a single currency.

HOW THE SYSTEM WORKED The mechanism that limited the fluctuations of EU members' currencies within a specified trading range (or *target zone*) was called the *exchange rate mechanism (ERM)*. Members were required to keep their currencies within 2.25 percent of the highest- and lowest-valued currencies. To illustrate, suppose that a weakening French franc was about to reach the 2.25 percent variation in its exchange rate with the German mark. The central banks of both France and Germany were to drive the value of the French franc higher—forcing the exchange rate away from the 2.25 percent fluctuation limit. How did they do so? By buying up French francs on currency markets, thereby increasing demand for the *franc* and forcing its value higher.

The EMS was quite successful in its early years. Currency realignments were infrequent, and inflation was fairly well controlled. But in late 1992, both the British pound and the Italian lira had been on the lower fringe of the allowable 2.25 percent fluctuation range with the German *mark* for some time. Currency speculators began unloading their pounds and lira. The central banks of neither Britain nor Italy had enough money to buy their currencies on the open market. As their currencies' values plummeted, they were forced to leave the ERM. The EMS was revised in late 1993 to allow currencies to fluctuate 15 percent up or down from the midpoint of the target zone. Although the Italian lira returned to the ERM in November 1996, the British pound remained outside the ERM. Many European nations moved to the euro as their currency (see Chapter 8), which eliminated the need for the ERM.

Of the three nations (Britain, Denmark, and Sweden) that qualify to use the euro but have opted out, only Denmark participates in what is called the *exchange rate mechanism II (ERM II)*.

The ERM II was introduced January 1, 1999, and continues to function today. The aim of ERM II is to support nations that seek future membership in the European monetary union (see Chapter 8) by linking their currencies to the euro. The euro acts as the center of a *hub and spokes* model, to which each currency is linked on a bilateral basis. The currencies of participating countries have a central rate against the euro with acceptable fluctuation margins of 15 percent, although narrower margins can be arranged. Future accession countries to the EU are obliged to join the single currency once they satisfy the criteria of the Maastricht Treaty.

> ⊘ **MyLab Management** Watch It The G20 and the Global Monetary and Financial Systems
>
> Apply what you have learned so far about international capital markets. If your instructor has assigned this, go to **www.pearson.com/mylab/management** to watch a video case to learn more about the international monetary system and the recent global financial crisis and answer questions.

Recent Financial Crises

Despite the best efforts of nations to head off financial crises within the international monetary system, the world has experienced several wrenching crises in recent years. Let's examine the most prominent of these.

DEVELOPING NATIONS' DEBT CRISIS By the early 1980s, certain developing countries (especially in Latin America) had amassed huge debts payable not only to large international commercial banks but also to the IMF and the World Bank. In 1982, Mexico, Brazil, and Argentina announced that they would be unable to pay interest on their loans. At the same time, many of these countries were also experiencing runaway inflation. Many countries in Africa were facing similar problems.

To prevent a meltdown of the entire financial system, international agencies stepped in with a number of temporary solutions to the crisis. Repayment schedules were revised to put off repayment further into the future. Then, in 1989, US Treasury Secretary Nicholas Brady unveiled the Brady Plan. The Brady Plan called for large-scale reduction of the debt owed by poorer nations, the exchange of old loans for new low-interest loans, and the making of debt instruments (based on these loans) that would be tradable on world financial markets. This last feature allowed a debtor country to receive a loan from an institution and then use it to buy special securities (called "Brady Bonds") on financial markets. Funds for these new loans came from private commercial banks and were backed by the IMF and the World Bank.

MEXICO'S PESO CRISIS Armed rebellion in the poor Mexican state of Chiapas and the assassination of a presidential candidate shook investors' faith in Mexico's financial system in 1993 and 1994. Capital flowing into Mexico was mostly in the form of stocks and bonds (portfolio investment) rather than factories and equipment (foreign direct investment). Portfolio investment fled Mexico for the United States as the Mexican peso grew weak and US interest rates rose. A lending spree by Mexican banks, coupled with weak banking regulations, also played a role in delaying the government's response to the crisis. In late 1994, the Mexican peso was devalued, forcing a loss of purchasing power on the Mexican people.

In response to the crisis, the IMF and private commercial banks in the United States stepped in with about $50 billion in loans to shore up the Mexican economy. Thus, Mexico's peso crisis contributed to an additional boost in the level of IMF loans. Mexico repaid the loans ahead of schedule and once again has a sizable reserve of foreign exchange.

SOUTHEAST ASIA'S CURRENCY CRISIS The roar of the "four tiger" economies and those of other high-growth Asian nations suddenly fell silent in the summer of 1997. For 25 years, the economies of five Southeast Asian countries—Indonesia, Malaysia, the Philippines, Singapore, and Thailand—had wowed the world with growth rates twice those of most other countries. Even though many analysts projected continued growth for the region, and even though billions of dollars in investment flooded in from the West, savvy speculators were pessimistic.

On July 11, 1997, the speculators struck, selling off Thailand's baht on world currency markets. The selling forced an 18 percent drop in the value of the baht before speculators moved on to the Philippines and Malaysia. By November, the baht had plunged another 22 percent, and every other economy in the region was in a slump. The shock waves of Asia's crisis could be felt throughout the global economy.

Suddenly, countries thought to be strong emerging market economies—"tigers" to be emulated by other developing countries—were in need of billions of dollars to keep their economies from crumbling. When the dust settled, Indonesia, South Korea, and Thailand all needed IMF and World Bank funding. As incentives for these countries to begin the long process of economic restructuring, IMF loan packages came with a number of strings attached. For example, the Indonesian loan package involved three long-term goals to help put the Indonesian economy on a stronger footing: (1) to restore the confidence of international financial markets, (2) to restructure the domestic financial sector, and (3) to support domestic deregulation and trade reforms.

What caused the crisis in the first place? Well, it depends on whom you ask. Some believe it was caused by an Asian style of capitalism. They say that blame lies with poor regulation, the practice of extending loans to friends and relatives who are poor credit risks, and a lack of transparency regarding the financial health of banks and companies. Others point to poor management of these nations' short-term debt obligations. Still others argue that persistent current account deficits in these countries are what caused the large dumping of these nations' currencies. What really caused the crisis is probably a combination of all these forces.[5]

RUSSIA'S RUBLE CRISIS Russia had a whole host of problems throughout the 1990s—some were constant, others were intermittent. For starters, Russia was not immune to the events unfolding across Southeast Asia in the late 1990s. As investors became wary of potential problems in other emerging markets worldwide, stock market values in Russia plummeted. Another problem contributing to Russia's issues was depressed oil prices. Because Russia depends on oil production for a large portion of its gross domestic product (GDP), the low price of oil on world markets cut into the government's reserves of hard currency. Also cutting into the government's coffers was an unworkable tax-collection system and a large underground economy—meaning that most taxes went uncollected.

There also was the problem of inflation. We learned earlier in this chapter how an expanded amount of money chasing the same amount of goods forces prices higher. This is exactly what happened when Russia released prices in 1992. As prices skyrocketed, people dug beneath their mattresses where they had stashed their rubles during times when there were no goods to purchase. We also saw earlier how inflation eats away at the value of a nation's currency. Russia saw inflation take its exchange rate from less than 200 rubles to the dollar in early 1992 to more than 5,000 to the dollar in 1995.

Then in early 1996, as currency traders dumped the ruble, the Russian government found itself attempting to defend the ruble on currency markets. As its foreign exchange reserves dwindled in a hopeless effort, the government asked for, and received, a $10 billion aid package from the IMF. In return, Russia promised to reduce its debt (which was averaging about 7 percent of GDP), collect taxes owed it, cease printing inflation-stoking sums of currency, and peg its currency to the dollar.

Things seemed to improve for a while, but then in mid-1998 the government found itself once again trying to defend the ruble against speculative pressure on currency markets. In a single day, the government spent $1 billion trying to prop up the ruble's value, forcing its hard currency reserves to shrivel to $14 billion. As it grew obvious that the government would soon be bankrupt, the IMF stepped in and promised Russia another $11 billion. But when it was alleged that some of the IMF loan had been funneled into offshore bank accounts, the IMF held up distribution of the money. On August 17, 1998, badly strapped for cash, the government announced that it would allow the ruble to devalue by 34 percent by the end of the year. It also declared a 90-day foreign-debt moratorium and announced a de facto default on the government's domestic bond obligations. On August 26, the Russian Central Bank announced that it would no longer be able to support the ruble on currency markets. In less than one month, its value fell 300 percent. Inflation shot up to 15 percent a month in August from 0.2 percent in July and reached 30 percent in the first week of September. By the time it was all over in late 1998, the IMF had lent Russia more than $22 billion.

Protestors hold an anti-austerity, pro-government demonstration outside the Greek parliament before a crucial euro zone finance ministers meeting. People were enraged by the tough fiscal measures imposed in order to obtain vital loans from the European Union. The fiscal plan reminded Greeks that being in the euro zone means abiding by the rules of the Stability and Growth Pact, which demands fiscal discipline. One placard in English reads, "We Are Not Merkel's Colony," referring to German Chancellor, Angela Merkel.

Kostas Koutsaftikis/Shutterstock

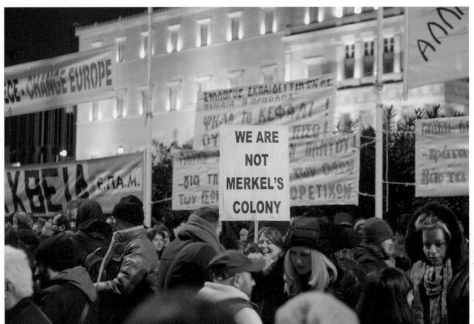

ARGENTINA'S PESO CRISIS Argentina was the star of Latin America in the early and mid-1990s. Yet by late 2001, Argentina had been in recession for nearly four years, mainly because of Brazil's devaluation of its own currency in 1999—making Brazil's exports cheaper on world markets. Meanwhile, Argentina's goods remained relatively expensive because its own currency was linked to a very strong US dollar through a currency board. As a result, Argentina saw much of its export business dry up and its economy slow significantly. By late 2001, the IMF had already promised $48 billion to rescue Argentina.

Things came to a head when the country began running out of money to service its debt obligations. The country finally defaulted on its $155 billion of public debt in early 2002, the largest default ever by any country. The government scrapped its currency board that linked the peso to the US dollar, and the peso quickly lost around 70 percent of its value on currency markets. The government, strapped for cash, seized the savings accounts of its citizens and restricted how much they could withdraw at a time.

Argentina has seen its economy ride a roller coaster of sorts since its 2001–2002 collapse. From 2001 through 2002, the economy shrank by 15 percent, unemployment shot up to 21 percent, and poverty engulfed 56 percent of its citizens. The government's plan of stimulating demand by raising wages, imposing price controls, keeping the peso low, and spending public funds worked for a time. But inflation soon reached double digits, hitting around 40 percent in 2016, cutting consumers' purchasing power and increasing poverty. Though the economy had again shrunk in 2016, leaders were hopeful that the country would turn the corner and return to growth in 2017.

Future of the International Monetary System

Recurring crises in the international monetary system are raising calls for a new system that is designed to meet the challenges of a global economy. Many believe that the vestiges of the IMF created by the Bretton Woods Agreement are no longer adequate to insulate the world's economies from disruptions in a single country or a small group of countries.

Meanwhile, leaders of many developing and newly industrialized countries are bemoaning what global capital has done to their economies. Although some call for the elimination of the IMF and its replacement by institutions not yet clearly defined, more likely will be revision of the IMF and its policy prescriptions. Efforts have already been made to develop internationally accepted codes of good practice to allow comparisons of countries' fiscal and monetary practices. Countries have also been encouraged to be more open and clear regarding their financial policies. Transparency on the part of the IMF is also being increased to instill greater accountability on the part of its leadership. The IMF also is increasing its efforts at surveillance of member nations' macroeconomic policies and is increasing its abilities in the area of financial-sector analysis.

Yet, orderly ways must still be found to integrate international financial markets so that risks are better managed. Moreover, the private sector must become involved in the prevention and resolution of financial crises. Policy makers are concerned with the way money floods into developing economies when growth is strong and then just as quickly heads for the exits at the first sign of trouble. Furthermore, some argue that because the IMF bails out debtor countries, private-sector banks do not exercise adequate caution when loaning money in risky situations—after all, the IMF will be there to pay off the loans of debtor countries. Greater cooperation and understanding among the IMF, private-sector banks, and debtor nations are needed.

QUICK STUDY 4

1. An exchange rate system in which currencies float against one another with governments intervening to stabilize currencies at target rates is called a *what*?
2. What do we call the arrangement whereby a nation lets its currency float within a margin around the value of another more stable currency?
3. A currency board is a monetary regime based on an explicit commitment to exchange domestic currency for *what*?

BOTTOM LINE FOR BUSINESS

Recent financial crises underscore the need for managers to fully understand the complexities of the international financial system. But this knowledge must be paired with vigilance of financial market conditions in order to manage businesses effectively. Here we focus on the main implications for business strategy and forecasting earnings and cash flows.

Implications for Business Strategy

Exchange rates influence all sorts of business activities for domestic and international companies. A *weak* currency (valued low relative to other currencies) lowers the price of a nation's exports on world markets and raises the price of imports. Lower prices make the country's exports more appealing on world markets. This gives companies the opportunity to take market share away from companies whose products are priced higher in comparison.

Although a government might devalue its currency to give domestic companies an edge over competition from other countries, devaluation reduces the buying power of the home country consumers. Devaluation might also allow inefficiencies to persist in domestic companies because it can lessen concern for production costs. A company improves its profits if it is selling in a country with a strong currency (one that is valued high relative to other currencies) while paying workers in a country with a weak currency. But companies that benefit from a temporary price advantage caused by exchange rates must not grow complacent about their own long-term competitiveness.

Forecasting Earnings and Cash Flows

Exchange rates also affect the amount of profit a company earns from its international subsidiaries. The earnings of international subsidiaries are typically integrated into the parent company's financial statements in the home currency. Translating subsidiary earnings from a weak host country currency into a strong home currency reduces the amount of these earnings when stated in the home currency. Likewise, translating earnings into a weak home currency increases stated earnings in the home currency.

Sudden, unfavorable movements in exchange rates can be costly for both domestic and international companies. On the other hand, stable exchange rates improve the accuracy of financial planning, including cash flow forecasts. Although companies can insure (usually by currency hedging) against potentially adverse movements in exchange rates, most available methods are too expensive for small and medium-sized businesses. Moreover, as the unpredictability of exchange rates increases, so too does the cost of insuring against the accompanying risk.

Managers also prefer movements in exchange rates to be predictable. Predictable exchange rates reduce the likelihood that companies will be caught off guard by sudden and unexpected rate changes. They also reduce the need for costly insurance against possible adverse movements in exchange rates. Rather than purchasing insurance, companies would be better off spending their money on more productive activities, such as developing new products or designing more-efficient production methods.

As we saw in this chapter, not only are a company's financial decisions affected by events in international financial markets, so too are production and marketing decisions. The next chapter begins our in-depth look at the main aspects of managing an international business. Our understanding of national business environments, international trade and investment, and the international financial system will serve us well as we embark on our tour of the nuances of international business management.

MyLab Management

Chapter Summary

LO10.1 Describe the importance of exchange rates to business activities.

- When a country's currency is *weak* (valued low relative to other currencies), the price of its exports on world markets declines (making exports more appealing on world markets) and the price of imports rises. A *strong* currency has the opposite effects.
- The intentional lowering of a currency's value by a nation's government is called *devaluation*. The intentional raising of a currency's value by a nation's government is called *revaluation*.
- The *efficient market view* says that prices of financial instruments reflect all publicly available information at any given time, whereas the *inefficient market view* says that they do not.
- *Fundamental analysis* uses statistical models based on fundamental economic indicators to forecast exchange rates. *Technical analysis* employs charts of past trends in currency prices and other factors to forecast exchange rates.

LO10.2 Outline the factors that help determine exchange rates.

- The *law of one price* says that when price is expressed in a common currency, an identical product must have an identical price in all countries. The theory of *purchasing power parity (PPP)* can be interpreted as the exchange rate between two nations' currencies that is equal to the ratio of their price levels.
- Inflation erodes purchasing power and affects exchange rates among currencies. Low interest rates lower borrowing costs and encourage spending and higher debt; high interest rates have the opposite effects.
- Because real interest rates are theoretically equal across countries, any interest rate difference between two countries must be due to different expected rates of inflation.
- A country experiencing inflation higher than that of another country should see the relative value of its currency fall.

LO10.3 Explain attempts to construct a system of fixed exchange rates.

- The *gold standard* required a nation to fix the value (price) of its currency to an ounce of gold, which also indirectly linked currencies to each other. Competitive devaluations among countries put an end to the gold standard.
- The *Bretton Woods Agreement* (1944) created an international monetary system based on the value of the US dollar and used the *gold standard* to link paper currencies to specific values of gold.
- The most important features of the Bretton Woods system were fixed exchange rates, built-in flexibility, funds for economic development, and an enforcement mechanism.
- The *International Monetary Fund (IMF)* regulates fixed exchange rates and enforces the rules of the international monetary system.

LO10.4 Describe efforts to create a system of floating exchange rates.

- The *Jamaica Agreement* (1976) endorsed a *managed float system* of exchange rates in which limited government intervention stabilized currencies at target exchange rates. The Plaza Accord and the Louvre Accord were later attempts to realign exchange rates to their targets.
- Today, a nation may "peg" its currency to another nation's currency that is more stable and more widely used internationally. Another option is for a country to use a currency board, which controls currency printing and helps cap inflation.

- The Exchange Rate Mechanism (ERM) of the European Union limited member countries' currencies within a target range to pave the way for adoption of the EU single currency, the euro. An ERM II helps a nation that has not adopted the euro to prepare for eventual adoption or to link its currency to the euro to reduce wild fluctuations.

Key Terms

Bretton Woods Agreement (p. 281)
currency board (p. 284)
devaluation (p. 272)
efficient market view (p. 273)
Fisher effect (p. 278)
fixed exchange-rate system (p. 280)
free float system (p. 284)

fundamental analysis (p. 274)
fundamental disequilibrium (p. 282)
gold standard (p. 280)
inefficient market view (p. 274)
international Fisher effect (p. 279)
international monetary system (p. 280)
Jamaica Agreement (p. 284)

law of one price (p. 275)
managed float system (p. 284)
revaluation (p. 272)
Smithsonian Agreement (p. 283)
special drawing right (SDR) (p. 282)
technical analysis (p. 274)

✪ TALK ABOUT IT 1

The financial booms and busts over recent years cause some people to call for a return to the gold standard. They point out that the gold standard reduced exchange-rate risk, imposed strict monetary policies on nations, and helped correct national trade imbalances.

10-1. Do you think a new gold standard could be successful today? Explain.
10-2. Do you think a global version of the European monetary system would work today? Explain.

✪ TALK ABOUT IT 2

When speculators sell a currency on a massive scale, a government is often forced to step in and spend billions of dollars supporting the currency's value on the open market. Some argue that currency speculators are "immoral" and say currency trading should only be allowed to facilitate deals between countries.

10-3. Is it ethical for global currency speculators to profit on a massive scale by betting against a currency, perhaps sending an entire economy into a tailspin?
10-4. Do you think that currency speculators perform a valuable service by correcting overvalued or undervalued currencies?

Ethical Challenge

You are the chair of an IMF task force. Your job is to reevaluate the policy of bailing out national governments that suffer major losses in the private sector in the name of protecting the value of the currency. Taxpayers in industrial countries typically foot the bill for IMF activities, with loans typically running into the many billions of dollars. Some critics call this system a kind of "remnant socialism" that rescues financial institutions and investors from their own mistakes with taxpayer money. Financial crises often originate as private-sector affairs, but then central banks step in and pledge foreign exchange reserves to shore up the currency.

10-5. Do you agree with the belief that the current system *privatizes* profits and then *socializes* losses if the government steps in with a bailout?
10-6. What sort of alternative can you envision to replace the current system, which often involves an IMF bailout?

Teaming Up

In groups of three or four, investigate the Greek debt crisis, which had a profound effect on Europe and the world. A seemingly small country with a population of 11 million in the heart of Europe revealed some of the underlying problems with the Eurozone and the inclusion of countries that were not politically or economically suited to a single currency. Share your ideas with the class from the perspective of travel agencies.

10-7. Briefly explain the reasons behind the Greek debt and economic crisis. What was behind it all?

10-8. What lessons from the Greek debt crisis could be learned by other developed countries?

10-9. What lessons from the Greek debt crises could be learned with regard to politics and government?

★ Market Entry Strategy Project

This exercise corresponds to the *MESP* online simulation. For the country your team is researching, integrate your answers to the following questions into your completed *MESP* report.

10-10. Is the nation a member of the International Monetary Fund?

10-11. Does it participate in a regional monetary system to manage exchange rates?

10-12. How have inflation and interest rates affected the nation's exchange rate with other currencies?

10-13. What impact has the country's exchange rate had on its imports and exports?

10-14. How has the exchange rate recently affected the activities of companies operating in the country and consumers' purchasing power?

10-15. What is the forecasted exchange rate for the year?

MyLab Management

★ Go to **www.pearson.com/mylab/management** for the following assisted-graded writing questions:

10-16. This chapter provided an overview of fixed and floating exchange rate systems and listed the advantages and disadvantages of each. Do you think the world will move toward an international monetary system of floating or fixed exchange rates in the future? Explain.

10-17. Some experts argue that the debt levels for some nations are so high that their entire external indebtedness, not just part, should be written off. What do you see as the pros and cons of this approach to debt relief?

Banking on Forgiveness

When James Wolfensohn became head of the World Bank, he bluntly admitted the bank had "screwed up" in Africa. Decades of loans had erected a vast modern infrastructure (dams, roads, and power plants) for Africa's poor, but the gap between rich and poor did not narrow. In fact, the policies of the bank and global financial regulators had created a new crisis in sub-Saharan Africa: These nations were now mired in debt they could not possibly repay. Africa's total debt at the time almost equaled the annual gross national product of the entire continent. For instance, in Mozambique, where 25 percent of all children die from infectious disease before the age of five, the government was spending twice as much paying off debt as it was spending on health care and education.

But just when many countries were receiving debt relief, the debate over aid versus loans arose again. Groups debated how to prevent economic collapses and debt problems in the developing world and how to use dwindling aid more efficiently. Some countries wanted to give more foreign aid but wanted the money to be given as grants to financially and politically stable nations. They also wanted World Bank funds to be given to poor nations as grants and not loans that nations would need to repay.

Other nations feared that giving the money away as grants would drain the World Bank's coffers, as well as their own. They acknowledged that they may not be able to do as much for the least-developed countries, but that the role of the World Bank, after all, is to act as a bank and not a donor. Support for this view was World Bank data that showed more than 95 percent of all loans are repaid and that poor nations are more careful with loans than they are with handouts.

For years, nongovernmental organizations (NGOs), such as advocacy group Oxfam International, had lobbied the Bank and the International Monetary Fund (IMF) to write off loans to their poorest borrowers, calling for "debt forgiveness" or "debt relief." Fortunately for the African people and their advocates, the new head of the bank put debt forgiveness at the top of his agenda.

In the fall of 1996, the World Bank and the IMF announced a plan to reduce the external debt of the world's poorest, most heavily indebted countries. The purpose of the plan, called the Heavily Indebted Poor Countries (HIPC) Debt Initiative, was to slash overall *debt stocks* by 50 percent, lower poor nations' *debt service,* and boost social spending in poor nations. The HIPC initiative identified countries in Africa, Latin America, Asia, and the Middle East that may qualify for debt reduction. But debt relief was not automatic. The international banking community used debt as both a carrot and

a stick: Whereas nations with good reform records obtained relief, those without reforms did not.

Then, in 2006, the world's largest international lending institutions launched the Multilateral Debt Relief Initiative (MDRI) to work alongside the HIPC initiative to help countries reach their debt-relief goals. By 2017, the 36 participating countries that received HIPC assistance had obtained a total debt relief of $99 billion from the IMF and other creditors. These countries saw their *debt stocks* reduced by 80 percent and their debt service as a percentage of GDP drop from 114 percent to 35 percent.

One success story is Uganda. Uganda was the first country declared eligible for assistance in 1997 and was the first to receive debt relief under the HIPC initiative in 1998. The decision to begin the program with Uganda was not an arbitrary one. While under the brutal dictatorship of Idi Amin, Uganda was treated as a pariah by creditors. But then President Yoweri Museveni led the country through a decade-long process of economic reform. Uganda became a model country, boasting a steady growth rate of around 5 percent, with coffee as its main export. By offering debt relief to Uganda, the World Bank and the IMF rewarded Uganda's exemplary track record by reducing its debt to the lowest possible level—about twice the value of its exports. Savings from the debt-relief program are pledged to improve health care and to make primary education available to all Ugandan families.

Thinking Globally

10-18. The World Bank and the IMF had once argued that the leniency of debt forgiveness would make it more difficult for themselves to borrow cheaply on the world's capital markets. If you were a World Bank donor, would you have supported the HIPC Debt Initiative or argued against it? Explain.

10-19. While working together on the HIPC Debt Initiative, things came to a standstill when the IMF gave a more optimistic forecast for Uganda's coffee exports than did the World Bank and so argued against the need for debt relief. Which organization do you think should play a greater role in aiding economic development? Explain.

Sources: "Heavily Indebted Poor Country (HIPC) Initiative," World Bank website (www.worldbank.org), October 10, 2016; "Debt Relief Under the Heavily Indebted Poor Countries (HIPC) Initiative," *Factsheet,* International Monetary Fund website (www.imf.org), March 24, 2014; *Heavily Indebted Poor Countries (HIPC) Initiative and Multilateral Debt Relief Initiative (MDRI)—Status of Implementation,* World Bank website (www.worldbank.org), May 19, 2010.

Chapter Eleven

International Strategy and Organization

Learning Objectives

After studying this chapter, you should be able to

11.1 Explain the company analysis techniques that precede strategy selection.

11.2 Describe the various strategies that companies use to reach their goals.

11.3 Outline the key issues behind the selection of organizational structure.

11.4 Describe various international organizational structures and types of work teams.

A Look Back

Chapter 10 explored the international monetary system. We examined the factors that affect the determination of exchange rates and discussed international attempts to create a system of predictable and stable exchange rates.

A Look at This Chapter

This chapter introduces us to the strategies used by international companies. We explore the different types of strategies available to international companies and important factors in their selection. We also examine the organizational structures that companies devise to suit their international operations.

A Look Ahead

Chapter 12 explains how managers screen and research potential markets and sites for operations. We identify the information required in the screening process and explain where managers can go to obtain such information.

MyLab Management

✪ IMPROVE YOUR GRADE!

When you see this icon ✪, visit **www.pearson.com/mylab/management** for activities that are applied, personalized, and offer immediate feedback.

Lidl UK: Britain's Fastest-Growing Discount Supermarket

Lidl started with a single store in Germany in the year 1973, but its operations have gradually expanded since its first store in the United Kingdom opened in 1994. Today, the discount supermarket has more than 700 stores and 12 regional distribution centers employing over 20,000 people across Great Britain. Lidl's "no-frills strategy"—offering a limited range of its own branded products at extremely competitive prices—resonated with its customers in the United Kingdom in the aftermath of the global financial recession of 2008. The company is committed to investing in its own brand ranges, although the retailer does work with fast-moving-consumer-goods giants like P&G to supply a few external branded goods.

davizro/123RF

Lidl incorporates a more price-sensitive focus within the discount supermarket industry while still making profits by selling 90 percent of its own branded products. Other supermarkets have attempted to catch up to this level of success; Tesco, for instance, announced a new chain of discount stores across the United Kingdom in its latest effort to compete with its rivals.

Lidl's no-frills, low-cost strategy has helped the retailer acquire a market share of 5.2 percent, as compared to 3.1 percent five years ago, becoming Britain's fastest-growing discount supermarket based on market share. Further, by forcing down price margins, Lidl has permanently changed the dynamics of the UK grocery market—in 2015, it was awarded the Grocer Gold Awards after beating Waitrose, Asda, and Aldi.

In order to sustain themselves (albeit as less-profitable entities), the big supermarkets in the United Kingdom have to incorporate low margins in their business model. Lidl, on the other hand, has low costs built into its business model already as it emphasizes bulk over brand and price over range. This means that Lidl offers a limited variety of its own branded products at a competitive price by volume; its competitors, on the other hand, offer a large product range at higher prices and low volume to meet their customers' needs. As you read this chapter, consider the creative strategies companies use to out-compete rivals and serve their customers.[1]

planning
Process of identifying and selecting an organization's objectives and deciding how the organization will achieve those objectives.

strategy
Set of planned actions taken by managers to help a company meet its objectives.

Planning is the process of identifying and selecting an organization's objectives and deciding how the organization will achieve those objectives. In turn, **strategy** is the set of planned actions taken by managers to help a company meet its objectives. The key to developing an effective strategy, then, is to define a company's objectives (or goals) clearly and to plan carefully how it will achieve those goals. This requires a company to undertake an analysis of its own capabilities and strengths in order to identify what it can do better than the competition. It also means that a company must carefully assess the competitive environment and the national and international business environments in which it operates.

A well-defined strategy helps a company compete effectively in increasingly competitive international markets. It serves to coordinate a company's various divisions and departments so that the company reaches its overall goals in the most effective and efficient manner possible. A clear, appropriate strategy focuses a company on the activities that it performs best and on the industries for which it is best suited. It keeps an organization away from a future of mediocre performance or total failure. An inappropriate strategy can lead a manager to take actions that pull a company in opposite directions or take it into industries it knows little about.

Managers confront similar concerns whether formulating a strategy for a domestic or an international company. Both types of firms must determine what products to produce, where to produce them, and where and how to market them. The biggest difference lies in complexity. Companies considering international production need to select from many potential countries, each likely having more than one possible location. Depending on its product line, a company that wants to market internationally might have an equally large number of markets to consider. Whether it is being considered as a site for operations or as a potential market, each international location has a rich mixture of cultural, political, legal, and economic traditions and processes. All these factors add to the complexity of planning and formulating strategy for international managers.

We begin this chapter by exploring important factors that managers consider when analyzing their companies' strengths and weaknesses. We examine the different international strategies and the corporate-, business-, and department-level strategies that companies implement. Next, we address the centralization versus decentralization decision and the issues of coordination and flexibility—key issues behind the selection of organizational structure. Finally, we explore the different types of organizational structures that companies use to coordinate their international activities.

11.1 Company Analysis

11.1 Explain the company analysis techniques that precede strategy selection.

The process of formulating a strategy permits managers to step back from day-to-day activities and get a fresh perspective on the current and future direction of the company and its industry. As shown in Figure 11.1, we regard strategy formulation as a three-stage process. Stages 1 and 2 involve company analysis and are discussed here. Stage 3 entails the actual selecting and formulating of strategies and is presented in the next major section titled "Strategy Formulation."

Company Mission and Goals

mission statement
Written statement of why a company exists and what it plans to accomplish.

Most companies have a general purpose for why they exist, which they express in a **mission statement**—a written statement of why a company exists and what it plans to accomplish. For example, one company might set out to supply the highest level of service in a *market segment*—a clearly identifiable group of potential buyers. Another might strive to be the lowest-cost supplier in its segment worldwide. The mission statement often guides decisions such as which industries to enter or exit and how to compete in chosen segments.

stakeholders
All parties, ranging from suppliers and employees to stockholders and consumers, who are affected by a company's activities.

TYPES OF MISSION STATEMENTS Mission statements often spell out how a company's operations affect its **stakeholders**—all parties, ranging from suppliers and employees to stockholders and consumers, who are affected by a company's activities. Some companies place corporate brands center stage and place the mission of creating well-liked brands above all else. The mission statements of other businesses focus on other issues, including superior shareholder returns, profitability, market share, and consumers. Still other companies define their mission to be socially responsible enterprises. For example, the mission statement of global integrated energy company, Tesla (www.tesla.com), is "to accelerate the world's transition to sustainable energy."[2]

Figure 11.1

Strategy-Formulation Process

The mission statement of an international business depends on (among other things) the type of business it is in, the stakeholders it is trying most to satisfy, and the aspect of business most important to achieving its goals. Yet companies must be sensitive to the needs of its different stakeholders in different nations. A company might need to balance the needs of stockholders for financial returns in the home nation, the needs of buyers for good value in a consumer market, and the needs of the public at large where it has a production facility.

Managers must also define the *objectives* they wish to achieve in the global marketplace. Objectives at the highest level in a company tend to be stated in the most general terms. An example of this type of objective is the following:

To be the largest global company in each industry in which we compete.

Objectives of individual business units in an organization tend to be more specific. They are normally stated in more concrete terms and sometimes even contain numerical targets. For example, such a mission statement could be stated as follows:

To increase the nutritious portion of our products 50 percent by 2024.

Objectives usually become even more precise at the level of individual departments and almost always contain numerical targets of performance. For example, the following could be the objective of a marketing and sales department:

To increase global market share by 5 percent in each of the next three years.

Core Competency and Value-Creation

Before managers formulate effective strategies, they must analyze the company, its industry (or industries), and the national business environments in which it is involved. They should also examine industries and countries being targeted for potential future entry. In this section, we address the company and its industries. We examine the business environment in the next section.

UNIQUE ABILITIES OF COMPANIES Although large multinational companies are often involved in multiple industries, most perform one activity (or a few activities) better than any competitor does. A **core competency** is a special ability of a company that competitors find extremely difficult or impossible to equal. It is not a skill; individuals possess skills. For example, an architect's ability to design an office building in the Victorian style is a skill. A core competency refers to multiple skills that are coordinated to form a single technological outcome.

core competency

Special ability of a company that competitors find extremely difficult or impossible to equal.

Although skills can be learned through on-the-job training and personal experience, core competencies develop over longer periods of time and are difficult to teach. At one point, Canon of Japan (www.canon.com) purchased expertise in optic technology but only later succeeded in developing a variety of products based on optic technology—including cameras, copiers, and semiconductor lithographic equipment. Likewise, Sony (www.sony.com) for decades relied on its core competency in miniaturizing electronic components in order to fortify its global leadership position in consumer electronics. These companies possessed unique abilities to create superior products through development of their core competencies.

How do managers actually go about analyzing and identifying their firms' unique abilities? Let's explore a tool commonly used by managers to analyze their companies—*value-chain analysis*.

value-chain analysis

Process of dividing a company's activities into primary and support activities and identifying those that create value for customers.

VALUE-CHAIN ANALYSIS Managers must select strategies consistent with their company's particular strengths and the market conditions the firm faces. Managers should also select company strategies based on what the company does that customers find valuable. This is why managers conduct a **value-chain analysis**—the process of dividing a company's activities into primary and support activities and identifying those that create value for customers.[3]

As we see in Figure 11.2, value-chain analysis divides a company's activities into primary activities and support activities that are central to creating customer value. *Primary activities* include inbound and outbound logistics, production (goods and services), marketing and sales, and customer service. Primary activities involve the creation of the product, its marketing and delivery to buyers, and its after-sales support and service. *Support activities* include business infrastructure, human resource management, technology development, and procurement (sourcing). Each of these activities provides the inputs and infrastructure required by the primary activities.

Each primary and support activity is a source of strength or weakness for a company. Managers determine whether each activity enhances or detracts from customer value, and they incorporate this knowledge into the strategy-formulation process. Analysis of primary and support activities often involves finding activities in which improvements can be made with large benefits.

Primary Activities When analyzing primary activities, managers often look for areas in which the company can increase the value provided to its customers. For example, managers might examine production processes and discover new, more-efficient manufacturing methods in order to reduce production costs and improve quality. Customer satisfaction might be increased by improving logistics management to shorten the time it takes to get a product to the buyer or by providing better customer service.

Companies might also lower costs by introducing greater automation into the production process. Computer maker Acer (www.acer.com) applied a fast-food production model to personal computer manufacturing. Rather than manufacture complete computers in Asia and ship them around the world, Acer builds components at plants scattered throughout the world. Those

Figure 11.2
Company Value Chain

components are then shipped to assembly plants, where computers are built according to customer specifications. Acer adopted this approach because there was no longer any value added in simply assembling computers. By altering its production and logistics processes, Acer developed a business model that created value for customers.

Support Activities Support activities assist companies in performing their primary activities. For example, the actions of any company's employees are crucial to its success. Production, logistics, marketing, sales, and customer service all benefit when employees are qualified and well trained. International companies can often improve the quality of their products by investing in worker training and management development. In turn, ensuring quality can increase the efficiency of a firm's manufacturing, marketing and sales, and customer service activities. Effective procurement (or sourcing) can locate low-cost, high-quality raw materials or intermediate products and ensure on-time delivery to production facilities. Finally, a sophisticated infrastructure not only improves internal communication but also supports organizational culture and each primary activity.

The in-depth analysis of a company that is inherent in the strategy-formulation process helps managers to discover their company's unique core competency and abilities and to identify the activities that create customer value. For a checklist of issues companies should consider in a self-analysis of whether it is ready to go global, see this chapter's Manager's Briefcase, titled "Ask Questions before Going Global."

A company cannot identify its unique abilities in a vacuum, separate from the environment in which it operates. The external business environment consists of all the elements outside a company that can affect its performance, such as cultural, political, legal, and economic forces; workers' unions; consumers; and financial institutions. Let's explore several of these environmental forces that affect strategy formulation.

NATIONAL AND INTERNATIONAL BUSINESS ENVIRONMENTS National differences in language, religious beliefs, customs, traditions, and climate complicate strategy formulation. Language differences can increase the cost of operations and administration. Manufacturing processes must sometimes be adapted to the supply of local workers and to local customs, traditions, and practices. Marketing activities sometimes can result in costly mistakes if they do not incorporate cultural differences. For example, a company once decided to sell its laundry detergent in Japan but did not adjust the size of the box in which it was sold. The company spent millions of dollars developing a detailed marketing campaign and was shocked when it experienced disappointing sales. It turned out that the company should have packaged the detergent in smaller containers for

---

MANAGER'S BRIEFCASE   Ask Questions before Going Global

It seems everywhere a business turns for advice these days it hears the mantra, "Go global." But a company needs a solid grasp of its capabilities and its product if it is going to be successful in global markets. Here is a brief checklist of issues for a business to consider:

- **Are You Ready?** Do you or your key personnel speak other languages? Have you or they lived in other cultures for extended periods? How long has your company been in business? What markets might need what your company sells? Can your business withstand the rough seas of global trade? What specific sales numbers are forecasted? Can you map your global business journey?
- **Is Your Product Ready?** Can your business capitalize on its strengths? Will you need to modify your product or your marketing approach? Will modifying the product or its marketing weaken your offering? Does your product satisfy all local safety standards and other regulations? Can your

product stand up to the competition and to the scrutiny of customers?
- **Is Each Department Ready?** Is your company's infrastructure capable of going global? Does each department (logistics, operations, marketing, sales, service, human resources, collections, etc.) have the resources to handle its international responsibilities? What is your company's financial strategy for international expansion? Can domestic sales support an initial period of money-losing international operations? Is everyone in the company committed to the international effort?
- **Is Your Strategy Ready?** Will your company's international effort conflict with or complement your overall business strategy? Will your company's foreignness be a hindrance, or can it be exploited profitably? Is your business capable of sustaining a lengthy international endeavor? How will your company break into long-established family networks and business relationships?

the Japanese market. Japanese shoppers prefer smaller quantities because they tend to walk home from the store and have smaller storage areas in tight living quarters.

Differences in political and legal systems also complicate international strategies. Legal and political processes often differ in target countries to such an extent that firms must hire outside consultants to teach them about the local system. Such knowledge is important to international companies because the approval of the host government is almost always necessary for making direct investments. Companies need to know which ministry or department has the authority to grant approval for a big business deal—a process that can become extremely cumbersome. For example, non-Chinese companies in China must often get approval to conduct business from several separate agencies. The process is further complicated by the tendency of local government officials to interpret laws differently than do bureaucrats in Beijing (the nation's capital).

Different national economic systems further complicate strategy formulation. Negative attitudes of local people toward the impact of direct investment can generate political unrest. Economic philosophy affects the tax rates that governments impose. Whereas socialist economic systems normally levy high taxes on business profits, free-market economies tend to levy lower taxes. The need to work in more than one currency also complicates international strategy. To minimize losses from currency fluctuations, companies must develop strategies to deal with exchange-rate risk.

Finally, apart from complicating strategy, the national business environment can affect the location in which a company chooses to perform an activity. For example, a nation that spends a high portion of its GDP on research and development (R&D) attracts high-tech industries and high-wage jobs and, as a result, prospers. By contrast, countries that spend relatively little in the way of R&D tend to have lower levels of prosperity.

> **QUICK STUDY 1**
>
> 1. A written statement of why a company exists and what it plans to accomplish is called a *what*?
> 2. A special ability of a company that competitors find extremely difficult or impossible to equal is called a *what*?
> 3. Value-chain analysis involves separating a company's activities into *what two categories* of activities?

11.2 Strategy Formulation

11.2 Describe the various strategies that companies use to reach their goals.

As we have seen, the strengths and special capabilities of an international company, along with the environmental forces it faces, strongly influence its strategy. Let's examine this third stage in the planning and strategy-formulation process.

Two International Strategies

Companies engaged in international business activities can approach the market using either a *multinational* or a *global* strategy. It is important to note that these two strategies do not include companies that export. Exporters do not have foreign direct investments in other national markets and should instead devise an appropriate export strategy (see Chapter 13). Let's now examine what it means for a company to follow a multinational or a global strategy.

multinational (multidomestic) strategy

Adapting products and their marketing strategies in each national market to suit local preferences.

MULTINATIONAL STRATEGY Some international companies choose to follow a **multinational (multidomestic) strategy**—a strategy of adapting products and their marketing strategies in each national market to suit local preferences. In other words, a multinational strategy is just what its name implies—a separate strategy for each of the multiple nations in which a company markets its products. To implement a multinational strategy, companies often establish largely independent, self-contained units (or subsidiaries) in each national market. Each subsidiary typically undertakes its own product research and development, production, and marketing. In many ways, each unit functions largely as an independent company. Multinational strategies are often appropriate for companies in industries in which buyer preferences do not converge across national borders, such as certain food products and some print media.

The main benefit of a multinational strategy is that it allows companies to monitor buyer preferences closely in each local market and to respond quickly and effectively to emerging buyer preferences. Companies hope that customers will perceive a tailored product as delivering greater value than do competitors' products. A multinational strategy, then, should allow a company to charge higher prices and/or gain market share.

The main drawback of a multinational strategy is that companies cannot exploit scale economies in product development, manufacturing, or marketing. The multinational strategy typically increases the cost structure for international companies and forces them to charge higher prices to recover such costs. As such, a multinational strategy is usually poorly suited to industries in which price competitiveness is a key success factor. The high degree of independence with which each unit operates also may reduce opportunities to share knowledge among units within a company.

GLOBAL STRATEGY Other companies decide that what suits their operations is a **global strategy**—a strategy of offering the same products using the same marketing strategy in all national markets. Companies that follow a global strategy often take advantage of scale and location economies by producing entire inventories of products or components in a few optimal locations. They also tend to perform product research and development in one or a few locations and typically design promotional campaigns and advertising strategies at headquarters. So-called global products are most common in industries characterized by price competition and, therefore, pressure to contain costs. They include certain electronic components, a wide variety of industrial goods such as steel, and some consumer goods such as paper and writing instruments.

global strategy
Offering the same products using the same marketing strategy in all national markets.

The main benefit of a global strategy is cost savings due to product and marketing standardization. These cost savings can then be passed on to consumers to help the company gain market share in its market segment. A global strategy also allows managers to share lessons learned in one market with managers at other locations.

The main problem with a global strategy is it can cause a company to overlook important differences in buyer preferences from one market to another. A global strategy does not allow a company to modify its products except for the most superficial features, such as the color of paint applied to a finished product or a small add-on feature. This can present a competitor with an opportunity to step in and satisfy any unmet needs of local buyers, thereby creating a niche market.

In addition to deciding whether the company will follow a multinational or a global strategy, managers must formulate strategies for the corporation, each business unit, and each department. Let's look closely at the three different levels of company strategy: *corporate-, business-, and department-level* strategies (see Figure 11.3).

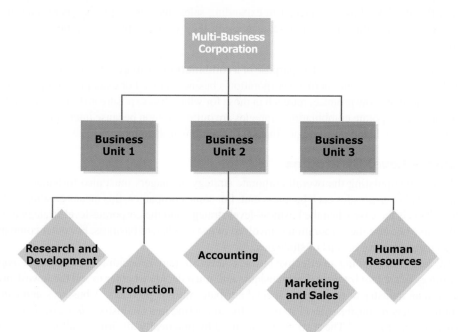

Figure 11.3
Three Levels of Company Strategy

Corporate-Level Strategies

Companies involved in more than one line of business must first formulate a *corporate-level strategy*. This means, in part, identifying the national markets and industries in which the company will operate. It also involves developing overall objectives for the company's different business units and specifying the role that each unit will play in reaching those objectives. The four key approaches to corporate strategy are *growth, retrenchment, stability*, and *combination*.

growth strategy

Strategy designed to increase the scale (size of activities) or scope (kinds of activities) of a corporation's operations.

GROWTH STRATEGY A **growth strategy** is designed to increase the scale or scope of a corporation's operations. *Scale* refers to the *size* of a corporation's activities, *scope* to the *kinds* of activities it performs. Yardsticks commonly used to measure growth include geographic coverage, number of business units, market share, sales revenue, and number of employees. *Organic growth* refers to a corporate strategy of relying on internally generated growth. For example, management at 3M (www.3m.com) strongly encourages entrepreneurial activity, often spinning off business units to nurture the best ideas and carry them to completion.

Other methods of growth include mergers and acquisitions, joint ventures, and strategic alliances (see Chapter 13). Companies use these tactics when they do not wish to invest in developing certain skills internally or when other companies already do what managers are trying to achieve. Common partners in implementing these strategies include competitors, suppliers, and buyers. Corporations typically join forces with competitors to reduce competition, expand product lines, or expand geographically. A common motivation for joining forces with suppliers is to increase control over the quality, cost, and timing of inputs.

retrenchment strategy

Strategy designed to reduce the scale or scope of a corporation's businesses.

RETRENCHMENT STRATEGY The exact opposite of a growth strategy is a **retrenchment strategy**—a strategy designed to reduce the scale or scope of a corporation's businesses. Corporations often cut back the scale of their operations when economic conditions worsen or competition increases. They may do so by closing factories with unused capacity and by laying off workers. Corporations can also reduce the scale of their operations by laying off managers and salespeople in national markets that are not generating adequate sales revenue. Corporations reduce the *scope* of their activities by selling unprofitable business units or those that are no longer directly related to their overall aims. Weaker competitors often resort to retrenchment when national business environments grow more competitive.

stability strategy

Strategy designed to guard against change and used by corporations to avoid either growth or retrenchment.

STABILITY STRATEGY A **stability strategy** is designed to guard against change. Corporations often use a stability strategy when trying to avoid either growth or retrenchment. Such corporations have typically met their stated objectives or are satisfied with what they have already accomplished. They believe that their strengths are being fully exploited and their weaknesses fully protected against. They also see the business environment as posing neither profitable opportunities nor threats. They have no interest in expanding sales, increasing profits, increasing market share, or expanding the customer base; at present, they want simply to maintain their current positions.

combination strategy

Strategy designed to mix growth, retrenchment, and stability strategies across a corporation's business units.

COMBINATION STRATEGY The purpose of a **combination strategy** is to mix growth, retrenchment, and stability strategies across a corporation's business units. For example, a corporation can invest in units that show promise, retrench in those for which less exposure is desired, and stabilize others. In fact, corporate combination strategies are quite common because international corporations rarely follow identical strategies in each of their business units.

Business-Level Strategies

In addition to stipulating the overall corporate strategy, managers must also formulate separate *business-level strategies* for each business unit. For some companies, this means creating just one strategy. This is the case when the business-level strategy and the corporate-level strategy are one and the same because the corporation is involved in just one line of business. For other companies, this can mean creating dozens of strategies.

The key to developing an effective business-level strategy is deciding on a *general competitive strategy in the marketplace*. Each business unit must decide whether to sell the lowest-priced product in an industry or to integrate special attributes into its products. A business unit can use one of three generic business-level strategies for competing in its industry—*low-cost leadership, differentiation*, or *focus*.[4] These strategies are used by practically all firms in all markets worldwide. Let's explore each of these strategies in detail.

LOW-COST LEADERSHIP STRATEGY A strategy in which a company exploits economies of scale to have the lowest cost structure of any competitor in its industry is called a **low-cost leadership strategy**. Companies that pursue the low-cost leadership position also try to contain administrative costs and the costs of their various primary activities, including marketing, advertising, and distribution. Although cutting costs is the mantra for firms that pursue a low-cost leadership position, other important competitive factors such as product quality and customer service cannot be ignored. Factors underlying the low-cost leadership position (efficient production in large quantities) help guard against attack by competitors because of the large upfront cost of getting started. The strategy typically requires a company to have a large market share because achieving low-cost leadership tends to rely on large-scale production to contain costs. One negative aspect of the low-cost leadership strategy is low customer loyalty—all else being equal, buyers will purchase from any low-cost leader.

A low-cost leadership strategy works best with mass-marketed products aimed at price-sensitive buyers. This strategy is often well suited to companies with standardized products and marketing promotions. Two global companies vying for the low-cost leadership position in their respective industries include Casio (www.casio.com) in sports watches and Texas Instruments (www.ti.com) in calculators and other electronic devices.

DIFFERENTIATION STRATEGY A **differentiation strategy** is one in which a company designs its products to be perceived as unique by buyers throughout its industry. The perception of uniqueness can allow a company to charge a higher price and enjoy greater customer loyalty than it could as a low-cost leader. But a perception of exclusivity, or meeting the needs of a small group of buyers, tends to force a company into a lower market-share position. A company using this strategy must develop a loyal customer base to offset its smaller market share and higher costs of producing and marketing a unique product.

One way products can be differentiated is by improving their reputation for *quality*. Ceramic tableware for everyday use is found at department stores in almost every country. But Japanese producer Noritake differentiates the ceramic tableware it makes (www.noritake.com) from common tableware by emphasizing its superior quality. The perception of higher quality allows manufacturers to charge higher prices for their products worldwide.

Other products are differentiated by distinctive *brand images*. Armani (www.armani.com) and DKNY (www.dkny.com), for example, are relatively pricey global clothiers appealing to a young, fashionable clientele. Each is continually introducing new textures and colors that are at once stylish and functional. Another example is Italian carmaker Alfa Romeo (www.alfaromeo.com), which does not compete in the fiercely competitive mass-consumer segment of the global

low-cost leadership strategy
Strategy in which a company exploits economies of scale to have the lowest cost structure of any competitor in its industry.

differentiation strategy
Strategy in which a company designs its products to be perceived as unique by buyers throughout its industry.

By analyzing its industry and assets, a company based in an emerging market can determine if its competitive edge is germane to the local market, or if it is transferable to other markets. Chinese appliance and electronics company, Haier, is taking the battle for market share to industrialized nations and is now one of the world's largest home appliances manufacturers. The company proudly displays its latest products at trade shows worldwide and competes well against the established competitors.

Kobby Dagan/Shutterstock

automobile industry. If it were to do so, it would have to be price-competitive and offer a wider selection of cars. Instead, Alfa Romeo offers a high-quality product with a brand image that rewards the Alfa Romeo owner with status and prestige.

Another differentiating factor is *product design*—the sum of the features by which a product looks and functions according to customer requirements. Special features differentiate both goods and services in the minds of consumers who value those features. Manufacturers can also combine several differentiation factors in formulating their strategies. For example, the designs of Casio (www.casio.com) and other makers of mass-market sports watches stress functionality. The sports watches of TAG Heuer (www.tagheuer.com) of Switzerland, on the other hand, offer class and style in addition to performance.

FOCUS STRATEGY A **focus strategy** is one in which a company focuses on serving the needs of a narrowly defined market segment by being the low-cost leader, by differentiating its product, or both. Increasing competition often means more products distinguished by price or differentiated by quality, design, and so forth. In turn, a greater product range leads to the continuous refinement of market segments. Today, many industries consist of large numbers of market segments and even smaller subsegments. For example, some firms try to serve the needs of one ethnic or racial group, whereas others, often entrepreneurs and small businesses, focus on a single geographic area.

Johnson & Johnson (J&J; www.jnj.com) is commonly thought of as being a single, large consumer-products company. In fact, it is a conglomerate of more than 250 operating companies that market an enormous variety of products to a wide array of market segments. Many individual J&J companies try to dominate their segments by producing specialty goods and services. In so doing, they focus on narrow segments by using either low-cost leadership or differentiation techniques.[5]

A focus strategy often means designing products and promotions aimed at consumers who are either dissatisfied with existing choices or who want something distinctive. Consider the highly fragmented gourmet coffee market. One extremely unusual brand of coffee called Luwak sells for up to $300 per pound! Apparently, luwaks (weasels on the Indonesian island of Java) eat coffee berries containing coffee beans. The beans "naturally ferment" as they pass through the luwaks and are later recovered. The beans are then washed, roasted, and sold around the world as a specialty coffee.[6]

Department-Level Strategies

Achieving corporate- and business-level objectives depends on effective departmental strategies that focus on the specific activities that transform resources into products. Formulation of *department-level strategies* brings us back to where we began our analysis of a company's capabilities that support its strategy: to the primary and support activities that create value for customers. After managers analyze these activities, they must develop strategies that exploit their firm's value-creating strengths.

PRIMARY AND SUPPORT ACTIVITIES Each department is instrumental in creating customer value through lower costs or differentiated products. This is especially true of departments that conduct *primary activities*. Manufacturing strategies are obviously important in cutting the production costs of both standardized and differentiated products. They are also crucial to improving product quality. Effective marketing strategies allow companies to promote the differences in their products. A strong sales force and good customer service contribute to favorable images among consumers or industrial buyers and generate loyal customers of both kinds. Efficient logistics in bringing raw materials and components into the factory and getting the finished product out the factory door can result in substantial cost savings.

Support activities also create customer value. For example, R&D identifies market segments with unsatisfied needs and designs products to meet them. Human resource managers can improve

---

focus strategy
Strategy in which a company focuses on serving the needs of a narrowly defined market segment by being the low-cost leader, by differentiating its product, or both.

efficiency and cut costs by hiring well-trained employees and conducting worker training and management development programs. Procurement tasks provide operations with quality resources at a reasonable cost. Accounting and finance (elements of a firm's infrastructure) must develop efficient information systems to assist managers in making decisions and maintaining financial control, thus having an impact on costs and quality in general.

There are important elements that drive the decisions of world-class companies with regard to strategy formulation. For example, the important *production* issues to consider are the number and dispersion of production facilities and whether to standardize production processes for all markets. The important *marketing* issue is whether to standardize either the physical features of products or their marketing strategies across markets. We present the strategic considerations of production and marketing activities in later chapters.

QUICK STUDY 2

1. What strategy involves adapting products and their marketing strategies to national markets to suit local preferences?
2. What is a benefit of using a global strategy?
3. Deciding on a general competitive strategy in the marketplace is the key to developing a *what*?

11.3 Issues of Organizational Structure

Organizational structure is the way in which a company divides its activities among separate units and coordinates activities among those units. If a company's organizational structure is appropriate for its strategic plans, it will be more effective in working toward its goals. In this section, we explore several important issues related to organizational structures and will examine several alternative forms of organization.

Centralization versus Decentralization

A vital issue for top managers is determining the degree to which decision making in the organization will be centralized or decentralized. *Centralized decision making* concentrates decision making at a high organizational level in one location, such as at headquarters. *Decentralized decision making* disperses decisions to lower organizational levels, such as to international subsidiaries.

Should managers at the parent company be actively involved in the decisions made by international subsidiaries? Or should managers intervene relatively little, perhaps, and only get involved in the most crucial decisions? Some decisions, of course, must be decentralized. If top managers involve themselves in the day-to-day decisions of every subsidiary, they are likely to be overwhelmed. For example, managers cannot get directly involved in every hiring decision or assignment of people to specific tasks at each facility. On the other hand, overall corporate strategy cannot be delegated to subsidiary managers because only top management is likely to have the appropriate perspective needed to formulate corporate strategy.

In our discussion of centralization versus decentralization of decision making, it is important to remember two points:

1. Companies rarely centralize or decentralize all decision making. Rather, they seek an approach that will result in the greatest efficiency and effectiveness.
2. International companies may centralize decision making in certain geographic markets while decentralizing it in others. Numerous factors influence this decision, including the need for product modification and the abilities of managers at each location.

With these points in mind, let's take a look at some specific factors that determine whether centralized or decentralized decision making is most appropriate.

WHEN TO CENTRALIZE Centralized decision-making helps coordinate the operations of international subsidiaries. This is important for companies that operate in multiple lines of business

11.3 Outline the key issues behind the selection of organizational structure.

organizational structure
Way in which a company divides its activities among separate units and coordinates activities among those units.

or in many international markets. It is also important when one subsidiary's output is another's input. In such situations, coordinating operations from a single, high-level vantage point is more efficient. Purchasing is often centralized if all subsidiaries use the same inputs in production. For example, a company that manufactures steel filing cabinets and desks will need a great deal of sheet steel. A central purchasing department will get a better bulk price on sheet steel than would subsidiaries negotiating their own agreements. Each subsidiary would then benefit by purchasing sheet steel from the company's central purchasing department at a lower cost than it would pay in the open market.

Some companies maintain strong central control over financial resources by channeling all subsidiary profits back to the parent for redistribution to subsidiaries based on their needs. This practice reduces the likelihood that certain subsidiaries will undertake investment projects when more promising projects at other locations go without funding. Other companies centrally design policies, procedures, and standards to encourage a single global organizational culture. This policy makes it more likely that all subsidiaries will enforce company rules uniformly. The policy also helps when companies transfer managers from one location to another because uniform policies can smooth transitions for managers and subordinates alike.

WHEN TO DECENTRALIZE Decentralized decision making is beneficial when fast-changing national business environments put a premium on local responsiveness. Decentralized decisions can result in products that are better suited to the needs and preferences of local buyers because subsidiary managers are in closer contact with the local business environment. Local managers are more likely to perceive environmental changes that managers at headquarters might not notice. By contrast, central managers may not perceive such changes or would likely get a secondhand account of local events. Delayed response and misinterpreted events could then result in lost orders, stalled production, and weakened competitiveness.

Participative Management and Accountability Decentralization can also help foster participative management practices. The morale of employees is likely to be higher if subsidiary managers and subordinates are involved in decision making. Subsidiary managers and workers can grow more dedicated to the organization when they are involved in decisions related to production, promotion, distribution, and pricing strategies.

Decentralization also can increase personal accountability for business decisions. When local managers are rewarded (or punished) for their decisions, they are likely to invest more effort in making and executing them. Conversely, if local managers must do nothing but implement policies dictated from above, they can attribute poor performance to decisions that were ill-suited to the local environment. When managers are held accountable for decision making and implementation, they typically delve more deeply into research and consider all available options. The results are often better decisions and improved performance.

Coordination and Flexibility

When designing the organizational structure, managers seek answers to certain key questions: What is the most efficient method of linking divisions to each other? Who should coordinate the activities of different divisions in order to achieve overall strategies? How should information be processed and delivered to managers when it is required? What sorts of monitoring mechanisms and reward structures should be established? How should the company introduce corrective measures, and whose responsibility should it be to execute them? To answer these types of questions, we must look at the issues of coordination and flexibility.

chains of command
Lines of authority that run from top management to individual employees and that specify internal reporting relationships.

STRUCTURE AND COORDINATION As we have seen, some companies have a presence in several or more national business environments while some firms manufacture and market products practically everywhere. Others operate primarily in one country and export to, or import from, other markets. Each type of company must design an appropriate organizational structure. Each needs a structure that clearly defines areas of responsibility and **chains of command**— the lines of authority that run from top management to individual employees and that specify internal reporting relationships. Finally, every firm needs a structure that brings together areas that require close cooperation. For example, to avoid product designs that make manufacturing more difficult and costly than necessary, most firms ensure that R&D and manufacturing remain in close contact.

STRUCTURE AND FLEXIBILITY Organizational structure is not permanent but is often modified to suit changes both within a company and in its external environment. Because companies usually base organizational structures on strategies, changes in strategy usually require adjustments in structure. Similarly, because changes in national business environments can force changes in strategy, they too will influence company structure. It is especially important to monitor closely the conditions in countries characterized by rapidly shifting cultural, political, and economic environments. Let's now explore four organizational structures that have been developed to improve the responsiveness and effectiveness of companies conducting international business activities.

QUICK STUDY 3

1. How a company divides its activities among separate units and coordinates activities among units is called *what*?
2. What type of decision making helps coordinate the operations of international subsidiaries?
3. What is a benefit of decentralized decision making in an organization?

11.4 Types of Organizational Structure

There are many different ways in which a company can organize itself to carry out its international business activities. But four organizational structures tend to be most common for the vast majority of international companies: division structure, area structure, product structure, and matrix structure.

11.4 Describe various international organizational structures and types of work teams.

International Division Structure

An **international division structure** separates domestic from international business activities by creating a separate international division with its own manager (see Figure 11.4). In turn, the international division is typically divided into units corresponding to the countries in which a company is active—say, Brazil, China, and France. Within each country, a general manager controls the manufacture and marketing of the firm's products. Each country unit typically carries out all of its own activities with its own departments, such as marketing and sales, finance, and production.

Because the international division structure concentrates international expertise in one division, divisional managers become specialists in a wide variety of activities such as foreign exchange, export documentation, and host government relations. By consigning international activities to a single division, a firm can reduce costs, increase efficiency, and prevent international activities from disrupting domestic operations. These are important criteria for firms new

international division structure
Organizational structure that separates domestic from international business activities by creating a separate international division with its own manager.

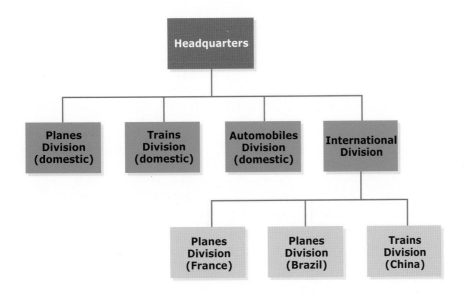

Figure 11.4
International Division Structure

to international business and whose international operations account for a small percentage of their total business.

An international division structure can, however, create two problems for companies. First, international managers must often rely on home-country managers for the financial resources and technical know-how that give the company its international competitive edge. Poor coordination between managers can hurt the performance not only of the international division but also of the entire company. Second, the general manager of the international division typically is responsible for operations in all countries. Although this policy facilitates coordination across countries, it reduces the authority of each country manager. Rivalries and poor cooperation between the general manager and country managers can be damaging to the company's overall performance.

International Area Structure

international area structure
Organizational structure that organizes a company's entire global operations into countries or geographic regions.

An **international area structure** organizes a company's entire global operations into countries or geographic regions (see Figure 11.5). The greater the number of countries in which a company operates, the greater the likelihood it will organize into regions—say, Asia, Europe, and the Americas—instead of countries. Typically, a general manager is assigned to each country or region. Under this structure, each geographic division operates as a self-contained unit, with most decision making decentralized in the hands of the country or regional managers. Each unit has its own set of departments—purchasing, production, marketing and sales, R&D, and accounting. Each unit also tends to handle much of its own strategic planning. Management at the parent-company headquarters makes decisions regarding overall corporate strategy and coordinates the activities of various units.

The international area structure is best suited to companies that treat each national or regional market as unique. It is particularly useful when there are vast cultural, political, or economic differences between nations or regions. When they enjoy a great deal of control over activities in their own environments, general managers become experts on the unique needs of their buyers. On the other hand, because units act independently, allocated resources may overlap, and cross-fertilization of knowledge from one unit to another may be less than desirable.

Global Product Structure

global product structure
Organizational structure that divides worldwide operations according to a company's product areas.

A **global product structure** divides worldwide operations according to a company's product areas. Figure 11.6 shows how a simplistic and fictional transportation company might be divided into planes, trains, and automobiles divisions. A computer company might be separated into divisions of Internet and Communications, Software Development, and New Technologies, for example. Each product division is then divided into domestic and international units. Each function—R&D, marketing, and so forth—is thus duplicated in both the domestic and international units of each product division.

The global product structure is suitable for companies that offer diverse sets of products or services because it overcomes some coordination problems of the international division structure.

Figure 11.5
International Area Structure

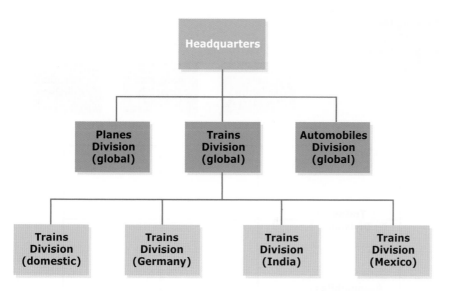

Figure 11.6
Global Product Structure

Because the primary focus is on the product, activities must be coordinated among a product division's domestic and international managers so they do not conflict.

Global Matrix Structure

A **global matrix structure** splits the chain of command between product and area divisions (see Figure 11.7). Each manager reports to two bosses: the president of the product division and the president of the geographic area. A main goal of the matrix structure is to bring together *geographic* area managers and *product* area managers in joint decision making. In fact, bringing together specialists from different parts of the organization creates a sort of team organization. The popularity of the matrix structure has grown among companies trying to increase local responsiveness, reduce costs, and coordinate worldwide operations.

global matrix structure
Organizational structure that splits the chain of command between product and area divisions.

The matrix structure resolves some of the shortcomings of other organizational structures, especially by improving communication among divisions and increasing the efficiency of highly specialized employees. At its best, the matrix structure can increase coordination while simultaneously improving agility and local responsiveness.

However, the global matrix structure suffers from two major shortcomings. First, the matrix form can be quite cumbersome. Numerous meetings are required simply to coordinate the actions of the various division heads, let alone the activities within divisions. In turn, the need for complex coordination tends to make decision making time consuming and slows the reaction time of the organization. Second, individual responsibility and accountability can become foggy in the matrix organization structure. Because responsibility is shared, managers can attribute poor performance to the actions of the other manager. Moreover, the source of problems in the matrix structure can be hard to detect and corrective action difficult to take.

There are other ways international companies can improve responsiveness and effectiveness. An increasingly popular method among international companies is the implementation of work teams to accomplish goals and solve problems. Let's explore in detail the use of work teams.

Work Teams

Globalization is forcing companies to respond more quickly to changes in the business environment. The formation of teams can be highly useful in improving responsiveness by cutting across functional boundaries—such as that between production and marketing—that slow decision making in an organization. Although a matrix organization accomplishes this by establishing cross-functional cooperation, companies do not always want to change their entire organizational structure in order to reap the benefits that cross-functional cooperation provides. In such cases, companies can implement several different types of teams without changing the overall company structure.

Work teams are assigned the tasks of coordinating their efforts to arrive at solutions and implementing corrective action. Today, international companies are turning to work teams on an unprecedented scale to increase direct contact between different operating units. Companies are

Figure 11.7
Global Matrix Structure

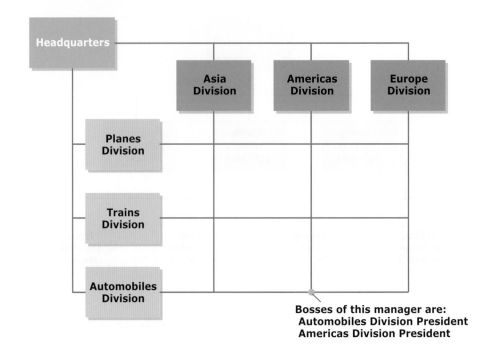

Bosses of this manager are:
Automobiles Division President
Americas Division President

even forming teams to design and implement their competitive strategies. Let's look at several different types of teams—self-managed teams, cross-functional teams, and global teams.

self-managed team

Team in which the employees from a single department take on the responsibilities of their former supervisors.

SELF-MANAGED TEAMS A **self-managed team** is one in which the employees from a single department take on the responsibilities of their former supervisors. When used in production, such teams often reorganize the methods and flow of production processes. Because they are "self-managed," they reduce the need for managers to watch over their every activity. The benefits of self-managed teams typically include increased productivity, product quality, customer satisfaction, employee morale, and company loyalty. In fact, the most common self-managed teams in many manufacturing companies are *quality-improvement teams*, which help reduce waste in the production process and, therefore, lower costs.

The global trend toward "downsizing" internal operations to make them more flexible and productive has increased the popularity of teams because they reduce the need for direct supervision. Companies around the world now employ self-managed teams in international operations. Yet, research indicates that cultural differences can influence resistance to the concept of self-management and the practice of using teams. Among other things, experts suggest that international managers follow some basic guidelines:[7]

- Use selection tests to identify the employees most likely to perform well in a team environment.
- Adapt the self-managed work-team concept to the national culture of each subsidiary.
- Adapt the process of integrating self-managed work teams to the national culture of each subsidiary.
- Train local managers at the parent company and allow them to introduce teams at a time they feel is most appropriate.

Similarly, the cultural differences discussed in Chapter 2 are important to managers who design teams in international operations. For example, certain cultures are more collectivist in nature. Some cultures harbor greater respect for differences in people's status. In some cultures, people believe the future is largely beyond their personal control. And some cultures display a so-called work-to-live mentality. Researchers say that in these cases conventional management should retain fairly tight authority over teams. But teams are likely to be productive if given greater autonomy in a culture where people are very hardworking.[8]

cross-functional team

Team composed of employees who work at similar levels in different functional departments.

CROSS-FUNCTIONAL TEAMS A **cross-functional team** is one composed of employees who work at similar levels in different functional departments. These teams work to develop changes in operations and are well suited to projects that require coordination across functions, such as reducing the time needed to get a product from the idea stage to the marketplace. International companies also use cross-functional teams to improve quality by having employees from purchasing, manufacturing, and distribution (among other functions) work together to address specific quality issues. For the same reason, cross-functional teams can help break down barriers between departments and reorganize operations around processes rather than by functional departments.

GLOBAL TEAMS Finally, large international corporations are creating so-called **global teams**— groups of top managers from both headquarters and international subsidiaries who meet to develop solutions to company-wide problems. For example, Nortel Networks (www.nortel.com) of Canada created a global team of top executives from Britain, Canada, France, and the United States that traveled to Asia, Europe, and North America looking for ways to improve product-development practices.

global team

Team of top managers from both headquarters and international subsidiaries who meet to develop solutions to company-wide problems.

Depending on the issue at hand, team members can be drawn from a single business unit or assembled from several different units. Whereas some teams are disbanded after resolving specific issues, others move on to new problems. The performance of global teams can be impaired by matters such as large distances between team members, lengthy travel times to meetings, and the inconvenience of working across time zones. Companies can sometimes overcome these difficulties, although doing so can be rather costly.

QUICK STUDY 4

1. What type of organizational structure tends to concentrate all international expertise in one division?
2. An organizational structure that divides worldwide operations according to a firm's product areas is called *what*?
3. What do we call a group of employees who work at similar levels in different departments?

A Final Word

Managers have the important and complicated task of formulating international strategies at the corporation, business unit, and individual department levels. Managers often analyze their companies' operations by viewing them as a chain of activities that create customer value (value-chain analysis). It is through this process that managers can identify and implement strategies suited to their companies' unique capabilities. The strategies that managers select then determine the firm's organizational structure. National business environments also affect managers' strategy and structure decisions, including whether to alter their products (standardization versus adaptation), where to locate facilities (centralized versus decentralized production), and what type of decision making to implement (centralized versus decentralized decision making).

The role of managers in formulating strategies and creating the overall organizational structure cannot be overstated. The strategies they choose determine the market segments in which their firms will compete and whether their firms will pursue low-cost leadership in their industry or will differentiate their products and charge a higher price. These decisions are crucial to all later activities of firms that are going international. They also influence how a company (1) enters international markets, (2) employs its human resources, and (3) manages its day-to-day production, marketing, and other operations.

MyLab Management™

Go to **www.pearson.com/mylab/management** to complete the problem marked with this icon .

Chapter Summary

LO11.1 Explain the company analysis techniques that precede strategy selection.
- Prior to strategy formulation managers must first undertake a careful analysis to identify a clear company mission and a well-defined set of objectives they want to achieve.
- Managers can identify company abilities that create customer value by using *value-chain analysis*, which divides a company's activities into primary activities and support activities that are central to creating value for customers.
- Managers must also analyze the cultural, political, legal, and economic environments for factors that can complicate strategy formulation.

LO11.2 Describe the various strategies that companies use to reach their goals.
- A *multinational strategy* is best when adapting products and marketing strategies to national markets and a *global strategy* is best when offering the same products using the same marketing strategy in all markets.
- *Corporate-level strategies* include: (1) *growth*—increase scale or scope of operations; (2) *retrenchment*—reduce the scale or scope of businesses; (3) *stability*—guard against change; and (4) *combination*—mix growth, retrenchment, and stability strategies across businesses.
- *Business-level strategies* include: (1) *low-cost leadership*—exploit economies of scale to have the lowest cost structure; (2) *differentiation*—design products perceived as unique in an industry; (3) *focus*—serve a narrow market segment through low-cost leadership, differentiation, or both.
- Achieving objectives depends on *department-level strategies* that focus on the specific *primary* or *support activities* that create customer value.

LO11.3 Outline the key issues behind the selection of organizational structure.
- *Organizational structure* is the way in which a company divides its activities among separate units and coordinates activities among those units.
- *Centralized decision making* occurs at a high level and helps coordinate operations of international subsidiaries. *Decentralized decision making* occurs at the subsidiary level and places a premium on local responsiveness.
- When designing structure managers must consider the degree of *coordination* needed among various groups within the firm and how much *flexibility* is required of the company's structure.
- Organizational structure must also define areas of responsibility and *chains of command*—lines of authority that specify internal reporting relationships.

LO11.4 Describe various international organizational structures and types of work teams.
- An *international division structure* creates a separate division with its own manager for international activities.
- An *international area structure* organizes a company's global operations into countries or geographic regions, with each division operating as a self-contained unit.
- A *global product structure* divides worldwide operations into product divisions, which are then divided into domestic and international units.
- A *global matrix structure* requires reporting to two bosses: the general manager of the product division and the general manager of the geographic area.
- *Work teams* coordinate their efforts to arrive at solutions and implement corrective action. Types of work teams are *self-managed teams, cross-functional teams,* and *global teams.*

Key Terms

chains of command (p. 306)
combination strategy (p. 302)
core competency (p. 297)
cross-functional team (p. 310)
differentiation strategy (p. 303)
focus strategy (p. 304)
global matrix structure (p. 309)
global product structure (p. 308)
global strategy (p. 301)

global team (p. 311)
growth strategy (p. 302)
international area structure (p. 308)
international division structure (p. 307)
low-cost leadership strategy (p. 303)
mission statement (p. 296)
multinational (multidomestic)
   strategy (p. 300)
organizational structure (p. 305)

planning (p. 296)
retrenchment strategy (p. 302)
self-managed team (p. 310)
stability strategy (p. 302)
stakeholders (p. 296)
strategy (p. 296)
value-chain analysis (p. 298)

✪ TALK ABOUT IT 1

Consider this statement: Cultures around the world are becoming increasingly similar, so companies should standardize both their products and global marketing efforts.

11-1. Do you agree or disagree with this line of reasoning? Explain.
11-2. Are there certain industries for which the statement might be more or less true?

✪ TALK ABOUT IT 2

List five products that you consumed (breakfast, chewing gum, etc.) or used (Wi-Fi Internet service, phone app, etc.) within the past 24 hours.

11-3. What strategy does the company behind each good or service employ: low-cost, differentiation, or focus?
11-4. For each company, explain what information helped you arrive at your answer.

Ethical Challenge

You are the CEO of a multinational corporation that has grown organically over the past 30 years. You know that your organizational structure is long overdue for a major change. The coordination of activities between the various units is not as good as it could be. Some parts of the organization are already centralized, such as administration; other parts, such as production, sales and marketing, and distribution, are largely decentralized. You want to consider the options carefully and make an assessment of their implications for the corporation.

11-5. How might centralization help to fully coordinate the operations of the organization? Who is likely to be affected by centralization?
11-6. Now consider the case for increased decentralization and where this option might, in fact, be beneficial to the organization. Will it mean more flexibility?

Teaming Up

In groups of three or four, think about an organization's global strategy and why growth may not always be the best choice. What is the point of having any other form of strategy? Assess other forms of strategy and suggest why they might be appropriate in certain cases. Once you have done this, share your thoughts with the rest of the class and try to get a consensus.

MyLab Management

⭐ Go to **www.pearson.com/mylab/management** for the following assisted-graded writing questions:

11-7. The elements that affect strategy formulation are different depending on whether a company's activities are primarily domestic or international. What are some of these elements?

11-8. Continuous advancements in technology alter the way international businesses are managed. Will technology change the fundamental strategies and structures of international companies, or can firms simply graft new strategies and structures onto existing ones?

PRACTICING INTERNATIONAL MANAGEMENT CASE

IKEA's Global Strategy

IKEA (www.ikea.com) is a nearly $40 billion global furniture powerhouse based in Sweden. With 389 stores in dozens of countries, the company's success reflects founder Ingvar Kamprad's "social ambition" of selling a wide range of stylish, functional home furnishings at prices so low that the majority of people can afford to buy them. The story of Kamprad's success is detailed in a book titled *IKEA: The Entrepreneur, the Business Concept, the Culture*. The store exteriors are painted with Sweden's national colors, bright blue and yellow. Shoppers view furniture in scores of realistic settings arranged throughout the cavernous showrooms.

In a departure from standard industry practice, IKEA's furniture bears names such as "Ivar" and "Sten" as well as model numbers. At IKEA, shopping is very much a self-service activity—after browsing and writing down the names of desired items in the showroom, shoppers pick their furniture off shelves, where they find boxes containing the furniture in kit form. One of the cornerstones of IKEA's strategy is having customers take their purchases home and assemble the furniture themselves. The typical IKEA store also contains a Swedish-cuisine restaurant, a grocery store called the Swede Shop, a supervised play area for children, and a baby-care room. IKEA's in-store eateries are so popular that 30 percent of restaurant customers say they went there only for the food. Figures like that have IKEA pondering expansion into stand-alone café's in city centers.

IKEA's approach to the furniture business enables it to rack up impressive growth in an industry in which overall sales are flat. Sourcing furniture from more than 1,500 suppliers in 50 countries helps the company maintain its low-cost position. IKEA has also opened stores in emerging markets, such as in Central and Eastern Europe. Because many consumers in those regions have relatively low purchasing power, the stores offer a smaller selection of goods, and some of the furniture is designed specifically for the cramped living styles typical in former Soviet bloc countries. Throughout Europe, IKEA benefits from the perception that Sweden is the source of high-quality products. In fact, one of the company's key selling points is its "Swedishness." IKEA also operates in emerging markets like Russia, where its core strategy and anticorruption policies have been effective.

Industry observers predict that the United States will eventually be IKEA's largest market. The company opened its first US store in Philadelphia in 1985 and today has dozens of outlets that generate billions of dollars in sales annually. IKEA's competitors take the company very seriously and say any industry player that ignores the future Walmart of home furnishings (as IKEA is sometimes called), does so at its own peril.

Some US customers, however, are irked to find popular items sometimes out of stock. Another problem is the long lines resulting from the company's no-frills approach. Although all customers appreciate receiving quality products at a fair price, some of them question whether drawbacks of the IKEA concept are worth the savings.

Goran Carstedt, president of IKEA North America, responds to such criticism by referring to the company's mission. He notes that IKEA's ability to keep prices low rests on the strategy of providing limited services. Customers return to IKEA despite having to make some small sacrifices because they value the company's low prices, he says. To keep them coming back, IKEA is spending millions on advertising to get its message across. Whereas common industry practice is to rely heavily on newspaper and radio advertising, two-thirds of IKEA's North American advertising budget is allocated for TV.

Incredibly, IKEA has also expanded into apartment building. The retail giant has more than 3,500 of its prefab homes throughout Sweden, Norway, Finland, and the United Kingdom. IKEA's BoKlok (meaning "smart living" in Swedish) apartments resemble IKEA's modern furniture. The apartments are designed with open-plan living spaces with high ceilings, windows on three sides, and, of course, pre-fitted IKEA kitchens.

Thinking Globally

11-9. When company founder Kamprad decided to expand into China, he based his decision on his own intuition, not on market research. Looking at IKEA's current performance in China, did Kamprad's decision pay off?

11-10. Relying on topics covered in this chapter, would you classify IKEA's approach as one of standardization or adaptation in markets around the world? Explain.

Sources: Jonathan Ringen, "Meatball Hero," *Fast Company*, May 2017, pp. 44–45; Dan Pontefract, "5 Principals of Purpose to Form a More Harmonious Society," B The Change website (www.bthechange.com), February 10, 2017; Jennifer Karmon, "IKEA's First Cultural Collaboration Is A Sharp Turn To The East: Sweden Meets China," Yahoo website (https://homes.yahoo.com/blogs/spaces), January 21, 2014; "The Corruption Eruption," *The Economist*, May 1, 2010, p. 73; Dianna Dilworth, "Ikea Enters UK's Housing Market," *Bloomberg Businessweek* (www.businessweek.com), April 20, 2007; Ikea website (www.ikea.com), selected reports.

Chapter Twelve

Analyzing International Opportunities

Learning Objectives

After studying this chapter, you should be able to

12.1 Explain the importance of examining basic appeal and national factors.

12.2 Describe how companies measure and select a market or site.

12.3 Identify the main sources of secondary market research data.

12.4 Describe common methods used to conduct primary market research.

A Look Back

Chapter 11 showed us how companies plan and organize themselves for international operations. We explored the different types of strategies and organizational structures that international companies use to accomplish their strategic goals.

A Look at This Chapter

This chapter begins with an explanation of why basic appeal and national factors are important when examining potential new markets and new sites for operations. Next, we describe how companies measure and select specific locations. We then discuss sources of secondary market research and methods of primary market research.

A Look Ahead

Chapter 13 describes the selection and management issues surrounding the different entry modes available to companies going international. We examine the importance of an export strategy for exporters and the pros and cons of each entry mode.

MyLab Management

⭐ IMPROVE YOUR GRADE!

When you see this icon ⭐, visit **www.pearson.com/mylab/management** for activities that are applied, personalized, and offer immediate feedback.

Starbucks Causes Global Jitters

SEATTLE, Washington—Starbucks (www.starbucks.com) began its global journey in 1996 with its first coffeehouse in Tokyo, Japan. Today, Starbucks has 24,000 retail stores in 70 countries, including the US market. Starbucks continues to cause jitters among its customers and competitors, and has no intention of slowing its global expansion.

Starbucks brought European-style coffee to the United States and then took its American-style coffeehouses to Europe. The coffee giant was right that paper-cupped lattes and nonsmoking venues could take on Europe's traditional cafés. Although in Britain since the late 1990s, Starbucks waited patiently before steaming into Zurich, Switzerland, in 2001 and into Paris, France, in 2004. Starbucks carefully researched Europe's markets before opening its first European café in Zurich and then branching out to other nations. With its multicultural and multilingual population, the Swiss market offered Starbucks a chance to educate itself on how to conduct business throughout Europe.

CandyBox Images/Shutterstock

It was years later that Starbucks introduced a coffee culture to tea lovers in China. Starbucks is encouraged by the fact that one-third of all Chinese households keep a jar of instant coffee on hand. Starbucks is trying to make coffee the drink of choice for the average 18 to 45-year-old Chinese consumer. Although ordinary Chinese do not consume a great deal of coffee China's population of 1.4 billion implies an enormous upside potential for growth. Starbucks plans to open 500 stores a year in China through 2021.

Starbucks rebounded strongly from a few tough years as a leaner version of its former self and renewed its focus on its core product, coffee. Starbucks' consistent socially responsible conduct and "Shared Planet" commitment earns it the loyalty and trust of customers. As you read this chapter, consider how companies research, analyze, and select the international markets they enter.[1]

Traditionally, companies have gotten involved in international business by entering familiar, nearby countries first. Managers often feel rather comfortable entering nearby markets because of their proximity and they likely have interacted with people from those cultures in the past. For example, companies in Canada, Mexico, and the United States often go international by entering one another's markets. Likewise, businesses in Asia often do business in one another's markets before pursuing investment opportunities outside the region.

Today, companies often formulate production, marketing, and other strategies as components of integrated plans. For example, to provide a continuous flow of timely information into the production process, many firms locate research and development (R&D) facilities near production sites abroad. Managers also find themselves analyzing locations as potential markets and as potential sites for operations simultaneously. When Mercedes (www.mercedes.com) introduced the M-class sport utility vehicle to the US market, it not only estimated the size of the potential market for the vehicle, but it simultaneously selected a suitable production site.

Increasing global competition means that companies must undertake high-quality research and analysis before selecting new markets and sites. Thus, companies are gaining a better understanding of both buyer behavior and business environments abroad. **Market research** is the collection and analysis of information used to assist managers in making informed decisions. This definition applies to the assessment of potential markets and sites for operations.

market research
Collection and analysis of information used to assist managers in making informed decisions.

Market research data on new markets helps managers design all aspects of marketing strategy and understand buyer preferences and attitudes. What works in France, for example, might not work in Singapore. Market research also gives a snapshot of local business conditions, such as employment levels, wage rates, and the state of the local infrastructure. It supplies managers with timely and relevant information so that they can anticipate market shifts, changes in regulations, and potential new competitors.

This chapter presents a systematic screening process for both markets and sites. We first describe important cultural, political, legal, and economic forces affecting the screening process. Next, we explore the specific types of information and analyses that help companies to make informed decisions regarding markets to enter and sites to select. We then explore the main sources of secondary market data and the most common methods for conducting primary market research firsthand.

12.1 Basic Appeal and National Factors

12.1 Explain the importance of examining basic appeal and national factors.

Two important issues concern managers during the market and site-screening process. First, they want to keep search costs as low as possible. Second, they want to examine every potential market and every possible location. To accomplish these two goals, managers can segment the screening of markets and sites into the following four-step process (see Figure 12.1):

1. Identify basic appeal.
2. Assess the national business environment.
3. Measure market or site potential.
4. Select the market or site.

This screening process involves spending more time, money, and effort on the markets and sites that remain in the later stages of screening. Expensive feasibility studies (conducted later in the process) are performed on a few markets and sites that hold the greatest promise. This approach creates a screening process that is cost effective yet does not overlook potential locations. This section covers the first two steps in the process and the next section presents the last two steps in the process.

Step 1: Identify Basic Appeal

We have already seen that companies go international either to increase sales (and thus profits) or to access resources. The first step in identifying potential markets is to assess the basic demand for a product. Similarly, the first step in selecting a site for a facility to undertake production, R&D, or some other activity is to explore the availability of the resources required.

DETERMINING BASIC DEMAND The first step in searching for potential markets means finding out whether there is a basic demand for a company's product. Important in determining this

Figure 12.1

Screening Process for Potential Markets and Sites

Step 4: Select the Market or Site
- Field trips
- Competitor analysis

Step 3: Measure Market or Site Potential
- Current sales, income elasticity, market potential indicator
- Quality of workforce, materials, infrastructure

Step 2: Assess the National Business Environment
- Language, attitudes, religious beliefs, traditions, work ethic
- Government regulation, government bureaucracy, political stability
- Fiscal and monetary policies, currency issues
- Cost of transporting goods, country image

Step 1: Identify Basic Appeal
- Suitability of climate, absolute bans
- Access to materials, labor, financing

basic appeal is a country's climate. For example, no company would try to market snowboards in Indonesia, Sri Lanka, or Central America because they receive no snowfall. The same product, on the other hand, is well suited for markets in the Canadian Rockies, northern Japan, and the Swiss Alps. Although this stage seems simple, it cannot be taken too lightly. A classic example is when, during its initial forays into international business, Walmart (www.walmart.com) found ice-fishing huts in its Puerto Rico inventory and no snowshoes at its stores in Ontario, Canada.

Certain countries also ban specific goods. Islamic countries, for instance, forbid the importation of alcoholic products, and the penalties for smuggling are stiff. Although alcohol is available on the planes of international airlines such as British Airways (www.ba.com) and KLM (www.klm.com), it cannot leave the airplane, and consumption cannot take place until the plane has left the airspace of the country operating under Islamic law.

DETERMINING AVAILABILITY OF RESOURCES Companies that require particular resources to carry out local business activities must be sure they are available. Raw materials needed for manufacturing either must be found in the national market or must be imported. Yet imports may encounter tariffs, quotas, or other government barriers. Managers must consider the additional costs of importing to ensure that total product cost does not rise to unacceptable levels.

The availability of labor is essential to production in any country. Many companies choose to relocate to countries where workers' wages are lower than they are in the home country. This practice is most common among makers of labor-intensive products—those for which labor accounts for a large portion of total cost. Companies considering local production must determine whether there is enough labor available locally for production operations.

Companies that hope to secure financing in a market abroad must determine the availability and cost of local capital. If local interest rates are too high, a company might be forced to obtain financing in its home country or in other markets in which it is active. On the other hand, access to low-cost financing may provide a powerful inducement to a company that is seeking to expand internationally. British entrepreneur Richard Branson opened several of his Virgin (www.virgin.com) Megastores in Japan despite its reputation as a tough market to crack. One reason for Branson's initial attraction to Japan was a local cost of capital that was roughly one-third the cost in Britain.

Markets and sites that fail to meet a company's requirements for basic demand or resource availability in Step 1 are removed from further consideration.

Step 2: Assess the National Business Environment

If the business environments of all countries were the same, deciding where to market or produce products would be rather straightforward. Managers could rely on data that report the performance of the local economy and analyze expected profits from proposed investments. But as we saw in earlier chapters, countries differ significantly in their cultures, politics, laws, and economies. International managers must work to understand these differences and to incorporate their understanding into market and site-selection decisions. Let's examine how domestic forces in the business environment actually affect the location-selection process.

CULTURAL FORCES Although countries display cultural similarities, they differ in language, attitudes toward business, religious beliefs, traditions, customs, and countless other ways. Some products are sold in global markets with little or no modification. These products include industrial machinery such as packaging equipment, consumer products such as toothpaste and soft drinks, and many other types of goods and services. Yet many products must undergo extensive adaptation to suit local preferences, such as books, magazines, ready-to-eat meals, and others.

Cultural elements can influence what kinds of products are sold and how they are sold. A company must assess how the local culture in a candidate market might affect the salability of its product. Consider Coca-Cola's (www.coca-cola.com) experience in China. Many Chinese take a traditional medicine to fight off flu and cold symptoms. As it turns out, the taste of this traditional medicine—which most people do not find appealing—is similar to that of Coke. Because of Coca-Cola's global marketing policy of one taste worldwide, the company had to overcome the aversion to the taste of Coke among Chinese consumers. It did so by creating a marketing campaign that associated drinking a Coke with experiencing a piece of American culture. What initially looked like an unattractive market for Coke became very successful through a carefully tailored marketing campaign.

Cultural elements in the business environment can also affect site-selection decisions. When substantial product modifications are needed for cultural reasons, a company might choose to establish production facilities in the target market itself. Yet serving customers' special needs in a target market must be offset against any potential loss of economies of scale due to producing in several locations rather than just one. Today, companies can minimize such losses through the use of flexible manufacturing methods. For example, a smartphone manufacturer that produces in multiple locations worldwide could ensure that each of its facilities could start producing any one of its phones for its different markets within 24 hours.

A qualified workforce is important to a company no matter what activity it is to undertake at a particular site. Also, a strong work ethic among the local workforce is essential to having productive operations. Managers must assess whether an appropriate work ethic exists in each potential country for the purposes of production, service, or any other business activity. An adequate level of educational attainment among the local workforce for the planned business activity is also very important. Although product-assembly operations may not require an advanced education, R&D, high-tech production, and certain services normally will require extensive higher education. If the people at a potential site do not display an appropriate work ethic or educational attainment, the site will be ruled out for further consideration.

POLITICAL AND LEGAL FORCES Political and legal forces also influence the market and site-location decision. Important factors include government regulation, government bureaucracy, and political stability. Let's take a brief look at each of these factors.

Government Regulation As we saw in earlier chapters, a nation's culture, history, and current events cause differing attitudes toward trade and investment. Some governments take a strong nationalistic stance, whereas others are quite receptive to international trade and investment. A government's attitude toward trade and investment is reflected in the quantity and types of restrictions it places on imports, exports, and investment in its country.

Government regulation can quickly eliminate a market or site from further consideration. First, it can create investment barriers to ensure domestic control of a company or industry. One way in which a government can accomplish this is by imposing investment rules on matters such as business ownership—for example, forcing foreign companies into joint ventures. Governments can extend investment rules to bar international companies entirely from competing in certain sectors of the domestic economy. The practice is usually defended as a matter of national security. Economic sectors commonly declared off-limits include TV and radio broadcasting, automobile manufacturing, aircraft manufacturing, energy exploration, military-equipment manufacturing, and iron and steel production. Such industries are protected either because they are culturally important, are engines for economic growth, or are essential to any potential war effort. Host governments often fear that losing control in these economic sectors means placing their fate in the hands of international companies.

Second, governments can restrict international companies from freely removing profits earned in the nation. This policy can force a company to hold cash in the host country or to reinvest it in new projects there. Such policies are normally rooted in the inability of the host-country government to earn the foreign exchange needed to pay for badly needed imports. For instance, Chinese subsidiaries of multinational companies must convert the local currency (*renminbi*) to their home currency when remitting profits back to the parent company. Multinationals can satisfy this stipulation only as long as the Chinese government agrees to provide it with the needed home-country currency.

Third, governments can impose very strict environmental regulations. In most industrial countries, factories that produce industrial chemicals as their main output or as byproducts must adhere to strict pollution standards. Regulations typically demand the installation of expensive pollution-control devices and close monitoring of nearby air, water, and soil quality. While protecting the environment, such regulations also increase short-term production costs. Many developing and emerging markets have far less strict environmental regulations. Regrettably, some companies are alleged to have moved production of toxic materials to emerging markets in order to take advantage of lax environmental regulations and, in turn, of lower production costs. Although such behavior is roundly criticized as highly unethical, it will occur less often as nations continue cooperating to formulate common environmental protection policies.

Finally, governments can also require that companies divulge certain information. Coca-Cola actually left India when the government demanded that it disclose its secret Coke formula as a requirement for doing business there. Coca-Cola returned only after the Indian government dropped its demand.

Government Bureaucracy A lean and smoothly operating government bureaucracy can make a market or site more attractive. On the other hand, a bloated and cumbersome system of obtaining approvals and licenses from government agencies can make it less appealing. In many developing

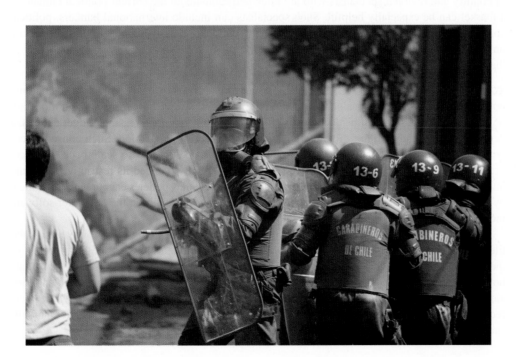

Stability can attract international business, but social unrest can severely disrupt operations and drive out international firms. Shown here, Chilean riot police disperse protesters during a student strike in downtown Santiago, Chile. Protesters were demanding that the government improve education quality. Riot police had to use a water cannon truck and tear gas to disperse demonstrators who burned cars, smashed windows, and damaged local storefronts.

Erlucho/Shutterstock

countries, what should be a relatively simple matter of obtaining a license to establish a retail outlet often means acquiring numerous documents from several agencies. The bureaucrats in charge of these agencies generally are little concerned with providing businesses with high-quality service. Managers must be prepared to deal with administrative delays and a maze of rules. For example, country managers for Millicom International Cellular (www.millicom.com) in Tanzania needed to wait 90 days to get customs clearance on the monthly import of roughly $1 million in cellular telephone equipment. Millicom endured this bureaucratic obstacle because of the local market's potential.

Companies will endure a cumbersome bureaucracy if the opportunity is sufficient to off-set any potential delays and expenses. Companies entering China cite the patience needed to navigate a maze of government regulations that often contradict one another, and they complain about the large number of permissions required from different agencies. The trouble stems from the fact that China is continually revising and developing its system of business law as its economy develops. But an unclear legal framework and inefficient bureaucracy are not deter-ring investment in China because the opportunities for both marketers and manufacturers are simply too great to ignore.

Political Stability Every nation's business environment is affected to some degree by political risk. As we saw in Chapter 4, political risk is the likelihood that a society will undergo political changes that negatively affect local business activity. Political risk can threaten the market of an exporter, the production facilities of a manufacturer, or the ability of a company to remove profits from the country in which they were earned.

The key element of political risk that concerns companies is *unforeseen political change*. Political risk tends to rise if a company cannot estimate the future political environment with a fair degree of accuracy. An event with a negative impact that is expected to occur in the future is not, in itself, bad for companies because the event can be planned for and necessary precautions taken. It is the unforeseen negative events that create political risk for companies.

Managers' perceptions of a market's political risk are often affected by their memories of past political unrest in the market. Yet managers cannot let past events blind them to future opportuni-ties. International companies must try to monitor and predict political events that threaten opera-tions and future profits. By investigating the political environment proactively, managers can focus on political risk and develop action plans for dealing with it.

But where do managers get the information to answer such questions? They may assign company personnel to gather information on the level of political risk in a country, or they may obtain it from independent agencies that specialize in providing political-risk services. The advice of country and regional specialists who are knowledgeable about the current political climate of a market can be especially helpful. Such specialists can include international bankers, political consultants, reporters, country-risk specialists, international relations scholars, political leaders, union leaders, embassy officials, and other local businesspeople currently working and living in the country in question.

ECONOMIC AND FINANCIAL FORCES Managers must carefully analyze a nation's economic policies before selecting it as a new market or site for operations. The poor fiscal and monetary policies of a nation's central bank can cause high rates of inflation, increasing budget deficits, a depreciating currency, falling productivity levels, and flagging innovation. Such consequences typically lower investor confidence and force international companies to scale back or cancel proposed investments. For instance, India's government finally reduced its restrictive trade and investment policies and introduced more-open policies. These new policies encouraged investment by multinationals in production facilities and R&D centers, especially in the computer software industry.

Currency and liquidity problems pose special challenges for international companies. Vola-tile currency values make it difficult for firms to predict future earnings accurately in terms of the home-country currency. Wildly fluctuating currency values also make it difficult to calculate how much capital a company needs for a planned investment. Unpredictable changes in currency values can also make liquidating assets more difficult because the greater uncertainty will likely reduce liquidity in capital markets—especially in countries with relatively small capital markets, such as Bangladesh and Slovakia.

In addition to their home government's resources, managers can obtain information about economic and financial conditions from institutions such as the World Bank, the International Monetary Fund, and the Asian Development Bank. Other sources of information include all types of business and economic publications and the many sources of free information on the Internet.

OTHER FORCES Transport costs and country image also play important roles in the assessment of national business environments. Let's take a brief look at each of these forces.

Cost of Transporting Materials and Goods The cost of transporting materials and finished goods affects any decision about where to locate manufacturing facilities. Some products cost very little to transport through the production and distribution process, whereas others cost a great deal. **Logistics** refers to management of the physical flow of products from the point of origin as raw materials to end users as finished products. Logistics weds production activities to the activities needed to deliver products to buyers. It includes all modes of transportation, storage, and distribution.

logistics
Management of the physical flow of products from the point of origin as raw materials to end users as finished products.

To realize the importance of efficient logistics, consider that global logistics is a $400 billion industry. We often think of the United States as an efficient logistics market because of its extensive interstate road system and rail lines that stretch from east to west. But because of overcrowded highways, 2 billion people-hours are lost to gridlock each year. That translates into $48 billion in lost productivity. Transport companies and cargo ports strenuously advertise their services precisely because of the high cost to businesses of inefficient logistics.

Country Image Because *country image* embodies every facet of a nation's business environment, it is highly relevant to the selection of sites for production, R&D, or any other activity. For example, country image affects the location of manufacturing or assembly operations because products must typically be stamped with labels identifying where they were made or assembled—such as "Made in China" or "Assembled in Brazil." Although such labels do not affect all products to the same degree, they can present important positive or negative images and boost or dampen sales.

Products made in relatively developed countries tend to be evaluated more positively than products from less-developed countries.[2] This relation is due to the perception among consumers that the workforces of certain nations have superior skills in making particular products. For example, consumer product giants Procter & Gamble (www.pg.com) and Unilever (www.unilever.com) have manufacturing facilities in Vietnam. But Vietnamese consumers tend to shun these companies' locally made Close-Up toothpaste and Tide detergent, instead seeking out identical products and brands produced in neighboring countries, such as Thailand. One Vietnamese shopper said that Tide from Thailand simply smells better to her. A general perception among Vietnamese consumers is that goods from Japan or Singapore are the best, followed by Thai goods. Unfortunately for Procter & Gamble and Unilever in Vietnam, many goods from other countries are smuggled in and sold on the black market, thereby denying the companies local sales revenue.

A country's image can be positive in one product class but negative in another. For example, the fact that Volkswagen's (www.volkswagen.com) new Beetle is made in Mexico for the US market has not hurt the Beetle's sales. But would affluent consumers buy a hand-built Rolls-Royce (www.rolls-roycemotorcars.com) automobile if it were produced in Bolivia? Because Rolls-Royce buyers pay for the image of a brilliantly crafted luxury car, the Rolls-Royce image probably would not survive intact if the company were to produce its cars in Bolivia.

Finally, note that country image can and does change over time. For example, "Made in India" has traditionally been associated with low-technology products such as soccer balls and many types of textile products. But today, world-class computer software companies increasingly rely on the software-development skills of engineers located in and around Madras and Bangalore in southern India.

Throughout our discussion of Step 2 of the screening process (assessing the national business environment), we have presented many factors central to traditional business activities. To explore issues specific to entering international markets successfully over the Internet, see the Manager's Briefcase, titled "Conducting Global e-Business."

MANAGER'S BRIEFCASE — Conducting Global e-Business

Generating sales in new geographic markets over the Internet is an increasingly popular method of expansion for large multinationals and entrepreneurs alike. Here are some issues managers should consider when entering new markets using the Internet.

Market Access

- **Infrastructure** Before investing heavily in e-business, investigate whether your potential customers have easy access to the Internet. Determine whether their government is developing advanced digital networks.
- **Content** Companies must be informed about the different policies of each country through which their information travels in order to avoid liability. Key topics are truth in advertising, fraud prevention, and violent, seditious, or graphic materials.
- **Standards** It is not always entirely clear which country has the power to establish standards of operations for e-business. Standards might be set up as trade barriers to keep international companies out of a domestic market.

Legal Issues

- **Privacy** One strength of e-business is that consumer data can be collected easily and used to generate sales. But consumer groups in some countries view the collection of such data as an invasion of privacy. Consumers are particularly vehement if they are unaware that this information is being collected and of how it is being used.
- **Security** Companies must ensure their data communications are safe from unauthorized access or modification. Security technology, such as encryption, password controls, and firewalls, still needs support from a global infrastructure.
- **Intellectual Property** International agreements govern and protect copyrights, databases, patents, and trademarks. Yet these issues will remain a global concern for e-business until a widely accepted legal framework is established for the Internet.

Financial Matters

- **Electronic Payments** Online use of credit cards remains a security concern for many consumers. Global electronic payment systems such as stored-value, smart cards, and other systems are in various stages of development and will alleviate many security issues.
- **Tariffs and Taxation** International policies regarding which party in an international e-business transaction owes taxes to which nation are not yet fully developed. Countries differ widely on how these matters should be treated.

✪ MyLab Management Watch It Companies Look at the Hispanic American Consumer

Apply what you have learned so far about identifying and assessing market potential. If your instructor has assigned this, go to **www.pearson.com/mylab/management** to watch a video case about companies marketing to Hispanic-American consumers and consumers in Mexico and answer questions.

QUICK STUDY 1

1. What is the first step in the screening process for potential markets and sites?
2. What forces should a company research when assessing a nation's business environment?
3. Evaluating a product from a certain country as superior to similar products from other countries is an example of *what* force at work?

12.2 Measure and Select the Market or Site

12.2 Describe how companies measure and select a market or site.

Markets and sites passing the first two steps in the screening process undergo further analysis in order for companies to arrive at a more manageable number of potential locations. In this section, we explore the factors that further influence the potential suitability of markets and sites for operations.

Step 3: Measure Market or Site Potential

Despite the presence of a basic need for a product and an adequately stable national business environment, potential customers might not be ready or able to buy a product for a variety of reasons. Despite the availability of resources, certain sites may be unable to supply a given company with the *level* of resources it needs. It is, therefore, crucial that management arrive at numerical estimates for each key success factor that contributes to a location's potential market size or its suitability as a site for operations.

MEASURING MARKET POTENTIAL As barriers to trade are reduced worldwide, companies are looking to increase sales in industrialized and emerging markets alike. But businesses can seldom create one marketing plan that will cover every market in which they sell their products. Nations enjoy different levels of economic development that affect what kinds of goods are sold, the manner in which they are sold, and their inherent features. Likewise, different levels of economic development require varying approaches to researching market potential. But how do managers estimate potential demand for particular products? Let's look at the factors managers consider when analyzing industrialized markets and then examine a special tool for analyzing emerging markets.

Industrialized Markets The information needed to estimate the market potential for a product in industrialized nations tends to be more readily available than for emerging markets. In fact, for the most-developed markets, research agencies exist for the sole purpose of supplying market data to companies. Euromonitor (www.euromonitor.com) is one such company with an extensive global reach in consumer goods. The company sells reports and does company-specific studies for many international corporations and entrepreneurs. Some of the information in a typical industry analysis includes the following:

- Names, production volumes, and market shares of the largest competitors
- Volume of exports and imports of the product
- Structure of the wholesale and retail distribution networks
- Background on the market, including population figures and key social trends
- Total expenditure on the product (and similar products) in the market
- Retail sales volume and market prices of the product
- Future outlook for the market and potential opportunities

The value of such information supplied by specialist agencies is readily apparent—these reports provide a quick overview of the size and structure of a nation's market for a product. Reports vary in their cost (depending on the market and product), but many can be had for around $750 to $1,500. The company also allows online purchase of reports in small segments for as little as $20 each. We discuss other sources for this type of market data later in this chapter.

Thus, companies that enter the market in industrialized countries often have a great deal of data available on that particular market. What becomes important then is the forecast for the growth or contraction of a potential market. One way of forecasting market demand is by determining a product's **income elasticity**—the sensitivity of demand for a product relative to changes in income. The income-elasticity *coefficient* for a product is calculated by dividing a percentage change in the quantity of a product demanded by a percentage change in income. A coefficient greater than 1.0 conveys an *income-elastic* product, or one for which demand increases more relative to an increase in income. These products tend to be discretionary purchases, such as computers, video games, jewelry, or expensive furniture—generally not considered essential items. A coefficient less than 1.0 conveys an *income-inelastic* product, or one for which demand increases less relative to an increase in income. These products are considered essential and include food, utilities, and beverages. To illustrate, if the income-elasticity coefficient for carbonated beverages is 0.7, the demand for carbonated beverages will increase 0.7 percent for every 1.0 percent increase in income. Conversely, if the income-elasticity coefficient for smartphones is 1.3, the demand for smartphones will increase 1.3 percent for every 1.0 percent increase in income.

income elasticity
Sensitivity of demand for a product relative to changes in income.

Emerging Markets The biggest emerging markets are more important today than ever. Nearly every large company engaged in international business is either already in or is considering entering the big emerging markets such as China and India. With their large consumer bases and rapid growth rates, they whet the appetite of marketers around the world. Although these markets are surely experiencing speed bumps along their paths of economic development, in the long term they cannot be ignored.

Companies considering entering emerging markets often face special problems related to a lack of information. Data on market size or potential may not be available, for example, because of undeveloped methods for collecting such data in a country. But there are ways companies can assess potential in emerging markets. One way is for them to rank different locations by developing a so-called *market-potential indicator* for each. This method, however, is only useful to companies considering exporting. Companies considering investing in an emerging market must look at other factors, which we examine next in the discussion of measuring site potential. The main variables commonly included in market-potential analyses are as follows:[3]

- *Market Size* This variable provides a snapshot of the size of a market at any point in time. It does not estimate the size of a market for a particular product but rather the size of the overall economy. Market-size data allows managers to rank countries from largest to smallest, regardless of a particular product. Market size is typically estimated from a nation's total population or the amount of energy it produces and consumes.
- *Market Growth Rate* This variable reflects the fact that, although the overall size of the market (economy) is important, so too is its rate of growth. It helps managers avoid markets that are large but shrinking and instead target those that are small but rapidly expanding. It is generally obtained through estimates of growth in gross domestic product (GDP) and energy consumption.
- *Market Intensity* This variable estimates the wealth or buying power of a market from the expenditures of both individuals and businesses. It is estimated from per capita private consumption and/or per capita gross domestic product (GDP) at purchasing power parity (see Chapter 4).
- *Market Consumption Capacity* The purpose of this variable is to estimate spending capacity. It is often estimated from the percentage of a market's population that is in the middle class, thereby concentrating on the core of an economy's buying power.
- *Commercial Infrastructure* This factor attempts to assess channels of distribution and communication. Variables may include the number of telephones, TVs, fax machines, or personal computers per capita; the density of paved roads or number of vehicles per capita; and the population per retail outlet. An increasingly important variable for businesses relying on the Internet for sales is the number of Internet hosts per capita. But because these data become outdated quickly, care must be taken to ensure accurate information from the most current sources.
- *Economic Freedom* This variable attempts to estimate the extent to which free-market principles predominate. It is typically a summary of government trade policies, government involvement in business, the enforcement of property rights, and the strength of the black market. A useful resource is the annual *Freedom in the World* report published by Freedom House (www.freedomhouse.org).
- *Market Receptivity* This variable attempts to estimate market "openness." One way it can be estimated is by determining a nation's volume of international trade as a percentage of GDP. If a company wants to see how receptive a market is to goods from its home country, it can ascertain the amount of per capita imports entering the market from the home country. Managers can also examine the growth (or decline) in these imports.
- *Country Risk* This variable attempts to estimate the total risk of doing business, including political, economic, and financial risks. Some market-potential estimation techniques include this variable in the market-receptivity variable. This factor is typically obtained from one of the many services that rate the risk of different countries, such as Political Risk Services Group (www.prsgroup.com).

After each of these factors is analyzed, they are assigned values according to their importance to the demand for a particular product. Potential locations are then ranked (assigned a market-potential indicator value) according to their appeal as a new market. As you may recall, we discussed several of these variables earlier in the book under the topics of national and international business environments. For example, *economic freedom* is shown in Map 3.1 (pages 110–111), *country risk* levels are shown in Map 4.2 (pages 138–139), and *market receptivity* (or openness) is shown in Map 5.1 (pages 158–159). Map 12.1 (pages 328–329) captures one other variable, *commercial infrastructure*, by showing the number of fixed-line and mobile phone subscribers per 1,000 people in each nation. This variable is an important indicator of a nation's overall economic development. Other variables that are also good proxies for this variable include the portion of a nation's roads that are paved or the number of personal computers, fax machines, and Internet hosts it has. One key cautionary note, however, is that emerging markets often either lack such statistics or, in the case of paved roads, international comparison is difficult.

MEASURING SITE POTENTIAL In this step of the site-screening process, managers must carefully assess the quality of the locally available resources. For many companies, the most important of these will be human resources—both labor and management. Wages are lower in certain markets because labor is abundant, relatively less skilled (though perhaps well educated), or both. Employees may or may not be adequately trained to manufacture a given product or to perform certain R&D activities. If workers are not adequately trained, the site-selection process must consider the additional money and time needed to train them.

Training local managers also requires a substantial investment of time and money. A lack of qualified local managers sometimes forces companies to send managers from the home market to the local market. This adds to costs because home-country managers must often receive significant bonuses for relocating to the local market. Companies must also assess the productivity of local labor and managers. After all, low wages tend to reflect low productivity levels of a workforce.

Managers should also examine the local infrastructure, including roads, bridges, airports, seaports, and telecommunications systems, when assessing site potential. Each of these systems can have a major impact on the efficiency with which a company transports materials and products. Of chief importance to many companies today is the state of a country's telecommunications infrastructure. Much business today is conducted through e-mail, and many businesses relay information electronically about matters such as sales orders, inventory levels, and production strategies, which must be coordinated among subsidiaries in different countries. Managers, therefore, must examine each potential site to determine how well it is prepared for contemporary communications.

Step 4: Select the Market or Site

This final step in the screening process involves the most intensive efforts to assess the remaining potential markets and sites—typically less than a dozen, sometimes just one or two. At this stage, managers normally want to visit each remaining location in order to confirm earlier expectations and to perform a competitor analysis. In the final analysis, managers normally evaluate each potential location's contribution to cash flows by undertaking a financial evaluation of a proposed investment. The specialized and technical nature of this analysis can be found in most textbooks on corporate finance.

FIELD TRIPS The importance of top managers making a personal visit to each remaining potential market or site cannot be overstated. Such trips typically involve attending strings of meetings and engaging in tough negotiations. The trip represents an opportunity for managers to see firsthand what they have so far seen only on paper. It gives them an opportunity to experience the culture, observe in action the workforce that they might soon employ, or make personal contact with potential new customers and distributors. Any remaining issues tend to be thoroughly investigated during field trips so that the terms of any agreement are precisely known in the event that a particular market or site is chosen. Managers can then usually return to the chosen location to put the terms of the final agreement in writing.

COMPETITOR ANALYSIS Because competitor analysis was covered in detail in Chapter 11, we offer only a few comments here. Intensely competitive markets typically put downward pressure on the prices that firms can charge their customers. In addition, intensely competitive sites for production and R&D activities often increase the costs of doing business. Naturally, lower prices and higher costs due to competitive forces must be balanced against the potential benefits offered by each market and site under consideration. At the very least, then, competitor analysis should address the following issues:

• Number of competitors in each market (domestic and international)
• Market share of each competitor
• Whether each competitor's product appeals to a small market segment or has mass appeal
• Whether each competitor focuses on high quality or low price
• Whether competitors tightly control channels of distribution

Map 12.1

**Fixed Lines and Mobile
Phones (per 1,000 People)**

**Fixed lines and mobile phones
(per 1,000 people)**

- more than 1,500
- 1,000–1,499
- 500–999
- 300–499
- 100–299
- less than 100
- no data available

- Customer loyalty commanded by competitors
- Potential threat from substitute products
- Potential entry of new competitors into the market
- Competitors' control of key production inputs (such as labor, capital, and raw materials)

So far, we have examined a model that many companies follow when selecting new markets or sites for operations. We have seen what steps companies take in the screening process, but we have yet to learn how they undertake such a complex task. Let's now explore the types of situations companies encounter when conducting research in an international setting and the specific tools used in their research.

QUICK STUDY 2

1. The sensitivity of demand for a product relative to changes in income is called *what*?
2. What variable is commonly included in a market potential indicator?
3. How important is it for top managers to pay a visit to a market or site before making a final decision?

12.3 Secondary Market Research

12.3 Identify the main sources of secondary market research data.

When trying to target specific population segments, marketing managers require highly detailed information. Fortunately, companies are often spared the time, money, and effort of collecting firsthand data for the simple reason that it has already been gathered. Companies can consult a variety of sources to obtain information on a nation's business environment and markets. The particular source that managers should consult depends on many factors, including the company's industry, the national markets they are considering, and how far along they are in the location-screening process.

secondary market research
Process of obtaining information that already exists within the company or that can be obtained from outside sources.

The process of obtaining information that already exists within the company or that can be obtained from outside sources is called **secondary market research**. Managers often use information gathered from secondary research activities to broadly estimate market demand for a product or to form a general impression of a nation's business environment. Secondary data are relatively inexpensive because they have already been collected, analyzed, and summarized by another party. Let's take a look at the main sources of secondary data that help managers make more-informed location-selection decisions.

International Organizations

There are excellent sources of free and inexpensive information about product demand in particular countries. For example, the *International Trade Statistics Yearbook* published by the United Nations (www.un.org) lists the export and import volumes of different products for each country. It also furnishes information on the value of exports and imports on an annual basis for the most recent five-year period. The International Trade Center (www.intracen.org), based in Geneva, Switzerland, also provides current import and export figures for more than 100 countries.

International development agencies, such as the World Bank (www.worldbank.org), the International Monetary Fund (www.imf.org), and the Asian Development Bank (www.adb.org), also provide valuable secondary data. For example, the World Bank publishes annual data on each member nation's population and economic growth rate. Today, most secondary sources supply downloadable data through the Internet or through traditional printed media.

Initial analyses of foreign market potential do not involve sending researchers to distant markets. Instead, companies acquire secondary market research. Obtaining secondary data is a cost-effective way to begin exploring potential markets. From its home base, a company can get an initial feel for buyer behavior in an unfamiliar market. Spanish clothing retailer, Zara, targets the growing middle classes with its more than 5,500 stores worldwide, like this store in Shanghai, China.

TonyV3112/Shutterstock

Government Agencies

Commerce departments and international trade agencies of most countries typically supply information about import and export regulations, quality standards, and the size of various markets. This data is normally available directly from these departments, from agencies within each nation, and from the commercial attaché in each country's embassy abroad. In fact, visiting embassies and attending their social functions while visiting a potential location are excellent ways of making contact with prospective future business partners.

Granted, the attractively packaged information supplied by host nations often ignores many potential hazards in a nation's commercial environment—governments typically try to present their countries in the best possible light. By the same token, such sources are prone to paint incomplete or one-sided portraits of the home market. It is important for managers to seek additional sources that take a more objective view of a potential location.

One source that takes a fairly broad view of markets is the Central Intelligence Agency's *World Factbook* (www.cia.gov). This source can be a useful tool throughout the entire market or site-screening process because of its wealth of facts on each nation's business environment. It identifies each nation's geography, climate, terrain, natural resources, land use, and important environmental issues in detail. It also examines each nation's culture, system of government, and economic conditions, including government debt and exchange-rate conditions. It also provides an overview of the quality of each country's transportation and communication systems.

The Trade Information Center (TIC; www.export.gov), operated by the US Department of Commerce, is a first stop for many importers and exporters. The TIC details product standards in other countries and offers advice on opportunities and best prospects for US companies in individual markets. It also offers information on federal export-assistance programs that can be essential for first-time exporters. Other TIC information includes the following:

- National trade laws and other regulations
- Trade shows, trade missions, and special events
- Export counseling for specific countries
- Import tariffs and customs procedures
- The value of exports to other countries

The Chilean Trade Commission within Chile's Ministry of Foreign Affairs has been particularly aggressive in recent years in promoting Chile to the rest of the world. ProChile (www.chileinfo.com) has 35 commercial offices worldwide. The organization assists in developing the export process, establishing international business relationships, fostering international trade, attracting investment, and forging strategic alliances. It offers a wealth of information on all of Chile's key industries and provides business environment information such as risk ratings. It also provides details on important trade regulations and standards of which exporters, importers, and investors must be aware.[4]

Commercial offices of the states and provinces of many countries also typically have offices in other countries to promote trade and investment. These offices usually encourage investment in the home market by companies from other countries and will sometimes even help companies in other countries export to the home market. For example, the Lorraine Development Corporation in Atlanta is the investment-promotion office of the Lorraine region of France. This corporation helps US companies evaluate location opportunities in the Lorraine region—a popular area for industrial investment. It supplies information on sites, buildings, financing options, and conditions in the French and European Union business environment and conducts 10 to 20 site-selection studies per year for investors.

Finally, many governments open their research libraries to businesspeople from all countries. For example, the Japanese External Trade Organization (JETRO; www.jetro.go.jp) in central Tokyo has a large library full of trade data that is available to international companies already in Japan. In addition, the JETRO website is useful for companies screening the potential of the Japanese market for future business activities from any location. The organization is dedicated to serving companies interested in exporting to or investing in Japan in addition to assisting Japanese companies in going abroad.

Industry and Trade Associations

Companies often join associations composed of firms within their own industry or trade. In particular, companies trying to break into new markets join such associations in order to make contact with others in their field. The publications of these organizations keep members informed about current events and help managers to keep abreast of important issues and opportunities. Many associations publish special volumes of import and export data for domestic markets. They frequently compile directories that list each member's top executives, geographic scope, and contact information such as phone numbers and addresses. Today, many associations also maintain informative websites. Two interesting examples are the websites of the National Pasta Association (www.ilovepasta.org) and the National Onion Association (www.onions-usa.org).

Sometimes industry and trade associations commission specialized studies of their industries, the results of which are then offered to their members at subsidized prices. These types of studies typically address particularly important issues or explore new opportunities for international growth. The National Confectioners Association (www.candyusa.com) of the United States, together with the state of Washington's Washington Apple Commission (www.bestapples.com), once hired a research firm to study the sweet tooth of Chinese consumers. The findings of the study were then made available to each organization's members to act on as they saw fit.

Service Organizations

Many international service organizations in fields such as banking, insurance, management consulting, and accounting offer information to their clients on cultural, regulatory, and financial conditions in a market. For example, the accounting firm of Ernst & Young (www.ey.com) publishes a "Doing Business In" series for most countries. Each booklet contains information on a nation's business environment, regulations regarding foreign investment, legal forms of businesses, labor force, taxes, and culture. Other companies provide specific and overall information on world markets. Managers can consult such organizations for specialized reports on market demographics, lifestyles, consumer data, buyer behavior, and advertising.

Internet

Companies engaged in international business are quickly realizing the wealth of secondary research information available on the Internet and the World Wide Web. These electronic resources are usually user friendly and have vast amounts of information.

LEXIS-NEXIS (www.lexisnexis.com) is a leading online provider of market information. This database of full-text news reports from around the world is updated continually. It also offers special services such as profiles of executives and products and information on the financial conditions, marketing strategies, and public relations of many international companies. Other popular online providers of global information include DIALOG (www.dialog.com) and Dow Jones (www.dowjones.com). Internet search engines such as Google (www.google.com) and Yahoo! (www.yahoo.com) are also helpful in narrowing down the plethora of information available electronically.

The Internet can be especially useful in seeking information about potential production sites. Because field trips to the most likely candidates are expensive, online information can be enormously helpful in saving both time and money. For example, you can begin a search for information on a particular country or region with most large online information providers. Narrowing your search to a more manageable list of subjects—say, culture, economic conditions, or perhaps a specific industry—can yield clues about sites that are promising and those that are not.

Problems with Secondary Research

The great benefit of secondary data is that it spares companies the time, money, and effort of collecting firsthand data for the simple reason that it has already been gathered. Yet, two problems with secondary data can arise when researching potential markets and sites.

AVAILABILITY OF DATA There tends to be plenty of excellent sources of secondary data in highly industrialized countries. This is especially true in Australia, Canada, Japan, Western Europe, the United States, and where government agencies and private research firms supply information. Two of these information suppliers are Nielsen (www.nielsen.com) and IRI (www.iriworldwide.com). Table 12.1 contains a listing of the top market research firms.

In many emerging and developing countries, however, previously gathered quality information is hard to obtain. Even when market data is available, its reliability is questionable. For example, analysts sometimes charge the governments of certain emerging markets with trying to lure investors by overstating estimates of gross income and consumption levels. In addition to deliberate misrepresentation, tainted information can also result from improper local collection methods and analysis techniques. But research agencies in emerging and developing markets that specialize in gathering data for clients in industrialized countries are developing higher-quality techniques of collection and analysis. For example, information supplier and pollster Gallup (www.gallup.com) is aggressively expanding its operations throughout Southeast Asia in response to the need among Western companies for more accurate market research.

COMPARABILITY OF DATA obtained from other countries must be interpreted with great caution. Because terms such as *poverty, consumption*, and *literacy* differ greatly from one country to another, such data must be accompanied by precise definitions. In the United States, for example, a family of four is said to be below the poverty line if its annual income is $24,600. The equivalent income for a family of four in Laos would place it in the upper class.

TABLE 12.1 Top Market Research Firms

Rank	Company Name	Country
1	Nielsen Holdings N.V.	United States/Netherlands
2	QuintilesIMS	United States
3	Kantar	United Kingdom/United States
4	IRI	United States
5	Ipsos	France/United Kingdom
6	Westat, Inc.	United States
7	GfK Group	Germany
8	The NPD Group, Inc.	United States
9	ICF	United States
10	Abt SRBI	United States

Source: Based on the 2017 "AMA Gold Report Top 50 Market Research Firms," American Marketing Association website (www.ama.org).

The different ways in which countries measure data also affect comparability across borders. For instance, some countries state the total quantity of foreign direct investment in their nations in terms of its *monetary value*. Others specify it in terms of the number of *investment projects* implemented during the year. But a single foreign direct investment into an industrialized nation can be worth many times what several or more projects are worth in a developing nation. To gather a complete picture of a nation's investments, researchers will often need to obtain both figures. Moreover, reported statistics may not distinguish between foreign direct investment (accompanied by managerial control) and portfolio investment (which is not accompanied by managerial control). Misinterpreting data because one does not know how they are compiled or measured can sabotage even the best marketing plans and production strategies.

QUICK STUDY 3

1. Obtaining information that already exists within or outside the company is called *what*?
2. What is a possible source of secondary research data?
3. What is a potential problem that can arise with the use of secondary research data?

12.4 Primary Market Research

12.4 Describe common methods used to conduct primary market research.

primary market research
Process of collecting and analyzing original data and applying the results to current research needs.

Although secondary information is very useful in the early stages of the screening process, sometimes more-tailored data on a location is needed. Under such circumstances, it might be necessary to conduct **primary market research**—the process of collecting and analyzing original data and applying the results to current research needs. This type of information is very helpful in filling in the blanks left by secondary research. Yet, it is often more expensive to obtain than secondary research data because studies must be conducted in their entirety. Let's explore some of the more common methods of primary research used by companies in the location-screening process.

Trade Shows and Trade Missions

trade show
Exhibition at which members of an industry or group of industries showcase their latest products, study activities of rivals, and examine recent trends and opportunities.

An exhibition at which members of an industry or group of industries showcase their latest products, study activities of rivals, and examine recent trends and opportunities is called a **trade show**. Trade shows are held on a continuing basis in virtually all markets and normally attract companies from around the globe. They are typically held by national or global industry trade associations or by government agencies. An excellent source of information about trade shows and exhibitions worldwide is Expo Central (www.expocentral.com).

Not surprisingly, the format and scope of trade shows differ from country to country. For example, because of its large domestic market, shows in the United States tend to be oriented toward business opportunities within the US market. In line with US culture, the atmosphere tends to be fairly informal. Conversely, because of the relatively smaller market of Germany and its participation in the European Union, trade shows there tend to showcase business opportunities in markets all across Europe and tend to be quite formal.

National culture plays a role in the extent to which companies take advantage of trade shows and other tools to become successful abroad. The entrepreneurial culture of the United States ensures that trade groups actively encourage small businesses to pursue international opportunities. To see how two small US companies pursued opportunities to go international, read this chapter's Culture Matters feature, titled "Is the World Your Oyster?"

trade mission
International trip by government officials and businesspeople that is organized by agencies of national or provincial governments for the purpose of exploring international business opportunities.

A **trade mission** is an international trip by government officials and businesspeople that is organized by agencies of national or provincial governments for the purpose of exploring international business opportunities. Businesspeople who attend trade missions are typically introduced both to important business contacts and to well-placed government officials.

Small and medium-sized companies often find trade missions very appealing for two reasons. First, the support of government officials gives them additional clout in the target country as well as access to officials and executives whom they would otherwise have little opportunity to meet. Second, although such trips can sometimes be expensive for the smallest of businesses, they are generally worth the money because they almost always reap cost-effective rewards. Trade missions to faraway places sometimes involve visits to several countries in order to maximize the return for the time and money invested. For instance, a trade mission for European businesspeople to Latin America may

CULTURE MATTERS   Is the World Your Oyster?

The business culture of every nation supports the international expansion efforts of its businesses to some degree. But what kinds of actions and information are useful to companies? Here are a few helpful pointers followed by two company examples:

- Small companies must first do lots of homework before jumping into the global marketplace. Going international is a long-term investment, and preparedness is a critical success factor. Companies must plan on investing a good deal of cash. A typical small business can expect to pay anywhere from $10,000 to $20,000 to perform basic market research, to attend a trade show, and to visit one or two countries.
- Lucille Farms, Inc., of Montville, New Jersey, produces and markets cheese products. Alfonso Falivene, Lucille's chief executive, is taking a cautious approach to going international. He recently joined the US Dairy Export Council, which offers members, among other things, international

trips to study new business opportunities and the competition. The council also offers its members a great deal of free information on international markets. Falivene says the council supplied market information that would have cost him thousands of dollars to obtain on his own.

- Meter-Man, Inc., of Winnebago, Minnesota, manufactures agricultural measuring devices. When Meter-Man decided to go international, it saw trade shows as a great way to gain market intelligence and establish contacts. At a five-day agricultural fair in Paris, company executives held 21 meetings with potential customers and sealed an agreement with a major distributor that covers the Parisian market for Meter-Man's products. Meter-Man's sales and marketing director was on a flight to a trade show in Barcelona, Spain, and struck up a conversation with the man next to him. The man wound up ordering $200,000 of Meter-Man's products and is today a major South American distributor for the company.

---

include stops in Argentina, Brazil, Chile, and Mexico. A trade mission to Asia for North American or European companies might include stops in China, Hong Kong, Japan, South Korea, and Thailand.

Interviews and Focus Groups

Although industry data are useful to companies early in the screening process for potential markets, subsequent steps must assess buyers' emotions, attitudes, and cultural beliefs. Industry data cannot tell us how individuals feel about a company or its product. This type of buyer information is required when deciding whether to enter a market and when developing an effective marketing plan. Therefore, many companies supplement the large-scale collection of country data with other types of research such as interviews with prospective customers. Interviews, of course, must be conducted carefully if they are to yield reliable and unbiased information. Respondents in some cultures might be unwilling to answer certain questions or may intentionally give vague or misleading answers in order to avoid getting too personal. For example, although individuals in the United States are renowned for their willingness to divulge all sorts of information about their shopping habits and even their personal lives, this is very much the exception among other countries.

An unstructured but in-depth interview of a small group of individuals (8 to 12 people) by a moderator in order to learn the group's attitudes about a company or its product is called a **focus group**. Moderators guide a discussion on a topic and interfere as little as possible with the free flow of ideas. The interview is recorded for later evaluation to identify recurring or prominent themes among the participants. This type of research helps marketers to uncover negative perceptions among buyers and to design corrective marketing strategies. Because subtle differences in verbal and body language could go unnoticed, focus group interviews tend to work best when moderators are natives of the countries in which the interview is held. Ironically, it is sometimes difficult to conduct focus groups in collectivist cultures (see Chapter 2) because people have a tendency to agree with others in the group. In such instances, it might be advisable to conduct a **consumer panel**—research in which people record in personal diaries information on their attitudes, behaviors, or purchasing habits.

focus group
Unstructured but in-depth interview of a small group of individuals (8 to 12 people) by a moderator in order to learn the group's attitudes about a company or its product.

consumer panel
Research in which people record in personal diaries information on their attitudes, behaviors, or purchasing habits.

Surveys

Research in which an interviewer asks current or potential buyers to answer written or verbal questions in order to obtain facts, opinions, or attitudes is called a **survey**. For example, if Saucony (www.saucony.com) wants to learn about consumer attitudes toward its latest women's running shoe, it could ask a sample of women about their attitudes toward the shoe. Verbal questioning could be done in person or over the telephone, whereas written questioning could be done in person, through the mail, or through forms completed at Saucony's website. The results would then be tabulated, analyzed, and applied to the development of a marketing plan.

survey
Research in which an interviewer asks current or potential buyers to answer written or verbal questions in order to obtain facts, opinions, or attitudes.

The single greatest advantage of survey research is the ability to collect vast amounts of data in a single sweep. But as a rule, survey methods must be adapted to local markets. For example, survey research can be conducted by any technological means in industrialized markets, such as over the telephone or the Internet. But telephone interviewing would yield poor results in Bangladesh because only a small percentage of the general population has telephones. Also, although a survey at a website is an easy way to gather data, it must be remembered that in less-industrialized nations users still represent mostly middle to upper-income households.

Written surveys can also be hampered by other problems. Some countries' postal services are unreliable to the point that parcels are delivered weeks or months after arriving at post offices, or they never arrive at all because they are stolen or simply lost. Naturally, written surveys are impractical to conduct in countries with high rates of illiteracy, although this problem can perhaps be overcome by obtaining verbal responses to spoken questions.

Environmental Scanning

environmental scanning

Ongoing process of gathering, analyzing, and dispensing information for tactical or strategic purposes.

An ongoing process of gathering, analyzing, and dispensing information for tactical or strategic purposes is called **environmental scanning**. The environmental scanning process entails obtaining both factual and subjective information on the business environments in which a company is operating or considering entering. The continuous monitoring of events in other locations keeps managers aware of potential business opportunities and threats. Environmental scanning contributes to making well-informed decisions and to the development of effective strategies. It also helps companies develop contingency plans for a particularly volatile environment.

Problems with Primary Research

Market research serves essentially the same function in all nations. A market's unique conditions and circumstances, however, can present difficulties that force adjustments in the way research is performed. Companies need to be aware of potential obstacles so that their research results are reliable.

Marketers who conduct research in unfamiliar markets must pay attention to the ways in which cultural variables influence information. Perhaps the single most important variable is language. For example, researchers unfamiliar with the language spoken in a market being investigated might be forced to rely on interpreters. Interpreters might unintentionally misrepresent certain comments or be unable to convey the sentiment with which statements are made.

Researchers might also need to survey potential buyers through questionnaires written in the local language. To avoid any misstatement of questions or results, questionnaires must be translated into the language of the target market and the responses then translated back into the researcher's language. Written expressions must be highly accurate so that results do not become meaningless or misleading. The potential to conduct written surveys is also affected by the illiteracy rates among the local population. A written survey is generally impossible to conduct in countries with high illiteracy rates. Researchers would probably need to choose a different information-gathering technique, such as personal interviews or observation of retail purchases.

Companies that have little experience in an unfamiliar market often hire local agencies to perform some or all of their market research. Local researchers know the cultural terrain. They understand which practices are acceptable and which types of questions can be asked. And they typically know whom to approach for certain types of information. Perhaps most importantly, they know how to interpret the information they gather and are likely to understand its reliability. But a company that decides to conduct its own market research must, if necessary, adapt its research techniques to the local market. Many cultural elements that are taken for granted in the home market must be reassessed in the host business environment.

QUICK STUDY 4

1. Collecting and analyzing original data and applying the results to current research needs is called *what*?
2. A trade show is the same thing as *what*?
3. A firm researching a very unfamiliar but potentially very profitable market might be best to do what?

A Final Word

To keep pace with an increasingly hectic and competitive global business environment, companies should follow a systematic screening process that incorporates high-quality research methods. This chapter provides a systematic way to screen potential locations as new markets or sites for business operations. But these issues constitute only the *first step* in the process of "going international." The next step involves actually accomplishing the task of entering selected markets and establishing operations abroad. In the following chapters, we survey the types of entry modes available to companies, how they acquire the resources needed to carry out their activities, and how they manage their sometimes far-flung international business operations.

MyLab Management

Go to **www.pearson.com/mylab/management** to complete the problems marked with this icon .

Chapter Summary

LO12.1 Explain the importance of examining basic appeal and national factors.
- The first step in exploring a potential new market is identifying basic product demand. Without basic demand there is no market.
- This step for assessing a new site for operations involves determining availability of resources for production, such as raw materials, labor, and capital. Without these factors a company may not be able to conduct its business.
- The second step involves examining the local culture, political, legal, and economic variables. Businesses seek nations with quality government bureaucracies, political stability, and sound monetary policies for both markets and sites.

LO12.2 Describe how companies measure and select a market or site.
- The third step is to measure the potential of each market by exploring a market's size and growth rate, and may involve calculating a *market-potential indicator*.
- This step for examining the suitability of a site for operations entails determining the availability of workers, managers, raw materials, and an adequate infrastructure.
- The fourth step involves visiting each remaining market or site to make a final decision. At this stage managers might perform a competitor analysis or a financial evaluation.

LO12.3 Identify the main sources of secondary market research data.
- Free or inexpensive information about product demand in a country can be obtained from *international organizations*, including international development agencies like the World Bank and the International Monetary Fund.
- *Government agencies*, such as commerce departments and international trade agencies, have information on import–export regulations, quality standards, and market size.
- *Industry and trade associations* often publish reports to keep managers abreast of important issues and opportunities.
- International *service organizations* in fields such as banking, insurance, consulting, and accounting offer their clients information on a market's cultural, regulatory, and financial conditions.

LO12.4 Describe common methods used to conduct primary market research.
- A *trade show* helps members of an industry showcase their latest products, see what rivals are doing, and learn about recent trends and opportunities.
- A *trade mission* takes government officials and businesspeople on international trips to explore business opportunities.
- *Interviews* help to assess potential buyers' emotions, attitudes, and cultural beliefs. A *focus group* is an in-depth interview designed to uncover attitudes about a company or its product.
- *Surveys* obtain potential customers' facts, opinions, or attitudes by asking written or verbal questions.
- The ongoing gathering, analyzing, and dispensing of information for tactical or strategic purposes is called *environmental scanning*.

Key Terms

consumer panel (p. 335)
environmental scanning (p. 336)
focus group (p. 335)
income elasticity (p. 325)

logistics (p. 323)
market research (p. 318)
primary market research (p. 334)
secondary market research (p. 330)

survey (p. 335)
trade mission (p. 334)
trade show (p. 334)

✪ TALK ABOUT IT 1

Western companies flooded into China when it opened its doors and allowed them to compete for market share in all sorts of industries. Yet, after several years many of these same companies either scaled back their operations in China or left the country entirely.

12-1. Where do you think these companies may have gone wrong in their analyses? Explain.
12-2. What role does the business media play in setting the tone for a nation's investment climate?

✪ TALK ABOUT IT 2

Sony's MiniDisc recorder/player was enormously successful in Japan but received a lukewarm welcome in the US market. When Sony attempted its third MiniDisc launch in the United States it thought it had the right formula because it had "found out what's in consumers' heads."

12-3. What type of research do you think Sony used to "get inside the heads" of its target market?
12-4. Do you think firms in certain cultures prefer to conduct certain types of market research? Explain.

Ethical Challenge

You are the CEO of a global healthcare corporation looking at the possibility of entering some new emerging markets. Market size and potential is actually quite hard to judge, so you need to look at some other way of working out their potential. Ethically, you will avoid markets that seem to have political or social problems as you do not wish your corporation to be tainted with accusations that you are prepared to operate anywhere to make a profit.

12-5. Decisions made about markets are based on secondary data. What ethical issues does this present?
12-6. Is it ethical to be focused on issues such as economic freedom when considering a market?
12-7. What is "country risk," and what types of factors are considered under this variable when assessing market potential? Is it a fair measurement?

Teaming Up

In groups of three or four, draw up a list of ten common consumer products that you may have purchased over the past few months. Where were they made? Did some state they were made or assembled at a specific location? Is there anything about the location of their manufacture that makes the product more or less attractive to you? Once you have completed your investigations, share your findings with the rest of the class.

MyLab Management

⭐ Go to **www.pearson.com/mylab/management** for the following assisted-graded writing questions:

12-8. This chapter opens with a profile of Starbucks Corporation, which opened its first store in Vietnam in 2013. What characteristics of the coffee and tea market in Vietnam do you think helped draw Starbucks into the country?

12-9. Some market researchers tout the benefits of "soft" market research data gathered using techniques such as focus groups and observation. Others argue the benefits of using "hard" data such as statistics on consumers' buying habits and figures on market size. When might each kind of data be preferred? Explain.

PRACTICING INTERNATIONAL MANAGEMENT CASE

Singapore Rises to Prominence in the World Market

Since becoming an independent nation in 1965, Singapore has been on the rise economically. Although it occupies a small geographical area, its busy port has aided Singapore in gaining economic power. The per capita GNP is one of the highest in the world. Major exports include electronics and chemicals, creating profits that allow for the purchase of raw materials that are not native to the country. As a result, Singapore relies heavily on a strategy similar to entrepôt trading, which involves importing raw materials and refining them into goods to be exported.

Singapore's economy is considered a free market, and it is developing at a very rapid pace. A strong educational system develops a large, skilled workforce, and the business environment up to this point has been relatively corruption-free. Government intervention is generally kept to a minimum, but the government has undertaken several measures to promote further economic growth. Heavy investment in the diversification of the economy—namely the promotion of tourism and funding of the pharmaceutical industry—has served the economy well. For example, the Marina Bay Sands Casino opened in April 2010, attracting many foreign tourists and providing plenty of job opportunities for Singapore citizens.

Things have not always been so easy for Singapore. The country hit an economic slump from 2000 to 2003 due to a series of events outside its control. An economic recession in the United States and the European Union had harmful effects on economic growth. The rebound, however, was a complete success, as Singapore posted a 7.5 percent growth in gross domestic product in 2007. The recovery went smoothly due to good economic strategy, a high percentage of skilled workers, and copious foreign investment. The assistance of government-linked corporations was also important in rebounding from the worldwide slump.

As the busiest trading hub in Southeast Asia, Singapore is the world's leading bunkering (refueling) port and second-largest container port. It is at the very heart of Asia's trading routes, in the same time zone as China and Western Australia. Singapore is home to some of the largest commodity trading companies, with a combined annual turnover in excess of $1 trillion. Singapore is well placed to take advantage of any upturn in global trade.

The number of wealthy residents of the country has risen at a rapid rate as a result of the general economic success. It has been estimated that by 2020, Singapore will have some 188,000 millionaires (*Wealth Insight*). This is an increase of 18 percent, 2 percent higher growth than Hong Kong. By 2015, Singapore's top 154,000 high-net-worth individuals had amassed some $806 billion. The economic climate of the world is changing, as smaller countries are becoming more powerful financially and closing in on larger countries with greater economic power. Globalization is providing the opportunity for countries like Singapore to step to the forefront of the trade market. If Singapore continues to employ the economic strategies it has up to this point, its future financial success is all but guaranteed.

Thinking Globally

12-10. As the economic adviser to the president of a small developing country, what lessons can you take from Singapore's economic approach that can be applied? Your country also has a functional, but not overly busy, port. What steps do you take to encourage trade with foreign countries?

12-11. Do you think that the economy of Singapore will be greatly affected by changes in the financial status of traditional economic superpowers? Why or why not? If the economy is affected, will it be positive or negative?

12-12. Why do you think the strategy of extended entrepôt trading—importing raw materials, refining them, then exporting them to foreign countries—is effective?

12-13. Is it possible for a country as small as Singapore to become a worldwide economic superpower? What factors must be considered in answering this question? In the new global economy, does the size of a country matter at all if the economic strategy is effective? Is having a busy port enough of an economic boost to lift a small country to economic prominence?

Sources: "Singapore Economy," EconomyWatch.com website (http://www.economywatch.com/world_economy/singapore/), December 18, 2008.

Chapter Thirteen

Selecting and Managing Entry Modes

Learning Objectives

After studying this chapter, you should be able to

13.1 Describe how companies use exporting, importing, and countertrade.

13.2 Explain the various methods of export/import financing.

13.3 Describe the different types of contractual entry modes.

13.4 Describe the various kinds of investment entry modes.

13.5 Outline key strategic factors in selecting an entry mode.

A Look Back

Chapter 12 explained how companies analyze international business opportunities. We learned how managers screen and research both potential markets and sites for operations.

A Look at This Chapter

This chapter introduces the different entry modes companies use to "go international." We discuss the important issues surrounding the selection and management of (1) exporting, importing, and countertrade; (2) contractual entry modes; and (3) investment entry modes.

A Look Ahead

Chapter 14 explains the international marketing efforts of companies. We identify the key elements that influence how companies promote, price, and distribute their products.

License to Thrill

LONDON, England—Marvel Enterprises (www.marvel.com) is a global character-based entertainment licensing company that over a span of 70 years developed a library of more than 5,000 characters. Shown here is Stan Lee, the creator of Spider-Man and a comic book writer, an editor, an actor, a producer, a publisher, and the former president and chairman of Marvel Comics.

Featureflash Photo Agency/Shutterstock

Marvel initially pursued licensing as a means to become more than just a comics and toy company, and it has already brought top comic-book characters—including Iron Man, Spider-Man, Blade, X-Men, and the Hulk—to the big screen with enormous success. The films do generate revenue for Marvel, but their main function is to popularize the company's comic-book characters.

Driving Marvel's earnings in recent years are its character-based licensing agreements for products such as lunchboxes, toys, and video games. Marvel's licensing business includes a deal with Hasbro (www.hasbro .com) to distribute action figures based on Marvel characters through the year 2017. Marvel earns royalties on all its toys sold worldwide (except Japan) through Hasbro. And Marvel's sale to Disney (www.disney .com) for $4.3 billion means that its characters are sure to take their adventures to even more movies, theme parks, and stores worldwide.

Marvel's 50/50 joint venture with Sony (www.sony.com) oversees all licensing and merchandising activities for the film *Spider-Man*, as well as Sony's animated TV series titled *Spider-Man*. Marvel moves constantly forward despite sales of its print comics being down somewhat. Marvel International, based in England, is developing the firm's licensing business in strategic international markets, which the company believes is largely untapped. As you read this chapter, consider why companies go international and when each market entry mode is appropriate.[1]

entry mode
Institutional arrangement by which a firm gets its products, technologies, human skills, or other resources into a market.

The decision of how to enter a new market abroad must take into account many factors, including the local business environment and a company's own core competency. An **entry mode** is the institutional arrangement by which a firm gets its products, technologies, human skills, or other resources into a market. Companies seeking entry into new markets for manufacturing and/or marketing purposes have many potential entry modes at their disposal. The specific mode chosen depends on many factors, including experience in a market, the amount of control managers desire, and the potential size of the market. In this chapter, we explore the following three categories of entry modes:

1. Exporting, importing, and countertrade
2. Contractual entry
3. Investment entry

13.1 Exporting, Importing, and Countertrade

13.1 Describe how companies use exporting, importing, and countertrade.

The most common method of buying and selling goods internationally is exporting and importing. Companies often import products in order to obtain less expensive goods or those that are simply unavailable in the domestic market. Companies export products when the international marketplace offers opportunities to increase sales and, in turn, profits. Companies worldwide (from both developed and developing countries) often see the United States as a great export opportunity because of the size of the market and the strong buying power of its citizens. Figure 13.1 showcases the top 10 exporters to the United States in terms of the value of goods sold.

Because this chapter focuses on how companies take their goods and services to the global marketplace, this first section concentrates on exporting. We then explain how companies use *countertrade* when cash transactions are not possible and discuss the main export/import financing methods. Because importing is a sourcing decision for most firms, it is covered in Chapter 15.

Why Companies Export

In the global economy, companies increasingly sell goods and services to wholesalers, retailers, industrial buyers, and consumers in other nations. Generally, there are three main reasons why companies begin exporting. First, many large companies use exporting to *expand total sales* when domestic markets become saturated. A greater sales volume lets a firm spread fixed production costs over a greater number of manufactured products, thereby lowering the cost of producing each unit of output. In short, this is a way to achieve economies of scale.

Second, exporting permits companies to *diversify sales*. In other words, they can offset slow sales in one national market (perhaps due to a recession) with increased sales in another. Diversified sales can level off a company's cash flow, making it easier to coordinate payments to creditors with receipts from customers.

Figure 13.1

Top Exporters to the United States

Source: Based on trade data on International Trade Administration website (www.trade.gov).

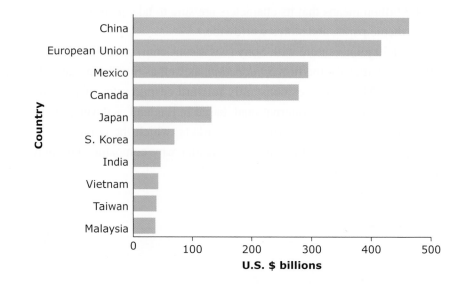

Third, companies can use exporting as a low-cost, low-risk way to *gain international business experience*. Owners and managers of small companies, which typically have little or no knowledge of how to conduct business in other cultures, use exporting to gain valuable international experience.

Developing an Export Strategy: A Four-Step Model

Companies are often drawn into exporting when customers in other countries solicit their goods. In this way, companies become aware of their products' international potential and get their first taste of international business.

Yet, a company should not fall into the habit of simply responding to random international requests for its products. A more logical approach is to research and analyze international opportunities and to develop a coherent export strategy. A business with such a strategy actively pursues export markets rather than sitting back and waiting for international orders to come in. Let's take a look at the four steps in developing a successful export strategy.

STEP 1: IDENTIFY A POTENTIAL MARKET To identify whether demand exists in a particular target market, a company should perform market research and interpret the results (see Chapter 12). Novice exporters should focus on one or only a few markets. For example, a first-time Brazilian exporter might not want to export simultaneously to Argentina, Britain, and Greece. A better strategy would likely be to focus on Argentina because of its cultural similarities with Brazil (despite having a different, though related, language). The company could then expand into more diverse markets after it gains initial international experience in a nearby country. The would-be exporter should also seek expert advice on the regulations and general process of exporting and on any special issues related to a selected target market.

STEP 2: MATCH NEEDS TO ABILITIES The next step is to determine whether the company is capable of satisfying the needs of the market. Suppose a market located in a region with a warm, humid climate for much of the year displays the need for home air-conditioning equipment. If a company recognizes this need but makes only industrial-sized air-conditioning equipment, it might not be able to satisfy demand with its current product. But if the company is able to use its smallest industrial air-conditioning unit to satisfy the needs of several homes, it might have a market opportunity. If there are no other options or if consumers want their own individual units, the company will likely need to design a smaller air-conditioning unit or rule out entry into that market.

STEP 3: INITIATE MEETINGS Holding meetings early in the process with potential local distributors, buyers, and others is a must. Initial contact focuses on building trust and developing a cooperative climate among all parties. The cultural differences between the parties will come into play already at this stage. Beyond building trust, successive meetings are designed to estimate the potential success of any agreement if interest is shown on both sides. At the most advanced stage, negotiations take place and details of agreements are finalized.

For example, a group of environmental technology companies in Arizona was searching for markets abroad. A delegation from Taiwan soon arrived in the Arizona desert to survey the group's products. Although days were busy with company visits, formal meetings, and negotiations, evenings were used for building relationships. There were outdoor barbecues, hayrides, line dancing, and frontier-town visits that gave the visitors a feel for local culture and history. To make their counterparts from Taiwan feel comfortable, nighttime schedules included visits to karaoke spots and Chinese restaurants where a good deal of singing took place. Follow-up meetings resulted in several successful deals.

STEP 4: COMMIT RESOURCES After all the meetings, negotiations, and contract signings, it is time to put the company's human, financial, and physical resources to work. First, the objectives of the export program must be clearly stated and should extend out at least three to five years. For small firms, it may be sufficient to assign one individual the responsibility for drawing up objectives and estimating resources. Yet, as companies expand their activities to include more products and/or markets, many firms discover the need for an export department or division. The head of this department usually has the responsibility (and authority) to formulate, implement, and evaluate the company's export strategy. See Chapter 11 for a detailed discussion of organizational design issues to consider at this stage.

Degree of Export Involvement

Companies of all sizes engage in exporting, but not all companies become involved in exporting to the same extent. Some exporting companies (usually entrepreneurs and small and medium-sized firms) perform few or none of the activities necessary to get their products into a market abroad. Instead, they use intermediaries that specialize in getting products from one market into another. Other exporting companies (usually only the largest companies) perform all of their export activities themselves, with an infrastructure that bridges the gap between the two markets. Let's take a closer look at the two basic forms of export involvement—direct exporting and indirect exporting.

direct exporting
Practice by which a company sells its products directly to buyers in a target market.

DIRECT EXPORTING   Some companies become deeply involved in the export of their products. **Direct exporting** occurs when a company sells its products directly to buyers in a target market. Direct exporters operate in many industries, including aircraft (Boeing; www.boeing.com), industrial equipment (John Deere; www.deere.com), apparel (Lands' End; www.landsend.com), and bottled beverages (Evian; www.evian.com). Bear in mind that "direct exporters" need not sell directly to *end users*. Rather, they take full responsibility for getting their goods into the target market by selling directly to local buyers and not going through intermediary companies. Typically, they rely on either local *sales representatives* or *distributors*.

Sales Representatives   A *sales representative* (whether an individual or an organization) represents only its own company's products, not those of other companies. Sales representatives promote those products in many ways, such as by attending trade fairs and by making personal visits to local retailers and wholesalers. They do not take title to the merchandise. Rather, they are hired by a company and normally are compensated with a fixed salary plus commissions based on the value of their sales.

Distributors   Alternatively, a direct exporter can sell in the target market through *distributors*, who take ownership of the merchandise when it enters their country. As owners of the products, distributors accept all the risks associated with generating local sales. They sell either to retailers and wholesalers or to end users through their own channels of distribution. Typically, distributors earn a profit equal to the difference between the price they pay and the price they receive for the exporter's goods. Although using a distributor reduces an exporter's risk, it also weakens an exporter's control over the price buyers are charged. A distributor who charges very high prices can stunt the growth of an exporter's market share. Exporters should choose, if possible, distributors who are willing to invest in the promotion of their products and who do not sell directly competing products.

indirect exporting
Practice by which a company sells its products to intermediaries who then resell to buyers in a target market.

INDIRECT EXPORTING   Some companies have few resources available to commit to exporting activities. Others simply find exporting a daunting task because of a lack of contacts and experience. Fortunately, there is an option for such firms. **Indirect exporting** occurs when a company sells its products to intermediaries who then resell to buyers in a target market. The choice of an intermediary depends on many factors, including the ratio of the exporter's international sales to its total sales, the company's available resources, and the growth rate of the target market. Let's take a closer look at several different types of intermediaries: *agents, export management companies,* and *export trading companies*.

agents
Individuals or organizations that represent one or more indirect exporters in a target market.

Agents   Individuals or organizations that represent one or more indirect exporters in a target market are called **agents**. Agents typically receive compensation in the form of commissions on the value of sales. Because establishing a relationship with an agent is relatively easy and inexpensive, it is a fairly common approach to indirect exporting. Agents should be chosen very carefully because terminating an agency relationship if problems arise can be costly and difficult. Careful selection is also essential because agents often represent several indirect exporters simultaneously. Agents might focus their promotional efforts on the products of the company paying the highest commission rather than on the company with the better products.

export management company (EMC)
Company that exports products on behalf of indirect exporters.

Export Management Companies   A company that exports products on behalf of an indirect exporter is called an **export management company (EMC)**. An EMC operates contractually, either as an agent (being paid through commissions based on the value of sales) or as a distributor (taking ownership of the merchandise and earning a profit from its resale).

An EMC will usually provide additional services on a retainer basis, charging set fees against funds deposited on account. Typical EMC services include gathering market information, formulating promotional strategies, performing specific promotional duties (such as attending trade fairs), researching customer credit, making shipping arrangements, and coordinating export documents. It is common for an EMC to exploit contacts predominantly in one industry (say, agricultural goods or consumer products) or in one geographic area (such as Latin America or Southeast Asia). Indeed, the biggest advantage of an EMC is usually a deep understanding of the cultural, political, legal, and economic conditions of the target market. Its staff works comfortably and effectively in the cultures of both the exporting and the target nation. The average EMC tends to deploy a wide array of commercial and political contacts in order to facilitate business activities on behalf of its clients.

Perhaps the only disadvantage of hiring an EMC is that the breadth and depth of its service can potentially hinder the development of the exporter's own international expertise. But an exporter and its EMC typically have such a close relationship that an exporter often considers its EMC as a virtual exporting division. When this is the case, exporters learn a great deal about the intricacies of exporting from their EMC. Then, after the EMC contract expires, it is common for a company to go it alone in exporting its products.

Export Trading Companies A company that provides services to indirect exporters in addition to activities directly related to clients' exporting activities is called an **export trading company (ETC)**. Whereas an EMC is restricted to export-related activities, an ETC assists its clients by providing import, export, and countertrade services; developing and expanding distribution channels; providing storage facilities; financing trading and investment projects; and even manufacturing products.

European trading nations first developed the ETC concept centuries ago. More recently, the Japanese have refined the concept, which they call *sogo shosha*. The Japanese ETC can range in size from small, family-run businesses to enormous conglomerates such as Mitsubishi (www.mitsubishi.com), Mitsui (www.mitsui.com), and ITOCHU (www.itochu.co.jp). An ETC in South

export trading company (ETC)

Company that provides services to indirect exporters in addition to activities related directly to clients' exporting activities.

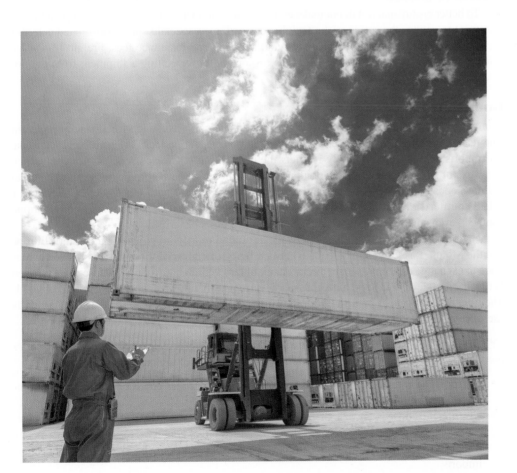

Owners of small to medium-sized businesses are often unsure of how to begin exporting. Obstacles can include a lack of time, international market knowledge, export logistics, and legal issues. For help, a novice exporter can benefit by employing a *freight forwarder*, a specialist in export-related activities that can help exported merchandise get to its port of destination securely. Here, a machine loads a shipping container onto a freight train in Doncaster, England, for delivery to the Felixstowe docks from which it will be exported.

123RF.com

Korea is called a *chaebol* and includes well-known companies such as Samsung (www.samsung .com) and Hyundai (www.hyundaigroup.com).

Japanese and South Korean ETCs have become formidable competitors because of their enormous success in gaining global market share. These Asian companies quickly came to rival the dominance of the largest US multinational corporations, which lobbied US lawmakers for assistance in challenging Asian ETCs in global markets. The result was the Export Trading Company Act passed in 1982. Despite this effort, the ETC concept never really caught on in the United States. Operations of the typical ETC in the United States remain small and are dwarfed by those of their Asian counterparts. One reason for the lack of interest in the ETC concept in the United States relative to that in Asia is that governments, financial institutions, and companies have much closer working relationships in Asia. The formation of huge conglomerates that engage in activities ranging from providing financing to manufacturing to distribution is easier to accomplish there. By contrast, the regulatory environment in the United States is wary of such cozy business arrangements, and the lines between companies and industries are more clearly drawn.

Avoiding Export and Import Blunders

It is understandably easy for companies that are new to exporting to make mistakes. First, many businesses fail to conduct adequate market research before exporting. In fact, many companies begin exporting by responding to unsolicited requests for their products. If a company enters a market in this manner, it should quickly devise an export strategy to manage its export activities effectively and not strain its resources.

Second, many companies fail to obtain adequate export advice. National and regional governments are often willing and able to help managers and small-business owners understand and cope with the vast amounts of paperwork required by each country's export and import laws. Naturally, more experienced exporters can be extremely helpful as well. They can help novice exporters avoid embarrassing mistakes by guiding them through unfamiliar cultural, political, and economic environments.

To better ensure that it will not make embarrassing blunders, an inexperienced exporter might also want to engage the services of a **freight forwarder**—a specialist in export-related activities such as customs clearing, tariff schedules, and shipping and insurance fees. Freight forwarders also can pack shipments for export and take responsibility for getting a shipment from the port of export to the port of import.

freight forwarder
Specialist in export-related activities such as customs clearing, tariff schedules, and shipping and insurance fees.

Countertrade

Companies are sometimes unable to import merchandise in exchange for financial payment. The reason is either that the government of the importer's nation lacks the hard currency to pay for imports or that it intentionally restricts the convertibility of its currency. Fortunately, there is a way for firms to trade by using either a small amount of hard currency or even none at all. Selling goods or services that are paid for, in whole or in part, with other goods or services is called **countertrade**. Although countertrade often requires an extensive network of international contacts, even smaller companies can take advantage of its benefits.

Nations that have long used countertrade are found mostly in Africa, Asia, Eastern Europe, and the Middle East. A lack of adequate hard currency often forced those nations to use countertrade to exchange oil for passenger aircraft and military equipment. Today, because of insufficient hard currency, developing and emerging markets frequently rely on countertrade to import goods. The greater involvement of firms from industrialized nations in those markets is expanding the use of countertrade.

countertrade
Practice of selling goods or services that are paid for, in whole or in part, with other goods or services.

TYPES OF COUNTERTRADE There are several different types of countertrade: *barter, counterpurchase, offset, switch trading,* and *buyback.* Let's take a brief look at each of these.

- **Barter** is the exchange of goods or services directly for other goods or services without the use of money. It is the oldest known form of countertrade.
- **Counterpurchase** is the sale of goods or services to a country by a company that promises to make a future purchase of a specific product from that country. This type of agreement is designed to allow the country to earn back some of the currency that it paid for the original imports.

barter
Exchange of goods or services directly for other goods or services without the use of money.

counterpurchase
Sale of goods or services to a country by a company that promises to make a future purchase of a specific product from the country.

- **Offset** is an agreement that a company will offset a hard-currency sale to a nation by making a hard-currency purchase of an unspecified product from that nation in the future. It differs from a counterpurchase in that this type of agreement does not specify the type of product that must be purchased, just the amount that will be spent. Such an arrangement gives a business greater freedom in fulfilling its end of a countertrade deal.
- **Switch trading** is countertrade whereby one company sells to another its obligation to make a purchase in a given country. For example, in return for market access, a firm that wants to enter a target market might promise to buy a product for which it has no use. The company then sells this purchase obligation to a large trading company that makes the purchase itself because it has a use for the merchandise. If the trading company has no use for the merchandise, it can arrange for yet another buyer who needs the product to make the purchase.
- **Buyback** is the export of industrial equipment in return for products produced by that equipment. This practice usually typifies long-term relationships between the companies involved.

Countertrade can provide access to markets that are otherwise off-limits because of a lack of hard currency. It can also cause headaches. Much countertrade involves commodity and agricultural products such as oil, wheat, or corn—products whose prices on world markets tend to fluctuate a good deal. A problem arises when the price of a bartered product falls on world markets between the time that a deal is arranged and the time at which one party tries to sell the product. Fluctuating prices generate the same type of risk encountered in currency markets. Managers might be able to hedge some of this risk on commodity futures markets similar to how they hedge against currency fluctuations in currency markets (see Chapter 9).

offset

Agreement that a company will offset a hard-currency sale to a nation by making a hard-currency purchase of an unspecified product from that nation in the future.

switch trading

Practice in which one company sells to another its obligation to make a purchase in a given country.

buyback

Export of industrial equipment in return for products produced by that equipment.

> ### QUICK STUDY 1
>
> 1. What are the four steps, in order, involved in creating an export strategy?
> 2. When a company sells its products to intermediaries who then resell to buyers in a target market it is called *what*?
> 3. What is the name of a specific type of countertrade?

13.2 Export/Import Financing

International trade poses risks for both exporters and importers. Exporters run the risk of not receiving payment after their products are delivered. Importers fear that delivery might not occur once payment is made for a shipment. Export/import financing methods designed to reduce these risks include *advance payment, documentary collection, letter of credit,* and *open account* (see Figure 13.2). Let's explore each of these methods.

13.2 Explain the various methods of export/import financing.

Figure 13.2

Risk of Export/Import Financing Methods

Advance Payment

Export/import financing in which an importer pays an exporter for merchandise before it is shipped is called **advance payment**. This method of payment is common when two parties are unfamiliar with each other, the transaction is relatively small, or the buyer is unable to obtain credit because of a poor credit rating at banks. Payment normally takes the form of a wire transfer of money from the bank account of the importer directly to that of the exporter. Although prior payment eliminates the risk of nonpayment for exporters, it creates the complementary risk of nonshipment for importers—importers might pay for goods but never receive them. Thus, advance payment is the most favorable method for exporters but the least favorable for importers.

Documentary Collection

Export/import financing in which a bank acts as an intermediary without accepting financial risk is called **documentary collection**. This payment method is commonly used when there is an ongoing business relationship between two parties. The documentary collection process can be broken into three main stages and nine smaller steps (see Figure 13.3).

1. Before shipping merchandise, the exporter (with its banker's assistance) draws up a **draft (bill of exchange)**—a document ordering the importer to pay the exporter a specified sum of money at a specified time. A *sight draft* requires the importer to pay when goods are delivered. A *time draft* extends the period of time (typically 30, 60, or 90 days) following delivery by which the importer must pay for the goods. (When inscribed "accepted" by an importer, a time draft becomes a negotiable instrument that can be traded among financial institutions.) This stage includes Steps 1 and 2 in Figure 13.3.

2. Following creation of the draft, the exporter delivers the merchandise to a transportation company for shipment to the importer. The exporter then delivers to its banker a set of documents that includes the draft, a *packing list* of items shipped, and a **bill of lading**—a contract between the exporter and shipper that specifies merchandise destination and shipping costs. The bill of lading is proof that the exporter has shipped the merchandise. An international ocean shipment requires an *inland bill of lading* to get the shipment to the exporter's border and an *ocean bill of lading* for water transport to the importer nation. An international

Figure 13.3
Documentary Collection Process

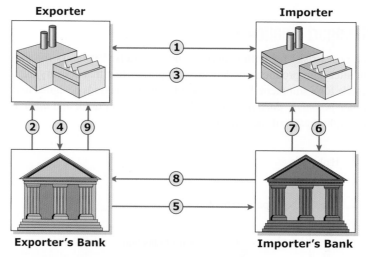

(1) **Exporter/importer contract to sell/buy goods**

(2) **Exporter's bank gives draft to exporter**

(3) **Exporter ships goods to importer**

(4) **Exporter delivers documents to its bank**

(5) **Exporter's bank sends documents to importer's bank**

(6) **Importer delivers payment to its bank**

(7) **Importer's bank gives bill of lading to importer**

(8) **Importer's bank pays exporter's bank**

(9) **Exporter's bank pays exporter for goods**

air shipment requires an *air way bill* that covers the entire international journey. This stage includes Steps 3 and 4 in Figure 13.3.

3. After receiving appropriate documents from the exporter, the exporter's bank sends the documents to the importer's bank. After the importer fulfills the terms stated on the draft and pays its own bank, the bank issues the bill of lading (which becomes title to the merchandise) to the importer. This stage includes Steps 5 through 9 in Figure 13.3.

Documentary collection reduces the importer's risk of nonshipment because the packing list details the contents of the shipment and the bill of lading is proof that the merchandise has been shipped. The exporter's risk of nonpayment is increased because, although the exporter retains title to the goods until the merchandise is accepted, the importer does not pay until all necessary documents have been received. Although importers have the option of refusing the draft (and, therefore, the merchandise), this action is unlikely. Refusing the draft—despite all terms of the agreement being fulfilled—would make the importer's bank unlikely to do business with the importer in the future.

Letter of Credit

Export/import financing in which the importer's bank issues a letter pledging to pay the exporter when the exporter fulfills the terms listed in the letter is called **letter of credit**. A letter of credit is typically used when parties to a transaction are not familiar with each other, when an importer's credit rating is unknown or questionable, when the exporter needs a letter of credit to obtain its own financing for the shipment, and when a market's own regulations require it.

The most common type of letter of credit is an *irrevocable letter of credit*, which allows the bank issuing the letter to modify its terms only after obtaining the approval of both exporter and importer. Banks will normally issue a letter of credit only after an importer has deposited on account a sum equal in value to that of the imported merchandise. Sometimes a bank will waive this requirement for its most reputable importers. But if it does so the bank remains obligated to pay the exporter if the exporter fulfills the terms stated in the letter of credit. This stage includes Steps 1 and 2 in Figure 13.4.

letter of credit

Export/import financing in which the importer's bank issues a letter pledging to pay the exporter when the exporter fulfills the terms listed in the letter.

Figure 13.4
Letter of Credit Process

1. Exporter/importer contract to sell/buy goods
2. Importer applies for letter of credit
3. Importer's bank issues letter of credit to exporter's bank on importer's behalf
4. Exporter's bank informs exporter of letter of credit
5. Exporter ships goods to importer
6. Exporter delivers documents to its bank
7. Exporter's bank delivers documents to importer's bank
8. Importer's bank sends payment to exporter's bank
9. Importer pays its bank for value of goods
10. Importer's bank delivers documents to importer

Once the importer's bank issues a letter of credit it sends the letter to the exporter's bank, which informs the exporter that a letter of credit has been opened in its favor. If the exporter believes it can fulfill the obligations as stated in the letter it will ship the merchandise. The exporter and its freight forwarder then deliver a documentary packet to its bank. This packet typically includes an invoice, packing list, draft, bill of lading, certificate of origin, certificate of insurance, and more. This stage includes Steps 3 through 6 in Figure 13.4.

The exporter's bank then delivers the letter of credit and documentary packet to the importer's bank for review. When the importer's bank is satisfied that the terms of the letter have been met, it sends payment to the exporter's bank, which then credits the exporter's account. The importer pays its bank (or makes provision for future payment) and, in return, receives the documentary packet that includes title to the merchandise. This stage includes Steps 7 through 10 in Figure 13.4.

The letter of credit reduces the importer's risk of nonshipment (as compared with advance payment) because the importer receives proof of shipment before it makes payment. Although the exporter's risk of nonpayment is slightly increased (over advance payment), overall risk is low because the exporter relies on the creditworthiness of the importer's bank, not the importer itself.

For a fee, an exporter can request its bank to 'confirm' the letter of credit, thereby adding the creditworthiness of the exporter's bank to the pledge made by the importer's bank. This provides added confidence of payment for the exporter because if the importer's bank cannot make payment (perhaps due to government controls on its currency, for example) the exporter's bank pledges to make payment. This then is called a *confirmed irrevocable letter of credit*.

Open Account

open account

Export/import financing in which an exporter ships merchandise and later bills the importer for its value.

Export/import financing in which an exporter ships merchandise and later bills the importer for its value is called **open account**. Because some receivables may not be collected, exporters should reserve shipping on open account only for their most trusted customers. This payment method is often used when the parties are very familiar with each other or for sales between two subsidiaries within an international company. The exporter simply invoices the importer (as in many domestic transactions), stating the amount and date due. This method reduces the risk of nonshipment faced by the importer under the advance payment method.

By the same token, the open account method increases the risk of nonpayment for the exporter. Thus, open account is the least favorable for exporters but the most favorable for importers. For some insights on how exporters can increase the probability of getting paid for a shipment, see the Manager's Briefcase feature, titled "Collecting International Debts."

MANAGER'S BRIEFCASE   Collecting International Debts

What is the point of working hard to make an international sale if the buyer does not pay? There are seldom easy answers when an exporter is stuck without payment. Here are several pointers on what businesses can do to reduce the likelihood of not receiving payment:

- Knowledge of the market you are exporting to is your first and best defense. Understanding its culture, the language spoken, and its legal system is ideal. You should also understand if there is typically a payment lag for business debts and customary debt-collection procedures.
- Be aware of countries that commonly cause problems when it comes to debt collection. Regularly consult the many free sources of information available on the Internet to learn which countries are problems. Avoid doing business with them and seek markets elsewhere.
- Both parties clearly understanding the payment terms in your export sales agreement is essential to preventing later collection problems. Also, be sure the buyer knows precisely when payment is to be issued.
- Do not wait too long to begin collecting a past-due account. Exporters who delay will likely never receive payment. Begin with firmly worded communications via phone, fax, e-mail, and letter.
- Consult an international trade attorney or hire an international debt-collection agency if necessary. If you are encouraged to accept arbitration as a way to resolve the issue, do so, as this often poses your best chance of seeing at least partial payment.

1. Export/import financing that presents the most risk for exporters is called *what*?
2. Export/import financing in which a bank acts as an intermediary without financial risk is called *what*?
3. Export/import financing in which the importer's bank issues a document stating that the exporter will get paid when it fulfills the terms of the document is called *what*?

13.3 Contractual Entry Modes

The products of some companies simply cannot be traded in open markets because they are *intangible*. Thus, a company cannot use importing, exporting, or countertrade to exploit opportunities in a target market. Fortunately, there are other options for this type of company. A company can use a variety of contracts—*licensing, franchising, management contracts*, and *turnkey projects*—to market highly specialized assets and skills in markets beyond its nations' borders.

13.3 Describe the different types of contractual entry modes.

Licensing

Companies sometimes grant other firms the right to use an asset that is essential to the production of a finished product. **Licensing** is a contractual entry mode in which a company that owns intangible property (the *licensor*) grants another firm (the *licensee*) the right to use that property for a specified period of time. Licensors typically receive royalty payments based on a percentage of the licensee's sales revenue generated by the licensed property. The licensors might also receive a one-time fee to cover the cost of transferring the property to the licensee. Commonly licensed intangible property includes patents, copyrights, special formulas and designs, trademarks, and brand names. Thus, licensing often involves granting companies the right to use *process technologies* inherent to the production of a particular good. For example, Hitachi, of Japan, licensed technology to be used in the recycling of plastics from Duales System Deutschland of Germany.

An *exclusive license* grants a company the exclusive rights to produce and market a property, or products made from that property, in a specific geographic region. The region can be the licensee's home country or can extend to worldwide markets. A *nonexclusive license* grants a company the right to use a property but does not grant it sole access to a market. A licensor can grant several or more companies the right to use a property in the same region.

Cross licensing occurs when companies use licensing agreements to exchange intangible property with one another. For example, Fujitsu (www.fujitsu.com) of Japan signed a five-year cross-licensing agreement with Texas Instruments (www.ti.com) of the United States. The agreement allowed each company to use the other's technology in the production of its own goods—thus lowering research and development (R&D) costs. The very extensive arrangement covered all but a few semiconductor patents owned by each company. Because asset values are seldom exactly equal, cross licensing also typically involves royalty payments from one party to the other.

licensing

Practice by which one company owning intangible property (the licensor) grants another firm (the licensee) the right to use that property for a specified period of time.

cross licensing

Practice by which companies use licensing agreements to exchange intangible property with one another.

ADVANTAGES OF LICENSING There are several advantages to using licensing as an entry mode into new markets. First, licensors can use licensing to finance their international expansion. Most licensing agreements require licensees to contribute equipment and investment financing, whether by building special production facilities or by using existing excess capacity. Access to such resources can be a great advantage to a licensor who wants to expand but lacks the capital and managerial resources to do so. And because it need not spend time constructing and starting up its own new facilities, the licensor earns revenues sooner than it would otherwise.

Second, licensing can be a less risky method of international expansion for a licensor than other entry modes. Whereas some markets are risky because of social or political unrest, others defy accurate market research for a variety of reasons. Licensing helps shield the licensor from the increased risk of operating its own local production facilities in markets that are unstable or hard to assess accurately.

Third, licensing can help reduce the likelihood that a licensor's product will appear on the black market. The side streets of large cities in many emerging markets are dotted with tabletop vendors eager to sell bootleg versions of computer software, Hollywood films, and recordings of internationally popular musicians. Producers can, to some extent, foil bootleggers by licensing local companies to market their products at locally competitive prices. Royalties will be lower than the profits generated by sales at higher international prices, but lower profits are better than no profits at all—which is what owners get from bootleg versions of their products.

Finally, licensees can benefit by using licensing as a method of upgrading existing production technologies. For example, manufacturers of plastics and other synthetic materials in the Philippines attempted to meet the high standards demanded by the local subsidiaries of Japanese electronics and office equipment producers. To do this, D&L Industries of the Philippines upgraded its manufacturing process by licensing materials technology from Nippon Pigment of Japan.

DISADVANTAGES OF LICENSING There also are important disadvantages to using licensing. First, it can restrict a licensor's future activities. Suppose a licensee is granted the exclusive right to use an asset but fails to produce the sort of results that a licensor expected. Because the license agreement is exclusive, the licensor cannot simply begin selling directly in that particular market in order to meet demand itself nor can it contract with another licensee. A good product and lucrative market, therefore, do not guarantee success for a producer entering a market through licensing.

Second, licensing might reduce the global consistency of the quality and marketing of a licensor's product in different national markets. A licensor might find the development of a coherent global brand image an elusive goal if each of its national licensees can operate in any manner it chooses. Promoting a global image might later require considerable amounts of time and money in order to change the misconceptions of buyers in the various licensed markets.

Third, licensing might amount to a company "lending" strategically important property to its future competitors. This is an especially dangerous situation when a company licenses assets on which its competitive advantage is based. Licensing agreements are often made for several years and perhaps even a decade or more. During this time, licensees often become highly competent at producing and marketing the licensor's product. When the agreement expires, the licensor might find that its former licensee is capable of producing and marketing a better version of its own product. Licensing contracts can (and should) restrict licensees from competing in the future with products based strictly on licensed property. But enforcement of such provisions works only for identical or nearly identical products, not when substantial improvements are made.

Franchising

franchising

Practice by which one company (the franchiser) supplies another (the franchisee) with intangible property and other assistance over an extended period.

Franchising is a contractual entry mode in which one company (the *franchiser*) supplies another (the *franchisee*) with intangible property and other assistance over an extended period. Franchisers typically receive compensation as flat fees, royalty payments, or both. The most popular franchises are those with widely recognized brand names, such as Mercedes (www.mercedes.com), McDonald's (www.mcdonalds.com), and Starbucks (www.starbucks.com). In fact, the brand name or trademark of a company is normally the single most important item desired by the franchisee. This is why smaller companies with lesser-known brand names and trademarks have greater difficulty locating interested franchisees.

Franchising differs from licensing in several ways. First, franchising gives a company greater control over the sale of its product in a target market. Franchisees must often meet strict guidelines on product quality, day-to-day management duties, and marketing promotions. Second, although licensing is fairly common in manufacturing industries, franchising is primarily used in service industries such as auto dealerships, entertainment, lodging, restaurants, and business services. Third, although licensing normally involves a one-time transfer of property, franchising requires ongoing assistance from the franchiser. In addition to the initial transfer of property, franchisers typically offer start-up capital, management training, location advice, and advertising assistance to their franchisees.

Companies based in the United States dominate the world of international franchising. US companies perfected the practice of franchising in their large, homogeneous domestic market with low barriers to interstate trade and investment. Yet franchising is growing in the European Union, with the advent of a single currency and a unified set of franchise laws. Many European managers with comfortable early-retirement packages have discovered franchising to be an appealing second career.

Despite projections for robust growth, European franchise managers often misunderstand the franchising concept. One example is when Holiday Inn's franchise expansion in Spain was moving more slowly than expected. According to the company's development director in Spain, Holiday Inn found that it needed to convince local managers that Holiday Inn did not want to "take control" of their hotels.[2] In some Eastern European countries, local managers do not understand why they must continue to pay royalties to brand and trademark owners. Franchise expansion in Eastern European markets also suffers from a lack of local capital, high interest rates, high taxes, bureaucratic obstacles, restrictive laws, and corruption.[3]

ADVANTAGES OF FRANCHISING There are several important advantages of franchising. First, franchisers can use franchising as a low-cost, low-risk entry mode into new markets. Companies following global strategies rely on consistent products and common themes in worldwide markets. Franchising allows them to maintain consistency by replicating the processes for standardized products in each target market. Many franchisers, however, will make small modifications in products and promotional messages when marketing specifically to local buyers.

Second, franchising is an entry mode that allows for rapid geographic expansion. Firms often gain a competitive advantage by being first in seizing a market opportunity. For example, Microtel Inns & Suites (www.microtelinn.com) of Atlanta, Georgia, is using franchising to fuel its international expansion. Microtel is boldly entering Argentina and Uruguay and eyeing opportunities in Brazil and Western Europe. Rooms cost around $75 per night and target business travelers who cannot afford $200 per night.[4]

Finally, franchisers can benefit from the cultural knowledge and know-how of local managers. This helps lower the risk of business failure in unfamiliar markets and can create a competitive advantage.

DISADVANTAGES OF FRANCHISING Franchising can also pose problems for both franchisers and franchisees. First, franchisers may find it cumbersome to manage a large number of franchisees in a variety of national markets. A major concern is that product quality and promotional messages among franchisees will not be consistent from one market to another. One way to ensure greater control is by establishing in each market a so-called *master franchisee*, which is responsible for monitoring the operations of individual franchisees.

Second, franchisees can experience a loss of organizational flexibility in franchising agreements. Franchise contracts can restrict their strategic and tactical options, and they may even be forced to promote products owned by the franchiser's other divisions. For years PepsiCo (www.pepsico.com) owned the well-known restaurant chains Pizza Hut, Taco Bell, and KFC. As part of their franchise agreements with PepsiCo, restaurant owners were required to sell only PepsiCo beverages to their customers. Many franchisees worldwide were displeased with such restrictions on their product offerings and were relieved when PepsiCo spun off the restaurant chains.

French hypermarket chain, Carrefour S.A., was founded in 1959 in the alpine town of Annecy in southeastern France. Today, nearly 12,000 stores in more than 30 countries carry one of the company's several banners. The company could not have achieved its growth without the use of franchising. Shown here are the Carrefour counters in Chongqing, China. Franchising helps Carrefour ensure that individual stores meet company guidelines on matters such as company policies, product offerings, and service. Can you think of other industries that employ franchising?

Pcruciatti/Shutterstock

Management Contracts

management contract

Practice by which one company supplies another with managerial expertise for a specific period of time.

Under the stipulations of a **management contract**, one company supplies another with managerial expertise for a specific period of time. The supplier of expertise is normally compensated with either a lump-sum payment or a continuing fee based on sales volume. Such contracts are commonly found in the public utilities sectors of developed and emerging markets. Two types of knowledge can be transferred through management contracts—the specialized knowledge of technical managers and the business-management skills of general managers.

ADVANTAGES OF MANAGEMENT CONTRACTS Management contracts can benefit organizations and countries. First, a firm can award a management contract to another company and thereby exploit an international business opportunity without having to place a great deal of its own physical assets at risk. Financial capital can then be reserved for other promising investment projects that would otherwise not be funded.

Second, governments can award companies management contracts to operate and upgrade public utilities, particularly when a nation is short of investment financing. That is why the government of Kazakhstan contracted with a group of international companies called ABB Power Grid Consortium to manage its national electricity-grid system for 25 years. Under the terms of the contract, the consortium paid past wages owed to workers by the government and invested more than $200 million during the first three years of the agreement. The Kazakhstan government had neither the cash flow to pay the workers nor the funds to make badly needed improvements.

Third, governments use management contracts to develop the skills of local workers and managers. ESB International (www.esb.ie) of Ireland signed a three-year contract not only to manage and operate a power plant in Ghana, but also to train local personnel in the skills needed to manage it at some point in the future.

DISADVANTAGES OF MANAGEMENT CONTRACTS Unfortunately, management contracts also pose two disadvantages for suppliers of expertise. First, although management contracts reduce the exposure of physical assets in another country, the same is not true for the supplier's personnel: Political or social turmoil can threaten managers' lives.

Second, suppliers of expertise may end up nurturing a formidable new competitor in the local market. After learning how to conduct certain operations, the party that had originally needed assistance may be capable of competing on its own. Firms must weigh the financial returns from a management contract against the potential future problems caused by a newly launched competitor.

Turnkey Projects

turnkey (build–operate–transfer) project

Practice by which one company designs, constructs, and tests a production facility for a client firm.

When one company designs, constructs, and tests a production facility for a client, the agreement is called a **turnkey (build–operate–transfer) project**. The term *turnkey project* is derived from the understanding that the client, who normally pays a flat fee for the project, is expected to do nothing more than simply "turn a key" to get the facility operating. The company awarded a turnkey project completely prepares the facility for its client.

Similar to management contracts, turnkey projects tend to be large-scale and often involve government agencies. But unlike management contracts, turnkey projects transfer special process technologies or production-facility designs to the client. They typically involve the construction of power plants, airports, seaports, telecommunication systems, and petrochemical facilities that are then turned over to the client. Under a management contract, the supplier of a service retains the asset—the managerial expertise. For example, Telecommunications Consultants India constructed telecom networks in both Madagascar and Ghana—two turnkey projects worth a combined total of $28 million.

ADVANTAGES OF TURNKEY PROJECTS Turnkey projects provide benefits to providers and recipients. First, turnkey projects permit firms to specialize in their core competencies and to exploit opportunities that they could not undertake alone. Exxon Mobil (www.exxonmobil.com) awarded a turnkey project to PT McDermott Indonesia (www.mcdermott.com) and Toyo Engineering (www.toyo-eng.co.jp) of Japan to build a liquid natural gas plant on the Indonesian island of Sumatra. The providers are responsible for constructing an offshore production platform, laying a 100-kilometer underwater pipeline, and building an on-land liquid natural gas refinery. The $316 million project is feasible only because each company contributes unique expertise to the design, construction, and testing of the facilities.

Second, turnkey projects allow governments to obtain designs for infrastructure projects from the world's leading companies. For instance, Turkey's government enlisted two separate consortiums of international firms to build four hydroelectric dams on its Coruh River. The dams combine the design and technological expertise of each company in the two consortiums. The Turkish government also awarded a turnkey project to Ericsson (www.ericsson.com) of Sweden to expand the country's mobile telecommunication system.

DISADVANTAGES OF TURNKEY PROJECTS Among the disadvantages of turnkey projects is the fact that a company may be awarded a project for political reasons rather than for technological know-how. Because turnkey projects are often of high monetary value and awarded by government agencies, the process of awarding them can be highly politicized. When the selection process is not entirely open, companies with the best political connections often win contracts, usually at inflated prices—the costs of which are typically passed on to local taxpayers.

Second, like management contracts, turnkey projects can create future competitors. A newly created local competitor could become a major supplier in its own domestic market and perhaps even in other markets where the supplier operates. Therefore, companies try to avoid projects in which there is danger of transferring their core competencies to others.

> **QUICK STUDY 3**
>
> 1. What is the name of a specific type of contractual entry mode?
> 2. What is it called when companies use agreements to exchange intangible property?
> 3. A disadvantage of both management contracts and turnkey projects is *what*?

13.4 Investment Entry Modes

Investment entry modes entail direct investment in plant and equipment in a country coupled with ongoing involvement in the local operation. Entry modes in this category take a company's commitment in a market to a higher level. Let's explore three common forms of investment entry: *wholly owned subsidiaries, joint ventures*, and *strategic alliances*.

13.4 Describe the various kinds of investment entry modes.

Wholly Owned Subsidiaries

As the term suggests, a **wholly owned subsidiary** is a facility entirely owned and controlled by a single parent company. Companies can establish a wholly owned subsidiary either by forming a new company and constructing entirely new facilities (such as factories, offices, and equipment) or by purchasing an existing company and internalizing its facilities. Whether an international subsidiary is purchased or newly created depends to a large extent on its proposed operations. When a parent company designs a subsidiary to manufacture the latest high-tech products, it typically must build new facilities. The major drawback of creation from the ground up is the time it takes to construct new facilities, hire and train employees, and launch production.

Conversely, finding an existing local company capable of performing marketing and sales will be easier because special technologies are typically not needed. By purchasing the existing marketing and sales operations of an existing firm in the target market, the parent can have the subsidiary operating relatively quickly. Buying an existing company's operations in the target market is a particularly good strategy when the company to be acquired has a valuable trademark, brand name, or process technology.

wholly owned subsidiary
Facility entirely owned and controlled by a single parent company.

ADVANTAGES OF WHOLLY OWNED SUBSIDIARIES There are two main advantages to entering a market using a wholly owned subsidiary. First, managers have complete control over day-to-day operations in the target market and access to valuable technologies, processes, and other intangible properties within the subsidiary. Complete control also decreases the chance that competitors will gain access to a company's competitive advantage, which is particularly important if it is technology-based. Managers also retain complete control over the subsidiary's output and prices. Unlike licensors and franchisers, the parent company also receives all profits generated by the subsidiary.

Second, a wholly owned subsidiary is a good mode of entry when a company wants to coordinate the activities of all its national subsidiaries. Companies using global strategies view each of their national markets as one part of an interconnected global market. Thus, the ability to exercise complete control over a wholly owned subsidiary makes this entry mode attractive to companies that are pursuing global strategies.

DISADVANTAGES OF WHOLLY OWNED SUBSIDIARIES Wholly owned subsidiaries also present two primary disadvantages. First, they can be expensive undertakings because companies must typically finance investments internally or raise funds in financial markets. Obtaining the necessary funds can be difficult for small and medium-sized companies but relatively easy for the largest companies.

Second, risk exposure is high because a wholly owned subsidiary requires substantial company resources. One source of risk is political or social uncertainty or outright instability in the target market. Such risks can place both physical assets and personnel in serious jeopardy. The sole owner of a wholly owned subsidiary also accepts the risk that buyers will reject the company's product. Parent companies can reduce this risk by gaining a better understanding of consumers prior to entering the target market.

Joint Ventures

Under certain circumstances, companies prefer to share ownership of an operation rather than take complete ownership. A separate company that is created and jointly owned by two or more independent entities to achieve a common business objective is called a **joint venture**. Joint venture partners can be privately owned companies, government agencies, or government-owned companies. Each party may contribute anything valued by its partners, including managerial talent, marketing expertise, market access, production technologies, financial capital, and superior knowledge or techniques of research and development. For example, Suzuki Motor Corporation, of Japan, formed a joint venture with the government of India to manufacture a small-engine car specifically for the Indian market.

joint venture

Separate company that is created and jointly owned by two or more independent entities to achieve a common business objective.

JOINT VENTURE CONFIGURATIONS As we see in Figure 13.5, there are four main joint venture configurations.[5] Although we illustrate each of these as consisting of just two partners, each configuration can also apply to ventures of several or more partners.

Forward Integration Joint Venture Figure 13.5(a) outlines a joint venture characterized by *forward integration*. In this type of joint venture, the parties choose to invest together in *downstream* business activities—activities further along in the "value system" that are normally performed by others. For instance, two household appliance manufacturers opening a retail outlet in a developing country would be a joint venture characterized by forward integration. The two companies now perform activities normally performed by retailers further along in the product's journey to buyers.

Backward Integration Joint Venture Figure 13.5(b) outlines a joint venture characterized by *backward integration*. In other words, the joint venture signals a move by each company into *upstream* business activities—activities earlier in the value system that are normally performed by others. Such a configuration would result if two steel manufacturers formed a joint venture to mine iron ore. The companies now engage in an activity that is normally performed by mining companies.

Buyback Joint Venture Figure 13.5(c) outlines a joint venture whose input is provided by, and whose output is absorbed by, each of its partners. A *buyback joint venture* is formed when each partner requires the same component in its production process. It might be formed when a production facility of a certain minimum size is needed to achieve economies of scale but neither

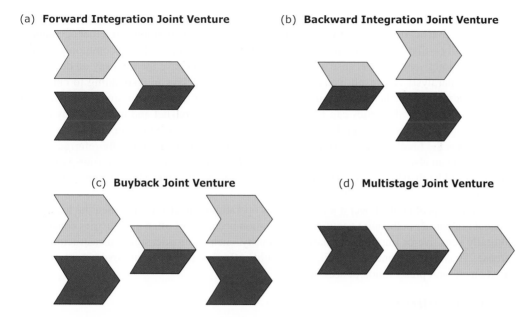

(a) **Forward Integration Joint Venture**

(b) **Backward Integration Joint Venture**

(c) **Buyback Joint Venture**

(d) **Multistage Joint Venture**

Figure 13.5

Alternative Joint Venture Configurations

Source: Peter Buckley and Mark Casson, "A Theory of Cooperation in International Business," in Farok J. Contractor and Peter Lorange (eds.), *Cooperative Strategies in International Business*, (Lexington, MA: Lexington Books, 1988), pp. 31–53.

partner alone enjoys enough demand to warrant building it. However, by combining resources, the partners can construct a facility that serves their needs while achieving savings from economies of scale production. For instance, this was one reason behind the $500 million joint venture between Chrysler (www.chrysler.com) and BMW (www.bmw.com) to build small-car engines in Latin America. Each party benefited from the economies of scale offered by the plant's annual production capacity of 400,000 engines—a volume that neither company could absorb alone.

Multistage Joint Venture Figure 13.5(d) outlines a joint venture that features downstream integration by one partner and upstream integration by another. A *multistage joint venture* often results when one company produces a good or service required by another. For example, a sporting goods manufacturer might join with a sporting goods retailer to establish a distribution company designed to bypass inefficient local distributors in a developing country.

ADVANTAGES OF JOINT VENTURES Joint ventures offer several important advantages to companies going international. Above all, companies rely on joint ventures to reduce risk. Generally, a joint venture exposes fewer of a partner's assets to risk than would a wholly owned subsidiary—each partner risks only its own contribution. That is why a joint venture entry might be a wise choice when market entry requires a large investment or when there is significant political or social instability in the target market. Similarly, a company can use a joint venture to learn about a local business environment prior to launching a wholly owned subsidiary. In fact, many joint ventures are ultimately bought outright by one of the partners after it gains sufficient expertise in the local market.

Second, companies can use joint ventures to penetrate international markets that are otherwise off-limits. Some governments either require nondomestic companies to share ownership with local companies or provide incentives for them to do so. Such requirements are most common among governments of developing countries. The goal is to improve the competitiveness of local companies by having them team up with and learn from international partner(s).

Third, a company can gain access to another company's international distribution network through the use of a joint venture. The joint venture between Caterpillar (www.caterpillar.com) of the United States and Mitsubishi Heavy Industries (www.mitsubishi.com) of Japan was designed to improve the competitiveness of each against a common rival, Komatsu (www.komatsu.com) of Japan. While Caterpillar gained access to Mitsubishi's distribution system in Japan, Mitsubishi got access to Caterpillar's global distribution network—helping it to compete more effectively internationally.

Finally, companies form international joint ventures for defensive reasons. Entering a joint venture with a local government or government-controlled company gives the government a direct stake in the venture's success. In turn, the local government will be less likely to interfere if it means that the venture's performance will suffer. This strategy can also be used to create a more "local" image when feelings of nationalism are running strong in a target country.

DISADVANTAGES OF JOINT VENTURES Among its disadvantages, joint venture ownership can result in conflict between partners. Conflict is perhaps most common when management is shared equally—that is, when each partner supplies top managers in what is commonly known as a "50–50 joint venture." Because neither partner's managers have the final say on decisions, managerial paralysis can result, causing problems such as delays in responding to changing market conditions. Conflict can also arise from disagreements over how future investments and profits are to be shared. Parties can reduce the likelihood of conflict and indecision by establishing unequal ownership, whereby one partner maintains 51 percent ownership of the voting stock and has the final say on decisions. A multiparty joint venture (commonly referred to as a *consortium*) can also feature unequal ownership. For example, ownership of a four-party joint venture could be distributed 20–20–20–40, with the 40-percent owner having the final say on decisions.

Second, loss of control over a joint venture's operations can also result when the local government is a partner in the joint venture. This situation occurs most often in industries considered culturally sensitive or important to national security, such as broadcasting, infrastructure, and defense. Thus, a joint venture's profitability could suffer because of local government motives based on cultural preservation or security.

Strategic Alliances

strategic alliance
Relationship whereby two or more entities cooperate (but do not form a separate company) to achieve the strategic goals of each.

Sometimes companies who are willing to cooperate with one another do not want to go so far as to create a separate, jointly owned company. A relationship whereby two or more entities cooperate (but do not form a separate company) to achieve the strategic goals of each is called a **strategic alliance**. Similar to joint ventures, strategic alliances can be formed for relatively short periods or for many years, depending on the goals of the participants. Strategic alliances can be established between a company and its suppliers, its buyers, and even its competitors. In forming such alliances, sometimes each partner purchases a portion of the other's stock. In this way, each company has a direct stake in its partner's future performance. This decreases the likelihood that one partner will try to take advantage of the other.

ADVANTAGES OF STRATEGIC ALLIANCES Strategic alliances offer several important advantages to companies. First, companies use strategic alliances to share the cost of an international investment project. For example, many firms are developing new products that not only integrate the latest technologies but also shorten the life spans of existing products. In turn, the shorter life span is reducing the number of years during which a company can recoup its investment. Thus, many companies are cooperating to share the costs of developing new products. For example, Toshiba (www.toshiba.com) of Japan, Siemens (www.siemens.com) of Germany, and IBM (www.ibm.com) of the United States shared the $1 billion cost of developing a facility near Nagoya, Japan, to manufacture small, efficient computer memory chips.

Second, companies use strategic alliances to tap into competitors' specific strengths. Some alliances formed between Internet portals and technology companies are designed to do just that. For example, an Internet portal provides access to a large, global audience through its website, while the technology company supplies its know-how in delivering, say, music over the Internet. Meeting the goal of the alliance—marketing music over the Web—requires the competencies of both partners.

Finally, companies turn to strategic alliances for many of the same reasons that they turn to joint ventures. Some businesses use strategic alliances to gain access to a partner's channels of distribution in a target market. Other firms use them to reduce exposure to the same kinds of risks from which joint ventures provide protection.

DISADVANTAGES OF STRATEGIC ALLIANCES Perhaps the most important disadvantage of a strategic alliance is that it can create a future local or even global competitor. For example, one partner might be using the alliance to test a market and prepare the launch of a wholly owned subsidiary. By declining to cooperate with others in the area of its core competency, a company can reduce the likelihood of creating a competitor that would threaten its main area of business. Likewise, a company can insist on contractual clauses that constrain partners from competing against it with certain products or in certain geographic regions. Companies are also careful to protect special research programs, production techniques, and marketing practices that are not committed to the alliance. Naturally, managers must weigh the potential for encouraging new competition against the benefits of international cooperation.

As in the case of joint ventures, conflict can arise and eventually undermine cooperation. Alliance contracts are drawn up to cover as many contingencies as possible, but communication and cultural differences can still arise. When serious problems crop up, dissolution of the alliance may be the only option.

QUICK STUDY 4

1. What is the name of a specific type of investment entry mode?
2. A wholly owned subsidiary is a facility owned and controlled by *what*?
3. What is the name of a specific type of joint venture?
4. A strategic alliance is similar to a joint venture except for that it doesn't involve *what*?

13.5 Strategic Factors in Selecting an Entry Mode

The choice of entry mode has many important strategic implications for a company's future operations.[6] Because enormous investments in time and money can go into determining an entry mode, the choice must be made carefully. Let's now examine several key factors that influence a company's international entry mode selection.

13.5 Outline key strategic factors in selecting an entry mode.

Selecting Partners for Cooperation

Every company's goals and strategies are influenced by both its competitive strengths and the challenges it faces in the marketplace. Because the goals and strategies of any two companies are never exactly alike, cooperation can be difficult. Moreover, ventures and alliances often last many years, perhaps indefinitely. Therefore, partner selection is a crucial ingredient for success.

Every partner must be firmly committed to the goals of the venture or agreement. Many companies engage in cooperative forms of business, but the reasons behind each party's participation are never identical. Sometimes, a company stops contributing to a venture once it achieves its own objectives. Detailing the precise duties and contributions of each party through prior negotiations can go a long way toward ensuring continued cooperation.

Although the importance of locating a trustworthy partner seems obvious, partners should be selected cautiously. Companies can have hidden agendas. Sometimes they try to acquire more from cooperation than their partners realize. If a hidden agenda is discovered, trust can break down and virtually destroy an agreement. Trust is so important that firms naturally prefer to partner with firms that they have had a favorable experience with in the past. However, such arrangements are much easier for large multinational corporations than for small and medium-sized companies with little international experience and few international contacts.

In an international arrangement, each party's managers must be comfortable working with people of other cultures and with traveling to (even perhaps living in) other cultures. As a result, cooperation will go more smoothly and the transition in work life and personal life will be easier for managers. Each partner's managers should also be comfortable working with, and within, one another's *corporate* culture. For example, although some companies encourage the participation of subordinates in decision making, others do not. Such differences often reflect differences in national culture, and when managers possess cultural understanding, adjustment and cooperation are likely to run more smoothly.

Above all, a suitable partner must have something valuable to offer. Firms should avoid cooperation simply because they are approached by another company. Rather, managers must be certain that they are getting a fair return on their efforts. And they should evaluate the benefits of a potential international arrangement just as they would any other investment opportunity. For some key considerations in negotiating international agreements, see the Culture Matters feature, titled "Negotiating Market Entry."

CULTURE MATTERS | Negotiating Market Entry

Global business managers negotiate the terms of many deals. A cooperative atmosphere between potential partners depends on both parties viewing contract negotiations as a success. Managers should be aware of the negotiation process and the roles played by culture and other influential factors:

- **Stage 1: Preparation** Negotiators must have a clear vision of what the company wants to achieve. Negotiation will vary depending on whether the proposed business arrangement is a one-time deal or just the first phase of a lengthy partnership.
- **Stage 2: Opening Positions** Discussions begin as each side states its opening position, which is each side's most favorable terms. Positions might emerge gradually to leave negotiators room to maneuver.
- **Stage 3: Hard Bargaining** The relative power of each party is key in the outcome of negotiations. Direct conflict is likely at this stage, and culture plays a role. For example, Chinese negotiators will likely try to avoid conflict and may call off talks if conflict erupts.

- **Stage 4: Agreement and Follow-Up** Negotiations reaching this stage are a success. Whereas Western negotiators view signing contracts as the end of negotiations, most Asian negotiators see contracts as the start of a flexible relationship.

Two key elements influence international business negotiations:

- **Cultural Elements** Negotiating styles differ from culture to culture. Successful negotiations in Asian cultures mean protecting the other party from losing face (being embarrassed or shamed) and meeting the other party halfway. Yet, negotiators in Western cultures typically hope to gain many concessions with little concern for embarrassing the other party.
- **Political and Legal Elements** Negotiators may have political motives. A rigid public position might be taken to show the company or government officials back home that they are working in the company's or nation's interest. Also, consumer groups and labor unions might lobby government officials to ensure that a proposed agreement benefits them.

Cultural Environment

As we saw in Chapter 2, the dimensions of culture—values, beliefs, customs, languages, religions—can differ greatly from one nation to another. In such cases, managers can be less confident in their ability to manage operations in the host country. They can be concerned about the potential not only for communication problems but also for interpersonal difficulties. As a result, managers may avoid investment entry modes in favor of exporting or a contractual mode. On the other hand, cultural similarity encourages confidence and thus the likelihood of investment. Likewise, the importance of cultural differences diminishes when managers are knowledgeable about the culture of the target market.

Political and Legal Environments

As mentioned earlier in this chapter, political instability in a target market increases the risk exposure of investments. Significant political differences and levels of instability cause companies to avoid large investments and to favor entry modes that shelter assets.

A target market's legal system also influences the choice of entry mode. Certain import regulations, such as high tariffs or low quota limits, can encourage investment. A company that produces locally avoids tariffs that increase product cost; it also does not have to worry about making it into the market below the quota (if there is one). But low tariffs and high quota limits discourage market entry by means of investment. Also, governments may enact laws that ban certain types of investment outright. For many years, China had banned wholly owned subsidiaries by non-Chinese companies and required that joint ventures be formed with local partners. Finally, if a market is lax in enforcing copyright and patent laws, a company may prefer to use investment entry to maintain control over its assets and marketing.

Market Size

The size of a potential market also influences the choice of entry mode. For example, rising incomes in a market encourage investment entry modes because investment allows a firm to prepare for expanding market demand and to increase its understanding of the target market. High domestic demand in China is attracting investment in joint ventures, strategic alliances, and wholly owned subsidiaries. On the other hand, if investors believe that a market is likely to remain relatively small, better options might include exporting or contractual entry.

Production and Shipping Costs

By helping to control total costs, low-cost production and shipping can give a company an advantage. Accordingly, setting up production in a market is desirable when the total cost of production there is lower than in the home market. Low-cost local production might also encourage contractual entry through licensing or franchising. If production costs are sufficiently low, the international production site might even begin supplying other markets, including the home country. An additional potential benefit of local production might be that managers could observe buyer behavior and modify products to better suit the needs of the local market. Lower production costs at home make it more appealing to export to international markets.

Companies that produce goods with high shipping costs naturally prefer local production. Contractual and investment entry modes are viable options in this case. Alternatively, exporting is feasible when products have relatively lower shipping costs. Finally, because they are subject to less price competition, products for which there are fewer substitutes or those that are discretionary items can more easily absorb higher shipping and production costs. In this case, exporting is a likely selection.

International Experience

Most companies enter the international marketplace through exporting. As companies gain international experience, they tend to select entry modes that require deeper involvement. But this means businesses must accept greater risk in return for greater control over operations and strategy. Eventually, they may explore the advantages of licensing, franchising, management contracts, and turnkey projects. After businesses become comfortable in a particular market, joint ventures, strategic alliances, and wholly owned subsidiaries become viable options.

This evolutionary path of accepting greater risk and control with experience does not hold for every company. Whereas some firms remain fixed at one point, others skip several entry modes altogether. Advances in technology and transportation are allowing small companies to leapfrog several stages at once. These relationships also vary for each company depending on its product and the characteristics of home and target markets.

> **QUICK STUDY 5**
>
> 1. When selecting a partner for cooperation it is important to remember *what*?
> 2. What factors may discourage an investment entry mode?
> 3. What factors may encourage an investment entry mode?

A Final Word

This chapter explained important factors in selecting entry modes and key aspects in their management. We studied the circumstances under which each entry mode is most appropriate and the advantages and disadvantages that each provides. The choice of which entry mode(s) to use in entering international markets matches a company's international strategy. Some companies will want to use entry modes that give them tight control over international activities because they are pursuing a global strategy. Meanwhile, other companies might not require an entry mode with central control because they are pursuing a multinational strategy. The entry mode must also align well with an organization's structure.

MyLab Management

Go to **www.pearson.com/mylab/management** to complete the problems marked with this icon .

Chapter Summary

LO13.1   Describe how companies use exporting, importing, and countertrade.

- Exporting can be a low-cost, low-risk way for a company to expand sales, diversify sales, or gain international experience.

- A successful export strategy involves (1) identifying a potential market, (2) matching needs to abilities, (3) initiating meetings, and (4) committing resources.
- *Direct exporting* is when a company sells its products directly to buyers in a target market. *Indirect exporting* occurs when a company sells its products to intermediaries who then resell to buyers in a target market.
- *Countertrade* is selling goods or services that are paid for with other goods or services; it can take the form of (1) *barter*, (2) *counterpurchase*, (3) *offset*, (4) *switch trading*, and (5) *buyback*.

LO13.2 Explain the various methods of export/import financing.

- With *advance payment* an importer pays an exporter for merchandise before it is shipped.
- *Documentary collection* calls for a bank to act as an intermediary without accepting financial risk.
- Under a *letter of credit*, the importer's bank issues a letter pledging to pay the exporter when the exporter fulfills the terms listed in the letter.
- Under *open account*, an exporter ships merchandise and later bills the importer for its value.

LO13.3 Describe the different types of contractual entry modes.

- *Licensing* is when a company that owns intangible property (the *licensor*) grants another firm (the *licensee*) the right to use that property for a specified period of time.
- *Franchising* occurs when one company (the *franchiser*) supplies another (the *franchisee*) with intangible property and other assistance over an extended period.
- A *management contract* is when one company supplies another with managerial expertise for a specific period of time. It can transfer two types of knowledge—the specialized knowledge of technical managers and the business-management skills of general managers.
- A *turnkey (build–operate–transfer) project* is when one company designs, constructs, and tests a production facility for a client.

LO13.4 Describe the various kinds of investment entry modes.

- A *wholly owned subsidiary* is entirely owned and controlled by a single company.
- A separate company created and jointly owned by two or more independent entities to achieve a common business objective is called a *joint venture*.
- Joint ventures can involve *forward integration* (investing in downstream activities), *backward integration* (investing in upstream activities), a *buyback joint venture* (input is provided by and output is absorbed by each partner), and a *multistage joint venture* (downstream integration by one partner and upstream integration by another).
- A *strategic alliance* is a relationship in which two or more entities cooperate (but do not form a separate company).

LO13.5 Outline key strategic factors in selecting an entry mode.

- The need for trust and valuable inputs makes careful partner selection crucial to success.
- Managers less confident in their abilities in unfamiliar cultures may avoid investment entry modes in favor of exporting or a contractual mode.
- Political differences and instability can cause companies to favor entry modes that limit investment and protect assets.
- Producing locally is desirable when total production cost in a market is lower than at home and when shipping costs are high.
- Companies tend to first go abroad by exporting and to later select entry modes that require deeper involvement.

Key Terms

advance payment (p. 348)
agents (p. 344)
barter (p. 346)
bill of lading (p. 348)
buyback (p. 347)
counterpurchase (p. 346)
countertrade (p. 346)
cross licensing (p. 351)
direct exporting (p. 344)
documentary collection (p. 348)

draft (bill of exchange) (p. 348)
entry mode (p. 342)
export management company (EMC)
  (p. 344)
export trading company (ETC) (p. 345)
franchising (p. 352)
freight forwarder (p. 346)
indirect exporting (p. 344)
joint venture (p. 356)
letter of credit (p. 349)

licensing (p. 351)
management contract (p. 354)
offset (p. 347)
open account (p. 350)
strategic alliance (p. 358)
switch trading (p. 347)
turnkey (build–operate–transfer)
  project (p. 354)
wholly owned subsidiary (p. 355)

✪ TALK ABOUT IT 1

Not all companies go international by first exporting, then using contracts, and then investing in other markets as they gain international experience.

13-1. How (if at all) do you think a company's product influences the process of going international?

13-2. How (if at all) will technology affect the process of going international? Explain.

✪ TALK ABOUT IT 2

Imagine you overhear two of your colleagues talking and one says to the other, "Companies should use investment entry modes whenever possible because they offer the greatest control over business operations."

13-3. Do you agree or disagree with this statement? Explain.

13-4. Are there times when other market entry modes offer greater control? Explain.

Ethical Challenge

You are the CEO of a company based in Abu Dhabi that imports fresh dates from South Africa to be processed at a site each in the United Arab Emirates, Saudi Arabia, Lebanon, Oman, and Kuwait. The imports are essential to provide sufficient product outside the harvest period in the Middle East. It is a complicated process that involves separating the bulk shipments that arrive at the port of Mina Zayed into consignments for each of the processing plants before they can be transported by bulk container. The decision has been made to process the dates in South Africa, close the processing plants in the Middle East, and ship the dates ready-packed directly to the market. You intend to establish a joint venture with a South African processer.

13-5. Do you think that your two companies can establish a common CSR policy that will guide a joint venture before operations commence?

13-6. What ethical issues might arise in taking the decision to launch a joint venture?

13-7. How would your key target markets in the Middle East react to your decision to move processing from the Middle East to South Africa?

Teaming Up

This project is designed to introduce you to the complexity of presentations and to help develop your presentation skills.

Background: In groups of three or four, choose a type of business, either product- or service-related, that is common in your country. You need to choose one that is not usually associated with franchising. Remember that franchising is all about creating a model business opportunity that can be replicated and run successfully in another geographical area. In many cases, the brand name is very important and part of the attraction of the franchise opportunity. Consider how you would describe the type of business, the advantages of using the brand name and the way of business, and how it might work in another country. Remember that beyond selling a basic package of materials—perhaps products—you are selling an intangible product to potential franchisees. You can choose a manufacturing- or a service-based business to franchise, and you should also be clear about the ongoing support and the kind of payment you would expect from a franchisee.

Activity: Break into teams of three or four persons. Give yourselves an hour to frame the franchise opportunity and to create some visuals to support your presentation. Once you are ready you should then present your franchise opportunity to the rest of the class. What is their reaction to the presentation and opportunity; do they think it would work in an overseas location? Groups should take it in turns to present their franchise choice, and at the end of the presentations, the class should vote to indicate which of the presentations were most effective and would work best.

MyLab Management

⭐ Go to **www.pearson.com/mylab/management** for the following assisted-graded writing questions:

13-8. Governments influence the international flow of trade and foreign direct investment in many varied ways including, for example, by forming regional economic groups. Identify two market entry modes and answer the question: how might each be affected by the actions of governments?

13-9. Consider the rush of western firms into China to launch their franchise systems there because of China's enormous population. If you were planning to launch your company's fast-food franchise in China, what factors might you need to give special consideration? Explain.

Telecom Ventures Unite the World

The world of telecommunications is changing. The era of global e-commerce is here, driven by new technologies such as broadband and wireless Internet access that make possible video telephone connections and high-speed data transmission. Annual worldwide revenues for telecommunications services total $600 billion, with international companies accounting for 20 percent of the business.

Market opportunities are opening around the world as post, telephone, and telegraph (PTT) monopolies are undergoing privatization. Since 1998, telecom deregulation has been taking place in earnest in Europe. Meanwhile, governments in developing countries are boosting investments in infrastructure improvements to increase the number of available telephone lines. The demand for telephone service is growing at a sharp pace; international telephone-call volume more than doubled over a recent six-year period. The net result of these changes is the globalization of the telecommunications industry. As William Donovan, a vice president at Sea-Land Service, said recently, "I don't want to have to talk to a bunch of different PTTs around the world. I don't want to have to go to one carrier in one country and a second in another just because it doesn't have a presence there."

Several alliances and joint venture partnerships formed between companies hoping to capitalize on the changed market and business environment. France Telecom, Deutsche Telekom, and Sprint created Global One to bring international telecommunications services to multinational companies. As part of the deal, Sprint sold 10 percent of its stock to each of its French and German partners. One hurdle for the company was how to integrate the three partners' communication networks into a unified whole. Also, start-up costs were high, and the need to communicate in three different languages created some friction among personnel. Early on, lengthy negotiations were required to reach agreement about the value each partner brought to the venture. A former Global One executive noted, "There is no trust among the partners." Other problems included equipment and billing incompatibilities resulting from distribution agreements with telephone monopolies in individual countries. And then there were the financial losses that prompted Sprint chairman William T. Esrey to install Sprint executive Gary Forsee as CEO and president of Global One.

AT&T also depends on various partnership strategies as entry modes. WorldPartners began as an alliance of AT&T, Kokusai Denshin Denwa (KDD) of Japan, and Telecom of Singapore. The goal was to provide improved telecommunications services for companies conducting business globally. Today, WorldPartners is composed of 10 companies, including Telecom New Zealand, Telestra (Australia), Hong Kong Telecom, and Unisource.

Unisource is itself a joint venture that originally included Sweden's Telia AB, Swiss Telecom PTT, and PTT Telecom Netherlands. Later, Telefonica de España became an equal equity partner in Unisource. Unisource and AT&T then agreed to form a 60–40 joint venture known as AT&T–Unisource Communications to offer voice, data, and messaging services to businesses with European operations. AT&T would have preferred to form a joint venture with the French or German telephone companies. Yet European regulators, concerned about AT&T's strong brand name and enormous size, refused to approve such a deal.

There was strong logic for the deal. AT&T–Unisource CEO James Cosgrove explained from headquarters near Amsterdam in Hoofddorp that to be competitive in Europe a telecom company needs to have a base there and offer global solutions. Despite the fact that there are five corporate parents, a sense of equality and congeniality has developed. CEO Cosgrove explained that after working together for two years, the parent companies realized that their own success is tied to the success of the shared venture. The presence of Telefonica de España in the alliance was especially significant for AT&T because of the Spanish company's strong influence in Latin America. Unfortunately, the alliance was weakened when Telefonica decided to ally itself with Concert Communications. To fill the void, AT&T and Italy's Stet announced a new alliance that would expand communication services to Latin America as well as Europe.

The third major telecommunications alliance, Concert Communications, was formed when British Telecommunications PLC bought a 20-percent stake in MCI Communications. Again, the goal of the alliance was to offer global voice and data network services to global corporations.

Thinking Globally

13-10. What strengths did AT&T bring to its joint venture with Unisource?

13-11. Can you think of any potential complications that could have arisen in the AT&T–Unisource joint venture?

13-12. Assess the formation of Global One, Unisource, and other partnerships in this case. What strategic factors might have influenced the entry mode choices that these firms made?

Sources: Barbara Martinez, "Sprint Names Its Long-distance Chief to Run Loss-Beset Global One Venture," *Wall Street Journal,* February 17, 1998, p. B20; Jennifer L. Schenker and James Pressley, "European Telecom Venture with Sprint Hasn't Become the Bully Some Feared," *Wall Street Journal,* December 23, 1997, p. A11; Alan Cane, "Unisource Partners to Strengthen Ties," *Financial Times,* June 4, 1997, p. 13 Gautam Naik, "Unisource Expected to Merge Operations," *Wall Street Journal,* June 4, 1997, p. B6.

Chapter Fourteen

Developing and Marketing Products

A Look Back

Chapter 13 explained the pros and cons of international entry modes and when each one is most appropriately used. We also described management issues with regard to each entry mode and the important strategic factors in their selection.

A Look at This Chapter

This chapter explores how globalization and differences in national business environments impact the development and marketing of products internationally. We examine the many variables that must be considered when creating product, promotional, distribution, and pricing strategies.

A Look Ahead

Chapter 15 explains how companies launch and manage their international production efforts. Again, an emphasis is placed on how environmental variables affect production strategies.

MyLab Management

✪ IMPROVE YOUR GRADE!

When you see this icon ✪, visit **www.pearson.com/mylab/management** for activities that are applied, personalized, and offer immediate feedback.

Wings for Life

VIENNA, Austria—When Dietrich Mateschitz traveled to Asia on business, he got a taste of some popular energy drinks. Sensing opportunity, he brought a sample of the drinks back to Austria and in 1987 started Red Bull (www.redbull.com). Red Bull Energy Drink is now available in more than 171 countries, and sales are in excess of 6 billion cans of the raging stuff each year.

Red Bull is identical in every market in which it is sold. Each slender red, blue, and silver can contains caffeine, carbohydrates, vitamins, and the amino acid taurine. That is music to the ears of club goers, who swear by the drink's ability to keep them going till dawn. Sales are soaring among this crowd partly due to the word-of-mouth advertising the company gets from loyal customers. Around the world, Red Bull recruits "brand ambassadors," who hand out free samples at events, and hires "student managers," who spread the word about the beverage and drink it on campuses.

Nadezda Murmakova/Shutterstock

Red Bull is also racking up double-digit revenue growth with creative TV ads. The ads display the company's "Red Bull Gives You Wings" tagline as cartoon characters float into the air after downing a can of the sweet drink. Red Bull also sponsors top athletes in racing and sporting events, including snowboarding, hang-gliding, skateboarding, and many kinds of daredevil stunts. Shown here, a Red Bull sponsored pilot performs a stunt at an airshow in Pribram, Czech Republic.

The company does not seem to mind that some people complain about Red Bull's extreme sweetness. A spokesperson says it's not meant to be a taste drink; either you love it or you hate it. Although Denmark, Norway, and Uruguay ban the drink because of its contents, it seems that many other people are happily running with the bull. Red Bull is hugely popular across Asia, particularly in Thailand where Mateschitz first discovered it, and in China, where enormous market potential has led to a dispute over control of the brand there. As you read this chapter, think about the many ways in which products are marketed around the world.[1]

So far throughout this book we have seen that globalization affects industries and products in different ways and to varying degrees. Some companies can take advantage of globalization's effects and create a single product that is marketed identically around the world. As we saw in this chapter's opening company profile, Red Bull markets an identical energy drink in the same manner in more than 171 countries. The products of other firms, however, require physical changes to suit the tastes of consumers abroad. Products of still other companies need different marketing campaigns to reflect the unique circumstances of local markets.

Companies that cannot sell the same product abroad as at home must create new products, modify promotional campaigns, or adjust their marketing strategies in some other way. Yet, how do managers decide when their marketing strategies can remain the same or if they need modification? This dilemma is referred to as the standardization-versus-adaptation decision.

In a well-known article, US researcher Theodore Levitt argued that companies should market the same products in the same way in all countries because the world is becoming standardized and homogeneous.[2] Technology, claimed Levitt, was causing people's needs and preferences to converge throughout the world. He urged companies to reduce production and marketing costs by standardizing both the physical features of their products and their strategies for marketing them. But standardization is just one of a number of strategies with which firms successfully go international and it may not always be the most appropriate strategy. A company may be better off adapting its strategy to the local market.

Consumers in different national markets often demand products that reflect their unique tastes and preferences. Cultural, political, legal, and economic characteristics have a great deal to do with the preferences of both consumers and industrial buyers. Recall from Chapter 2 that a culture's aesthetics involves, among other things, preferences for certain colors. Ohio-based Rubbermaid (www.rubbermaid.com) considers aesthetics when it markets its household goods internationally. The company offers its products in an assortment of materials (from plastics to metal), colors (from white and neutral tones to bright reds and blues), and features (from no lids and open tops to lids that seal tightly) depending, in part, on the market in question.

Certain products do appeal to practically all cultures. Although it is not a traditional Asian drink, red wine is sweeping across Asia. Driving demand are medical studies reporting the health benefits of red wine and the fact that red is considered good luck in many Asian cultures. Many Asians now choose red wine at restaurants because of its image as the beverage of choice for the sophisticated and successful. Today in Beijing, fashionable young people also give red wine as a housewarming present instead of the traditional favorites of their parents and grandparents.

With this brief introduction, let's now take an in-depth look at issues that are relevant to international marketing strategy. In this chapter, we describe how marketing internationally differs in terms of how companies create their product strategies, promote and advertise a product, decide on a pricing strategy, and design distribution channels. Throughout the chapter, we examine how globalization on one hand and national differences on the other influence international marketing activities.

14.1 Developing Product Strategies

14.1 Describe the factors to consider in developing international product strategies.

Marketing activities that span time zones and cultures can test the most seasoned marketing managers. When a company decides to "go international," managers have many options at their disposal when it comes to standardizing or adapting their products. Let's examine some of the factors that influence the standardize-versus-adapt decision as well as several other international product strategy issues.

Laws and Regulations

Companies must often adapt their products to satisfy laws and regulations in a target market. People's tastes also vary across markets, and taste in chocolate is no exception to the rule. A so-called Chocolate War erupted in the European Union (EU) as it tried to standardize member countries' product content regulations. On one side stood the so-called cocoa purists, including Belgium, France, Germany, Spain, Italy, the Netherlands, Luxembourg, and Greece. Opposite stood Britain, Denmark, Portugal, Austria, Finland, and Sweden—nations who permit manufacturers to add vegetable fats to chocolate products. The purists argued not only that European advertising should be restricted to using the word *chocolate* for 100-percent cocoa products but also that the term *milk chocolate* be outlawed altogether. They wanted nonpure products labeled something like "chocolate with milk and noncocoa vegetable fats."

The fact that many developing countries have fewer consumer protection laws creates an ethical issue for some companies. Ironically, lower levels of education and less buying experience mean that consumers in developing countries are more likely to need protection. However, many governments impose fewer regulations in order to hold down production costs and consumer prices. Unfortunately, this can be an invitation for international distributors to withhold full information about products and their potential dangers.

Cultural Differences

Companies also adapt their products to suit local buyers' product preferences, which are rooted in culture. Häagen-Dazs (www.haagendazs.com) is an international company that prides itself on its ability to identify the taste preferences of consumers in target markets. It then modifies its base product with just the right flavor to make a product that satisfies consumers' needs. Following years of trial and error developing secret formulas and conducting taste tests, Häagen-Dazs finally launched its green-tea flavor ice cream throughout Japan. The taste is that of *macha* tea—an elite strain of green tea that has been used in elaborate Japanese ceremonies for centuries. Green-tea ice cream was an instant hit and one day may even surpass Häagen-Dazs' perennial flavor champion in Japan—vanilla.

Not all companies need to modify their product to the culture; instead, they may need to identify a different cultural need that it satisfies. Altoids (www.altoids.com), for example, is a British product that has been used for 200 years to soothe upset stomachs. But the company identified a different use for its product in the United States. Because of its strong flavor, Altoids is sold in the US market as a breath mint and has pushed aside weaker-flavored candies.

Brand and Product Names

Several issues related to a company's brand name are important concerns for the day-to-day activities of international managers. A **brand name** is the name of one or more items in a product line that identifies the source or character of the items. When we see a product labeled with a particular brand name, we assign to that product a certain value based on our past experiences with that brand. That is why a brand name is central to a product's personality and the image that it presents to buyers. It informs buyers about a product's source and protects both customer and producer from copycat products. Brand names help consumers to select, recommend, or reject products. They also function as legal property that owners can protect from trespass by competitors.

brand name
Name of one or more items in a product line that identifies the source or character of the items.

A brand name is central to a product's personality and to how buyers perceive it. The brands of all types of global companies blend into the urban surroundings in almost every nation. Shown here a young man rides a moped for McDonald's delivery service in Guangzhou, China. A strong brand is essential for a global company whether its industry is fast food, delivery services, mobile phones, financial services, or computer software. What are some of the reasons why having a global brand image is so important today?

TonyV3112/Shutterstock

Indeed, a strong brand can become a company's most valuable asset and primary source of competitive advantage. A consistent worldwide brand image is increasingly important as more consumers and businesspeople travel internationally than ever before. An inconsistent brand name can confuse existing and potential customers. Although companies normally keep their brand names consistent across markets, they can create new product names or modify existing ones to suit local preferences.

Companies also need to review the image of their brand from time to time and update it if it seems old-fashioned. One classic example is that of Lipton (www.lipton.com). The company wanted people to think of Lipton tea as an alternative to colas and other soft drinks. Since the 1890s, Lipton had as its mascot Sir Thomas J. Lipton, the tea maker's founder. But in a major overhaul of the brand, all references to Mr. Lipton were removed because he gave the product a dated image—young people thought of Lipton tea as a drink for their parents' generation. To breathe new life into the brand, Lipton booted the founder in favor of "Tom," a sassy young Briton.

SELECTING INTERNATIONAL BRAND AND PRODUCT NAMES Whether they are standardized or adapted locally, products in international markets need carefully selected names. All company and product brand names (like all nouns) are made up of *morphemes*—semantic elements, or language building blocks, such as the *van* in *advantage*. NameLab (www.namelab.com) is an identity-consulting firm that uses more than 6,000 morphemes to develop new product names. NameLab points out that because most Western languages stem from the same linguistic source—Indo-European—companies can create brand names having similar meanings in these nations. *Accu*, for example, connotes *accuracy* in both Western and Japanese cultures. Thus Honda (www.honda.com) named its upscale car division Acura. Other names that are constructed to have similar connotations in many languages or to embody no cultural bias include Compaq (www.compaq.com), Kodak (www.kodak.com), and Sony (www.sony.co.jp).[3] After they choose a name, companies can survey local native speakers about their reactions to it. These techniques help companies reduce the likelihood of committing potential marketing blunders.

Brand names seldom offend people in international markets, but product names can be highly offensive if they are not carefully researched and selected. Clarks Shoes (www.clarks.com), a British shoe company, once gave a name to a line of shoes that was offensive to the Hindu religious community in Britain. Consequently, the company issued a statement in the British press apologizing for naming some of its products with the names of the Hindu Gods Vishnu and Krishna and for offending the British Hindu community. In the future, Clarks Shoes promised to carry out more extensive marketing research before naming its products.

Other times, product names must be changed, not because they are offensive, but because they mislead consumers. Consider the problem faced by the British beverage and chocolate producer Cadbury Schweppes (www.cadburyschweppes.com). When Swiss chocolate manufacturers sued on the grounds that the public was being misled into thinking that Cadbury's Swiss Chalet bar was genuine Swiss chocolate, the company was forced to withdraw the product from the marketplace. A British court confirmed that the name and packaging of the product—the "Swiss" part of the name and the image of a snow-capped Swiss Alp—were likely to mislead consumers.

National Image

The value customers obtain from a product is heavily influenced by the image of the country in which it is designed, manufactured, or assembled. We consider the influence of a country's name when thinking of Italian shoes, German luxury cars, and Japanese electronics. This image can be positive for some products but negative for others. For example, the best Russian caviar and vodkas have reputations of quality around the world. But how do you feel about Russian automobiles or computers? Attaching "Russia" to certain products is beneficial, whereas attaching it to others could be detrimental.

Because it affects buyers' perceptions of quality and reliability, national image is an important element of product policy. Yet, national image can and does change slowly over long periods of time. Decades ago, Japanese products were considered to be of poor quality and rather unreliable. A national effort toward quality improvement and the installation of quality-control procedures by companies has earned Japan a national image for precision and quality products. Once vehicles for budget-conscious consumers, Japanese cars now include some of the finest-built luxury automobiles in the world.

Likewise, years ago Taiwan was known for basic, no-frills items such as toys and industrial products of all sorts. But today, many of Taiwan's industries possess a reputation for innovation—designing products that reflect decades of investing in people's research and engineering skills. One company that benefited from an intense devotion to research and development (R&D) is Taiwanese bicycle manufacturer Giant (www.giant-bicycles.com). The company began in Taichung, Taiwan, nearly three decades ago producing bikes under the brand names of other companies. But when the company began to manufacture under its own brand name, it carved itself a solid niche in the mountain bike market. Giant's innovation in using lightweight materials and creating groundbreaking designs even earned it sponsorship of Spain's world-champion racing team. Today, high-tech products—and even those not traditionally thought of as high tech (such as bikes)—stamped "Made in Taiwan" command respect in global markets.

> ✪ **MyLab Management** Watch It Marketing a Movie Globally
>
> Apply what you have learned so far about adapting products for international markets. If your instructor has assigned this, go to **www.pearson.com/mylab/management** to watch a video case about how and why the US-movie industry adapts films for other markets and answer questions.

Counterfeit Goods and Black Markets

In Chapter 3 we discussed how companies are trying to protect their intellectual property and trademarks from counterfeit goods. Recall that *counterfeit goods* are imitation products passed off as legitimate trademarks, patents, or copyrighted works—products that normally enjoy legal protection. Because developing nations often are weakest in enforcing such legal protections, they normally have the most active counterfeiting markets. Countries that top the list for the portion of their markets comprised of counterfeits include China, India, Russia, Thailand, and Turkey.

Counterfeiting is common among highly visible brand-name consumer goods, including watches, perfumes, clothing, movies, music, and computer software. Counterfeit products are typically sold to consumers on what is called the black market—a marketplace of underground transactions that typically appears because a product is either illegal (such as counterfeits) or tightly regulated. Tabletop vendors working the back streets of the world's largest cities represent the retail side of the black market. For example, in Sofia, the capital of Bulgaria, you can buy one CD-ROM that contains 50 software applications for $10; buying all the official versions of these products would cost about $5,000. In Estonia's Kadaka flea market, you can find the full Microsoft Office (www.microsoft.com) software bundle for around $18—about one-fiftieth of its official selling price. Increasingly, engineered industrial components such as aircraft parts, medicines, and other pharmaceutical products are also becoming targets of counterfeiters.

Counterfeit goods can damage buyers' image of a brand when the counterfeits are of inferior quality—which is nearly always the case. Buyers who purchase an item bearing a company's brand name expect a certain level of craftsmanship and, therefore, satisfaction. But when the product fails to deliver on the expectations, the buyers are dissatisfied, and the company's reputation is tarnished. Japanese motorcycle manufacturers recently saw their sales in China fall sharply, because people were buying near-replicas of their products at discounts of up to 40 percent of the originals. But the counterfeiting problem is more serious today because the Chinese producers are now exporting their cycles to other Asian nations. Yamaha (www.yamaha-motor.com), Japan's second-largest motorcycle producer, is considering legal action against one Chinese company. Yamaha officials say that the Chinese company's products resemble its own models right down to the Yamaha name stamped on the side.

Shortened Product Life Cycles

Companies traditionally managed to extend a product's life by introducing it into different markets consecutively. They did this by introducing products in industrialized countries and only later marketing them in developing and emerging markets. Thus, while a product's sales are declining in one market, they might be growing in another.

Advances in telecommunications, however, have alerted consumers around the world to the latest product introductions. Consequently, consumers in developing and emerging markets also demand the latest products and are not happy with receiving what is yesterday's fad in the highly developed nations. Also, the rapid pace with which technological innovation occurs today is shortening the life cycles of products. The actions of international companies themselves actually helped to create this situation. Companies are undertaking new-product development at an increasingly rapid pace and are thus shortening the life cycles of their products.

> ### QUICK STUDY 1
>
> 1. Deciding whether to keep a marketing strategy the same or to modify it abroad is also known as the *what*?
> 2. What factors influence a company's international product strategy?
> 3. What product characteristic is more likely than others to offend people in another culture?

14.2 Creating Promotional Strategies

14.2 Outline the international promotional strategies and methods available to firms.

promotion mix
Efforts by a company to reach distribution channels and to target customers through communications, such as personal selling, advertising, public relations, and direct marketing.

pull strategy
Promotional strategy designed to create buyer demand that will encourage distribution channel members to stock a company's product.

push strategy
Promotional strategy designed to pressure distribution channel members to carry a product and to promote it to final users of the product.

Promotion mix comprises a company's efforts to reach distribution channels and target customers through communications, such as personal selling, advertising, public relations, and direct marketing. Not surprisingly, promotional activities often receive the greatest attention among marketers because many people, even professionals, tend to equate *marketing* with *promotion*. After we examine two general promotional strategies, we discuss the complications that can arise in international advertising and communications.

Push and Pull Strategies

There are two general promotional strategies that companies can use to get their marketing message across to buyers. Companies can rely completely on just one of these strategies or use them in combination. A promotional strategy designed to create buyer demand that will encourage distribution channel members to stock a company's product is called a **pull strategy**. In other words, buyer demand is generated in order to "pull" products through distribution channels to end users. Creating consumer demand through direct marketing techniques is a common example of a pull strategy. For example, when Procter & Gamble (www.pg.com) encountered distribution difficulties when trying to introduce Rejoice hair-care products into Asia, the company opted to generate grassroots consumer demand. The company hired a fleet of trucks to drive through village squares and hand out free trial packages to potential end users.

By contrast, a **push strategy** is a promotional strategy designed to pressure distribution channel members to carry a product and promote it to final users. Manufacturers of products commonly sold through department and grocery stores often use a push strategy. For example, manufacturer's sales representatives are constantly calling on Walmart (www.walmart.com) to encourage it to stock the manufacturer's product and give it good visibility. Push strategies are also used for office products, including computers and office furniture. A company's international sales force is the key to successfully implementing a push strategy abroad. For insights into how companies can better manage their salespeople in other cultures, see the Manager's Briefcase, titled "Managing an International Sales Force."

Whether the push or pull strategy is most appropriate in a given marketing environment depends on several factors:

- *Distribution System* Implementing a push strategy can be difficult when distribution channel members (such as distributors) wield a great deal of power relative to that of producers. It can also be ineffective when distribution channels are lengthy: The more levels of intermediaries that there are, the more distribution channel members there are who must be convinced to carry a product. In such cases, it might be easier to create buyer demand using a pull strategy than to persuade distributors to stock a particular product.
- *Access to Mass Media* Developing and emerging markets typically have fewer available forms of mass media for use in implementing a pull strategy. Accordingly, it is difficult to increase consumer awareness of a product and to generate product demand. Many

MANAGER'S BRIEFCASE | Managing an International Sales Force

Today, companies reap a greater portion of their revenues from international sales. How can you become a better global manager of your company's international sales force? Here are some helpful hints on improving the effectiveness of your company's representatives abroad:

- **Know the Sales Scene** Your company should conduct research before hiring and managing an international sales force, then should formulate a targeted sales strategy and empower your sales force to meet their performance targets. The amount of compensation, as well as the way in which it is delivered, varies from country to country. For example, in the United States a greater portion of salary is based on commission than it is in Europe. Know the salary structure and incentive plans of salespeople with similar jobs at local companies.

- **Research the Customer** Do not assume that customers abroad have the same needs and preferences as customers at home. Investigate what potential buyers want and how much they are willing to pay. When ECA International (a market information provider) tried to expand into Asia, it was unsuccessful time and again. The company learned through its sales force that potential customers wanted to buy research piece by piece rather than buy a membership in the company. ECA was able to sell its memberships in Asia after it adapted its methods to suit local buyers.

- **Work with the Culture** John Wada, sales and marketing director for cross-cultural management company IOR, explained that motivating salespeople means setting attainable goals within the context of the local culture. Your company should seek answers to a host of questions: Do people in the local culture feel differently about work teams and competition than your sales force at home? How about schedules and deadlines? Are you moving into a culture where "time is of the essence" or one where time is less important? Your company and its local sales force must understand what is expected of one another.

- **Learn from Your Representatives** If your salespeople believe they are pushing products that bear no relationship to the local market, their performance will suffer. "I'd do a great job," so the story goes, "but the product just won't sell here." Salespeople may begin focusing on critiquing products rather than selling them. Involve your sales reps in the R&D process so that they have a better sense of what is going on with the product. Perhaps bring your sales force to the home office to learn about your business so they understand their vital link in your company's chain of business activities. Finally, top managers should visit the local office to better comprehend the needs of local customers.

Sources: Based on Charlene Marmer Solomon, "Managing an Overseas Sales Force," *World Trade*, Global Sales and Technology Special Section, pp. S4–S6.

---

consumers in these markets cannot afford cable or satellite TV, or perhaps even glossy magazines. In such cases, advertisers might turn to billboards and radio. At other times, gaining wide exposure can be difficult because existing media have only local, as opposed to national, reach. For example, Indonesia did not launch its first nationwide TV station until 1994. Yet in other situations, advertising certain products on certain media is unlawful. For example, companies that enter Canada or the United States cannot use TV or radio to advertise tobacco products.

- *Type of Product* A pull strategy is most appropriate when buyers display a great deal of brand loyalty toward one particular brand name. In other words, brand-loyal buyers know what brand of a product they want before they go shopping. On the other hand, push strategies tend to be appropriate for inexpensive consumer goods characterized by buyers who are not brand loyal. Low brand loyalty means that a buyer will go shopping for a product not knowing which brand is best, and simply will buy one of those carried by the retailer or wholesaler. A push strategy is also suited to industrial products because potential buyers usually need to be informed about a product's special features and benefits.

International Advertising

International advertising differs a great deal from advertising in domestic markets. Managers must rely on their knowledge of a market to decide whether an ad is suitable for the company's international promotional efforts. Cultural similarities can mean that ads need only slight modification for different nations, whereas cultural differences may mean that entirely new ads must be created.

Coca-Cola's (www.cocacola.com) classic experience in creating an ad to appeal to the people of China illustrates the problems that can arise when developing specialized ads. Coca-Cola's desire to create a Coke ad that looked authentically Chinese drew a commercial crew to Harbin, a city in northeast China. But during the journey to Harbin the bus carrying the crew that was filming the commercial stalled. When the driver lit a fire under the gas tank to thaw the fuel, the horrified crew scrambled off the bus, thinking it might explode. The crew stood in biting, sub-zero temperatures until the bus was once again running—the director's frostbitten nose bears the scars of the adventure. Then, when a local older man hired to be in the ad had trouble following the director's instructions, local villagers pointed out why—he was deaf. Finally, the crew had to trudge around in knee-deep snow first to get a field of frozen red pinwheels to spin and then to reorient the whole set so that the wind (which was blowing in an unfavorable direction) could spin the pinwheels. But it appears that Coke's efforts at creating an ad depicting people celebrating Chinese New Year in the traditional manner in a picturesque village paid off, as local viewers said the ad touched them emotionally. The localized ads exemplify Coke's "think local, act local" mantra, which was pioneered by Chairman Douglas Daft as part of an effort to remake Coke into the nimble marketer it once was.[4]

Let's now explore some of the factors involved in the decision of whether to standardize or adapt advertisements.

STANDARDIZING OR ADAPTING ADVERTISEMENTS The vast majority of advertising that occurs in any one nation is produced solely for that domestic audience. But companies that advertise in multiple markets must determine the aspects of the advertising campaign that can be standardized across markets and those that cannot. Companies that do market their products across national boundaries try to contain costs by standardizing as many aspects of their campaigns as possible. However, companies seldom standardize all aspects of their international promotions for a variety of reasons, including differences in culture and laws.

Firms that standardize advertising often control campaigns from the home office. This policy helps them to project consistent brand images and promotional messages across all markets—the aim of a global strategy (see Chapter 11). Companies can achieve consistency by standardizing their basic promotional message, creative concepts, graphics, and information content. After a company decides to pursue a global marketing strategy, it naturally tries to get the most for its advertising expenditure.

One way companies can reach a global audience is to sponsor global sporting events, such as the Olympics, World Cup Soccer, and Formula One automobile racing. These types of events receive heavy media coverage and are often telecast simultaneously in multiple nations. Even posting banners around the venues of such events can boost recognition of a company's brand name by exposing it to perhaps millions of viewers around the world. Viewers in 102 countries see the banners of companies that sponsor Formula One automobile racing.

CASE: THE ELUSIVE EURO-CONSUMER The continuing integration of nations belonging to the European Union is causing many marketers to dream of a day when they can standardize

Players compete for the ball during the World Cup Final game between Argentina and Germany in Rio de Janeiro, Brazil. The global broadcast of the World Cup every four years offers companies a chance to put their messages before an audience totaling 30 billion cumulative viewings. The brands of global companies are plastered on signs around the perimeters of playing fields and are seen worldwide during matches. Advertising by each individual sporting goods company can total hundreds of millions of dollars during the World Cup.

Jefferson Bernardes/Shutterstock

their advertising to appeal to a so-called Euro-consumer. But the Euro-consumer remains a rare, mythical creature that eludes even the world's most clever advertisers.

Some well-known international advertising agencies have tried a pan-European advertising approach only to fail because of national differences. Consider the experience of the acclaimed Leo Burnett Company (www.leoburnett.com) when it took on the goal of creating a single European campaign for United Distillers' Johnnie Walker (www.johnniewalker.com) whiskey. It took many painful tests and revisions before the ad could be rolled out. In the original ad, the tag line read "The Water of Life" and showed a man attending "the running of the bulls" in Pamplona, Spain. After narrowly escaping being trampled by the bull, the man celebrates with a glass of Johnnie Walker Red Label. But in many countries, the Pamplona setting raised hackles because people said, "The Spanish don't know anything about making good whiskey." Tests of the ad in Germany showed it would not work because to Germans it seemed simply reckless—not a widely admired trait there. Jenny Vaughn, worldwide brand director for Johnnie Walker, explained that in Germany a bull run was out of the question because a goldfish can't even be shown in a fish bowl on German television. The tagline "Water of Life" was baffling or sent the wrong message in many languages so the line was changed to "Taste Life." Then a voice-over in the ad was incorrectly translated in one language as "when your life flashes in front of you, make sure it's worth watching." In every market, either the words didn't make sense or the meaning was lost. In Italy, the line was totally discarded. In Germany, attempts at translation proved so maddening that the line was replaced with "Live every day as if it were your last."

Europe's many languages certainly create thorny translation issues for marketers. Thus, the most successful pan-European ads are those that contain a great deal of visuals, have few written or spoken words, and focus on the product and consumer. One such ad is that for TAG Heuer (www.tagheuer.com) watches, which positions the company's product as competitive and a winner. In the ad, a swimmer is shown racing a shark and a hurdler is shown leaping an oversize razor blade. The highly visual ad gets across the company's message that it is a winner.

Blending Product and Promotional Strategies

When companies extend their marketing efforts internationally, they develop communication strategies that blend product and promotional strategies.[5] A company's communication strategy for a particular market takes into account the nature of the product being marketed and the promotion mix to market it. After we discuss the marketing communication process, we examine five product/promotional methods companies use and the appropriate situation for each.

COMMUNICATING PROMOTIONAL MESSAGES The process of sending promotional messages about products to target markets is called **marketing communication**. Communicating the benefits of a product can be more difficult in international business than in domestic business for several reasons. Marketing internationally usually means translating promotional messages from one language into another. Marketers must be knowledgeable of the many cultural nuances that can affect how buyers interpret a promotional message. A nation's laws that govern the promotion of products in another country can also force changes in marketing communication.

Marketing communication is typically considered a circular process, as shown in Figure 14.1. The company with an idea it wishes to communicate is the source of the communication. The idea is *encoded* (translated into images, words, and symbols) into a *promotional message* that the company is trying to get across. The promotional message is then sent to the *audience* (potential buyers) through various *media*. Media commonly used by companies to communicate their promotional messages include radio, TV, newspapers, magazines, billboards, and direct mailings. After the audience receives the message, they decode the message and interpret its meaning. Information in the form of *feedback* (purchase or nonpurchase) then flows back to the source of the message. The decoding process by the audience can be disrupted by the presence of *noise*—anything that disrupts the audience's ability to receive and interpret the promotional message. By ignoring important cultural nuances, companies can inadvertently increase the potential for noise that can cloud the audience's understanding of their promotional message. For example, language barriers between the company and potential buyers can create noise if a company's promotional message is translated incorrectly into the local language.

marketing communication
Process of sending promotional messages about products to target markets.

Figure 14.1

**Marketing
Communication Process**

Source: Based on Courtland L. Bovee, John
V. Thill, George P. Dovel, and Marian Burk
Wood, *Advertising Excellence* (New York,
NY: McGraw-Hill, 1995), p. 14.

PRODUCT/COMMUNICATIONS EXTENSION (DUAL EXTENSION) This method extends the same home-market product and marketing promotion into target markets. Under certain conditions, it can be the simplest and most profitable strategy. For example, because of a common language and other cultural similarities, companies based in English-speaking Canadian provinces can sell the same product with packaging and advertising in the US market—provided the product is not required by the US government to carry any special statements or warnings. The Canadian companies contain costs by developing a single product and one promotional campaign for both markets. Yet it is important for Canadian companies not to ignore any subtle cultural differences that could cause confusion in interpreting the promotional message.

As the information age continues to knit the world more tightly together, this dual extension method will probably grow more popular. Today, consumers in seemingly remote parts of the world are rapidly becoming aware of the latest worldwide fads and fashions. But this strategy appears to be better suited for certain groups of buyers, including brand-conscious teenagers, business executives, and wealthy individuals. The strategy also tends to be better suited for companies that use a global strategy with their products, such as upscale personal items with global brand names—examples include Rolex (www.rolex.com) watches, Hermes (www.hermes.com) scarves and ties, and Chanel (www.chanel.com) perfumes. It can also be appropriate for global brands that have mass appeal and that cut across all age groups and social classes—such as Canon (www.canon.com), Mars (www.mars.com), and Samsung (www.samsung.com). The strategy also is useful to companies that are the low-cost leaders in their industries: One product and one promotional message keep costs down.

PRODUCT EXTENSION/COMMUNICATIONS ADAPTATION Under this method, a company extends the same product into target markets but alters its promotion. Communications require adaptation because the product satisfies a different need, serves a different function, or appeals to a different type of buyer. Companies can adjust their marketing communication to inform potential buyers that the product either satisfies their needs or serves a distinct function. This approach helps companies contain costs because the good itself requires no alteration. Altering communications can be expensive, however, especially when cultural differences among target markets are significant. Filming altered ads with local actors and on location can add significantly to promotional costs.

One company that changes its promotional message for international markets is the Japanese retailer Muji (www.muji.net). Muji offers a wide variety of goods, including writing materials, clothing, and home furnishings inspired by a central theme rooted in centuries of Japanese culture—the simplicity of everyday life. Muji's philosophy is one of selling unbranded quality goods, and reflects the company's goal of producing functional Japanese minimalist products for the masses. Its target market in Japan is the average school-aged child and young adult. But Muji's European stores use a different promotional message. Muji's European customers tend to be older and see themselves as sophisticated and stylish buyers of the company's products. In

Europe, Muji's promotional message focuses on the respectability of its brand name—clearly different from its message in Japan. Also, the company's European customers are not simply buying a product (as do its Japanese customers); they are buying into the traditional Japanese concept of simplicity.[6]

Low economic development can require that communications be adapted to suit local conditions. In developing countries (such as rural parts of India and China), TV and radio coverage are limited, and development of the Web is years behind that of developed nations. Marketers in those countries must use alternative techniques, including door-to-door personal selling and regional product shows or fairs.

On the other hand, companies in Europe and North America and certain Asian countries can rely on a modern telecommunications system to reach millions of consumers through TV, radio, and the World Wide Web. In these markets, it is common for companies to adapt their websites to each national market. To read about how a business can tailor a website to suit local culture, see this chapter's Culture Matters feature, titled "Localizing Websites."

PRODUCT ADAPTATION/COMMUNICATIONS EXTENSION Using this method, a company adapts its product to the requirements of the international market while retaining the product's original marketing communication. There are many reasons why companies need to adapt their products. One might be to meet legal requirements in the local market. Moreover, governments can require that firms use a certain amount of local materials, labor, or some other resource in their local production process. If the exact same materials or components are not available locally, the result can be a modified product.

This method can be costly because appropriately modifying a product to suit the needs of local buyers often means the company must invest in production facilities in the local market. If each national market requires its own production facility, cost savings provided by economies of scale in production can be elusive. Still, a company can implement this strategy successfully if it sells a differentiated product for which it can charge a higher price to offset the greater production costs.

PRODUCT/COMMUNICATIONS ADAPTATION (DUAL ADAPTATION) This method adapts both the product and its marketing communication to suit the target market. The product itself is adapted to match the needs or preferences of local buyers. The promotional message is adapted to explain how the product meets those needs and preferences. Because both production and marketing efforts must be altered, this strategy can be expensive; therefore, it is not very common. It can be implemented successfully, however, if a sufficiently large and profitable market segment exists.

CULTURE MATTERS | Localizing Websites

When going global with an Internet presence, the best strategy may be to localize as much as possible. Online customers often want an experience that corresponds to their cultural context offline. Here are a few tips for perfecting an online presence:

- **Choosing Colors.** A black-and-white website is fine for many countries, but in Asia visitors may think you are inviting them to a funeral. In Japan and across Europe, websites in pastel color schemes often work best.
- **Selecting Numbers.** Many Chinese-speaking cultures consider the number *4* unlucky, although *8* and *9* symbolize prosperity. Be careful that your web address and phone numbers do not send the wrong signal.
- **Watching the Clock.** If marketing to countries that use the 24-hour clock, adjust times stated on the site so it reads, "Call between 9:00 and 17:00," instead of "Call between 9 a.m. and 5 p.m."

- **Avoiding Slang.** English in Britain is different from that in the United States, Spanish in Spain is different from that in Mexico, and French in France is different from that in Quebec. Avoid slang to lessen the potential negative impact of such differences.
- **Waving the Flag.** Using national flags as symbols for buttons that access different language versions of your site should be done carefully. Mexican visitors to your site may be put off by a Spanish flag to signify the site's Spanish-language version, for example.
- **Doing the Math.** Provide conversions into local currencies for buyer convenience. For online ordering, be sure your site calculates any shipping costs, tax rates, tariffs, and so on. Also allow enough blanks on the order form to accommodate longer international addresses.
- **Getting Feedback.** Finally, talk with customers to learn what they want to accomplish on your website. Then, thoroughly test the site to ensure that it functions properly.

PRODUCT INVENTION This method requires that an entirely new product be developed for the target market. Product invention is often necessary when many important differences exist between the home and target markets. One reason for product invention is that local buyers cannot afford a company's current product because of low purchasing power. For example, Honda (www.honda.com) developed a car called the City for budget-conscious buyers in Southeast Asia and Europe.

Product inventions can also arise because of a lack of adequate infrastructure needed to operate certain products. One day, London inventor Trevor Baylis was watching a TV documentary on the difficulty of educating Africans about AIDS because much of the continent did not have the electricity infrastructure or batteries to operate radios. Baylis set to work and developed the Freeplay windup radio—30 seconds of cranking keeps it going for 40 minutes. Baylis and several South African businessmen then formed a company called Bay-Gen Power Corporation in Cape Town, South Africa. The radio was first sold only to relief agencies working in developing nations. But due mostly to word of mouth, it has become popular worldwide among hikers, environmentalists, and even hip shoppers looking for eco-friendly appliances.

QUICK STUDY 2

1. A strategy that pressures channel members to carry and promote a product is called a *what*?
2. Firms that standardize international advertising often control campaigns from *where*?
3. The process of sending promotional messages about products to target markets is called *what*?

14.3 Designing Distribution Strategies

14.3 Explain the factors to consider when designing international distribution strategies.

Planning, implementing, and controlling the physical flow of a product from its point of origin to its point of consumption is called **distribution**. The physical path that a product follows on its way to customers is called a *distribution channel*. Companies along this channel that work together in delivering products to customers are called *channel members* or *intermediaries*. Bear in mind that manufacturers of goods are not the only producers who need distribution channels. Service providers, such as consulting companies, health-care organizations, and news services, also need distribution (or delivery) systems to reach their customers. In the business of delivering news services over the World Wide Web, channel members involved in getting news from the newsroom to the reader can include, among others, Internet service providers and search engine suppliers.

Companies develop their international distribution strategies based on two related decisions: (1) how to get goods *into* a country and (2) how to distribute goods *within* a country. We presented the different ways companies get their products into countries in Chapter 13. Here we focus on distribution strategies within countries.

distribution
Planning, implementing, and controlling the physical flow of a product from its point of origin to its point of consumption.

Designing Distribution Channels

Managers consider two overriding concerns when establishing channels of distribution: (1) the amount of *market exposure* a product needs and (2) the *cost* of distributing a product. Let's look at each of these concerns.

DEGREE OF EXPOSURE In promoting its product to the greatest number of potential customers, a marketer must determine the amount of exposure needed. An **exclusive channel** is one in which a manufacturer grants the right to sell its product to only one or a limited number of resellers. An exclusive channel gives producers a great deal of control over the sale of their product by wholesalers and retailers. It also helps a producer to constrain distributors from selling competing brands. In this way, an exclusive channel creates a barrier that makes it difficult or impossible for outsiders to penetrate the channel. For example, in most countries new-car dealerships reflect exclusive distribution—normally, Mitsubishi dealerships cannot sell Toyotas, and General Motors dealers cannot sell Fords.

exclusive channel
Distribution channel in which a manufacturer grants the right to sell its product to only one or a limited number of resellers.

When a producer wants its product to be made available through as many distribution outlets as possible, it prefers to use an **intensive channel**—one in which a producer grants the right to sell its product to many resellers. An intensive channel provides buyers with location convenience

intensive channel
Distribution channel in which a producer grants the right to sell its product to many resellers.

because of the large number of outlets through which a product is sold. It does not create strong barriers to channel entry for other producers, however. Nor does it provide much control over reseller decisions, such as what competing brands to sell.

Large companies whose products are sold through grocery stores and department stores typically take an intensive channel approach to distribution. The obstacle for small companies that choose an intensive channel approach is gaining shelf space—especially companies with lesser-known brands. The increasing global trend toward retailers developing their own *private-label brands* (brands created by retailers themselves) exacerbates this problem. In such cases, retailers tend to give their own brands prime shelf space and give lesser-known brands poorer shelf locations that are up high or near the floor.

CHANNEL LENGTH AND COST *Channel length* refers to the number of intermediaries between the producer and the buyer. In a *zero-level channel*—which is also called direct marketing—producers sell directly to final buyers. A *one-level channel* places only one intermediary between the producer and the buyer. Two intermediaries make up a *two-level channel*, and so forth. In general, the greater the number of intermediaries in a channel, the more costly it becomes. This happens because each additional member adds a charge for its services onto the product's total cost. This is an important consideration for companies that sell price-sensitive consumer products, such as candy, food, and small household items, which usually compete on the basis of price. As we saw in Chapter 11, companies that sell highly differentiated products can charge higher prices because of their products' distinctiveness; therefore, they have fewer problems using a channel of several levels.

Influence of Product Characteristics

The value of a product relative to its weight and volume is called its **value density**. Value density is an important variable in formulating distribution strategies. As a rule, *the lower a product's value density, the more localized the distribution system*. Most commodities, including cement, iron ore, and crude oil, have low value-density ratios—they're heavy but not particularly "valuable" if gauged in, say, shipping weight per cubic meter. Relative to their values, the cost of transporting these goods is high. Consequently, such products are processed or integrated into the manufacturing process at points close to their original locations. Products with high value-density ratios include emeralds, semiconductors, and premium perfumes. Because the cost of transporting these products is small relative to their value, they can be processed or manufactured in the optimal location and then shipped to market. Because Johnson & Johnson's (www.jnj.com) Vistakon contact lenses have high value density, the company produces and inventories its products in one US location and serves the world market from there.

value density
Value of a product relative to its weight and volume.

When products need to be modified for local markets, companies can design their distribution systems accordingly. Caterpillar (www.cat.com) redesigned its distribution system so that it doubles as the final component in the company's production system. Each national market carries a range of optional product components for Caterpillar's lift trucks. The company ships partially completed lift trucks, along with optional parts, to distribution warehouses in each target market. After a buyer decides what options it desires, final assembly takes place. Caterpillar's distribution warehouses now extend the company's assembly line—allowing the company to maintain or improve service at little cost.

Special Distribution Problems

A nation's distribution system develops over time and reflects its unique cultural, political, legal, and economic traditions. Although each nation's distribution system has its own unique pros and cons, it is the negative aspects of distribution that pose the greatest threat to the business activities of international companies. In some countries, risks arise mostly from the potential for theft and property damage. In others, it is simply the lack of understanding that creates uncertainty and risk. Let's look at two special problems that can affect a company's international distribution activities.

LACK OF MARKET UNDERSTANDING Companies can experience a great deal of frustration and financial loss simply by not fully understanding the local market in which they operate. In one now-classic case, Amway Asia Pacific Ltd., the Asian arm of US-based Amway (www .amway.com), learned the hard way about the pitfalls of overestimating the knowledge of distributors in emerging markets. The company has a worldwide policy of giving distributors a full refund on its soaps and cosmetics if the distributor's customers are dissatisfied—even if the returned containers are empty. But the policy had some bizarre results shortly after Amway entered China. Word of the guarantee spread quickly. Some distributors repackaged the products in other containers, sold them, and took the original containers back to Amway for a refund. Others scoured garbage bins, gathering bags full of discarded bottles. In Shanghai, returns were beginning to total $100,000 a day. Amway's Shanghai chief Percy Chin admitted that the firm's policy was, perhaps, too lax. Amway soon changed its refund policy to allow a refund only for bottles at least half full.[7]

THEFT AND CORRUPTION   A high incidence of theft and corruption can present obstacles to distribution. The distribution system in Russia reflects its roughly 75-year experiment with communism. When Acer Computers (www.acer.com) decided to sell its computers in Russia, it built production facilities in Russia's stable neighbor, Finland, because the company was leery of investing directly in Russia. Acer also considered it too risky to navigate Russia's archaic distribution system on its own. In three years' time, a highway that serves as a main route to get goods overland from Finland to Russia saw 50 Finnish truckers hijacked, two drivers killed, and another two go missing. Acer solved its distribution problem by selling its computers to Russian distributors outside its factory in Finland. The Russian distributors, who understood how to negotiate their way through Russia's distribution system, would then deal with any distribution problems in Russia.[8]

> **QUICK STUDY 3**
>
> 1. What type of channel grants the right to sell a product to many resellers?
> 2. In terms of channel length, direct marketing is also known as a *what*?
> 3. A product with a low value density tends to have a distribution system that is more *what*?

14.4 Developing Pricing Strategies

14.4 Describe the two main international pricing strategies and factors to consider.

The pricing strategy that a company adopts must match its overall international strategy. The product of a company that is the low-cost leader in its industry usually cannot be sold at a premium price because it likely has few special features and stresses functionality rather than uniqueness. On the other hand, a company that follows a differentiation strategy usually can charge a premium price for its product because buyers value the product's uniqueness. Let's now examine two pricing policies (*worldwide pricing* and *dual pricing*) that companies use in international markets and then explore the important factors that influence managers' pricing decisions.

Worldwide Pricing

worldwide pricing
Policy in which one selling price is established for all international markets.

A pricing policy in which one selling price is established for all international markets is called **worldwide pricing**. In practice, a worldwide pricing policy is very difficult to achieve. First, production costs differ from one nation to another. Keeping production costs the same is not possible for a company that has production bases within each market it serves. As a result, selling prices often reflect these different costs of production.

Second, a company that produces in just one location (to maintain an equivalent cost of production for every product) cannot guarantee that selling prices will be the same in every target market. The cost of exporting to certain markets will likely be higher than the cost of exporting to other markets. In addition, distribution costs differ across markets. Where distribution is efficient, selling prices might well be lower than in locations where distribution systems are archaic and inefficient.

Third, the purchasing power of local buyers must be taken into account. Managers might decide to lower the sales price in a market so that buyers can afford the product and the company can gain market share.

Finally, fluctuating currency values also must be taken into account. When the value of the currency in a country where production takes place rises against a target market's currency, the product will become more expensive in the target market.

Dual Pricing

Because of the problems associated with worldwide pricing, another pricing policy is often used in international markets. A pricing policy in which a product has a different selling price in export markets than it has in the home market is called **dual pricing**. When a product has a higher selling price in the target market than it does in the home market (or the country where production takes place), it is called *price escalation*. It is commonly the result of the reasons just discussed—exporting costs and currency fluctuations.

But sometimes a product's export price is lower than the price in the home market. Under what circumstances does this occur? Some companies determine that domestic market sales are intended to cover all product costs (such as expenses related to R&D, administration, and overhead). They then require exports to cover only the *additional* costs associated with exporting and selling in a target market (such as tariffs). In this sense, exports are considered a sort of "bonus."

To apply dual pricing successfully in international marketing, a company must be able to keep its domestic buyers and international buyers separate. Buyers in one market might cancel orders if they discover that they are paying a higher price than are buyers in another market. If a company cannot keep its buyers separate when using dual pricing, buyers could potentially undermine the policy through *arbitrage*—buying products where they are sold at lower prices and reselling them where they command higher prices. As is often the case, however, the higher selling price of a product in an export market often reflects the additional costs of transportation to the local market and any trade barriers of the target market, such as tariffs. For arbitrageurs to be successful, the profits they earn must be enough to outweigh these additional costs.

dual pricing
Policy in which a product has a different selling price (typically higher) in export markets than it has in the home market.

Factors That Affect Pricing Decisions

Many factors have an important influence on managers' pricing decisions. We devote the following discussion to four of the most important—transfer prices, arm's length pricing, price controls, and dumping.

TRANSFER PRICES Prices charged for goods or services transferred among a company and its subsidiaries are called **transfer prices**. It is common for parent companies and their subsidiaries to buy from one another. For example, the parent company often licenses technologies to its subsidiaries in return for royalties or licensing fees. Subsidiaries prefer this route to buying on the open market because they typically receive lower prices. Parent companies then buy finished products from subsidiaries at the stated transfer price.

transfer price
Price charged for a good or service transferred among a company and its subsidiaries.

At one time, companies enjoyed a great deal of freedom in setting their transfer prices. Subsidiaries in countries with high corporate tax rates would reduce their tax burdens by charging a low price for their output to other subsidiaries. The subsidiary lowered the taxes that the parent company must pay by reducing its profits in the high-tax country. Likewise, subsidiaries in countries with low tax rates would charge relatively high prices for their output.

Transfer prices followed a similar pattern based on the tariffs of different nations. Subsidiaries in countries that charged relatively high tariffs were charged lower prices to lower the cost of the goods in the local market. This pattern of transfer prices helped large corporations with many subsidiaries to manage their global tax burden better and to become more price-competitive in certain markets.

ARM'S LENGTH PRICING Increased regulation of transfer-pricing practices today is causing reduced freedom in manipulating transfer prices. Many governments now regulate internal company pricing practices by assigning products approximate transfer prices based on their free-market price. Therefore, most international transfers between subsidiaries now occur at a so-called **arm's length price**—the free-market price that unrelated parties charge one another for a specific product.

arm's length price
Free-market price that unrelated parties charge one another for a specific product.

Another factor that is increasing the use of arm's length pricing is pressure on companies to be good corporate citizens in each of their target markets. Developing and emerging markets are hurt most by lost revenue when international companies manipulate prices to reduce tariffs and corporate taxes. They depend on the revenue for building things such as schools, hospitals, and infrastructure, including telecommunications systems and shipping ports. These items in turn benefit international companies by improving the productivity and efficiency of the local business environment. Indeed, some international companies have even developed codes of conduct specifying that transfer prices will follow the principle of arm's length pricing.

price controls

Upper or lower limits placed on the prices of products sold within a country.

PRICE CONTROLS Pricing strategies must also consider the potential for government **price controls**—upper or lower limits placed on the prices of products sold within a country. Upper-limit price controls are designed to provide price stability in an inflationary economy (one in which prices are rising). Companies that want to raise prices in a price-controlled economy must often apply to government authorities to request permission to do so. Companies with good contacts in the government of the target market might be more likely to get a price-control exemption. Those unable to obtain an exemption will typically try to lessen the impact of upper-limit price controls by reducing production costs.

By contrast, lower-limit price controls prohibit the lowering of prices below a certain level. Governments sometimes impose lower-limit price controls to help local companies compete against the less expensive imports of international companies. Other times, lower-limit price controls are designed to ward off price wars that could eliminate the competition and thereby give one company a monopoly in the domestic market.

DUMPING We detailed the practice of dumping in Chapter 6 when discussing government involvement in international trade. Recall that *dumping* occurs when the price of a good is lower in export markets than it is in the domestic market. Accusations of dumping are often made against competitors from other countries when inexpensive imports flood a nation's domestic market. Although charges of dumping normally result from deliberate efforts to undercut the prices of competitors in the domestic market, changes in exchange rates can cause unintentional dumping. When a country's government charges another nation's producers of dumping a good on its market, antidumping tariffs are typically imposed. Such tariffs are designed to punish producers in the offending nation by increasing the price of their products to a fairer level.

QUICK STUDY 4

1. What makes a worldwide pricing policy difficult to achieve in practice?
2. To apply dual pricing successfully, how must a firm treat its domestic and international buyers?
3. Parent firms and subsidiaries often transfer products among themselves at a price called *what*?

A Final Word

Despite the academic debate over globalization and the extent to which companies should standardize their international marketing activities, many companies continue to adapt to local conditions. Sometimes this takes the form of only slightly modifying promotional campaigns; at other times it can require the creation of an entirely new product. The causes of alterations in promotional aspects of marketing strategy can be cultural, such as language differences. They can also be legal, such as requirements to produce locally so as to help ease local unemployment or to spur local industry around the production facility. Other companies are able to reap the rewards of standardization and centralized production that can result from the ability to sell one product worldwide. In the next chapter, we take an in-depth look at the factors that influence the development of production strategies and the types of decisions managers must make along the way.

MyLab Management

Go to **www.pearson.com/mylab/management** to complete the problems marked with this icon .

Chapter Summary

LO14.1 Describe the factors to consider in developing international product strategies.
- Companies may standardize products in certain categories, but adapt to unique tastes and preferences in others for reasons of culture and regulations.
- Companies may keep their brand names consistent across all markets but create new product names or modify existing ones to suit local preferences.
- The image of the nation in which a company designs, manufactures, or assembles a product can influence buyer perception of quality and reliability.
- Counterfeit goods of inferior quality damage buyers' image of a brand. Shortened product life cycles affect decisions of when to market internationally.

LO14.2 Outline the international promotional strategies and methods available to firms.
- A *pull strategy* creates buyer demand that encourages channel members to stock a product, whereas a *push strategy* pressures channel members to carry and promote a product.
- *Product/communications extension (dual extension)*: same product and promotion abroad.
- *Product extension/communications adaptation*: same product but altered promotion abroad.
- *Product adaptation/communications extension*: adapted product but original promotion abroad.
- *Product/communications adaptation (dual adaptation)*: adapted product and promotion abroad.
- *Product invention*: entirely new product and new promotion abroad.

LO14.3 Explain the factors to consider when designing international distribution strategies.
- An *exclusive channel* grants the right to sell a product to one or a limited number of resellers. This strategy gives wholesalers and retailers significant control over sales.
- An *intensive channel* grants the right to sell a product to many resellers, which offers less control over reseller decisions.
- *Channel length* refers to the number of intermediaries between the producer and the buyer. Longer channels generally mean higher distribution costs, which may not be appropriate for price-sensitive products.
- Special distribution problems that generate uncertainty and risk for successful product distribution are a lack of market understanding and the potential for theft and corruption.

LO14.4 Describe the two main international pricing strategies and factors to consider.
- *Worldwide pricing* is the strategy of using one selling price for all international markets and is difficult to achieve in practice.
- *Dual pricing* means having a different selling price in export markets than in the home market.
- Exporting costs and currency fluctuations can cause *price escalation*, which raises a product's selling price abroad relative to the home market or where it is produced.
- A product's *transfer price*, *arm's length price*, and *price controls* can all raise or lower its price in international markets.

Key Terms

arm's length price (p. 381)
brand name (p. 369)
distribution (p. 378)
dual pricing (p. 381)
exclusive channel (p. 378)

intensive channel (p. 378)
marketing communication (p. 375)
price controls (p. 382)
promotion mix (p. 372)
pull strategy (p. 372)

push strategy (p. 372)
transfer price (p. 381)
value density (p. 379)
worldwide pricing (p. 380)

✪ TALK ABOUT IT 1

So far in this book we've seen many product markets where global convergence is taking place. But we've also seen many product markets that are resisting homogenization and are retaining their national distinctiveness.

14-1. Thinking of a product that is moving toward convergence, how will convergence influence the marketing manager's job?

14-2. Thinking of a product that is resisting convergence, what is the cause of the resistance?

✪ TALK ABOUT IT 2

Critics of the tobacco industry allege that in developing markets cigarette manufacturers create special tobacco blends that contain additives to give an extra "kick." If true, such practices put the "standardization-versus-adaptation" issue in an unusual perspective.

14-3. If tobacco companies adapt their products in this way, do you think this practice is ethical?

14-4. Can you think of companies in other industries that change the contents of their products to appeal to buyers?

Ethical Challenge

Challenges are just another opportunity, or so they say. As the sole distributor in your region for a very well-known and successful branded consumer product, you are certainly facing a challenge right now, but where is the opportunity? Sales are great because demand is high due to the saturation advertising. The problem is that you are out of stock. It pains you every day to turn away dozens of customers. The prospect of new stock is some weeks into the future. Meanwhile, your employees have little to do, your store is virtually empty, and cash flow is drying up. Then a contact in the same business offers you a solution. He can provide you with the stock you need. Sure, it has foreign packaging, but you cannot ask him about that. The price is great too.

14-5. These are probably counterfeit or parallel imports. Could they damage your long-term business?

14-6. Is it wise to buy the counterfeits?

14-7. Why are some countries far more likely to have a thriving counterfeit market than others? Suggest some likely countries with a major problem.

Teaming Up

In groups of three or four, think about brands that are available around the world. You may have travelled and noticed that brands are cheaper, more expensive, or roughly the same price. Think about those brands and consider the following questions, then share your answers with the class.

14-8. What is worldwide pricing? Did you find any examples of these (they are often found in retail chains)?

14-9. What is dual pricing? Give some examples of these. What are the different types of dual pricing?

14-10. What are transfer prices? How are these prices used by subsidiaries of multinational business organizations?

MyLab Management

✪ Go to **www.pearson.com/mylab/management** for the following assisted-graded writing questions:

14-11. Price escalation can present serious problems for companies exporting using a worldwide pricing policy. It can drive a product's price up high enough to make it uncompetitive in a market abroad. How might a company combat the effects of price escalation?

14-12. Certain organizations regularly attack advertisers for their promotional methods, charging them with creating wants as opposed to helping satisfy needs. What could the advertising industry do to make itself a smaller target for such criticisms? Explain.

PRACTICING INTERNATIONAL MANAGEMENT CASE

Psychology of Global Marketing

It's no secret that marketers use a good dose of psychology in both designing and implementing their promotional campaigns—or at least it should not be. But some people, including Gary Rushkin of Washington, DC-based Commercial Alert (www.commercialalert .org), argue that parents are being duped. He says that parents do not realize the sophisticated techniques that marketers can use to entice demand. Rushkin's organization was behind a letter signed by 60 US psychologists that was sent to the American Psychological Association (www.apa.org) that complained of advertising methods aimed at children.

What was the cause of their fury? Apparently, it was an article by Dr. James McNeal appearing in *Marketing Tools* magazine that described what is called a projective completion test. Suppose a children's TV program is a hit and boys are buying the company's toy that is tied to the program but girls aren't. To find out why, a company assembles a group of girls. They are given a picture of a boy and girl watching the program in which the boy is asking the girl, "Why do you like watching this program?" The girls' answers help provide clues to how the company can modify its marketing strategy to appeal to girls. Dr. McNeal says the method is common sense and sound science. Critics argue the opposite and say that insights into human psychology should be used for healing and not for advertising to kids. The American Psychological Association admits that there are currently no guidelines for psychologists working in advertising.

Advertising executives are not just busy creating TV ads. Over a recent one-year period, the number of children's websites with no advertising dropped from 10 percent down to 2 percent. In what forms do the promotions appear? One tool is *games*. Roughly 55 percent of all children and teens' websites feature games. Ellen Neuborne told her six-year-old that he could choose a candy at the supermarket checkout. With a pack of Sweet Tarts in hand, he broke into a little song-and-dance about the sweets. When asked if that was from the TV commercial he said that it was from the Sweet Tarts Internet game. With the use of such games, companies get to spend an extended period of time with kids—far more than they get from a TV ad.

Another tool is *e-mail*. The US Children's Online Privacy Act forbids companies from using e-mail to sell to kids under age 13 without parental permission. But companies get around the problem by having kids e-mail each other. For example, children can go to the website (www.sesameworkshop.org) and e-mail a greeting card to a friend that features a Sesame Street character. And then there are the *chat rooms*. Brian Rubash is manager for technical marketing at Tiger electronics (www.tigertoys.com), a division of toy-maker Hasbro (www.hasbro.com). He says that he regularly signed on to a newsgroup he found on Yahoo! (www.yahoo.com) to offer product news and to answer questions about the i-Cybie robotic dog the company was launching.

European nations have some of the strictest regulations covering marketing to children. However, nations belonging to the European Union (EU) have widely varying rules. For example, Greece bans all TV ads for war toys and bans ads for all other toys between 7 a.m. and 10 p.m. The Dutch-speaking part of Belgium bans TV advertising within five minutes of the start and end of children's programs. Sweden bans all ads aimed at children under age 12. This means that when kids in Sweden watch the Pokémon cartoon series, they do not hear the closing jingle "Gotta catch'em all" that plays elsewhere.

But the problem for the Swedes (and others with more restrictive bans) is that they can only enforce their laws on programs originating from within the country. They have no power of enforcement over programs broadcast from other nations or from satellite transmissions. That is why the Swedes are pushing for a common restrictive policy toward advertising aimed at children. Although an outright ban like Sweden's is unlikely, partial bans such as that in place in Belgium could be implemented.

To forestall stricter EU–wide legislation, advertisers could initiate voluntary limits themselves. In fact, the World Health Organization called on private companies to self-regulate in the area of advertising to children. This is an especially timely request given the rising incidences of childhood obesity and diabetes. Between 2005 and 2009, 52 companies in the food industry created thirteen pledges on food marketing to children. Two pledges were global in scope, nine were country-specific, and three were in the soft drinks and fast-food industries.

Yet, marketers defend their actions. Advertising executive Geoffrey Roche of Toronto, Canada, dismissed the idea that psychologists have the power to alter consumers' minds to any large extent, especially not one that is harmful. Dr. Curtis Haugtvedt, president of the Society for Consumer Psychology, says that although evidence of the negative aspects of advertising does exist, ads can also benefit kids. Haugtvedt also stresses the role of parental guidance in helping kids to become responsible consumers and to not allow them to make such decisions independently.

Thinking Globally

14-13. If you were Stephan Loerke, of the World Federation of Advertisers, how would you argue for the EU to not enact more strict advertising laws?

14-14. Do you personally agree with the case you made above?

14-15. Thinking of a specific product sold in industrialized nations, do you think it could create wants more than it satisfies needs if it were marketed in a developing country?

Sources: Corinna Hawkes and Jennifer L Harris, "An Analysis of the Content of Food Industry Pledges on Marketing to Children," *Public Health Nutrition* 14(8), 2011, pp. 1403–1414; Ellen Neuborne, "For Kids on the Web, It's an Ad, Ad, Ad, Ad World," *Bloomberg Businessweek* (www.businessweek.com), August 12, 2001; Brandon Mitchener, "Banning Ads on Kids' TV," *Wall Street Journal Europe*, May 22, 2001, p. 25 James MacKinnon, "Psychologists Act against Ad Doctors," Adbusters website (www.adbusters.org).

Chapter Fifteen

Managing International Operations

Learning Objectives

After studying this chapter, you should be able to

15.1 Describe the elements to consider when formulating production strategies.

15.2 Outline the issues to consider when acquiring physical resources.

15.3 Identify the key production matters that concern managers.

15.4 Explain the potential ways to finance business operations.

A Look Back

Chapter 14 explored the influence of globalization on international marketing activities. We also examined how differences in national business environments impact the development of marketing strategies.

A Look at This Chapter

This chapter examines how companies launch and manage their international production efforts. We analyze how companies acquire the materials and products they need and how aspects of the business environment affect production strategies. We also look briefly at how companies finance their activities.

A Look Ahead

Chapter 16 examines how international companies manage their human resources. Topics include international staffing policies, recruitment, training, compensation, labor relations, and culture shock.

MyLab Management

✪ IMPROVE YOUR GRADE!

When you see this icon ✪, visit **www.pearson.com/mylab/management** for activities that are applied, personalized, and offer immediate feedback.

Amazon: From a Garage to the Globe

SEATTLE, Washington—In 1995, recognizing a worldwide demand for books, Jeff Bezos traded his Wall Street firm for his garage to launch Amazon. Set up as an online marketplace, Amazon initially catered solely to customers in the United States, but two decades later, it is the leading market e-retailer worldwide, controlling about 16 percent of the global e-commerce market.

Today, Amazon's operations across the globe include more than 100 fulfillment centers and warehouses that support global sales in more than 100 countries. Moreover, its product offering has expanded well beyond books to include 480 million products, covering everything from kitchenware to computer software. It has 15 country-specific sales websites and software development centers in over eight countries.

Kristoffer Tripplaar/Alamy Stock Photo

While Amazon's revenue is largely derived from the sale of goods via its website and as a global online marketplace for third-party sellers, these are not its only sources of income. In 2006, the company began offering its Amazon Web Services cloud-computing platform. The service is available to businesses in North America, South America, Asia, and Europe and reflects Amazon's ability to use its assets and IT expertise to provide business-to-business services globally. Although much of Amazon's operations are financed by its profits, this is not its only source of finance; in 2017, the company sold corporate bonds totalling $16 billion in value.

Having diverse international operations is not without its problems. For example, Amazon's own Echo, produced by Foxconn in China, is beset by controversies about working conditions in offshore facilities and income disparities between those on the factory floor in China and those in the boardroom in Seattle. This can be a costly public-relations issue for a tech giant like Amazon.

Amazon's success is thanks to tremendous planning in its operations, involving considerations such as where to produce and source products from, the volume of products required, and where to establish its many global facilities. The Kindle is a case in point: the limited production and US-only launch of the original Kindle in 2007 was meant to assess the demand of an e-reader, and the subsequent international launch of the Kindle 2 when the first-generation Kindle proved successful illustrates the methodical approach Amazon takes to planning its international operations.

The same is true for any global business—such decisions warrant a great deal of attention and consideration. As you read this chapter, consider how companies structure their global production facilities and how they finance all of their business activities.[1]

Whether an international company's production activity involves manufacturing a product or providing a service, it must acquire many resources before beginning operations. Where will it get the raw materials or components it needs to perform its production activities? How much production capacity is needed? Will the company construct or buy new facilities? How large must its service centers be? Where will it get the financial capital it needs? The answers to these questions are complex and interrelated.

This chapter begins by examining important issues to consider when formulating international production strategies. The topics covered include decisions about whether to centralize or decentralize production and whether production will be standardized or adapted to national markets. In the process, we draw linkages to earlier discussions, including overall corporate strategy and marketing strategy. We then describe how companies acquire the resources they need to accomplish their production goals. We explain how firms acquire fixed (or tangible) assets, including production facilities, offices, equipment, and materials. We also consider several key production concerns, such as international logistics and total quality management. We then explain important factors influencing managers' decisions about whether to expand or reduce operations abroad. We close by taking a brief look at how companies finance their international production operations and other activities.

15.1 Production Strategy

15.1 Describe the elements to consider when formulating production strategies.

Production operations are important to achieving a company's strategy. Careful planning of all aspects of production helps companies cut costs (to become low-cost leaders) or design new products and product features necessary for a differentiation strategy. Among the important strategic issues that managers must consider are planning for production capacity, the location of facilities, production processes to be used, and the layout of facilities.

Capacity Planning

capacity planning
Process of assessing a company's ability to produce enough output to satisfy market demand.

The process of assessing a company's ability to produce enough output to satisfy market demand is called **capacity planning**. Companies must estimate global demand for their products as accurately as possible. If the capacity being used is greater than the expected market demand, a company may need to scale back production by perhaps reducing the number of employees or work shifts at some facilities. Yet, countries have different laws regulating the ability of employers to eliminate jobs. So, depending on the country, a firm may or may not need to give advance notice of layoffs or plant closings. On the other hand, if market demand is growing, managers must determine in which facilities to expand production or whether additional facilities are needed to expand capacity. Rather than miss out on potential sales, a company might contract with other producers to meet the excess demand until new facilities are up and running.

Capacity planning is also extremely important for service companies. For example, a hotel chain moving into a new geographic market must estimate the number of rooms that its facilities should contain. It must also determine whether a facility will be used for conventions and the like and the number of meeting rooms it must build. Videoconferencing facilities might be added if local firms require them to keep in touch with geographically dispersed operations.

Facilities Location Planning

facilities location planning
Selecting the location for production facilities.

Selecting the location for production facilities is called **facilities location planning**. Companies often have many potential locations around the world from which to choose a site for production, R&D, or some other activity. Aspects of the business environment that are important to facilities location planning include the cost and availability of labor and management, raw materials, component parts, and energy. Other key factors include political stability, the extent of regulation and bureaucracy, economic development, and the local culture, including beliefs about work and important traditions.

Reducing production costs by taking advantage of lower wages in another country is often essential to keeping a company's products competitively priced. This is especially important when the cost of labor contributes greatly to total production costs. But the lower wages of a nation's workforce must be balanced against its potentially lower productivity. Worker productivity tends to be lower in most developing nations and some emerging markets as compared with developed nations.

Although most service companies must locate near their customers, they must still consider a wide variety of customers' needs when locating facilities. Are convenience and being located in a high-traffic area important to customers? Such a location is clearly important for some companies, including restaurants, banks, and cinemas. For other service businesses, such as consulting companies or public utilities, a convenient location is less important.

Supply issues are also important in location planning. For any one mode of transportation, the greater the distance between production facilities and target markets the longer it takes for customers to receive shipments. In turn, companies must compensate for delays by maintaining larger inventories in target markets—adding to storage and insurance costs. Shipping costs are also greater when production occurs away from target markets. Transportation costs are one of the driving forces behind the globalization of the steel industry. Shipping costs for steel can run $40 to $50 per ton—a significant amount when steel sells for $400 to $500 per ton. By building steel mills in countries where their customers are located, steel producers significantly reduce their transportation costs.

Automobile makers from Japan and Germany invested in production facilities inside the United States for some of the reasons just identified. For example, Toyota (www.toyota.com) and other Japanese automobile companies manufacture cars in the United States to offset the risks from currency fluctuations, to defuse political concerns about the United States' trade deficit with Japan, and to be closer to customers. BMW (www.bmw.com) of Germany assembles automobiles in the United States for similar reasons. For one, the past strength of Germany's currency made German products more expensive on world markets. Another reason is that Germany is home to the world's highest paid workers—the average hourly income is approximately $32. Finally, German companies were attracted by the lower cost of land and concessions, including tax breaks offered by state governments eager to attract industry.

LOCATION ECONOMIES Selecting highly favorable locations often allows a company to achieve **location economies**—economic benefits derived from locating production activities in optimal locations. Location economies result from the right mix of the kinds of elements previously described. To take advantage of location economies, companies either undertake business activities themselves in a particular location or obtain products and services from other companies located there. Location economies involve almost any business activity that companies in a particular location perform very well, such as R&D or providing advertising services.

The following examples illustrate the extent to which service and manufacturing companies exploit location economies. One company designed its precision ice hockey equipment in Sweden, obtained financing from Canada, assembled it in Cleveland and Denmark, and marketed it in

location economies
Economic benefits derived from locating production activities in optimal locations.

Companies do an enormous amount of planning for operations when undertaking international business. As business grows increasingly global, supply chains grow longer and more complex. Shown here, a forklift loads trucks at a port for inland transport of containers. Sourcing components from abroad and sending finished goods to other nations means examining the ports through which goods will flow.

Weerasak Saeku/Shutterstock

North America and Europe. This equipment incorporated alloys whose molecular structure was researched and patented in Delaware and fabricated in Japan. Airplane manufacturer Boeing (www.boeing.com) designed aircraft in the state of Washington and Japan, assembled it in Seattle with tail cones made in Canada, special tail sections made in China and Italy, and engines made in Great Britain. As a final example, one company's advertising campaign was conceived in Great Britain, filmed in Canada, dubbed in Great Britain, and edited in New York.[2]

The key fact to remember is that *each production activity generates more value in a particular location than it could generate elsewhere*. Productivity is a very important (although not the only) factor in determining the value that a location adds to a certain economic activity. Two resources—labor and capital—heavily influence the productivity of a location.

Granted, to take advantage of location economies, managers might need to familiarize themselves with vastly different customs and traditions. Political and legal differences can force firms to retain outside consultants or to train corporate lawyers in local traditions. Language differences might mean translating important documents on an ongoing basis. For these reasons, companies sometimes hire other companies in a location to perform an activity for them.

CENTRALIZATION VERSUS DECENTRALIZATION An important consideration for production managers is whether to centralize or decentralize production facilities. *Centralized production* refers to the concentration of production facilities in one location. With *decentralized production*, facilities are spread over several locations and could even mean having one facility for each national business environment in which the company markets its products—a common policy for companies that follow a multinational strategy. Companies often centralize production facilities in pursuit of low-cost strategies and to take advantage of economies of scale—a typical policy for companies that follow a global strategy. By producing large quantities of identical products in one location, the companies cut costs by reducing the per-unit cost of production.

Transportation costs and the physical landscape also affect the centralization-versus-decentralization decision. Because they usually sell undifferentiated products in all their markets, low-cost competitors generally do not need to locate near their markets in order to stay on top of changes in buyer preferences. That is why low-cost producers often choose locations with the lowest combined production and transportation costs. But even these firms must balance the cost of getting inputs into the production process and the cost of getting products to markets. Key factors in the physical environment that affect the transport of goods are the availability of seaports, airports, or other transportation hubs.

Conversely, companies that sell differentiated products may find decentralized production the better option. By locating separate facilities near different markets, they remain in close contact with customers and can respond quickly to changing buyer preferences. Closer contact with customers also helps firms develop a deeper understanding of buyer behavior in local cultures.

When close cooperation between R&D and manufacturing is essential for effective differentiation, both activities are usually conducted in the same place. Yet, new technologies are giving companies more freedom to separate these activities. Today's rapid speed of communications allows a subsidiary and its home office to be large distances from each other.

Process Planning

process planning

Deciding the process that a company will use to create its product.

Deciding on the process that a company will use to create its product is called **process planning**. The particular process to be used is typically determined by a firm's business-level strategy. For example, low-cost strategies normally require large-scale production because producers want the cost savings generated by economies of scale. A company that mass-produces snowboards for average skiers will typically use a highly automated production process that integrates advanced computer technology. Differentiation strategies, however, demand that producers provide extra value by offering customers something unique, such as superior quality, added features, or special brand images. Companies that handcraft snowboards for professionals will rely not on automated production but on skilled craftspeople. The company will design and produce each snowboard to suit the habits and special needs of each individual snowboarder. For such a company, service is a major component of the production process.

Availability and cost of labor in the local market is crucial to process planning. If labor in the host country is relatively cheap, an international company will likely opt for less technology and for more labor-intensive methods in the production process—depending on its particular product and strategy. But again, the availability of labor and the level of wages in the local market must be balanced against the productivity of the local workforce.

STANDARDIZATION VERSUS ADAPTATION Another important issue in production strategy is deciding whether the production process will be standardized for all markets or adapted to manufacture products modified for different markets. For example, low-cost leadership often dictates automated, standardized production in large batches. Large production batches reduce the cost of producing each unit, thus offsetting the higher initial investment in automation. And production costs are reduced further as employees improve performance by repeating their activities and learning new procedures that would, for example, help minimize errors and waste.

But differentiation often demands decentralized facilities designed to improve local responsiveness. Because decentralized production facilities produce for one national market or for a regional market, they tend to be smaller. This tends to eliminate the potential to take advantage of economies of scale and therefore increases per-unit production costs. Similarly, the smaller market share that a differentiation strategy targets normally requires relatively smaller-scale production. Differentiating a product by incorporating certain features desired by customers requires more costly manufacturing processes. R&D costs also tend to be higher for products with special product designs, styles, and features.

Facilities Layout Planning

Deciding the spatial arrangement of production processes within production facilities is called **facilities layout planning**. Consider the fact that in Japan, Singapore, and Hong Kong, the supply of land is limited and its cost is high. Companies that locate in these markets must use the available space wisely by designing compact facilities. Conversely, in countries such as Canada, China, and the United States, an abundance of space reduces the cost of building facilities in many locations. Because land is cheaper, companies have more flexibility in designing facilities.

facilities layout planning
Deciding the spatial arrangement of production processes within production facilities.

More importantly, facility layout depends on the type of production process a company uses, which in turn depends on a company's business-level strategy. For instance, rather than producing mass quantities of computers to be stored in inventory, Compaq (www.compaq.com) competes by manufacturing computers as it receives orders from individual customers. To implement this business strategy, Compaq executives decided to replace mass-assembly lines with three-person work cells. In production trials at a plant in Scotland, output increased 23 percent as compared with the previous best assembly line. In addition, output per square foot went up 16 percent—a significant increase in the efficiency within the facility.

> **QUICK STUDY 1**
>
> 1. Assessing a firm's ability to produce enough output to satisfy demand is called *what*?
> 2. Location economies can arise from the optimal execution of *what*?
> 3. What typically determines the process that a firm uses to create its product?

15.2 Acquiring Physical Resources

Before an international company begins operations, it must acquire a number of physical resources. For example, managers must answer questions that include, Will the company make or buy the components it needs in the production process? What will be the sources of any required raw materials? Will the company acquire facilities and production equipment or build its own? In this section, we present the main elements that managers need to consider when answering these types of questions.

15.2 Outline the issues to consider when acquiring physical resources.

Make-or-Buy Decision

The typical manufacturing company requires a wide range of inputs into its production process. These inputs typically enter the production line either as raw materials that require processing or as components needing only assembly. Bear in mind, too, that a component may require minor adjustments or other minor processing before it goes into production. Deciding whether to make a component or to buy it from another company is called the **make-or-buy decision**. Each option has its own set of advantages and disadvantages.

make-or-buy decision
Deciding whether to make a component or to buy it from another company.

Dell Computer Corporation perfected the art of outsourcing. The company designs and builds computing systems for consumers and companies, but it does not build the computer components itself. This production strategy made Dell a model of efficiency in the personal computer (PC) industry and allowed it to deliver custom-made PCs in just three days, whereas most of its rivals measured their delivery times in weeks. Do you think outsourcing will continue to gain acceptance in the future?

Humphery/Shutterstock

vertical integration

Extension of company activities into stages of production that provide a firm's inputs (backward integration) or absorb its output (forward integration).

REASONS TO MAKE **Vertical integration** is the process by which a company extends its control over additional stages of production—either inputs or outputs. When a company decides to make a product rather than buy it, it engages in "upstream" activities (production activities that come before a company's current business operations). For example, an automobile manufacturer that decides to manufacture its own window glass is engaging in a new upstream activity.

Lower Costs Above all, companies make products rather than buy them in order to reduce total costs. Generally, the manufacturer's profit is the difference between the product's selling price and its production cost. When a company buys a product, it rewards the manufacturer by contributing to the latter's profit margin. Yet, a company often undertakes in-house production when it can manufacture a product for less than it must pay another business to produce it. Thus, in-house production allows a company to lower its own production costs.

For example, a computer motherboard is the physical foundation of a personal computer to which the microprocessor, memory chips, and other components are attached. This critical component accounts for about 40 percent of a personal computer's total cost. Compaq discovered that it could produce motherboards itself for $25 less than its Asian suppliers and save two weeks' shipping time in the process.

Small companies are less likely than large ones to make rather than buy, especially when a product requires a large financial investment in equipment and facilities. But this rule of thumb might not necessarily hold if the company possesses a proprietary technology or some other competitive advantage that is not easily copied.

Greater Control Companies that depend on others for key ingredients or components give up a degree of control. Making rather than buying can give managers greater control over raw materials, product design, and the production process itself—all of which are important factors in product quality. In turn, quality control is especially important when customers are highly sensitive to even slight declines in quality or company reputation.

In addition, persuading an outside supplier to make significant modifications to quality or features can be difficult. This is especially true if modifications entail investment in costly equipment or if they promise to be time-consuming. If just one buyer requests costly product adaptations or if there is reason to suspect that a buyer will eventually take its business elsewhere, a supplier may be reluctant to undertake a costly investment. Unless that buyer purchases in large volumes, the cost of the modifications may be too great for the supplier to absorb. In such a case, the buyer simply may be unable to obtain the product it wants without manufacturing it in-house. Thus, companies maintain greater control over product design and product features if they manufacture components themselves.

Finally, making a product can be a good idea when buying from a supplier means providing the supplier with a firm's key technology. Through licensing agreements (see Chapter 13), companies often provide suppliers in low-wage countries with the technologies needed to make their products. But if a company's competitive advantage depends on that technology, the licensor could inadvertently be creating a future competitor. When controlling a key technology is paramount, it is often better to manufacture in-house.

REASONS TO BUY The practice of buying from another company a good or service that is part of a company's value-added activities is called **outsourcing**. Outsourcing results from continuous specialization and technological advancement. For each successive specialization of its operations process, a manufacturer requires greater skill and knowledge than it did before. By outsourcing, a company can reduce the degree to which it is vertically integrated and the overall amount of specialized skills and knowledge that it must possess.

outsourcing
Practice of buying from another company a good or service that is part of a company's value-added activities.

Outsourcing has become extremely popular in the business of computer manufacturing. Component makers—including Intel (www.intel.com) in microprocessors, Seagate (www.seagate.com) in hard drives, US Robotics (www.usr.com) in modems, and Mitsumi (www.mitsumi.com) in DVD drives—supply big and small manufacturers worldwide. Computer companies buy components from these manufacturers, assemble them in their own facilities, and sell completed systems to consumers and businesses. A related practice in the computer industry is known as "stealth manufacturing," which calls for outsourcing the actual assembly of the computers themselves, plus the job of shipping them to distributors and other intermediaries.

A new and interesting type of outsourcing seems to be increasingly popular. The online forum called InnoCentive (www.innocentive.com) connects companies and institutions seeking solutions to difficult problems using a global network of more than 145,000 creative thinkers. These engineers, scientists, inventors, and businesspeople with expertise in life sciences, engineering, chemistry, math, computer science, and entrepreneurship compete to solve some of the world's toughest problems in return for significant financial awards. InnoCentive is open to anyone, is available in seven languages, and pays cash awards that range from as little as $2,000 to as much as $1 million.[3]

Many companies buy when buying is the lower-cost option. When a firm cannot integrate vertically by manufacturing a product for less than a supplier can, it will typically outsource. Let's explore some other reasons why companies prefer to buy rather than make.

Lower Risk In earlier chapters, we described many types of risks faced by companies that construct and staff facilities in other countries. For example, recall that political risk is quite high in certain markets. Social unrest or open conflict can threaten physical facilities, equipment, and employee safety.

One way a company can eliminate the exposure of assets to political risk in other countries is simply by refusing to invest in plants and equipment abroad. It can instead purchase products from international suppliers. This policy also eliminates the need to purchase expensive insurance coverage that is needed when a company undertakes production in an unstable country. Yet, this policy will not completely shield the buyer from all potential disruptions—political instability can cause delays in the timely receipt of needed parts. Indeed, even under normal circumstances, the longer delivery times involved in international outsourcing can increase the risk that the buyer will not meet its own production schedule.

Greater Flexibility Maintaining sufficient flexibility to respond to market conditions is increasingly important for companies everywhere. Making an in-house product that requires large investments in equipment and buildings often reduces flexibility. By contrast, companies that source products from one or more outside suppliers gain flexibility. In fact, added flexibility is the key factor in a fundamental change in attitude toward outsourcing, which many managers now regard as a full-fledged strategy for change rather than a limited tactical tool for solving immediate problems.

Maintaining flexibility is important when the national business environments of suppliers are volatile. Buying from several suppliers, or establishing production facilities in more than one country, allows a company to outsource products from one location if instability erupts in another. The same is true during periods of great volatility in exchange rates. Exchange-rate movements can increase or decrease the cost of importing a product from a given country. By buying from multiple suppliers located in several countries, a company can maintain the flexibility needed to change sources and reduce the risk associated with sudden swings in exchange rates.

Companies also maintain operational flexibility simply by not having to invest in production facilities. Unencumbered by investment in costly production equipment and facilities, a firm can alter its product line very quickly. This capability is especially important for products with small production runs or those with highly uncertain potential. Furthermore, a company can obtain financial flexibility if its capital is not locked up in plants and equipment. It can then use excess financial capital to pursue other domestic or international opportunities. Outsourcing can also free a company from having to invest in R&D and then to earn a return on that investment.

Market Power Companies can gain a great deal of power in their relationships with suppliers simply by becoming important customers. In fact, sometimes a supplier can become a sort of hostage to one particular customer. This situation occurs when a supplier becomes heavily dependent on a company that it serves with nearly all of its production capacity. If the main buyer suddenly begins outsourcing elsewhere, the supplier will have few other customers to whom it can turn. This situation gives the buyer significant control in dictating quality improvements, forcing cost reductions, and making special modifications.

Barriers to Buying For various reasons, companies sometimes face obstacles when buying products from international suppliers. First, the government of the buyer's country may impose import tariffs designed to improve the nation's balance of trade. Tariffs can add anywhere from 15 to 50 percent to the cost of a component that a manufacturer needs from abroad.

Second, the services provided by intermediaries increase the cost of buying abroad. Obtaining letters of credit, arranging physical transportation, and obtaining insurance all add to the final cost that a manufacturer pays for a product supplied from abroad. Although these expenses are currently lower than they have ever been, they can significantly increase total product cost. If high enough, they can negate any advantage of buying from an international supplier.

✪ MyLab Management Watch It Toyota Outsourcing and Logistics

Apply what you have learned so far about acquiring physical resources. If your instructor has assigned this, go to **www.pearson.com/mylab/management** to watch a video case about how Toyota sources components for its automobile production system and answer questions.

Raw Materials

Decisions about the selection and acquisition of raw materials are important to many different types of manufacturers. The twin issues of quantity and quality drive many of these decisions. First, some industries and companies rely almost exclusively on the quantity of locally available raw materials. This is most true for companies involved in mining, forestry, and fishing. There must be an adequate supply of iron ore, oil, lumber, or fish to justify the large financial investment required to build processing facilities.

Second, the quality of raw material has a huge influence on the quality of a company's end product. For instance, food-processing companies must examine the quality of the locally grown fruit, vegetables, grains, and any other ingredients. Beverage companies must assess the quality of the local water supply. Some markets may require large financial investments to build water-purifying facilities. Elsewhere (such as much of the Middle East), the only local water source may be seawater that must be desalinized.

Fixed Assets

fixed (tangible) assets
Company assets such as production facilities, inventory warehouses, retail outlets, and production and office equipment.

Most companies must acquire **fixed (tangible) assets**—such as production facilities, inventory warehouses, retail outlets, and production and office equipment—in the host country. Many companies have the option of either (1) acquiring or modifying existing factories or (2) building entirely new facilities—called a *greenfield* investment. Considering either option involves many individuals within the company. For example, production managers must verify that an existing facility (or an empty lot) is large enough and will suit the company's facility layout needs. Site-acquisition experts and legal staff must guarantee that the proposed business activity abides by local laws. Public relations staff must work with community leaders to ensure that the company does not jeopardize the rights, values, and customs of the local population.

Finally, managers must make sure that the local infrastructure can support the firm's proposed on-site business operations. Also, factory and office equipment is likely to be available locally in most newly industrialized and developed markets, but not in developing markets. Thus, managers must assess both the cost in tariffs that will be imposed on imported equipment and the cost in time and effort that will be required to import it.

QUICK STUDY 2

1. Vertical integration is the process by which a company extends its control over *what*?
2. Why might a company make a product in-house rather than buy it?
3. Why might a firm buy a product rather than make it in-house?

15.3 Key Production Concerns

In Chapter 11, we presented how the number and location of manufacturing facilities can affect company strategy and organizational structure. At this point, there remain just several issues to discuss related to manufacturing operations. In this section, we first examine how companies maximize quality and minimize shipping and inventory costs. Then we take a brief look at the important reinvestment-versus-divestment decision.

15.3 Identify the key production matters that concern managers.

Quality Improvement Efforts

Companies strive toward quality improvement for two reasons: costs and customer value. First, quality products help keep production costs low because they reduce waste in valuable inputs, reduce the cost of retrieving defective products from buyers, and reduce the disposal costs that result from defective products. Second, some minimum level of acceptable quality is an aspect of nearly every product today. Even companies that produce low-cost products try to maintain or improve quality, as long as it does not erode their position in what is typically a price-competitive market or market segment. A company that succeeds in combining a low-cost position with a high-quality product can gain a tremendous competitive advantage in its market.

Improving quality is also important for a company that provides services—whether as its only product or in conjunction with the goods it manufactures and markets. Managing quality in services is complicated by the fact that a service is created and consumed at the same time. For this reason, the human interaction between the employee who delivers the service and the buyer is important to service quality. Still, activities that must be conducted prior to the actual delivery of a service are also important. For example, it is important that a restaurant be clean and have on hand the ingredients it needs to prepare the meals on its menu. Likewise, a bank can provide high-quality service only if employees arrive for work on time and interact professionally with customers.

Let's take a brief look at two movements that inspire the drive toward quality: total quality management and International Standards Organization (ISO) 9000 certification.

TOTAL QUALITY MANAGEMENT Company-wide commitment to meet or exceed customer expectations through continuous quality improvement efforts and processes is called **total quality management (TQM)**. TQM also places a great deal of responsibility on each individual to be focused on the quality of his or her own output—regardless of whether the employee's activities are based in the factory, in administration, or in management.

By continuously improving the quality of its products, a company can differentiate itself from rivals and attract loyal customers. The TQM philosophy initially took hold in Japan, where electronics and automobile firms applied TQM techniques to reduce costs and thereby gain significant market share around the world through price competitiveness and a reputation for quality. It was not until US and European companies lost a great deal of market share to their Japanese rivals that they embraced TQM principles.

total quality management (TQM)

Company-wide commitment to meet or exceed customer expectations through continuous quality improvement efforts and processes.

ISO 9000 The ISO 9000 is an international certification that companies get when they meet the highest quality standards in their industries. Firms in the European Union are leading the way in quality certification. But both European and non-European companies alike are working toward certification in order to ensure access to the European marketplace. To become certified, companies must demonstrate the reliability and soundness of all business processes that affect the quality of their products. Many companies also seek ISO 9000 certification because of the message of quality that certification sends to prospective customers. For information on how companies can blend TQM principles and the drive toward ISO 9000 certification, see the Manager's Briefcase, titled "World-Class Standards."

Shipping and Inventory Costs

Shipping costs can have a dramatic effect on the cost of getting materials and components to the location of production facilities. When the cost of getting inputs into the production process is a large portion of the product's total cost, producers tend to locate close to the source of those inputs. Shipping costs are affected by many elements of a nation's business environment, such as its general level of economic development, including the condition of seaports, airports, roads, and rail networks.

It used to be that producers would buy vast quantities of materials or components and store them in large warehouses until they were needed in the production process. Storing great amounts of inventory for production, however, is costly in terms of insuring them against damage or theft and the rent or purchase price of the warehouse needed to store them.

Because companies have far better uses for the money tied up in such inventory, they developed better inventory management techniques. A production technique in which inventory is kept to a minimum and inputs to the production process arrive exactly when they are needed (or *just in time*) is called **just-in-time (JIT) manufacturing**. Although the technique was originally developed in Japan, it quickly spread throughout manufacturing operations worldwide. JIT manufacturing drastically reduces the costs associated with large inventories. It also helps reduce wasteful expenses because defective materials and components are spotted quickly during production. Under traditional systems, defective materials or components were sometimes discovered only after being built into finished products.

just-in-time (JIT) manufacturing

Production technique in which inventory is kept to a minimum and inputs to the production process arrive exactly when they are needed.

MANAGER'S BRIEFCASE World-Class Standards

In today's competitive environment, many companies are applying TQM principles. For companies doing business internationally, ISO 9000 certification is becoming increasingly important. But the ISO 9000 standards do not specify how a company should develop its quality processes. Rather, ISO requires each company to define and document its own quality processes and show evidence of implementing them. The following is a framework describing how TQM and ISO 9000 principles can be linked to enhance a company's capability for delivering quality products or services.

The main principles of TQM include the following:

- **Delight the Customer** Companies must strive to be the best at what customers consider most important. This can change over time, so business owners must be in close touch with customers.
- **Use People-Based Management** Systems, standards, and technology cannot, in and of themselves, guarantee quality. The key is to provide employees with the knowledge of what to do and how to do it and to provide feedback on performance.
- **Provide Continuous Improvement** TQM is not a short-term quick fix but is a continual process. Achieving major

breakthroughs is less important than smaller, incremental improvements.
- **Create Management by Fact** Quality management and improvement requires that managers clearly understand how consumers perceive the performance of a company's goods and services. Rather than trusting "gut feelings," obtain factual information, and share it with employees.

Companies can link these TQM principles to ISO 9000 standards in three ways:

- **Process Definition** The existing business process must be defined. Once defined, it must be satisfying to key stakeholders, and it must "delight the customer."
- **Process Improvement** To achieve positive results, everyone within the organization should use the defined process properly; otherwise, a company may need to adjust its policies.
- **Process Management** Management and employees must possess factual knowledge about process details in order to manage them properly.

Sources: Based on G. K. Kanji, "An Innovative Approach to Make ISO 9000 Standards More Effective." *Total Quality Management*, February 1998, pp. 67–79.

Reinvestment versus Divestment

Companies maintain the current level of operations when no new opportunities are foreseen. Yet, changing conditions in the competitive global marketplace often force managers to choose between *reinvesting* in operations and *divesting* them.

Companies often reinvest profits in markets that require long payback periods as long as the long-term outlook is good. This is often the case in developing countries and large emerging markets. For example, corruption, red tape, distribution problems, and a vague legal system present challenges for non-Chinese companies. But because long-term returns on their investments are expected, Western companies reinvest heavily in China despite what are sometimes uncertain short-term profits. Most of these companies invest in production facilities to take advantage of a low-cost labor pool and low-cost energy.[4]

Companies scale back their international operations when it becomes apparent that making operations profitable will take longer than expected. Again, China serves as a good example. Some companies were lured to China by the possibilities for growth offered by 1.2 billion consumers; however, some had to scale back ambitions that had been based on overly optimistic marketing plans.

Companies usually decide to reinvest when a market is experiencing rapid growth. Reinvestment can mean either expanding in the market itself or expanding in a location that serves the growing market. Investing in expanding markets is often an attractive option because potential new customers usually have not yet become loyal to the products of any one company or brand. It can be easier and less costly to attract customers in such markets than it is to gain a share of markets that are stagnant or contracting.

Yet, problems in the political, social, or economic sphere can force a company either to reduce or to eliminate operations altogether. Such problems are usually intertwined with one another. For example, in recent years some Western companies pulled their personnel out of Indonesia because of intense social unrest stemming directly from a combination of political problems (discontent with the nation's political leadership), economic difficulties, and terrorist attacks.

Finally, companies invest in the operations that offer the best return on their investments. That policy often means reducing or divesting operations in some markets, even though they may be profitable, in order to invest in more profitable opportunities elsewhere.

QUICK STUDY 3

1. Why might a company strive for quality improvement?
2. The international certification that a company gets when it meets the highest quality standards in its industry is called *what*?
3. Under what conditions might a company reinvest earnings in its operations?

15.4 Financing Business Operations

Companies need financial resources to pay for a variety of operating expenses and new projects. They must buy raw materials and component products for manufacturing and assembly activities. At certain times, they need large sums of capital, whether for expanding production capacity or entering new geographic markets. But companies also need financing to pay for all sorts of activities in addition to those related to production. They must pay for training and development programs and compensate workers and managers. Businesses must pay advertising agencies for helping the company promote its goods and services. They must also make periodic interest payments to lenders and perhaps reward stockholders with dividends.

But all companies have a limited supply of resources at their disposal to invest in current operations or new endeavors. So where do companies obtain needed funds? Generally, organizations obtain financial resources through one of three sources:

15.4 Explain the potential ways to finance business operations.

1. Borrowing (debt)
2. Issuing equity (stock ownership)
3. Internal funding

Borrowing

International companies (like domestic companies) try to get the lowest interest rates possible on borrowed funds. However, this objective is more complex on a global scale. Difficulties include exchange-rate risk, restrictions on currency convertibility, and restrictions on the international flow of capital.

Borrowing locally can be advantageous, especially when the value of the local currency has fallen against that of the home country. Suppose a Japanese company borrows from US banks for investment in the United States. Let's say that one year later the US dollar has fallen against the Japanese *yen*—in other words, fewer *yen* are now needed to buy one dollar. In that case, the Japanese company can repay the loan with fewer *yen* than would have been required if the value of the dollar had not fallen.

But companies are not always able to borrow funds locally. Often, they are forced to seek international sources of capital. This is sometimes the case when a subsidiary is new to the market and has not yet built a reputation with local lenders. In such cases, a parent firm can help a subsidiary acquire financing through a so-called **back-to-back loan**—a loan in which a parent company deposits money with a host-country bank, which then lends the money to a subsidiary located in the host country.

For example, suppose that a Mexican company forms a new subsidiary in the United States but that this subsidiary cannot obtain a US bank loan. The Mexican parent company can deposit Mexican *pesos* in the branch of a US bank in Mexico (see Figure 15.1). The US bank's home office then lends dollars to the subsidiary in the United States. The amount of money lent in dollars will be equivalent to the amount of pesos on deposit with the US bank's Mexican branch. When the US subsidiary repays the loan in full, the parent company withdraws its deposit (plus any interest earned) from the US bank's Mexican branch.

back-to-back loan

Loan in which a parent company deposits money with a host-country bank, which then lends the money to a subsidiary located in the host country.

Issuing Equity

Recall from Chapter 9 that the *international equity market* consists of all stocks bought and sold outside the home country of the issuing company. Companies issue such stock primarily to access pools of investors with funds that are unavailable domestically. Yet, getting shares listed on another country's stock exchange can be a complex process. For one thing, complying with all the rules and regulations governing the operation of a particular stock exchange costs a great deal of time and money. Only large companies, therefore, tend to list shares on multiple exchanges.

Figure 15.1

Mexico—United States Back-to-Back Loan

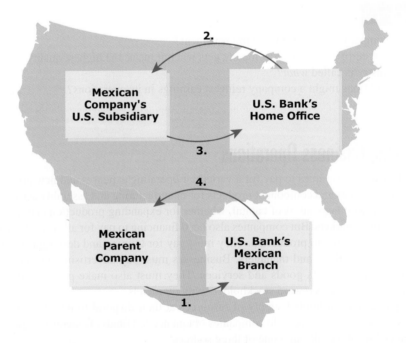

1. **Mexican parent company deposits pesos in U.S. bank's branch in Mexico.**
2. **U.S. bank's home office lends dollars to Mexican company's subsidiary in the United States.**
3. **Mexican subsidiary repays the dollar loan.**
4. **Mexican parent company withdraws peso deposit plus interest.**

ISSUING AMERICAN DEPOSITORY RECEIPTS To maximize international exposure (and to access funds), non–US companies often list themselves on US stock exchanges. Non–US companies can list shares directly in the United States by issuing **American Depository Receipts (ADRs)**—certificates that trade in the United States and that represent a specific number of shares in a non–US company. Large US banks, such as Citibank (www.citibank.com), issue ADRs that then trade on the New York Stock Exchange (www.nyse.com), the computerized National Association of Securities Dealers Automated Quotation system (www.nasdaq.com), and the over-the-counter (OTC) market. As we saw in the company profile at the start of this chapter, Japan-based Toyota (www.toyota.co.jp) accesses US investors by issuing ADRs.

International companies also make use of Global Depository Receipts (GDRs). These are similar in principle to ADRs but are listed and traded in London and Luxembourg. Companies from India aggressively issue GDRs to circumvent stringent listing requirements in their home market.[5]

Advantages of ADRs Companies gain several important advantages through ADRs. First, investors who buy ADRs pay no currency-conversion fees. By contrast, if a US investor were to purchase the shares of a non–US company on another country's stock exchange, he or she would incur the expense of converting currencies. Avoiding such expenses, plus the added convenience of paying in dollars, encourages US investors to buy ADRs. Second, there are no minimum purchase requirements for ADRs, as there sometimes are for shares of a company's stock.

Third, companies offer ADRs in the United States to appeal to mutual funds. Investment laws in the United States limit the amount of money that a mutual fund can invest in the shares of companies not registered on US exchanges. US mutual fund managers were forced to sell shares of German software producer SAP (www.sap.com) when they appreciated in price. Some fund managers pleaded with SAP America to get ADRs, so SAP complied. Listing ADRs in the United States also allowed the company to reward employees with discounted shares of company stock—something that it could not have done otherwise because companies are barred from awarding shares in unregistered companies to employees in the United States.[6]

VENTURE CAPITAL Another source of equity financing for entrepreneurial start-ups and small businesses is **venture capital**—financing obtained from investors who believe that the borrower will experience rapid growth and who receive equity (part ownership) in return. Those who supply the venture with the capital it needs are called *venture capitalists*. Although there is often substantial risk associated with new, rapidly expanding enterprises, venture capitalists invest in them because they can also generate very large returns on investment.

Venture capitalists with deep pockets now have a global reach. Nevertheless, many small companies around the world confront real obstacles when trying to obtain financing. Entrepreneurs in the United States, however, tend to have a relatively easier time financing activities and expansion because of a culture that values entrepreneurship. The culture of the United States is individual-oriented and rewards individual business risk-taking with financial rewards. For some key strategies that entrepreneurs use to find international investors, see the Culture Matters feature, titled "Financing Business from Abroad."

EMERGING STOCK MARKETS Naturally, companies from countries with emerging stock markets face certain problems. First, emerging stock markets commonly experience extreme volatility. An important contributing factor is that investments into emerging stock markets are often so-called *hot money*—money that can be quickly withdrawn in times of crisis. By contrast, *patient money*—foreign direct investment in factories, equipment, and land—cannot be pulled out as readily. Large and sudden sell-offs of equity are signs of market volatility that characterize many emerging stock markets. Such large sell-offs occur because of uncertainty regarding the nation's future economic growth.

Second, companies that issue equity on their countries' emerging stock markets are often plagued by poor market regulation. This can allow large local companies to wield a great deal of influence over their domestic stock markets. As long as powerful domestic shareholders dominate such exchanges, international investors will likely hesitate to enter. The root of the problem often lies in regulation that favors insiders over international investors.

Internal Funding

Ongoing international business activities and new investments can also be financed internally, whether with funds supplied by the parent company or by its international subsidiaries.

American Depository Receipt (ADR)

Certificate that trades in the United States and that represents a specific number of shares in a non-US company.

venture capital

Financing obtained from investors who believe that the borrower will experience rapid growth and who receive equity (part ownership) in return.

CULTURE MATTERS   Financing Business from Abroad

Small-business financing is becoming more global as national economies become interwoven and as technology eases communication. To simply gain a position in the relatively safe US market, for example, an international investor may accept a lower rate of return. Here are some tips from entrepreneurs who found international capital for their companies:

- **Business School International Programs.** Instructors of international business courses often have contacts in both education and industry abroad. To break into this network, perhaps visit your local college and take an executive education course or join a program in which you can work closely with entrepreneurial advisers.
- **Your Country's Commerce Department.** Ask about potential international markets to which your product might be appealing. Developing, emerging, and highly developed countries all have needs in practically every economic

sector. Your nation's commerce department can help in your preliminary scouting of opportunities, as can your country's embassies.

- **Leverage Your Contacts.** Tap the professionals with whom you work—especially attorneys and accountants with international ties. Long before you start pursuing overseas investors, consider asking a respected executive with international experience to serve on your board of directors.
- **Industry Events in Other Countries.** Do this to increase your contacts and exposure. Your specific trade association should be able to provide you with a schedule of shows taking place in other countries.
- **Hire an Intermediary to Find Capital.** These types of intermediaries can help locate funding from international venture-capital firms, banks, and other lending institutions. They also can help expanding businesses get capital from financial institutions in other parts of the world.

INTERNAL EQUITY, DEBT, AND FEES Spin-off companies and new subsidiaries typically require a period of time before they become financially independent. During this period, they often obtain internal financing from parent companies.

Many international subsidiaries obtain financial capital by issuing equity, which as a rule is not publicly traded. In fact, equity is often purchased solely by the parent company, which obviously enjoys great influence over the subsidiary's decisions. If the subsidiary performs well, the parent earns a return from the appreciating share price that reflects the increased valuation of the company. If the subsidiary decides to pay stock dividends, the parent company can also earn a return in this way. Parent companies commonly lend money to international subsidiaries during the start-up phase and when subsidiaries undertake large new investments. Conversely, subsidiaries with excess cash often lend money to parent or sister companies that need capital.

revenue

Money earned from the sale of goods and services.

REVENUE FROM OPERATIONS Money earned from the sale of goods and services is called **revenue**. This source of capital is the lifeblood of international companies and their subsidiaries. If a company is to succeed in the long term, it must at some point generate sufficient internal revenue to sustain day-to-day operations. At that point, outside financing is required only to expand operations or to survive lean periods—say, during seasonal sales fluctuations.

As we saw in earlier chapters, international companies and their subsidiaries also internally generate revenues through so-called *transfer prices*—prices charged for goods or services transferred among a company and its subsidiaries. Companies set subsidiaries' transfer prices high or low, according to their own goals. For instance, often companies pursue transfer pricing aggressively when they wish to minimize taxes in a high-taxation country. Transfer pricing can be used if there are no national restrictions on the use of foreign exchange or on the repatriation of profits to home countries. Figure 15.2 summarizes the internal sources of capital for international companies and their subsidiaries.

Capital Structure

capital structure

Mix of equity, debt, and internally generated funds used to finance a company's activities.

The **capital structure** of a company is the mix of equity, debt, and internally generated funds that it uses to finance its activities. Firms try to strike the right balance among financing methods to minimize risk and the cost of capital.

Debt requires periodic interest payments to creditors such as banks and bondholders. If the company defaults on interest payments, creditors can take the company to court to force it to pay—even forcing it into bankruptcy. On the other hand, in the case of equity, only holders of certain types of preferred stock (which companies issue sparingly) can force bankruptcy because of default. As a rule, then, companies do not want to carry too much debt in relation to equity that can increase their risk of insolvency. Debt still appeals to companies in many countries, however,

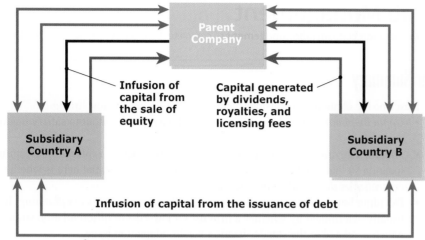

Figure 15.2
Internal Sources of Capital for International Companies

because interest payments can be deducted from taxable earnings—thus lowering the amount of taxes the firm must pay.

The basic principles of capital structure do not vary from domestic to international companies. But research indicates that multinational firms have lower ratios of debt to equity than domestic firms. Why is this so? Some observers cite increased political risk, exchange-rate risk, and the number of opportunities available to multinational companies as possible explanations for the difference. Others suggest that the debt-versus-equity option depends on a company's national culture. But this suggestion has come under fire because companies from all cultures want to reduce their cost of capital. Moreover, many large international companies generate revenue from a large number of countries. How does one determine the "national culture" of these companies?

National restrictions can influence the choice of capital structure. These restrictions include limits on the international flows of capital, the cost of local financing versus the cost of international financing, access to international financial markets, and controls imposed on the exchange of currencies. The choice of capital structure for each of a company's international subsidiaries—and, therefore, its own capital structure—is a highly complex decision.

QUICK STUDY 4

1. In general, through what source do companies obtain financial resources?
2. A common way for non-US companies to access US capital markets is to issue *what*?
3. A firm's mix of equity, debt, and internally generated funds that it uses to finance its activities is called *what*?

A Final Word

Whether an international company's production activity involves manufacturing a product or providing a service, it must acquire many resources before beginning operations. It needs to resolve issues such as where it will get raw materials or components, how much production capacity it needs, whether to construct or buy new facilities, what the size of its service centers will be, and where it will get financing. The answers to these questions are complex and interrelated.

This chapter discussed important issues to consider when formulating international production strategies, including planning for production capacity, the location of facilities, production processes to be used, and the layout of facilities. We also discussed the decision that companies face of whether to centralize or decentralize production and whether production will be standardized or adapted to national markets. In the process, we saw how production issues are linked to earlier discussions of overall corporate strategy and marketing strategy. We closed the chapter with a discussion of how companies finance their international production operations and other activities.

MyLab Management

Go to **www.pearson.com/mylab/management** to complete the problems marked with this icon .

Chapter Summary

LO15.1   Describe the elements to consider when formulating production strategies.
- *Capacity planning* helps a company to produce enough output to satisfy market demand.
- *Facilities location planning* is at its best when production is placed in an optimal location so that it achieves *location economies*. Also, essential here is whether to *centralize* or *decentralize* production.
- Deciding how a company will create its product is called *process planning*. It is usually determined by whether a firm uses a low-cost or differentiation strategy, which is related to the standardization versus adaptation issue.
- Deciding the spatial arrangement of production processes within facilities, called *facilities layout planning*, depends on the type of production process a company employs.

LO15.2   Outline the issues to consider when acquiring physical resources.
- The *make-or-buy* decision is a choice for or against greater *vertical integration*—the process of extending control over additional stages of production.
- A firm that chooses to *make* a particular product or component often does so to take advantage of lower costs or to achieve greater control.
- *Outsourcing* can provide greater flexibility while reducing exposure to exchange-rate fluctuations and other risks.
- Key issues facing firms producing locally are the *quantity* and *quality* of locally available raw materials.
- Companies can either (1) acquire or modify existing factories or (2) build entirely new facilities.

LO15.3   Identify the key production matters that concern managers.
- *Total quality management (TQM)* is a company-wide commitment to meet or exceed customer expectations through continuous quality improvement efforts and processes.
- International Standards Organization (ISO) 9000 certification is awarded to firms that meet the highest quality standards in their industries.
- *Just-in-time (JIT) manufacturing* is a technique in which inventory and its cost are minimized and inputs to the production process arrive exactly when needed.
- Companies often *reinvest* in operations when a market is expected to provide a large return or when a market is growing rapidly.
- Companies often *divest* when (1) profitability is delayed; (2) problems arise in the political, social, or economic sphere; or (3) other, more profitable opportunities arise.

LO15.4   Explain the potential ways to finance business operations.
- In *back-to-back loans*, parent firms loan money to subsidiaries by depositing money in host-country banks.
- Foreign companies can access the US capital market by issuing *American Depository Receipts (ADRs)*—certificates that trade in the United States and that represent a specific number of shares in a non–US company.
- *Venture capital* is a source of equity for entrepreneurial start-ups and small businesses.
- Parent companies and their subsidiaries can obtain *internal funding* through (1) a swapping of debt or equity and (2) charging one another royalties and licensing fees.
- *Revenue* from ongoing operations can help finance company expansion.

Key Terms

American Depository Receipt (ADR) (p. 399)
back-to-back loan (p. 398)
capacity planning (p. 388)
capital structure (p. 400)
facilities layout planning (p. 391)

facilities location planning (p. 388)
fixed (tangible) assets (p. 394)
just-in-time (JIT) manufacturing (p. 396)
location economies (p. 389)
make-or-buy decision (p. 391)
outsourcing (p. 393)

process planning (p. 390)
revenue (p. 400)
total quality management (TQM) (p. 395)
venture capital (p. 399)
vertical integration (p. 392)

✪ TALK ABOUT IT 1

Companies around the world are increasingly committing themselves to attaining ISO certification in a variety of areas, including quality and pollution minimization.

15-1. Do you think this is the start of a long-term trend toward global standardization of product and process standards? Explain.

15-2. Do you think that someday all companies and their products will need certification in order to conduct international business? Explain.

✪ TALK ABOUT IT 2

The United States is home to some of the world's leading computer software companies, most of which commonly outsource software development to other countries, including Egypt, India, Ireland, Israel, Malaysia, Hungary, and the Philippines.

15-3. Why do you think these countries became suppliers to the software industry?

15-4. Do you think that development of the industry in these countries is a threat to companies in the United States? Explain.

Ethical Challenge

You are the CEO of a manufacturing company. You manufacture all the parts needed to make a small range of products, but you have lacked investment over the past few years. A new contract from a major retailer offers you the opportunity to expand your output, but your production manager tells you that the equipment will not be able to cope. In short, you need to invest at least half the amount that the whole contract is worth with the retailer. Essentially, this would mean your factory would be working for 18 months just to pay for the new machinery. There is another clear and more straightforward alternative. You could buy all of the parts from a number of overseas suppliers and convert the factory into an assembly plant for a fraction of the cost.

15-5. Suggest two good reasons why you should still manufacture.

15-6. What are the implications of taking the outsourcing route instead of manufacturing?

15-7. Why is outsourcing abroad considered a lower-risk option compared to running a manufacturing facility?

Teaming Up

In groups of three or four, consider how a business could raise funds to make an investment in a business opportunity. You should think about the three key sources of funding. Once you have done this, share your suggestions with the rest of the class.

15-8. How does a business go about borrowing funds? Is debt a good idea?

15-9. What are the processes and implications of issuing equity or stock ownership to the business?

15-10. How would a business be able to achieve internal funding?

MyLab Management

⭐ Go to **www.pearson.com/mylab/management** for the following assisted-graded writing questions:

15-11. When technology companies went bust in the early 2000s, many pundits declared e-business dead. But as we can tell nearly two decades later, e-business is here to stay. Do you think an Internet retailer requires fewer physical, financial, and human resources than a traditional retailer or just as many? Explain.

15-12. Many companies seek to cut costs and improve quality by introducing techniques such as just-in-time and quality circles. But the results often fall short of those achieved at top companies with sterling quality reputations, such as Toyota. Why do you think this is the case?

PRACTICING INTERNATIONAL MANAGEMENT CASE

Toyota's Strategy for Production Efficiency

Toyota Motor Corporation (www.toyota-global.com) commonly appears in most rankings of the world's most respected companies. One reason for Toyota's strong showing in such rankings is that the company always seems to maintain profitability in the face of economic downturns and slack demand. Another reason is that leaders in a wide range of industries have high regard for Toyota's management and production practices.

Toyota first began producing cars in 1937. In the mid-1950s, a machinist named Taiichi Ohno began developing a new concept of automobile production. Today, the approach known as the Toyota Production System (TPS) has been intensely studied and widely copied throughout the automobile industry. Ohno, who is addressed by fellow employees as *sensei* ("teacher and master"), followed the lead of the family that founded Toyota (spelled Toyoda) by exhibiting high regard for company employees. Ohno also believed that mass production of automobiles was obsolete and that a flexible production system that produced cars according to specific customer requests would be superior.

It was at Toyota that the well-known just-in-time approach to inventory management was developed and perfected. Implementing just-in-time required *kanban*, a simple system of colored paper cards that accompanied the parts as they progressed down the assembly line. *Kanban* eliminates inventory buildup by quickly telling the production personnel which parts are being used and which are not. The third pillar of the TPS was quality circles, groups of workers who discussed ways to improve the work process and make better cars. Finally, the entire system was based on *jidoka*, which literally means "automation." As used at Toyota, however, the word expresses management's faith in the worker as a human being and a thinker.

A simple example illustrates the benefits of Toyota's system. Toyota dealerships found that customers kept returning their vehicles with leaking radiator hoses. When a team of workers at the US plant where the vehicle was made was asked to help find a solution, they found the problem was the clamp on the radiator hose. In assembly, the clamp is put over the hose, a pin on the side is pulled out, and the hose is secured. But sometimes the operator would forget to pull out the pin. The hose would remain loose and would leak. The team installed a device next to the line that contains a funnel and electric eye. If a pin is not tossed into the funnel (passing the electric eye) every 60 seconds, the device senses that the operator must have forgotten to pull the pin and stops the line. As a result, a warranty problem at the dealerships was eliminated, customer dissatisfaction was reduced, and productivity was increased.

Nearly 50 years after the groundwork for the TPS was first laid, the results speak for themselves. Toyota's superior approach to manufacturing has been estimated to yield a cost advantage of $600 to $700 per car due to more efficient production, plus another $300 savings per car because fewer defects mean less warranty repair work. Ohno's belief in flexible production can also be seen in the fact that Toyota's Sienna minivan is produced on the same assembly line in Georgetown, Kentucky, as the company's Camry models. The Sienna and Camry share the same basic chassis and 50 percent of their parts. Out of 300 different stations on the assembly line, Sienna models require different parts at only 26 stations. Toyota expects to build one Sienna for every three Camrys that come off the assembly line.

Thinking Globally

15-13. Chrysler engineers helped Toyota develop its Sienna minivan. In return, Toyota provided input on automobile production techniques to Chrysler. Why do you think Chrysler was willing to share its minivan know-how with a key competitor?

15-14. Considering financial, marketing, and human resource management issues, what other benefits do you think Toyota obtains from its production system?

Sources: Christoph Rauwald, "Toyota Loses Global Sales Crown to VW as US Trade Barriers Loom," *Automotive News* (www.autonews.com), January 30, 2017; Hirotaka Takeuchi, Emi Osono, and Norihiko Shimizu, "The Contradictions That Drive Toyota's Success," *Harvard Business Review*, June 2008, pp. 96–104; David Welch, "What Could Dull Toyota's Edge," *Bloomberg Businessweek*, April 28, 2008, p. 38.

Chapter Sixteen

Hiring and Managing Employees

Learning Objectives

After studying this chapter, you should be able to

16.1 Explain the three types of staffing policies that companies use.

16.2 Describe the key human resource recruitment and selection issues.

16.3 Summarize the main training and development programs that firms use.

16.4 Explain how companies compensate managers and workers.

16.5 Describe the importance of labor–management relations.

A Look Back

Chapter 15 examined how companies launch and manage their international production efforts. We also briefly explored how companies finance their various international business operations.

A Look at This Chapter

This final chapter examines how a company acquires and manages its most important resource—its employees. The topics we explore include international staffing policies, recruitment and selection,

training and development, compensation, and labor–management relations. We also learn about culture shock and how employees can deal with its effects.

Leaping Cultures

SANTA CLARA, California—Intel (www.intel.com) created the world's first micro-processor in 1971. Today, annual revenue is $59 billion, around 78 percent of which is earned outside the United States. Intel is the world's largest maker of computer chips and is a leading manufacturer of computer, networking, and communications products. The company is also at the leading edge of creating the next-generation computing power needed for self-driving vehicles.

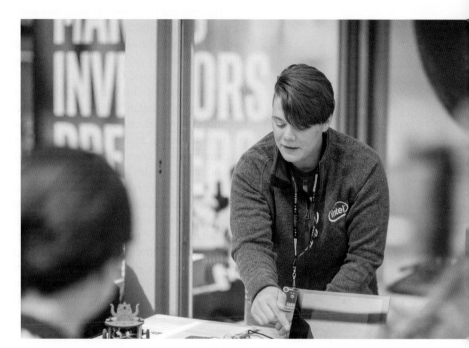

With 106,000 employees worldwide, Intel must deal with many issues when managing people. The company must answer some important questions when selecting people to manage each of its local facilities in dozens of countries. Can a qualified manager be found locally? If so, what salary should Intel pay the local manager? Or will a manager need to be sent from the United States or from a facility in another nation? If so, what should Intel pay that individual? Intel's compensation and benefits packages vary greatly from one country to another because of different practices around the world.

David Gilder/Shutterstock

There is also the issue of culture. Although the depth of cultural knowledge required of various employees differs, Intel wants all its employees to be culturally astute. Its culture-specific training courses teach employees how business differs across cultures. Intel says its training is designed to develop employees' knowledge, awareness, and skills to ensure their effectiveness and productivity. It is also supposed to help employees identify strategies for successfully doing business in other countries and with people from other countries.

From tech-support reps working long distance with customers abroad to globetrotting executives, many Intel employees regularly rely on their cross-cultural communication skills. As you read this chapter, consider all the human resource issues that arise when international companies manage their employees around the world.[1]

human resource management (HRM)
Process of staffing a company and ensuring that employees are as productive as possible.

expatriates
Citizens of one country who are living and working in another.

Perhaps the most important resource of any successful business is the people who comprise it. If a company gives its human resource management practices the importance they deserve, it can have a profound impact on performance. Highly trained and productive employees who are proficient in their duties allow a company to achieve its business goals both domestically and internationally. **Human resource management (HRM)** is the process of staffing a company and ensuring that employees are as productive as possible. It requires managers to be effective in recruiting, selecting, training, developing, evaluating, and compensating employees and in forming good relationships with them.

International HRM differs considerably from HRM in a domestic setting because of differences in national business environments. There are concerns over the employment of **expatriates**—citizens of one country who are living and working in another. Companies must deal with many issues when they have expatriate employees on job assignments that could last several years. Some of these issues are related to the inconvenience and stress of living in an unfamiliar culture. In the company profile at the start of this chapter, we saw how Intel enrolls its employees in culture-specific training courses to prepare them for doing business internationally.

Training and development programs must often be tailored to local practices. Some countries, such as Germany and Japan, have extensive vocational-training schools that turn out graduates ready to perform their jobs proficiently. Finding well-qualified nonmanagerial workers in those markets is relatively easy. By contrast, developing a production facility in many emerging markets requires far more basic training of workers. For example, workers in China work hard and tend to be well educated. But because China lacks an advanced vocational training system like those in Germany and Japan, Chinese workers tend to require more intensive on-the-job training. Recruitment and selection practices must also be adapted to the host nation's hiring laws. Hiring practices regarding nondiscrimination among job candidates must be carefully monitored so that the company does not violate such laws. And companies that go abroad to lower labor expenses must adjust pay scales and advancement criteria to suit local customs.

Because culture is so important to international business, we studied culture early (Chapter 2) and returned repeatedly to the topic throughout this book. Culture is also central to this final chapter's discussion of how international companies manage their employees. We begin by discussing the different types of human resource staffing policies that international companies use. Then, we learn about the important factors that affect recruitment and selection practices internationally. We explore the many different types of training and development programs companies can use to improve the effectiveness of their employees. We also examine the compensation policies of international companies. We close the chapter with a discussion of the importance of labor–management relations around the world.

16.1 International Staffing Policies

16.1 Explain the three types of staffing policies that companies use.

staffing policy
Customary means by which a company staffs its offices.

ethnocentric staffing
Staffing policy in which individuals from the home country manage operations abroad.

The customary means by which a company staffs its offices is called its **staffing policy**. Staffing policy is greatly influenced by the extent of a firm's international involvement. There are three main approaches to the staffing of international business operations: *ethnocentric*, *polycentric*, and *geocentric*. Although we discuss each of these approaches as being distinct from one another, companies often blend different aspects of each staffing policy in practice. The result is an almost infinite variety of international staffing policies among international companies.

Ethnocentric Staffing

In **ethnocentric staffing**, individuals from the home country manage operations abroad. This policy tends to appeal to companies that want to maintain tight control over decision making in branch offices abroad. Accordingly, those companies try to formulate policies designed to work in every country in which they operate. But note that firms generally pursue this policy in their international operations for top managerial posts—implementing it at lower levels is often impractical.

ADVANTAGES OF ETHNOCENTRIC STAFFING Firms pursue this policy for several reasons. First, locally qualified people are not always available. In developing and newly industrialized countries, there is often a shortage of qualified personnel that creates a highly competitive local labor market.

Second, companies use ethnocentric staffing to re-create local operations in the image of home-country operations. Especially if they have climbed the corporate ladder in the home office, expatriate managers tend to infuse branch offices with the corporate culture. This policy is important for companies that need a strong set of shared values among the people in each international office—such as firms implementing global strategies. For example, Mihir Doshi was born in Bombay, but his family moved to the United States in 1978. Doshi graduated from New York University and became a naturalized US citizen in 1988. In 1995, he became executive director of Morgan Stanley's (www.morganstanley.com) operations in India. He says that although he is very American, in India he can adapt to being Indian. Meanwhile, Morgan Stanley gets somebody who can instill the company culture in India.[2]

By the same token, a system of shared values is important when a company's international units are highly interdependent. For instance, fashioning branch operations in the image of home-office operations can also ease the transfer of special know-how. This advantage is particularly valuable when that know-how is rooted in the expertise and experience of home-country managers.

Finally, some companies feel that managers sent from the home country will look out for the company's interests more earnestly than will host-country natives. Japanese companies are notorious for their reluctance to place non-Japanese managers at the helm of international offices. And when they do appoint a foreigner, they often place a Japanese manager in the office to monitor important decisions and report back to the home office. Companies that operate in highly nationalistic markets and those worried about industrial espionage also typically find an ethnocentric approach appealing.

DISADVANTAGES OF ETHNOCENTRIC STAFFING Despite its advantages, ethnocentric staffing has its negative aspects. First, relocating managers from the home country is expensive. The bonuses that managers often receive for relocating plus relocation expenses for entire families can increase the cost of a manager several times over. Likewise, the pressure of cultural differences and long periods away from relatives and friends can contribute to the failure of managers on international assignments.

Second, an ethnocentric policy can create barriers for the host-country office. The presence of home-country managers in the host country might encourage a "foreign" image of the business. Lower-level employees might feel that managers do not really understand their needs because they come from another culture. Occasionally they are right: Expatriate managers sometimes fail to integrate themselves into the local culture. And if they fail to overcome cultural barriers, they typically fail to understand the needs of their local employees and those of their local customers.

Sending a manager from the home country to run things in a host country (ethnocentric staffing) can send the wrong message to local employees. To avoid this, a multinational might hire an individual from the host country to manage operations (polycentric staffing). And at still other times, a company may send the best-qualified individual regardless of nationality to manage operations abroad (geocentric staffing). Each approach can be the best one depending on the particular circumstances.

Monkey Business Images/Shutterstock

Polycentric Staffing

polycentric staffing
Staffing policy in which individuals from the host country manage operations abroad.

In **polycentric staffing**, individuals from the host country manage operations abroad. Companies can implement a polycentric approach for top- and mid-level managers, for lower-level staff, or for nonmanagerial workers. It is well suited to companies who want to give national units a degree of autonomy in decision making. This policy does not mean that host-country managers are left to run operations in any way they see fit. Large international companies usually conduct extensive training programs in which host-country managers visit home offices for extended periods. This exposes them to the company's culture and specific business practices. Small and medium-sized companies can find this policy expensive, but being able to depend on local managers who fully understand what is expected of them can far outweigh any costs.

ADVANTAGES AND DISADVANTAGES OF POLYCENTRIC STAFFING Polycentric staffing places managerial responsibility in the hands of people who are intimately familiar with the local business environment. Managers with deep cultural understanding of the local market can be an enormous advantage. They are familiar with local business practices and can read the subtle cues of both verbal and nonverbal language. They need not overcome any cultural barriers created by an image of being an outsider, and they tend to have a better feel for the needs of employees, customers, and suppliers.

Another important advantage of polycentric staffing is elimination of the high cost of relocating expatriate managers and families. This benefit can be extremely helpful for small and medium-sized businesses that cannot afford the expenses associated with expatriate employees.

The major drawback of polycentric staffing is the potential for losing control of the host-country operation. When a company employs natives of each country to manage local operations, it runs the risk of becoming a collection of discrete national businesses. This situation might not be a problem when a firm's strategy calls for treating each national market differently. It is not a good policy, however, for companies that are following global strategies. If these companies lack integration, knowledge sharing, and a common image, performance will surely suffer.

Geocentric Staffing

geocentric staffing
Staffing policy in which the best-qualified individuals, regardless of nationality, manage operations abroad.

In **geocentric staffing**, the best-qualified individuals, regardless of nationality, manage operations abroad. The local operation may choose managers from the host country, from the home country, or from a third country. The choice depends on the operation's specific needs. This policy is typically reserved for top-level managers.

ADVANTAGES AND DISADVANTAGES OF GEOCENTRIC STAFFING Geocentric staffing helps a company develop global managers who can adjust easily to any business environment—particularly to cultural differences. This advantage is especially useful for global companies trying to break down nationalistic barriers, whether between managers in a single office or between different offices. One hope of companies using this policy is that a global perspective among its managers will help them seize opportunities that may otherwise be overlooked.

The downside of geocentric staffing is the expense. Understandably, top managers who are capable both of fitting into different cultures and being effective at their jobs are highly prized among international companies. The combination of high demand for their skills and their short supply inflates their salaries. Moreover, there is the expense of relocating managers and their families—sometimes every year or two.

QUICK STUDY 1

1. A firm that staffs its operations abroad with home-country nationals uses a staffing policy called *what*?
2. Polycentric staffing is when a company staffs its operations with people from *where*?
3. Geocentric staffing is typically reserved for *whom*?

16.2 Recruiting and Selecting Human Resources

Naturally, companies try to recruit and select qualified managers and nonmanagerial workers who are well suited to their tasks and responsibilities. But how does a company know the number of managers and workers it needs? How does it recruit the best available individuals? How does it select from the pool of available candidates? In this section, we explore some answers to these and other important questions about recruiting and selecting employees.

16.2 Describe the key human resource recruitment and selection issues.

Human Resource Planning

Recruiting and selecting managers and workers requires **human resource (HR) planning**—the process of forecasting a company's human resource needs and its supply. The first phase of HR planning involves taking an inventory of a company's current human resources—that is, collecting data on every employee, including educational background, special job skills, previous jobs, language skills, and experience living abroad.

human resource planning
Process of forecasting a company's human resource needs and its supply.

The second phase of HR planning is estimating the company's future HR needs. For example, consider a firm that plans to sell its products directly to buyers in a new market abroad. Will it create a new operation abroad and staff it with managers from the home office, or will it train local managers? Will it hire its own local sales force, or will it hire a distributor? Likewise, manufacturing or assembling products in an international market requires factory workers. A company must decide whether to hire these people itself or to subcontract production to other producers—thus eliminating the need for it to hire the workers. For additional issues that companies should consider when staffing internationally, see the Manager's Briefcase feature, titled "Growing Global."

As we noted in previous chapters, this decision frequently raises ethical questions. The general public is becoming increasingly well informed about the fact that global companies make extensive use of subcontractors in low-wage nations. Of concern is the question of whether subcontractors are taking advantage of "sweatshop" labor. But publicity generated by allegations of workplace abuse caused many firms to establish codes of conduct, and they stepped up efforts to ensure compliance. For example, Apple (www.apple.com) sent a team of investigators to China to look into charges of sweatshop-like conditions at a company manufacturing Apple's iPod. The company that Apple investigated was a division of the world's largest contract electronics manufacturer, Hon Hai Precision Industry.[3]

MANAGER'S BRIEFCASE Growing Global

Going global successfully requires experience and business acumen. It can also strain a company's resources of time, money, and people. Here is some advice on human resource issues to consider when expanding internationally:

- **Don't Rely Solely on Home-Country Expatriates** Sending employees from the home country to manage host-country operations is not always best, according to Joseph Monti, a partner at Grant Thornton (www.grantthornton.com). Although they know the company and its products, home-country employees often lack experience and contacts in the local culture. Monti says a better strategy may be to hire a local general manager and bring support staff in from the United States as needed.
- **Contacts Do Not Guarantee Contracts** Relationships are more important than contracts, says Virginia Kamsky, CEO of Kamsky Associates, Inc. (www.kamsky.com). But she cautions that companies should not assume that business will flow in just because they hire a government official's

son. Kamsky says that companies will do better to hire people with the right attitude and excellent people skills.
- **Treat Your Employees Abroad as You Want to Be Treated** People are pretty much the same everywhere in the world, says Jeff Dzuira, director of international sales at Ferris Manufacturing (www.polymem.com). Treating employees fairly and respecting the local culture demonstrates honesty and builds goodwill. This will create a bond of trust that can grow into profitable relationships.
- **Employ the Web in Your Search** One of the largest employment websites is Monster (www.monster.com). It has branches in 22 countries and literally millions of résumés and is larger than ever since its merger with HotJobs. Employers can also post job announcements on the website at Overseas Jobs (www.overseasjobs.com). Of course, there are many more websites out there, and undertaking an aggressive job search or recruitment drive on the Internet is becoming increasingly common.

Another example on this topic involves Levi Strauss (www.levistrauss.com). When apparel contractors in Bangladesh admitted that they hired children, Levi Strauss demanded that they comply with local regulations. Unfortunately, it turned out that many of the underage workers were their families' sole sources of support. Levi's struck a deal: Contractors agreed to continue paying wages to the youngsters while they went to school, and then they would be rehired when they reached age 14. Levi's paid for them to attend school until they came of age.

In the third phase of HR planning, managers develop a plan for recruiting and selecting people to fill vacant and anticipated new positions, both managerial and nonmanagerial. Sometimes, a firm must also make plans for reducing its workforce—a process called *decruitment*—when current HR levels are greater than anticipated needs. Planning for decruitment normally occurs when a company decides to discontinue manufacturing or selling in a market. Unfortunately, the decision by global companies to shift the location of manufacturing from one country to another can also result in lost jobs. Let's now take a closer look at the recruitment and selection processes.

Recruiting Human Resources

recruitment
Process of identifying and attracting a qualified pool of applicants for vacant positions.

The process of identifying and attracting a qualified pool of applicants for vacant positions is called **recruitment**. Companies can recruit internally from among their current employees or look to external sources.

CURRENT EMPLOYEES Finding an international manager among current employees is easiest for a large company with an abundance of internal managers. Likely candidates within the company are managers who were involved in previous stages of an international project—say, in *identifying* the new production site or potential market. It is likely that these individuals have already made important contacts inside the host country and that they have already been exposed to its culture.

RECENT COLLEGE GRADUATES Companies also recruit from among recent college graduates who have come from other countries to attend college in the firm's home country. This is a particularly common practice among companies in the United States. Over a one-year period, these new hires receive general and specialized training and then are given positions in their native countries. As a rule, they learn about the organization's culture and the way in which it conducts business. Most important, perhaps, is their familiarity with the culture of the target market, including its customs, traditions, and language.

LOCAL MANAGERIAL TALENT Companies can also recruit local managerial talent. Hiring local managers is common when cultural understanding is a key job requirement. Hiring local managers with government contacts can speed the process of getting approvals for local operations. In some cases, governments force companies to recruit local managers so that they can develop their own internal pools of managerial talent. Governments sometimes also restrict the number of international managers that can work in the host country.

NONMANAGERIAL WORKERS Companies typically recruit locally for nonmanagerial positions because there is often little need for highly specialized skills or training. However, a specialist from the home country is typically brought in to train people chosen for more demanding positions.

Firms also turn to the local labor market when governments restrict the number of people allowed into the host country for work purposes. Such efforts are usually designed to reduce unemployment among the local population. On the other hand, countries sometimes permit the importation of nonmanagerial workers. Kuwait, a wealthy oil-producing country in the Middle East, has brought in large numbers of nonmanagerial workers for its blue-collar and technical jobs. Many of these workers come from Egypt, India, Lebanon, Pakistan, and the Philippines in search of jobs or higher wages.

Selecting Human Resources

selection
Process of screening and hiring the best-qualified applicants with the greatest performance potential.

The process of screening and hiring the best-qualified applicants with the greatest performance potential is called **selection**. The process for international assignments includes measuring a person's ability to bridge cultural differences. Expatriate managers must be able to adapt to a new way of life in the host country. Conversely, native host-country managers must be able to work effectively with superiors who have different cultural backgrounds.

In the case of expatriate managers, cultural differences between home country and host country are important factors in their potential success. Culturally sensitive managers increase the likelihood that a company will achieve its international business goals. Recruiters can assess cultural sensitivity by asking candidates questions about their receptiveness to new ways of doing things and questions about racial and ethnic issues. They can also use global aptitude tests to assess an employee's readiness for an international assignment.

It is also important to examine the cultural sensitivity of each family member who will be going to the host country. The ability of a family member (particularly a spouse) to adapt to a new culture can be a key factor in the success or failure of an expatriate manager.

> ✪ **MyLab Management** Watch It Root Capital Human Resource Management and Operations
>
> Apply what you have learned so far about recruiting and selecting employees. If your instructor has assigned this, go to **www.pearson.com/mylab/management** to watch a video case about human resource management at Root Capital and answer questions.

Culture Shock

Successful international managers typically do not mind, and often enjoy, living and working outside their native lands. In extreme cases, they might even be required to relocate every year or so. These individuals are capable of adapting quickly to local conditions and business practices. Such managers are becoming increasingly valuable with the emergence of markets in Asia, Central and Eastern Europe, and Latin America. They are also helping to create a global pool of managers who are ready and willing to go practically anywhere on short notice. The size of this pool, however, remains limited because of the difficulties that many people experience in relocating to unfamiliar cultures.

Living in another culture can be a stressful experience. Selecting managers comfortable traveling to and living in unfamiliar cultures, therefore, is an extremely important factor when recruiting for international posts. Set down in the midst of new cultures, many expatriates experience **culture shock**—a psychological process affecting people living abroad that is characterized by homesickness, irritability, confusion, aggravation, and depression. In other words, they have trouble adjusting to the new environment in which they find themselves. *Expatriate failure*—the early return by an employee from an international assignment because of inadequate job performance—often results from cultural stress. The higher cost of expatriate failure is convincing many companies to invest in cultural-training programs for employees sent abroad. For a detailed look at the culture-shock process and how to reduce its effects, see the Culture Matters feature, titled "A Shocking Ordeal."

culture shock
Psychological process affecting people living abroad that is characterized by homesickness, irritability, confusion, aggravation, and depression.

Reverse Culture Shock

Ironically, expatriates who successfully adapt to new cultures often undergo an experience called **reverse culture shock**—the psychological process of readapting to one's home culture. Because values and behavior that once seemed natural now seem strange, reverse culture shock may be even more disturbing than culture shock. Returning managers often find that either no position or merely a "standby" position awaits them in the home office. Companies often do not know how to take full advantage of the cross-cultural abilities developed by managers who have spent several potentially valuable years abroad. It is not uncommon for expatriates to leave their companies within a year of returning home because of difficulties blending back into the company culture.

reverse culture shock
Psychological process of readapting to one's home culture.

Moreover, spouses and children often have difficulty leaving the adopted culture and returning home. For many Japanese employees and their families, reentry into Japanese culture after a work assignment in the United States can be particularly difficult. The fast pace of business and social life in the United States, plus the relatively high degree of freedom and independence for women, contrasts with life in Japan. Returning Japanese expatriates can find it difficult to adjust back to life in Japan after years of living in the United States.

DEALING WITH REVERSE CULTURE SHOCK The effects of reverse culture shock can be reduced. Home-culture reorientation programs and career-counseling sessions for returning managers and their families can be highly effective. For example, the employer might bring the entire family home for a short stay several weeks before the official return. This kind of trip allows returnees to prepare for at least some of the reverse culture shock that may await them.

CULTURE MATTERS   A Shocking Ordeal

Culture shock typically occurs during stays of a few months or longer in an unfamiliar culture. It begins on arrival and normally occurs in four stages (although not all people go through every stage):

- **Stage I** The "honeymoon" typically lasts from a few days to a few weeks. New arrivals are fascinated by local sights, pleasant hospitality, and interesting habits. They are thrilled about their opportunity and are optimistic about prospects for success. Yet this sense of security is often false because, so far, interactions with locals are similar to those of a tourist.
- **Stage II** This stage lasts from a few weeks to a few months; in fact, some people never move on to Stage 3. Unpredictable quirks of the culture become annoying and even maddening. Visitors begin mocking the locals and regarding the ways of their native cultures as superior. Relationships with spouses and children suffer, and depression, perhaps even despair, sets in.
- **Stage III** Emotions hit bottom and recovery begins. Cynical remarks cease as visitors begin to learn more about the local culture, interact more with locals, and form friendships.
- **Stage IV** Visitors not only better understand local customs and behavior but actually appreciate many of them. They now treat differences as "unique" solutions to familiar problems in different cultural contexts. Reaching this stage is a sign that the expatriate has adapted well and that success in his or her international assignment is likely.

Here are some steps that prospective expatriates can take to reduce the burden of culture shock during an international assignment:

- Undergo extensive psychological assessment to ensure that both you and your family members are emotionally able to handle the assignment.
- Obtain knowledge of the local culture (especially its language) and critically examine your own cultural biases before leaving home.
- If possible, visit the assigned country, mingling with local people and getting a feel for your future assignment. Ask about local educational, financial, and health-care services.
- After you are inside a culture, meet with others—both natives and expatriates—to discuss your negative and positive experiences.
- Most important: Relax, be adventurous, take a worldly perspective, and keep your sense of humor.

Good career development programs can help companies retain valuable managers. Ideally, the career development plan is worked out before the employee goes abroad and is revised before his or her return. Some companies work with employees before they go abroad to plan career paths of up to 20 years within the company. Mentors who have previously gone abroad and had to adjust on returning home can also be assigned to returning managers. The mentor becomes a confidant with whom the expatriate manager can discuss particular problems related to work, family, and readjusting to the home culture.

QUICK STUDY 2

1. The process of forecasting a company's human resource needs and its supply is called *what*?
2. When recruiting employees, from where can companies attract qualified applicants?
3. Culture shock is a psychological process that affects people who live *where*?

16.3 Training and Development

16.3 Summarize the main training and development programs that firms use.

After a company recruits and selects its managers and other employees, it normally identifies the skills and knowledge that employees have and those that they need in order to perform their duties. Employees who lack the necessary skills or knowledge can then be directed into specific training or development programs.

Approximately 300,000 US citizens live outside the United States on international assignments, in addition to hundreds of thousands more who travel abroad on business for stays of up to several weeks. Some of the many costs of relocating an employee for a long-term international assignment include moving expenses and ongoing costs for things such as housing, education, and cost-of-living adjustments. That is why many companies realize the need for in-depth training and development programs if they are to get the maximum productivity from managers posted abroad.

As companies increasingly reach out to the world to obtain services, they are turning to online training (eTraining) programs that teach skills immediately relevant to employees' jobs. These programs include administrative training, human resources training, compliance training, and training in frontline issues such as the consumer benefits of a new product. The appeal of eTraining to international companies is its consistency: eTraining delivers a consistent message in the same way to an infinite number of employees. By contrast, employees receiving other types of training in diverse settings worldwide can go away with many different perceptions or biases. Workplace eTraining is not perfect: It can be difficult to engage people online and to teach soft skills, such as appropriate facial expressions and tone of voice. But its ability to flexibly train large groups cost-effectively makes it a viable alternative to traditional training methods.[4]

Methods of Cultural Training

Ideally, everyone involved in business should be culturally literate and prepared to go anywhere in the world at a moment's notice. Realistically, many employees and many companies do not need or cannot afford to be entirely literate in another culture. The extent of a company's international involvement demands a corresponding level of cultural knowledge from its employees. Companies whose activities are highly international need employees with language fluency and in-depth experience in other countries. Meanwhile, small companies or those new to international business can begin with some basic cultural training. As a company increases its international involvement and cross-cultural contact, employees' cultural knowledge must keep pace.

As we see in Figure 16.1, companies use many methods to prepare managers for an international assignment. These methods tend to reflect a manager's level of international involvement. The goal is to create informed, open-minded, flexible managers with a level of cultural training appropriate to the duties required of them.

ENVIRONMENTAL BRIEFINGS AND CULTURAL ORIENTATIONS *Environmental (area) briefings* constitute the most basic level of training—often the starting point for studying other cultures. Briefings include information on local housing, health care, transportation, schools, and

Figure 16.1

International Assignment Preparation Methods

climate. Such knowledge is normally obtained from books, films, and lectures. *Cultural orientations* offer insight into social, political, legal, and economic institutions. Their purpose is to add depth and substance to environmental briefings.

CULTURAL ASSIMILATION AND SENSITIVITY TRAINING *Cultural assimilation* teaches the culture's values, attitudes, manners, and customs. So-called guerrilla linguistics, which involves learning some phrases in the local language, is often used at this stage. It also typically includes role-play exercises: The trainee responds to a specific situation and is evaluated by a team of judges. This method is often used when someone is given little notice of a short stay abroad and wishes to take a crash course in social and business etiquette and communication. *Sensitivity training* teaches people to be considerate and understanding of other people's feelings and emotions. It gets the trainee "under the skin" of the local people.

LANGUAGE TRAINING The need for more thorough cultural preparedness brings us to intensive *language training*. This level of training entails more than memorizing phrases for ordering dinner or asking directions. It gets a trainee "into the mind" of local people. The trainee learns more about why local people behave as they do. This is perhaps the most critical part of cultural training for long-term assignments.

A survey of top executives found that foreign-language skills topped the list of skills needed to maintain a competitive edge. According to the survey, 31 percent of male employees and 27 percent of female employees lacked foreign-language skills. To remedy this situation, many companies either employ outside agencies that specialize in language training, or they develop their own programs. Employees at 3M Corporation (www.3m.com) developed a third way. They created an all-volunteer "Language Society" composed of current and retired employees and family members. About 1,000 people are members, and the group offers classes in 17 languages taught by 70 volunteer employee teachers. The society meets 45 minutes per week and charges a nominal $5 membership fee. Officials at 3M say that the society nicely complements the company's formal language education program.[5]

FIELD EXPERIENCE *Field experience* means visiting the culture, walking the streets of its cities and villages, and becoming absorbed by it for a short time. The trainee gets to enjoy some of the unique cultural traits and to feel some of the stresses inherent in living in the culture.

Finally, remember that spouses and children also need cultural training. Training for them is a good investment because the alternatives—an international "commuter marriage" or an expatriate failure—are both psychologically and financially expensive options.

Compiling a Cultural Profile

Cultural profiles can be quite helpful in deciding whether to accept an international assignment. The following are some excellent sources for constructing a cultural profile:

- **CultureGrams** Published by ProQuest, this guide can be found in the reference section of many libraries. Frequent updates make *CultureGrams* (www.culturegrams.com) a timely source of information. Individual sections profile each culture's background and its people, customs, courtesies, and society. A section titled "For the Traveler" covers details such as required entry visas and vaccinations.
- **Country Studies Area Handbooks** This series explains how politics, economics, society, and national security issues are related to one another and are shaped by culture in more than 70 countries. Handbooks tend to be politically oriented because they are designed for US military personnel. The *Country Studies Area Handbooks* are available on the Web at the Library of Congress website (http://lcweb2.loc.gov/frd/cs/cshome.html).
- **Background Notes** These notes contain much relevant factual information on human rights and related issues in various countries. Yet because they are published by the US Department of State (www.state.gov), they take a US political perspective.

Information can also be obtained by contacting the embassies of other countries in your home nation. People with firsthand knowledge and specific books and films are also good sources of information. After you are inside a country, you'll find your home country's embassy a good source of further cultural advice. Embassies maintain networks of home-nation professionals who work in the local culture, some with many years of experience on which you can draw.

Nonmanagerial Worker Training

Nonmanagerial workers also have training and development needs. This is especially true in some developing and newly industrialized countries where people have not even completed primary school. Even if the workforce is fairly well educated, workers may lack experience working in industry. In such cases, companies that do business abroad can train local workers in how to work on an assembly line or to cultivate business leads to make sales. The need for such basic-skills training continues to grow as companies increasingly explore opportunities in emerging markets.

In many countries, national governments cooperate with businesses to train nonmanagerial workers. Japan and Germany lead the world in vocational training and apprenticeship programs for nonmanagerial workers. Students who are unable or unwilling to enter college can enter programs paid for by the government and private industry. They undergo extensive practical training that exposes them to the cutting-edge technologies used by the country's leading companies. For example, Germany's Mittelstand is a network of three million small and medium-sized companies that account for about two-thirds of the country's jobs. Mittelstand companies provide 80 percent of Germany's apprenticeships. Although they typically employ fewer than 100 people, many Mittelstand companies are export powerhouses.

> ### QUICK STUDY 3
>
> 1. What constitutes the most basic level of cultural training?
> 2. What type of training is said to get one "into the mind" of the local people?

16.4 Employee Compensation

Essential to good international HRM is a fair and effective compensation (reward) system. Such a system is designed to attract and retain the best and brightest employees and to reward them for their performance. Because a country's compensation practices are rooted in its culture and legal and economic systems, determining compensation can be complicated. For example, base pay accounts for nearly all employee compensation in some countries. In others, bonuses and fringe benefits account for more than half of a person's compensation.

16.4 Explain how companies compensate managers and workers.

Managerial Employees

Naturally, compensation packages for managers differ from company to company and from country to country. Good packages are fairly complicated to design, for several reasons. Consider the effect of *cost of living,* which includes factors such as the cost of groceries, dining out, clothing, housing, schooling, health care, transportation, and utilities. Quite simply, it costs more to live in some countries than in others. Moreover, within a given country, the cost of living typically varies from large cities to rural towns and villages. Most companies add a certain amount to an expatriate manager's pay to cover greater cost-of-living expenses. On the other hand, managers who are relocating to lower cost-of-living countries are typically paid the same amount that they were receiving at the home office—otherwise, they would be financially penalized for accepting an international job assignment.

Companies must cover other costs incurred by expatriate managers even when the cost of living abroad is lower than at home. One important concern for relocating managers is the quality of local education. In many cases, children cannot immediately enter local classes because they do not speak the local language. In such instances, most companies pay for private-school education.

BONUS AND TAX INCENTIVES Companies commonly offer managers inducements to accept international postings. The most common is a financial bonus. This bonus can be in the form of a one-time payment or an add-on to regular pay—generally 15 to 20 percent. Bonuses for managers who are asked to go into a particularly unstable country or one with a very low standard of living often receive *hardship pay.*

Managers can also be attracted by another income-related factor. For example, the US government permits citizens working abroad to exclude $102,100 of "foreign-earned income" from their

Here, a multi-cultural group of men and women warm up before taking part in a sporting event along the banks of the Kallang River in Singapore. The small island nation has a large expatriate community that offers networking opportunities and acts as a support network for foreigners who relocate there. Multinational companies must adjust the compensation of their expatriate employees in Singapore because it is one of the most expensive places in the world to live.

Diyben/Shutterstock

taxable income in the United States—even if it was earned in a country with no income tax. But earnings over that amount are subject to income tax, as are employee benefits such as free housing.

CULTURAL AND SOCIAL CONTRIBUTORS TO COST Culture also plays an important role in the compensation of expatriate managers. Some nations offer more paid holidays than others. Many offer free medical care to everyone living and working there. Granted, the quality of locally available medical care is not always good. Many companies, therefore, have plans to take seriously ill expatriates and family members home or to nearby countries where medical care is equal to that available in the home country.

Companies that hire managers in the local market might encounter additional costs engendered by social attitudes. For instance, in some countries employers are expected to provide free or subsidized housing. In others, the government obliges employers to provide paid maternity leaves of up to one-and-a-half years. Government-mandated maternity leaves vary significantly across European countries. Although not all such costs need to be absorbed by companies, they do tend to raise a country's cost of doing business.

Managers recruited from within the host country generally receive the same pay as managers who work for local companies. Yet they often receive perks not offered by local firms. And some managers are required to visit the home office at least several times per year. If time allows, many managers will make these into short vacations by taking along their families and adding a few extra days onto the length of the trip.

Nonmanagerial Workers

Two main factors influence the wages of nonmanagerial workers. First, their compensation is strongly influenced by increased cross-border business investment. Employers can relocate fairly easily to nations where wages are lower. In the home country, meanwhile, workers must often accept lower wages when an employer gives them a choice of accepting the reduction or watching their jobs move abroad. This situation is causing a trend toward greater equality in workers' pay around the world. This equalizing effect encourages economic development and improvement in workers' lives in some nations at the expense of workers in other nations.

The freedom with which an employer can relocate differs from country to country, however. Although firms in some countries are allowed to move with little notice, in others they are highly restricted. Some countries force companies to compensate workers who lose their jobs because of relocation. This policy is common in European countries that have erected extensive social safety nets for unemployed workers.

Second, the greater mobility of labor today affects wages. Although labor laws in Europe are still more stringent than in the United States, the countries of the European Union (EU) are abolishing the requirement that workers from one EU nation must obtain visas to work in another. If workers in Spain cannot find work at home or if they feel that their current pay is inadequate, they are free to move to another EU country where unemployment is lower (say, Great Britain). A problem that plagues some European countries today is that they seem to be creating a group of people who are permanently unemployed.

1. A manager who goes to work in an unstable country might receive a bonus called *what*?
2. Some factors that contribute to the compensation of expatriate managers include *what*?

16.5 Labor–Management Relations

The positive or negative condition of relations between a company's management and its workers (labor) is referred to as **labor–management relations**. Cooperative relations between labor and management can give a firm a tremendous competitive advantage. When management and workers realize they depend on one another, the company is often better prepared to meet its goals and to surmount unexpected obstacles that may crop up. Giving workers a greater stake in the company—say, through profit-sharing plans—is one way to increase morale and generate commitment to improved quality and customer service.

Because relations between laborers and managers are human relations, they are rooted in culture and are often affected by political movements in a market. Large international companies tend to make high-level labor decisions at the home office because it gives them greater control over their network of production operations around the world—yet lower-level decisions are often left to managers in each country. In effect, this policy places decisions that have a direct impact on workers' lives in the hands of experts in the local market. Such decisions might include the number of annual paid holidays, the length of maternity leave, and the provision of day-care facilities. Localizing such management decisions tends to contribute to better labor–management relations because managers familiar with local practices are better equipped to handle matters that affect workers personally.

16.5 Describe the importance of labor–management relations.

labor–management relations
Positive or negative condition of relations between a company's management and its workers.

Importance of Labor Unions

The strength of labor unions in a country where a company has operations is important to its performance and can even affect the selection of a location. Developing and emerging markets in Asia are a popular location for international companies. Some Asian governments appeal to international companies to locate facilities in their nations by promising to keep labor unions in check. But companies also find developed nations attractive if, for whatever reason, a cooperative atmosphere exists between company management and labor unions. In some Asian countries, especially Japan, a cultural emphasis on harmony and balanced interests discourages confrontation between labor and management.

Ireland became a favorite location for a toehold in the European Union (EU). The main attractions are productive labor, lower wages, and a reduced likelihood of disruptive strikes. Labor unions are not as strong there as they are on the continent, particularly in France and Germany. Nevertheless, Germany has not been immune to the trend of falling union membership. Union membership has dropped off in Germany over the past decade from about 12 million to about 8 million workers. The main reason for the decline is the lack of interest in union membership in the former East German territories. In addition, labor unions comprise only about 9 percent of the labor force in the United States today, compared with 36 percent 50 years ago.

Despite declines in union membership, labor in Germany exercises a good deal of power over management decisions. In fact, under a plan called *codetermination*, German workers enjoy a direct say in the strategies and policies of their employers. This plan allows labor representatives to participate in high-level company meetings by actually voting on proposed actions.

INTERNATIONAL LABOR MOVEMENTS The global activities of unions are making progress in areas such as improving the treatment of workers and reducing incidents involving child labor. But the efforts of separate national unions to increase their cooperation are somewhat less successful. Although unions in one nation might want to support their counterparts in another country, generating grassroots support is difficult for two reasons. First, events taking place in another country are difficult for many people to comprehend. Distance and cultural difference make it hard for people to understand others who live and work elsewhere.

Second, whether they realize it or not, workers in different countries sometimes compete against one another. For example, today firms can relocate internationally rather easily. Thus, labor unions in one country might offer concessions to attract the jobs that will be created by a new production facility. In this way, unions in different nations can wind up competing against one another. Some observers argue that this phenomenon creates downward pressure on both wages and union power worldwide.

QUICK STUDY 5

1. Because labor-management relations are human relations they are rooted in *what*?
2. German workers have a direct say in the strategies and policies of their employers under a plan called *what*?

A Final Word

This chapter concludes our survey of international business. We studied how firms, ranging from small and medium-sized businesses to large global companies, hire and manage their most important resource—their employees. We covered a great deal of territory in our tour of international business. We hope we piqued your interest in the global marketplace and in the activities of all types of international companies. Yet our learning does not end here. Each of us will continue to be exposed to international business in our daily lives—whether as consumers or as current or future business managers. We will continue to expand our knowledge of other national cultures, the international business environment, and how companies manage their international operations. We wish you well on your continued journey through this fascinating and dynamic subject!

MyLab Management

Go to **www.pearson.com/mylab/management** to complete the problems marked with this icon .

Chapter Summary

LO16.1   Explain the three types of staffing policies that companies use.
- *Ethnocentric staffing* is when a firm staffs its operations outside the home country with home-country nationals. It can give a company tight control over subsidiary decision making.
- *Polycentric staffing* is when a company staffs its operations with host-country natives. It can give subsidiaries some autonomy in decision making.
- *Geocentric staffing* is when a company staffs its operations with the best-qualified individuals, regardless of nationality. It is typically reserved for top-level managers.

LO16.2   Describe the key human resource recruitment and selection issues.
- Large companies often recruit international managers from within the ranks of existing employees, but smaller companies may need to hire outside managers.
- International students who have graduated from colleges abroad can be hired, trained locally, and posted in their home countries.

- Local managerial talent may be recruited in the host country to hire people with an understanding of the local culture and political system. This is often required when a company engages extensively in manufacturing or marketing abroad.
- *Culture shock* is the psychological process affecting people living abroad and is characterized by homesickness, irritability, confusion, aggravation, and depression. *Reverse culture shock* is the psychological process of readapting to one's home culture.

LO16.3 Summarize the main training and development programs that firms use.
- Cultural training can reduce the effects of culture shock and reverse culture shock.
- *Environmental briefings* and *cultural orientations* provide insight on local housing, health care, and political, economic, and social institutions.
- *Cultural assimilation* and *sensitivity training* explain the local values, attitudes, and customs, and help one to understand local feelings and emotions.
- *Language training* provides specific, practical skills that teach employees to communicate in the local language.
- *Field experience* involves a visit to the culture to begin growing accustomed to it.

LO16.4 Explain how companies compensate managers and workers.
- An effective compensation policy takes into account local cultures, laws, and practices. Key issues include base pay, bonuses, and fringe benefits.
- Managerial compensation packages may need adjustment to reflect the local cost of living and, perhaps, the cost of education.
- *Bonus payments* or hardship pay may be needed to entice managers to accept international assignments.
- Nonmanagerial compensation levels can be influenced by prevailing wage rates in the local market, and by wages in other countries as well.

LO16.5 Describe the importance of labor–management relations.
- *Labor–management relations* are the positive or negative condition of relations between company management and its workers.
- Good labor–management relations can help a company meet its goals and surmount unexpected obstacles.
- Labor–management relations are rooted in culture and are often affected by political movements in the local market.
- The strength of labor unions where a company operates can affect its performance and can affect site-selection decisions.

Key Terms

culture shock (p. 413)
ethnocentric staffing (p. 408)
expatriates (p. 408)
geocentric staffing (p. 410)

human resource management (HRM)(p. 408)
human resource planning (p. 411)
labor–management relations (p. 419)
polycentric staffing (p. 410)

recruitment (p. 412)
reverse culture shock (p. 413)
selection (p. 412)
staffing policy (p. 408)

✪ TALK ABOUT IT 1

Many Japanese companies use ethnocentric staffing policies in international operations despite the difficulties that this policy can cause companies.

16-1. Why do you think Japanese companies prefer to have Japanese in top management positions?
16-2. If you were working as a consultant for a Japanese company, would you recommend that it change this policy? Explain.

✪ TALK ABOUT IT 2

Culture shock is the psychological difficulties experienced when living in an unfamiliar culture, and is characterized by homesickness, irritability, confusion, aggravation, and depression.

16-3. If you have ever experienced culture shock, in which country did it occur?

16-4. What did you do to overcome the shock or lessen its effects? Explain.

Ethical Challenge

You have been appointed to run a manufacturing plant in an overseas location by your company. The building is a shell, and you have time to carefully consider your hiring options. Having done this before, your natural inclination is to bring in experienced managers from countries you know and trust. In the past, you hired only locals and it was a disaster as you did not understand the culture, customs, and ways of working. This time, it is your intention to put someone you can trust between them and you. You may encounter some resistance from HR if you go ahead with this plan.

16-5. It would seem that ethnocentric staffing is your preferred way forward. Is ethnocentric staffing justifiable on ethical grounds?

16-6. Your approach was polycentric the previous time. Why might this approach not work in all instances?

Teaming Up

In groups of three or four, put yourselves in the role of the HR department of a global business that is being set up for the first time in a new overseas location. The business has a fundamental understanding of the location; they have been working with distributors and stockists there for some years. Now they want a permanent presence there and need carefully considered advice.

16-7. What are your thoughts about hiring local managerial talent?

16-8. What about existing employees? Where should we look internally to find potential managerial talent that could operate well overseas?

16-9. Perhaps you should recruit people directly out of university. Is that a good idea?

MyLab Management

 Go to **www.pearson.com/mylab/management** for the following assisted-graded writing questions:

16-10. Home country expatriates manage operations abroad in ethnocentric staffing, and the best qualified candidate from anywhere manages operations in geocentric staffing. What are some key reasons for keeping expatriate managers in top positions?

16-11. Suppose a company decides that it has made a mistake by hiring local personnel in a key Asian country. What are some potential problems that it will face if it decides to install or reinstate expatriate managers in these positions?

PRACTICING INTERNATIONAL MANAGEMENT CASE

BP: Challenges in Global Staffing

Finding, recruiting, training, and fulfilling human resource requirements are big challenges for companies that operate globally. British Petroleum (BP), the 100-year-old leading oil and gas company and the world's third-largest energy company, is constantly involved in hiring and managing employees with an extensive range of expertise and capabilities all around the world. Operating in more than 80 countries, BP implements various staffing policies to ensure that its operations continue to run smoothly. As discussed below, BP also needs to keep a watchful eye over staff turnover!

In July 2010, BP sued six former members of its energy team in Singapore over what BP claimed was a misuse of confidential information. The information was said to favor BP's regional rival in Singapore, Shenzhen Brightoil Group, helping it gain a strategic advantage over BP in the Asian market. After the unusual resignation of six employees with no solid explanation, BP began to investigate the circumstances of the resignations and discovered that they had acted wrongfully by compiling a list of grievances based on old emails and text messages.

The six people sued by BP were Quek Chin Thean, formerly Global Head of Residues Trading; Simon Cheong, Legal Manager; Paul John Bradshaw, Head of Operations Eastern Hemisphere; John Foo, Trading Manager; Clarence Chang, Regional Marine Sales Manager; and Laura Kuan, Executive Assistant. It was claimed that they targeted and recruited BP staff to join Shenzhen Brightoil Group. Quek Chin Thean, who was a well-respected manager in BP's trade section, had been hired locally by BP in 1992 and was accused of recruiting three U.S.-based colleagues to Shenzhen Brightoil Group. John Foo, Paul John Bradshaw, and Laura Kuan were also suspected of making unauthorized downloads from BP's computer networks.

BP also believed that the employees took advantage of the information to which they had access by sharing BP's commercial strategies and trading confidential information with the ultimate aim of setting up a Singapore-based oil-trading firm. According to BP, the unauthorized disclosure of such information would greatly damage the security of BP's strategies. BP also argued that its customers were being diverted to Shenzhen Brightoil, which was considered a deliberate act of sabotage. Furthermore, BP insisted that the six employees directly helped Shenzhen Brightoil Group while they were still employed by BP, contradicting the terms of their employment contracts. The six denied all accusations against them in August 2010.

The case was extremely important for BP as its Singapore office works in the Asian oil-trading hub, which has a very competitive job market. BP has many rivals in the region including large corporations such as Mercuria Energy Ltd., Noble Group Ltd., Standard Chartered Ltd., Citigroup Inc., Société Générale SA, and Trafigura Beheer BV, which are hiring coal, oil, and natural gas traders in Asia amid rising demand in the region for energy. BP argued that it lost the opportunity to address any human-resource issues and stem the loss of its staff as a result of the sudden and mass resignations of many of its valuable employees.

Thinking Globally

16-12. What advantages did BP expect in hiring local managers in an emerging market like Southeast Asia?

16-13. What challenges did BP face by hiring local people in its office in Singapore?

16-14. Suppose a company decides that it has made a mistake by hiring local personnel in a key Asian country. What are some potential problems that it will face if it decides to install or reinstate expatriate managers in these positions?

Sources: C. Russell and J. Carrigan, "BP Sues Six Former Staff for Misusing Confidential Information," *Bloomberg Businessweek* website (www.businessweek.com), July 23, 2010; Tan A. "BP Ex-Employees Deny Wrongdoing in Singapore Lawsuit," *Bloomberg Businessweek* website (www.businessweek.com), August 2, 2010.

Endnotes

Chapter 1

1. "Ray-Ban: The History of the Top-Selling Eyewear Brand Worldwide," Luxottica (www.luxottica.com); Paddy Maddison, "The History of Ray-Ban," The Idle Man (theidleman.com); Phil Wahba, "How Ray-Ban Sunglasses Recovered Their Luxury Identity," *Fortune*, January 27, 2016 (fortune.com); "Annual Report 2017," Luxottica (www.luxottica.com).

2. "Fortune Global 500: The 500 Largest Corporations in the World," (fortune.com/global500), July 2016; *World Trade Statistical Review 2016* (Geneva, Switzerland: World Trade Organization, October 2016), (www.wto.org), pp. 14 and 15.

3. "The Retreat of The Global Company," *The Economist*, January 28, 2017, pp. 18–22.

4. "Fortune Global 500: The 500 Largest Corporations in the World," (www.fortune.com/global500), July 2016.

5. Vellus Products Company website (www.vellus.com).

6. Weekend in Italy website (en.firenze.waf.it), select articles.

7. This comparison between the first and second ages of globalization is drawn from Thomas L. Friedman, *The Lexus and the Olive Tree* (New York: Anchor Books, 2000), pp. xvi–xix.

8. "Economics A-Z," *The Economist* (www.economist.com).

9. Brundtland Commission, *Our Common Future* (New York: Oxford University Press, 1997).

10. Yvo de Boer et al., *Expect the Unexpected: Building Business Value in a Changing World* (Amstelveen, Netherlands: KPMG International Cooperative, 2012).

11. *The Simpsons* website (www.thesimpsons.com).

12. "Why Even Win-Win Trade Deals Are Tough," *The Economist* (www.economist.com), February 2, 2017; "A Limited Doha Round Trade Deal Is Agreed in Indonesia," *The Economist* (www.economist.com), March 19, 2014.

13. iMeet website (www.pgi.com/imeet).

14. Innocentive website (www.innocentive.com).

15. For a discussion of each item of data contained in this index, see the detailed explanation of the KOF Index (http://globalization.kof.ethz.ch).

16. Naomi Klein, "Outsourcing the Friedman," Naomi Klein's website (www.naomiklein.org).

17. The results of these two studies are reported in Daniel W. Drezner, "Bottom Feeders," *Foreign Policy* (www.foreign policy.com), November 1, 2000.

18. M. Lundberg and L. Squire, *The Simultaneous Evolution of Growth and Inequality* (Washington, DC: World Bank, 1999).

19. David Dollar and Aart Kraay, *Growth Is Good for the Poor* (Washington, DC: World Bank, 2001), available at www.worldbank.org.

20. Studies cited in *Poverty in an Age of Globalization* (Washington, DC: World Bank, 2000).

21. As reported in "A Wealth of Data," *The Economist*, July 31, 2010, p. 62.

22. *World Economic Outlook* (Washington, DC: International Monetary Fund, April 2008), Figure in Box 5.1, "Financial Openness and GDP Growth," available at www.imf.org.

23. "Why the War on Poverty Is about To Get Harder," *The Economist* (www.economist.com), May 3, 2017.

24. "Undermining Sovereignty and Democracy," *The Ten Year Track Record of the North American Free Trade Agreement* (Washington, DC: Public Citizen's Global Trade Watch, 2004).

25. Stephen Krasner, "Sovereignty," *Foreign Policy*, January/February 2001, pp. 20–29.

Chapter 2

1. Larissa Faw, "Haribo Imports UK Campaign To America," *MediaPost Agency Daily* (www.media-post.com), February 20, 2017; Lorraine Mirabella, "German Gummi Bear Maker Aims for Bigger Share of US Market," *Baltimore Sun* (www.baltimoresun.com), April 7, 2012; Hans Greimel, "Gummi Bears Solve a Sticky Problem," *International Herald Tribune*, April 17, 2001, p. 14 Haribo website (www.haribo.com).

2. Alibaba website (www.alibaba.com), various company reports.

3. "IKEA Apologizes for Catalog Aimed at Ultra-Orthodox Jews," Fox News website (www.foxnews.com), February 18, 2017.

4. "Edoardo Campanella and Marta Dassù, "A Future of the English-Speaking Peoples: Lie Back and Think of the Anglosphere," *Foreign Affairs* website (www.foreign affairs.com), February 21, 2017.

5. "Rethinking the Welfare State," *The Economist*, June 4, 2016, p. 12.

6. Florence Kluckhohn and F. L. Strodtbeck, *Variations in Value Orientations* (Evanston, IL: Harper & Row, 1961).

7. Hofstede's original study has been criticized as having a Western bias, ignoring subcultures, and being outdated, as it was conducted in the 1960s and 1970s. See R. Mead, *International Management: Cross-Cultural Dimensions* (Oxford: Basil Blackwell, 1994), pp. 73–75.

8. Geert Hofstede, "The Cultural Relativity of Organizational Practices and Theories," *Journal of International Business Studies*, Fall 1983, pp. 75–89; Geert Hofstede's website (www.geert-hofstede.com).

9. Discussion based on the discussion by Geert Hofstede at (http://geerthofstede.com/dimension-data-matrix); and Matthew Maclachlan, "Indulgence vs. Restraint–The 6th Dimension," (www.communicaid/.com), January 11, 2013.

Chapter 3

1. Lauren Thomas, "Pepsi Doubles Down On 'Guilt-Free' Options In Effort To Boost Sales," CNBC website (www.cnbc.com), April 26, 2017; "PepsiCo's 2025

Sustainability Agenda Designed to Meet Changing Consumer, Societal Needs," *Sustainable Brands* website (www.sustainablebrands.com), October 17, 2016; "PepsiCo, Clinton Foundation To Source Cashew From India," *Odisha Sun Times* (www.odishasuntimes.com), May 23, 2014; "Cola Wars, Continued: Good for You, Not for Shareholders," *The Economist* (www.economist.com), March 15, 2012; PepsiCo website (www.pepsico.com), various reports.

2. Annette Weisbach, "Why Germans Want out of Google's Street View," CNBC website (www.cnbc.com), August 14, 2010.

3. Claire Miller and Kevin O'Brien, "Germany's Complicated Relationship with Google Street View," *New York Times* website (bits.blogs.nytimes.com), April 23, 2013.

4. "Economic and Financial Indicators," *The Economist*, May 13, 2017, p. 80.

5. *BSA Global Software Survey* (Washington, D.C.; Business Software Alliance, May 2016), pp. 8–9, available at www.bsa.org/globalstudy.

6. Ron Nurwisah, "Indonesian Smoking Toddler Cuts Back to 15 Cigarettes Daily," *National Post* (www.nationalpost.com), June 9, 2010.

7. Daniel Franklin, "Just Good Business," *The Economist*, Special Report on Corporate Social Responsibility, January 19, 2008, pp. 3–6.

8. Milton Friedman, "The Social Responsibility of Business Is to Increase Its Profits," *New York Times Magazine*, September 13, 1970, pp. 32–33, 122, 126.

9. Levi-Strauss website (www.levistrauss.com).

10. Daniel Franklin, "A Stitch in Time," *The Economist*, Special Report on Corporate Social Responsibility, January 19, 2008, pp. 12–14.

11. Starbucks website (www.starbucks.com).

12. Fair Trade USA website (www.fairtrade.org).

13. Carbon Footprint website (www.carbonfootprint.com).

14. Heather Green and Kerry Capell, "Carbon Confusion," *Bloomberg Businessweek* (www.businessweek.com), March 6, 2008.

15. Michelle Conlin, "Sorry, I Composted Your Memorandum," *Bloomberg Businessweek*, February 18, 2008, p. 60.

16. Alissa Walker, "Spin the Bottle," *Fast Company*, June 2008, pp. 54–55.

17. Jack Ewing, "The Wind at Germany's Back," *Bloomberg Businessweek*, February 11, 2008, p. 68.

Chapter 4

1. Celia Chen, "Foxconn Posts 50 per cent Revenue Growth in December on iPhone X Shipments," *South China Morning Post,* January 12, 2018 (www.scmp.com); "Foxconn Technology Group's Revenue (Hon Hai Precision Industry) Worldwide from 2005 to 2017 (in Trillion New Taiwan/Billion U.S. Dollars)," Statistica, 2018 (www.statista.com); Robin Moh, "World's Largest Electronic OEM Foxconn Applies for China A-share Market List, Raising to Pivot?" KrASIA, May 16, 2018 (kr-asia.com); "Inside China's Ruling Party," BBC News (news.bbc.co.uk); Sherisse Pham, "How Much Has the U.S. Lost from China's IP Theft?" CNNMoney, March 23, 2018 (money.cnn.com).

2. Daniel S. Levine, "Got a Spare Destroyer Lying Around? Make a Trade: Embracing Counter Trade as a Viable Option," *World Trade*, June 1997, pp. 34–35.

3. "Teachers Paid in Vodka," *BBC* website (www.bbc.co.uk).

4. Data obtained from Organisation for Cooperation and Development (OECD), "Statistics" section (www.oecd.org).

5. "Argentina's Expropriation of Energy Company Only Isolates Country," *Globe and Mail* (www.theglobeandmail.com), April 18, 2012.

6. Shell website (www.shell.com).

7. Donald Clarke, "Has China Restored Private Land Ownership? The Implications of Beijing's New Policy," *Foreign Affairs* (www.foreignaffairs.com), May 16, 2017.

8. "First Break All the Rules," *The Economist*, April 17, 2010, pp. 6–8.

Chapter 5

1. Richard Kestenbaum, "Is Walmart Good or Bad for America? The Question May Be Outdated," *Forbes* (www.forbes.com), May 18, 2017; Stephanie Clifford and Stephanie Rosenbloom, "With Backdrop of Glamour, Wal-Mart Stresses Global Growth," *New York Times* (www.nytimes.com), June 4, 2010; Andrew Winston, "Wal-Mart's New Sustainability Mandate in China," *Bloomberg Businessweek* (www.businessweek.com), October 28, 2008; Walmart website (www.walmart.com), select fact sheets.

2. "Getting on the Fast Track: Small Business and International Trade," Small Business Survival Committee website (www.sbsc.org).

3. *International Trade Statistics 2013* (Geneva: World Trade Organization, November 2013), Tables I.7 and I.9, available at www.wto.org.

4. "Business in China: High Seas, High Prices," *The Economist* (www.economist.com), August 7, 2008.

5. Adam Smith, *The Wealth of Nations*, first published in 1776.

6. David Ricardo, *The Principles of Political Economy and Taxation*, first published in 1817.

7. Bertil Ohlin, *Interregional and International Trade* (Cambridge, MA: Harvard University Press, 1933).

8. Wassily Leontief, "Domestic Production and Foreign Trade: The American Capital Position Re-Examined," *Economia Internationale*, February 1954, pp. 3–32.

9. Raymond Vernon and Louis T. Wells Jr., *Economic Environment of International Business*, 7th ed. (Upper Saddle River, NJ: Prentice Hall, 1991).

10. Sébastien Miroudot and Norihiko Yamano, "Towards Measuring Trade in Value-Added and Other Indicators of Global Value Chains," Presentation at the World Bank, June 9–10, 2011.

11. Ingenico website (www.ingenico.com), select reports and press releases.

12. Elhanan Helpman and Paul Krugman, *Market Structure and Foreign Trade* (Cambridge, MA: MIT Press, 1985).

13. For a detailed discussion of the first-mover advantage and its process, see Alfred D. Chandler, *Scale and Scope* (New York: Free Press, 1990).

14. Michael E. Porter, *The Competitive Advantage of Nations* (New York: Free Press, 1990).

15. Michael E. Porter, "Clusters and the New Economics of Competition," *Harvard Business Review* (November–December 1998), pp. 77–90.

Chapter 6

1. Kaushik Basu, "Winners and Losers in Textile Shake-up," BBC News, March 2, 2005, (news.bbc.co.uk); BGMEA, "Members List" (www.bgmea.com); K. Saha, "Governance and Trade: A Mixed-Method Analysis of Governance Impact on Bangladeshi Apparel Trade Performance," PhD thesis, Birmingham City University, 2018; "Textiles Monitoring Body (TMB) The Agreement on Textiles and Clothing," World Trade Organization (www.wto.org).
2. "What You Don't Know About NAFTA," *Bloomberg Businessweek* (www.businessweek.com), March 18, 2008.
3. "The Chaebol Conundrum," *The Economist*, April 3, 2010, pp. 14–15.
4. "Signs of the Zeitgeist," *The Economist*, May 29, 2010, p. 52.
5. These facts on the WTO are drawn from the WTO website (www.wto.org).
6. "Why Even Win-Win Trade Deals Are Tough," *The Economist* (www.economist.com), February 2, 2017.

Chapter 7

1. Sam McEachern, "California Answers VW's $800M Dieselgate Settlement To Build ZEV Infrastructure," *Hybridcars.com* (www.hybridcars.com), May 25, 2017; Karl Brauer, "All-New 2015 Golf Represents the Future of Volkswagen in the US," *Forbes* (www.forbes.com), June 11, 2014; Alex Taylor III, "Das Auto Giant," *Fortune*, July 23, 2012, pp. 150–155; Volkswagen website (www.vw.com), select reports.
2. This section draws on information contained in the *World Investment Report 2016* (Geneva, Switzerland: UNCTAD, June 2016), Chapter 1.
3. Raymond Vernon and Louis T. Wells Jr., *Economic Environment of International Business*, 7th ed. (Upper Saddle River, NJ: Prentice Hall, 1991).
4. John H. Dunning, "Toward an Eclectic Theory of International Production," *Journal of International Business Studies*, Spring–Summer 1980, pp. 9–31.
5. For an excellent discussion of the economic benefits provided by particular geographic locations, see Paul Krugman, "Increasing Returns and Economic Geography," *Journal of Political Economy*, June 1991, pp. 483–499.

Chapter 8

1. Naomi Gordon, "Here's Why Nestlé's Milkybars Are About to Taste Different," *The Guardian* (www.theguardian.com), March 7, 2017; Toby Webb, "Nestlé + Greenpeace: A Model for Sustainable Sourcing of Palm Oil?" Triple Pundit website (www.triplepundit.com), May 19, 2012; Tom Mulier, "Nestlé Targets Malnutrition to Fight Danone's Gains," *Bloomberg Businessweek* (www.businessweek.com), January 18, 2010; Nestlé website (www.nestle.com), select reports and fact sheets.
2. *NAFTA after Five: The Impact of the North American Free Trade Agreement on Australia's Trade and Investment*, Australian Department of Foreign Affairs and Trade (www.dfat.gov.au/geo/americas/nafta).
3. "The ECB's Bond-Buying Plan," *The Economist*, September 15, 2012, p. 68.
4. Data obtained from United States–Mexico Chamber of Commerce website (www.usmcoc.org); *North American Free Trade Agreement (NAFTA)*, Office of the United States Trade Representative website (www.ustr.gov/trade-agreements/free-trade-agreements/north-american-free-trade-agreement-nafta).
5. Data obtained from Industry of Canada Strategis website (www.strategis.ic.gc.ca); *North American Free Trade Agreement (NAFTA)*, Office of the United States Trade Representative website (www.ustr.gov/trade-agreements/free-trade-agreements/north-american-free-trade-agreement-nafta).
6. Data obtained from Office of the United States Trade Representative website (www.ustr.gov).
7. Data obtained from the AFL-CIO website (www.aflcio.org).
8. *NAFTA: Myth vs. Facts*, Office of the United States Trade Representative (www.ustr.gov), March 2008.
9. Office of the United States Trade Representative (www.ustr.gov), select reports; US Government Export Portal (www.export.gov), select reports.

Chapter 9

1. Dave Their, "The Nintendo Switch Seems to Continue Its Most Bizarre Sales Streak," *Forbes* (www.forbes.com), May 28, 2017; Leo Lewis and Kana Inagaki, "Nintendo To Ramp up Production of Switch as Demand Soars," *Financial Times* (www.ft.com), May 28, 2017; Kyo Sasaki, "Analyst: Nintendo Will Ship 4 Million Wii U Consoles to Retail," Wii U Daily website (www.wiiudaily.com), July 26, 2012; Martyn Williams, "Nintendo Records a Loss as DS Sales Plummet," *Bloomberg Businessweek* (www.businessweek.com), July 29, 2010; Matt Vella, "Wii Fit Puts the Fun in Fitness," *Bloomberg Businessweek* (www.businessweek.com), May 21, 2008; Nintendo website (www.nintendo.com), various articles and annual reports.
2. "Assessing the Damage," *Euromoney* (www.euromoney.com).
3. Bank for International Settlements website (www.bis.org), Foreign Exchange Statistics section.
4. CME Group website (www.cmegroup.com).
5. Philadelphia Securities Exchange website (www.phlx.com).

Chapter 10

1. Adam Samson, "Morgan Analysts Boost Euro Forecast; See Currency at $1.18 by Year-End," *Financial Times* (www.ft.com), June 5, 2017; "The Euro: The Flight from Spain," *The Economist*, July 28, 2012, p. 10 Bradley Davis, "Euro Weakens as Debt Jitters Outweigh Data," *Wall Street Journal* (www.wsj.com), June 17, 2010; "Emergency Repairs," *The Economist*, May 15, 2010, pp. 77–79; "The Euro in the World," European Commission website (www.ec.europa.eu).
2. "The Big Mac Index: Calories and Currencies," *The Economist*, July 28, 2012, p. 66; "When the Chips Are Down," *The Economist*, July 24, 2010, p. 72.
3. International Monetary Fund website (www.imf.org), select reports.
4. *SDR Valuation*, International Monetary Fund website (www.imf.org).
5. Robert N. McCauley and Jens Zukunft, "The Asian Financial Crisis: International Liquidity Lessons," *BIS Quarterly Review* (www.bis.org), June 9, 2008.

Chapter 11

1. "About Lidl Supermarket," Lidl UK (www.lidl.co.uk); Mintel, "Supermarkets UK—November 2017," Mintel Academic (academic.mintel.com); Murad Ahmed and Scheherazade Daneshkhu, "Tesco to Launch New Chain of Discount Stores," *Financial Times*, July 23, 2018 (www.ft.com); "Market Share of Grocery Stores in Great Britain from August 2012 to August 2017," Statista, www.statista.com; Emma Featherstone, "Lidl Remains UK's Fastest-Growing Supermarket as Sector Enjoys 17 Months of Sales Growth," *The Independent*, October 17, 2017 (www.independent.co.uk); "Grocer of the Year Award," Lidl UK (www.lidl.co.uk); Adam Gale, "Why Aldi and Lidl Will Keep on Growing," Management Today, May 1, 2018 (www.managementtoday.co.uk); Steve Burt, Leigh Sparks, and Christoph Teller, "Retailing in the United Kingdom—a Synopsis," *European Retail Research*, vol. 24 (no. 1), 2010, pp. 173–194.
2. Tesla website (www.tesla.com).
3. For an excellent discussion of this approach, see Michael E. Porter, *On Competition* (Boston: Harvard Business School Press, 2008).
4. The discussion of these strategies is based on Michael E. Porter, *Competitive Strategy* (New York: Free Press, 1980), pp. 34–46.
5. Johnson & Johnson website (www.jnj.com).
6. Norimitsu Onishi, "From Dung to Coffee Brew with No Aftertaste," *New York Times* (www.nytimes.com), April 17, 2010.
7. Bradley L. Kirkman and Debra L. Shapiro, "The Impact of Cultural Values on Employee Resistance to Teams," *Academy of Management Review*, vol. 22 (no. 3), 1997, pp. 730–757.
8. Ibid.

Chapter 12

1. Emily Bary, "Starbucks Wants to Change Habits in China," *Barrons* (www.barrons.com), June 9, 2017; Elaine Lyerly and Melia Lyerly, "Why Cause Marketing Is Smart Strategy," *Gaston Gazette* (www.gastongazette.com), March 26, 2016; Alistair Dawber, "British Rebound Gave Starbucks a Lift," *Bloomberg Businessweek* (www.businessweek.com), January 22, 2010; "Starbucks Fact Sheet" (www.starbucks.com), February 2008; Starbucks website (www.starbucks.com), select reports.
2. Johny K. Johansson, Ilkka A. Ronkainen, and Michael R. Czinkota, "Negative Country-of-Origin Effects: The Case of the New Russia," *Journal of International Business Studies*, vol. 25 (no. 1), pp. 157–176.
3. This discussion is based on S. Tamer Cavusgil, "Measuring the Potential of Emerging Markets: An Indexing Approach," *Business Horizons*, January–February 1997, pp. 87–91; "Market Potential Indicators for Emerging Markets," Michigan State University CIBER (http://ciber.bus.msu.edu).
4. Information obtained from the ProChile website (www.chileinfo.com).

Chapter 13

1. Nicole LaPorte, "Marvel Rules the Universe," *Fast Company*, May 2017, pp. 60–67, & 68; Asher Elbein, "The Real Reasons for Marvel Comics' Woes," *The Atlantic* (www.theatlantic.com), May 24, 2017; Erik Larson, "Marvel Sues over Copyright Claims by Artist's Heirs," *Bloomberg Businessweek* (www.businessweek.com), January 8, 2010; Ronald Grover, "Iron Man Spawns a Marvel of a Movie Studio," *Bloomberg Businessweek* (www.businessweek.com), April 29, 2008; Marvel website (www.marvel.com), select reports.
2. David Ing, "Spain Proves Tough to Crack," *Hotel & Motel Management*, vol. 212 (no. 15), p. 8.
3. Laura Gatland, "Eastern Europe Eagerly Accepts US Franchisors," *Franchise Times*, vol. 3 (no. 9), p. 17.
4. Frank H. Andorka Jr., "Microtel Introduces New-Construction Plan," *Hotel & Motel Management*, vol. 212 (no. 13), p. 1.
5. This classification is made in Peter Buckley and Mark Casson, "A Theory of Cooperation in International Business," in Farok J. Contractor and Peter Lorange (eds.), *Cooperative Strategies in International Business* (Lexington, MA: Lexington Books, 1988), pp. 31–53.
6. This section is based in part on Franklin R. Root, *Entry Strategies for International Markets* (Lexington, MA: Lexington Books, 1987), pp. 8–21.

Chapter 14

1. "Red Bull Owner Locks Horns over Drink's Future in China," *Financial Times* (www.ft.com), June 8, 2017; Alex Duff, "Red Bull's Mark Webber Wins Spanish Formula One Race," *Bloomberg Businessweek* (www.businessweek.com), May 9, 2010; Rob Taylor, "Red Bull Drink Lifts Stroke Risk: Australian Study," *Reuters* (www.reuters.com), August 14, 2008; Red Bull website (www.redbull.com), select reports.
2. To read the original, classic article, see Theodore Levitt, "The Globalization of Markets," *Harvard Business Review*, May–June 1983, pp. 92–102.
3. NameLab, Inc., website (www.namelab.com).
4. Alessandra Galloni, "Coca-Cola Tests the Waters with Localized Ads in Europe," *Wall Street Journal* (www.wsj.com), July 18, 2001.
5. This section draws on the classic discussion of these strategies in Warren J. Keegan, *Global Marketing Management*, 5th ed. (Upper Saddle River, NJ: Prentice Hall, 1995), pp. 489–494.
6. Muji website (www.muji.com), select reports.
7. Craig S. Smith, "In China, Some Distributors Have Really Cleaned Up with Amway," *Wall Street Journal*, August 4, 1997, p. B1.
8. "Laptops from Lapland," *The Economist*, September 6, 1997, pp. 67–68.

Chapter 15

1. "E-commerce Market Share of Leading E-Retailers Worldwide in 2016, Based on GMV," Statistica (www.statista.com); "Net Sales Revenue of Amazon from 2004 to 2017 (in Billion U.S. Dollars)," Statistica (www.statista.com); Jeff Desjardins, "Breaking Down How Amazon Makes Money," Visual Capitalist, December 19, 2017, www.visualcapitalist.com; "AWS Global Infrastructure," AWS (aws.amazon.com); Gethin Chamberlain, "Underpaid and Exhausted: The Human Cost of Your Kindle," *The Guardian*, June 9, 2018 (www.theguardian.com); "Amazon

Seals $16bn Corporate Bond Sale," *Financial Times*, August 15, 2017 (www.ft.com).

2. This classic example is found in Robert B. Reich, *The Work of Nations* (New York: Vintage Books, 1992), p. 112.

3. InnoCentive website (www.innocentive.com).

4. Stefanie Olsen, "Venture Money Flows in India and China," *Bloomberg Businessweek* (www.businessweek .com), August 22, 2008.

5. "Depositary Receipts Hit Record Trading Volume in First Half of 2008," *Reuters* (www.reuters.com), July 14, 2008.

6. Andy Serwer, "It's Big. It's German. It's SAP," *Fortune*, September 7, 1998, p. 191.

Chapter 16

1. Patrick Moorhead, "Intel Absolutely a Player to Be Reckoned with in Autonomous Driving Technology," *Forbes* (www.forbes.com), May 25, 2017; "Global 500," *Fortune*, July 21, 2008, pp. 156–182; Peter Burrows, "High-Tech's 'Sweatshop' Wakeup Call," *Bloomberg Businessweek* (www.businessweek.com), June 14, 2006; Intel website (www.intel.com), select reports.

2. Barry Newman, "Expat Archipelago: The New Yank Abroad Is the 'Can-Do' Player in the Global Village," *Wall Street Journal*, December 12, 1995, p. A12.

3. Arik Hesseldahl, "Fixing Apple's 'Sweatshop' Woes," *Bloomberg Businessweek* (www.businessweek.com), June 28, 2006.

4. Mathew Simond, "Can Online Learning Be Cost-Effective?" *EzineArticles* (www.ezinearticles.com), March 3, 2008; Nina Silberstein, "On-the-Job Training Goes Online," *Online Degrees*, Fall/Winter 2007, pp. 30–32.

5. Stephen Dolainski, "Are Expats Getting Lost in the Translation?" *Workforce*, February 1997, pp. 32–39.

Glossary

Absolute advantage. Ability of a nation to produce a good more efficiently than any other nation.

Ad valorem tariff. Tariff levied as a percentage of the stated price of an imported product.

Administrative delays. Regulatory controls or bureaucratic rules designed to impair the flow of imports into a country.

Advance payment. Export/import financing in which an importer pays an exporter for merchandise before it is shipped.

Aesthetics. What a culture considers "good taste" in the arts, the imagery evoked by certain expressions, and the symbolism of certain colors.

Agents. Individuals or organizations that represent one or more indirect exporters in a target market.

American Depository Receipt (ADR). Certificate that trades in the United States and that represents a specific number of shares in a non-US company.

Antidumping duty. Additional tariff placed on an imported product that a nation believes is being dumped on its market.

Antitrust (antimonopoly) laws. Laws designed to prevent companies from fixing prices, sharing markets, and gaining unfair monopoly advantages.

Arm's length price. Free-market price that unrelated parties charge one another for a specific product.

Attitudes. Positive or negative evaluations, feelings, and tendencies that individuals harbor toward objects or concepts.

Back-to-back loan. Loan in which a parent company deposits its money with a host-country bank, which then lends the money to a subsidiary located in the host country.

Balance of payments. National accounting system that records all receipts coming into the nation and all payments to entities in other countries.

Barter. Exchange of goods or services directly for other goods or services without the use of money.

Base currency. The denominator in a quoted exchange rate, or the currency that is to be purchased with another currency.

Berne Convention. International treaty that protects copyrights.

Bill of lading. Contract between an exporter and a shipper that specifies merchandise destination and shipping costs.

Body language. Language communicated through unspoken cues, including hand gestures, facial expressions, physical greetings, eye contact, and the manipulation of personal space.

Bond. Debt instrument that specifies the timing of principal and interest payments.

Born global firm. Company that adopts a global perspective and engages in international business from or near its inception.

Brain drain. Departure of highly educated people from one profession, geographic region, or nation to another.

Brand name. Name of one or more items in a product line that identifies the source or character of the items.

Bretton Woods Agreement. Agreement (1944) among nations to create a new international monetary system based on the value of the US dollar.

Buyback. Export of industrial equipment in return for products produced by that equipment.

Capacity planning. Process of assessing a company's ability to produce enough output to satisfy market demand.

Capital account. National account that records transactions involving the purchase and sale of assets.

Capital market. System that allocates financial resources in the form of debt and equity according to their most efficient uses.

Capital structure. Mix of equity, debt, and internally generated funds used to finance a company's activities.

Capitalism. Belief that ownership of the means of production belongs in the hands of individuals and private businesses.

Carbon footprint. Environmental impact of greenhouse gases (measured in units of carbon dioxide) that results from human activity.

Caste system. System of social stratification in which people are born into a social ranking, or caste, with no opportunity for social mobility.

Centrally planned economy. Economic system in which a nation's land, factories, and other economic resources are owned by the government, which plans nearly all economic activity.

Chains of command. Lines of authority that run from top management to individual employees and that specify internal reporting relationships.

Civil law. Legal system based on a detailed set of written rules and statutes that constitute a legal code.

Class system. System of social stratification in which personal ability and actions determine social status and mobility.

Clearing. Process of aggregating the currencies that one bank owes another and then carrying out the transaction.

Combination strategy. Strategy designed to mix growth, retrenchment, and stability strategies across a corporation's business units.

Common law. Legal system based on a country's legal history (tradition), past cases that have come before its courts (precedent), and how laws are applied in specific situations (usage).

Common market. Economic integration whereby countries remove all barriers to trade and to the movement of labor and capital among themselves and set a common trade policy against nonmembers.

Communication. System of conveying thoughts, feelings, knowledge, and information through speech, writing, and actions.

Communism. Belief that social and economic equality can be obtained only by establishing an all-powerful Communist Party and by granting the government ownership and control over all types of economic activity.

Comparative advantage. Inability of a nation to produce a good more efficiently than other nations but an ability to produce that good more efficiently than it does any other good.

Compound tariff. Tariff levied on an imported product and calculated partly as a percentage of its stated price and partly as a specific fee for each unit.

Confiscation. Forced transfer of assets from a company to the government without compensation.

Consumer panel. Research in which people record in personal diaries information on their attitudes, behaviors, or purchasing habits.

Convertible (hard) currency. Currency that trades freely in the foreign exchange market, with its price determined by the forces of supply and demand.

Copyright. Property right giving creators of original works the freedom to publish or dispose of them as they choose.

Core competency. Special ability of a company that competitors find extremely difficult or impossible to equal.

Corporate social responsibility. Practice of companies going beyond legal obligations to actively balance commitments to investors, customers, other companies, and communities.

Counterpurchase. Sale of goods or services to a country by a company that promises to make a future purchase of a specific product from the country.

Countertrade. Practice of selling goods or services that are paid for, in whole or in part, with other goods or services.

Countervailing duty. Additional tariff placed on an imported product that a nation believes is receiving an unfair subsidy.

Cross licensing. Practice by which companies use licensing agreements to exchange intangible property with one another.

Cross rate. Exchange rate calculated using two other exchange rates.

Cross-functional team. Team composed of employees who work at similar levels in different functional departments.

Cultural diffusion. Process whereby cultural traits spread from one culture to another.

Cultural imperialism. Replacement of one culture's traditions, folk heroes, and artifacts with substitutes from another.

Cultural literacy. Detailed knowledge about a culture that enables a person to work happily and effectively within it.

Cultural trait. Anything that represents a culture's way of life, including gestures, material objects, traditions, and concepts.

Culture shock. Psychological process affecting people living abroad that is characterized by homesickness, irritability, confusion, aggravation, and depression.

Culture. Set of values, beliefs, rules, and institutions held by a specific group of people.

Currency arbitrage. Instantaneous purchase and sale of a currency in different markets for profit.

Currency board. Monetary regime based on an explicit commitment to exchange domestic currency for a specified foreign currency at a fixed exchange rate.

Currency controls. Restrictions on the convertibility of a currency into other currencies.

Currency futures contract. Contract requiring the exchange of a specified amount of currency on a specified date at a specified exchange rate, with all conditions fixed and not adjustable.

Currency hedging. Practice of insuring against potential losses that result from adverse changes in exchange rates.

Currency option. Right, or option, to exchange a specified amount of a currency on a specified date at a specified rate.

Currency speculation. Purchase or sale of a currency with the expectation that its value will change and generate a profit.

Currency swap. Simultaneous purchase and sale of foreign exchange for two different dates.

Current account deficit. When a country imports more goods and services and pays more abroad than it exports and receives from abroad.

Current account surplus. When a country exports more goods and services and receives more income from abroad than it imports and pays abroad.

Current account. National account that records transactions involving the export and import of goods and services, income receipts on assets abroad, and income payments on foreign assets inside the country.

Customs union. Economic integration whereby countries remove all barriers to trade among themselves and set a common trade policy against nonmembers.

Customs. Habits or ways of behaving in specific circumstances that are passed down through generations in a culture.

Debt. Loan in which the borrower promises to repay the borrowed amount (the principal) plus a predetermined rate of interest.

Demand. Quantity of a good or service that buyers are willing to purchase at a specific selling price.

Democracy. Political system in which government leaders are elected directly by the wide participation of the people or by their representatives.

Derivative. Financial instrument whose value derives from other commodities or financial instruments.

Devaluation. Intentionally lowering the value of a nation's currency.

Developed country. Country that is highly industrialized and highly efficient, and whose people enjoy a high quality of life.

Developing country. Nation that has a poor infrastructure and extremely low personal incomes. Also called less-developed countries.

Differentiation strategy. Strategy in which a company designs its products to be perceived as unique by buyers throughout its industry.

Direct exporting. Practice by which a company sells its products directly to buyers in a target market.

Distribution. Planning, implementing, and controlling the physical flow of a product from its point of origin to its point of consumption.

Documentary collection. Export/import financing in which a bank acts as an intermediary without accepting financial risk.

Draft (bill of exchange). Document ordering an importer to pay an exporter a specified sum of money at a specified time.

Dual pricing. Policy in which a product has a different selling price (typically higher) in export markets than it has in the home market.

Dumping. Exporting a product at a price either lower than the price that the product normally commands in its domestic market or lower than the cost of production.

E-business (e-commerce). Use of computer networks to purchase, sell, or exchange products; to service customers; and to collaborate with partners.

Eclectic theory. Theory stating that firms undertake foreign direct investment when the features of a particular location combine with ownership and internalization advantages to make a location appealing for investment.

Economic development. Increase in the economic well-being, quality of life, and general welfare of a nation's people.

Economic system. Structure and processes that a country uses to allocate its resources and conduct its commercial activities.

Economic transition. Process by which a nation changes its fundamental economic organization and creates new free-market institutions.

Economic union. Economic integration whereby countries remove barriers to trade and the movement of labor and capital among members, set a common trade policy against nonmembers, and coordinate their economic policies.

Efficient market view. View that prices of financial instruments reflect all publicly available information at any given time.

Embargo. Complete ban on trade (imports and exports) in one or more products with a particular country.

Emerging markets. Newly industrialized countries plus those with the potential to become newly industrialized.

Entry mode. Institutional arrangement by which a firm gets its products, technologies, human skills, or other resources into a market.

Environmental scanning. Ongoing process of gathering, analyzing, and dispensing information for tactical or strategic purposes.

Equity. Part ownership of a company in which the equity holder participates with other part owners in the company's financial gains and losses.

Ethical behavior. Personal behavior in accordance with guidelines for good conduct or morality.

Ethnocentric staffing. Staffing policy in which individuals from the home country manage operations abroad.

Ethnocentricity. Belief that one's own ethnic group or culture is superior to that of others.

Eurobond. Bond issued outside the country in whose currency it is denominated.

Eurocurrency market. Market consisting of all the world's currencies (referred to as "Eurocurrency") that are banked outside their countries of origin.

European monetary union. European Union plan that established its own central bank and currency.

Exchange rate. Rate at which one currency is exchanged for another.

Exchange-rate risk (foreign exchange risk). Risk of adverse changes in exchange rates.

Exclusive channel. Distribution channel in which a manufacturer grants the right to sell its product to only one or a limited number of resellers.

Expatriates. Citizens of one country who are living and working in another.

Export management company (EMC). Company that exports products on behalf of indirect exporters.

Export trading company (ETC). Company that provides services to indirect exporters in addition to activities related directly to clients' exporting activities.

Exports. Goods and services sold abroad and sent out of a country.

Expropriation. Forced transfer of assets from a company to the government with compensation.

Facilities layout planning. Deciding the spatial arrangement of production processes within production facilities.

Facilities location planning. Selecting the location for production facilities.

Factor proportions theory. Trade theory stating that countries produce and export goods that require resources (factors) that are abundant and import goods that require resources in short supply.

First-mover advantage. Economic and strategic advantage gained by being the first company to enter an industry.

Fisher effect. Principle that the nominal interest rate is the sum of the real interest rate and the expected rate of inflation over a specific period.

Fixed (tangible) assets. Company assets such as production facilities, inventory warehouses, retail outlets, and production and office equipment.

Fixed exchange-rate system. System in which the exchange rate for converting one currency into another is fixed by international agreement.

Focus group. Unstructured but in-depth interview of a small group of individuals (8 to 12 people) by a moderator in order to learn the group's attitudes about a company or its product.

Focus strategy. Strategy in which a company focuses on serving the needs of a narrowly defined market segment by being the low-cost leader, by differentiating its product, or both.

Folk custom. Behavior, often dating back several generations, that is practiced by a homogeneous group of people.

Foreign bond. Bond sold outside the borrower's country and denominated in the currency of the country in which it is sold.

Foreign Corrupt Practices Act. Law that forbids US companies from bribing government officials or political candidates in other nations.

Foreign direct investment (FDI). Purchase of physical assets or a significant amount of the ownership (stock) of a company in another country to gain a measure of management control.

Foreign exchange market. Market in which currencies are bought and sold and their prices determined.

Foreign trade zone (FTZ). Designated geographic region through which merchandise is allowed to pass with lower customs duties (taxes) and/or fewer customs procedures.

Forward contract. Contract that requires the exchange of an agreed-on amount of a currency on an agreed-on date at a specified exchange rate.

Forward market. Market for currency transactions at forward rates.

Forward rate. Exchange rate at which two parties agree to exchange currencies on a specified future date.

Franchising. Practice by which one company (the franchiser) supplies another (the franchisee) with intangible property and other assistance over an extended period.

Free float system. Exchange-rate system in which currencies float freely against one another, without governments intervening in currency markets.

Free trade area. Economic integration whereby countries seek to remove all barriers to trade among themselves but where each country determines its own barriers against nonmembers.

Free trade. Pattern of imports and exports that occurs in the absence of trade barriers.

Freight forwarder. Specialist in export-related activities such as customs clearing, tariff schedules, and shipping and insurance fees.

Fundamental analysis. Technique that uses statistical models based on fundamental economic indicators to forecast exchange rates.

Fundamental disequilibrium. Economic condition in which a trade deficit causes a permanent negative shift in a country's balance of payments.

GDP or GNP per capita. Nation's GDP or GNP divided by its population.

General Agreement on Tariffs and Trade (GATT). Treaty designed to promote free trade by reducing both tariffs and nontariff barriers to international trade.

Geocentric staffing. Staffing policy in which the best-qualified individuals, regardless of nationality, manage operations abroad.

Global matrix structure. Organizational structure that splits the chain of command between product and area divisions.

Global product structure. Organizational structure that divides worldwide operations according to a company's product areas.

Global strategy. Offering the same products using the same marketing strategy in all national markets.

Global team. Team of top managers from both headquarters and international subsidiaries who meet to develop solutions to company-wide problems.

Globalization. Trend toward greater economic, cultural, political, and technological interdependence among national institutions and economies.

Gold standard. International monetary system in which nations link the value of their paper currencies to specific values of gold.

Gross domestic product (GDP). Value of all goods and services produced by a domestic economy during a one-year period.

Gross national product (GNP). Value of all goods and services produced by a country's domestic and international activities during a one-year period.

Growth strategy. Strategy designed to increase the scale (size of activities) or scope (kinds of activities) of a corporation's operations.

Hofstede framework. Framework for studying cultural differences along five dimensions, such as individualism versus collectivism and equality versus inequality.

Human development index (HDI). Measure of the extent to which a government equitably provides its people with a long and healthy life, an education, and a decent standard of living.

Human resource management (HRM). Process of staffing a company and ensuring that employees are as productive as possible.

Human resource planning. Process of forecasting a company's human resource needs and its supply.

Imports. Goods and services purchased abroad and brought into a country.

Income elasticity. Sensitivity of demand for a product relative to changes in income.

Indirect exporting. Practice by which a company sells its products to intermediaries who then resell to buyers in a target market.

Industrial property. Patents and trademarks.

Inefficient market view. View that prices of financial instruments do not reflect all publicly available information.

Intellectual property. Property that results from people's intellectual talent and abilities.

Intensive channel. Distribution channel in which a producer grants the right to sell its product to many resellers.

Interbank interest rates. Interest rates that the world's largest banks charge one another for loans.

Interbank market. Market in which the world's largest banks exchange currencies at spot and forward rates.

Interest arbitrage. Profit-motivated purchase and sale of interest-paying securities denominated in different currencies.

International area structure. Organizational structure that organizes a company's entire global operations into countries or geographic regions.

International bond market. Market consisting of all bonds sold by issuing companies, governments, or other organizations outside their own countries.

International business. Commercial transaction that crosses the borders of two or more nations.

International capital market. Network of individuals, companies, financial institutions, and governments that invest and borrow across national boundaries.

International division structure. Organizational structure that separates domestic from international business activities by creating a separate international division with its own manager.

International equity market. Market consisting of all stocks bought and sold outside the issuer's home country.

International Fisher effect. Principle that a difference in nominal interest rates supported by two countries' currencies will cause an equal but opposite change in their spot exchange rates.

International Monetary Fund. Agency created to regulate fixed exchange rates and to enforce the rules of the international monetary system.

International monetary system. Collection of agreements and institutions that govern exchange rates.

International product life cycle. Theory stating that a company begins by exporting its product and then later undertakes foreign direct investment as the product moves through its life cycle.

International product life cycle. Theory stating that a company will begin by exporting its product and later undertake foreign direct investment as the product moves through its life cycle.

International trade. Purchase, sale, or exchange of goods and services across national borders.

Jamaica Agreement. Agreement (1976) among IMF members to formalize the existing system of floating exchange rates as the new international monetary system.

Joint venture. Separate company that is created and jointly owned by two or more independent entities to achieve a common business objective.

Just-in-time (JIT) manufacturing. Production technique in which inventory is kept to a minimum and inputs to the production process arrive exactly when they are needed.

Kluckhohn–Strodtbeck framework. Framework for studying cultural differences along six dimensions, such as focus on past or future events and belief in individual or group responsibility for personal well-being.

Labor–management relations. Positive or negative condition of relations between a company's management and its workers.

Law of one price. Principle that an identical item must have an identical price in all countries when the price is expressed in a common currency.

Legal system. Set of laws and regulations, including the processes by which a country's laws are enacted and enforced and the ways in which its courts hold parties accountable for their actions.

Letter of credit. Export/import financing in which the importer's bank issues a letter pledging to pay the exporter when the exporter fulfills the terms listed in the letter.

Licensing. Practice by which one company owning intangible property (the licensor) grants another firm (the licensee) the right to use that property for a specified period of time.

Lingua franca. Third or "link" language understood by two parties who speak different native languages.

Liquidity. Ease with which bondholders and shareholders may convert their investments into cash.

Lobbying. Policy of hiring people to represent a company's views on political matters.

Local content requirements. Laws stipulating that a specified amount of a good or service be supplied by producers in the domestic market.

Location economies. Economic benefits derived from locating production activities in optimal locations.

Logistics. Management of the physical flow of products from the point of origin as raw materials to end users as finished products.

Low-cost leadership strategy. Strategy in which a company exploits economies of scale to have the lowest cost structure of any competitor in its industry.

Make-or-buy decision. Deciding whether to make a component or to buy it from another company.

Managed float system. Exchange-rate system in which currencies float against one another, with governments intervening to stabilize their currencies at particular target exchange rates.

Management contract. Practice by which one company supplies another with managerial expertise for a specific period of time.

Manners. Appropriate ways of behaving, speaking, and dressing in a culture.

Market economy. Economic system in which most of a nation's land, factories, and other economic resources are privately owned, either by individuals or businesses.

Market imperfections. Theory stating that when an imperfection in the market makes a transaction less efficient than it could be, a company will undertake foreign direct investment to internalize the transaction and thereby remove the imperfection.

Market power. Theory stating that a firm tries to establish a dominant market presence in an industry by undertaking foreign direct investment.

Market research. Collection and analysis of information used to assist managers in making informed decisions.

Marketing communication. Process of sending promotional messages about products to target markets.

Material culture. All the technology used in a culture to manufacture goods and provide services.

Mercantilism. Trade theory that nations should accumulate financial wealth, usually in the form of gold, by encouraging exports and discouraging imports.

Mission statement. Written statement of why a company exists and what it plans to accomplish.

Mixed economy. Economic system in which land, factories, and other economic resources are rather equally split between private and government ownership.

Multinational (multidomestic) strategy. Adapting products and their marketing strategies in each national market to suit local preferences.

Multinational corporation (MNC). Business that has direct investments abroad in multiple countries.

National competitive advantage theory. Trade theory stating that a nation's competitiveness in an industry depends on the capacity of the industry to innovate and upgrade.

Nationalism. Devotion of a people to their nation's interests and advancement.

Nationalization. Government takeover of an entire industry.

New trade theory. Trade theory stating that (1) there are gains to be made from specialization and increasing economies of scale, (2) the companies first to market can create barriers to entry, and (3) government may play a role in assisting its home companies.

Newly industrialized country (NIC). Country that has recently increased the portion of its national production and exports derived from industrial operations.

Normal trade relations (formerly "most favored nation status"). Requirement that WTO members extend the same favorable terms of trade to all members that they extend to any single member.

Offset. Agreement that a company will offset a hard-currency sale to a nation by making a hard-currency purchase of an unspecified product from that nation in the future.

Offshore financial center. Country or territory whose financial sector features very few regulations and few, if any, taxes.

Open account. Export/import financing in which an exporter ships merchandise and later bills the importer for its value.

Organizational structure. Way in which a company divides its activities among separate units and coordinates activities among those units.

Outsourcing. Practice of buying from another company a good or service that is part of a company's value-added activities.

Over-the-counter (OTC) market. Decentralized exchange encompassing a global computer network of foreign exchange traders and other market participants.

Patent. Property right granted to the inventor of a product or process that excludes others from making, using, or selling the invention.

Planning. Process of identifying and selecting an organization's objectives and deciding how the organization will achieve those objectives.

Political economy. Study of how a country manages its affairs by using its political, economic, and legal systems.

Political risk. Likelihood that a society will undergo political change that negatively affects local business activity.

Political system. Structures, processes, and activities by which a nation governs itself.

Political union. Economic and political integration whereby countries coordinate aspects of their economic and political systems.

Polycentric staffing. Staffing policy in which individuals from the host country manage operations abroad.

Popular custom. Behavior shared by a heterogeneous group or by several groups.

Portfolio investment. Investment that does not involve obtaining a degree of control in a company.

Price controls. Upper or lower limits placed on the prices of products sold within a country.

Primary market research. Process of collecting and analyzing original data and applying the results to current research needs.

Private sector. Segment of the economic environment comprising independently owned firms that seek to earn profits.

Privatization. Policy of selling government-owned economic resources to private operators.

Process planning. Deciding the process that a company will use to create its product.

Product liability. Responsibility of manufacturers, sellers, individuals, and others for damage, injury, or death caused by defective products.

Promotion mix. Efforts by a company to reach distribution channels and to target customers through communications, such as personal selling, advertising, public relations, and direct marketing.

Property rights. Legal rights to resources and any income they generate.

Pull strategy. Promotional strategy designed to create buyer demand that will encourage distribution channel members to stock a company's product.

Purchasing power parity (PPP). Relative ability of two countries' currencies to buy the same "basket" of goods in those two countries.

Purchasing power. Value of goods and services that can be purchased with one unit of a country's currency.

Push strategy. Promotional strategy designed to pressure distribution channel members to carry a product and to promote it to final users of the product.

Quota. Restriction on the amount (measured in units or weight) of a good that can enter or leave a country during a certain period of time.

Quoted currency. The numerator in a quoted exchange rate, or the currency with which another currency is to be purchased.

Rationalized production. System of production in which each of a product's components is produced where the cost of producing that component is lowest.

Recruitment. Process of identifying and attracting a qualified pool of applicants for vacant positions.

Regional economic integration (regionalism). Process whereby countries in a geographic region cooperate to reduce or eliminate barriers to the international flow of products, people, or capital.

Representative democracy. Democracy in which citizens elect individuals from their groups to represent their political views.

Retrenchment strategy. Strategy designed to reduce the scale or scope of a corporation's businesses.

Revaluation. Intentionally raising the value of a nation's currency.

Revenue. Money earned from the sale of goods and services.

Reverse culture shock. Psychological process of readapting to one's home culture.

Secondary market research. Process of obtaining information that already exists within the company or that can be obtained from outside sources.

Secular totalitarianism. Political system in which leaders rely on military and bureaucratic power.

Securities exchange. Exchange specializing in currency futures and options transactions.

Securitization. Unbundling and repackaging of hard-to-trade financial assets into more liquid, negotiable, and marketable financial instruments (or *securities*).

Selection. Process of screening and hiring the best-qualified applicants with the greatest performance potential.

Self-managed team. Team in which the employees from a single department take on the responsibilities of their former supervisors.

Smithsonian Agreement. Agreement (1971) among IMF members to restructure and strengthen the international monetary system created at Bretton Woods.

Social group. Collection of two or more people who identify and interact with each other.

Social mobility. Ease with which individuals can move up or down a culture's "social ladder."

Social stratification. Process of ranking people into social layers or classes.

Social structure. A culture's fundamental organization, including its groups and institutions, its system of social positions and their relationships, and the process by which its resources are distributed.

Socialism. Belief that social and economic equality is obtained through government ownership and regulation of the means of production.

Special drawing right (SDR). IMF asset whose value is based on a "weighted basket" of five currencies.

Specific tariff. Tariff levied as a specific fee for each unit (measured by number, weight, etc.) of an imported product.

Spot market. Market for currency transactions at spot rates.

Spot rate. Exchange rate requiring delivery of the traded currency within two business days.

Stability strategy. Strategy designed to guard against change and used by corporations to avoid either growth or retrenchment.

Staffing policy. Customary means by which a company staffs its offices.

Stakeholders. All parties, ranging from suppliers and employees to stockholders and consumers, who are affected by a company's activities.

Stock. Shares of ownership in a company's assets that give shareholders a claim on the company's future cash flows.

Strategic alliance. Relationship whereby two or more entities cooperate (but do not form a separate company) to achieve the strategic goals of each.

Strategy. Set of planned actions taken by managers to help a company meet its objectives.

Subculture. A group of people who share a unique way of life within a larger, dominant culture.

Subsidy. Financial assistance to domestic producers in the form of cash payments, low-interest loans, tax breaks, product price supports, or other forms.

Supply. Quantity of a good or service that producers are willing to provide at a specific selling price

Survey. Research in which an interviewer asks current or potential buyers to answer written or verbal questions in order to obtain facts, opinions, or attitudes.

Sustainability. Development that meets the needs of the present without compromising the ability of future generations to meet their own needs.

Switch trading. Practice in which one company sells to another its obligation to make a purchase in a given country.

Tariff-quota. Lower tariff rate for a certain quantity of imports and a higher rate for quantities that exceed the quota.

Tariff. Government tax levied on a product as it enters or leaves a country.

Technical analysis. Technique that uses charts of past trends in currency prices and other factors to forecast exchange rates.

Technological dualism. Use of the latest technologies in some sectors of the economy coupled with the use of outdated technologies in other sectors.

Theocracy. Political system in which a country's religious leaders are also its political leaders.

Theocratic law. Legal system based on religious teachings.

Theocratic totalitarianism. Political system under the control of totalitarian religious leaders.

Total quality management (TQM). Company-wide commitment to meet or exceed customer expectations through continuous quality improvement efforts and processes.

Totalitarian system. Political system in which individuals govern without the support of the people, tightly control people's lives, and do not tolerate opposing viewpoints.

Trade creation. Increase in the level of trade between nations that results from regional economic integration.

Trade deficit. Condition that results when the value of a country's imports is greater than the value of its exports.

Trade diversion. Diversion of trade away from nations not belonging to a trading bloc and toward member nations.

Trade mission. International trip by government officials and businesspeople that is organized by agencies of national or provincial governments for the purpose of exploring international business opportunities.

Trade show. Exhibition at which members of an industry or group of industries showcase their latest products, study activities of rivals, and examine recent trends and opportunities.

Trade surplus. Condition that results when the value of a nation's exports is greater than the value of its imports.

Trademark. Property right in the form of words or symbols that distinguish a product and its manufacturer.

Transfer price. Price charged for a good or service transferred among a company and its subsidiaries.

Turnkey (build–operate–transfer) project. Practice by which one company designs, constructs, and tests a production facility for a client firm.

United Nations (UN). International organization formed after World War II to provide leadership in fostering peace and stability around the world.

Value added tax (VAT). Tax levied on each party that adds value to a product throughout its production and distribution.

Value density. Value of a product relative to its weight and volume.

Value-chain analysis. Process of dividing a company's activities into primary and support activities and identifying those that create value for customers.

Values. Ideas, beliefs, and customs to which people are emotionally attached.

Vehicle currency. Currency used as an intermediary to convert funds between two other currencies.

Venture capital. Financing obtained from investors who believe that the borrower will experience rapid growth and who receive equity (part ownership) in return.

Vertical integration. Extension of company activities into stages of production that provide a firm's inputs (backward integration) or absorb its output (forward integration).

Vertical integration. Extension of company activities into stages of production that provide a firm's inputs (backward integration) or that absorb its output (forward integration).

Voluntary export restraint (VER). Unique version of export quota that a nation imposes on its exports, usually at the request of an importing nation.

Wholly owned subsidiary. Facility entirely owned and controlled by a single parent company.

World Bank. Agency created to provide financing for national economic development efforts.

World Trade Organization (WTO). International organization that enforces the rules of international trade.

Worldwide pricing. Policy in which one selling price is established for all international markets.

Name Index

Subject Index

Page references in italics indicate illustrations; page references in bold indicate tables, and page references in bold italics indicate maps.